1999

The Historical Jesus
in the
Twentieth Century

1900–1950

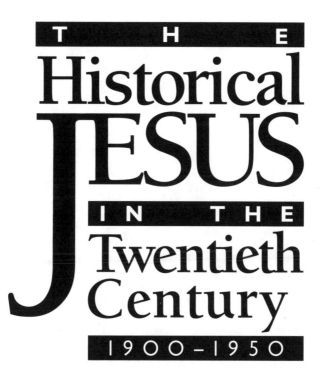

THE
Historical
JESUS
IN THE
Twentieth
Century
1900–1950

Walter P. Weaver

TRINITY PRESS INTERNATIONAL
Harrisburg, Pennsylvania

Trinity Press International, P.O. Box 1321, Harrisburg, PA 17105
Trinity Press International is a division of the Morehouse Group

Library of Congress Cataloging-in-Publication Data
Weaver, Walter P.
      The historical Jesus in the twentieth century, 1900–1950 / Walter
  P. Weaver
          p.   cm.
      Includes bibliographical references.
      ISBN 1-56338-280-6 (pbk. : alk. paper)
      1. Jesus Christ – Biography – History and criticism.   I. Title.
  BT301.9.W43   1999
  232.9′08′09041– dc21   99-29794

Printed in the United States of America

99   00   01   02   03   04   10   9   8   7   6   5   4   3   2   1

This book is for
Peggy
Wife and Companion
All along this path

Contents

PREFACE

In the sixth edition of Albert Schweitzer's famous work — essentially the second edition (1913) of the original *Von Reimarus zu Wrede* — Schweitzer composed a new preface (translated into English for the third English edition) in which he disclaimed any intention of further revisions of his work and said that he would leave it to others to introduce "order into the chaos of modern lives of Jesus, which I performed for the earlier period."

With some trepidation three of us have undertaken his challenge, though not without some serious qualification. Herewith is presented the first volume; the second comes from Ernst Baasland, formerly of the Norwegian Lutheran School of Theology at Oslo and now bishop of Stavanger, and will cover the years 1951–80. The third and last volume will be by James H. Charlesworth of Princeton Theological Seminary and will go from 1981 to the end of the century.

Our work does not simply emulate Schweitzer's model, though it does pay considerable homage to his in various ways, not least among them that now three are required to continue what one did before. But also Schweitzer seemed to aim at exhaustive coverage, leaving nothing out that was remotely worth mentioning. In fact, he only managed to master the German situation, at least in his first edition; in the second he cast a somewhat larger net, probably responding to an initial greater interest in his work in England especially than in Germany. There is the further problem that the sheer weight of material across several continents since his time would likely intimidate even Schweitzer. And no one can ever be certain that he or she has managed to cover every base; there is always the haunting suspicion that something important has been left aside, some small pamphlet residing in an obscure journal somewhere, or even something considered by another to be vitally important. Choices are inevitable in an enterprise such as this one and they must be exercised in the process of a comfortable acquisition of the material. Not all of that acquisition is reproduced in the main body of the work, but what is given here has proposed itself for inclusion only out of a sifting process bred of a continual conversation with the material itself.

I have also declined to include commentaries as a general rule, not because they are unimportant, but because of the rather obvious problem involved in their reproduction. A few instances have been treated in very special cases.

The impression that remains with me after completing this work is that our usual views of the "Quests" of the historical Jesus do not do justice to the actual history. We have grown accustomed to appealing to the "Old Quest–No Quest–New Quest–Third Quest," but we may have to reconsider, for the common language represents a distinctively German perspective for the most part. To say so is not to offer denigration or denial entirely, for it is essentially the case that Germany has provided the most adventurous and often most stimulating movements in the story. But others have also their own contributions, and part of the goal here has been to tell a more inclusive story. That should not be seen as deliberate rectification, but of an effort to locate the reality of the matter. Perhaps the British, the Americans, the French, the Dutch, and the Scandinavians have not always pressed the same limits as the Germans, but something distinctive was nevertheless going on there that deserves a memorial and here is given a voice.

Something needs to be said about procedures. Generally, in this volume I have refrained from repeating what can be found in Schweitzer, except some matters especially from the second edition, which was never translated into English, and some references to material in the original edition. To some extent the practices of the sources summarized here have been modified; for example, the designations of b.c. and a.d. have been changed to b.c.e. and c.e. The common mode of speaking in gendered terms that was characteristic of most of the sources in the time period covered has generally not been repeated, except in the case of direct quotations.

As to documentation, Schweitzer took up the policy of summarizing his sources without specific attribution. I have done likewise, except that most direct quotations are referenced in the main body of the text parenthetically. Other material is footnoted as appropriate. There is also to be found a substantial body of biographical information collected as a biographical appendix, but only occasionally incorporated into the main narrative. To do so would have encumbered that narrative greatly, but biography is not a matter of indifference either, so the reader may be advised to look in the appendix for further information. Some degree of biographical material is inserted where I considered it appropriate to do so — an entirely subjective judgment.

ACKNOWLEDGMENTS

This book had its origin in some conversations with James H. Charlesworth and subsequently inaugurated its journey during a six-month sabbatical at the Center of Theological Inquiry at Princeton. I am grateful to that splendid institution for its hospitable ethos that wisely nurtures the scholarly process. Access to the Princeton Seminary library was obviously a marvelous asset. Other libraries have also contributed: the library and staff at Florida Southern College, its director, Andrew Pearson, and staff persons Randall MacDonald, Mary Flekke, Nora Galbraith, and Beth Watson, all of whom performed graciously to meet my seemingly endless requests for books; the Duke Divinity School library, to which I made occasional visits; and the libraries at the University of Florida and the University of South Florida, who were largely unaware of my visits to access their resources. And to those persons, family and otherwise, who contributed to a fund to sustain the original sabbatical, I also record my thanks: Florida Southern College; my parents, the late Dr. L. Stacy Weaver and Mrs. Elizabeth H. Weaver; and the late Janie D. Weaver. A special thanks also goes to my brother, Dr. Charles H. Weaver, and his wife, Nancy, for their hospitality on some of those forays into North Carolina. To Methodist College in Fayetteville, North Carolina, I express my appreciation to become the first Samuel J. and Norma Womack Lecturer, where major parts of the chapter on Schweitzer were given. And finally I tender some appreciation to the members of the Department of Religion and Philosophy at Florida Southern College, my co-conspirators in the kindly business of subverting young minds, who read some of the material and have always been unfailing good friends and colleagues.

ABBREVIATIONS

AJT	American Journal of Theology
ATR	Anglican Theological Review
ExpTim	Expository Times
HibJ	Hibbert Journal
HTR	Harvard Theological Review
JBL	Journal of Biblical Literature
JR	Journal of Religion
JTS	Journal of Theological Studies
LQR	London Quarterly Review
PSTJ	Perkins (School of Theology) Journal
RB	Revue biblique
RGG	Religion in Geschichte und Gegenwart
TLZ	Theologische Literaturzeitung
TRu	Theologische Rundschau
ZNW	Zeitschrift für die neutestamentliche Wissenschaft
ZTK	Zeitschrift für Theologie und Kirche

PROLOGUE

January 1, 1900. The year rolled over with a smile.

By the reckoning in England and America, it was counted as the last year in the old century, but it somehow seemed even more portentous than what followed, pointing to a near eschatological fervor of expectation; whether from God or not was left to be told. Yet if the western world was less than certain that God was in his heaven, it was at least sure that all was well upon the earth. The *New York Times*, reporting on the revelry in New York accompanying the end of the old and the onset of the new in the preceding evening, noted the large gatherings around St. Patrick's Cathedral and lamented the use of some newfangled double horns, more strident than the old ones, and praised the sturdy custom of the ships in the harbor sounding their whistles and bells to mark the new time. The *Times* also reported a concert by Ignacy Paderewski the evening before at Carnegie Hall, and summarized sermons given a day earlier, a Sunday as it happened, in the city's leading churches and, on the Sabbath, in the synagogues. The sermons were delivered in eloquent speech, indulged in a large amount of retrospection, and generally urged people to rise to still greater levels of human achievement. Father M. J. Lavelle of St. Patrick's declared that the preceding century "was the most remarkable century in the history of the world. The material progress that had been made was astounding, but the spiritual progress was equally remarkable."[1] Father Lavelle spoke for an entire generation.

The *Times* also reported on various celebrations around the world, noting that the Kaiser (Emperor William in the *Times*' parlance) and his empress had appeared before large gatherings in the Lustgarten in Berlin. Guns fired, church bells pealed, and roman candles went up; divine worship was conducted, after which the worshipers went to White Hall "which was illuminated like fairyland and decorated with symbols typifying a bright future."[2] The *Times* observed that the Germans also marked the event as the onset of the new century, lending it an aura of greater significance. In Great Britain the welcoming of the new was marred by the brutish little war going on in South Africa, with the British troops chasing the Boers further into the interior of the continent to make the land safer for the exploitation of its gold. The *Times* of London gave most of its news reporting to coverage of the war; the new year was barely noticeable, but the

---

1. *New York Times*, January 1, 1900, 7.
2. Ibid., 2.

1

edition of January 2 also urged the reform of the army that it might be fit to do whatever the empire needed.

Still other tiny dark clouds danced at the party: Wilhelm of Germany thought it might be well for him and his country to begin building up his navy, and in brief remarks he quoted Frederick William the First: "When one in this world wants to decide something with the pen he does not do it unless supported by the strength of the sword."[3] Already the British had seized one of his ships in Delagoa Bay harbor, claiming that it held among its cargo contraband intended for the Boers. And even in America, perhaps the most conspicuously buoyant of all places,[4] the remembrance of its own shortlived war with Spain (1898) was still fresh; a few voices were being raised in horror at the continuing toll of human life taken in subduing the Philippines — some estimates ran to 600,000 or more Filipinos, though no one really knew. It was sufficient to call forth a condemnation from one of the country's leading wits and authors, Mark Twain.[5] Yet what could stand before the insistent call of Manifest Destiny arising once more?

But as a whole there was a commonality among the inhabitants of western culture, a shared feeling that their world was rapidly evolving, by some mysterious, unacknowledged Darwinian hand, into something yet greater and grander. Humankind's aspirations seemed to know no limits. Science had opened all doors, and it could only be a matter of more time, more effort, before the untold tales of the universe unfolded. The nineteenth-century struggle against nature seemed largely over; even if things like natural disasters — storms and the like — occasionally exercised their fury, that was a mere trifle, an inconvenience to be temporarily endured.

Science and its child, technology, had gained the day. The new century would quickly yield further advances: in 1903 the Wright brothers would change transport forever with their modest flight from the dunes of Kitty Hawk, North Carolina; Einstein's special theory of relativity appeared in 1905, the general theory in 1916; Max Planck already in 1900 had begun formulating the quantum theory. Communications were advancing; the ground for later radio and television was laid in the discoveries of the Scottish physicist James Clerk Maxwell regarding magnetic properties and the German Heinrich Hertz about the char-

---

3. *New York Times*, January 2, 1900, 1. The Kaiser addressed officers of the military, as reported in both *Times* editions of January 2, 1900, and, consistent with the Hohenzollern piety and conviction of divine right, he laced his speech with religious language, asserting that the German people found favor with God in the buildup of the army and would surely do so with the same process of building up the navy. The *Times* of London gave the full text of the Kaiser's brief address in its edition of January 2, 1900.

4. The noticeable American optimism was connected especially with a robust economy. The *Times* reported on the state of the world economy and expressed a good bit of boasting about the prospects for American business, the latter slightly blurred only by those worrisome trusts that threatened the nature of free competition.

5. The references are from an article, "The Spanish-American War," in *Compton's Interactive Encyclopedia* (CD-ROM, 1994).

acter of electromagnetic wave propagation. The wireless invention of the Italian Marconi had already made possible instant communication, first effectively used among ships traveling the seas. The automobile was racing through various model stages, with 8,000 registrations in America alone in the year 1900; insights into the age of the universe and the origins of human beings were advancing rapidly, as also the psychoanalytic theories of Sigmund Freud were widely challenging all assumptions about human behavior. And that tormentor of all things religious and currently cultural, Friederich Nietzsche, had himself died in 1900, though his legacy was only beginning.[6]

As to that uncertainty about God in his heaven, everyone knew that there were certain things "modern men" did not any longer accept; one of them was surely the simplistic notion of a kindly transcendent deity presiding from his heaven and interjecting his miraculous doings for the benefit of his beloved children. Of course the popular view might have been just exactly that, but then such views hardly counted among the true makers of culture, and perhaps even the sophisticated were convinced as to their being beloved of God. In the year 1900 there appeared a work about Jesus, of no consequence for genuine *Leben-Jesu-Forschung*, but nevertheless paradigmatic of the ethos at the time.[7] It was by Newell Dwight Hillis, pastor of Plymouth Church, Brooklyn, and alleged that a new era was at hand, that the culture had just passed through a destructive one in which everything was questioned and taken apart. The late nineteenth century, the good pastor argued, was a second-rate era intellectually, and it was time for a renewal, which he thought lay at hand. "The most striking fact in modern life is the growing reverence for the teachings and character of Jesus Christ" (xi), he said, and — the same in another way — "The waxing fame of Christ is the most striking fact of our era" (45). All civilization bows to Christ, the world's greatest intellect, most outstanding character, and just about everything. The new culture will then certainly be based upon a representation of the life and work of Christ to the world. A knowledge of and relatedness to Jesus will constitute the basis of renewal, not submission to a transcendent God. In short, a generous Christ for a benevolent world.

The threads of theological liberalism are easily recognizable in this comfortable picture. Ritschlianism compressed for the masses has the sound of triviality. But Ritschlianism was not trivial. It commanded the assent of some of the greatest minds, especially, of course, in Germany. Adolf von Harnack, the consummate Ritschlian, had just released *Das Wesen des Christentums* (1900;

---

6. A general sociocultural survey is Alan Bullock, ed., *The Twentieth Century: A Promethean Age* (New York: McGraw-Hill, 1971); also the collection of essays in the British series by C. B. Cox and A. E. Dyson, eds., *The Twentieth Century Mind: History, Ideas, and Literature in Britain*, 2 vols (London: Oxford University Press, 1972). A good sociocultural church history is Howard C. Kee et al., *Christianity: A Social and Cultural History* (New York: Macmillan, 1991).

7. Newell Dwight Hillis, *The Influence of Christ in Modern Life* (New York: Hodder and Stoughton, 1900). Plymouth Church had a lengthy history of distinguished liberal ministers; Lyman Abbott served there 1888–99, and before him was Henry Ward Beecher, 1845–87.

translated in 1903 as *What Is Christianity?*).[8] This work would be so influential that it would become shorthand for the liberal Ritschlian position;[9] nearly a century later Harnack's characterization of the gospel as the message that has to do "with the Father only, and not the Son" has become a cliché. The liberal position assumed the disparity between Jesus and Paul, and was staked on a certain reading of the historical Jesus that Harnack had very pithily summarized.

Indeed, Germany was well supplied with the brightest intellects and their name was legion: Kaftan, Herrmann, Troeltsch, Holtzmann (H. J. and Oskar), Bousset, Windisch, Rade, Jülicher, Heitmüller, Weiss, Wrede. And waiting in the wings was a new generation, with the likes of Dibelius, Bultmann, Schmidt, and Bauer. Even a young Karl Barth, later to remove himself from the school, worked as assistant to Martin Rade in editorship of *Die Christliche Welt*, the popular organ of the Ritschlian school. It is hard to imagine a more creative, energetic time, or a more powerful collection of intellects to carry it forth.

Not only the sciences but the arts as well mirrored this sense of a new epoch turning over and the creative energy inspired by it. In 1900 Picasso came for the first time to Paris, and in 1904 settled there. Paris was the center for artists of all sorts and experimentation was the impulse decreed by the muses. Avant-gardism had already arrived there, probably could be dated from the Impressionism Exhibition of 1874, the neo-impressionism of Seurat, and the post-impressionism of Van Gogh, Cézanne, and Gauguin. The Italian futurist Filippo Tommaso Marinetti (1876–1944) traveled extensively around Europe and Russia espousing the idea that the past must be destroyed in order to build a new world of the arts, and his ideas, though not creating such a world, in some sense represented it.

The modern era in art is often dated to 1905, when the Fauves exhibited their work in the Salon d'Autumne, led by Henri Matisse, whose painting "The Joy of Living" seems to herald the new age. Even more representative was no doubt Picasso's "Les Demoiselles d'Avignon" (1907), presaging the evolution of cubism, however shortlived the latter proved to be. Similar movements occurred in Germany, leading to German expressionism (Emil Nolde) and the group known as "Die Brücke." These developments expressed both an attempt to fashion a new art consistent with the new world rising largely though science and technology, and at the same time to react against that world through the rediscovery of primitivistic influences.

The unity of these movements can best be seen in a micro-instance in the case of the Russian impresario Sergei Diaghilev (1872–1929). Diaghilev came to Paris and created the Ballets Russes and involved in it an astounding collection of artists and performers of all sorts. At one time or another, sometimes simultaneously, he commissioned work from Picasso, Jean Cocteau, Matisse, Stravinsky,

8. Adolf von Harnack, *What Is Christianity?*, trans. Thomas Bailey Saunders (New York: Putnam's, 1903); reprinted with introduction by Rudolf Bultmann, Fortress Texts in Modern Theology (Philadelphia: Fortress Press, 1986).

9. The Ritschlians and the liberals were not necessarily the same thing; as a practical matter most liberals were Ritschlians and vice-versa.

Satie, Ravel, and numerous others. (Stravinsky's famous *The Rite of Spring* was the result of one such commission.) He was inspired by the vision of ballet as the unifying element in all the arts, and he sought to join together all the avant-garde arts at the time, with nearly amazing success.

Similar movements occurred in literature and the theater, with contributions from Ibsen, Shaw, Mann, Gide, Kafka, Joyce, and far too many others to identify. Even Broadway was not exempt, pushing the limits of the acceptable, like *Sapho,* condemned by the *New York Journal* for its "cold-blooded bid for the sensual approval of foolish people."[10] Ethel Barrymore and Maude Adams were prominent names. And in 1903 a new entry in the entertainment field showed signs of growing up with the appearance of *The Great Train Robbery.* Film was on its way, however painfully, to maturation, and would in 1912 produce — not without controversy — a life of Jesus, filmed on location in Palestine.[11]

Architecture also stretched its possibilities, with the Chicago architect Louis Sullivan masterminding the creation of the skyscraper, a kind of modern, secularized ziggurat. Sullivan's student was Frank Lloyd Wright, whose influence on modern architecture would become profound.[12] His notion of "organic architecture," of designing structures that harmonized with and seemed to grow out of their environment, still resonates in a much-later world more ecologically conscious. Of course, there were analogous movements in Europe, especially in Germany and Vienna, with the work of architects like Otto Wagner and his pupils Adolf Loos and Josef Hoffmann, and Peter Behrens, whose pupil Walter Gropius in 1919 turned the art school at Weimar into the Bauhaus, perhaps the most important center for the new modern style.

Music was less convulsed by free experimentation; the classical mood was retained in the works of Gustav Mahler and the early Richard Strauss, the latter moving in his middle period toward the powerful romanticism represented by Richard Wagner. In France Maurice Ravel and Claude Debussy prevailed, but soon into the twentieth century matters would change. Arnold Schoenberg (1874–1951), a Viennese initially under Wagner's spell, found a quite different direction; his *Pierre lunaire* of 1912 courted the boundaries of experimentalism. So striking were his early works that riots broke out at their production in 1905 and 1908. But above all Schoenberg's later discovery of the twelve-tone system of composition, the fruit of his quest for logic and "unity," led to atonality and the equation of dissonance with consonance. Like Stravinsky he fled Europe in the 1930s and spent the remainder of his life in the United States.

This same vigor of creative effort is manifested in the major centers of theo-

---

10. In the series by the editors of Time-Life, *This Fabulous Century, 1900–1910,* 8 vols. (New York: Time-Life Books, 1969), 1:256. A popular rather than an academic series, though the factual matter ought to be reliable.

11. An account of this "cinematograph" is given in the *Literary Digest* 45 (August 10, 1912): 227–28.

12. The largest single-site collection of his architecture is my own institution, Florida Southern College, in Lakeland, Florida.

logical study, though with clearly varying differences depending on the tradition and localized culture. There are, in fact, quite noticeable differences in scholarly style among the practitioners of biblical and theological scholarship. The Germans were undoubtedly the furthest advanced into historical method and its criticism of the material. There was a conspicuous degree of pride in practicing a scientific methodology and some polite disdain for those who did not. An example of a "life" of Jesus popular at the time will serve as illustration. A work by James Stalker, a pastor of the Scottish Free Church at Aberdeen, Scotland, it underwent various revisions and editions over a nearly thirty-year period, including translation into German with four different editions of the translation.[13] Stalker was clearly aware of the work being done in Germany; in the preface to the 1909 version he noticed Albert Schweitzer's 1906 book and the many lives of Jesus it surveyed, and observed with a sniff Schweitzer's virtual silence on all but German works: "But it can only be attributed to the enthusiasm of youth when the author speaks as if Germany had worked singlehandedly at this problem and as if the whole world were now waiting for the verdict at her lips" (5). Stalker meant to bow to no one on the Continent, and his work certainly went its own way. A brief summary will suffice.

The birth stories were taken as historical records and problems smoothly resolved; for example, it was after the presentation in Jerusalem that the magi visited the family in Bethlehem, where they had returned intending to reside, but Herod's plot caused them to flee to Egypt. Later, at the beginning of his ministry, Jesus came to know himself as the messiah, though Stalker declined to name a point in the ministry. "I cannot trust myself," he said, "even to think of a time when He did not know what his work in this world was to be" (22).

Stalker described the historical setting, with the Pharisees depicted as unvarnished legalists in an all-too-characteristic fashion, and the whole society described as possessing an "awful degradation" (31). Jesus came as a reformer first, not as the militant messiah expected at the time.

The baptism was Jesus' mode of entrance onto his messianic work, certainly not an act of repentance. He suffered temptation to be an easily winning messiah, but refused that in order to hold to the plan that he had from the start: to establish the kingdom of God in the hearts of individuals through the power of love and truth.

The ministry lasted three years; the first was a time of obscurity, largely in Judea; the second was a time of public favor; and the third a time of opposition. John's order prevailed here, and Stalker assumed, again with Johannine help, that Jesus must have been for a time a colleague of the Baptist.

The second year was in Galilee. The miracles attracted crowds. Stalker only hinted here and there that some miracles might be explained by the impact of Jesus' personality. Jesus spoke in short sayings and parables, the latter illustrations

---

13. James Stalker, *The Life of Jesus Christ* (New York: Fleming H. Revell, 1880, 1891; new and rev. ed., 1909).

of truths. His message was of the kingdom, the new era, the messianic age. The kingdom was not material, but an inner one of character and communion with the Father. Still the "center and soul of His preaching was Himself" (74).

Jesus was unexcelled in his demonstration of love, graciousness, sinlessness, and his unparalleled equal treatment of all.

The third year consisted of six months in Galilee with little success. The Pharisees, full of harsh legalism, were hardened against Jesus, for he did not conform to their picture of the messiah. The Sadducees were equally as bad, and only interested in Jesus when he seemed to threaten the public good. They despised his lowly origins and the company he kept (he went among sinners because he meant to save them).

Jesus went to Jerusalem to make atonement for sin. A crowd assembled, hearing of the raising of Lazarus. Only his followers — not the Jerusalemites — took part. The last days in Jerusalem were described by Stalker on a day-by-day basis. Matthew 23 showed Jesus' "pent-up criticism of a lifetime" (114) and marked the final breach with the Pharisees. Judas betrayed Jesus because he (Judas) loved money. Jesus knew he was about to die. The last supper was a passover, though Stalker combined John and the synoptics with no particular notice of a problem in chronology.

Two trials were described, a civil and an ecclesiastical one; all was a great mockery of justice. The Jewish authorities took Jesus to Pilate. It was the nation's suicide, according to Stalker. Jesus was accused of blasphemy; hence, the Jews were at fault. The Sanhedrin led the procession to Calvary; Jesus spoke his seven words from the cross. Crucifixion was for slaves and revolutionaries, and though Jesus died as the former, he really died bearing the sins of the world.

The proof of the resurrection lies in the changed lives of the originally disbelieving disciples. The conclusion wound down the book with more rapturing over Jesus' greatness and influence on the world.

Stalker's work was reviewed by Wilhelm Baldensperger in the 1900 edition of the *Theologische Rundschau*.[14] It was, he said, mostly a summary of the four gospels, from a largely nonhistorical standpoint, though possessing a certain literary "dressing" that commended it to the contemporary reading public. In Baldensperger's view the work lacked any serious understanding of the nature of the sources for writing a life of Jesus. Later Schweitzer would characterize it as a "liberal-edifying" life of Jesus, though the designation "liberal" stretches credibility.[15] Nevertheless, the response at the critical level to Stalker suggests that his work was not to be taken with much seriousness and no significant contribution was to be expected from it. For his part Stalker seemed bent on keeping to his own independent path.

---

14. *TRu* (1900): 342–44.
15. The second edition of his famous 1906 book: see Albert Schweitzer, *Geschichte der Leben-Jesu-Forschung* (Tübingen: J. C. B. Mohr [Paul Siebeck], 1913), 578 n. 1 (hereafter *Geschichte*). More in chapter 1.

In fact, Stalker's work presents an example of the kind of English-language "life" typical in the Victorian era, a type analyzed very ably by Daniel L. Pals,[16] and characterized by the expectation that such "lives" would contain a degree of edifying or faith-inducing material. The opposite was practiced in the circles of German liberal scholarship, where the ideal was scholarly objectivity and where *Lehrfreiheit und Lernfreiheit* undergirded the whole notion of the university. At least, that was the formal state of things; typically a distinction was made between "scientific" and "practical" work and supposedly the two never crossed. The reality was more that theological struggles were carried forth exegetically; the scholarship, while maintaining its integrity, was also the locus for contentions of a quite practical nature.[17] In short, the Germans often did theology and called it *Wissenschaft*, while the British did *Wissenschaft* and called it theology. The Americans had no name for what they did and it is probably fair to say that critical American scholarship was still in its infancy.[18]

Nevertheless, an amazing degree of interchange was occurring among the leading centers of theological study. The British were keenly aware of what was being manufactured in Germany, though perpetually cast a suspicious eye at it. The British would allow nothing to immigrate that was not carefully scrutinized, rather like an old dog pawing at a piece of uncertain beef, not sure whether he was willing to digest it. The scene in America was more composite; some places kept apace with everything occurring in Europe, particularly at places like Yale, Union, Harvard, the lately come University of Chicago, and much less happily at Princeton.[19] There was a noticeably less degree of reciprocity from the German side, with exceptions, such as Ernst von Dobschütz and his later successor at Halle, Hans Windisch, who were sensitive to currents in England and America.[20]

---

16. Daniel L. Pals, *The Victorian "Lives" of Jesus*, Trinity University Monograph Series in Religion 7 (San Antonio: Trinity University Press, 1982).

17. See the comments of Walter Lowrie in the introduction to Schweitzer's *The Mystery of the Kingdom of God: The Secret of Jesus' Messiahship and Passion*, trans. with introduction by Walter Lowrie (New York: Dodd, Mead, 1914). The often acrimonious *Streit* over the question of the historicity of Jesus in the first part of the twentieth century also demonstrates what Teutonic passions could be aroused. On this debate see chapter 2.

18. These are, of course, oversimplifications, but they convey a general "feel" for differences that are real and have something to do with the way in which scholarship functions culturally. Americans certainly strove for scholarly objectivity, to the point that the publications of, say, the Society of Biblical Literature and Exegesis (in the *Journal of Biblical Literature*) seemed eerily oblivious to the actual world. This phenomenon was noted by Ernest W. Saunders in his history of SBL, *Searching the Scriptures: A History of the Society of Biblical Literature, 1880–1980*, Biblical Scholarship in North America 8 (Chico, Calif.: Scholars Press, 1982).

19. There was a conspicuous tendency at Princeton to defend and explicate a conservative Reformed tradition, with people like Geerhardus Vos, Benjamin Warfield, J. G. Machen, and others who would be instrumental in the fundamentalist controversies of the early twentieth century. The overpowering influence of Charles Hodge at Princeton continued well into the twentieth century. A convenient history is William K. Selden, *Princeton Theological Seminary: A Narrative History, 1812–1992* (Princeton: Princeton University Press, 1992).

20. Certainly there were others: Carl Clemen, Harnack's student Gustav Krüger, and the *Altetestamentler* Karl Budde. But von Dobschütz and Windisch were the most consistent interpreters of the Anglo-American scene.

German criticism, however, was clearly well advanced beyond all others. At the turn of the century the British were still engaged in a debate over the extent to which "modernism" was going to be allowed to prevail. Some articles appearing at the turn of the century in the *London Quarterly Review* demonstrate the nature of the debate.

In an article reviewing both *A Dictionary of the Bible*, edited by James Hastings, and *Encyclopedia Biblica*, edited by T. K. Cheyne, W. T. Davison asked whether there was a "silent revolution" going on and whether criticism had displaced the old reverence for the Bible as the authoritative Word of God.[21] He found evidence of it especially in Cheyne's *Encyclopedia*, which seemed to him most influenced by German scholarship. That need not affect the authority of the Bible, if properly conducted, and might even strengthen it, said Davison, but we have to know where to draw the limits. He mentioned archaeology, textual criticism, questions of introduction, even the admission of "legends" in the Old Testament and refusal to engage in an unrealistic harmonizing. Davison's comparison of the two dictionaries showed that the Hastings work was more moderate, more inclined to assign historical trustworthiness, and less suspicious of the supernatural. But both implied the revolution, especially when compared with the 1863 Smith's Bible Dictionary. Davison himself remarked that the

> principle of free inquiry, untrammeled by any preconceived doctrine of "inspiration" or any theories concerning what "revelation" ought to contain, or how far the records of the Scriptures must agree in detail — the charter, that is, of criticism — is of inestimable value, and must be accepted as the necessary postulate of all Bible study to-day. (15)

Still, Davison saw the *Encyclopedia* as tending toward too radical a criticism. There was too much novelty, a departure too far from tradition. The time has come, he said, for criticism to make the Bible as revelation of God in history more illuminating. It is a good time for progress. "Much of the work that has already been done has been of great value to sound exegesis, and has widened the thoughts while not impairing the faith of Christian students of the Bible." For "God, who guides His Church and honours His Word, will make His truth to prevail."[22] So it would seem that, in the end, criticism cannot be downed, but

---

21. W. T. Davison, "The Progress of Biblical Criticism," *LQR* (1900): 1–24, reviewing James Hastings, ed., *A Dictionary of the Bible* (Edinburgh: T. & T. Clark, 1899) and T. K. Cheyne, ed., *Encyclopedia Biblica* (London: A. & C. Black, 1899). Pals also has a good discussion of the conditions obtaining in Great Britain in the first decade of the twentieth century (*Victorian "Lives" of Jesus*, 165–200), noticing many of the articles mentioned here.

22. Davison, "The Progress of Biblical Criticism," 23–24. In a later review of the English translation of Harnack's *What Is Christianity?* Davison put the matter of British-German attitudes even more exactly. Harnack, said Davison, was "the learned and eloquent corypheus of the Ritschlian school," and added, "a large proportion of readers in Berlin will shrug their shoulders because Harnack believes too much, whilst here, we are glad to think, the great majority will regret that he believes so little" (*LQR* [1901]: 168).

is a little like a petulant child who needs to be restrained and made to serve a higher (theological) interest.

In the same issue an article by Alexander Brown asked whether the ordinary church people were not now at risk because the higher criticism had come into the church itself and the old belief in the infallibility of the Bible was under fire.[23] Brown wished that the critics would agree on something, then come at the laity. "We cannot afford to change the authorship of the sacred books every quarter of a century" (72). Nevertheless some things were more important than others, he said; textual criticism was to be admitted, as indeed was criticism of scriptural texts that seemed to suggest an immoral action on God's behalf, especially as seen in the Old Testament. The Bible was not only a progressive revelation of God, but likewise of persons. Many things were being outgrown. A necessary criticism ought to apply, but with patience and tenderness. The Bible is really about religious things, about God, not a few trivial points of history, geography, or natural science.

The concern for how scholarly activity "plays" in the church and among the laity is evident. There exists also a concession to the rights of criticism, but its rights are still to be subordinated to the expectations of faith. Wherever possible, accommodation is to be sought, but there is no willingness visible to concede an open field to criticism.

Nor should we think that German scholarship was only sensitive to its setting within the university and indifferent to the circumstances of church and society. An instructive piece by Richard Lempp, commissioned by the *Harvard Theological Review* in 1910 to account for the German situation to American readers, described the church as faced with the urgent issue of its relation to the culture: "Can the church, which up to the eighteenth century had been the chief promoter and embodiment of culture, remain and be preserved over against a culture which has now become independent, or is this independent modern culture destined to sweep the church away?"[24] Germany, he said, differed from England and America, where the culture was largely friendly to the church, but a new secular culture, very powerful, threatened the hegemony of the church. It is a struggle likely to disturb the western world for some time to come.

Lempp noted that the growth of secularism had led to efforts to strengthen the institutional church, following the model of Calvinistic and American life.

---

23. Alexander Brown, "How Does It Stand with the Bible?" *LQR* (1900): 71–82.

24. Richard Lempp, "Present Religious Conditions in Germany," *HTR* 3 (1910): 85–124. Lempp gave the material as lectures at the Harvard Summer School of Theology on July 12–13, 1909. A second Lempp article describing conditions after the war identified him as a student in the Harvard Divinity School in 1908–9 who received the S.T.B. degree in 1909. He went back to Germany and received his Ph.D. at Tübingen, became a pastor in 1912, and served as a chaplain from 1914 to 1918 in the war and was recalled in 1918 to become court preacher to the king of Württemberg and teacher in a newly founded seminary at Stuttgart. He lost his post at the abdication of the king and at the time of the second article was secretary of the *Evangelischer Volksbund für Württemberg*, an association for promoting Christian unity and other activities. See Lempp, "Church and Religion in Germany," *HTR* 14 (1921): 30 n.

The best of German church life was the associations, such as "Inner Mission," working among the poor, and the Gustav Adolf League, ministering to Protestants living among Catholics. Four groups could be found in the churches: (1) liberals, who attempted "to reconcile Christianity and modern culture into a higher, rational religion" (95); (2) Ritschlians who constituted the majority of the professors and related to the orthodox church, but stood for freedom of theological scholarship and freedom for ministers; (3) the *Evangelische Vereinigung,* standing for moderate progress; and (4) the Positive Union, or orthodox party, smallest among professors but largest among ministers as well as the greatest number of the laity.

The situation gave rise to conflict, heresy trials, and problems for ministers in preaching. Church unity was at risk, not only from within, but also from the influence of English and American denominations, or sects, such as Methodists, Baptists, Adventists, and Christian Scientists, who tended to reject all modern culture. All German Protestants were united in their opposition against Rome. The Pope's Syllabus of 1864 condemned modern culture as full of errors and rejected freedom of conscience and toleration. The encyclical of 1907 reiterated papal opposition to all reform.

About 60 percent of the populace might be considered friendly to the church, while the media-makers tended to be hostile. Only 10 percent of educated Protestant men attended church and many persons considered the Christian religion itself to be outmoded and outgrown. The conservatives could hardly determine the future, as they had little grasp on modern culture. The "Ultramontanes"[25] were even more backward, trying to force medieval culture on the twentieth century. The social democrats, or Marxists, saw religion as a private affair and were interested in economic matters. The socialists sought to destroy religion and they were having some success, though peasants still tended to baptize and have funerals in the church. Morals were also affected by the socialist program; morality was scoffed at as an illusion. The socialists made progress among the young: chastity was considered a "ridiculous prudery by girls as well as young men."[26]

Friedrich Naumann, who was formerly with Adolf Stöcker and then parted from him because of Stöcker's paternalism and orthodoxy, founded the National Social party.[27] There was a new wave of social enthusiasm from 1890 to 1894 comparable to that in America. But the movement subsided because Naumann did not win any socialists to his party, then Naumann himself changed, seeing that a great industrial development was necessary, accompanied by imperial poli-

---

25. A term widely used then to refer to those who looked beyond the mountains, the Alps (ultra, montes), for authority from Rome.

26. Lempp, "Present Religious Conditions in Germany," 109.

27. Stöcker was court preacher at Berlin. He advocated a vigorous socialist position, but unfortunately his identification of Jewish leaders of industry with repressive capitalism led him into a virulent anti-Semitism.

cies, more colonies, and the buildup of the navy.[28] In fact, Naumann concluded that politics could not be Christian since it was a power struggle and therefore Christianity could not supply the aims of politics or solve existing political problems.

For Lempp, a new realism had arisen. Germany had created a new empire, and made great progress in industry and the arts. Naturalistic art like that of the poets Ibsen and Hauptmann and painters like Liebermann had at the same time revealed the cruelties of society and its realities. Philosophy, marked by agnostic positivism, monism, or materialism, treated everything as accidental products of the causal mechanism and had no idea of God. Religion seemed outgrown. The results of criticism had become widely known and removed belief in the trustworthiness of Christian fundamentals. Religion had vanished from the minds of the educated and the culturally elite. Said Lempp:

> Moral weakness and cynicism pervade large numbers of the educated; and when in the later eighties and the nineties of the nineteenth century the old optimism in regard to technical and political success gave way to the painful discovery of the inner demoralization and shallowness of life, German culture of the so-called *fin de siècle* really became in many respects a decadent civilization.[29]

Lempp suspected, however, that the worst of it was over, that the naturalism of the nineteenth century was abating, that a neo-romanticism was appearing. The faith in the sufficiency of modern secular culture seemed to be shaken. Especially Nietzsche had aroused great interest chiefly among the young. His gospel of the superman attracted many, producing the proclamation that God was dead along with unbounded individualism and immorality. "The 'Congregation of Nietzsche,' as they call themselves, have undertaken a campaign to overthrow the Christian religion" (119). Lempp gave it as his judgment that Nietzsche had destroyed naturalism, but his long-term influence would not be the death of Christianity, for his whole concern was with the welfare of the soul, his thinking a seeking after God.

It was startling, said Lempp, that Harnack's *What Is Christianity?* should command such a wide audience, that a book like Frenssen's *Hilligenlei* should sell 150,000 copies.[30] That showed a widespread popular interest, but it seemed more

---

28. This buildup of the navy, which we noticed as reported in the *Times* of both New York and London, was also supported by various members of the elite intellectual community, including Harnack. The later support of the Kaiser's war policy by the group of academics in the "Declaration of the 93," which compelled Karl Barth's separation from liberalism, also contained the name of Harnack as well as some of the conservative theologians such as Seeberg and Schlatter, not to mention the physicist Max Planck.

29. Lempp, "Present Religious Conditions in Germany," 117.

30. Described in Schweitzer's *Quest of the Historical Jesus: A Critical Study of Its Progress from Reimarus to Wrede*, trans. W. Montgomery (London: A. & C. Black, 1910), 307–9. Frenssen was a pastor who abandoned the church and its ministry and became a novelist. He trained in places like Tübingen and Berlin, but had no real interest in theology. An English account of his work is *Gustav Frenssen, Village Sermons by a Novelist*, trans. with account of the author and his work by T. F. Kinloch (New York: D. Appleton, 1924). The English translation of *Hilligenlei* is *Holy Land*, trans. M. L. Hamilton (Boston: D. Estes, 1906).

aesthetic than religious. Naturalism was outgrown; orthodoxy was gone forever. "Today, therefore," said Lempp, "culture with its immanence and religion with its transcendence must try to come to an understanding. If they do not succeed, modern culture and the Christian church will separate for all time; if they do succeed, there is a possibility of union."[31]

This article aptly brings together many of the issues and themes that pervaded the German setting at that time by one who saw it firsthand. What was dominant and recurring was the meeting of religion and culture and the necessity for accommodation with the "modern" world. This theme actually runs, in one form or another, throughout the whole of western culture, though in most respects what was occurring in Germany was significantly ahead of developments in other countries, and the issue of the relation of Christianity and culture was felt most intensely there. The secularization process was obviously further advanced there than in other citadels of western society.[32]

A few characterizations will briefly extend these observations to other areas.

Kirsopp Lake described the situation in Holland at the turn of the century from his own personal participation in it.[33] Lake characterized a contention in Holland resembling those elsewhere between the modernists or liberals and the "fundamentalists." The liberals controlled the University of Leiden and partly Groningen, while Utrecht was under control of the more conservative aristocrats and of the party politically called "Historical Christian." Conflict was engendered by the ambitions of Abraham Kuijper, who was utterly disliked by the liberals and modernists, and who founded his own private university in Amsterdam called the Free University. Following a power struggle with liberals, Kuijper also became minister of education and was responsible for filling positions in the faculties of the national universities. An important theological position held by a Professor van Malen was vacated through bad health; the faculty proposed the name of Wilhelm Bousset and Kuijper refused, hoping to kill off the modernist movement with the substitution of his own candidate. A struggle ensued, with faculty and Kuijper deadlocked. The result was compromise, with all turning toward England for a candidate. Rendel Harris was selected and accepted but quickly withdrew; the names of F. C. Burkitt, F. C. Conybeare, and R. H. Charles were proposed, but all refused. Lake was then chosen and, to his regret apparently, accepted. He became caught up between factions of competing moderns, he said, much to his surprise and dismay, with the primary issue the question of the historicity of Jesus, a matter disturbing Germany especially, but much of the western

---

31. Lempp, "Present Religious Conditions in Germany," 121–22.

32. Pals, in chap. 5 of *Victorian "Lives" of Jesus,* characterizes the British situation as moving strongly in that same direction in the first decade of the twentieth century, with the consequence that authors of lives of Jesus could no longer presume a ready-made audience for their productions.

33. The essay is a chapter entitled, "Albert Schweitzer's Influence in Holland and England," in a Schweitzer *Festschrift, The Albert Schweitzer Jubilee Book,* ed. A. A. Roback with J. S. Bixler and George Sarton (Cambridge, Mass.: Sci-Art Publishers, 1945; Westport, Conn.: Greenwood Press, 1970), 427–39. Lake was at the time Professor Ordinarius of Early Christian Literature and New Testament Exegesis at Leiden, later returned to England, then to Harvard.

theological world in the first decades of the twentieth century (see chap. 2). Lake related how Schweitzer's work dropped into that setting and influenced the debate through its attachment to the historicity of Mark-plus-Matthew and consequently indirectly sided with those who advocated the historical figure of Jesus as portrayed in the Markan account.

What is of interest at this point is not the particulars of the debate going on, but the witness to the same struggles over modernity and its implications for theological work. There was a universality among the western countries in facing the same cultural issues, much of which stemmed directly from the German setting, but to a degree was also simply the common property of all at the turn of the century.

A similar situation prevailed in Scandinavia, though we shall use Norway as the instance. In the *Journal of Theological Studies* for 1903 appeared an article by J. Beveridge detailing what begins to sound like an all-too-familiar debate.[34] It gave some account of a controversy in Norway going on for some time, Beveridge said; the article's title was taken from a book of the same name by Bishop Heuch of Christiansand in 1902 calling attention to rationalistic tendencies within the Norwegian church.

Heuch was the apostle of orthodoxy, standing for old Lutheran dogmatism. A book by a clergyman, J. H. H. Brochmann of the Cathedral Church of Christiansand, calling for a restatement of the doctrine of the Law and grace, first brought down wrath from Heuch. Thv. Klaveness, a liberal, defended Brochmann, as did Professor Mmydberg of Uppsala, Sweden. The bishop condemned the book as containing pernicious heresy. Klaveness also provoked controversy, asserting that contemporary men did not go to church; they were men of modern culture and the church did not speak to them. They were, said Klaveness, repelled by certain dogmas, such as the Trinity, christology, and the atonement. A great gulf has arisen between church and culture. The church should emphasize the fatherly God who wants his children to come to him, that is, what Jesus preached. Sin, too, ought not to be forgotten, but total depravity could be abandoned as unthinkable for modern men.

This work provoked the bishop to issue his book *Against the Stream*.[35] The controversy aroused a great deal of interest, while Heuch himself was apparently regarded by many as a kind of hero, and was even fêted by the king. He went out after nearly every "liberal" mind he could find, against any and every attempt to make a bridge between modern culture and Christian faith, against anything that was "an echo from extreme German theology" (15). Biblical criticism was an obvious target. Faith only can arise by the power of the Word; we cannot be dependent on the results of scientific study. Said Heuch: "If we are to be the slaves of men, then it would be better to believe the Pope than the theologians. For the Pope is only one, and his teaching is ever the same; but the theologians are as

---

34. J. Beveridge, "'Against the Stream,'" *JTS* 5 (1903): 1–21.
35. Bishop Heuch, *Against the Stream* (Christiania, 1902).

numerous as the flies in summer and so are their scientific results" (17). As for the bishop himself, "I believe because it is absurd," he said, echoing Kierkegaard, and claimed that his opponents were secretly rationalists who were prepared to convert the gospel into mere morality. But, Beveridge reported, while there were some indications that "the waves of rationalism from Germany are lapping the Norwegian strand, not one priest or theological professor in Norway is to-day a complete rationalist" (19). The bishop had won some kind of victory, though no more than temporarily stanching the tides of criticism and "modernism" in the church and university.

Roman Catholic scholarship was a nonparticipant in these developments, indeed, could not have been without breaching various papal directives against modernism.[36] Rome was not prepared to condescend to "modernism," nor would it for some years to come. Historical criticism was an unwelcome visitor in the Roman house, and "lives" of Jesus were simply not possible in any critical sense.

There were, however, a nameable number of Roman Catholic "modernists," such as Alfred Loisy in France, and George Tyrrell and Baron Friederich von Hügel in England. Loisy relinquished the priesthood in 1907 and was finally excommunicated in 1908. Tyrrell was dismissed from the Jesuits in 1906 and died an untimely death from Bright's disease (nephritis) in 1909. Von Hügel retained his relationship with the church even at the price of his hope to reconcile modernism with his traditional faith. He was not, however, ordained, a fact that likely saved him from the Curia.

Loisy had a career in rural parishes and at the Institut Catholique in Paris before coming under an official cloud. He was deprived of his chair in 1893 and went to the Dominican Convent of Neuilly from 1894 to 1899; his book, *The Gospel and the Church*, which was his response to Harnack and ostensibly a defense of the Catholic faith, nevertheless brought him into still further trouble.[37] His refusal to submit to authority worsened his circumstance and led to his excommunication. His position would ultimately become even more radical, with little to be known or said about the historical Jesus.[38] He died in 1940, after an extensive publication career.

Tyrrell, on the other hand, was an Irish priest who had come from the Anglican tradition originally and made a conversion to Catholicism; he contemplated a re-conversion at one point, but never did.[39] Unlike the calmer von Hügel, Tyrrell was passionate and made of the stuff of martyrs. His best-known work,

---

36. The first papal directive was in 1864; *Pascendi* appeared in 1907. A convenient translation of the latter is to be found as an appendix in the reissue of the work by Alfred Loisy, *The Gospel and the Church*, trans. L. P. Jacks with a new introduction by R. Joseph Hoffmann (Buffalo, N.Y.: Prometheus Books, 1988). The original French version was 1902.

37. Loisy, *The Gospel and the Church*, 25 n. 31.

38. See chap. 5.

39. His friend von Hügel said that he would rather see Tyrrell become an atheist than an Anglican (in Maude Petre, *Von Hügel and Tyrrell: The Story of a Friendship* [New York: E. P. Dutton, 1927] 173). See also von Hügel's memorial to Tyrrell in "Father Tyrrell: Some Memorials of the Last Twelve Years of His Life," *HibJ* 8 (1909–10): 233–52.

Christianity at the Crossroads, was published posthumously.[40] It shows positive influence from his reading of Schweitzer's work, which he saw as supportive of
Catholic supernaturalism; with that he coupled a critique of Harnack, embodied in the oft-quoted statement, "The Christ that Harnack sees, looking back
through nineteen centuries of Catholic darkness, is only the reflection of a liberal
Protestant face, seen at the bottom of a deep well" (49).

The works of both Loisy and Tyrrell were chronicled by Maude Petre, a common link with them and von Hügel, and lifelong friend of all. She was herself
a committed modernist and, though required to assent to the Encyclical *Pascendi* of Pius X, refused to do so, for which she paid the penalty of a "local"
excommunication, not able to receive communion in her own diocese and deprived of graveside rites at her death. Having early in life joined an order, the
sisterhood of "The Daughters of Mary," she was heavily involved in promoting
the causes of the poor and orphanages, until she came into contact with Tyrrell
in 1900 and he became her cause, so to speak. She composed works on both
Tyrrell and Loisy, though both themselves also left their autobiographies.[41] Petre
herself probably best summed up the three persons who greatly occupied her life:
"von Hügel was cautious, and he was also correct. Loisy was, on the whole, correct, but he was only cautious in detail, not in his general policy; and Tyrrell, of
course, was neither cautious nor correct."[42]

Her disaffection with the church led to relinquishing her leadership of the
sisterhood to which she had fallen heir. To critics of her seeming unorthodoxy,
she replied, "I could never do less for man in order to think more of God."[43]
All four of these figures were strikingly powerful persons who were caught in the
struggle between the forces of the new world and the resistance of an institution
that did not know how to yield.

A different path was taken by M.-J. Lagrange, the founder of the École
Biblique and its organ the *Revue biblique.* Lagrange was a superior scholar and
fully conversant with the directions taken in liberal Protestantism and historical methodology generally. Yet he was clearly constrained by the dogmas of his
church and in particular the papal directives and opinions of the Pontifical Biblical Commission (PBC). It would have been difficult in any case to deviate very

40. George Tyrrell, *Christianity at the Crossroads* (London: Longmans Green, 1909), introduction
by Maude Petre, reissued in 1963 by George Allen and Unwin (London), with a foreword by A. R.
Vidler.
41. Maude Petre, *Alfred Loisy: His Religious Significance* (Cambridge: University Press, 1944); and
Autobiography and Life of George Tyrrell (London: E. Arnold, 1912); *Von Hügel and Tyrrell.* Her own
story was told in her *My Way of Faith* (London: Dent, 1937), while she also gave an account of
modernism in *Modernism, Its Failure and Its Fruits* (London: T. C. and A. C. Jack, 1918). Loisy's
own accounts are his *Memoires pour servir à l'histoire de notre temps* (Paris: Emile Nourry, 1930–31),
3 vols.; and also *My Duel with the Vatican: The Autobiography of a Catholic Modernist,* trans. Richard
Wilson Boynton (New York: E. P. Dutton, 1924). Petre's review of the autobiography is in *HibJ* 29
(1930–31): 655–66. An Anglican sympathizer was A. Leslie Lilley, *Modernism: A Record and Review*
(London: Pitman and Sons, 1908).
42. Petre, *Alfred Loisy,* 31.
43. From the biographical notes on Maude Petre by James A. Walker in *Alfred Loisy,* x.

far from the official statements of the PBC that were regularly published in the *Revue biblique*. But Lagrange managed to maintain his position as an obedient son of the church while also cultivating a serious level of scholarship.[44] Not until 1942 and the issuance of *Divino afflante Spiritu* by Pius XII — in part a monument to Lagrange's influence — was there a greater freedom that would truly open up the field of critical biblical study for Roman Catholic scholars.

A little-known event that also encapsulated the spirit of the times was the Fifth World Congress of Free Christians and Other Religious Liberals held at Berlin in August of 1910. Under the sponsorship of the American Unitarians, the Congress brought together people from all the world's religions and fostered a dialogue across confessional divisions. An account of the meeting was given by the executive secretary, Charles W. Wendte, who also headed the American delegation of some 200 persons and spoke in fluent German and French to various of the meetings. The names of participants reads like a "who's who" of theological and biblical studies: Rade, Harnack, Bousset,[45] Troeltsch, Weinel, Gunkel, von Soden, Wendt, among Germans; Bacon, Peabody, Rauschenbusch, among Americans; J. Estlin Carpenter and C. G. Montefiore from England; A. Sabatier (French Ritschlian) and Etienne Giran among others. Large numbers of persons registered as delegates and still more of a lively Berlin public attended. Harnack, for example, spoke to over a thousand people on a Saturday morning at 8:30; his subject was "The Double Gospel in the New Testament."[46] No subject seemed beyond bounds; all world religions, large and small, were allowed in. Women, too, held a session on their position and their hopes.[47] The least attractive meeting was on temperance; not even the discourse of Rauschenbusch in fluent German could redeem it from a scanty crowd. It was a subject that stretched even German liberalism too far.

Just as impressive in Wendte's account of the meeting were the affairs surrounding it, with gracious hosting from the Germans as the foreign delegates traveled up and down the land. The whole event was suffused with a sense of genuine neighborliness, of a Christmas-like peace on earth among persons of good will. Only two discordant notes were sounded in Wendte's report: one, that the subject of relations between Jews and Christians was such a "ticklish" one in Germany that outside speakers had to be recruited, among them the distinguished Jewish scholar C. G. Montefiore from England; the other, that a

---

44. See Richard Murphy, ed., *Lagrange and Biblical Renewal*, Aquinas Institute Studies No. 1 (Chicago: Priory Press, 1966); also Jerome Murphy-O'Connor, *The École Biblique and the New Testament: A Century of Scholarship (1890–1990)* (Göttingen: Vandenhoeck and Ruprecht, 1990). See chap. 8 for more on Lagrange and Catholic lives of Jesus.

45. The Bousset essay is reproduced below, chap. 2, 64–65.

46. This and all the proceedings were published as *Fifth International Congress of Free Christianity and Religious Progress,* ed. Charles Wendte (London: Williams and Norgate, 1911). Harnack's essay is on 99–107. Many of the essays were subsequently published as separate pamphlets, including Harnack's and Bousset's.

47. Among them the spouse of Heinrich Weinel, who herself held a Ph.D. in religion, and a number of other women speakers, mostly of the Unitarian-Universalist persuasion.

discussion between liberals and orthodox brought forth a man "grim of visage and harsh in voice and manner" from the orthodox side who seemed to share little of the liberal spirit.[48] Emphasizing theological differences was not in the program. Nevertheless, the overwhelming sense taken from this Congress was that the western world was mending its differences, that a new world order lay close at hand, a time when old ruptures would heal and lions would lie down with lambs.

American optimism, as we noted at the outset, was pervasive; the leaders of business and industry and government were tirelessly — and often boringly — raising the cup to the grand gods of commerce and profit. Said Sen. Albert J. Beveridge of Indiana:

> God has marked the American people as His chosen nation to finally lead in the regeneration of the world. This is the divine mission of America, and it holds for us all the profit, all the glory, all the happiness possible to man. We are trustees of the world's progress, guardians of its righteous peace.[49]

It was a time for making fortunes, often of obscene display of the same. One of the gaudier places was Newport, Rhode Island, part-time social home of the exceedingly rich. Among the mansions — referred to vacuously as "cottages" — was one belonging to Cornelius Vanderbilt; called the Breakers, it contained seventy rooms and a seemingly endless amount of ornamentation and material goods. Over the library mantelpiece was the slogan, "Little do I care for riches." The extremely wealthy must have had a sense of self-parody.

Women, too, were looking for change and a new day. The suffrage movement was being widely pressed, even by women still bound in corsets and bonnets and to home and hearth, though not for some years would the movement crystallize into legislation (Norway, 1913; Germany, 1919; United States, 1920; England, 1928). Margaret Sanger was bravely raising the issue of contraception and suffering persecution for it at the hands of the moral inquisition led by Anthony Comstock and his New York Society for the Suppression of Vice. But the typewriter and other such things also encouraged the movement of women from the traditional home role into the business environment (though still not as executives). And even the homemaker was experiencing relief from daily choring, with helpful gadgets from Sears-Roebuck. The most public American woman had to be Alice Roosevelt, daughter of Teddy (himself a bully president for a bully period); Alice's free-spiritedness — she even smoked in public! — suggested possibilities open to the more liberated woman. Teddy was supposed to have said indulgently, if in the sexist manner of his time, "I can do one of two things. I

---

48. From Wendte's account in his "Summary and Appreciation" of the Congress published separately by the American Unitarian Association (Boston, 1910). It was a reprint from the *Christian Register*.

49. This and other factual matters from *This Fabulous Century*, 1:30.

can be President of the United States, or I can control Alice. I cannot possibly do both."[50]

Even sport reflected the times. Baseball was the most widely attended sport; the first World Series was played in 1903. But football was growing; its nature seemed to coincide with the energetic optimism of the time, so much so that it would be better to characterize it as ferociously competitive. In 1905 nineteen players in high school and college were killed by the harshness of play, forcing educators to set more stringent rules.

If there was a symbol typifying the spirit of the age until at least the First World War, it would have been the *Titanic*. This gigantic ship, proclaimed as invincible, met its fate in the icy north Atlantic running against an unseen iceberg while its passengers, so assured of their safety by the highest levels of technology, had no notion of their impending doom. The story is widely known and often told, more recently through the discovery of the ship's final resting place and also in the form of a highly popular film likely to find a permanent place in epic film-making. It is a story that stands in a sense for the whole period with its blustering confidence in the works of humankind and sense of superiority over the powers of the natural world. Unbridled arrogance contempted by the gods: Aeschylus could not have done it better.

The general American optimism had its counterpart in the social gospel movement at the close of the nineteenth century and the opening of the twentieth. This story is too well known to bear any repeating here; major figures were Shailer Mathews at Chicago, Francis Peabody at Harvard, and, of course, Walter Rauschenbusch at Rochester. Its creed was embodied in the 1908 statement of the Federal Council of the Churches of Christ in America, largely defending the rights of the working poor, demanding such things as abolition of child labor, better wages and conditions for workers, and one day off a week — issues that spotlighted a darker underside to the dominating capitalistic system. Rauschenbusch's classic statement of the social gospel's theology, *A Theology for the Social Gospel*, was issued in 1917, as Americans were entering the Great War and just two years before Karl Barth's *Römerbrief*.[51] Its repetition of liberal theological themes of suspiciously Teutonic origin foredoomed it to failure at the time and its author to a sad condemnation that doubtless contributed to an early death in 1918.

And yet not everyone in American biblical scholarship had come to terms with historical-critical method. A model instance would be that of George Holley Gilbert, Professor of New Testament Literature and Interpretation at the

---

50. *This Fabulous Century*, 1:180. The matter of fathers "controlling" their daughters was already under some serious questioning. Something at the popular level of cultural clash can be seen in a tiny article in the *New York Times* of January 6, 1900, 1, reporting that a Dutch Reformed pastor, Rev. William Burton of Kingston, New York, chastised his congregation for men smoking and women wearing corsets. No man, he said, should marry "a woman who laced." In retaliation his house was burned, but he continued to preach anyway, to nearly empty benches.

51. Walter Rauschenbusch, *A Theology for the Social Gospel* (New York: Macmillan, 1917).

Chicago Theological Seminary. Gilbert had written a life of Jesus in 1896 that
strongly resembled its English counterparts in the latter part of the nineteenth
century, with a mix of scholarship and a significant degree of pietistic oratory.
By 1912 he had issued a work with quite a different sound.[52] To read the later
one after the first is like crossing some kind of divide. In the former Gilbert was
undecided about the synoptic problem, still supporting a view of the mutual independence of the three gospels, each having written sources. Variations were
due to different eyewitnesses in the life of Jesus. The historical reliability of the
gospels was verified over the centuries by Christian experience and, though the
gospels did not agree in all details, they did so in the main. The fourth gospel was
also a trustworthy source. The fact that it differed from the others actually tes-
tified to its independent reliability; it had to come from someone with authority
to differ. Its picture was basically in harmony with that of the synoptics.

Jesus' message was of the kingdom of heaven, the divine rule in the hearts
of men. It has a future element, the end of the age, heaven as the abode of the
blessed. The present element is preeminently ethical and spiritual. It is not political; Jesus the king witnessed to the rule of truth. Repentance is the introduction
to life in the kingdom, while ethics and prayer are the life of the kingdom. Jesus
was conscious of his union with God and of being the messiah of Israel. Son of
man was his own peculiar self-designation, a title for messiah. His speech about
the coming of the Son of man in judgment and power was realized in the triumph of the gospel at Pentecost and the success of the Christian movement.
And so on and on.

In the 1912 version Gilbert acknowledged his conversion from a simplistic
view of the sources of the life of Jesus to the newer one, from accepting that
they were supplementary accounts to their being of less than historical value.
He predicted that the newer view would lead to an unsettling of faith as some
"attempt to support the tottering heritage of devout but unscientific ages."[53] He
acknowledged the influence of Ernest DeWitt Burton of the University of Chicago, virtually tantamount to acknowledging German influence, for Chicago was
quite sensitive to German developments.

Gilbert presumed the Markan hypothesis, with some insightful remarks on
the nature of the presentations by the various evangelists and the Logia source.
Some of the material peculiar to Matthew and Luke did not pass Gilbert's sense
of authenticity. Analysis of John led to the conclusion that it was "not history
and not biography, but a profound philosophical meditation in which the facts
of the life of Jesus are treated with sovereign freedom" (71). Other sources did
not deserve consideration. The historical times were described, fairly detailed
and competently.

---

52. The original work was George Holley Gilbert, *The Student's Life of Jesus* (New York: Macmillan, 1896; 3d ed., 1902). The book continued over a lengthy period of years to be revised and
reissued. Also appearing in the same vein was *The Revelation of Jesus* (New York: Macmillan, 1899).
The later one was *Jesus* (New York: Macmillan, 1912).

53. Gilbert, *Jesus*, ix.

Gilbert began with the Logia source and obviously considered it the oldest and best. He went on to Mark, looking for data about Jesus' origin and early life. Not much was found. Jesus was from Nazareth, a carpenter, he had brothers and sisters, but there was not much basis for expecting him to appear as a teacher. He went public with the appearance of John the Baptist. Baptism was his calling as a prophet, followed further along as the messiah to bring the kingdom. The wilderness experience had a basis in history; it denoted his communion with God. The temptation was authentic and showed Jesus' rejection of popular ideas of messiahship and instead his acceptance of prophetic messiahship.

What did Jesus think of himself? The Logia source suggests that he saw himself as the revealer of God and giver of the knowledge of God (Matt. 11:27 par.). He thought of himself as a prophet, but differently in that he possessed *complete* knowledge of God. Elsewhere he was seen as a teacher, even Son of man, but Gilbert saw this as equivalent to messiah of the end with no special significance.

The kingdom had various emphases. Sometimes it was the rule of God in man's heart, sometimes Jesus spoke of it as present especially in his own self, as the new age when the kingdom was made known uniquely through himself. Gilbert found these views in the Logia source; in the common tradition of the synoptists — the triple tradition — some similar things appeared, such as imitating Jesus, the ministering of the Son of man, the admission of children, the requirement of service. The material peculiar to Matthew and Luke was examined with similar result. Gilbert seemed especially fond of Luke 17:20–21, the idea of the kingdom "within." The kingdom had nothing to do with the prevailing notion of an external, political entity. Gilbert judged the future-coming Son of Man sayings to be not prominent or of special importance to Jesus, and to mention only a judgment in general. The real content of Jesus' teaching was the fatherhood of God. "We may say that Jesus' ideal for his people flowered out of the fatherhood of God, as that had been apprehended by him in his own spiritual life" (167).

Gilbert attempted to construct a chronology of Jesus' career. He largely followed the Markan tradition; Jesus preached his message, anticipated his death, and was condemned in Jerusalem for being a blasphemer. Death ended the story.

A separate part took up the legendizing of Jesus. The birth and infancy stories appeared here, as did certain elements of the ministry, such as calming the storm and walking the sea. Some healings were allowed, occurring through the influence of the mind. Legendary material increased with time, though the Logia source was relatively free of it. What about the resurrection? From his examination of various sayings Gilbert concluded that Jesus said nothing about a bodily resurrection. The rising after three days referred to the triumph of his cause. The tomb stories contained many contradictions and differences, and had no particular value, but certainly we can say that some people, such as Paul, had visions of Christ. It was a spiritual vision; a physical resurrection was not to be entertained.

There is little startling about Gilbert's work; for the most part the second book marks the author's initiation into the movement of liberal lives of Jesus and thereby also his commitment to a more seriously critical method. But this modest contribution to American work on the historical Jesus gains significance by marking a passage of sorts — from critical-edifying to purely critical. It is as though in the space of a dozen years the author had moved into a new time; with him there seemed to pass also an old era.

So when the new century was formally welcomed on January 1, 1901 (at least in England and America), it was in effect already well launched; a new world was coming into being, a time of unrestricted progress, of daunting new technologies, powers, and opportunities. Perhaps God was in his heaven after all. Or perhaps not. It must have seemed, in any case, marvelously exciting to be alive in the western world at the turning of the century.

This sense of hopefulness is maintained still in the reportage of the new century, though not quite as robustly as in the celebrations already described. Nevertheless, the *Times* of London quoted extensively from the sermon of the Archbishop of Canterbury, who offered the judgment that the opportunity was never greater to evangelize the world and to seek a reconciliation between science and the revealed Word. The *Times* opined its hope that the empire would prosper, noting again the necessity to strengthen the army, while the navy was already sufficient for the needs of the empire. The Boer War continued to occupy the news columns; it would not be resolved until 1902, and its presence still furnished a dampening influence on the general circumstances accompanying the appearance of a new century.[54]

The *New York Times* reported celebrations similar to those of the previous year, only gaudier: a literally "electric" moment with lights flashing, bombs thundering, rockets ascending, the Sousa band playing. The president of the city council spoke on the steps of City Hall — the mayor perversely declining to attend — and noted that the achievements of science and civilization were "not less than marvelous," while a chorus of peculiarly eclectic musical taste managed to perform both "America" and "The Hallelujah Chorus." As before, sermons in leading churches were quoted, the Rev. Dr. R. S. MacArthur of the Calvary Baptist Church observing that the combination of science and religion would make the twentieth century "voiceful with praise and radiant with the glory of God." The *Times* expressed its editorial judgment that the nineteenth century was a "century of marvels" and celebrated the enlargement of democratic freedom everywhere (although noticing with some regret that the Philippine insurrection was not yet over).[55] Missing from the accounts of both *Times* was any notice of observances in other countries. Unmistakably present was the same expectation of great things still to come.

---

54. *Times* of London, January 1, 1900, 4. Others quoted included the Canons of St. Paul's Cathedral and Westminster Abbey, the former giving thanks for moral as well as material progress, while the latter had the temerity to complain of problems of poverty and forces hostile to religion, and the like. The *Times*' editorializing is on p. 11.

55. *New York Times*, January 1, 1901, 1–2. The *Times*' editorial comments are on p. 8.

But not everyone agreed.

There was in Strassburg a young man, 25 years of age, who was living at St. Thomas College in a room overlooking a tranquil garden, working on the dissertation for his licentiate in theology, and thinking dissident thoughts.[56] Some time later he would recall that he had attended a social gathering in Berlin in 1899 when a chance remark in the noisy talk caught his attention, someone observing that the current generation was but a group of epigoni, mere imitators of their predecessors. The thought quite agreed with what had been going through the mind of the young man, but which he had lightly mentioned among his acquaintances. He was convinced that his civilization, that civilization of European origin over which so many hallelujahs were being sung, was declining, that his own time was an unworthy one. The ground of his thought was that his *Kultur* lacked a *Weltanschauung*, a philosophical underpinning that would give everything depth and meaning and worthfulness. Such thoughts were heresy at the time, and the young man would not fully unfold them until some years later in his life.

The young man with unpopular thoughts was Albert Schweitzer; the subject of his theological dissertation was the Lord's Supper, to which he appended also a sketch of the life of Jesus as an entrée to grasping what the Supper was about originally. The sketch appeared in 1901 and began, concurrently with the new century, a new era in biblical studies of the life of Jesus.

---

56. I follow the German spelling of Strassburg here, otherwise when Alsace was under French control.

Chapter 1

ALBERT SCHWEITZER

Albert Schweitzer. *Aus meinem Leben und Denken*. Hamburg: R. Meiner Verlag, 1931. English trans., *Out of My Life and Thought: An Autobiography*, trans. C. T. Campion. New York: Henry Holt, 1933.

———. *Das Messianitäts- und Leidensgeheimnis: Ein Skizze des Lebens Jesu*. Tübingen: J. C. B. Mohr, 1901. English trans., *The Mystery of the Kingdom of God: The Secret of Jesus' Messiahship and Passion*, trans. with introduction by Walter Lowrie. New York: Dodd, Mead, 1914.

———. *Die psychiatrische Beurteilung Jesu*. Tübingen: J. C. B. Mohr, 1913. English trans., *The Psychiatric Study of Jesus*, trans. with introduction by Charles R. Joy. Boston: Beacon Press, 1948.

———. *Geschichte der Leben-Jesu-Forschung*. Tübingen: J. C. B. Mohr (Paul Siebeck), 1913. 2d ed. of *Von Reimarus zu Wrede*, significantly expanded and retitled in the fashion to which Schweitzer subsequently preferred to refer to it. This edition has never been translated into English as such, though Walter Lowrie included extensive quotations from the new parts of the conclusion in his introduction to *The Mystery of the Kingdom of God*, and later Henry Clark provided a complete translation of the new portions of the conclusion in his work, *The Ethical Mysticism of Albert Schweitzer* (Boston: Beacon Press, 1962), appendix 2, 195–205. The sixth edition of 1951 contained a new preface that was translated into English and included in the third English edition of the *Quest*.

———. *Von Reimarus zu Wrede: Eine Geschichte der Leben Jesu Forschung*. Tübingen: J. C. B. Mohr, 1906. English trans., *The Quest of the Historical Jesus: A Critical Study of Its Progress from Reimarus to Wrede*, trans. W. Montgomery. London: Adam and Charles Black, 1910. Since reprinted many times, with the English version from Macmillan Press (1968) containing a new introduction by James M. Robinson. Johns Hopkins University Press has announced a new paperback reissue of the English translation.

Few persons have so impressed the power of their life on their times as Albert Schweitzer. To inquire into his life is like entering into a spiraling tunnel, so many are the personalities deeply resident there, and all dwelling comfortably with one another. Theologian, philosopher, musician, medical doctor, missionary: such were the many vocations to which he responded, and he performed them all, usually simultaneously, with seeming ease. To pronounce the name of Schweitzer is virtually to invoke a saint, a thought that Schweitzer himself might have found odd, but which many people in the twentieth century would think appropriate.[1] Whether they would continue to do so if they were fully conversant with the character of his authentic thought is yet another question.

Born on January 14, 1875, at Kayserberg in Upper Alsace, the second of five children, Schweitzer was the son and grandson (his mother's father) of a pastor. In 1916 his mother was killed by cavalry horses[2] on the road between Günsbach, where the Schweitzers lived, and Weierim-Tal, and his father died of natural causes in 1925. Schweitzer's studies took him through the gymnasium, where, he later said, he was not an especially good student, and then on to the university at Strassburg. Along the way there were opportunities to pursue his work in music at the organ, beginning at the age of 5; by the age of 9 he played at the church service for the first time. At Strassburg he took up the study of philosophy and theology together and there also first encountered the leading New Testament scholar of that time, H. J. Holtzmann, whose work the young Schweitzer would soon find fault with, though keeping his youthful opinions at first to himself. There is not a little irony in the dedication of his first major work of New Testament scholarship, the *Skizze des Lebens Jesu,* to Holtzmann, as this work signified an end of the approaches to the life of Jesus represented at that time by Holtzmann.

Nevertheless, Schweitzer reported a great appreciation for Holtzmann, who on his part evidently saw something in the young man who had become his student. At the same time Schweitzer began his own independent inquiry into the life of Jesus, stimulated first by reading Holtzmann's commentary on Mark. He found in Mark certain deficiencies in the account of Jesus' activity which seemed to him remedied only by noticing what was reported in Matthew 10–11, especially the story of the mission-journey of the disciples. At the time of this discovery Schweitzer was serving his required one year of military training, and had formed the habit of carrying his Greek New Testament with him in his haversack. It was while on maneuvers that he came upon the stimulating section in Matthew's chapter 10 that provided for him the clue to the understanding of the historical Jesus. He was at the time 19 years old.[3]

So a very young, obviously precocious Schweitzer, while in the field for military maneuvers, came upon the secret of the historical Jesus, all in opposition to his revered teacher. Few stranger places have served as a locus of revelatory

---

1. In the First United Methodist Church in Lakeland, Florida, there are — typically — stained-glass windows with scenes portraying biblical characters and saints old and new. Among the new is one of Albert Schweitzer. I do not know how Schweitzer would evaluate his enshrinement in glass in a church in Florida, but I would guess that he might find in it a strangeness comparable to an encounter with the historical Jesus.

2. Schweitzer gives no more than the merest statement of this tragedy in his autobiography, but what happened was that a soldier's horse, out of control, came galloping suddenly around a bend in the road where Frau Schweitzer was walking, and she was unable to get out of the way. The horse knocked her down, she struck the back of her head and was fatally wounded. A fuller account is taken from Louis Schweitzer's diary and recounted in James Brabazon, *Albert Schweitzer: A Biography* (New York: G. P. Putnam's Sons, 1975), 266.

3. The data used here are taken from Schweitzer's *Out of My Life and Thought: An Autobiography,* trans. C. T. Campion (New York: Henry Holt, 1933), chap. 1, 13–23 (hereafter *Life and Thought*).

events. He went on to stand for the first theological examination at Strassburg, writing on the Lord's Supper in Schleiermacher, the New Testament, and the Reformers. Out of that inquiry came the stimulus that led to his first book, to which was attached also the *Skizze,* his initial public foray into the problem of the historical Jesus. It was published in 1901; Schweitzer was 26 years old. His intention was to provide a fuller "life" of Jesus at a subsequent point, but what materialized was instead the major work on *Leben-Jesu-Forschung* in 1906. Schweitzer found himself captivated by the problems of the life of Jesus and set about trying to understand them by investigating their history. He composed this work from the abundant collection of books in the Strassburg library; he brought them all home and piled them up in stacks by chapter in his living room. All who came to visit, including the cleaning lady, had to weave their way through the piles, for no one was allowed to disturb them until the writing was finished.[4] At the end of this work Schweitzer reiterated his constructive view of Jesus' ministry to be found in the earlier *Skizze* and elaborated it somewhat more fully.

Schweitzer's Jesus

What was it that Schweitzer discovered on a rest day from his military activity in the village of Guggenheim? The idea presented itself that Jesus in his journey-discourse to his disciples was not expecting some natural kingdom in this world, as Holtzmann and others seemed to think, according to the ethicizing interpretations of liberalism, but rather a supernatural kingdom bringing with it the endtime. The text seemed further to indicate that Jesus himself had not hitherto been thought of as the messiah, but rather as the forerunner, a role that Jesus himself seemed to ascribe to John the Baptist. Jesus only spoke of a future appearance of the Son of man. These ideas would in time coalesce into a full-blown — or, as Schweitzer would doubtless prefer — *konsequente* (thoroughgoing) eschatological interpretation of the career of Jesus.[5]

Schweitzer was fully aware that a "life" of Jesus cannot be constructed from the sources available for knowledge of Jesus. Only something of the last months of his career can be known, and a picture of that brief compass can be retrieved only from Mark with the help of Matthew. John was clearly not to be considered at all, and since Luke largely reproduces the material in Mark and Matthew, it, too, may be overlooked. Schweitzer's comment on Luke was: "Wherever it

---

4. Reported in his *Life and Thought,* 58. The abundance of "lives" of Jesus in the Strassburg library, so Schweitzer reported when he offered the work for publication to J. C. B. Mohr, was due to the fact that publishers had supplied many volumes after 1870 when the Strassburg library burned. See Hans Walter Bähr, ed., *Albert Schweitzer: Letters 1905–1965,* trans. Joachim Neugroschel (New York: Macmillan, 1992), 6.

5. In the following characterization of Schweitzer's picture of the historical Jesus I use *Mystery of the Kingdom of God,* as well as *Quest of the Historical Jesus,* with appropriate supplementation from *Geschichte der Leben-Jesu-Forschung.* There is also a handy summary of his views contained, unexpectedly, in *The Psychiatric Study of Jesus,* trans. with introduction by Charles R. Joy (Boston: Beacon Press, 1948).

goes beyond them [i.e., Mark and Matthew] it makes us a doubtful contribution, which moreover is without any great significance for the criticism of Jesus and so can be left out of consideration" (*Psychiatric Study*, 46). Basically, then, Schweitzer was using Mark with contributions from Matthew. His suspicions about the reliability of Mark alone had much to do with the preference given that gospel in the liberal school of the day, a preference owing in the first place to its chronological priority as the first source behind the synoptic tradition.

It is also apparent that Schweitzer's presentation of the historical Jesus was formed in continual debate with the prevailing pictures of Jesus provided by the predominant liberalism of the time. His method, like that of Strauss before him, was confrontational (if not Hegelian), and calculated to destroy what seemed to him highly erroneous and nonhistorical. That liberal view rested on four assumptions:

1. The life of Jesus falls into two contrasting epochs, an earlier, successful period of activity, followed by a retreat to the north, and a second, later journey to Jerusalem characterized by hostility and eventually death;

2. The passion story has been influenced by Pauline atonement theories;

3. The kingdom of God is conceived as an ethical society of service to humanity, a theme that dominates the passion narrative; and

4. The success of the passion depended on the disciples understanding the kingdom in this sense and acting on it; the passion-idea then must have communicated this ethical element.[6]

These are all taken apart one at a time and replaced with the eschatological interpretation.

Schweitzer rejected the notion, prevalent at the time, of two contrasting periods in Jesus' career: first a happy time of success in Galilee, broken by increasing opposition to him, causing a "flight" to the north (Mark 7:24ff.), then the decisive journey to Jerusalem with its hostility from the authorities, eventuating in Jesus' death. The moral kingdom of Jesus' proclamation came up against implacable opposition. Schweitzer agreed that there were two periods in Jesus' career, but no one can grasp them without supplementing Mark with Matthew. There never was anything resembling a "development" in Jesus' ideas, however, and no amount of attempted psychologizing about the "evolution" of his thought, as in liberalism, can grasp the key to his activity. In Schweitzer's view the evidence suggested that the Galilean period was mixed, success and opposition, but that Jesus in any case held steadfastly from the start to the finish to the expectation of the eschatological kingdom. At his baptism he knew himself to be the messiah of the eschatological kingdom, but only revealed his messiahship to the disciples at Caesarea-Philippi, after disclosing it initially to the inner circle of three at the Transfiguration. His proclamation included the ethical demand for repentance,

---

6. Schweitzer's summary, from *Mystery of the Kingdom of God*, 63–64.

the moral renewal that according to general expectation would help bring about the kingdom. In that sense Jesus' ethic goes with his eschatology. In that sense also the ethical demand as embodied in the Sermon on the Mount, for example, constituted an interim ethic, a demand seeming to be appropriate only as preparation for the soon-to-arrive eschatological kingdom.

Jesus sent his disciples out on a mission to proclaim this eschatological kingdom, apparently expecting it to occur before their return (Matt. 10:23). He spoke of the Son of man's appearance at the coming of the kingdom, by which he meant to refer to his own installation as messiah publicly in the eschatological kingdom. The disciples returned, reporting success, but still the kingdom failed to appear. The success was a sign that the apocalyptic expectation was basically correct, only something more was needed. This something more was the subject of Jesus' deliberation at his "flight" north; upon his return he determined that an atonement was necessary, an act of repentance on behalf of all the people. This constituted the second period in his activity, the decision to go to Jerusalem to force the issue of the kingdom, so to speak, by offering his own life as an atonement for all the people. The apocalyptic expectation required that there be a period of "messianic tribulation," or woes just before the End. Jesus decided that he must take upon himself the suffering associated with the period of tribulation as an act of atonement, a "ransom for many," as Mark put it (Mark 10:45). Consequently, those who see a Pauline influence in the sacrificial statements have misunderstood; these come from Jesus himself and disclose his apocalyptic understanding of his mission.

Schweitzer's handling of the suffering Son of man sayings runs in the same direction. The suffering of the Son of man is the necessity of his mission, laid upon him by the divinely ordained course of apocalyptic events. Schweitzer interpreted the saying, "The Son of man must suffer and will then rise from the dead," to mean "As the one who is to be Son of man at the resurrection of the dead I must suffer" (*Mystery*, 193). Here Schweitzer engaged in a little sleight of hand himself, forcing the verse to refer to the general resurrection of the dead rather than Jesus' own forthcoming resurrection. He also designated as "unhistorical" all Son of man passages where Jesus alluded to himself as such prior to Caesarea-Philippi (or the Transfiguration, in the case of the three), except where he spoke of the Son of man as coming in the future. Jesus is now the messiah (=Son of man), but will be disclosed as such only at the coming of the eschatological kingdom. That is his "secret."

With this line of interpretation Schweitzer tore apart the liberal consensus: there never was a Jesus who cavorted around Galilee happily winning converts with his message about an ethical kingdom of human service; the service of which he spoke was the necessary repentance providing moral renewal as preparation for the supernatural kingdom. There never was opposition that drove Jesus to consider the eschatological idea; the latter was present from the beginning and determined everything. Not Paul but Jesus first came to think of his deed as sacrificial, as atonement for all people, as filling the expectation of messianic tribulation just before the End. The same applies to the passion of Jesus; it has nothing to do with inauguration of the new ethical kingdom, but rather is itself the last deed that was to bring forth the eschatological kingdom.

The last days in Jerusalem marked Jesus' course as a way of failure. He entered the city according to his own plan of messianic action, though the crowd only took him for Elijah, the forerunner. The entry for Jesus was messianic, but not for the people. Jesus then plotted how he might provoke the authorities to put him to death, attacking the temple and the Pharisees. The expected kingdom did not appear, though Jesus held a final meal in anticipation of it, even as he had earlier in Galilee fed the crowds symbolically such a meal. The secret of the messiahship came out through Judas' betrayal and led to Jesus' capture and condemnation. Jesus was condemned before the Sanhedrin as a blasphemer and Pilate was induced to have him executed. The "fickle" crowd was persuaded by the priests who went among them with their accusations of blasphemy. Schweitzer's story then seems to conclude almost abruptly:

> At midday of the same day — it was the 14th Nisan, and in the evening the Paschal lamb would be eaten — Jesus cried aloud and expired. He had chosen to remain fully conscious to the last. (*Quest*, 395)

The second edition of 1913 ends slightly more modestly:

> Around midday of the same day Jesus cried out and expired. He had refused the offer of a narcotic (Mark 15:23) in order to maintain clear consciousness to the end. (*Geschichte*, 443)

Either way, Schweitzer knew the mind of Jesus, even at the point of death. It is all the more surprising how little attention he devoted to explanation of the trial and the reasons for the condemnation of Jesus. How facilely he accepted the Markan claim of "blasphemy," with hardly a protest. Is it so obvious that someone claiming to be messiah would be convicted of blasphemy? Evidently to Schweitzer the idea that Jesus deliberately forced his own death overpowered and perhaps even muted too many other questions. All the other players in the drama have merely bit roles, consigned to virtual silence.

Not so surprising, but equally instructive, is Schweitzer's own silence with regard to the empty tomb stories, not to mention "resurrection." He likely would have agreed that these do not belong to the domain of the historian,[7] but it is also true that for Schweitzer the Easter tradition had no special significance. He remarked in the preface to the *Skizze* that the Christian faith stands by the question of Jesus' messianic consciousness. If Jesus did not hold himself to be the messiah, then "this means the death blow to the Christian faith." That is to say, if faith in Jesus as messiah only comes from the early church, then Christian faith has lost its ground, for "the judgment of the early Church is not binding upon us" (*Mystery*, 5–6). Presumably only what Jesus said would be binding. That would seem at best to downplay the resurrection-faith of the early church.

---

7. Discussion in Brabazon, *Albert Schweitzer*, 131.

The Immediate Response to Schweitzer

That Schweitzer's work inspired great controversy is well known. That eventually his work, modified in various ways, came to dominate the twentieth-century view of the historical Jesus is also self-evident. It is less well known that the immediate impact of his work was something short of revolutionary.

When the *Skizze* appeared in 1901, it actually gained only modest attention. A review by Georg Hollmann in *Theologische Literaturzeitung* basically approved of Schweitzer's emphasis on the eschatological interpretation of Jesus, but withheld final judgment pending appearance of the promised full "life" of Jesus.[8] There were, of course, points of contention (Hollmann saw no connection between Jesus' preaching of repentance and his conviction of his death as instrumental in bringing about the kingdom), but generally the review seemed not to regard Schweitzer's work as scandalous or somehow out of bounds.

Heinrich Weinel was more blunt.[9] The work was false in just about every respect, wrongly interpreting its texts (betrayal of Judas, feeding by the sea), and showed almost total lack of source criticism. Its views were superficial and signified a "squeezing of Jesus into the paragraphs of Weber's Jewish theology" (244). Weinel thought, nevertheless, that the author was gifted with rational power, only more so on the side of systematizing logic than of historical comprehension. Noting that Schweitzer had dedicated his book to Holtzmann, Weinel hoped that the student might yet learn something of the prudence and profundity of his revered teacher.

In the introduction to his translation of the *Skizze* (*Mystery*), Walter Lowrie referred to the "scant attention" paid to Schweitzer's work in Germany, as well as the "passive hostility" it received and attributed this to the way in which Schweitzer attacked the prevailing liberalism of the day. Schweitzer's work, he said, "was met by something like a conspiracy of silence." Much the same occurred with reference to the *Quest*, though there Schweitzer compelled attention by the force of the book, even if his views still were largely ignored. Writing in 1914 Lowrie could say: "The translator knows of no prominent scholar in Germany who has cordially welcomed Schweitzer's view, nor of any that has thoroughly and ably opposed it." Lowrie then characterized a different reception in England, mostly attributable to William Sanday and F. C. Burkitt, and especially among the younger men at Cambridge and Oxford. He added that Ernst von Dobschütz came to England as a kind of emissary to attempt to discredit Schweitzer, causing Sanday to back off from his earlier enthusiasm. In America, Lowrie reported, "the whole question has been simply ignored."[10]

Indeed, there is truth in Lowrie's depiction. When *Von Reimarus zu Wrede*

---

8. Georg Hollmann, review of Schweitzer's *Das Messianitäts-und Leidensgeheimnis: Ein Skizze des Lebens Jesu*, TLZ 27 (1902): 466–69.

9. Heinrich Weinel, review of Schweitzer's *Das Messianitäts-und Leidensgeheimnis: Ein Skizze des Lebens Jesu*, TRu 15 (1902): 242–45.

10. Lowrie, introduction to Schweitzer, *Mystery of the Kingdom of God,* 17–19, 21.

appeared, there was also a review in *Theologische Literaturzeitung*,[11] this time by Paul Wernle, and the tone was not very friendly. Wernle chided Schweitzer for a false title: the book should have been called *From Reimarus to Schweitzer*, he said, for even Wrede belonged to the "monstrous field strewn with corpses of the great life-of-Jesus battle" as the sole survivor; and he further faulted Schweitzer — perhaps with justice — for not taking account of the influence of the English deists on Reimarus (as well as the influence of Voltaire et al.). Wernle complained that Schweitzer's work was more criticism than history, and from the eschatological point of view of the author. Wernle then undertook a detailed critique of many of Schweitzer's key moves in the text of the New Testament, such as his appeal to Matthew 10–11. Wernle's own view was that the whole is a composition of the evangelist, the individual parts of which could be traced to Mark 6, 13, and Luke 10, 12. The passages came from the primitive community, not from Jesus, he said, against Schweitzer's attribution of them to the historical Jesus. Wernle thought that Schweitzer lacked an elementary sense of the nature of tradition-historical laws, and consequently his own reconstruction of Jesus was without foundation. We have nothing, Wernle said, that does not come through the community some thirty to forty years after the death of Jesus. He characterized Schweitzer's view of the sources as *phantastiche Quelleninterpretation*, and wondered whether, theologically, Schweitzer's picture of an error-prone Jesus would not merely stir up a new theme for scandal for modern theology to have to deal with. It was a less than flattering appraisal.

Equally blunt was Adolf Jülicher. He entitled the first chapter of his work, where he reviewed Schweitzer's *Von Reimarus zu Wrede*, "The Epoch 1901."[12] It was a sarcastic title, based on Schweitzer's observation that his and Wrede's work (*Das Messiasgeheimnis in den Evangelien*) first appeared at the same time, 1901, both in agreement, though in different ways, on opposition to the modern lives of Jesus. "Therefore for him 1901 is the year of the Epoch," said Jülicher (8). That very much summed up the tone of the review.

Jülicher began by observing that "for some months the shrill cry has sounded in our hearing: 'There is nothing more negative than the result of the investigation into the life of Jesus'" (1). He was, of course, quoting Schweitzer, and went on to say that Schweitzer's cry came not from pain, but was a *Jubelruf*, a joyous cry. What Schweitzer was out to do, according to Jülicher, was to destroy modern liberal theology. Citing Schweitzer's lament that the modern picture of Jesus had no power to awaken the spiritual life of the country, Jülicher complained that Schweitzer seemed to think that no one had been concerned about such things before the "Schweitzer era," as he called it. And, in any case, he asked,

---

11. Paul Wernle, review of Schweitzer's *Von Reimarus zu Wrede: Eine Geschichte der Leben Jesu Forschung*, TLZ 31 (1906): 502–6.

12. Adolf Jülicher, *Neue Linien in der Kritik der evangelischen Überlieferung* (Giessen: Alfred Töpelmann, 1906). The review of Schweitzer's *Von Reimarus zu Wrede* is in the first chapter, 1–13. Lowrie (*Mystery of the Kingdom of God*, 19) characterized Jülicher's treatment of Schweitzer's work, correctly I think, as "supercilious."

was it right to decide the validity of a historical thesis on the basis of the appeal it had attained in the life of the people?

After summarizing the basic lines of Schweitzer's theory, Jülicher said, "The Jesus whom Schweitzer proclaims as the Jesus of the gospels has sprung from his own head, fully formed before he [Schweitzer] entered into the details of the sources; and worthy of wonder is only the artistry with which our author composes his bizarre tapestry out of threads of old tradition." Jülicher accused Schweitzer of choosing the least reliable traditions, such as indications of time, place, and the connection of sayings, and of a "violation of the law and rule of historical inquiry." He basically faulted Schweitzer for not having done his work, not attending to detail, for being a bad historian who was not entitled even to a rebuttal, since he was practicing "dogmatic, not historical criticism" (5–6).[13]

Jülicher's judgment: "So I can only with regret state that the best-read and most intrepid critic of the Life-of-Jesus Research so unambiguously shows, in the same book from which we can and will learn worthy new and different things, that he has learned nothing from the whole history."[14] He then quoted Loisy to the effect that progress in criticism comes by evolution, not revolution, and went on to scold Schweitzer for allying himself with Wrede, who, in Jülicher's view, did not intend to found a "school" of any sort (in reaction to Schweitzer's characterization of the "schools" of thoroughgoing eschatology and thoroughgoing skepticism). Schweitzer, he said, issued pronouncements from his throne rather than undertaking the necessary work of the critic. Progress in research can only come through a refinement in historical method, not through the denial of all methods.

It was a polemical rather than analytical response, something like a wounded cat striking back. Jülicher declined to engage in the details of debate with Schweitzer. The review leaves the impression that Schweitzer was one of the outsiders trying to get in the club, but never really belonged, and was not likely to.

---

13. This reference to Schweitzer's work as historian seemed typical among liberal critics. Hans Windisch did not review Schweitzer's work until 1909 (*Von Reimarus zu Wrede*, TRu 12:146–62). While he expressed some sarcasm similar to that of Jülicher, referring to the "new aeon" represented by the thoroughgoing eschatological interpretation, beyond which no further development was permitted, still he gave a more temperate assessment, praising Schweitzer's stunning work, its poetic character, though at the same time finding fault with its lack of patience and calm characteristic of the objective historian. The work, he said, was much influenced by the temperament of its author, but nevertheless characterized it as a "wunderbare Gemisch von Wissenschaft und Dichtung" (146). He also faulted Schweitzer for lumping together people like Schenkel, Weizsäcker, Holtzmann, Keim, Beyschlag, and B. Weiss as just "liberals," and quarreled with Schweitzer for putting himself and Weiss together as the "Konsequenters" over against everybody else before them, who were merely "the halt and blind." Cf. also D. Paul Melhorn, review of *Von Reimarus zu Wrede* in *Protestantische Monatshefte* 11 (1907): 372–75, who acclaimed Schweitzer's literary gifts, but had reservations about the thoroughly eschatological approach and disagreed that we in our time should not have the right to reinterpret the message of Jesus.

14. Jülicher, *Neue Linien in der Kritik der evangelischen Überlieferung*, 7.

I know of no specific response of Schweitzer to these particular reviews,[15] but he did, in the second edition of his work, notice that his reception elsewhere seemed warmer than among his own colleagues in Germany. He also took account of English-American works for the first time in a section added to the second edition, noting that his *Leben-Jesus-Forschung* had created a lively *Auseinandersetzung* in those countries to a degree it did not in Germany. He cited F. C. Conybeare alleging that Schweitzer's work had created in England the greatest impression of all the works of theology in Germany.[16] As sympathizers he specifically mentioned William Sanday and F. C. Burkitt,[17] and as opponents of the eschatological interpretation he named C. Emmet, G. Abbott, H. B. Sharman, B. W. Bacon, Percy Gardner, and E. C. Dewick. Each got from Schweitzer in the main body of the text a single sentence or so, all in a short paragraph (*Geschichte*, 593–94).

The lukewarm, even hostile reception accorded Schweitzer in his own country is understandable. He had trampled all over the fondest flowers of the liberals, quite deliberately at that, and they would not return his deed with thanks. But why would England, not exactly noted as the home of radical theology, find any comfort in Schweitzer's views? The answer is revealing.

In an essay on "The Present Position of Liberal Theology in Great Britain," J. Warschauer first quoted von Dobschütz to the effect that the views of Schweitzer met with approval in England but not in Germany, where even Schweitzer's friends found his views one-sided and declined to follow him.[18] Warschauer agreed and argued that the reason for the kinder English reception was that the eschatological theory was a "godsend" to the opponents of liberalism, that is, a weapon against the liberal historical-critical appropriation of the historical Jesus in the struggle against dogma. Said Warschauer, *"The eschatological hypothesis was welcomed in England because it seemed to signify the failure of liberal*

---

15. In a letter to George Seaver (*Albert Schweitzer: The Man and His Mind* [New York: Harper, 1947], 197 n. 1), Schweitzer said that he habitually declined to respond to critics: "I have never allowed myself to become involved in controversy. I have never debated the question with my critics. I have simply exposed the problem." Schweitzer mentioned Jülicher's work in the *Geschichte* (590), but made no specific response to Jülicher's criticisms.

16. *Geschichte*, 562 n. 1, citing F. C. Conybeare, *History of New Testament Criticism* (London, 1910).

17. Sanday in his *The Life of Christ in Recent Research* (New York: Oxford University Press, 1907), and Burkitt in "The Eschatological Idea in the Gospel," in *Cambridge Biblical Essays*, ed. H. B. Swete (London: Macmillan, 1909), 193–213.

Sanday's reviews of Schweitzer are found especially in chaps. 2–4. He commended Schweitzer's work and acknowledged its influence on his own presentation. In reality, Sanday had some differences with Schweitzer, while acknowledging also areas of agreement, especially on the tendency to overpsychologize, to read modernisms into Jesus' message. He seemed particularly impressed with what looked like Schweitzer's reclaiming of the historical trustworthiness of the gospels, though even there he thought that Schweitzer was not consistent.

Sanday also noticed Jülicher's review of Schweitzer and pronounced it unjust (168). In chap. 7 he observed that Schweitzer's real significance lay in the dissatisfaction felt in Germany with regard to the dominant liberalism.

18. Joseph Warschauer, "The Present Position of Liberal Theology in Great Britain," *AJT* 16 (1912): 333–58.

Christianity" (351; italics his). It allowed orthodoxy to rescue the Christ of the creeds. It is not easy to imagine Schweitzer being invoked as defender of the orthodox faith.[19]

Some reviewers seemed not very interested. G. E. Ffrench, reviewing the English translation of Schweitzer's book, after observing that Schweitzer was an advocate of the eschatological solution to Jesus' life, came to the judgment that "the historical part of his work is of great value, but his own contribution to the discussion will help only in a limited degree to the readjustment of our ideas which is necessary from time to time."[20] So much for prophetic insight.

Ffrench also saw that Schweitzer depicted Jesus as a "deluded enthusiast" and wondered whether the "Jesus of the German theologians" could have "grown into the Christ who supplied the motive power to the grand history of Christian missions" (206). The concern for the picturing of a Christ who cannot be accommodated in modern theology is evident.

The classic British sense of "balance" also asserted itself. Even Sanday, who had at first been a sponsor of Schweitzer, began to back off his earlier endorsement, as Lowrie noted. In an article only a year or so after the English translation of Schweitzer's work appeared, Sanday observed that Schweitzer had given the "strongest impulse" to the apocalyptic interpretation, but the pendulum was beginning to swing back. After acknowledging his own role in endorsing Schweitzer too strongly, Sanday claimed that the problem with Schweitzer was his extremism — a product of his "youthful impetuosity and enthusiasm."[21]

Sanday sounded just a bit like a father admonishing an errant child whom he had first allowed too much freedom. He thought, he said, that apocalyptic was a good starting point, but it was used and changed by Jesus himself as applied to his conception of himself and his mission, for example, the kingdom was not only future as in apocalyptic, but also present; the Son of man conception was modified by Jesus through the addition of the suffering servant idea. Schweitzer's mistake, according to Sanday, was to apply his theory too rigorously.

A similar fate awaited Schweitzer in America, if somewhat more belatedly. Lowrie was not quite accurate in picturing a total indifference in America, though one looks in vain in, for example, the *Journal of Biblical Literature* for even a modest review of any edition of Schweitzer's works. There was in that journal, to borrow a famous phrase from Schweitzer, a "silence all around" (*Quest,*

---

19. Schweitzer later recalled in his autobiography (*Life and Thought,* 63) that his appeal for F. C. Burkitt was of the scientific kind, while Sanday's "Catholic type of piety" seemed to find comfort in his (Schweitzer's) views, i.e., as a critique of the modernizing liberal portrait of Jesus. Schweitzer made no comment on Sanday's subsequent withdrawal.

20. G. E. Ffrench, review of *The Quest of the Historical Jesus: A Critical Study of Its Progress from Reimarus to Wrede,* by Albert Schweitzer, *HibJ* 9 (1910–11): 203–6.

21. William Sanday, "The Apocalyptic Element in the Gospels," *HibJ* 10 (1911–12): 83–109. Sanday offered the candid admission that "the freshness and force of the style perhaps attracted me somewhat unduly" and that he was less aware of the "audacity and exaggeration" of Schweitzer's own constructions. I also follow here the standard if erroneous use of the word "apocalyptic" as a noun in English — very common at the time. See below, chap. 8.

368).[22] Elsewhere, William Adams Brown of Union Theological Seminary, in an article entitled, "The Place of Christ in Modern Theology," thought that the current eschatological interpretation was but an eddy in the currents of scholarship that would soon run its course and a sense of balance and proportion would be restored.[23] His main point was that Jesus was a moral model.

Shirley Jackson Case, in reviewing a number of works on Jesus, seemed remarkably restrained and only commented on the "state of suspense" on the eschatological question.[24] Frank Porter, reviewing a work of Shailer Mathews, noted that the eschatological view had many advocates, especially in Germany.[25] He counted Mathews among them and said there were two possible means of escaping the critical situation posed by the thoroughgoing eschatology: either question the extent of the eschatological element in the mind of Jesus or look for a foundation beneath the eschatological one. He noted that Mathews also emphasized the element of presentness in the kingdom-concept of Jesus. Said Porter:

> The messianic apocalyptic element was beyond doubt of great significance in the beginnings of Christianity, and has a large place in the New Testament. We must, unquestionably, clear it away in order to adapt New Testament teachings to our own times, and the clearing must be done by such thorough-going distinctions between form and substance as are here attempted. [114, referring to Mathews, who found permanency or substance in the form of apocalyptic thought]

A somewhat more sober assessment was given by Francis Peabody in the *Harvard Theological Review.* The effect of Schweitzer's work, he said, could be compared to Baur and *Tendenz* criticism, a clarifying principle "likely to remain a permanent factor in critical research."[26] But still he rejected the notion of an interim ethic in Jesus' teaching and declined to allow the eschatological element to dominate the ethical. And even though Schweitzer listed Benjamin W. Bacon as among his critics, Bacon was somewhat more nuanced, characterizing

---

22. It is true that *JBL* was not doing regular reviews at the time, but one might have expected at least an article somewhere on the debate stirred up by Schweitzer. Not until 1922 did the Society hold a symposium on eschatology. A similar silence prevailed elsewhere, e.g., *Revue biblique.*

23. William Adams Brown, "The Place of Christ in Modern Theology," *AJT* 16 (1912): 31–50.

24. *AJT* 16 (1912): 296–99, reviewing E. F. Scott, *The Kingdom and the Messiah,* C. W. Emmet, *The Eschatological Question in the Gospels; and Other Studies in Recent New Testament Criticism,* and von Dobschütz's *The Eschatology of the Gospels.* Case typically reviewed books with little personal judgment. His own later work, however, clearly demonstrates that he had come to terms with the eschatological interpretation. While I have not come across a direct review by Case of Schweitzer, Case's lecture notes, housed in the archives at Florida Southern College, clearly show his knowledge of Schweitzer's work at an early point. Case's life and work are accounted for especially in chaps. 3–4.

25. Frank Porter, review of Mathews, *The Messianic Hope in the New Testament, AJT* 10 (1906): 111–15.

26. Francis Peabody, "New Testament Eschatology and New Testament Ethics," *HTR* 2 (1909): 50–57. A few years afterward Warner F. Gookin, reviewing H. Latimer Jackson, *The Eschatology of Jesus, HTR* 8 (1915): 559–61, chided Jackson for not taking account of Schweitzer's issues, which he has "forced upon us" (561). So clearly Schweitzer's work had made its impact.

Schweitzer's book as "a great and epoch-making book," marking an epoch be-cause "it issues so well the summons to another trial balance on the work of the documentary critics, and itself responds to it so badly."[27] Basically Bacon thought Schweitzer did well on the history of interpretation, and not so well on his reconstruction.

It is clear enough that questions of the relevance of the eschatological Jesus to Christian faith were very much an issue driving the response to Schweitzer. The eschatological interpretation was certainly already under discussion, but no one until Schweitzer had applied it so consistently as an explanation of the public ministry of Jesus. It was that thoroughness that set Schweitzer apart and, at first, seemed to threaten his work with oblivion. He was too one-sided, many said.[28] A one-sided man can be safely ignored.

The journal articles portrayed what seems like a peaceful academic com-munity, pursuing its vocation in the quiet hallways and offices of the campus, composing little studies on the grammar of the Bible, its language, history, and historical circumstances. The Jesus of liberal theology is largely dominant, and scholarship seems not quite to be aware that a bomb has dropped in its gar-den. Most of the German gardeners have fled away; a few of the English and Americans stayed to admire the hole.

Among the latter were some surprises parallel to those found in England. A review article in the *Princeton Theological Review* by Geerhardus Vos illustrates the point and shows precisely the ground on which the more orthodox found an ally, or thought they did, in Schweitzer.[29] Vos specifically liked Schweitzer's seem-ing restoration of the supernatural, the emphasis on predestinarianism, even the atonement (Jesus chose to die), and above all the antiliberal attack on the then-current "lives" of Jesus with their psychologizing and idea of a "development" in the life of Jesus. It is clear that Vos saw in Schweitzer a potential way of overcom-ing the prevailing liberal theology of the day. He thought that Schweitzer had helped rescue Jesus from being desupernaturalized, which for him was equivalent to being de-eschatologized. An eschatological Jesus was a supernatural Jesus, down to and including the fact that he chose his own death deliberately as an act of atonement "for many."[30] In short, Vos could see Schweitzer restor-ing the dogmatic Christ. Christological dogma was the underlying issue. Never

---

27. Benjamin W. Bacon, "A Turning Point in Synoptic Criticism," *HTR* 1 (1908): 63, 65.

28. Cf. also H. A. A. Kennedy, "The Life of Jesus in the Light of Recent Discussions," *AJT* 11 (1907): 150–57, reviewing Schweitzer's *Von Reimarus zu Wrede.* He found Schweitzer's alliance with Weiss unfortunate "for the balance and proportion of the book" (154).

29. Geerhardus Vos, review of Schweitzer's *Quest of the Historical Jesus, PTR* 9 (1911): 132–41.

30. It is evident that Vos was not simply uncomfortable with the eschatological interpretation of Jesus' preaching of the Kingdom, for in earlier review articles he had expressed a critique of a different sound. Cf. *PTR* 1 (1903): 298–303, where he reviewed Paul Wernle, *Die Reichsgotteshoffnung in den Ältesten Christlichen Dokumenten und bei Jesus,* and complained about the danger of the hyper-eschatological interpretation devaluing Jesus' ethic, since, for Vos, the Kingdom is "the supreme religious ideal" (303). Vos showed himself to be very concerned with the "doctrinal consciousness of Jesus" in *PTR* 4 (1906): 262, reviewing Shailer Mathews, *The Messianic Hope in the Gospels.* It seems that it was not the eschatological interpretation itself, but the christological dogma that was at stake.

mind that a lot of other things came with the package, including a Jesus who died as a failure with respect to his own vision. But it was the thoroughly eschatological view of Schweitzer which commended itself to those concerned about the future of dogma.

Schweitzer had after all not been the first to introduce the eschatological interpretation of Jesus' work; already the little pamphlet of Johannes Weiss had established that debate.[31] What Schweitzer did was to provide a consistent interpretation of Jesus from the perspective of eschatology. Everything was to be explained with this one key. That was both the promise and the threat of his project, depending on one's own stance. The sheer power of the presentation lay in its artistry, its literacy, its forcefulness. Not everyone was prepared to accept that picture but, strangely enough, the ones in England and America who warmed to it most readily were those with a dogmatic agenda, who felt that Schweitzer's interpretation offered a wall against the tide of modern liberal theology. Schweitzer surely must have been a bit chagrined by his inclusion among the orthodox, though nowhere did he say so. For the Jesus whom he "resurrected" from history gave no real consolation to the practitioners of the Christ-dogma, though Schweitzer did indeed find in his eschatological Jesus some inspiration. How he did so we must also consider, but first one other observation about the first reactions to Schweitzer.

Characteristic of these reactions to Schweitzer was an apparent lack of interest in one of the most conspicuous features of the "old quest" to which Schweitzer had called attention at the conclusion to his survey of *Leben-Jesu-Forschung*. That was the degree to which every succeeding generation of portrayals of Jesus had simply manufactured a Jesus who was an image of the generation manufacturing the picture. All of them simply read their own philosophical assumptions into the teaching of Jesus. So successively there appeared the Jesus of rationalism, the romantic Jesus, the liberal Jesus, and so on. And while Schweitzer himself noticed this phenomenon, it does not seem to have occurred to him that he, too, might have been engaged in a similar process.

But other spirits also fluttered about in the company of Schweitzer's eschatological one, and they must, at some near point, come into the light. Already the question of the theological significance of the eschatological Jesus had jumped to the fore. This question impressed itself on Schweitzer's mind as well. How did he respond to it?

The Theological Question

It seems evident that Schweitzer was aware from the start of his discovery of the eschatological interpretation that it would raise great problems for traditional

---

31. Johannes Weiss, *Die Predigt Jesu vom Reiche Gottes* (Göttingen: Vandenhoeck and Ruprecht, 1892); English trans., *Jesus' Proclamation of the Kingdom of God*, trans. Richard Hyde Hiers and David Larrimore Holland, Lives of Jesus (Philadelphia: Fortress Press, 1971).

Christian faith. The *Skizze* already contained some of his moves toward an interpretation of the significance of the eschatological Jesus. At the end of this work Schweitzer tried to relate the eschatological Jesus to the modern world. Attempting to justify the liberal, noneschatological reinterpretation of Jesus' death as a kind of consecration of his sacrifice for the ethical kingdom, Schweitzer wrote favorably, "Our modern view of Jesus' death is true, true in its inmost nature, because it reflects his ethical-religious personality in the thought of our time" (*Mystery*, 250).[32] But then he added:

> This Jesus [the eschatological Jesus] is far greater than the one conceived in modern terms; he is really a super-human personality. With his death he destroyed the form of his "Weltanschauung," rendering his own eschatology impossible. Thereby he gives to all peoples and to all times the right to apprehend him in terms of their thoughts and conceptions, in order that his spirit may pervade their "Weltanschauung" as it quickened and transfigured the Jewish eschatology. (251)

The task of theology is "to found our Christian view of the world solely upon the personality of Jesus Christ, irrespective of the form in which it expressed itself in his time. He himself has destroyed this form with his death. History prompts theology to this unhistorical step." In the postscript he could assert that the purpose of his work had been simply "*to depict the figure of Jesus in its overwhelming heroic greatness and to impress it upon the modern age and upon the modern theology*" (italics his). To do that we must return to his time and "be forced to lay our faces in the dust, without daring even to wish to understand his nature. Only then can the heroic in our Christianity and in our 'Weltanschauung' be again revived" (252, 274–75).

There is here a great deal of reference to our *Weltanschauung*, or worldview (Lowrie declining to translate the term), and to our efforts to shape it somehow with the help of the figure of Jesus. In fact, Schweitzer seemed concerned from the outset with what he perceived as the failure of the culture of his own time, with a decline in the civilization of western Europe.[33] The problem was for him how to find the ethical energy to revitalize that culture. These views were elab-

---

32. This seemingly favorable evaluation of the liberal Jesus recalls Johannes Weiss, who had in his 1892 essay demolished that picture as historically wrong, but himself had then announced his preference for it theologically. See his comments in the foreword to the second edition of *Die Predigt Jesu vom Reiche Gottes* (2d ed., 1900; 3d ed., 1964, ed. Ferdinand Hahn with a preface by Rudolf Bultmann translated for the English translation [ibid.]), xi. I believe what Schweitzer meant is that Jesus, by his deliberate death, has ended the apocalyptic picture, the expectation of imminent End, simply because it did not happen and still has not happened. However, what remains is the Jesus of the powerful will, now freed from the dogma of apocalyptic.

33. He noted this in his autobiography (*Life and Thought*, esp. 173–75 and the discussion in the epilogue, 254–83). The confluence of all these interests, and especially the significance of the conclusion to the second edition of Schweitzer's *Geschichte*, were first called to my attention in a perceptive article by David Dungan, "Albert Schweitzer's Disillusionment with the Historical Reconstruction of the Life of Jesus," in the *PSTJ* 29 (Spring 1976): 27–48. I do not know whether this article subsequently appeared in a form available to a wider audience.

orated at more length in the conclusion to the second edition of his work, the
Geschichte der Leben-Jesu-Forschung.[34]

The possibility of knowing Jesus was not confined to the experts:

> To know Jesus and to understand Him requires no preliminary erudition. Nor is it
> necessary that we know the details of His public ministry or be able to reconstruct
> a "life of Jesus." His very being, that which He is and wills, manifests itself in a few
> of His lapidary sayings and thrusts itself upon us. We know Him without knowing
> much about Him, and we sense His eschatological significance even without having
> a scholarly knowledge of this concept. (195)

For Schweitzer the elemental matter has to do with the will, which is timeless
and points to that which is irreducible in persons. What is important about the
historical Jesus is his will, not his worldview, which is subject to change, as with
any person. Jesus' worldview was, of course, late-Jewish apocalypticism, which is
no longer relevant, but the will of Jesus expressed in that form still is relevant.
The question is how to translate the will of Jesus into modern terms so that its
vitality and power can continue to invigorate our own civilization. The previous
attempts to do so have weakened the will expressed in Jesus' apocalyptic thinking. Better to leave Jesus in his mode, said Schweitzer, to conserve the power
of the will expressed in it. What Jesus did was to express his ethical will in the
conceptual materials of his age; he did so in a penetrating and powerful way,
and that is his significance still for us, for we would not have had that clarification without the impact of his personality. That is still his importance, the
impact of his will upon our time and culture. The historical Jesus, with his eschatological conditionedness, is a stranger to our time because we do not grasp
the drive toward fulfillment, perfection, in his ethical will. We attempt to modernize the stranger. We lack the same "willing and hoping and longing" that he
possessed. Thus Schweitzer: "Only in so far as the conceptual materials of an
age are charged with ethical-eschatological vitalities does that age have a real
and living relationship to Jesus. This means that its world-view must exhibit the
equivalent of the will and hope which were central for Him; that is, it must be
dominated by the thoughts which are found in Jesus' concept of the Kingdom
of God" (198–99).

Schweitzer repeated his assessment of his own time as a time of stagnation,
even retrogression, in civilization. The will of Jesus was not allowed to infuse
the culture. There was no striving after that moral perfection of humankind that
Schweitzer attributed to Jesus. He saw as possible a kind of direct hermeneutical
significance in this will of Jesus expressed in his eschatological expectation of
the kingdom of God:

> We possess only so much of Him as we permit Him to preach to us of the Kingdom
> of God.... The only thing that matters is this: that the significance of the concept
> of the Kingdom of God for our world-view is the same as it was for Him, and that

---

34: In this summary I use Henry Clark's translation in *The Ethical Mysticism of Albert Schweitzer*
(Boston: Beacon Press, 1962) with any emendations noted.

we experience in the same way that He did the urgency and the power of that concept. (201)

This occurred, for Schweitzer, in a *"will to will understanding* of Jesus, for in this the essence of the world-view is communicated" (201; italics Clark's). There was, for Schweitzer, a kind of automatic translation of Jesus' word to us, a bridging of the hermeneutical gap that seems to occur somewhat mystically. Schweitzer added that the moral perfecting of the world can, of course, occur only as a consequence of our own ethical striving, not as a result, as Jesus expected, of a divine intervention. What is important is that we share the same vision. Schweitzer seemed to rank some things in Jesus' worldview as historically conditioned, such as his predestinarianism, his devaluing of work and property, and so on. But we should focus ourselves on that which is "self-authenticating" (202; *Zwingende*) in Jesus, and actually no lengthy learning is required to do so. Even the "interim" nature of Jesus' ethic is no drawback, for we must learn to purify ourselves inwardly and be free from the world, which is what Jesus' eschatological ethic points us to.

Schweitzer added that Jesus' contribution was to focus and present powerfully this eschatological ethic. None of that needs to be considered the result of some special revelation, however, for such ideas lie within us all and are "given with the ethical will." He further added that, if he should be accused of being merely rational and moralistic,[35] then he would reply that salvation in any case comes to "being set free from the world and from ourselves through a fellowship of the will with Jesus, and being filled with power and peace and courage for life." Then: "Let no one forget that Jesus Himself was essentially a rationalist and a moralist. That He was conditioned by late-Jewish metaphysics is incidental."[36]

Schweitzer characterized our relationship to Jesus as "mystical" insofar as it encompasses this will-to-will union. In this sense Schweitzer was willing to describe Christianity as a "Jesus-mysticism," if not a "Jesus-cult" (204). In this sense also something like community would appear to be possible as the fellowship of all those whose wills are united to Jesus' will. It was from this perspective of will joined to will[37] that Schweitzer wrote the oft-quoted paragraph at the end of the first edition, which was retained unaltered in the second:

---

35. Later Schweitzer would simply accept the designation of "rationalist" (*Life and Thought*, 257).

36. Clark, *Ethical Mysticism of Albert Schweitzer*, 203. This conditionedness of Jesus' message, and the necessity to restate it in modern terms, Schweitzer has always maintained. In his autobiography (*Life and Thought*, 68), he wrote: "We of to-day do not, like those who were able to hear the preaching of Jesus, expect to see a Kingdom of God realizing itself in supernatural events. Our conviction is that it can only come into existence by the power of the spirit of Jesus working in our hearts and in the world. The one important thing is that we shall be as thoroughly dominated by the idea of the Kingdom, as Jesus required his followers to be." In the *Geschichte* (595) Schweitzer said that the point of designating Jesus' ethic as "interim" was to affirm that Jesus' moral demands had in view the approaching kingdom and the judgment, that therefore Jesus actually had no ethic of the kingdom, which presupposed a circumstance in which human beings would be free of temptation and sin, like the angels.

37. This is Schweitzer's own explanation of the passage as set out in his *Life and Thought*, 71–72.

He comes to us as One unknown, without a name, as of old, by the lakeside, He came to those men who knew Him not. He speaks to us the same word: "Follow thou me!" and sets us to the tasks which He has to fulfill for our time. He commands. And to those who obey Him, whether they be wise or simple, He will reveal Himself in the toils, the conflicts, the sufferings which they shall pass through in His fellowship, and, as an ineffable mystery, they shall learn in their own experience Who he is. (205, preserving intact the translation of the 1910 English edition)

This passage has given much consolation to pious Christians across the years, but it is more than doubtful whether they have been reading it as Schweitzer intended it. For him the historical Jesus was a heroic figure, the one who lay "hold of the wheel of the world to set it moving on that last revolution which is to bring all ordinary history to a close" (*Quest*, 369), as he said in another of those oft-quoted texts. And if this Jesus was wrong in his calculation about the coming of the kingdom, it must simply be admitted, for we cannot do otherwise than remain devoted to truth, pleasant or otherwise. That does not invalidate Jesus' message, which must be removed in any case from its apocalyptic bindings that are no longer valid in the modern world.[38] What matters about Jesus is that he imposed his will on history (or at least attempted to, heroically), and as such he strode giant-like across the events that have shaped our past and present. That is his greatness, and it is this emulation of the will of Jesus, the spirit of Jesus, which can still shape our own time and culture, if only we allow it to do so.

Under that same inspiration Schweitzer himself returned to medical school and went to Africa to found a hospital. His choice of service to the Africans was in particular moved by the past history of injustices done them, though he had held in his mind for years the general plan of spending the first thirty years of his life in scholarship and the arts, and then doing something in the service of humanity, moved by Jesus' own ethical vision.[39] So in the end it was the ethical will of Jesus, somehow directly communicated to us across the barrier of the

---

38. See Schweitzer's discussion in his *Life and Thought*, 72–73. In fact, for Schweitzer it is a positively good thing that the apocalyptic worldview has perished, leaving only the ethic of Jesus as a spiritual force to move us. The ethic has been already freed from dogma, the dogma of the apocalyptic worldview.

39. Ibid., 227–28. It is a misperception that Schweitzer left his theological career out of some sense of disillusionment. Cf. the statement in the introduction to the work of the Jesus Seminar, *The Five Gospels: The Search for the Authentic Words of Jesus*, new translation and commentary by Robert W. Funk, Roy W. Hoover, and the Jesus Seminar, Polebridge Press Book (New York: Macmillan, 1993):

Schweitzer saw Jesus' ethic as only an "interim ethic" (a way of life good only for the brief period before the cataclysmic end, the eschaton). As such he found it no longer relevant or valid. Acting on his own conclusion, in 1913 Schweitzer abandoned a brilliant career in theology, turned to medicine, and went out to Africa where he founded the famous hospital at Lambaréné out of respect for all forms of life. (3)

It is true that in a sense Schweitzer thought the "interim ethic" of Jesus could not be simply transported into our own time, though by his own reckoning he went to Africa to do something in the spirit of Jesus. He certainly did not go there moved by the ethic of reverence for life, since he only came to that position after being in Africa for some time.

years, which remained normative for Schweitzer. This "ethical eschatology" of Jesus, as he had from the first called it, continued to function authoritatively, even though originally of an "interim" nature, for still in every age it is necessary to have that will that is able to set aside the world and pursue a different vision.

Later, of course, Schweitzer would evolve his thought into "reverence for life," an idea that came to him while he was floating upriver on a small steamboat in Africa.[40] His concern at the time, perhaps even all the time, was the problem of civilization, how to unite the ethics of the will-to-live with the will-to-progress in civilization. He believed that he found the answer in this "reverence for life," in which every will-to-live recognizes the right of every other will-to-live and regards all life as sacred. His reflections on this subject eventuated in publication of the various works on civilization climaxing years of concern for the philosophical questions of ethical life-and-world affirmation.[41] While it might seem that "reverence for life" can hardly be derived from the historical Jesus, in Schweitzer's mind they were quite compatible, both rooting in the idea of the human will.[42] It was because Christianity could and did separate Jesus' ethic from his life-and-world negating apocalyptic worldview, however, that progress in civilization could occur.

Schweitzer had finished his *Von Reimarus zu Wrede* while in his first year of medical studies, at the same time continuing to lecture in theology and to play concerts on the organ. It was a formidable course. In 1913 he finished his medical studies with submission of his thesis on the *Psychiatric Study of Jesus*, while at the same time issuing the second edition of *Geschichte der Leben-Jesu-Forschung*. The second edition was about 240 pages longer than the original and updated the literature through 1912. It included expanded material on the question of languages (Aramaic) and parallels in rabbinic literature and in Buddhism, and summarized the psychiatric issues that would appear more fully in *The Psychiatric Study of Jesus*.[43] But by far the dominant part of the additions — two large chapters — was given over to a characterization of the discussion, which at the time in Germany roused quite a storm, over the historicity of Jesus. This issue, which seems now so outlandish, nevertheless stirred great passions in the first part of the century and now and again arises phoenix-like to plague studies of the historical Jesus.[44]

---

40. *Life and Thought*, 180.

41. *Verfall und Wiederaufbau der Kultur* (Munich: C. H. Beck, 1923); *Kultur und Ethik* (Munich: C. H. Beck, 1923). The two have been brought together in a single English volume, *The Philosophy of Civilization*, trans. C. T. Campion (New York: Macmillan, 1949).

42. Cf. *Life and Thought*, 270, where Schweitzer characterized his ethic of reverence for life as the "ethic of Love widened into universality." Schweitzer always maintained that our contemporary ethic has to be evolved rationally out of our own circumstances.

43. It is noteworthy that Schweitzer should feel compelled to take up a defense of Jesus' sanity, since he himself was partly responsible for raising the question with his thoroughgoing eschatological Jesus who anticipated the imminent end of the world and thought of himself as the One to come on the clouds of heaven.

44. This issue is accounted for in chaps. 2 and 8.

The remainder of Schweitzer's incredible career need not be laid out here and is generally well known in any case. His work at Lambaréné was interrupted by the Great War and he himself was taken prisoner as a German. He was later allowed to return to his hospital and build it up over the years. He received international admiration and support for his conspicuous devotion, including the Nobel prize in 1951. He died in 1965 and was buried at Lambaréné.

There are questions left by all great figures and Schweitzer is no exception. We could inquire into the sources behind his portrayal of Jesus, whence came this picture of the heroic Jesus, the Jesus of the powerful will. Not from Carlyle, according to Schweitzer's own evaluation,[45] though Nietzsche might be a candidate.[46] It should also again be acknowledged that Schweitzer, in fact, as the liberals had critically objected, did little to advance our understanding of the sources for knowledge of Jesus. His powerful presentation accepted the essential historicity of the sources (Mark, Matthew) and perhaps, as already noted, even delayed further analysis of the nature of the oral tradition underlying these sources. This understanding was already in hand at Schweitzer's time, but its further evolution into *Formgeschichte* did not appear until the period beyond the Great War. Schweitzer was quite willing to await the verdict of history on his *konsequente Eschatologie* and especially seemed to regard all efforts at distinguishing the genuine and the ungenuine in the tradition as arbitrary.[47] Certainly Schweitzer's work shaped the discussion for years to come and posed powerfully several of the lingering problems of *Leben-Jesu-Forschung*: the question of the nature and extent of the eschatological element in Jesus' message; the issue of Jesus' messianic consciousness; and the seemingly unresolvable problem of the Son of man. And, finally, perhaps also Schweitzer's own life inspires speculation about still another kind of question: In the end did Schweitzer really model himself after Jesus, or did he model Jesus after himself?

---

45. In his *Life and Thought*, where he gives it as his judgment that Carlyle's book was "not a profound book" (111).

46. I do not know of any explicit acknowledgment on Schweitzer's part, but B. H. Streeter once remarked that Schweitzer's Jesus reminded us "of the Superman of Nietzsche wearing Galilean robes." Certainly Schweitzer's own life incorporated Nietzschean motifs: a "superman" figure, the powerful individual set against the culture, driven by the power of uniquely creative thought. The reference to Streeter comes from Brabazon, *Albert Schweitzer* (141) with attribution to A. M. Hunter in Robert Davidson and A. R. C. Leaney, *Biblical Criticism*, Pelican Guide to Modern Theology 3 (Harmondsworth, England: Penguin, 1970), 256.

47. See, for example, the statement in the *Geschichte* (597), where he disavowed all such efforts and concluded: "Sooner or later the time will come when the simple and natural will be recognized as the true." For further consideration see chap. 2.

Chapter 2

THE NONHISTORICAL JESUS

Liberalism mounted its own death watch. It was not undone by Schweitzer, though he intended to wound it mightily, for he saw its picture of Jesus as simply false historically, and theologically lacking the power to inform the culture.[1] But liberalism exposed itself to attack from all sides: from the orthodox for its abandonment of christology, but also from the radical left for its core attachment to the historical Jesus. What enabled the left-wing critique of the very historicity of Jesus was liberalism's own criticism of its sources, which had advanced to such a point that it became questionable whether a real figure actually lay behind those sources. That was already implicit in the position of the liberals who were, however, unwilling to take that step, and were certainly not compelled to do so. But they had opened the door wide enough to allow others to enter.

This debate over the historicity of Jesus became intense in the first decade of the twentieth century and spread from Germany into Holland, England, and America. It peaked around 1910 with a public conference in the Zoological Gardens in Berlin and began to taper off thereafter.[2] It was, in fact, an acrimonious debate, with historical and theological issues intertwined, and it was also apparent that the liberals had brought the matter, to their regret apparently, upon themselves. Of course, it is also true that this questioning of the very existence of Jesus as a historical figure was not really new, having gone back as far at least as the eighteenth-century Frenchmen Charles François Dupuis and Constantin François Volney, and wound its way down through Bruno Bauer and Albert Kalthoff, as Schweitzer had originally described and, in his greatly expanded second edition, had more extensively discussed.[3] While it does not seem merited to give so large an accounting of the issue as it claimed in its own time, it is worthwhile to survey it modestly through the lens of its primary advocates and attempt to understand why biblical scholarship had come to such a pass.

---

1. In fact, his critique of the Ritschlians was especially sharp. It was they who separated religion from philosophy and thus drove theology into the impasse it had reached in the first decade of the twentieth century. See *Geschichte,* esp. 512–13.

2. The transcript of this conference was published by the Deutschen Monistenbundes as *Hat Jesus gelebt?* (Berlin: Verlag des Deutschen Monistenbundes, 1910). The issue never really died, but subsided and did not quite attain the visibility it once enjoyed.

3. *Quest of the Historical Jesus,* 313ff; *Geschichte,* chaps. 22–23.

45

The Discussion of the Sources

Two matters go together here: the understanding of the sources (the gospels) for the life of Jesus, and the quest for the criteria of authenticity. Already by the turn of the century the Markan hypothesis was well in hand, at least in Germany, and the understanding of the oral nature of the material underlying even the synoptics was far advanced. There was a decided tendency to favor the antiquity of the "Logia" (Q) source and, as is widely known, to prefer Mark as the most reliable source. It is certainly not the case that Form Criticism came along after World War I and produced great skepticism about the nature of the sources, for that skepticism already existed and was guided by the assumption that the community after Jesus had preserved the material about him and had at the same time profoundly influenced it.[4] A look at some standard publications influential at the time will show something of the reasons for the debate.

Paul Wernle, whom we encountered in reviewing reactions to Schweitzer, composed a short work on the sources that aptly summarizes the prevailing view in the liberalism of the day.[5] Interestingly, Wernle observed in the preface:

> There is great danger of each one of us shaping his own Jesus in his own image, and ascribing to Jesus those thoughts and feelings which dwell, perhaps unsuspected, in the depths of his own soul. Then the voice which comes to us from the central point of history is merely the echo of our own.[6]

He then asserted that we are on the edge of a great New Age and the question is whether Jesus had anything to say to us. But first we need to form a correct impression of the sources for knowledge of Jesus — thus Wernle's justification for his little book.

The sources outside the New Testament have essentially no value for the historian; Paul is scanty, and the Apocrypha is worthless. Only the gospels count, and John, though perhaps preserving some old traditions (for example, date of the crucifixion), also raises great difficulties and should be largely omitted. Among the synoptics, Mark is the primary source along with the Logia. Matthew and Luke are secondary, conflated sources. Mark was basically a compiler, with perhaps some written material behind the gospel, but primarily the material was oral. Mark compiled his work with the dominant theological idea of demonstrating Jesus as Son of God–messiah, utilizing miracles as proofs. Earlier stages of the Markan tradition are difficult to analyze. Mark may be by that John Mark mentioned by Papias.

---

4. This assertion does not deny that the Markan outline was still credited generally and only fell apart with the success of the work of Wrede and later K. L. Schmidt, at least in Germany. Form Criticism would later certainly radicalize what was already present.

5. Paul Wernle, *Sources of Our Knowledge of the Life of Jesus*, trans. Edward Lummis (London: Philip Green, 1905). It was aimed at a popular audience apparently, but is a useful summary. Similar judgments are expressed in Adolf Jülicher, *An Introduction to the New Testament*, trans. Janet Penrose Ward (London: Smith, Elder, 1904), with more emphasis if anything on the impact of oral tradition on the transmission of the Jesus-material.

6. Wernle, *Sources of Our Knowledge of the Life of Jesus*, ix.

The Logia source has no known order, and could also be the source referred to by Papias. Its author could have been an eyewitness, though the work clearly had a literary history before it fell into the hands of Matthew and Luke. Its historical value is high. There is also special material found in Matthew and Luke, though it has also been interpreted by the different writers of the gospels.

No biography or life of Jesus is possible; no development can be detected, and differing Galilean and Jerusalem periods are not valid. No overall plan of a life can be seen from the gospels collectively. The Christian community greatly influenced the picture. Of particularly complex problems such as the Son of man, Wernle asked, somewhat plaintively, "In the 'Son of Man' problem, shall we ever gain a clear insight into Jesus' own position?" (158). What we have in the gospels is largely the faith of the community, though we can still know something of Jesus' teaching and what he thought about the great questions (God, who is man, and so on).

In a short work entitled *Jesus in Modern Criticism: A Lecture*, the Zurich professor Paul Schmiedel set himself the task of describing an absolute residue of texts that could be called historical and that guaranteed the historicity of Jesus of Nazareth.[7] These texts came to be called "Schmiedel's pillars" or pillar passages, and their assertion proved to be a tempting target for the deniers of Jesus' historicity. Schmiedel also observed the tendency to remake Jesus in one's own image, though he also did not find it necessary for Christian faith for everyone to become good historians. However, for those who did not wish to believe contrary to the findings of criticism, he thought it helpful to set forth what could be known with certainty about Jesus as a basis for erecting a more complete picture.

The nine pillar passages were: Mark 3:21, 3:31–35, 6:5, 8:12 (par. Matt. 12:39=Luke 11:29), 10:18, 13:32, 15:34; Matt. 11:5, 12:32, 16:5–12. The primary consideration for Schmiedel was whether some text expressed something contrary to the interests of the community and therefore argued for the authenticity of the text.[8] These passages would guarantee that such a figure as Jesus existed, that some irreducible minimum could be known with certainty about him, and on this basis a wider picture could be constructed, provided that it did not contradict the pillar passages. Schmiedel then proceeded to show just how he might flesh out such a picture. Unfortunately, few paid much attention to his positive moves, for he had created the impression that the undermining of the pillar passages would constitute a serious challenge to the very historical existence of Jesus himself.

As a third instance we can also take one of the standard handbooks at the

---

7. Paul Schmiedel, *Jesus in Modern Criticism: A Lecture*, trans. Maurice A. Canney (London: A. & C. Black, 1907). The original was an article in *Protestantische Monatshefte* (1906): 257–82, and afterwards separately published as *Die Person Jesus im Streite der Meinungen der Gegenwart* (Leipzig: Heinsius, 1906). Schmiedel was Professor of New Testament at Zurich. His views were also mediated to English-speaking readers through his contributions to the *Encyclopaedia Biblica*.

8. Schmiedel had to do some figurative interpreting here and there, such as in the feeding stories (crowds were fed with teaching), or the reply to John (referred to spiritual healings, and so on).

time, the *Biblische Theologie des Neuen Testaments* of Heinrich Weinel, which compactly summarized the grasp of the sources at the time and, equally important, the criteria for determining authenticity as well as what was inextricably bound up with that issue, the question of the way in which Jesus could be distinguished from his environment.[9] The sources are, first of all, the first three gospels; the Markan hypothesis is assumed. Mark is a chronologically ordered account of Jesus' deeds and suffering, providing proofs of his messiahship through his miracles, prophecies, and other signs. Behind it lie older, fundamental groups of narratives arranged by catchword. The form of Mark used by Matthew and Luke was different from that known to us. In addition is the Logia source, the non-Markan material found in Matthew and Luke. The order is better preserved in Luke. It is a kind of catechism like the Didache and is probably identical to the collection of sayings of the Lord mentioned by Papias and said to be translated by Matthew from Aramaic. In addition, there are valuable materials preserved independently by Matthew and Luke. Some apocryphal material, such as the gospel of the Hebrews, is to be noticed. John is of minor importance. Weinel's summary was much the same as Wernle's and everyone else's, the conventional wisdom in the liberal school.

As to determining what is authentic, Weinel said, first, the most historically worthy is that which has dual attestation: Mark and L (Logia), or one of these and special Matthean or Lukan material. What comes from the later tendencies or convictions of the Christian movement should be excluded, though this cannot be converted into its opposite, that is, that everything explainable from a tendency of the early community should be construed as inauthentic. If nothing speaks against something that Jesus also could have thought, then that tradition is to be maintained.

But most essential is what was original with Jesus. "The fundamental matter is what is new, original. Not what Jesus shares with his people and his time is what has had historic significance, but rather what he possesses that goes beyond that" (42). Weinel added that this was the way in which to characterize and conceive every historical phenomenon.

In the third edition of 1921, Weinel emphasized the latter more strongly. There is material attributed to Jesus that is in fact not his personally and essentially but is only Jewish and temporal. Jesus must be seen in relation to the highest religions of the ancient world. Only so can the peculiarity of his religion stand out. Certainly Jesus did not appear to found a new religion or church; nevertheless, a new religion came with him: a new God-faith, a new ideal for humankind, a new valuation of the world and a new redemption for humankind, redemption from sin and guilt, and the power for a new life that also overcomes suffering.

---

9. Heinrich Weinel, *Biblische Theologie des Neuen Testaments: Die Religion Jesu und des Urchristentums; Grundriss der theologischen Wissenschaften*, Dritter Teil, Zweiter Band (Tübingen: J. C. B. Mohr [Paul Siebeck], 1911). The key discussion is on 40–42.

That can only come clear when our presentation does not remain within the frame-work of the old Jewish concepts, in which Jesus also carried the new that he brought, rather when, in continuation of the religious-historical consideration, it shows how the new religion is distinguished from the preceding ones (45).[10]

We would today recognize that Weinel was operating with a form of the cri-terion of multiple attestation and the principle of dissimilarity, with the primary focus on the impact exerted by the early Christian community on the Jesus-tradition. While he did not specifically extend the criteria to include Jesus' difference from Judaism, he did insist that the true understanding of a histor-ical person could occur only when we have determined that figure's originality or distinctiveness.

So the sources were already being subjected to severely critical evaluation, so much so that the question could arise as to just how much of a historical figure actually lay behind them. This was the door opened by the liberal criticism, and through it marched the likes of Arthur Drews, William Benjamin Smith, and John M. Robertson. While not the only participants in this debate over the historicity of Jesus, they were the figures attracting the widest attention, and we will use them as paradigm of the whole discussion.[11]

Arthur Drews

Arthur Drews, who would become the most notorious spokesman for the de-niers of Jesus' historicity, was a philosophy professor at the Karlsruhe Technical Institute, seemingly an unlikely place and he an unlikely person to arouse such a noisy controversy. But Drews had a knack for catching the public's atten-tion and, to be polite about it, for tweaking the collective beard of the liberal theologians. Born in 1865 at Petersen, Holstein, he studied at the Universities of Munich, Berlin, Heidelberg, and Halle. He earned his philosophy degree at Halle, became privat docent at Karlsruhe in 1896 and professor in 1898. He pub-lished a variety of works on Kant, Hegel, Schilling, Nietzsche, and Wagner, and also turned his interest to gospel criticism. He was not trained in that area — a matter of continual carping from the liberal critics[12] — but had acquainted him-self especially with the works of the *religionsgeschichtliche Schule* and made full

---

10. F. C. Burkitt also advocated the notion of "double attestation," by which he meant authenti-cation from the two earliest sources (Mark and Q). See his *The Gospel History and Its Transmission* (Edinburgh: T. & T. Clark, 1906), esp. 147ff., with a listing of passages. Later Burkitt would also emphasize (1) Jewish and Palestinian topography; (2) knowledge of Aramaic or signs of its use; and (3) Jewish thought. See *The Earliest Sources for the Life of Jesus,* new and rev. ed. (London: Constable, 1922). All these criteria emphasized Jesus' belonging within Judaism.

11. There was, as noted in the prologue, a Dutch school of radical critics who adopted a similar posture. There were also other German critics, such as the Assyriologist Pèter Jensen at Marburg, whose broad position was that Christianity was based on a form of the Gilgamesh myth.

12. Johannes Weiss, for example, referred to him as a "self-appointed historian" who relished his alleged role as a martyr and was even not above comparing himself to D. F. Strauss. See Weiss's comments in the preface to his *Jesus von Nazareth Mythus oder Geschichte? Eine Auseinandersetzung mit Kalthoff, Drews, Jensen* (Tübingen: J. C. B Mohr [Paul Siebeck], 1910). Drews's biographical data are from *Wer Ist's?* (1928).

advantage of what he found there. It is scarcely an exaggeration to say that the liberal theologians contributed the materials with which the radical critics would build their house. The analogizing of Jesus to his environment led first to the question whether there was anything novel about Jesus, as Weinel had asked, and then whether there was anything historical about Jesus. And the logical end would be whether the historicity of Jesus was necessary to Christian faith at all.

In the preface to the first and second editions of his work Drews noted that his purpose was to show that everything about the historical Jesus had a mythical character and thus it was not necessary to presuppose that a historical figure ever existed.[13] Paul certainly was necessary for the foundation of Christianity, but not Jesus. And so: "Consequently it is self-deceit to make the figure of this 'unique' and 'mighty' personality, to which a man may believe he must on historical grounds hold fast, the central point of religious consciousness" (19). It is apparent that the struggle was being directed against the Jesus of liberal theology.

Something of the flavor of the debate was given in the preface to the third edition, in which Drews complained of not being given serious scientific consideration, and referred to the various attacks on him, charges of dilettantism, and the public meetings over his work:

> I am left perfectly cold by personal slanders, anonymous threats, and pious corrections, meetings of protest in which the Minister of Public Worship takes part with obbligato trombone choirs and professions of faith, as well as by the uproar of the multitude roused to fanaticism in this manner by the "guardian of their souls." They are everything except refutations. (24–25)

What was his work all about?

It proposed the theory of a pre-Christian Jesus cult. The hellenistic world was a time of syncretism, of longing for redemption. The Jews had come under the influence of Persian dualistic thought; the messiah, formerly an expectation of a royal ruler, now became associated with the endtime, the Son of man, the Danielic ruler-redeemer (=Saoshyant or Mithras), mingled with the Philonic notion of the Logos or Word, and Stoic Reason, or Wisdom, the mediator between humankind and God. The desire for communion with God manifested itself in various sect groups, such as Therapeutai, Essenes, Mandeans, Gnostics, and Jewish apocalyptic groups. The messianic figure of the latter rooted in a Joshua-Jesus figure, an ancient Ephraimitic sun god connected with Passover and circumcision. Evidence points toward this Joshua as a messianic figure (cf. Zechariah). Through various verbal gymnastics Drews connected this Joshua-Jesus with the Therapeutai (=Jason=healer) and through Epiphanius with the Essenes=Jessenes=Nazarenes, also mentioned by Acts. Epiphanius thus witnesses to a pre-Christian Jesus healing deity, an original Joshua cult of the sun god.

---

13. Arthur Drews, *The Christ Myth*, trans. C. Delisle Burns, from the 3d German ed. (London: T. Fisher Unwin, 1910; reprint, New York: Prometheus Books, 1998).

The suffering, dying-rising savior god has many antecedents in the ancient world, in Judaism (Deutero-Isaiah), in the fertility cults everywhere seen, in human sacrifice and the scapegoat idea, the deified man dying for all, or in the Persian practice of the "beardless one," a mock figure sent through the streets and allowed to collect from the shopkeepers freely within a specified time, or be ruthlessly beaten by the crowd. He presumably represented the departure of winter or was intended to hasten its departure. Such stands behind the Esther story. It was not too far to the idea of a suffering messiah whose death would be efficacious for his people. The Ephraimitic Joshua must have been a similar figure. Connections with the Jesus cult can be seen in the Arabian tradition that the mother of Joshua was named Mirzam (=Mariam=Maria); also, the name of the mother of Adonis, another similar figure, was Myrrha. Even Plato knew of the idea of the "just man" spending his life in unacknowledged persecution; similarly with the Pharisees.

Other elements in the Jesus myth have parallels: the birth stories (flight into Egypt=Horus fleeing on an ass from Seth; slaughter of the innocents=weeping over Tammuz or Adonis; magi=astrological figures, stars, symbolic of the winter solstice). Other parallels were drawn to the Hindu Agni (=fire deity), whose birth was celebrated in terms reminiscent of Jesus (the fire god enters in darkness and concealment, gives light at the time of the solstice); the priests greet his birth with rejoicing and gifts (such as myrrh). There are further parallels in the Krishna and Buddha mythologies, the latter likely gained from the former and then mediated to Christianity. Drews speculated how this might have happened through trade and commerce, or was perhaps mediated through Mandean and Persian sources. As to Jesus' supposed parents, Joseph was originally a god, like Kinyras, father of Adonis, and was said to have been an artisan, inventor of the hammer and lever, and the like. Hermes' father was also an artisan. Mary, too, is Maya, mother of Agni, also Myrrha, mother of Adonis, Semiramis, mother of Babylonian Marduk, and Mirzam, mother of Joshua, and even Merris (according to Eusebius), the Egyptian princess who found Moses in a basket.

The baptism also can be referred to its astrological sources. John the Baptist is not a historical figure; he conceals the Babylonian water god Ea (Oannes), whose worship includes baptism as a representation of the course of the sun as it makes its way through the constellations of the water-carrier and the fishes. John's depiction as Elijah confirms this interpretation, as Elijah himself was a form of the sun god (=Helios=German Heljas=Ossetic Ilia).

Fire worship also accounts for the practices at the sacrament of the supper. Again the parallels come from the Rigveda, the Agni story wherein the priests prepare sacred food (a cake, symbolic of all solid food, and the soma, a cup symbolic of all liquid). Agni dwelled invisibly in these substances and the communers were taken up into his life. The worshiper also provided sacrificial gifts, so worshiper and god both were given to one another as sacrificial offering. Antecedents also are evident in Judaism: at the show bread the priests laid twelve cakes on the altar for Aaron and sons; Joshua the sun god was also accompa-

nied in crossing the Jordan by twelve assistants, originally the journey of the sun
through the twelve signs of the Zodiac. And more widely are the agreements
with the mystery cults (Mithras, Saoshyant, Saos, son of Zeus, Dionysus, Jason,
Demeter). So: Jason, Joshua, Jesus. It is all the same.

Jesus as the lamb of God also has its roots in the Agni tales in which Agni
entered the constellation of the ram (=spring, or lamb), paralleled in the Jewish pasch. Thus lamb and light go together, as in the Gospel of John. The cross
originally had no connection with death on a gibbet, but was a cult sign (Tau)
going back into Egypt, Assyria, and Persia, a magic sign such as can even be
seen in the Old Testament story of Moses holding up his arms for victory over
the Amalekites, or is associated with deities as varied as Serapis and Thor. It is
a sun symbol, the creative force of nature and new life. The idea of the gibbet
arose from the fact that the same words were used for crucifixion and its material (*stauros, xulon*),[14] and since the Jewish paschal lamb was said to be skewered
lengthwise and crosswise, the notion of the "skewered" messiah on the gibbet
must have arisen among the Christians. Most of the other features of "crucified"
were added under the influence of Psalm 22. Originally Christ was depicted before the cross as symbol of life and resurrection, as in the mysteries. Medieval
times first depicted him as on the cross, a crucified figure.

A second part of the book took up the Christian Jesus. The Jesus myth had
been in existence a very long time in one form or another, but it was only in the
appearance of the tentmaker of Tarsus, Paul, that a Jesus community separated
from Judaism took root. Said Drews, in a revealing way: "The first evidence
of such a consciousness, and also the first brilliant outline of a new religion
developed with Jesus as its central idea, lies in the epistles of the tent-maker of
Tarsus, the pilgrim apostle Paul."[15]

Aside from the questionableness of which letters may be ascribed to Paul,
what do they tell us of a real historical Jesus? Nothing, answered Drews (sayings, references to James, are community rules, allusions to any "brother"). In
fact, Paul's Jesus is a completely divine figure, a "purely divine personality, a
heavenly spirit without flesh and blood, an unindividual superhuman phantom"
(180). Where did all this come from? The Hellenistic world was already satu-
rated with such cults. Drews examined Tarsus, the place of Stoicism and mystery
cults, and concluded that when Paul, with his Jewish background, first heard of
a Jewish god Jesus, he must have reacted with hostility when he saw how it all
was being syncretized. But then "on a sudden there came over him as it were
enlightenment," said Drews (187). What if all the claims of the mysteries were
so? And despairing of his own ability to secure the righteousness required by
the Law, Paul was struck by the notion of the self-sacrificing god, the messiah
to come, who had already come and accomplished through his shameful death/

---

14. I take it that Drews referred to the use of σταυρόω in its sense of driving a stake or impaling;
ψύλον can also be shorthand for a crucifixion.

15. Drews, *The Christ Myth,* 165.

glorious resurrection what humans could not accomplish for themselves. So "the moment in which this idea flashed through Paul's mind was the moment of the birth of Christianity as Paul's religion" (189).

Everything else followed. Paul invented the notion of Incarnation; no historical personality was really necessary. In fact, the Christ is but an

> idea of the human race conceived as a personality, the Platonic idea of Humanity personified, the ideal man as a metaphysical essence; and so in his fate the fate of all mankind is fulfilled. . . . It is clearly the Platonic idea of humanity, and nothing else. (197)

What about the Jesus of the gospels? Drews used the results of criticism against the critics. John has no value, Mark is the source of the other two, and is itself of questionable historical worth. Wrede was invoked as help. If Mark is discarded, only the Q or Logia source remains. But even here questions abound. In the end Drews, examining the optimism of the liberals about recovering a historical Jesus from such accounts, said,

> Everywhere there is the same half-comic, half-pathetic drama: on the one hand the evangelical authorities are depreciated and the information is criticized away to such an extent that hardly anything positive remains from it; on the other hand there is a pathetic enthusiasm for the so-called "historical kernel." Then comes praise for the so-called critical theology and its "courageous truthfulness," which, however, ultimately consists only in declaring evident myths and legends to be such. (226)

The secular testimony to Jesus (Tacitus and others) was also declared to be of no value. Drews then took up objections to the thesis of the denial of Jesus' historicity, finding nothing whatsoever historical in the gospel stories of Jesus. Everything has its counterpart somewhere in mythology. Schmiedel's "pillars," the embarrassing passages, could also have been invented in the service of producing a likely picture of the god incarnate. Not a single saying can with certainty be traced back to a historical figure. So:

> Can we then think that the supporters of an "historical" Jesus are right in treating it as nothing more than a "crude sin against all historical methods," as something most monstrous and unscientific, if one draws the only possible inference from the result of the criticism of the Gospels, and disputes the existence at any time of an historical Jesus? (252)

The gospels are only "the expression of the consciousness of a community" (264).

The embodiment of the god Jesus as a human figure is traceable back to the conflicts of the early community. The Jerusalem church needed to assert its authority as apostles and to demonstrate it through descent from an actual historical figure, just as the bishops of Rome even today claim legitimacy from that same figure. Christianity developed from Gnosticism, with which it also subsequently came into conflict and competition. This conflict led it to stronger assertion of the real humanness of its Jesus over against Gnosticism. The Fourth Gospel especially witnesses to that development.

For Drews the religious life of the present cannot be served by the historical Jesus of liberalism. Rather, what matters is to hold to the notion of redemption, the idea of the God-man with which Christianity began. God became man so that man might become god. Man can and should become God through the agency of his moral activity. To attain victory over the world, to anticipate triumph over suffering, to overcome the limits of the finite in God-consciousness — that is to preserve the essence of Christianity and, not incidentally, to assure the triumph of a monism with a religious consciousness.

Certainly Drews was not an old-fashioned village atheist, attacking the very notion of a deity or religion itself as outmoded; he was, rather, contending for a different Christianity (or, more broadly, a different religious consciousness), contending against the insufficiency of the liberal version. But his critics were also right: his work was based on *Religionsgeschichte* gone amuck, with the most appalling connections drawn among items that had no natural kinship.

William Benjamin Smith

If Arthur Drews seemed strange in a role urging something resembling a reform of Christianity, then William Benjamin Smith was all the more so. Born in 1850 in Kentucky, Smith moved with his family to Missouri where he grew up on a farm, his father later killed by Union soldiers. Academically talented but largely impoverished, Smith graduated from the University of Kentucky, receiving an M.A. and teaching at the university in geology, zoology, and botany. The Greek and Latin he acquired in the university were extended by his own studies to include Hebrew, French, German, and Italian, and later Assyrian. Contact with critical developments in Old Testament led him to a position of skepticism, and he studied a year in Germany at Göttingen, receiving his doctorate in 1879 with honors. He occupied positions at Fayette College, Missouri, came to chair the Department of Physics at the University of Missouri, and in 1885 moved to Tulane University where he taught mathematics. He continued his interest in biblical studies and in 1906 published, with the sponsorship of Paul Schmiedel of Zurich, *Der vorchristliche Jesus*.[16] Schmiedel did not agree with his work, but was sufficiently impressed with it to provide for it an introduction and assure its reception in Germany. This work was never completely translated into English, but the substance of Smith's views were made available later in his *Ecce Deus*.[17]

Smith was self-consciously contending against the all-too-human or "purely human" Jesus of liberalism. Neither, however, did he care for the eschatological figure. His judgment about Schweitzer's Jesus:

---

16. William Benjamin Smith, *Der vorchristliche Jesus: Vorstudien zur Entstehungsgeschichte des Urchristentums* (Jena: Verlagt bei Eugen Diederichs, 1906; 2d ed., 1911). According to Schmiedel Smith wrote to him saying, "My vocation is mathematics, my avocation is theology" (v).

17. William Benjamin Smith, *Ecce Deus: Studies of Primitive Christianity* (Chicago: Open Court Publishing, 1912). The biographical data are from Smith's posthumous work, *The Birth of the Gospel: A Study of the Origin and Purport of the Primitive Allegory of the Jesus*, ed. Addison Gulick (New York: Philosophical Library, 1957). See the preface by the editor.

> Of all the "Jesus-shapes," this seems the least lovely and the most inadequate....
> [It] is, indeed, the *reductio ad absurdum* of the liberal purely human hypothesis;
> while its logical successor, the psychopathic theory of Binet-Sanglé and his peers,
> is the *reductio ad nauseam.* (xviii)

What Smith proposed instead was a symbolic interpretation of the data.

What lies behind the New Testament is the cult of the Jesus. Tradition in-sists that what we have to do with is the god-man. Smith wished to resolve this dilemma into a choice: either Jesus was a deified man or the Jesus was a humanized God. He opted for the latter, liberalism the former. He wished to contest the liberal assertion of a unique personality at the core of Christianity. It was not true, he thought, that great historical movements have at their center some specific personality, some individual (for example, the French Revolution). Christianity was in fact sycretic. Its only unifying item was worship of Jesus as god. If Jesus were merely a man, then nothing would be left. The real secret of Christianity was monotheism, worship of the one god under the name of the Jesus; it was a protest against polytheism.

Christianity was then a Jesus cult directed against polytheism and for mono-theism. As such it found it necessary to mask itself and so spoke in symbols. The whole message has to be decoded, which is what Smith proposed to do. His mode of argumentation can be seen in a single example. In the scene where Jesus sends the disciples on their mission (Mark 3:14–15; Matt. 10:1; Luke 10:17–20) and they return proclaiming victory over Satan who fell "like lightning from heaven," Smith asked:

> What else can this be but the fall of polytheism, the victory of monotheism? If
> such be not the meaning of these verses, then what is their meaning? What other
> possible significance, that is not trivial, can they have? Can any rational man for
> a moment believe that the Saviour sent forth his apostles and disciples with such
> awful solemnity to heal the few lunatics that languished in Galilee? (57)

So a cult grew up with the goal of making known everywhere the one god. Nat-urally this god would have revealed himself to the cult, just precisely as a man. And that is how Jesus is pictured. From that insight imagination could and did run riotously wild, producing various gospels. Help was available in many forms, from Plato's just man to the mystery religions everywhere, but the germinating idea was the principle of oneness, the monotheistic impulse. The first Christians or proto-Christians were Gnostics. Certain texts were illuminated in this light: Acts 10:38 does not refer to a human being, but to the gnostic redeemer on his cosmic journey through the universe to earth.

Gospel texts that seem to point to a human Jesus, such as reference to his human emotions, were eyed by Smith in a symbolic way. For example, Mark 10:21 says that Jesus "loved" the rich young man. But, says Smith, the rich young man is "nothing else than Faithful Israel" (98) and not a real person at all. And what about all those multitudes Jesus was said to have healed of their various maladies? All is just spiritual: He healed them of their paganism, false worship, and polytheism.

So a historical interpretation, which would see a real historical figure, is not necessary. The symbolic covers every case. In Mark 16:51–52 the young man is not, as Julius Wellhausen thought, merely a neighborhood *Kind* who heard the rumpus and ran out of his bed to see what was the matter in the scuffling. Rather, the barely clothed young man recalls descriptions of the angels and Old Testament models (Ezekiel, Daniel); he is, in fact, the "Angel-Self of Jewish anthropology, the Persian *ferhouer*. . . . a kind of astral body that 'follows along with' the Jesus, robed in fine linen to abate its intolerable splendour. The soldiers try to seize it, but it flees away naked, leaving only the linen investiture behind" (113). So there was no human Jesus who was arrested; such a thought would have been impossible for Mark. It was only the "garment" of flesh he has put on. The "real" one fled away "naked," as disembodied spirit.

But surely Paul spoke of a historical figure. Questionable, said Smith, and examined the Pauline "quadrilateral," the four epistles supposed to be unquestionably from Paul. Even if those be granted to Paul, the interpretation of them remains arguable.

Smith was unmoved by the argument of a vivid personality behind the gospel record. If that is so, he claimed, then no one has yet been able to say what that personality was. And it is not clear that the depiction of such was the purpose of the evangelists anyway.

Smith also took up the pillars of Schmiedel. A single instance (Mark 10:18) will suffice: "Why do you call me good? None is good save God alone." Schmiedel argued that such verses showed the human figure of Jesus, since it is inconceivable that these words would simply have been made up by the community that worshiped him. But, asked Smith, with some justification, why would this community have handed down just such traditions if they could not make sense of them in light of their own views?[18] The whole is a symbolism and the main phrase meant, "One is the good," that is, a veiled allusion to the monotheistic doctrine. And even if the Jesus were disclaiming goodness, it would only be relative to the Father's goodness.

And so on. With the disintegration of the pillars, the historical Jesus has disappeared.

The extrabiblical evidence likewise gave little comfort to the supporters of historicity. Speaking of the notices in Tacitus and Josephus, Smith observed that the liberal scholars themselves did not quite agree as to their value, H. von Soden extolling Tacitus and Daniel Chwolson[19] defending Josephus, with each detracting from the other. Smith then wrote:

---

18. Here Smith touched a problem for all authenticity judgments based on the claim that a tradition is more reliable when it cuts against the grain of the interests of the community that preserved it. At the same time, as especially Form Criticism would insist, no tradition was preserved that did not serve that same interest. The two assumptions necessarily stand in some tension with each other.

19. Reference was to the German Jewish scholar Daniel Chwolson.

> To track down the endless inaccuracies and fallacies of such hasty superficialities
> would be a weary and bootless task, like chasing field-mice in autumn: stamp them
> out here, and lo they stir the soil yonder! In this case to be just would be cruel;
> one can afford to be generous, and to pass over these *Flugschriften* as too flighty for
> detailed notice, and as not representing their authors properly. (230)

In his own assessment he found nothing that would be incontestably original
and hence supportive of the historicity of Jesus (the reference to James is likely a
reference to a "class of earnest Messianists" [237], while the absence of any mention of a Neronian persecution in Christian literature tells against the originality
of the allusions in Tacitus).

He took up the concept of the kingdom of God and chided the liberals for
emphasizing Luke 17:20–21, "The kingdom is within you." He quoted Wellhausen as translating *Innerhalb von euch* and interpreting the text with primary
emphasis on the inner kingdom, the one in the human heart. He agreed that the
kingdom was not a future entity either, but affirmed that it was an organization,
in fact, the Christian community, the society in which the Jesus was worshiped as
the one God. Thus the preaching of repentance in preparation for the kingdom
in the synoptics is the demand to change one's mind and accept the message of
the monotheistic God.

It is obvious that Smith had difficulty being taken seriously, in part because
of his methodology and in part due to his lack of credentials in the field. He
appeared to be merely a dilettante, a mathematician poaching on the historian's
turf. That judgment had some validity, but on the other hand Smith was remarkably well versed in the texts and in the literature surrounding the controversy.
It is likely also that he was not fully understood; in a pamphlet his publisher put
out accompanying his work, Smith gave it as his judgment that he had at no
time ever asserted that Jesus was mythical.

> My uniform contention has been that Jesus, the Christ, was, and is, divine, essential
> God, an Aspect or Person of the One Deity....I have everywhere affirmed his
> reality and divinity and substantial Godhead in the most explicit terms used by any
> critic since the birth of criticism.[20]

Disingenuous, perhaps, as he affirmed rather carefully the existence of the
Christ-figure, but just as carefully avoided any affirmation of the "historical
Jesus." That may be also because to do so would be to consent to the picture
as constructed by the "liberals." Just so does it become all the clearer the extent
to which ideological issues were driving the whole debate, and the degree to
which the program of liberalism had itself generated the controversy.

---

20. From a flyer put out by the publisher of Smith's work in America (Open Court Publishing
Company). It is located in the Shirley Jackson Case archives at Florida Southern College along with
Smith's critical response to Case's work.

John M. Robertson

A somewhat different case is presented by the third member of the "unholy"
trinity, John M. Robertson.[21] Robertson was one of those classic British-Scottish
dissenters known as freethinkers. Born in 1856 (d. 1933) he had little formal
education, having left school at the age of 13, never to return; yet his learning,
acquired on his own, was prodigious and in a wide variety of humanistic fields.
He worked throughout his life primarily as a writer, a sometime journalist, and
a sometime politician, having been elected to Parliament in 1906 — as a Liberal
naturally — and he served until 1918. He made various lecture tours to the
United States and married an American woman from Iowa. His writings included
two classics on free thought (1899, 1929), a number of works of literary criticism
that compared favorably with Matthew Arnold, and, of course, rather extensive
works in religious history.

His work is contained largely in three volumes: *Christianity and Mythology;
Pagan Christs: Studies in Comparative Hierology;* and *The Historical Jesus: A Survey
of Positions.*[22]

The first book was a variation of the thesis pursued by Drews — who, indeed, was probably dependent on both Robertson and Smith[23] — an independent
investigation into the sources and nature of myths. After an extended discussion of preceding works on the origins of myths, Robertson attended to the
current debate as represented by Drews, referring to the meeting in Berlin
under the auspices of the German Society of Monists (*Monistenbund*) on January 31–February 1, 1910, stimulated by the paper by Drews entitled, "Is Jesus a
Historical Personality?" Robertson quoted von Soden as referring to him as "an
Englishman (not the celebrated one) who has no great name among us." Robertson added that "I may be permitted to offer the rev. professor my condolences on
the fact that he is under a similar drawback in England, and to express the hope
that both of us may nevertheless continue to hold up our heads." Of Schweitzer
he said that his work "is considerably further removed from the traditional belief
than from this negation thereof."[24]

Robertson surveyed the history of myth-interpretation up to that point
in time, with the claim that his own was scientific, using an evolutionary,
sociological-anthropological approach. Myths are explanations of otherwise uncomprehended phenomena. A myth is "simply a false hypothesis...which once
found easy credence" (xviii). The substantial bulk of the book was given to consideration of the relationship between the Christ and Krishna myths. Robertson

21. His biography in the *Dictionary of National Biography* was rather flatteringly composed by the
eminent economist and political scientist Harold J. Laski.

22. Robertson, *Christianity and Mythology* (London: Watts, 1900; 2d ed., 1910); *Pagan Christs:
Studies in Comparative Hierology* (London: Watts, 1903; 2d ed., 1911); and *The Historical Jesus: A
Survey of Positions* (London: Watts, 1916).

23. Schweitzer said that Drews simply took over Smith's notion of a pre-Christian Jesus cult, and
also referred to Drews as simply an epigonist — something dreadful in the Schweitzerian scheme of
things. See *Geschichte,* 505.

24. Robertson, *Christianity and Mythology,* xv, xvi.

wished to dispute that the Krishna myth was derived from or somehow based on the Christ myth. He favored the antiquity of the Krishna myth, though not necessarily direct dependence. In some cases Buddhism was the mediator; in others, it was a complex of myths widely available in the Greco-Roman world. In short, Christianity was manufactured out of preexisting materials.

The third major part of the work characterized the gospel myths. Robertson rejected the then-prevailing idea (Herbert Spencer, James Frazer) that behind myths of origin are actual historical personages. In Robertson's view it is only the ethical content of a given religion that continues to commend that religion to modern persons as having a historical basis in some actual figure. But that is no proper ground for a critical belief. Myths of doctrine also abound (Solomon, Moses).

Robertson then turned his attention to gospel myths, such as the virgin birth (pagan, astrological), and other details of the birth narratives (cave and stable, massacre of the innocents), Jesus in the temple (precocious child theme), upbringing at Nazareth (no Nazareth then), the temptation (Buddha parallels), water-wine story (Dionysus), temple-scourging (Egyptian), walking on the sea (parallels in the Poseidon myth), and healings. Even the figures of Paul, Peter, and Judas (betrayal myth of Joseph; mystery drama) came under the same line of interpretation, as did also the Lord's Supper (mystery drama), and so on right through the crucifixion, cross, and resurrection. The teaching was subjected to the same analysis. All is mythical or at best contradictory. How can the same figure claim to be "meek and lowly in heart" and "a greater than Solomon" all at the same time? Or that he has nowhere to lay his head and yet has come eating and drinking? In fact, there must have been many Jesuses with teaching from different sects clashing and resounding now all in the same record. Jesus as savior was no different. Such was a widespread notion at that time. Jesus as mediator, as logos, was all too familiar, just like Mithra, Marduk, and the emperor-god. The John the Baptist cult points to a pre-Christian cult of Jesus, likely located in Mandaism.

In short, all is a congery of myth. The Christian cult was the work of many, mostly anonymous, though certainly some, such as Paul, should be given extra credit. But there was not much of value in the record anyway:

> Had they [the gospels] been the moral marvel they are said to be, they should have prevented the decay which fell upon a world enlightened by them. . . . They [the gospels] are absolutely devoid of the species of light which alone could have arrested that decay. Of political science they show no trace; they implicitly endorse slavery, as does Paul, and their doctrines of a speedy end of the world, and of salvation by blind faith, were the virtual frustration of all the better precepts they contained. If the scrupulous Stoicism of Marcus Aurelius, gravely bent on his public duty, could not arrest Roman dissolution, much less could the gospels do so. (435)

Robertson considered various objectors. Among these he counted Schweitzer as "affirmative" and gave on the whole a thankful estimate of Schweitzer's work for pointing out all the problems in constructing a "life" of Jesus, for being a "destroyer" to the orthodox, but of course also found Schweitzer's Jesus equally problematic: "In the end he does but yield us a new psychological romance, utterly recalcitrant to the bulk of the record" (458).

Robertson at that point was less focused on the liberal debate that was being carried on in Germany. He had no agenda to retain Christianity in some other form. He was, at all appearances, an old-style rationalist contending against orthodoxy. In fact, his inclusion in the company of Drews and Smith seemed at first a little strange.

The second volume, *Pagan Christs*, goes some distance further in endorsing Drews's notion of the existence of a pre-Christian Jesus cult, a Joshua-Jesus cult of a sun god,[25] with the nearest pagan analogies to the suffering messiah in the Prometheus myth. The gospels are mystery plays, dramas. Jesus is a pagan savior god, like Dionysus, Osiris, or Aesclepius. A sacrificial meal was eaten, followed by the mystery drama. Robertson traced out the idea of human sacrifice and its role in religions. This was embodied in the eucharist, though real human sacrifices stand back of it, lost in the primitive beginnings. A special ancestry lies in Mithraism.

Something of Robertson's program can be seen in the following:

> Religious belief has been historically associated with both the progress and the paralysis of civilisation; and the just inference is that, so far from its being *the* principle of betterment, it is simply a form of fallacious mental activity, which may either be countervailed by truer forms or may countervail them. . . . There is thus no reason to doubt that in savage as in civilized times the forces of organized religion have been arrayed against the forces of betterment, social as well as intellectual, with but a dubious record on the side of moralisation. (386–87)

Robertson's position hardened still more in the third volume, *The Historical Jesus: A Survey of Positions*. There is no value, he said, in the approaches taken by his critics, in merely "bragging" on Jesus, or elevating him above all others. A considerable effort was expended in replying to the critics. He seemed kindly disposed toward Schmiedel, even while disagreeing with him. Christianity, he reiterated, originated in a rite, not a message, in agreement with his previous view that the ritual existed first, then the teachings were created to justify the existence of the practice.

Robertson delighted in the findings of the critical scholars. The primitive gospel was the Logia source (Q), but it had no passion narrative, which was appended later (Mark). Thus it is demonstrable that there was a different origin for the passion story; it was narrative of the mystery drama, having nothing to do with the teaching material originally. But neither contained anything historical. The usual theories of composition of the gospels are either to be rejected, or they simply do not support the notion of historicity. What is seen, whether Logia or gospel, is the clash of competing sects and different views of the Jesus. Oral tradition does not solve the problem either; it is used to account for the

---

25. Robertson, *Pagan Christs*, 162–67.

different versions of Jesus, but actually they are often contradictions, leaving the historian nowhere to go. The weakness of the critics can be seen in their treatment of the healings. Most of the critics waffle, talking about psychic processes and the like. The evidence for a trial is no better. There were two groups in the early church, Judaizers and Gentiles; the former needed an execution by the Romans, the latter prosecution by the Jews. Hence the trial was shaped to those ends. It is a mystery play.

Alfred Loisy's Jesus was essentially a liberal Jesus, a bundle of contradictions as well — an eschatologist with an ethical bent. There could also be no comfort in the appeal to Paul on the issue of Jesus' historicity. Sketching the history of this debate, Robertson saw D. F. Strauss as a halfway house, holding on to the historicity of Jesus. Schweitzer's work gained some approval, though Robertson disagreed with the assessment of Bauer, who misused the myth theory, even misunderstood myth, since he attributed the whole gospel to the creation of a single individual. Of Schweitzer:

> What his book mainly demonstrates is the laborious futility of the age-long discussion maintained by the professional theologians of Germany.... Dr. Schweitzer's Jesus has, indeed, disciples for no assignable reason, but he is expressly declared to be no Teacher, even as Wrede's Teacher is expressly declared to be no Messiah. The joint result is to leave the ground tolerably clear for the scientific myth theory, of which Dr. Schweitzer has not come within sight, having omitted to inquire about it.[26]

Robertson agreed with Schweitzer that the choice was between the eschatological and the liberal Jesus. Having satisfied himself that the liberal one is indefensible, Robertson then took up Schweitzer's eschatological one. He scorned Schweitzer's picture of a Jesus who claimed a secret messiahship, who entered the city as Elijah, fooling the crowd, and was betrayed by Judas, who merely reported what was easily known and who was accompanied by the charade of priests who persuaded the fickle crowd that here was an unworthy who deserved death for claiming to be the secret messiah. "Dr. Schweitzer seems to realize all absurdities save his own," said Robertson (203). And, after quoting Schweitzer on the nonexistence of the liberal Jesus and the affirmation of his own Jesus from whom the "mighty spiritual force" went forth, Robertson ended:

> "Loves me, loves me not," as the little girls say in counting the flower petals. We seem entitled to suggest in the interests of simple science, as distinguished from Germanic *Kultur*, that temperament might perhaps usefully be left out of the debate; and that the question what Jesus stands for may be left over till we have settled whether the film presented to us by Dr. Schweitzer can stand between us and a scientific criticism which assents to all of his verdict save the reservation in favour of his own thesis. (204)

The conclusion made it clear that Robertson was simply working from the perspective of the rationalist or freethinker, with no theological goal in mind. In his

---

26. Robertson, *Historical Jesus*, 197, 199.

view as well most of the gospel material had already been attributed to myth by the critics themselves; his work only took it a step further. Robertson was clearly a competent polemicist with an impressive learning; but like Drews much of his erudition was inchoate, lacking any interpretive power, and his grasp of the Jesus tradition seemed far more elementary than that of his critics.

Schweitzer's Assessment

Schweitzer had devoted a great deal of space in his second edition to the *Streit* over the historicity of Jesus, summarizing the literature and analyzing the issues involved. In his *Geschichte* he devoted two large chapters to the relevant material and the debate (chaps. 22–23), locating its origins in the investigations of the *religionsgeschichtliche Schule* and in the failure of modern theology, going back at least to Hegel and the marriage of Christian faith and "history" — in Schweitzer's view a fatal move carried forth in the Ritschlian school. Religion, as he seemed never to weary of saying, ought to be grounded in a philosophy or metaphysics that would not leave faith vulnerable to the vicissitudes of historical science. Drews and the others simply took advantage of the position to which the modern theology had exposed itself.

Schweitzer found little to praise in the controversy, saying that it did the twentieth century no honor and had elements of sheer demagoguery about it, especially in the public rallies and slogans and appeals to the masses. For Schweitzer the most important issue was the religious-philosophical one. Christianity would likely always have to reckon with the possibility of Jesus' non-historicity: What would be left for it should Jesus' historical existence have to be given up? The historical figure of Jesus could then only be an element in religion, not its foundation. That is why religion needs a metaphysics, a basic view of the nature and meaning of being that is independent of history and transmitted traditions. Otherwise religion would remain a slave of history. It was this failure, to repeat, that was most perceptible in the Ritschlian school and brought on the question of Jesus' historicity and, not so incidentally, betrayed the liberal impulse and opened the door again to orthodoxy.

Here Schweitzer took up the thesis of Breslau professor G. Wobbermin, perhaps based on Martin Kähler's earlier distinction between "historic" and "historical" (*geschichtlich* and *historisch*).[27] Christian faith is tied to the "historic"

---

27. Kähler's work in 1892, not noticed by Schweitzer, was *The So-Called Historical Jesus and the Historic Biblical Christ*, trans. and ed. with introduction by Carl E. Braaten, Seminar Editions (Philadelphia: Fortress Press, 1962). Discussion of Wobbermin in *Geschichte*, 521. An insightful discussion of the tensions within the Ritschlians, notably between the older Ritschlians and the younger "leftist" group (*religionsgeschichtliche Schule*), with attention to Troeltsch's and Wobbermin's essays also is to be found in George Rupp's *Culture-Protestantism: German Liberal Theology at the Turn of the Twentieth Century*, American Academy of Religion Studies in Religion 15 (Atlanta: Scholars Press, 1977), esp. chaps. 2–3.

(*geschichtlich*) Jesus, the one persisting throughout history, the "spirit" of Jesus, and not the historical (*historisch*) Jesus. Schweitzer had no sympathy for that distinction, labeling it an "artful piece of modern scholasticism" that could provide no answer to the question of the relation of Christian faith to the historical Jesus. Similarly, he remained unimpressed with either the social-psychological analysis of Ernst Troeltsch or the "symbolic" interpretation of Wilhelm Bousset.[28] For Schweitzer it was a simple issue of whether the historical Jesus, the Jesus of the two oldest gospels, has significance for us today or not. If so, it is not necessary to clothe him in symbols (Bousset); if not, then such symbols would in fact only become his grave clothes. Nor is it saying much for Jesus that he remains relevant only as the head of a cultic community (Troeltsch).[29] Schweitzer did find some importance in the positions of Troeltsch and Bousset: they could not, as leading theologians, find much more significance in the historical particularity of Jesus' personality than the deniers of Jesus' historical existence. All the more strange that they were so concerned to maintain it.

Neither was Schweitzer much impressed with Schmiedel's pillars or the criteria of authenticity articulated by Weinel, failing to see how such a distinction between what comes from the church and what comes from Jesus could be maintained — in the two oldest gospels those distinctions are at bottom empty words. Such efforts can only be minimally satisfactory. Schweitzer maintained his view consistently that the two oldest gospels must simply be taken *en bloc* and judged authentic or inauthentic. He then undertook an analysis of the deniers' use of research into Gnosticism and other hellenistic elements in constructing their case for a Jesus-cult antedating Christianity. None of it provided any demonstration that a genuine historical personality did not lie behind the records and, Schweitzer concluded, to the extent that the hypotheses of Jesus' nonhistoricity distanced themselves from the "noisy polemic with 'theology'" and engaged in "genuine proofs," just so did they show themselves to be "impracticable hypotheses" (564).

But, in fact, the essays by Troeltsch and Bousset are worth more consideration than Schweitzer seemed to give them, not only for the merit of their own thought, but also as illuminating the extent to which the liberal theology of the day was driven by its own works and the inexorableness of its own logic.

---

28. Troeltsch in *Die Bedeutung der Geschichtlichkeit Jesu für den Glauben* (Tübingen: J. C. B. Mohr [Paul Siebeck], 1911); a translation appeared as "The Significance of the Historical Existence of Jesus for Faith," in *Ernst Troeltsch: Writings on Theology and Religion,* trans. and ed. Robert Morgan and Michael Pye (Louisville: Westminster/John Knox Press, 1977). The translation is by Robert Morgan. Bousset's essay was *Die Bedeutung der Person Jesu für den Glauben* (Berlin: Schöneberg, 1910), published in English by Williams and Norgate in 1911 as a separate pamphlet as "The Significance of the Personality of Jesus for Belief," no translator given. The pamphlet was extracted from the large volume referred to earlier (see prologue, n. 46).

29. It is perhaps not too surprising that Schweitzer would not be attracted to Troeltsch's way of thinking, for Schweitzer was himself driven by the conception of the creative individual exercising the power of rational thought to achieve solutions to civilization's need.

Wilhelm Bousset

Bousset's essay appeared as an address at the Fifth International Congress for Free Christianity and Religious Progress held at Berlin in August of 1910.[30] He began by observing that, indeed, little can be known about the Jesus of history, even discounting the current denials of his historicity:

> Our knowledge of the real facts of His life is so little that it could be written on a slip of paper. The teaching or the Gospel of Jesus is a web often not to be disentangled, woven of the tradition of His community, and of possibly true words of the Master. What the Gospels tell us about the peculiar self-consciousness of Jesus, and its forms and therefore about His innermost life, is overshadowed by the dogma of His community.[31]

Such knowledge provides little ground for the basing of faith, and it is surely questionable whether the certainty of faith ought to reside in the uncertainties of historical research. Of course, that is little problem for the positive theology,[32] as can be seen in the Halle theologian Martin Kähler who showed that it needed only the data of the death and resurrection and perhaps a supernatural beginning.[33] Modern theology [liberalism] took up a different stance, coming from Schleiermacher, an antirational position basing itself on "history" and locating everything in the historical personality of Jesus, which Schleiermacher supposed he had found truly in the Gospel of John. The nineteenth century followed in his train. But this line has driven theology to its present impasse: "History resolutely pursued to its end points of necessity beyond itself."[34]

Bousset then entered upon some analysis of the position of historicism in his own time in the work of Ritschl in particular, for whom the personality of Jesus lay at the center, and who thought to find in Jesus the prophet and founder of the kingdom of God. But Ritschl only took from Jesus the most striking things, the things that seemed to support the notions already brought to the text. So criticism pointed out that the matters thought to be of prime importance were only implanted there ourselves; and while there may well be many things of eternal significance in the message and life of Jesus, criticism itself is hardly in a position to make such a judgment. So when hope of discovering what is of substance in the teaching itself is abandoned, faith falls back on the most insubstantial thing of all, the historical personality of Jesus himself that seems to defy categorization. One can then simply be content with the picture of Jesus through

---

30. Above, prologue, 17 n. 46.

31. Bousset, "Significance of the Personality of Jesus for Belief," pamphlet, 4, or book, 209. Future page citations to Bousset's work will have the pamphlet page number followed by a slash and the book page number (e.g., 4/209).

32. This terminology applies to orthodox Protestant thinking.

33. Doubtless Bousset was referring to the now well-known essay by Martin Kähler, referred to earlier (n. 27 above). The confluence of this comment with the later position developed by Bultmann is quite remarkable (excepting the reference to the supernatural birth). Of course Bousset would characterize this positive position as based on a "phantastic [sic] mythical-dogmatic interpretation of the life of Jesus by Paul" (4/209).

34. Bousset, 6/211.

pious contemplation, in which case the question continually arises whether this faith-picture bears any relation to history; it necessarily becomes tied to further questions about Jesus' own messianic consciousness, again bringing forth uncertainty. Or one can have recourse to the idea that Jesus was the originating impulse of Christian faith and so abandon the connection basically between current religious life and history, but at the price again of a questionable basis for such a contemporary religious life. So again the pursuit of history points beyond itself, and what it points to is reason itself.

For Bousset religion is an essential and primordial element in reason itself; it does not arise from something outside human nature or some supernatural revelation. Neither are religious ideas scientific theorems or deducible from logical premises. Rather, they are

> final truths which can only be pointed to as a constituent part of our reason but which as expressions of a fundamental faculty which defies all rational analysis can never be proved. Reflection can not produce this faculty by proving it, can only make us conscious of its existence and its peculiarity. Religion does not acquire life by rational reflection, in fact it is preexistent to it. (11/216)

That is because religion has to do with meaning and value, unlike natural science or even historical science. Religion attempts to comprehend the totality of things, the world-reality in its wholeness, and it asserts the meaningfulness of this reality. Practical belief, however, does not depend directly on these reflections of reason, but rather lives from symbols and pictures, parables and poetry. The aesthetic sense and the religious sense are in this respect very close to one another. Thus, for example, Jesus can depict the kindness and power of God as Father through invoking the image of the lilies of the field.

The religious consciousness has evolved over centuries, beginning with a sense of awe or horror and dependence (Schleiermacher), proceeding through selection of symbols to higher ends, and culminating in great historical personalities. So Jesus finds his role here, in line with other great figures (prophets and the like). These remain at the symbolic level and have their function there. As such Jesus as historical figure is not crucial; what is crucial is Jesus as symbol:

> At this point therefore all depends on the symbol and the picture, not on final truth and reality. This lies beyond the symbols in the unalterable God-given profundities of human reason, in the eternal worth of the "ideas." The symbol serves as illustration not as demonstration. (15/220)

At this level even the Fourth Gospel remains truthful, however much it has been refuted as history by criticism. Bousset added,

> And even if Science should pass the ultimate verdict that Jesus never existed, yet faith can not be lost, for it rests upon its own eternal foundations; and moreover the figure of Jesus in the Gospels would remain in spite of it, though only as a great fiction, yet as fiction of eternal symbolic significance. (16/220–21)

Bousset did not think that Jesus was not a historical figure, but the loss of his historicity could not affect the significance for faith of his "facticity" as symbol.

Ernst Troeltsch

Troeltsch had no interest in attempting to demonstrate the existence of Jesus as a historical figure and, indeed, regarded the current debate as "ludicrous."[35] However, there is a continuing issue of whether historical criticism must be severed from Christian faith or whether there is some necessary relationship between the two. Conceived from the perspective of orthodox Christianity, there is no problem; the dogmatic Christ rules everywhere and his reality is assumed. It is also not a problem for many modern persons for whom religion is simply a matter of individuals who may have an inner relationship to Christianity but for whom the church has no particular significance. This position is traceable back to the beginnings of modern criticism and on down through Hegel and Strauss and the modern Ritschlians; it rests on the separation of person and principle, on recognition that religious faith ought to arise from history but not be dependent upon it. Once the Christian idea was secured, it might be loosed from its original moorings in history (Hegel; cf. Strauss). Since then there are "halfway houses" providing solutions (liberalism), claiming some necessity for a relationship to a historical person in order to establish the Christian idea of redemption, that is, while faith may be assured of its redemptive efficacy, its arousal is tied to the historical personality of Jesus, if not to any particular collection of his sayings or miracles, which may have become problematic (so Schleiermacher, Ritschl, Herrmann). Whether the emphasis falls on the total personality of Christ, as evidenced in the gospels (especially John), to create the certainty of faith (Schleiermacher), or his authority to provide assurance of forgiveness (Ritschl), or the power of his personality to effect assurance of the forgiving grace of God (Herrmann), in every case an *idea* of God tied to the historical personality of Jesus lies at the core and provides the act of redemption, not a cosmic, salvific event.

Implicit is the assumption, unacceptable to the modern world, that only in Christ is there salvation. And equally questionable, rendered so by modern criticism, is the further assumption that Jesus' historical personality can be grasped at all. Furthermore, historical investigation of the origins of Christianity only raises more difficulties for faith, and tends to demonstrate the historical contingency of Christianity, that it is altogether a product of its time and culture and has no claim to uniqueness. But such "christocentricism" invests our own time and place with a value it has no right to and will not be agreed to in the modern world. The reaction is the current relativizing of the historical Jesus, even to the extent of denying his historicity. For many it is not valid to connect the Christian idea so irretrievably to the historical figure of Jesus. "For them," said Troeltsch,

> Jesus is then the historical starting-point of Christian life and culture, his picture is pedagogically significant or a symbol of Christianity, but an inner conceptually necessary connexion of the Christian idea to the personality of Jesus is no longer there for countless people. (190)

35. *Ernst Troeltsch: Writings*, trans. and ed. Morgan and Pye, 184.

The problem, then, is really only applicable to those who wished to maintain both historical criticism and Christianity as a religion of redemption in some way, only to those who (like Troeltsch himself) wished to acknowledge the claims of the modern world and at the same time preserve the religious powers of Christianity. Troeltsch repeated his argument that a genuine and indissoluble connection between Christian faith and the historical person of Jesus only exists for orthodox Christian faith, on the one hand, and, less clearly so in the mediating position represented by Schleiermacher-Ritschl-Herrmann. Ritschlianism gave rise to the *religionsgeschichtliche Schule* by the violence it did to the text historically in appealing to a wrongful picture of Jesus as its authority; it also assumed, by its inextricable link to Jesus, that persons were unable to do anything to effect their own salvation. In other words, the tie to the historical figure of Jesus concealed an implicit doctrine of original sin, that is, only in the Christian culture can the power of the figure be mediated. Such a thought can get nowhere in the modern world, where the twin assumptions of an earlier "contaminated" humanity and a later one needing "decontamination" are meaningless. Modern thought presupposes only the development of the human spirit in the past and its endless possibilities for development in the future.

All that seems to be left is then either a purely factual historical Jesus or a symbolic one, one who might have given rise to the Christian idea but who may not any longer be necessary for it. But that way seems to have no future and, in fact, religious sentiment seems to be prevailing only in the traditional churches. Troeltsch suggested that therein may lie a clue to the real character of the issue at stake. The modern solution ignores the fact of religious community, the necessity for gathering around a cultic head and carrying forth the actualizing of God in cult and worship:

> This lack of community and cult is the real sickness of modern Christianity and contemporary religious practice generally. It is what makes it so impermanent and chaotic, so dependent on who happens to be there, so much an amateur thing for enthusiasts, so much a matter of world-view and the intellect. It has no dominant center from which it can be nourished, but just as many centers as there are sensitive individual seekers. But it is not just that modern religion has become chaotic and indefinite. It is also feeble and insipid because it lacks the effect which a total spirit and fellowship has upon the individual, with its power to encourage and sustain, intensify and diversify, and above all to set practical goals for the like-minded group. (194)

In religions prophets and founders function as archetypes, sources of power and authority. That is why Christ has this central position and Christianity cannot survive without the Christ of the cult. So for social-psychological reasons the connection with Jesus is absolutely necessary. A new religion would require a new figure. A noncultic Christianity would be "mere illusion" (197). For this reason historical criticism is not a matter of indifference. Those who are content with a Jesus who is simply a mythical embodiment of an idea or symbol are not likely to join communities anyway, and neither will believers be satisfied with such. For believers God cannot be an idea or possibility but is a "holy reality" (197). It is therefore consequential that their faith is connected to one who truly struggled, lived, conquered, and died.

It is therefore impossible to dismiss criticism. Faith cannot establish facts, though it can interpret them. And although the details about the figure of Jesus may not be knowable, the general outline of his teaching and his historical factuality can be established and must be by means of historical research. That might not have been necessary in a prehistorical age, but such no longer exists. If this means that faith cannot be delivered from the hands of the scholars and professors, then we must admit to a certain dependence there, at least "a dependence upon the general feeling of historical reliability produced by the impression of scientific research" (199). And in a scientific world this dependence should not be a matter for lamentation, for faith cannot exempt itself from that world.

And, too, it must be remembered that this dependence does not occur in a vacuum, that what is known and treasured about Jesus has a long history in his community. His significance is seen in the preparation of the Old Testament community, the psalms and the prophets, as well as in the history of Christianity since. In that respect Jesus is "not the only historical fact that is significant for our faith" (201), though his factuality and knowability remain essential to the continuance of Christianity. Troeltsch concluded his essay with noticing some differences, however modest, between himself and the Schleiermacher-Ritschl-Herrmann line (his emphasizes the significance of community, builds on the necessity of religious communities for a cultic center, is not tied to some implied idea of original sin, and therefore is open to other religious redemptive communities with cultic heads).

Bousset's desire to deliver faith from the vagaries of criticism would find many echoes down the road of the twentieth century, and Troeltsch's emphasis on community would especially resonate in American circles. But the two of them also disclose the outer limits of possibilities within a broadly liberal frame of reference: either take refuge in a symbolic Jesus or lean faith onto the works of the scholars and professors. Bousset's general posture offered a real alternative, short of the position of Drews and company, without fleeing from critical studies in the name of faith. It doubtless owed something to Kant, while also there is no surprise in Karl Barth's listening darkly to Troeltsch's essay as it was delivered in its original shape as a lecture.[36]

It bears noticing that the preoccupation in both the Troeltsch and Bousset essays was with *religion* as such. There was a kind of phenomenological concern with religion, its character and its significance, with Christianity as subset, so to speak, of the larger phenomenon of religion. "Modernism" was concerned with "religion," with its nature and importance, and especially with justifying its

---

36. Robert Morgan in ibid., 258 n. 29, referring to Barth's *Theology and Church* (London: SCM Press, 1962), 60–61.

continued existence in the modern world.[37] This, too, found a decided rejection in the movement associated with the name of Karl Barth, who wished to speak again *theologically* of God.

Other Contributors

The historicity debate was represented on the Anglo-American scene most ably by Shirley Jackson Case, with contributions also from the rationalist F. C. Conybeare and the more orthodox Friedrich Loofs.[38] Numerous articles also appeared, though we will only observe something of Case's reportage.[39]

After characterizing the liberalism from which the historicity debate sprang, Case then provided some of the history of the problem, noting the contributions of the French in Charles Dupuis and Constantin Volney (end of eighteenth century), Karl Bahrdt and Karl Venturini in Germany, Charles Hennell in England, as well as the influence of D. F. Strauss and Bruno Bauer. He then listed the main opponents in Germany (Arthur Drews, Albert Kalthoff, Peter Jensen, Samuel Lublinski), in England (J. M. Robertson, G. R. S. Mead, Thomas Whittaker), in Holland (Gerardus J. P. J. Bolland), in France (Charles Virolleaud), Italy (Emilio Bossi), Poland (Andrzej Niemojewski), and America (W. B. Smith). There were, said Case, two questions about the radical position: Does it successfully treat the traditional evidence, and does it propose a believable reconstruction of Christian origins?

The parallels so fluidly used by the deniers hardly prove anything more than that the writers of the New Testament were persons of their own time. Furthermore, the parallels are often scraped up from almost anywhere. Paul is a case in point. The letters are usually dismissed as all pseudepigraphic with, however, no real argument for that position. That is characteristic of the whole radical position: assertion without real argument.

As to the second question, how well the reconstruction of Christian origins went on, Case was equally critical: Not well. Evidence for a pre-Christian Jesus cult is slender. The Joshua idea of Drews does not hold up. Epiphanius is not really supportive, as Drews supposed (because of Epiphanius's equation of early

37. As a specific instance we can notice, on the American scene, the formation of the *Journal of Religion* in 1921 as a union of the *American Journal of Theology* and *Biblical World*, both products of the Chicago Divinity School. A journal dealing with *religion* was more attuned to the focus of modernity. A scan of the journals at the time, certainly well into the twenties and thirties, reveals this rather widespread phenomenological and "religious" interest in "religion."

38. F. C. Conybeare in *The Historical Christ* (London: Watts, 1914); Loofs in *What Is the Truth about Jesus Christ? Problems of Christology* (Edinburgh: T. & T. Clark, 1913). Also T. J. Thorburn, *The Mythical Interpretation of the Gospels: Critical Studies in the Historic Narratives*, Bross Library 7 (New York: Scribner's, 1916).

39. Shirley Jackson Case, *The Historicity of Jesus: A Criticism of the Contention That Jesus Never Lived, a Statement of the Evidence for His Existence, an Estimate of His Relation to Christianity* (Chicago: University of Chicago Press, 1912). Case's book was preceded by his own articles, "The Historicity of Jesus," "Is Jesus a Historical Character?," and "Jesus' Historicity: A Statement of the Problem," all in *AJT* 15 (1911): 20–42, 205–27, and 265–68, respectively. On Case generally see chap. 4.

Christians with Philo's therapeutai and existence of a pre-Christian group of Nazarees). The hypothesis of a pre-Christian Jesus myth does not convince.

Case then set forth the evidence for Jesus' historicity. He acknowledged the nature of the earliest sources, Mark and Q, which show signs of interpreting and representing the interests of the early communities behind them. But none of that need mean, however, that no historically reliable data are present. We need to be careful, however, and to find as most historical what is most difficult dogmatically for the early interpreters, or what is not linked to their dogmatic or apologetic interests.

Examination of Paul reveals little interest in the historical Jesus, but we cannot interpret his relative silence as ignorance. And even Paul was not completely silent; there are passages where most likely Paul was asserting something traditional about Jesus. Not only did Paul exist, but the existence of Jesus was critically important for his theology.

The gospel evidence supports what is inferred from Paul concerning a real figure behind the community pictures given there, especially to be seen where the text goes contrary to the interests of the community (the recollection that the disciples did not understand Jesus, that his family considered him crazy, that he was baptized by John). And what we know of the message of Jesus embedded there cannot be derived from non-Christian sources or from such as Paul. Where did it come from?

> Not from some fortuitous concourse of abstract ideas crystallizing of themselves above the heads of men and falling upon them as snow from the clouds. Great thoughts do not come to humanity that way. They are rather the product of some great soul, reacting upon the actual problems of his world.[40]

The primitive community itself is also evidence for the existence of Jesus. Objectors think it is unimaginable for Jesus' contemporaries, who thought of him as human like themselves, now to be worshiping him as a god. Not necessarily so, said Case. The transition to exalted messiah was effected instantly by the resurrection experiences.

Was Jesus then the founder of Christianity? We could say it was the resurrection faith, but even here this faith was connected with the disciples' memory of Jesus. It was Jesus they saw in their ecstatic visions, not someone or something else. Indeed, Case wished to link the personality of Jesus closely with the resurrection faith:

> The impress his personality left upon them contained an element of vitality, interpreted by them in terms of resurrection faith, which was more enduring than all their former messianic expectations, and in turn became the basis of a new messianic hope. Thus the secret of Jesus' influence upon the disciples must ultimately be sought in the content of his own religious life during the period of his association with them. In the last analysis it was his power as a religious individual that

---

40. Case, *Historicity of Jesus*, 233.

made possible the early faith; the personal religion of Jesus was the foundation of the disciples' religion about Jesus. (280–81)

A general characterization of Jesus and his message followed, along with some suggestions as to Jesus' continuing relevance in the current world. Jesus is "more than a pattern to be copied, he is a demonstration of spiritual power to be felt today by those who have received the unction of his spirit" (342). So then for Case, as for liberalism in some broad sense, the personality of Jesus was this spiritual power that emanated from him and is attainable and repeatable in one's own life.

The denial of Jesus' historicity has never convinced any large number of people, in or out of technical circles, nor did it in the first part of the century. At the same time this seemingly odd moment in Jesus studies never quite seems to vanish forever, and it would reappear shortly in the works of Paul-Louis Couchoud and some others, whom we shall notice in another context.[41] It is a lurking monster present wherever critical studies are recognized and proceed, and for that reason an accompaniment to a generally "liberal" commitment to critical methodology. The nonhistorical Jesus is then as much a creation of the liberal impulse as is the historical Jesus. Christian orthodoxy has no real interest in either, is barely threatened by the former, and cannot awaken the latter.

But liberalism stirred other passions as well, some of them to its detriment. And other eventful processes were being set in motion: a soil was being prepared that would bring forth a harvest of silence, of seed falling on barren ground, on hard, unproductive ground, and a ghastly war was brewing that would grind all other mills to a garish halt.

---

41. Below, chap. 8.

Chapter 3

THROUGH THE GREAT WAR

In accounting for the literature from 1907 through 1912 Schweitzer included more non-German works, though still admittedly with fairly scant notice. In fact, he observed that not much work had been done in the area at all due to the preponderance of interest in the historicity question, and he declared that the two most important works in the time period were those of Alfred Loisy and Max Maurenbrecher.[1] There were also certain issues that seemed to continue as open questions, among them the debate over the eschatological element and the matter of Jesus' messianic consciousness, even though Schweitzer himself clearly felt he had gotten hold of the right solution. But not everyone agreed, and in English-speaking countries especially this and related issues went on apace, not apart from the German setting but in awareness of it without simply emulating it.

In England everyone awaited William Sanday's life of Jesus, though in vain, for he never wrote it. Perhaps the issues had overtaken him and there was too much now to be decided, too much rendered uncertain by the force of Schweitzer's work and the newer debates over historicity and the like. In any case lives of Jesus did indeed begin to diminish; ones that appeared take on different shapes, though it seems clear that the lines laid out by liberalism continued to predominate through the time of the First World War.

In England a burning issue was the Jesus or Christ question; its importance was personified in the devotion of a separate volume to it in 1909 by the prestigious *Hibbert Journal*, under the title *Jesus or Christ?* The debate paralleled the Jesus-Paul controversy in Germany,[2] and, in fact, drew contributions from Germany's theologians. Harnack would reformulate essentially the same question in 1910 in his lecture at the Fifth International Congress of Free Christianity and Religious Progress under the title, "The Double Gospel in the New Testament."[3] The underlying issue was christological: Was Jesus the God-man of traditional orthodoxy or simply a man like other men, even if an extraordinary man? The essay stimulating the discussion in the *Hibbert Journal Supplement 1909* was provided by a Rev. R. Roberts, who wondered how it was that a divine Jesus could

---

1. See below, 79ff.

2. Summary of pertinent texts in W. G. Kümmel's *The New Testament: The History of the Investigation of Its Problems*, trans. S. McLean Gilmour and Howard C. Kee (Nashville: Abingdon Press, 1972), esp. 288ff.

3. As described above, p. 17, n. 46. Harnack's essay is on 99–107 of the *Proceedings* and was also issued as a separate pamphlet published in 1911 by Norgate and Williams, London.

at the same time be characterized by obviously untrue propositions, such as belief in demons, or could lack concern for social and political issues of great moment, such as rapacious acquisition or the subordination of women.[4] The Jesus known by means of critical study hardly seems reconcilable with the Christ of tradition. Responses came from Heinrich Weinel, Paul Schmiedel, Benjamin Bacon, and other notables. Weinel continued to urge the superiority of Jesus' moral teaching, and in a similar way also Schmiedel (Fatherly love is Jesus' most precious thing), though neither would admit to using the traditional language of the God-man. Bacon traced out the division between the synoptic Jesus and Paul, but concluded that the division cannot but be allowed to stand, and the philosophers and theologians of the church will ever have to manage it.

It is clear enough that the ancient conundrum personified by the two-nature theory had never vanished and was now renewed in the face of a growing, relentless criticism. "Modernism" was compelling all things ancient to give account of themselves. Among liberals the customary Christ was receding in favor of his historical counterpart.

Nevertheless, there was a diminishing of lives of Jesus in the time just before and during the Great War. There was a virtual consensus that a "life" of Jesus could not be constructed anyway, even though a picture of his teaching was available. English-language works about Jesus continued to appear, without establishing yet a particular genre. America was still assimilating the liberal Jesus; Oskar Holtzmann's life of Jesus was issued in translation in 1904 and enjoyed a good readership for some time.[5] It is, in fact, striking how well liberal lives persisted even in the face of trenchant criticism by Schweitzer; in America they continued well into the middle decades of the twentieth century. At the same time certain other, older works, like those of Renan, Edersheim, Smith, Farrar, Fairbairn, and Seeley, continued to be reissued regularly, some of them also right on up to the middle of the century.[6]

A variety of lesser, non-German works made their appearance in the early

---

4. The essay was entitled "Jesus or Christ: An Appeal for Consistency" (270–82). A separate response to Roberts was issued by J. Warschauer, *Jesus or Christ?* (London: James Clark, 1909). Warschauer argued that Christianity rested on the *unique* personality of its Founder. Uniqueness here was invoked to support the concept of the incarnate Jesus. Warschauer also criticized Kalthoff and Robertson. Loisy also joined the discussion with his essay, "Remarques sur le volume 'Jésus ou le Christ,'" *HibJ* 8 (1910): 473–95, in both French and English versions.

5. Oskar Holtzmann, *The Life of Jesus*, trans. J. T. Bealby and Maurice A. Canney (London: A. & C. Black, 1904).

6. Renan's *Life of Jesus* has appeared in many editions and was frequently reprinted; one in my possession is *Life of Jesus* (New York: Howard Wilford Bell, 1904). See also Alfred Edersheim, *The Life and Times of Jesus the Messiah*, 8th rev. ed. (New York: Longmans, Green, 1904); Frederick Farrar, *The Life of Christ* (New York: E. P. Dutton, 1874); John R. Seeley, *Ecce Homo: A Survey of the Life and Work of Christ* (Boston: Roberts Brothers, 1866); A. M. Fairbairn, *Studies in the Life of Christ*, 14th ed. (London: Hodder and Stoughton, 1907); David Smith, *The Days of His Flesh: The Earthly Life of Our Lord and Saviour Jesus Christ*, 8th ed. (New York: George H. Doran, n.d.); later was his *The Historic Jesus* (London: Hodder and Stoughton, 1912). Not much of a critical nature can be found in these English works, though there is at the same time a wealth of historical detail and other data. Cogent analyses can be found in Pals's work (prologue, n. 16).

part of the century. Two English writers, W. H. Bennett and J. M. Thompson, declined to attempt a life in the usual sense, but nevertheless produced pictures of Jesus based on Mark.[7] Bennett set himself the task of visualizing the Gospel of Mark from the perspective of one who had not read it previously, imagining his reader as a modern liberal Jew who had no real knowledge of Jesus and the gospels. He then embarked on a kind of commentary on the text, often an uncritical one more moved by homiletical than historical concerns. Some examples: the kingdom is the "new dispensation of righteousness and prosperity" established by God;[8] Mark's controversy stories are taken at face value; the parable of the sower is about the failure of Jesus' preaching; the mustard seed speaks of the kingdom growing from small beginnings; Jesus overruled the law of Moses, leading to the church as an independent organization; Jesus traveled to Jerusalem bent on sacrificing himself and fully aware of his coming destiny. Yet some defensive explanations are also offered: the historical ground of the Transfiguration can no longer be penetrated; the disciples took the ass at the entrance so as to protect the owner who was not complicit in helping Jesus; Jesus refurbished Jewish ideas in expressing the little apocalypse. But there is also no notice of problems over the Passover meal or any questions raised about the trial. Yet there is a certain literary elegance now and then in the book, as befits its more sermonic interests.

Thompson's book located itself theologically within the doctrine of the Incarnation and as such sought to explore seriously the human side of Jesus and thereby also to acknowledge the necessity and value of historical criticism. Thompson based his picture on Mark, giving "slices" of Jesus' "life," but also referred often to the other synoptic gospels. Mark was taken as emanating from Peter and also gained priority as the source for Matthew and Luke. Some of Thompson's "slices" were: Jesus' family and friends had no idea of his coming eminence; Jesus was a disciple of John the Baptist, he came from the country and shared that mentality; it was Jesus' realization that John was Elijah that led to his own self-discovery; he taught by question-answer, metaphor, and parable; the most original sayings are those connected with an act;[9] miracles were Jesus' way of doing good; his mind held many of the same ignorances as his contemporaries'; he spoke and acted like a prophet, though the expectation of the imminent kingdom and Parousia were unfulfilled; he quoted scripture and believed in demons and Satan; he had an eschatological outlook. Socially, Jesus came from a modest class himself, was one of the poor, and seemed to lead a movement hostile to the Judean authorities. He found wealth inherently de-

---

7. W. H. Bennett, *The Life of Christ According to St. Mark* (London: Hodder and Stoughton, 1907); and J. M. Thompson, *Jesus According to S. Mark,* 2d ed. (New York: E. P. Dutton, 1910). Bennett was Professor, Hackney College and New College, London and Sometime Fellow of St. John's College, Cambridge; Thompson was Fellow and Dean of Divinity, S. Mary Magdalen College, Oxford, and Examining Chaplain to the Bishop of Gloucester.

8. Bennett, *Life of Christ,* 13.

9. Anticipating the paradigm (apophthegm) in Form Criticism.

structive, saw marriage as a temporary expedient, forbade divorce, and displayed little interest in politics (the Caesar saying points to the kingdom swallowing up the things of Caesar). The kingdom would be religiously and individually based and was entirely future, prepared for in the present. It was a messianic kingdom purged of political meaning and outside the present order. So Jesus accepted the status quo socially. He was not ascetic, but did demand self-sacrifice and saw sin as an evil intention.

Jesus maintained silence about himself up to Caesarea-Philippi, where his messiahship was then opened to the disciples. It was something that gradually evolved. He knew himself as a leader who asked for devotion to himself, but came to claim the title of Son of man only in connection with his passion. The baptism was the turning point, though immediately thereafter until Caesarea-Philippi his view slowly developed. He was primarily a prophet and the Son of man references applied to humankind generally. Later the ransom saying advanced his idea of the messiah and at the last supper he viewed his death as "the price of the kingdom,"[10] with himself thereafter as the one to come in a glorified state to inaugurate the final kingdom.

Rush Rhees, the Professor of New Testament Interpretation at the Newton Theological Institution, issued his *The Life of Jesus of Nazareth: A Study* in 1900;[11] it broke no new ground, but showed the author's awareness of critical questions, even though he constructed his own picture from all four gospels. He acknowledged the validity of the two-document hypothesis. The Old Testament scholar C. A. Briggs, whose denomination subjected him to a heresy trial,[12] offered some insights, as he saw it, on the life of Jesus.[13] Abandoning strictly Markan chronology and taking his clues where he could find them, Briggs concluded that there was a Galilean ministry before the arrest of John the Baptist and that, further, while five pairs of disciples were absent on a mission in Galilee Jesus went with James and John to Jerusalem and at other intervals with Thomas and Matthew to Perea. Events in the gospels were moved around according to this scheme. Briggs's proposal seems not to have stirred much interest.

More conservative is the work of the Baptist scholar A. T. Robertson, whose *Epochs in the Life of Jesus: A Study of Development and Struggle in the Messiah's Work*[14] went about its presentation with all four gospels in hand as well, and as though all were of equal value. Robertson's better work lay in his meticulous attention to details of Greek grammar.

---

10. Thompson, *Jesus According to S. Mark*, 267.

11. Rush Rhees, *The Life of Jesus of Nazareth: A Study* (New York: Scribner's, 1900).

12. 1892–93. The issue was primarily Briggs's allegiance to critical methodology and denial of verbal inerrancy, even of autographs. Along with his defender, Henry P. Smith, Briggs as well as Union Seminary was condemned by the General Assembly of the Presbyterian Church in 1893, though the seminary kept him in his post anyway. He became an episcopal priest in 1899.

13. C. A. Briggs, *New Light on the Life of Jesus* (New York: Scribner's, 1904). Briggs was at the time Edward Robinson Professor of Biblical Theology at Union Theological Seminary in New York.

14. A. T. Robertson, *Epochs in the Life of Jesus: A Study of Development and Struggle in the Messiah's Work* (New York: Scribner's, 1907).

Of somewhat greater interest is the book of the Amsterdam pastor Etienne Giran, whose *Jesus of Nazareth: An Historical and Critical Survey of his Life and Teaching*[15] follows a recognizable liberal path; its Jesus transformed the material at hand — kingdom of heaven — into an individual, internal affair, and emphasized the idea of God as Father and people as his children. Giran offered the original notion that, at the end, the authorities had Jesus' body removed because they did not wish his tomb to become a shrine. He proposed the further opinion that if Jesus had not died on the cross, the churches would have long ago killed him anyway. Today we must find him in his spirit and personality.

The book of W. B. Selbie, *The Life and Teaching of Jesus Christ*, though short, nevertheless sounds themes that echoed for years; it recognizes the two-document hypothesis and the lesser value of John.[16] Jesus' message was the familiar one of the fatherly God and brotherly children; the kingdom was both present and future; women were included in Jesus' activity; Jesus died as servant-messiah. William Bancroft Hill of Vassar College wrote his book primarily for students.[17] An appendix includes a rather learned essay on the history of "lives" of Jesus in German, French, and English literature, but the other parts of the book are characterized by a fair amount of dilating on Jesus' greatness.

A more substantive work would be Nathaniel Schmidt's *The Prophet of Nazareth*.[18] Schmidt first gave an accounting of the christologizing of Jesus and how this picture came under attack in the Enlightenment, utilizing much of the material that Schweitzer would unfold in his more famous publication a year later. He then unveiled a lengthy characterization of the messianic hope, with its roots in the Old Testament, and traced it on through the intertestamental literature, including the concept of the Son of man in Daniel, Enoch, and 4 Ezra. Along the way he noted the standard of authenticity (from Schmiedel) that said whatever contradicts the church's veneration for Jesus likely is genuine. His examination of the Son of man texts led to the conclusion that Jesus did not speak of himself as Son of man, but only of "man" in general (Matt. 10:23, Schweitzer's key text, was dismissed as reflecting the missionary outlook of the Jewish-Christian church). Even the suffering sayings were suspect. Schmidt found no real reason to think that Jesus ever claimed to be the messiah. The Son of man coming on the clouds of heaven was invented by the Christians; Son of God was not a messianic title, was never used by Jesus nor was he ever addressed that way. Jesus used "son" only in an ethical sense and it applied to everyone. The Logos-idea of John has nothing to do with the historical figure of Jesus.

---

15. Etienne Giran, *Jesus of Nazareth: An Historical and Critical Survey of His Life and Teaching*, trans. E. L. H. Thomas (London: The Sunday School Association, 1907).

16. W. B. Selbie, *The Life and Teaching of Jesus Christ*, Century Bible Handbooks (New York: Hodder and Stoughton, 1908).

17. William Bancroft Hill, *Introduction to the Life of Christ* (New York: Scribner's, 1911).

18. Nathaniel Schmidt, *The Prophet of Nazareth* (New York: Macmillan, 1905). Schmidt was Professor of Semitic Languages and Literature at Cornell University and Director of the American School of Archaeology in Jerusalem.

A discussion of the sources showed that little could be gained from Paul, and the synoptic history is complex. Here Schmidt departed from the nearly universal consensus of the priority of Mark and opted for the Griesbach hypothesis; still, he gave some worthy analysis of the characteristics of each gospel. He concluded that the sources would be the synoptics, John (rarely), the Gospel of the Hebrews, and scattered other references.

On the life of Jesus Schmidt basically followed Matthew. The birth stories are legend; Jesus had parents Mary and Joseph, though nothing is known of his childhood. He was a carpenter, a house builder, not a rabbi or teacher. Socially, he was from the poor and identified with them and the oppressed. He was sympathetic with Essenism, but was not an Essene. He associated with John the Baptist, though the baptism story was shaped by the later church. Probably Jesus was identifying with the prophetic movement. He preached that the kingdom was at hand, when God would reign and bring happiness. Therefore all should repent. Jesus also healed and exorcized demons. His fame spread, even as he breached the sabbath laws, made disciples, criticized the Law, and uttered much of the collection known as the Sermon on the Mount. His attacks on Pharisaism brought enmity. Other miracles were rationalized, for example, Jairus's daughter was only comatose.

After Caesarea Philippi Jesus determined to go to Jerusalem. The larger teaching from Luke was utilized on the journey. The entrance into the city was fashioned by the evangelists into a messianic one. The real event leading to Jesus' death was his attack on the temple. Like an old prophet he criticized the sacrificial system and antagonized the hierarchy. He was arrested and given an illegal trial, then sent to Pilate who condemned him as an insurgent. The Jews are not to be blamed today for what the conservatives did to Jesus then.

Jesus' ministry was perhaps a year in length. He died on Friday, Nisan 14, the date uncertain.

A separate section took up Jesus' teaching, which bears no relation to the creeds and teaching of the church. His teaching revolved around two points: the kingdom of heaven and the Father in heaven. The kingdom is the reign of God, of heaven, a future fact, and especially for the poor and suffering and outcasts. It means a righteous life in a new social order. Jesus' ethics could be seen as transitory, as guidance until the kingdom should come [Schweitzer before Schweitzer]. The ethical emphasis was on active love and being children of the Father. There were no sacraments instituted by Jesus and he said nothing about faith in himself. His influence has been wide nevertheless, through the expectation of his return as messiah which, of course, never happened. His elevation into the trinity and its impact was traced by Schmidt in brief compass.

Today, said Schmidt, criticism is winning the day; science prevails. Jesus can still inform and lead us with his high moral ideals. Even though Jesus expected a new social order to appear at any time, there seemed to be also an element of gradualism in his teaching.

Schmidt's work shows the impact of liberalism certainly, though it is a work accomplished with some degree of independence — even if, as in the case of the synoptic problem, against the prevailing winds — and also with a large measure of critical awareness. The treatment of Jesus as a nonmessianic prophet with no claim to be the Son of man was not customary at the time, especially among Americans, a view that still echoes nearly a century later. Also, Schmidt's evident concern to argue the necessity of criticism and to explicate the history of *Leben-Jesu-Forschung* seemed to indicate that those things could not yet be everywhere assumed on the American scene. .

The distinguished Yale scholar C. F. Kent worked primarily in the Old Testament, but also set forth a "life" of Jesus.[19] It was largely developed along customary liberal lines, with primary focus on Mark and Q as sources (Mark uses Peter's memories, Q is probably Papias's logia), though also recognizing that each evangelist had distinctive themes to elaborate, and that behind all lay a period of oral tradition. The gospels were written to meet the needs of the community, to address missionary requirements and those of Greek-speaking Christians. John is of secondary value and was acquainted with all the synoptics as well as with Paul's writing.

The birth narratives have religious value only; Jesus was born c. 6 B.C.E., and knew Hebrew and Greek in addition to Aramaic. His visit to the temple at age 12 is historical; as an adult he worked as a builder, perhaps a repairer of the mud houses and a maker of furniture. He was attracted to John the Baptist, was himself baptized (a turning point), an experience in which he saw himself as Son of God with a mission suggested by Deutero-Isaiah. He worked for a time in Judea, then went to Galilee after John's arrest. John's later question to him from prison led him to assert his work as servant. His kingdom was spiritual, in the hearts and lives of people. So the "master builder" went to work in Galilee to bring people in touch with God, to realize their own sonship and human brotherhood. He also meant to rescue the synagogue from its "dogmatic and ceremonial restrictions" (78) imposed by the Pharisees.

Kent's story then played out according to the Markan order, with critical incursions into the narrative, especially at points such as the healings and other miracles. Jesus did not really wish to be a miracle worker; some things were the impact of his personality, and ancients were generally ignorant of natural laws. So in the storm-stilling Jesus was addressing the disciples with his command, "Peace, be still"; in the feeding story Jesus fed the spiritually hungry who shared their bread with others. Demoniacs were insane persons. But above all Jesus was a teacher of charming personality and great method. He was a master of metaphor and taught in parables (word pictures), which sometimes approached allegory. His concept of God reaches back to the prophets, but he entertained no nationalism and regarded everyone as equal before God. The kingdom is primarily moral and spiritual; maybe Jesus held to a final rule imposed by God, but

---

19. Charles Foster Kent, *The Life and Teachings of Jesus According to the Earliest Records* (New York: Scribner's, 1913). Kent was then the Woolsey Professor of Biblical Literature.

his emphasis was on the present. Only at the end of his life did he look to a future vindication. The core of his ethic was the love commandment; he did not legislate for the nation, but only for individuals and he was not a social reformer, though it could be said that he intended a commonwealth of persons regarding each other as brothers and governed by love. There are some social implications of other matters in his teaching (wealth, divorce, caring for the poor).

Jesus went to Jerusalem to protest the misdeeds of the priests and Pharisees, but his attack on the temple was disastrous, for it led to his death. He spoke of the apocalypse only after being abandoned and faced with martyrdom. John is correct on the dating of the last supper, but Paul's account is the earliest and suggests a meal occurring before Passover. Luke's trial account is superior to the others; Annas carried out the conspiracy resulting in Jesus' death. The charge to Pilate was that Jesus claimed the messiahship. Luke correctly interprets Jesus' last words from the cross. The disciples' recovery of faith and courage witnesses to the reality of the resurrection. Peter saw Jesus, though as an inner spiritual experience.

Schweitzer on Loisy and Maurenbrecher

Bracketing out for now the more popular works on Jesus, there are few lives of Jesus, particularly of any consequence, right on through the war period.[20] Schweitzer, as mentioned, observed that the most significant works were those of Alfred Loisy and Max Maurenbrecher.[21] We may briefly note these two works by drawing again on Schweitzer's summary.

Loisy, said Schweitzer, was an opponent of Wrede. If Jesus had not been condemned on the basis of his own admission to the messiahship, then the whole gospel story is inconceivable. What led to his death if not his own confession? How did the disciples arrive at the notion he was resurrected and would come again on the clouds of heaven? The disciples assumed his messiahship because they were persuaded of it beforehand. To Loisy Jesus began as a preacher of the kingdom of heaven, but held to his messiahship from the beginning. Yet Loisy also acknowledged the eschatological character of Jesus' activity; Jesus expected to become the messiah when the kingdom was revealed (as the prophet of Nazareth, he was not yet the messiah).

By Schweitzer's reckoning Loisy has not accounted for the problems in the modern historical pictures of Jesus. He did not appreciate the information that Jesus went north after the animosity of Herod and the scribes. Loisy presup-

---

20. The popular works are treated separately. See chapter 9.

21. *Geschichte,* 567. That of Loisy is *Les Évangiles synoptiques,* 2 vols. (Chez L'Auteur; Ceffonds, Près Montier-en-du [Haute-Marne], 1907–8); Maurenbrecher's is *Von Nazareth nach Golgotha: Untersuchungen über die weltgeschichtlichen Zusammenhänge des Urchristentums* (Berlin: Schöneberg, 1909). Schweitzer's discussion of Loisy is on 567–70 and that of Maurenbrecher on 570–76. The work by Loisy is a massive commentary on the whole synoptic tradition with a summary of Jesus' ministry, 1:203–53.

posed that after the success of the sending out of the disciples the popular mood turned against Jesus. Jesus, fearless, was led to the conclusion that his destiny lay in Jerusalem and at Passover where many would gather. Loisy did not explain how Peter at Caesarea-Philippi came to recognize Jesus as the messiah, or what Judas betrayed to the priests. He described the entrance into Jerusalem as the activity of Jesus' own followers, and assumed that the disciples held to Jesus' messianic majesty. Jesus' saying about the superiority of the messiah to David's son meant that the coming lord would surpass any Israelite king in greatness and power. Jesus, so Schweitzer quoted Loisy as saying, "n'allait pas à Jérusalem pour y mourir; it y allait pour préparer, au riske de sa vie, l'avènement de Dieu" (*Geschichte*, 569). The predictions of the suffering and death are not authentic; the same applies to the words about the saving significance of his death. Mark, said Loisy, was trying to prove the messiahship of Jesus, using such things as miracles, demon recognition, and the empty tomb. Mark was a disciple of Paul, not Peter, which is why Peter comes off so badly. Much else comes from Paul: the atonement, predestination, condemnation of the Jews, and the understanding of parables as intended to confuse.

But, Schweitzer asked in conclusion, What use is it to reject Wrede while at the same time maintaining a no less thoroughgoing criticism of the oldest narrative material?[22]

Maurenbrecher received somewhat more favorable treatment.[23] He was attempting to attain a new conception of the life of Jesus; his point of departure was the observation that the religion of early Christianity was something other than the teaching of Jesus, insofar as the dying and resurrected One is the object of faith — a subject absent from his own preaching. The disciples created Christianity since it was they who brought together the myth of the dying-rising God-man with the historical Jesus. This myth was found not only in the pagan world, but in Jewish apocalyptic as well, for example, in Daniel. There the saints must suffer for three and one-half time periods; accordingly, the fourth must be the last kingdom. Therefore the Son of man of Daniel must pass through death and resurrection to attain to the final rule. Jesus' emergence on the third day from the tomb proves that we are here dealing with this myth of the Son of man. It goes back to Babylonian sources (Marduk) and to other Asia Minor and Persian syncretistic ideas. So Maurenbrecher took his ideas from the *religionsgeschichtliche Schule*. Wrede provided a basis with his theory that Jesus made no messianic claim or predictions of the death and resurrection. Maurenbrecher accepted as original only Jesus' prophecies of the Son of man in the third person, without reference to himself.

Yet the eschatological element was recognized; Jesus expected the near End. We have to suppose some small time in his ministry and some huge expectation

22. Schweitzer's summaries tended to focus on the issues that were critical for his own presentation, as indeed he evaluated his references from the same perspective.

23. Maurenbrecher was a *Hilsprediger* in 1900 in Zwickau, was brought to Berlin by Friedrich Naumann and in 1903 left the National Socialist Party and attached himself to social democracy.

to account for his public activity. At the same time Maurenbrecher endowed Jesus with proletarian thoughts, as Kalthoff did. The poor are the sharers in the kingdom of God; the struggle with the Pharisees contained social motives (loosening of the Law, Sabbath observance), though Jesus was not a socialist revolutionary. He was an eschatological prophet for whom all depended on divine intervention.

After John's death Jesus appeared, working for a time in Capernaum. The hostility of Herod and the scribes caused him to flee. He went into the Decapolis but had little success. A bad experience in Nazareth crystalized his hope; he fled north and began to speak of his suffering and death. At Caesarea-Philippi he experienced something like a vision (the Transfiguration is its historical expression). This, plus a sense of the woes of the End, brought him to Jerusalem. There he got carried away and uttered a remark about the temple stones being overthrown, which gave his opponents an opportunity to move against him. He was seized as a blasphemer and brought to his condemnation and death.

Jesus did not believe he had to die. He was deeply surprised that the kingdom had not come. His experience was expressed at the last supper; at that point a melancholic impatience appeared in lieu of joy. Arrest and judgment came swiftly. The disciples fled, but found new courage in Galilee. There they remembered that Jesus had spoken of the Son of man, which was to them a source of comfort. Then the disciples suddenly discovered that this thought also explained the undeserved death of their master. He had been speaking earlier to them about his own destiny and he was himself the Son of man. Visions of the resurrected One confirmed their new faith.

This new faith brought them back to Jerusalem, where their preaching made new followers. It was now a message about the suffering-dying God-man, a figure the hearers would have known from centuries of such redeemer figures. Thus began the new religion.

It was a work of great skill, said Schweitzer, but still beset with all the difficulties accompanying the modern reconstructions, including Wrede's. In the end it failed to make any advance in the life of Jesus.

Wilhelm Heitmüller

Scholarly "lives" after Schweitzer — in Germany especially — seem to become more difficult to locate than the elusive historical Jesus. The little work by Wilhelm Heitmüller is worthy of some attention.[24] It was an expanded edition of his article on "Jesus Christ" in the *Religion in Geschichte und Gegenwart* of 1912. The article evidently caused him some problems with ecclesiastical authorities, so he issued it to a wider audience.

The work made no pretense at being a "life" of Jesus, but dealt with certain issues in Jesus' public activity, his personality, and his message. The historicity

---

24. Wilhelm Heitmüller, *Jesus* (Tübingen: J. C. B. Mohr [Paul Siebeck], 1913).

debate claimed some modest attention: the evidence (Tacitus, Suetonius, apocryphal material, Paul, though not necessarily Josephus) speaks for a historical
personality. As to the sources, they consist of the New Testament gospels, which
are not written from a purely historical interest, but for edification, for faith.
John has so re-formed the tradition that it has but slender value, maybe whatever agrees with the synoptic material. Matthew and Luke use Mark and Q for
their own purposes. The difference from John is thus a matter of degree, but
the degree is significant, for the synoptics are bound closer to the tradition and
reshape it without destroying it. Yet even Mark has to be revalued; the view
that it contains old community recollections and that the author did not in-
trude himself much cannot be sustained. Mark has a point of view, serves the
Christian mission, and has no real chronological outline or more than general
geographical references. Mark was a naive folklorist from whom we can get reliable material only in his individual traditions, narratives, and words. Q likewise
owes its origin to the needs and practical uses of the community. It consists of
sayings and discourses and is meant to express the purposes of the community
as opposed to merely reproducing Jesus' preaching. Much the same applies to M
and L, which are to be thought of as independent material, not written sources.
All this material circulated orally, passing through many hands. Even the oldest
of it shows the influence of the Easter faith, with the oldest levels bringing us to
the early community's picture of Christ around the year 60. Is there something
behind that?

Here Heitmüller briefly cited the answer of the deniers like Drews, but the
opinion still holds that Jesus himself and the gospel tradition are the "shell and
kernel" (33) of the tradition to be held together. Examples such as Mark 3:21,
14:32–42, 50, which go contrary to the interests of the community, point to
reliable tradition. These encourage trust generally in the tradition.

What, then, are the criteria by which to judge the authenticity of the material? The oldest is that which runs against or does not correspond to the faith,
theology, cult, or ethics of the early community. This can be extended to include
everything in organic connection with it. Also what is characteristic and original
can be considered with great care. We should especially be wary of the faith of
the earliest Christianity. To it belongs faith in Jesus' messiahship, his near coming, suffering, and resurrection, and the miraculous power of Jesus. Q is more
worthy than Mark, but a modest picture at best is to be expected.

The birth stories have no value; the historian cannot pronounce on the cor-
rectness of holding to the virgin birth (it is not in Paul, Mark, or Q, and Mark
3:21 shows a different view, as do John 1:45, 62). The genealogies are apologetic. Galilee was the locus of Jesus' activity and probably lasted no more than
a year. There is uncertainty over the date of his birth (4 B.C.E. likely) or death
(30 or 31). He probably died on a Friday, though whether it was 14 or 15 Nisan
is uncertain.

As to miracles, the historian knows that Jesus as the messiah would be presented that way; such belongs to religious heroes, among both Jews and Gentiles

alike. The best of the miracle tradition is Jesus as a healer; modern medicine recognizes the influence of the nervous system and other psychic factors. The "almost magical, compelling power of his personality (*Persönlichkeit*) over persons" (70) was grounded in his own faith in God's miracle-power, in his experience of and relationship to God.

Jesus had a human consciousness (prayed to God), as well as a high sense of calling — he spoke prophetic words, contested the law (broke its framework), and exceeded the prophetic consciousness. He was mediator of a peculiar revelation of God (Matt. 11:25–27=Luke 10:21ff.). "Son" means that Jesus and God stand in a special relationship of trust and love. This consciousness of Jesus, said Heitmüller, is mysterious, uncanny (*unheimlich*; 71). Yet we do not know whether Jesus saw his own person as significant religiously; there are hints to that effect (Mark 13:22), but more important is his assertion that no one stands between men and God, not even himself. He preaches grace and forgiveness; he does not ask for faith in himself.

It seems likely that Jesus did claim to be messiah and was condemned as such. But how did he think of it? Various ideas were at hand (Son of David, Son of God, Son of man). Jesus denied fulfilling the nationalistic hope and apparently did not use "Son of God" of himself. "Son of man" is more controversial. Some instances only mean "man" generally, while others are of two types: suffering and heavenly coming. There is an inclination to introduce the term where there was none originally and therefore perhaps this carries back to the very beginning. Yet we cannot exclude the possibility that Jesus spoke of the heavenly messianic man (cf. Enoch), perhaps in limited circles and only at the end of his life, as one who would come on the clouds or who must suffer and die (though even the latter could have arisen after his own crucifixion). He then would have spoken in a limited way of the accomplishment of his work even in the face of something terrible at the end, and the community later expanded the sayings. These are possibilities, no more. It is just as possible that the community introduced everything into his mouth. As to how and when Jesus had come to faith in his messianic majesty, the oldest tradition says it was at his baptism. There are problems with that; Caesarea-Philippi points toward the end of his activity. We do not really know. What is certain is the prophetic consciousness. How the different elements resided together in his consciousness remains an insolvable psychological puzzle.

Jesus began with John, a prophet of judgment, and was likely influenced by him, though we know nothing specific. The baptism is authentic, and Jesus also proclaimed the kingdom and summoned people to repentance. His activity was that of teacher and healer, though he was not a professional scribe. His healings show the defeat of Satan and preparation for God's rule. He sought the tormented, the down and out, and was a friend of tax collectors and sinners. He also directed himself against the official theologians and their piety. It was this kind of attack that led him to the cross. His own followers were the little people, the fishermen, workers, and women. He so impressed his personality on them that death itself could not obscure what he meant to them. Whether he chose twelve is uncertain but possible.

How long he was in Galilee we do not know. He traveled in gentile areas and came to Caesarea-Philippi. He was confessed as messiah, and more and more the messianic idea must have acted on his consciousness thereafter. He went to Jerusalem perhaps because he had to end his calling there, to seek out the enemy in his lair. He must have known the danger. The number of his followers, the temple attack, and the entry into Jerusalem were the occasion of enmity toward Jesus. Judas betrayed his location.

As to Jesus' trial, the tradition is muddled. Possibly blasphemy was originally found in the word about destroying the temple. Jesus was brought to Pilate who may have attempted to release him (Barabbas), but allowed him to be taken with two other law-breakers.

So Jesus died, but a community appeared, founded on the personality of Jesus. He was the gospel, not some knowledge or enlightenment that he brought. His personality was the new and creative thing he introduced into history. To be sure, it was not the whole personality, but the religious one. It comes enclosed in the faith of the community that it created, but we see its features, especially in Jesus' words and in its religious and ethical disposition or feeling.

Most characteristic of Jesus was his total focus on God, the "saturation of his being with Religion" (108). So massive was this focus that nothing else mattered — neither citizenship, the state, social life, politics, science, knowledge, nor culture, but only God. His distance from the world is not world-denial (he was known as a glutton and a drunkard); the duties of social community are assumed — marriage, the Caesar-saying — but what matters is unmediated experience of God. The powerful and saving God is also the Father who seeks and saves sinners, and to love God is also to love the neighbor. All that connects with Jesus' self-consciousness, for as Son he is revealer of God. Whether he claimed to be messiah or even the man from heaven is peripheral.

The kingdom of God and its nearness lay at the heart of Jesus' proclamation. Likely he began with a message of repentance in view of the kingdom's coming, yet that was for him a point of departure, not the kernel. What was central was what has always been central in religion: the God-man relationship.

Jesus' God-concept was from Judaism, yet he accomplished its ethicizing. "Father" was especially significant. "The whole depth and innerness of his faith is held together in this word" (123). It was not new with Jesus, but it was given new weight.

Jesus taught not national religion but individualism. Herein also lies the seed of universalism, even if the pagan-mission words are inauthentic (maybe Matt. 10:6 and 10:23 are genuine). Jesus was free from Jewish nationalism.

The will of God is the basis for ethical behavior, but also the thought of judgment shadows the ethical teaching of Jesus. The kingdom is near; therefore judgment is near. Jesus was against Pharisaic morality, which is negative, characterized by "not" doing and avoiding sin rather than doing good. The Pharisees focused on purity and ceremonial position. They were casuistic; Jesus asserted the unconditional nature of ethical responsibility. For Jesus the will of God is in the Law, but primarily in the twofold commandment of love of God and the neighbor. The neighbor is everyone who needs help; love is nondiscriminating, noncalculating, forgiving.

Jesus' ethic was strange, paying no attention to matters of state, culture, or justice. Customarily the explanation of this strangeness is linked to Jesus' expectation of the kingdom of God, the End, but the true understanding lies in Jesus' individualism. Next to the relationship of the individual to God, all other family, social, and cultural relations fade.

The kingdom is the rule of God, the ruling, reigning God. There are elements of both present and future in Jesus' proclamation, but he especially emphasized the kingdom as present. If he thought of himself as messiah, then also the Rule of God came with that and was effective at the same time. Yet he also did not paint in glowing colors the picture of the future rule, as in messianic Judaism. He did deny knowing the time of the End, only that it comes in this generation (Mark 9:1), suddenly and uncalculatingly. Resurrection and judgment belong to it.

What was new in Jesus' preaching? Much in his teaching has parallels in Jewish or Greco-Roman sources. Still he gives a new way to God, a new religious ideal. So said Heitmüller:

> The exclusive predominance of life in God; the absolute elevation and sovereignty of the ethical demand; the insoluble binding together of religion and ethics; the unremitting ethicising of the representation of God, who as the righteous Judge represents the ethical demand and still in extravagant love wills to forgive sinners; the freeing of piety from all national and juridical burden; piety as lowly, free trust, and ethics as love toward the neighbor: all that presents in its unity a religious ideal that in that world was new and unique. (147–48)

Even so, what was most creative was Jesus himself, his personhood, such that traditional piety could say that in him the divine life entered into history. This "personality" is still the source of life and the power of Christianity today. Its influence extended beyond Jesus' death; Jesus continued to exert his "personality" on his followers. According to Heitmüller "Jesus' personality was surrounded with an extraordinary grandeur [*Hoheit*], that from it an unaccustomed power radiated to his disciples, a power whose strength remained effective beyond his death and bound his own to him" (168).

Heitmüller's little work seems in some ways simply a warming-over of older liberal themes, with emphasis on the "personality" of Jesus, not merely his outward characteristics. There is a grasp of the oral nature of the tradition upon which Form Criticism would enlarge and systematize; and again there is visible the primary criterion of authenticity, that is, that which is set against the interests of the early church. The extension of the criteria that excluded Jesus' connection with his Judaic context is lacking, but there remains the insistence on Jesus' *uniqueness*, a consideration driven apparently by a defensive theology that needed a different ground for still attaching itself to Jesus and could only find that ground in a demonstration of something remarkable and unparalleled in historical experience.

As the Great War progressed, its casualties were not only measured in human lives, horrible as that was, but in lives of Jesus as well, and in the severe limitations placed upon the exchange of scholarly information as well as its production. Issues of the journal *Theologische Rundschau*, for example, regularly carried reviews by Hans Windisch of literature dealing with the *Leben und Lehre Jesu* up until 1917 when all publication ceased. In fact, the war itself imposed its own kind of nationalistic demand such that in 1915 a new section was added to the Life and Teaching section of the journal entitled "Jesus und der Krieg," so large had grown the literature, either in defense of the war or skeptical of it.[25] The same tendency prevailed in the current literature in other lands.[26] Much of it was hardly worthy of "scientific" scholarship; there was a conspicuous tendency to enlist Jesus in every army and send him off to war. Of this material James Moffatt's comment seems apropos and even understated: "The theology underlying current views on this topic is sadly in want of correction."[27]

Yet there were some works in that time period that deserve attention. Two in particular should be observed, both because of their "type" as lives of Jesus, and because each in its own way exemplified something characteristic. One was the widely read and often issued work by the Cambridge scholar T. R. Glover and the other was a not-as-well-known work by Paul Wernle, *Jesus*,[28] which Hans Windisch would later characterize as "the best detailed, scholarly, and yet popular exposition of the teaching and character of Jesus that we have in German."[29]

---

25. A similar emphasis can be seen in the *Theologische Literaturzeitung* in its section "Religiöse Kriegsliteratur."

26. F. J. Foakes-Jackson, ed., *The Faith and the War* (Macmillan, 1915); G. K. A. Bell, ed., *The War and the Kingdom of God* (London: Longmans, Green, 1915); reviews in *JTS* 17 (1916): 184–89; also see Joseph Crocker, "American's Bondage to the German Spirit," *HibJ* 13 (1915): 801–14; M. Epstein, "Some Recent German War Literature," *HibJ* 14 (1916): 15–29; J. P. Bang, "The Root of the Matter," *HibJ* 15 (1917): 1–17; A. S. Ferguson, "More German Sermons," *HibJ* 15 (1917): 18–24.

27. Moffatt, *HibJ* 14 (1916): 188.

28. T. R. Glover, *The Jesus of History* (London: Student Christian Movement, 1917), went through its 25th edition in 1948. Glover was a Fellow of St. John's College, Cambridge, and University Lecturer in Ancient History. The original edition of Paul Wernle's *Jesus* was 1916, but the one available to me was labeled a *Feldausgabe* and issued in 1917 (Tübingen: J. C. B. Mohr [Paul Siebeck]). I have difficulty imagining its appeal to a soldier.

29. Hans Windisch, "Literature on the New Testament in Germany, Austria, Switzerland, Holland, and the Scandinavian Countries, 1914–1920," *HTR* 15 (1922): 151. Windisch was reporting on the literature produced during the war that was generally unavailable to English-speaking countries. Earlier Windisch had reviewed the book in *TRu* (1917): 42–49, voicing some reservations about its deliberate religious interest.

T. R. Glover

Glover's book is the result of lectures given in India in 1915–16, with material also from various articles in journals. We seek to know Jesus, said Glover, because he has influenced our civilization more than any other and still does. People remain religious even in an age demanding scientific proofs. Some have spoken to the question of who Jesus was by asserting his nonhistoricity. Nonsense, said Glover, running briefly through some of the evidence (Tacitus, Suetonius, Paul, the very existence of the church itself). He then undertook a modest analysis of the sources (gospels). John is not to be considered. The synoptics have Mark as a basic source and one other (referring obliquely to Q); Peter allegedly stands behind Mark, while Luke was Paul's companion. The (synoptic) gospels are not biographies or firsthand documents, but they preserve genuine words and traditions ("essentially true and reliable records of a historical person").[30] They have a simplicity and plainness that speaks for their authenticity. Beyond that, they contain Aramaic phrases, stories contrary to the church's own interests, reflections of Jesus' own environment, and evidences of a marked personality. And, finally, it has to be remembered that the early church accepted the gospels, thereby authenticating them as genuine recollections corresponding to its own impression of Jesus.

We have to observe the canons of historical understanding: put Jesus in his time, try to understand his own intention and meaning in his words, grasp what was his experience, especially of God, and the nature of the thought behind his words. The danger of such study lies not in modernizing him too much, but in underestimating him, that is, not doing justice to a figure of such monumental impact upon history.

We know little of Jesus' childhood and youth. We assume some things from the nature of his teaching: parables of household, domestic, and rural life and the like. He was the oldest son of a widowed mother with four brothers and at least two sisters, and a carpenter by trade. He learned to use analogies from home life and nature, unlike Paul, who was more a citizen of the city. He learned at home and synagogue and certainly knew the Old Testament, though it is doubtful that he had formal education. He grew up and doubtless played games with children; the first word he learned was likely "Abba." His knowledge of human nature was gained by observation. Here Glover speculated imaginatively about what the young Jesus might have experienced, hypothesizing that he must surely have wandered to some of the caravan routes surrounding Nazareth and how

> it would be hard to believe that a bright, quick boy, with genius in him, with poetry in him, with feeling for the real and for life, never went down on to that road, never walked alongside of the caravans and took note of the strange people "from the east and from the west, from the north and from the south" (Luke xiii.29) — Nubians, Egyptians, Romans, Gauls, Britons, and Orientals. (29)

---

30. Glover, *Jesus of History*, 12.

We can learn something of the character of his mind from his teaching, his words. We notice his use of irony, his sense of humor; he had feelings and emotions, a broad compassion, with quickness of mind and grasp of a situation, sympathy for others, an instinct for fact and for God. Not all of his words and experiences were merely comforting, however; the temptation (which comes from Jesus himself) speaks otherwise, as does the saying about leaving the dead to bury the dead, and the word about the demon who was driven out only to return sevenfold. He was also a remarkable parabler who sounded a different note from most teachers. He had a mind not bound by authority and tradition, one that went to the heart and was direct. He was a no-nonsense person whose personal power was felt far and wide.

Jesus came into a hard world. Infanticide, slavery, and crucifixion were signs of that hardness. As Horace once reported: " 'I have been good,' said the slave. 'Then you have your reward,' said the poet; 'you will not feed the crows on the cross' " (*Epistles*, 1.16.48). Judaism expected its messiah, but there were many variations. Men despaired of the present and hoped for a better future. Judaism taught virtue for the sake of reward, but misunderstood God: Was God only the Judge, the law-giver? Jesus set himself the task of repairing that misunderstanding, of compelling a rethinking of God and of engendering a new relation to God. Not sacrifice and cult, but relationship and total commitment were his demand. Such a demand was universal in its implication. Jesus had to re-create the language of God, as in his praying, for example; he sought to explore God anew through the models of friendship and love. This is essentially the meaning of Incarnation (friendship and identification).

The disciples were impulsive and simple, like Peter, but Jesus treated them as friends. His method of teaching was not complex; it was intended for the simple and plain. It was characterized by the arresting phrase, its language fresh. Jesus' presence was actively transforming for the disciples. "The greatest miracle in history seems to me the transformation that Jesus effected in those men," said Glover (88–89).

Jesus profoundly changed the world's thinking about God. We do not know where his teaching on God came from, for his internal development is unavailable to us. He is not mystical, yet lived in closest communion with God. God knows, cares, and acts providentially. He is Father and also the King on his throne who rules over all. God manifests great interest in the individual, imparting his love and generosity. (His rain falls on the good and the evil alike.) Even the enemy is included. The parables of the pearl and treasure point to finding God as ruler and giving up everything to have that. The seed and leaven point to growth in knowledge of God.

Jesus was not an ascetic, but taught a different holiness. Men should expect an answer to prayer, for God is the good Father who wishes to give to his children. Such lies at the heart of Jesus' faith and Christian faith. It is life based on God, a thought-out life, marked by complete dedication and obedience to God.

Jesus had great compassion for crowds and for persons. He went to Jerusalem and experienced compassion for the city. He also healed the sick, though we cannot pronounce on any one case. He endorsed work and did not condemn money, but rather said what could be done with it. He did not explain pain, but sympathized with suffering. His new sympathy for women altered their position in the world. The same could be said for his attitude toward children. He also emphasized tenderness, while always speaking against a life of drift, a nonthought-out life, or a life of nonfaith. He believed in humanity's possibilities; this faith in the individual and his worth is the ground of democracy. Yet Jesus had no illusions about human weaknesses or wasted lives.

Jesus had a connection with John the Baptist, though it is not clear exactly what that was, for the difference is evident. John was the preacher of judgment. Jesus also knew to take sin seriously — warning others about it, especially condemning the Pharisees, hypocrites, and those who were lax. For Jesus sin was not merely external or environmental, but came from the heart and was involved in the very nature of man.

Jesus chose the cross. What did he intend by that? The answer involves what he meant by the kingdom of God. It is something new, a new life, a new beginning, a new knowledge of God. All time and existence are involved. Jesus thought his death would achieve something, but he was not obsessed with the idea of his own speedy return on the clouds of heaven (Schweitzer). He meant to achieve salvation: forgiveness and acceptance with the Father. He went to Jerusalem out of love for men and for God, to make plain the love of God to people. "It was his love of men and women and his faith in God that took him there" (178). Only through the cross could he bring the reality of God to men.

At the crucifixion the disciples ran away; later they are found preaching Jesus. Something decisive happened. "Great results have great causes," said Glover (178). The evidence for the resurrection is not in the record of the tomb, but in the lives of the disciples.

The last part of the book asked about the old Roman empire, described it and its religions, and wondered how it all was lost. It had, said Glover, an unexamined life, it was not reasonable, it had no real faith, and no morals in religion. Indeed, its religion created fear and gave no hope of immortality. The church triumphed over it, refusing to compromise. How?

> If I may invent or adapt three words, the Christian "out-lived" the pagan, "out-died" him, and "out-thought" him. He came into the world and lived a great deal better than the pagan; he beat him hollow in living. (213)

Ultimately, love was the solution. The slave, women, everyone attained a new status. The secret was Jesus himself; he brought a new fortitude in the face of death.

Glover concluded his work reviewing Jesus' impact on the past and how Jesus might still be approached. We are now living in the scientific age, where everything is tested and retested and subject to verification. Accordingly, the best way to find out about Jesus is through experience. One should begin there and see where it leads, rather than assume some a priori theory of his nature.

This book enjoyed a wide popularity in England and also in America. Some of that was attributable to its readability; it was written with a degree of eloquence and literary quality. In fairness to the book, it is not possible in a compact summary to communicate its "feel." Glover was also evidently fairly well informed on the issues of critical scholarship, but those were clothed, as it were, in vestments of word and even devotion that rendered them, if not null, at least unobtrusive. Certainly, the work was not aimed at scholars, though it presupposed scholarship. It really did nothing to advance life-of-Jesus research, though if that standard were raised as a criterion by which to judge any work on Jesus, then booksellers would go begging for an audience. It says rather more about the special English way of presenting scholarly matters in a vivid way that communicates without risking too serious a level of offense. If nevertheless we should ask about the underlying scholarship, we would conclude that (1) biographies of Jesus are not possible, though we can know his message and even something of his inner thoughts; (2) the gospels, largely excluding John, are fundamentally reliable, though decisions as to authenticity are permissible and even necessary; (3) miracles are problematic and largely not susceptible to verification, though it is clear that Jesus healed; and (4) the strictly eschatological interpretation of Jesus is inadequate.

Paul Wernle

Not altogether dissimilar in intent is the book on Jesus by Paul Wernle. Though written during the war, it claimed (in the preface) to have no relation to that event, but was rather a scientific work that wished to see Jesus in his own time and among his own people and to see what he had to say to his own time.

Two things are needed for appropriate inquiry; one is proper use of the sources. The basic ones are Mark, written for gentile Christians, the Sayings Collection (*Spruchsammlung*), written for Jewish Christians, and pieces of tradition found in Matthew and Luke. Behind that lies a longer period of oral tradition. We have to seek the oldest parts in order to form a picture. There is no certainty from the picture thus constructed.

The second consideration is the religious. Historical work can determine the genuine from the nongenuine, but it cannot tell us the final religious value of Jesus. Jesus can only be made truly understandable by the religious appreciation of him, more precisely, the psychological-religious. The historian also needs something Jesus-like in himself in order to grasp what Jesus was about. And even if he knew everything about the historical Jesus, he still would not attain to Jesus.

The book differed from the usual life of Jesus in that it dealt largely with themes in Jesus' message, rather an anticipation of form-critical procedure;[31] only in the last chapter was much said at all about events in Jesus' life, and there the passion narrative was dominant. Five chapters formed the different themes: 1, on Jesus' background, "Volkstum und Eigenart";[32] 2, "Faith in God"; 3, "Mankind and the Demand of God"; 4, "The Message of the Coming Kingdom of God"; and 5, "Jesus the Christ."

The first part set out Jesus in his Judaic context. Jesus was unquestionably a Jew, rooted in the biblical faith of his people. Israel held special place for him although, in Wernle's view, Jesus overcame the nationalistic religion of his people. He accepted the temple and its cultus, the ordinances and commands of the Bible, and the general sacred history from Abraham down. The prophets were important for him and influences can be seen in his words. Daniel is obvious (Son of man), though there are problems of usage and meaning. Much was contributed by Christian scribal and especially apocalyptic expansions, though Jesus seems to have accepted the general picture of a coming final judgment and the contrast of the kingdom with hell as the destiny of those who do not accept the kingdom. Since the disciples stand in the same stream of ideas, it is difficult to separate their interests from those of Jesus.

But above all Jesus gained his faith in God from the Bible. In Israel he would have learned to name God as his Father and see himself as a child of God. God who chose Israel, created all things, and made covenant with his people was also an ethical God, demanding obedience, though also the last word he will speak to his people in the coming kingdom will be one of grace. It was a monotheistic faith, but also had room for the idea of Satan and the demonic, always subordinated to God.

We have therefore to seek Jesus as a biblical Jew to understand him. His individuality must be found within Judaism. Something of the negative side of his individuality can be described: he was not interested in money-making or possessions, or politics, and his views strongly contrasted with Pharisaic-scribal piety and views of the Law. Especially his God-consciousness (God as Father) stood out. That was something he held before he came under the influence of the Baptist, as was also the case with his future hope. The expectation of the kingdom came from the Jewish environment. Jesus seemed to assume that everyone knew of it, but he gave it greater seriousness. The last hour of decision had come; all stand before the great either/or: either life in eternity or consignment to hell. However, Jesus was no enthusiast (dwelling only in a blessed future), but was a realist as, for example, his parables show. He dealt with the actual world and knew well the heart of humankind. He spoke of family life, marriage, was

---

31. Troeltsch, in his review in *TLZ* (1916): 54–57, attributed the structure to dogmatics, and specifically the dogmatics of Herrmann.

32. It is difficult to render these terms in English; something like "National Identity and Particularity" might do, with the latter referring to Jesus' individuality. These terms later in the Hitler period bore also a more sinister meaning (something essentially "German" and "racial character").

himself a workman (*Maurer*), and above all had a heart for his brother, as shown especially in his concern for the fallen, the outcasts, the poor and deprived.

Jesus was baptized by John, a decisive step for Jesus, though we do not know what Jesus' baptism meant. It seems Jesus was attracted to John because he was a man of God bringing near the kingdom of God with divine authority, like an old prophet. But Jesus did not unfold John's movement, but himself appeared as a prophet of the kingdom.

The new message of Jesus was that the kingdom was near, but the basis of it was his faith in God. He did not offer a new doctrine of God, for his God-concept came out of his people Israel. Like an old prophet he broke with nationalism, not by affirming some other God than the God of Israel, but by taking that faith with great seriousness and by affirming that God will overthrow faithless Israel (destruction of the temple). Jesus' originality consisted not in some concept of God, but in how he explained and proclaimed the relationship to the old God of Israel.

Most prominent in Jesus' expectation was the present reign of God on the earth. In this connection Jesus taught God's providence and gave ethical instructions. God only is good; we experience his will in the demand of the Law. For Jesus this demand is primarily inner, in the attitude, the heart, the thoughts, and not simply deeds. Doing the will of the Father is the condition for entrance into the kingdom.

What about the idea of reward? Jesus certainly was no Kantian; he taught the idea of reward, as well as the idea of hell. Still the emphasis for Jesus was on the love, the goodness, the compassion of God our Father in heaven who always gives us what we need — not a sentimental love, but one that has in hand suffering and death, judgment and hell, and can accomplish the separation of humankind from evil on the basis of this love.

Jesus was not a modern socialist and directed his message to the individual. He differed from Judaism, which tied God's goodness to the Law. For Jesus law and grace are united in the one God before whom all stand in judgment and demand, gift and forgiveness. In Judaism one must already belong to the righteous, those who observe the Law, in order to experience God's love, whereas for Jesus the love is directed especially to the hopeless and lost, sinners and tax collectors.

The kingdom is not an ethical postulate that comes by our work or demand, but by God's will, a gift from above. The last word is God's love that blesses his children. The core of Jesus' gospel is God the Father and his children.

What was new in Jesus' message was the degree of seriousness with which the old was taken. So Jesus' message of God's love for sinners (grace) assumed a new shape (parables). Even more was Jesus' proclamation that the God he preached was already making a beginning by the inbreaking of the kingdom in the present in great powers and miracles. Wernle was willing to call this the "prophetic and messianic element in Jesus' faith in God."[33]

---

33. Wernle, *Jesus*, 100.

The kingdom of God meant heaven, eternity on earth. Jesus lived and breathed in the face of this eternal community with God, this being-in-blessedness. Jesus was not concerned with the betterment of society, but with eternal welfare for the brother and oneself. So Jesus was no moral teacher in the usual sense; he cared not for questions of state, family, and the like. He could not entirely avoid them, but directed himself to eternal matters. "Jesus was not a Jewish teacher of morality, but a prophet of the coming of God" (105).

Jesus was fundamentally conservative with respect to the Jewish Bible. Yet there was a contention with scribes and Pharisees over the *understanding* of the Law, the correct understanding of the will of God. Both appealed to the Law, no doubt, but what was at stake was the entrance into the kingdom, the conditions for entering the kingdom. Wernle saw that as a struggle of autonomy and heteronomy, freedom versus human commands. Jesus was not like a rabbi bound to tradition before him, and did not speak like a scribe, but rather spoke with authority, as tradition remembered. He appealed to the Spirit within himself and enjoyed the freedom of the children of God (no fasting, practice of sabbath freedom, association with sinners and tax collectors, attack on the temple). He had an inner certainty not comprehensible to the scribes or, for that matter, to Christians decades later. His ethical consciousness was disclosed in this autonomy that broke through Jewish nationalism.

A related point was that Jesus broke through the practices of holiness at the time to get to the central point of ethics. No washing and purifying for Jesus; what matters is the internal — a track that Paul would complete with abandonment of the Law. There was no special holy sphere for Jesus. This contrasting answer of Jesus and the Pharisees to the question about the will of God was an essential ground for the origin of Christianity as a new religion.

Jesus did not overturn the Law, but sharpened and internalized it. He also simplified it: the variety of codes in the Bible led to the search for a center point; Jesus found it in the love commandment. What is not from love falls away, nationalistic and ceremonial alike. Jesus overcame that which is Jewish in the Law from within. This ethical perspective connects with the eschatological expectation: now is the time of the approaching kingdom, now the children of God live in purity, now things like oath-swearing, resistance, divorce, and retaliation are revoked. It is a sharpening, an intensification, a completion of the Law, and a more stringent demand than that in Judaism or the Old Testament. All that matters is how to stand in the final Judgment, how to obey the perfect will of God.

Jesus was thus distinguished from all social or political work of a reformer. He fostered a religious individualism. Thus it can be said that he overcame or surpassed the Jewish Law not by rejection, but by redirecting it to individuals and their preparation for eternity. Jesus was certainly not an ascetic, nor was he a proletarian agitator; his concern for the poor and oppressed was individual and connected to the moment of the inbreaking kingdom. Nor was he a socialist with a plan of organization; rather, the kingdom was near and demanded service as the rule of the community.

Thus Jesus had no social ethic. The depreciation of family and relatives, the restoration of marriage to its original rights — all was tied to the eschatological situation of the coming kingdom. Jesus was also hard on the rich, but that too was religiously based. On the other side, the poor were not valued for their moral excellence, but simply because of their need. They are also the ones who receive the news of the kingdom because they have nothing and can only look with joy to the future. Poverty will persist until the coming of the kingdom of God, then all relationships on earth will be made new; until then it would have been foolish for Jesus to direct all his energies to eliminating poverty.

Likewise Jesus had little to say about the state and justice. He was no revolutionary seeking to replace one legal system with another; he directed his disciples toward the personal and internal. In that sense Jesus was conservative; he eschewed all political and power struggles. For him there were two kingdoms: one a kingdom of compulsory obedience and the other a kingdom of free will and the service of love. Jesus had no program of political revolution.

That the last hour has come gives Jesus' message its special character; he demanded the either/or toward his person. Is God at work or is Satan? Just here Jesus is distinguishable from the later Christian mission, which also spoke of the nearness of the end and the approaching judgment. But Jesus with his special powers was living only this once in history; one faced this either/or directly. Later this decision was converted to the dogmatic decision by the Christian community. Jesus likely thought of a transformed body in the kingdom, like Paul, or as in the transfiguration scene (later, but it reflects Jesus' view of the inbreaking kingdom). The beatitudes also aptly describe those who long for the kingdom: the meek, hungry, those thirsting for righteousness, the mourning, the pure in heart. The kingdom is also judgment and hell. Now all is a mixture, later there will be separation. The kingdom and eternal life are the same, blessedness for individuals.

The kingdom has an ethical character. Those who enter it are the purified, people of love and peace, sincerity, and compassion. New in Jesus is this ideal world where the people of this character are the citizens of the kingdom, where brother serves brother and no one is exalted above another. The mystery of the inbreaking kingdom is also tied to Jesus' person; where he is and acts there is the beginning of the kingdom. Therefore the mystery of the kingdom hangs together with the messianic mystery and is inseparable from it. The kingdom is both a there and a not-there; there are little beginnings, but the kingdom is not there in its full unfolding.

What did Jesus think of the fact that the kingdom did not come? The tradition shows Jesus earlier speaking of the inbreaking kingdom and later of the future kingdom only. Did he change? There is not a word of that in the tradition. Both still stand, the inbreaking kingdom and still the future one in face of powerful forces of opposition. Jesus must have experienced the contradiction that the reverse of his messianic expectations came to pass: the one who announced the kingdom to his people was driven to the cross, that instead of the new wonderful world the one who spoke in the name of God himself experienced death and the force of these powers. Later Christianity sweetened the terrible event by interpreting it as the final sacrificial offering for sin, but it is doubtful that Jesus saw it as such. We do not know whether he lost hope in the coming of the kingdom; the cry of despair might point that way, but nevertheless Jesus also set his hope on eternity, and that is the abiding element in his expectation. "The true kingdom of God is eternity, into which we all sooner or later will enter" (269).

Wernle agreed with Harnack: Jesus did not preach himself but the Father only. He preached the kingdom, the will of God, and trust in the heavenly Father. He was not an ascetic like John, he lived in the world and went about in the company of sinners and tax collectors and disreputable women. He even practiced forgiveness of sin; a "man" has authority on earth to forgive sins, he claimed. Later tradition ascribed that authority specifically to Jesus. He functioned as a God-representative to his contemporaries. He was to them free, a helper, their brother and servant.

He also was said to be a wonder-worker, but not the usual one, for he acted out of others' need. It is hard today to know how much of the miracle tradition goes back to Jesus; everything comes to us through the miracle faith of the Christians. It seems certain that Jesus healed, and he expected childlike trust and faith, without which no miracle could occur. Some healings were doubtless psychic; all show the importance of the trust that Jesus elicited.

The question of his identity must have been a passionate one for those who came in touch with him. If we ascribe truth to Peter's confession we have also to go a step further and allow that Jesus may have taken the biblical messianic hope to himself. Both nationalistic and mythical elements existed in the messianic hope, which gave a freedom to emphasize one or the other. The national was the Son of God, the one who would do miracles and provide signs from heaven. There was also the Son of man, the world judge. That introduced contradictions in the messianic expectation: one from David's line, but also a heavenly judge.

But what would a messianic claim have meant for Jesus? Jesus was entirely unpolitical; Rome was not the enemy. Yet it is clear that Jesus was condemned on the basis of being king of the Jews and making a messianic claim, but what that meant to him is another question. He was a quite new and different king, whose greatness consisted of his service and help. He was also a Jewish king without Jews, who more and more excluded themselves.

There was also this expectation of the coming of the "man," but only at the last times of Jesus (cf. the trial, the promise of coming on the clouds of heaven). Many scholars think that is all after Jesus' time. But probably it is the "nevertheless" set over against the destruction of Jesus' earthly course. It comes from the biblical faith in which Jesus lived.

There were only two ways in which one might become messiah: by political conquest or elevation by God's power. For Jesus the first was excluded, so only the second was possible. Yet Jesus did not wait for divine power to elevate him, but went into society with love and service for others. This was the great and new thing in his messianic thought. He met the need and pain of his people. In short, he made a savior-calling out of a messianic-calling. To call Jesus savior is to give him the title that he created by his deed. So while there may be traces of the old messianism, the world lives from his new messianism. As such he is God's representative who acts in God's stead and unites the divine and human in himself. "The new thing above all consists in the fact that he appeared as the one entrusted by God, as the one who knew the heart and will of God and could bring God's nearness and love for mankind" (328). This was a new meaning for the ancient messianic and Son of God titles. He probably became aware of that calling at his baptism. The secrecy theme (Mark) preserves the truth that Jesus did not openly claim the messianic title. Jesus did not demand faith in his messiahship, but he met it in his disciples.

The suffering messiah was foreign to Judaism. Scholars find it impossible that Jesus foresaw his suffering and death; he could not have cried out from the cross had he foreseen everything. But can it be that Jesus had no idea what was to befall him? That can hardly be so for one who knew well humankind and the powers that opposed God in the world. Yet Jesus' idea of the messiah possessed a new feature: not the old, lordly figure, but a tragic hero who finished in disgrace and shame. When did he get this idea? Probably not until after the entrance into the city and the temple scene, which are not acts of one anticipating a suffering end. It would not have been until he concluded that a suffering role was God's will for him (Gethsemane). But Jesus may have had intimations that something good would come of his suffering and death.

How did Jesus reckon with apparent destruction by his enemies? A Jesus who would abandon his soul to destruction is not Jesus as we have known him. The text refers to Psalm 110, but chiefly Jesus seems in the last days to have turned to Daniel, to the figure of the "man" to come on the clouds of heaven and exercise the judgment. Jesus had not thought at the beginning of this Danielic "man." In the earlier parts of the gospel this "man" referred to simply a human being and was used first in a special sense only after Caesarea-Philippi, according to Mark, who may have formed the sayings about the suffering Son of man. It is also possible Jesus from the beginning of his intimations about suffering may have occupied himself with Daniel and his "man" and sought consolation for his earthly humiliation in the heavenly coming. That is all uncertain, but the puzzle is how Jesus could speak of a coming "man" as though he were someone different and without saying anything about his own departure. It could be understood that the "man" is someone different, that is, Jesus himself when he is different from himself as the suffering one. The "secret" would be just that, that he the suffering one will be the one coming. That may seem strange to us, but how could Jesus believe that God would abandon him, or leave him desolate, him who brought persons to the kingdom? This was the "nevertheless" of his faith: However my enemies triumph over me, God will maintain me and present me as world judge. And soon, in this generation.

The Passion followed. Judas' betrayal is incomprehensible. At the Supper the form of the words are from Mark's community and its celebration. Perhaps Jesus simply said, "This is my body, this is my blood," in simple parallelism. The meaning would be: as you take bread and wine to nourish yourself, so take my body and blood for your inner nourishment; one would be a symbol for the other. Hold to me through these symbols; we will soon be together in the joy of the kingdom. Then came the final struggle. Jesus' whole work, his messianic activity, the kingdom of God, all were in question. His struggle was with God: Jesus' will to life, God's will to death. He must take the bitter from the hand of the Father.

Eyewitnesses cease with the arrest. Jesus was taken before the Sanhedrin and charged with being an enemy of the temple. It is not likely that he said *he* would destroy it, but he did appear in the temple and predict its destruction. What role he saw for himself is unknown; perhaps that was a promise of the coming kingdom. That was not a basis for bringing Jesus before Pilate, but a charge of being a messianic pretender was.

The disciples fled and returned to Galilee; only a pair of women, who bear the tradition of Jesus' last hours, were left in Jerusalem. The disciples lost faith, but in Galilee after a short time appearances occurred, with Peter the first to be convinced thereby of Jesus' resurrection. Then more appearances occurred, as recorded in 1 Corinthians 15. Then came reports that women had found the grave empty. From the appearances came the conviction that Jesus was not dead, but alive, made into the heavenly messiah, and would come again as the "man" in Daniel on the clouds of heaven.

The new Christian faith grew from the conviction that Jesus was now lord and messiah and would come again to bring the kingdom. Thereafter faith was directed to the person of Jesus and this confession became the criterion of Christian faith itself. There was both blessing and curse in that development. Dogma arose, along with submersion of the practical, of love of God and brother, to this new center of the religion. The doing of the will of God, love of the neighbor, receded in favor of confession to Jesus. It had a baneful effect; making confession to Jesus the critical test — whoever could babble a confession with the lips — (367) — and led to loss of humanity and a poverty of love and a sickness afflicting Christianity still. The good side was that the new religion took on the character of a personal relation of the heart to Jesus himself. It was not a religion of ideas and postulates but of a love for Jesus himself. Otherwise the loss of Jesus would have left an impoverished world, not having that peace and joy in human hearts. Thereby was preserved the new messianism Jesus brought into the world. Yet his own expectation of the kingdom on earth was not and still remains unfulfilled. In its place is faith in the exaltation of Jesus to heaven. Present for us still is, however, that he brought to us on earth the blessed presentness of God and His salvation, and has given us the Father in heaven and courage and joy to love the brothers:

> Thereby he has brought us the heavenly kingdom on earth — though not yet the perfect and eternal one — nevertheless the heavenly kingdom in the midst

of struggle and necessity, in the suffering and sin of earthly life, with an outlook
on the greater eternity and with the power and love of the God who is already
present. (368)

So ends the book with considerable sermonizing.

It is a repetitious book, replaying its themes regularly. It is also one whose
roots in the liberal tradition are still very much evident; Wernle's most eloquent waxing was reserved for the themes of God as our Father and our love
for everyone else as brother, even though there was also the most thoroughgoing application of the eschatological interpretation of the kingdom in Jesus'
message. There is much that sounds Schweitzerian: the messianic claim, expectation of the imminent kingdom with Jesus himself a messianic figure. And there
is much that is evocative of Heitmüller: the nonpolitical Jesus, the interest in
the ways that Jesus differed from his environment. But from another perspective,
the work is a kind of bridge from the older liberalism to what was yet to come
in the shape of Form Criticism. The nature of the oral tradition was recognized;
judgments of authenticity on the basis of the impact of the later community were
freely indulged, though lacking was any capacity to analyze the tradition in terms
of its oral forms. The Kierkegaardian *Entweder/Oder* appeared, as it would later
in Bultmann's *Jesus,* though Wernle's book as a whole has not the epoch-making
character of Bultmann's work.

Wernle's work was constructed from a safer base in Switzerland, but few other
worthwhile "lives" issued from countries enmeshed in the conflict, for the Great
War preempted all causes. Scholarship, too, was mesmerized by national peril
and driven to a period of pause, if not nevertheless a time of total inactivity.
There were movements afoot, but they only became visible at war's end.

Chapter 4

RESURRECTION AND DEATH
Jesus in the Twenties

The Great War ruined everything. No one could calculate the losses to scholarship in terms of lives that were wasted and would make no contribution. The optimistic hopes for world unity, the sense of pressing on toward some kind of beatific future, were all shattered. A highly civilized world had behaved in such a way as to vindicate the Darwinian claims regarding human ancestry. Theological studies were not exempt from the horror: K. L. Schmidt spoke of his war wounds in his significant book released in 1919; Rudolf Bultmann reported a brother lost in the war; the distinguished linguist J. H. Moulton was killed in a U-boat attack; and the harshest of feelings were engendered across national lines for quite some time.[1] Ernst Troeltsch is a case in point.

Troeltsch wrote to his friend Baron Friederich von Hügel about the conditions prevailing in Germany following the war. Von Hügel shared Troeltsch's painful report with his friend Norman Kemp Smith:

> Men are mad and set about to destroy what remains. Famine is already a widespread reality among us, and the situation will soon be desperate. People are now living off their old, stored-away possessions, such as clothing, shoes, etc. One cannot even imagine the future.... We are all grieving for our beloved dead. At the outbreak of the war my mother suffered a stroke induced by terror and died soon after. My father was broken and numbed by the loss. He lived just two years longer and died without ever comprehending the war. My sister lost her only son after two weeks of war service. My brother-in-law was shattered by this and died one year later! So it goes in these times. They are considered fortunate whom death has released from the madness of this world, and those who are left behind must earnestly stretch their love for fellow-man to be able to bear further existence among men.[2]

---

1. K. L. Schmidt, *Der Rahmen der Geschichte Jesu: Literarkritische Untersuchungen Ältesten Jesusüberlieferung* (Berlin: Trowitzsch and Sohn, 1919) ix; Bultmann's autobiographical statement, "Autobiographical Reflections," in *Existence and Faith,* trans. with introduction by Schubert Ogden, Living Age Books (New York: Meridian Books, 1960), 285. Moulton's death was reported by Hans Windisch, ZNW 20 (1921): 73.

2. Quoted in Lawrence F. Barmann, ed., *The Letters of Baron Friedrich von Hügel and Professor Norman Kemp Smith* (New York: Fordham University Press, 1981), 68, 70. Smith was a professor of philosophy at Edinburgh, also at one time at Princeton. This volume also contains a gold mine of biographical data about then-current figures in England–Scotland.

The correspondence between Kemp Smith and von Hügel also documents the efforts of the two to arrange a lecture tour for Troeltsch in England and Scotland, and, eventually, to extend him an invitation to be the Gifford lecturer. There was difficulty in every instance because of hostility aroused by the war; the tour was finally arranged, but Troeltsch died on February 1, 1923, before fulfilling it.[3]

Richard Lempp, whose report on conditions in Germany around 1910 we referred to earlier,[4] produced a similar article for the *Harvard Theological Review* in 1921.[5] This time it had a quite different tone, with some sense of anger at not only the terrible aftermath of the war, but also the bleak outlook occasioned by the Treaty of Versailles. There was also political unrest in the form of danger from the Bolsheviks and revolution. Churches' support of the war had led to some disaffection with them; little funding was available for the printing of theological works. The socialists and even the communists gained support, causing many to leave the churches. The problem of the relation of church and culture, of which Lempp had spoken earlier, remained unsolved. There was a need, he said, for some new prophet who can unite the old gospel with the new circumstance.[6]

In America the president of the Society of Biblical Literature and Exegesis, James A. Montgomery, offered his retrospective and prospective thoughts on the biblical disciplines,[7] suggesting that American scholars had been held captive to Germany and calling for an independent scholarship, with its own commentaries, dictionaries, and sources of journal publication.[8] Perhaps the war served as a catalyst, driving American scholarship to an independent course, though the lives of Jesus produced at that time, as we will see, do not necessarily reflect that kind of movement.

But certainly the circumstance in America was different; it is always so with the victors. The aftermath of the war marked the decade of the Roaring Twenties, a giddy period in which Americans indulged in whatever passions they could summon. The flapper, the Charleston, criminal gangs in pursuit of illegal liquor symbolized the time, even as expatriate literary figures like Ernest Hemingway fled the land for other shores. Religiously, it was the time also of another kind of warfare, cultural warfare, between the "modernists" and the fundamentalists —

---

3. No doubt some of this hostility was altogether understandable, given Troeltsch's support of the war in Germany. See Hans-Georg Drescher, *Ernst Troeltsch: His Life and Work*, trans. John Bowden (Minneapolis: Fortress Press, 1993), 249ff. Perhaps it is only surprising that some sense of reconciliation appeared as quickly as it did.

4. See above, prologue, n. 24.

5. Richard Lempp, "Church and Religion in Germany," *HTR* 14 (1921): 30–52.

6. The words had irony, for a prophet certainly arose — a false prophet — who exploited the conditions to produce an even more fearful nationalistic force in the ensuing decade of the thirties.

7. James A. Montgomery, "Present Tasks of Biblical Scholarship," *JBL* 38 (1919): 1–14. Saunders (in *Searching the Scriptures*) referred to Montgomery's address, reprinted in the journal, as a "declaration of independence" (30). Montgomery was professor in the Philadelphia Divinity School as well as the University of Pennsylvania and had been director of the American School of Oriental Research. His more famous pupil was William F. Albright.

8. *JBL* was printed in Leipzig from 1913 to 1934 (Saunders, *Searching the Scriptures*, 7 [prologue, n. 18]).

a decade punctuated at its navel by the Scopes trial (1925) and terminated by the Great Depression. It was probably the last era of innocence in America, and concurrently the time of greatest production for American lives of Jesus.

And yet even in Germany something was stirring during the dark years of the war, for shortly after its conclusion there appeared, almost by magic, three startling works — actually, four if we wish to venture beyond our limits — that signified a beginning and an end. The beginning was the onset of *Formgeschichte* and the end was the cessation of the heart of liberalism, its core attachment to the historical Jesus. The theological moment was, of course, Karl Barth's *Römerbrief* (1919), marking in a broad sense a return to the epistle over against the dominance of the gospel, or kerygma versus historical figure, and rejection of the so-called culture Protestantism associated with the Ritschlian school. In the same year appeared Martin Dibelius's *Die Formgeschichte des Evangeliums*[9] and K. L. Schmidt's *Der Rahmen der Geschichte Jesu*,[10] with both followed two years later by Rudolf Bultmann's *Die Geschichte der synoptischen Tradition*.[11] It is quite impossible to summarize these works, nor is it necessary, but some generalizations may be indulged.

Form Criticism

It is clear that Form Criticism did not erupt, as it were, out of nowhere, *ex nihilo*. Its antecedents lay in the liberal school, in the *religionsgeschichtliche* investigations of Hermann Gunkel[12] and in the recognition already existing of the oral character of the tradition. But the liberals were unable to do very much with this recognition until the development of a tool or method for analyzing that tradition. Bultmann himself traced its immediate antecedents to the work of Wilhelm Wrede and Julius Wellhausen, then to the pattern already set by Gunkel on the

---

9. Martin Dibelius, *Die Formgeschichte der Evangeliums* (Tübingen: J. C. B. Mohr [Paul Siebeck], 1919); English trans., *From Tradition to Gospel*, trans. Bertram Lee Woolf in collaboration with the author (New York: Scribner's, n.d. [1935?]). Also a few years later was the summary work, *Geschichte der urchristlichen Literatur*, Sammlung Göschen I: Evangelien und Apokalypten (Berlin: Walter de Gruyter, 1926). It included a description of wider issues (apocryphal literature, synoptic question, apocalypses).

10. As above, n. 1.

11. Rudolf Bultmann, *Die Geschichte der synoptischen Tradition*, FRLANT (Göttingen: Vandenhoeck and Ruprecht, 1921); English trans., *History of the Synoptic Tradition*, rev. ed., trans. John Marsh (Oxford: Basil Blackwell, 1963) (hereafter *History*). Usually included in early *formgeschichtliche* studies were also Georg Bertram, *Die Leidensgeschichte Jesu und der Christuskult: Eine formgeschichtliche Untersuchung* FRLANT (Göttingen: Vandenhoeck and Ruprecht, 1922); and Martin Albertz, *Die synoptischen Streitgespräche: Ein Beitrag zur Formengeschichte des Urchristentums* (Berlin: Trowitzsch, 1921).

12. Ludwig Köhler reported a conversation with Gunkel in which the latter suggested that his impact in the long term might be greater on New Testament research than Old: *Das Formgeschichtliche Problem des Neuen Testaments* (Tübingen: J. C. B. Mohr [Paul Siebeck], 1927), 7. The recognition of an earlier, oral period goes back still further, though it had become axiomatic by the period of the liberals. A short history of the predecessors is given by Erich Fascher, *Die formgeschichtliche Methode: Eine Darstellung und Kritik, Zugleich ein Beitrag zur Geschichte des synoptischen Problems* (Giessen: Alfred Töpelmann, 1924), 4–51.

Old Testament.[13] Bultmann then described his own procedure and how it agreed with or differed from that of Dibelius. Both moved out from the acknowledgment of a sociological principle, that is, that the tradition reflects and grows out of the life-setting of the community (*Sitz im Leben*); Dibelius attempted to reconstruct the history of the tradition by proceeding from the *Sitz im Leben* to the literary forms, while Bultmann began with the literary setting and inferred something about the life of the community. Still, both were doing approximately the same thing, except that Bultmann, in his own view, attached greater importance to the decision about the factuality or historicity of the tradition as it can be derived from form-critical analysis than did Dibelius. In consequence Bultmann concerned himself with what he designated as "the one chief problem of primitive Christianity, the relationship of the primitive Palestinian and Hellenistic Christianity" (5).

This latter point is of more than passing historical interest, for Bultmann's analysis of the synoptic tradition played also into his theological program. His analysis turned on the distinction between the hellenistic and palestinian churches; the former took over the tradition from the latter and hellenized it, which is to say, kerygmatized it. (What shows influence of this hellenistic kerygma cannot go back to Jesus, and so on.) Theologically, Bultmann would opt for the kerygma, the Easter kerygma of the hellenistic church (Paul, in his view), over against the position of the palestinian church with its Jesus-traditions. That is not to say that Bultmann's historical analysis was merely driven by his theological interest, though it is much less certain anymore whether this distinction between hellenistic and palestinian is not simply too neat and even convenient.

There were terminological differences between Dibelius and Bultmann — Dibelius preferring "paradigm" to Bultmann's "apophthegm," for example, as descriptions of the form of story that supplies a narrative context leading up to a striking saying. And Dibelius never failed to mention his description of the gospels as *klein Literatur*, or popular writing produced by nonliterary persons which therefore had qualities of naivete and lack of sophistication. The gospel writers were looked upon as primarily editors of an oral tradition or, in some cases, collections of existing smaller units of material. But essentially Dibelius and Bultmann were engaged in the same project of analyzing the forms of the tradition and pressing toward an understanding of that history in order to arrive at a judgment as to the oldest layer of tradition, which then presumably could be ascribed to Jesus himself.

K. L. Schmidt's work had a more modest ambition — not to encompass the whole synoptic tradition, but to investigate the chronological and topographical references in the synoptic tradition. These cannot first be treated as historical, since they constitute a literary problem in the synoptic tradition, and it is to the

---

13. Bultmann, *History*, 1–3.

literary analysis that Schmidt devoted his inquiry.[14] The results of this analysis with respect to the historicity of the gospel framework were almost entirely negative: there is no real historical framework of the life of Jesus, not even Mark's, the oldest, which serves the religious and missionary and apologetic purposes of the author. There remains, so the conclusion ran, "no life of Jesus in the sense of an unfolding biography, no chronological outline of the story of Jesus, but rather only individual stories, pericopes, which are set in a framework."[15] Schmidt's work then finished Wrede's earlier wrecking operations on the Gospel of Mark; Bultmann and Dibelius assembled the pieces sufficiently to allow at least a portrayal of the *message* of Jesus, if not a "life" or even an itinerary of his activity.[16]

Bultmann's Portrayal of Jesus

Bultmann's *Jesus* was published in 1926.[17] It was and still is a landmark work, standing like a tree silhouetted against a wilderness, with no real peers and few successors — not until Günther Bornkamm's book, which remains its lineal descendent.[18] The introduction set out the methodology, with its now-famous disclaimer that no life of Jesus is possible and, in particular, that "we can know almost nothing concerning the life and personality of Jesus, since the early Christian sources show no interest in either, are moreover fragmentary and often legendary; and other sources about Jesus do not exist."[19] This statement should, however, be seen not simply as a shocking affirmation of Bultmann's radical skepticism, but rather as a response to the liberalism in which he was himself trained and from which he came. There was nothing new in claiming that Jesus' life could not be written, but the statement disclaiming any interest in his "personality" needs some unpacking. The immediate background can be seen in something like Heitmüller's work that we examined earlier, where considerable interest was devoted to Jesus' *Persönlichkeit*.[20] This term approaches the meaning "personhood," and certainly goes beyond what in English we associate with the

---

14. It was in fact his *Habilitationschrift*, whose publication was delayed a few years by the war. For a later dissent from Schmidt's work from the English side, see C. H. Dodd's essay, "The Framework of the Gospel Narrative," *ExpTim* 43 (1931–32): 396–400. Dodd found that Mark transmitted pericopae with an itinerary along with an outline of the whole ministry.

15. Schmidt, *Der Rahmen der Geschichte Jesu*, 317.

16. Dibelius's works on Jesus will be considered in chapter 5.

17. Rudolf Bultmann, *Jesus* (Berlin: Deutsche Bibliothek, 1926). Interestingly, it was published as part of a series entitled The Immortals: The Spiritual Heroes of Mankind in Their Life and Significance, with Numerous Illustrations, vol. 1. One has to wonder whether the makers of this series appreciated how little Bultmann's book corresponded to the apparent intention of the series.

18. Günther Bornkamm, *Jesus of Nazareth*, trans. James M. Robinson with Irene and Fraser McLuskey (New York: Harper, 1960).

19. I follow generally the English translation, *Jesus and the Word*, trans. Louise Pettibone Smith and Erminie Huntress Lantero (New York: Scribner's, 1934), 8. The translation is quite literate, though something like "rule" or "reign" might have been better for *Herrschaft*.

20. Above, chap. 3, 81–86. Bultmann's own *History* was dedicated to his former teacher Heitmüller, whom he succeeded at Marburg.

word "personality," that is, individual characteristics of a person. That, too, no doubt is bracketed out by Bultmann's exclusion, but equally inaccessible to the historian for Bultmann is the "essence" or revelatory character of Jesus, which almost seems to lurk as a hidden item in the liberal preoccupation with the *Persönlichkeit* of Jesus. The assumption seems to be that there had to be something special about this Jesus, but having abandoned the christological portrayal as simply later theology of the community, the liberals could not quite say what that something was. It could only be hinted at, as something that lay embedded in his personality. Bultmann would have no more of that. For him the line between historical figure and kerygma of the community had broadened into a chasm, a boundary not easy to get over. To have it otherwise would expose the Easter kerygma to the uncertainties of the historian's labors.[21]

A second introductory item is Bultmann's statement of the criteria for determining authenticity. First to be excluded were matters of language or content that came from héllenistic Christianity; then the palestinian material itself could be evaluated on the basis of the elimination of whatever "betrays the specific interests of the church or reveals characteristics of later development."[22] Missing was any reference to the obverse side of what Norman Perrin would later call the "criterion of dissimilarity," the parallel material from Judaism. However, Perrin himself credited Bultmann with first practicing this criterion in relation to the assessment of the parables,[23] although an equally important statement lies in Bultmann's determination of the Logia of Jesus. After asserting that the most likely authentic Logia are to be found wherever we can see an eschatological mood or call to repentance (such as Mark 3:27, 8:35), or those that presuppose a new disposition (purity sayings, children), he then added:

> All these sayings, which admittedly are in part no longer specific examples of logia, contain something characteristic, new, reaching out beyond popular wisdom and piety and yet are in no sense scribal or rabbinic nor yet Jewish apocalyptic. So here if anywhere we can find what is characteristic of the preaching of Jesus.[24]

Nothing scribal, rabbinic, Jewish apocalyptic, or popular wisdom and piety: that about covers most anything Jewish. Certainly Bultmann was attempting to attain to what was *characteristic* of Jesus among the preserved Logia[25] and felt con-

---

21. These kinds of issues arose more sharply in the time of the so-called New Quest of the historical Jesus.

22. Bultmann, *Jesus and the Word*, 13.

23. Norman Perrin, *Rediscovering the Teaching of Jesus* (New York: Harper, 1967), 40, citing Bultmann's *History*, 205. The criterion was later elaborated by Ernst Käsemann clearly, without the Perrin title. Cf. Käsemann's programmatic essay, "The Problem of the Historical Jesus," in *Essays on New Testament Themes*, trans. W. J. Montague, Studies in Biblical Theology 41 (Naperville, Ill.: Alec R. Allenson, 1964), 37. The statement runs: "In only one case do we have more or less safe ground under our feet; when there are no grounds either for deriving a tradition from Judaism or for ascribing it to primitive Christianity, and especially when Jewish Christianity has mitigated or modified the received tradition, as having found it too bold for its taste."

24. Bultmann, *History*, 105.

25. It needs to be emphasized that only a single category, Logia, was under consideration, but the principle was capable of extension.

strained to exclude whatever had parallels from Judaism; he had no evident interest in developing a non-Jewish Jesus, though, like his liberal predecessors, he was interested in determining how Jesus differed from Judaism. Indeed, as Bultmann himself formulated the statement of criteria in the Jesus book, he hardly departed from the liberals — in fact, sounded very much like them (something new, not from the later community) — excepting only the radicality of the application.

In his presentation of Jesus, Bultmann first sketched out the background in Judaism, connecting the messianic movements of the time with the activity of both John the Baptist and Jesus. Neither was a political figure, though both were executed by the political authorities as leading such movements. Jesus appeared after John's death as an eschatological prophet; he anticipated the near kingdom, as can be seen in the messianic demonstration at the end, at the last supper, and at the takeover of the temple to purify it for the kingdom. The kingdom is imminent; the world stands at the "dawn" of the kingdom, which now casts its shadow into the present. The demons are being put to flight, Satan's rule is being challenged. Jesus then appeared with a message about this imminent end and preached repentance in preparation for it. Now is the last hour, now is the moment of decision: either/or, for or against the kingdom. This kingdom is therefore eschatological deliverance (*Heil*), something miraculous, something brought by God's power, supernatural, superhistorical. Jesus expected this grand eschatological drama to unfold — the Son of man appearing, the dead arising, the judgment with its consequences for heavenly glory or the torments of hell. Jesus, however, refused to engage in apocalyptic speculation, nor did he relate to the Jewish nationalistic hopes. Certainly the kingdom was for the Jewish people, and Jesus contemplated no gentile mission, yet also for him the Jew as such, like the Gentile as such, has no special claim before God. No human being actually has any claim; everyone alike is summoned to decision in the last hour.

The kingdom is not seen as already *present*, according to Bultmann, though it is so near that it completely determines the present and compels that either/or decision. It is in the act of decision that authentic humanity is achieved, and therefore every hour is the last hour insofar as persons are confronted with decision:

> If men are standing in the crisis of decision, and if precisely this crisis is the essential characteristic of their humanity, then every hour is the last hour, and we can understand that for Jesus the whole contemporary mythology is pressed into the service of this conception of human existence. Thus he understood and proclaimed his hour as the last hour.[26]

So Jesus operated with no humanistic valuations of humankind (intrinsic worthfulness) and, no matter how often he referred to Satan, his location of the essence of human existence in the *will* shows that ultimately the concept of Satan also belongs simply to that mythological picture with which Jesus operated.

---

26. Bultmann, *Jesus*, 52.

Jesus also appeared as a rabbi, a scribe who taught the Law. In fact, actually, he taught the will of God and sometimes set that over against the Law. He differed in significant ways from the usual rabbis; he went about with sinners and publicans, even had women among his followers, had special affection for children, and, while he obviously accepted the authority of scripture, he also differed from the usual Jewish legal piety. Obedience was the essence of such legalism, and while Jesus taught obedience, he differed from the Jewish ethic in that he conceived that obedience radically, requiring not the formal, outward unquestioning obedience, but that which assents internally. One must not do something obediently, but rather be obedient essentially. There is no reward for such obedience; there is only a reward for those who do not consciously seek one.

Jesus actually taught no ethics at all in the sense of a system of ordered values. He showed no interest in questions of state, society, the right, or world reform, but simply proclaimed the will of God as the only good. The demand to submit to the will of God also constitutes a crisis of decision, and it is this decision-character of the demand that links it to and unites it with Jesus' proclamation of the kingdom. That the demand of the will of God is the condition for entrance into the kingdom is true, to a degree, but the unity in Jesus' message lies in the demand for decision toward the present hour as the last hour, as seen in both the proclamation of the will of God and the kingdom. The theory of an interim ethic is to be rejected, for it assumes that Jesus thought of the demand as merely relative.

Jesus' conception of God was rooted in his Jewish background. God as Creator is transcendent and as Father is immanent. Judaism never managed to unify these two, though Jesus did, since he conceived radically both the idea of sin and of grace. The words about God's providence, even though perhaps not genuine, nevertheless reflect something characteristic of the teaching of Jesus. Jesus was not evidently concerned with the question of the justice of God or the problem of suffering in the world. Human beings have no right to expect an answer to their questions about the misfortunes of life. There is, however, no doubt that Jesus believed in miracles and himself was a practitioner of healing and exorcism. He refused to accredit himself by a miracle, and evidently understood his miracles to be signs of the imminence of the kingdom. Beyond that it is not worthwhile to attempt an explanation of the miracle stories. That Jesus assumed the omnipotence of God is evident, though what that means is that God is omnipotent only when He is so for me, in the realization of his omnipotence in my life. God is always distant for the unbeliever, always near to faith.

Jesus certainly believed in and practiced prayer, though how much of the Lord's Prayer goes back to him is indeterminable. It is at least characteristic. Prayer of petition meant just that, the request for God actually to do something. How is that reconcilable with the demand for unconditional obedience? The latter does not mean simply resignation, and petition contains obedience when it is expression of wishes. Jesus was in no case merely an ascetic. His praying involves the paradox of "trustful petition with the will to surrender" (188).

Jesus also taught the nearness of God in the form of divine forgiveness; in fact, unlike Judaism he conceived it radically. Man is absolutely a sinner (unlike Judaism which still assumed the possibility of human achievement or at the least the value of a person's repentance). For Jesus human beings have nothing meritorious to offer and can only be dependent on the pure gift of God's forgiveness. That is why he turned to the sinners and tax collectors, for they grasp more clearly the grace-character of the forgiving God. It is similar with children, who drew Jesus' approval. The later church attached this forgiveness to Jesus' own death (and resurrection) as the act of salvation. Jesus did not so speak — all such sayings are inauthentic — and insofar as the church has attempted to portray these "events" as demonstrable events of salvation in history it has gone astray. Jesus himself provided no provable demonstration of this salvation; it is event known only through his word, for which there is no proof. Nor was his own "personality" a ground for faith, and the only estimate of him that is consistent with his own view is that he was the bearer of a message, the word. Only as such did he claim to bring forgiveness. Whether he truly did and whether he was the bearer of a word from God were the decisions that faced his hearers.

So the book ends with never a word about "resurrection," which would in any case be inaccessible to the historians' gaze. Yet the book does contain more about what was characteristic of Jesus than is often assumed to be the case, without at the same time undertaking anything resembling a "life" or even a historical outline of Jesus' public activity. The overall impression, of course, remains of a work that has its primary focus on the *word*, the message of Jesus, with a degree of charity exercised toward even those traditions that may not be original with Jesus, but nevertheless reflect something characteristic of him.

So did Bultmann wrestle with the message of Jesus, and it must be admitted that the cleverness of it all is simply breathtaking. Everything that seems strange about Jesus was forthrightly acknowledged: he expected a cosmic, imminent end of the world, he practiced exorcisms and the like, held to the conception of Satan and his power. At the same time all this was wrestled out of Jesus and effectively "demythologized" into the existential Kierkegaardian call to decision. Even though Bultmann did not evidently have in hand yet the full Heideggerian existentialist analysis of *Dasein*,[27] he was already *unterwegs*, so to speak, in this

---

27. Applied most effectively to the theology of Paul, as in *Theology of the New Testament*, trans. Kendrick Grobel (New York: Scribner's, 1951), vol. 1, especially the characterization of the anthropological terms. The original was published in 1948 (*Theologie des Neuen Testaments* [Tübingen: J. C. B. Mohr (Paul Siebeck), 1948]). The message of Jesus is resummarized there as prolegomena to the *real* theology of the New Testament (Paul and John). It is there also that Bultmann repeated the seemingly precipitous statement that "Jesus' call to decision implies a christology," (1:43), when evidently he meant that Jesus' preaching implied a (messianic? eschatological? prophetic?) self-understanding, as opposed to a post-Easter Christian confession. The same was said much earlier (1929) in Bultmann's essay, "The Significance of the Historical Jesus for the Theology of Paul," in *Faith and Understanding*, trans. Louise Pettibone Smith; ed. with introduction by Robert W. Funk (New York:

Jesus-book. So a Jesus more to our liking finally emerges from the wrestling contest, and Bultmann's liberal lineaments become more evident in the endeavor to dress Jesus in some more fashionable clothing. The liberal soil of the work also showed itself in that the Jesus of those "lives" was also unrelentingly nonpolitical, socially uninvolved, ethically individualistic, and always Judaism-transcending.

At the same time Bultmann never did slink around apologizing for miracles or embarrassing stories; he never hesitated to call a legend by its proper name or to recognize a myth when he saw one. That was no doubt connected with his theology, which never rested on anything discoverable by the historian. Here it is only necessary to recall that Bultmann found himself quite comfortably in the company of Karl Barth, at least at the first, on the issue of what constitutes authentic Christian faith, which is certainly not to be mistaken for the endlessly altering opinions of the critics. On that Barth and Bultmann would always agree, even if later on they fell out over Bultmann's affinity for the existentialism of Heidegger.

Bultmann, in fact, never claimed that his portrayal of Jesus was a form of the kerygma;[28] it is at best the historian's reconstruction, something any historian might wish to do as presenting him with a possibility for his own self-understanding. That does not make it the specifically Christian *kerygma*, or proclamation of the crucified-risen One. And even if the portrayal of the historical figure and his message should nevertheless sound that way, that would only be because the two do stand in some sort of continuity, do both pose the issue of eschatological decision, the last-hour decision.[29]

Bultmann's picture of Jesus or, more precisely, his picture of the message of Jesus generated controversy. His apparent reduction of Jesus' ethic to the life of the individual drew some notice,[30] and the existentialist approach stirred a different approach to Jesus, such as that of Rudolf Otto.[31] But like Schweitzer before him, Bultmann had few successors, none immediately. It can be said with some fairness that it was really Bultmann and not so much Schweitzer whose work marked a period of "No Quest" (as it is widely referred to) in Germany. As

---

Harper, 1969), 220–46, esp. 237. Jesus saw himself as the bearer of the definitive word in the last hour and thus implied that the response to him was the decisive one for his hearers, but no explicit messianic consciousness was affirmed. The term "christology" here arouses levels of thought that Bultmann seemed not to intend.

28. The opposite, in fact. Cf. Hans Werner Bartsch, ed., *Kerygma and Myth: A Theological Debate*, 2 vols., trans. Reginald H. Fuller, Harper Torchbooks (New York: Harper and Brothers, 1961), 1:117.

29. On this see the issues documented in the 1929 essay (above) and further in Bultmann's later Heidelberg address, "The Primitive Christian Kerygma and the Historical Jesus," in *The Historical Jesus and the Kerygmatic Christ*, ed. and trans. Carl E. Braaten and Roy A. Harrisville (New York: Abingdon Press, 1964), 15–52.

30. One instance would be Edwyn Hoskyns's review of Bultmann's *Jesus*, JTS 28 (1927): 106–9, who spoke of the "devastating individualism" of the book.

31. Rudolf Otto, *Reich Gottes und Menschensohn: Ein religionsgeschichtlicher Versuch* (Munich: Beck, 1933); English trans., *The Kingdom of God and the Son of Man*, trans. Floyd V. Filson and Bertam Lee Woolf (Grand Rapids, Mich.: Zondervan, n.d.). Otto is dealt with below, chap. 5.

W. G. Kümmel observed, aside from the works of Bultmann and Otto, there was little else written about the historical Jesus until the early 1950s.[32]

Lives of Jesus then virtually ceased in Germany in the twenties. English production was also limited, and primarily it was the Americans who continued to compose works on Jesus through the decade. That may be related to the sociopolitical scene; works on Jesus seem to multiply where a more optimistic cultural mood seeds the social environment.

Two English books, however, are worthy of consideration, not so much because they indicated the future of research or even helped to decide the trend, but because they actually represent opposite ends of works on Jesus, and we may devote some attention to them. One was the moderately conservative work of the Anglican A. C. Headlam, bishop of Gloucester, and the other was the more radical book by Joseph Warschauer. We will look at each in turn.[33]

A. C. Headlam

Claiming to argue for the credibility of the gospels, Headlam accepted the Markan hypothesis and affirmed that it was based on Peter's recollections. In spite of some problems, Mark, dating around 64 or even earlier, is reliable: "Tradition may have coloured the record a little, but in the main there seems no reason why we should not accept it as authentic."[34]

Q is likely Papias's logia, Luke traveled with Paul and had additional good sources, and Matthew chose his material like a good historian and is largely blameless. John used all four sources and, though more of a theological work, also contains some good traditions.

Conditions at the time of Jesus were recounted: Herod and his sons, the procurators, education (most people were literate), but a rather sharp judgment was passed on the religion of the rabbis, characterized as "distorted in mind, in morals, in religion...a zeal for God...great earnestness and strong characters...vitiated by self-will, by narrowness and pedantry" (90). Jesus himself was synagogue-educated, but it is uncertain whether he could write or knew Greek. He came from the poor, was a carpenter, but had no rabbinic training; Greek influence can be seen among some Jews, though there is hardly any evidence of that in the gospels. Apocalyptic thought, however, was pervasive.

---

32. W. G. Kümmel, *Dreißig Jahre Jesusforschung (1950–1980)*, herausg. von Helmut Merklein (Bonn: Peter Hanstein Verlag, 1985), 1–2. The report of Ernst von Dobschütz ("Der heutige Stand der Leben-Jesu-Forschung," *ZTK*, n.f. [1924]: 64–84), recounted the certainties attained and the evolution of Form Criticism, and did not seem to know that there was a danger of the whole issue disappearing, and, in fact, argued for the necessity of the historical figure of Jesus for theology itself (an antidote to a new dogmatism).

33. Headlam's was *The Life and Teaching of Jesus the Christ* (London: John Murray, 1923); also published in the same year by Oxford. Warschauer's was *The Historical Christ* (London: T. Fisher Unwin, 1927).

34. Headlam, *Life and Teaching of Jesus the Christ*, 15.

Jesus shared the cosmology and belief systems of his time (angels, demons); he had no scientific knowledge. Jesus' roots were in the Old Testament, such as Daniel (kingdom), and Isaiah (suffering servant). It was Jesus, not the church, who took up these concepts and transformed them. His work was first connected with John the Baptist, himself an eschatological figure. No national privilege would avail in the coming judgment — only justice, mercy, and charity. Jesus' baptism by John constituted a great spiritual crisis for him (Jesus), the moment in which he knew himself to be the son and servant of God with a great mission. The story had to have come from Jesus himself. Schweitzer's thoroughgoing apocalypticizing, however, was excessive:

> It is...a cause of failure in many scholars that, instead of following their texts, they allow themselves to be overpowered by some mastering idea, and then pour the history into that mould. This is true in a marked manner of the modern eschatological interpretation. It has given a meaning to much which was obscure, and illuminated the whole period. But it is only one current of thought...imperfect generalizations must not dominate our history. (165)

Jesus preached in Galilee, attracting fame, and he also made astonishing claims. His behavior was shocking to some (consorting with sinners, tax collectors, and disreputable women). But then he came to save sinners.

He also performed exorcisms, which are cases of mental illness. Other healings may be attributable to psychosomatic causes, though all miracles cannot be ruled out a priori. Primary, however, was Jesus' teaching and spiritual power. Opposition to Jesus arose, for he practiced no fasting and was free in his sabbath observance. His purpose was to replace a formal religion with a spiritual one. His conflict with the scribes and rabbis led to his separation from the synagogue, signifying the beginning of the church, for it led to the selection of the twelve.

The Sermon on the Mount embodies Jesus' teaching; it is not a single discourse, but comes from a trustworthy source. The messianic kingdom would be especially for the poor and downtrodden, though Jesus' focus was primarily on spiritual blessings. He taught a new way, summed up in the love commandment, which emphasized principles, not rules and laws. The source was the Old Testament, but Jesus with "unerring touch" (221) extracted from it universal principles. By it everyone is made a brother, with no barriers of race or language. Jesus opposed the externalism and legalism of the Pharisees; religion is inward, spiritual. Primary themes were prayer and the fulfilling of the will of God the heavenly Father. The "golden rule" is the essence of Jesus' teaching.

The apocalyptic kingdom did not attract Headlam. The relevant texts, such as Mark 9:1 and Luke 22:29–30, are susceptible of various interpretations. Perhaps Jesus thought of the kingdom as the future dissemination of his teaching and message throughout the world. In any case the kingdom is not reducible to the individual or to the future; it is both present and social, though not political. It is individuals doing the will of God. "The Golden Age comes by each man acting rightly" (266).

The kingdom is traceable through the Old Testament, messianic thought, and the rabbinic texts. The failure of the hope brought about the apocalyptic expectation of a final divine intervention. There was a more elevated notion of a kingdom of righteousness and an eschatological one of a temporal, earthly nature. Jesus repudiated the latter version; many of the parables, such as the sower, suggest that the kingdom is already here, in the form of the message and the word of Jesus himself. It depends on growth in the hearts of persons; it is slow and secret, but will become great. So the kingdom can mean a principle of life and conduct, or Christianity as a process at work in the world of which the church is the visible manifestation, or the final consummation of all things. As present the kingdom signifies God's sovereignty or rule already effective — living by the will of God — even though as present it is imperfect and incomplete.

Jesus sent the disciples on a mission, where they had success. Afterward he withdrew to train them; when he returned to his mission the miracle of the loaves occurred (something wonderful happened and stirred up the people), and the crowd tried to make Jesus king (John). It was a time of danger and Jesus withdrew through Tyre and Sidon. After some months of instructing his disciples he made his way to Caesarea-Philippi, where he disclosed the idea of the suffering messiah. He could not accomplish his purpose without a break with Judaism that would result in his death.

It was Jesus and not the church who combined the idea of the messiah with the idea of the suffering servant. The Son of man was the messiah from heaven, the ruler in the final judgment. Jesus went to Jerusalem with these ideas. Here, however, Headlam's story ended rather abruptly, with no account of the trial, the crucifixion, or the tomb stories. Primarily Headlam was concerned to locate the founding of Christianity in the work and teaching of Jesus himself. It was not the church that created the message, but Jesus' message that created the church.

Headlam's work represents a type of life whose nineteenth-century ancestry was not so far removed as to be indiscernible; it was characterized by basic confidence in the gospel record, playing down the variations among the gospels, and finding even more in John than might have been expected. It disclosed the impact of a more serious criticism, but nevertheless continued to struggle against it while also acceding to it. Certain things were retained in the record that have come almost to be expected in the English tradition: the baptism of Jesus as the event that was formative for him; the kingdom as the rule of God, with presentness the important thing; emphasis on the ethical; on Jesus as suffering servant–Son of man messiah, fully in command and aware of it all; the chronological scheme available from Mark. The theological agenda was certainly not hidden; there was no pretense here of being some kind of purely objective, scientific historian. It was a work that aimed to be faithful historically and grammatically in the understanding of the times, the geography, and the sociopolitical setting, but an underlying inspiration theory seems to preclude a very stringent criticism. It was historiography in the service of faith.

Joseph Warschauer

Warschauer's name will not be so well known as others, but his book has something of a unique claim.[35] It aimed to give an account of Jesus entirely along the line of Schweitzer's eschatological theory; in that respect it is really unique, for while Schweitzer influenced just about everybody, he convinced just about nobody, and his imitators were practically nonexistent. I know only of this one work, dedicated in gratitude to Schweitzer and provided, like the English translation of Schweitzer's *Quest*, with a preface by F. C. Burkitt, himself a subscriber to much in Schweitzer, but no composer of a real "life" of Jesus.[36]

The introduction, quoting Martin Kähler that the gospels are "records of the passion extended backwards,"[37] observed that, though the material is scanty, we can find connections and development and order the story in its likely sequence. The purpose was to say (quoting Ranke) "what really happened."

Apocalyptic thought influenced Jesus. It arose in times of darkness when people despaired of the present and looked for divine deliverance. Warschauer gave the origins (Day of Yahweh, Daniel, Isaiah, postexile, Enoch). Jesus proclaimed the imminent kingdom, but not a nationalistic one. After his death the resurrection faith arose, and traditions such as the birth stories were told. The genealogies are of no historical value and hopelessly contradictory; the birth stories are valueless to the historian, as are the virgin birth narratives. Jesus was born in the natural way to Joseph and Mary in Nazareth. The date of his birth was probably between 15 and 4 B.C.E. Jesus grew up in Galilee, but we know nothing of his growth and development.

At the time of Jesus people expected the messiah, to be preceded by the coming of a forerunner. So people were first anticipating Elijah. John the Baptist, later put into this role by Jesus, was an ascetic who preached eschatological judgment and issued an ethical demand for repentance like an old prophet. It is likely he was killed for political reasons.

Stirred by apocalyptic expectations Jesus went to John and was baptized. It was a decisive moment for Jesus that he likely related to his disciples himself. Did he therein see himself as the messiah? Doubtless he experienced a call to some great work — he felt himself God's Son as a result — but it seems incredible that a Galilean artisan should at that time have seen himself as the most glorious figure in Israel. Jesus experienced conflict; the messianic secret reflects uncertainty about his messiahship.

---

35. The name may occasionally be found under the form Warshaw. The author was well known at the time, even though he held no academic post, but worked largely as a journalist and freelance writer. Nevertheless, he had degrees from Oxford (M.A.) and Jena (Ph.D.) and was obviously well informed.

36. Excepting only Burkitt's little work of 1932, *Jesus Christ: An Historical Outline* (see below, chap. 5). Burkitt's preface observed that Warschauer's work was written from the "modernist" perspective, i.e., one which recognizes that "our universe is governed by inexorable natural law, and what we know of the earlier history of this planet and of the men who live upon it puts the recorded traditions of Greeks and Hebrews equally into the region of fairy tales" (xi).

37. Warschauer, *The Historical Christ*, 2.

Problems abound in reconstructing the career of Jesus: chronological uncertainty and geographical confusion. He worked around the Sea of Galilee, especially Capernaum. He called disciples and was a healer; he practiced exorcism, or cure by suggestion. These "cures" are susceptible of naturalistic explanations (as example, Peter's mother-in-law had a nervous condition). Jesus also challenged the authorities, the ritual laws, and even the law of Moses itself. He associated with unclean characters, and he questioned sabbath practice.

Jesus also anticipated the imminent end. The disciples would sit on twelve thrones in the kingdom and would eat at Jesus' table in the kingdom. But while the form of his message was eschatological, the essence was ethical. The center was the fatherhood of God and humanity's relation to the Father. For Jesus the kingdom was not purely future, but had already begun, and indeed with his own coming.

Warschauer agreed with Schweitzer that the "mystery" of the kingdom was the "secret" that the kingdom is imminent. The parables give expression to that (mustard seed, sower, leaven, seed growing secretly). Human effort, as in sowing the word, is significant. The kingdom was to be taken with force (a good thing); in this sense the ethical in Jesus transformed the eschatological. His own plan was to call the kingdom into being by a heroic effort. Said Warschauer:

> It is open to us to see the essential truth of this conception, and its independence of those mere garments of eschatology which speedily dropped from it. . . . That that consummation did not appear *when* Jesus expected it, is a detail; that it can and will come only *in the way* He expected it, matters everything. Not in one glorious burst, but little by little, not along the lines of catastrophe, but of evolution, will the more perfect human society, with God as its Blessed and Only Potentate, be established.[38]

A short inserted appendix gave a review of parable interpretation, showing the influence of Jülicher: parables have a single point and are not allegorical.

It is not likely that Jesus claimed to be Son of God or Son of David either. Son of man is a different question. Jesus used the title, but in a future sense, in the third person when speaking of the advent of the Son of man, referring to himself in his future role. He could hardly have been foretelling an advent of someone who was already present. A development must have taken place in Jesus' thinking, and he only gradually came to that conclusion. He may have first looked on himself as the forerunner, and only after he had determined on his own death did he come to see himself as the future messiah. Caesarea-Philippi was the crucial point, after which Jesus began to speak of himself as the Son of man, the messiah-designate after his suffering death. This combination was Jesus' own revolutionary contribution to the doctrine of the messiah.

The nature miracles endured more rationalization from Warschauer (the storm stilling: Jesus slept, was roused and unhappy at the shouting and ranting

---

38. Ibid., 86.

of the disciples, rebuked them, and suddenly the storm itself ceased — a coinci-
dence that the superstitious disciples saw as a miracle). But in the end the most
important thing was the "power to revive dead souls" (121).

Jesus sent the apostles on a preaching mission (Matt. 10:23). Disappointment
at the results and pursuit by Herod led to further development in Jesus' thought,
that he must himself take on the sufferings of the apocalyptic birth pangs in
order to introduce the new age.

The core of the bread-and-fish stories is a messianic feeding in the wilderness,
with Jesus giving everybody a fragment. Afterward the people wanted to make
Jesus king, forcing him to withdraw further. In this period of withdrawal Jesus
began to formulate his plan of suffering in Jerusalem. Only by passing through
death could he return as the messiah in the supernatural kingdom, and only in
Jerusalem would that transpire.

Jesus' controversies with scribes were genuine, with Jesus opposing these
"puerilities of rabbinism" and thereby departing from the practice of the time,
indeed the Law itself, such that he "burnt his boats" with the officialdom and
set himself on a deadly course. Jesus "proclaimed a religion of the heart and of
the spirit against one of external rules and superstitious observance" and "openly
despised and defied the Law" (161, 163).

Warschauer declined to follow Schweitzer on the theory of the interim ethic;
the core of his teaching was that God is a Father and cares for the individual.
Said Warschauer:

> It was this fact — the Divine Fatherhood, and the consequences flowing there-
> from once it became a fact, and not merely a theory — which carried Him
> in instance after instance beyond the limitations of His age and race, rendered
> Him so unconscious of those limitations that He was not conscious of transcend-
> ing them. . . . Jesus the eschatologist is bounded in His vision by the affairs and
> aspirations of His own little nation; Jesus the moralist immediately becomes a uni-
> versalist, because He preaches a universal ethic, the inevitable inference from the
> universal Fatherhood of God. (172–73)

Jesus even transcended the Law (sabbath-observance, oaths, ritual of clean-
unclean). There was also a certain understandable degree of one-sidedness in
Jesus' teaching which was directed against the one-sidedness of his opponents,
for example, turning the other cheek, divorce, oaths, hating father and mother.
The scribes and Pharisees, on the other hand, were wholly concerned with exter-
nals, whereas Jesus simply "sweeps all this legal lumber away." His emphasis on
the internal was his "final breach with the Law" (178), and it was this attitude
that was not conditioned by his eschatological expectations.

Jesus went away to Tyre and Sidon, having finally antagonized most everybody by questioning the Law itself. He withdrew because he meant to die, but
not in Galilee and not at that time. He had to plan his way to Jerusalem. We
do not know how long this period was. The core of historicity beneath the layers of mythology and legend in the Transfiguration and Caesarea-Philippi scenes
indicates that Jesus disclosed his identity as the coming messiah (including his

prospective death) first to an inner core of three disciples, then afterwards to all (at Caesarea-Philippi). He initiated all the disciples when Peter blurted out his confession. The predictions of suffering and death and resurrection were there-fore historical, though the detailed form of the sayings was likely provided by the later church.

Jesus returned to Galilee, probably to gather his followers for the journey to Jerusalem. There was miscellaneous teaching along the way; Pauline influence on Mark can be seen in the ransom saying (Mark 9:45).

Regarding problems of the Jerusalem period, John's chronology is to be pre-ferred, with crucifixion on the day before Passover and the last supper celebrated earlier than in the synoptics. The entrance was messianic only to Jesus who meant to keep his messiahship a secret still, but the crowd saw him as Elijah. Jesus cleansed the temple on Tuesday, an act of challenge to the authorities; he was trying to get himself killed. It was a messianic act, a seizing of the kingdom by violence. Jesus got away with it, to his disappointment, for he wished to pro-voke the authorities to kill him then and there. The harsh sayings thereafter had the same intent. However, the authorities soon plotted to do away with him, now recalling also his earlier Galilean attacks on the Law. So there was good ground among both Pharisees and Sadducees as well to be rid of this troublemaker. His scathing attack as recorded in Matthew 24 sealed his doom.

The authorities needed an occasion to move against Jesus. Judas supplied that by disclosing to them that Jesus thought of himself as the future messiah; he gave away the secret. Judas sent Jesus to the cross, contrary to Jesus' own plan, which probably was originally to get himself killed on the spot, by stoning perhaps or by attack with a sword.

Warschauer resolved the Johannine–synoptic chronology conflict in favor of John. Jesus with the disciples ate the Passover on 13 Nisan, with the crucifixion on 14 Nisan, the day of preparation. The last supper was a messianic gathering, as with Schweitzer, while the sacramental use of bread and wine came from the later church on analogy with the mystery religions. Jesus' self-struggle in the garden had a historical core; perhaps his struggle was over a death he did not anticipate: crucifixion rather than by a quick blow or thrust.

Problems abound in the account of Jesus' trial. John probably has the better version in reporting that Jesus went first to the house of Annas and then to Caiaphas. There was probably not a trial at all before the Sanhedrin, but only a kind of consultation, to formulate something to take to Pilate. Blasphemy might have some basis in the claim that Jesus threatened the temple, but it was the admission of messianic status that condemned him.

The appearance before Pilate also has legendary characteristics (Pilate's wife's dream) and shows a tendency to exonerate the Romans and blame the Jews. Scripture has furnished much of the material for the trial as well as the cruci-fixion scene. It is doubtful there were any sympathizers of Jesus present; some women who followed from Galilee saw him from a distance, but the disciples had fled. What is historical is summed up as follows:

There remains the name of the place of crucifixion, Golgotha, though we cannot identify that most sacred spot on earth; the incident of the procession meeting Simon of Cyrene, and compelling him to carry the Master's cross; probably the humane offer to the Lord of a cup of medicated wine as an anaesthetic, and His refusal to drink it; the nature of the inscription on the cross, showing that Jesus was condemned to death on account of His misinterpreted claim to the messianic office; the crucifixion itself; the circumstance that there were with Him two others, who suffered as common malefactors; the unsympathetic comments of some of the spectators; the presence of some women disciples who watched the sad scene from afar; the division of His garments among the executioners; finally, the loud cry of pain with which He breathed His last. (340)

The stories of the aftermath are full of contradictions and confusion. Jesus was saved from the burial of a common criminal by the intervention of Joseph, who gave a hasty burial just before the Sabbath intervened. Matthew's stolen-body story is incredible. The empty tomb stories are equally contradictory. There is nothing in Paul. Jesus did speak of his resurrection, but probably only minimally, with not so much detail as the predictions suggest, and he likely did not say anything about appearing to his disciples during that interval between his death and the appearance of the kingdom that he anticipated so quickly. The disciples expected the public, world-transforming event of the kingdom, not private appearances.

What really happened at the tomb? The women came upon a young man who told them they were looking in the wrong place for the body — perhaps he had seen them there two days earlier — and directed them to another tomb. The women in fear, in the semidarkness, in their nervousness and stressed condition, fled away, perhaps afraid of being recognized, and for the time being said nothing to anyone. Thereafter, with the words, "He is not here" in their memory, they would have concluded that he was risen and would have begun to have visions of Jesus. Mary was a likely one for such visions, though the appearances probably began in Galilee (cf. John 21). Further legendary elaborations occurred. In time the Parousia was displaced by the notion of Jesus' continual spiritual presence, and that remains the truth of the matter.

The book then ended with the usual sermonic flourishes but, significantly, Warschauer said that Jesus' "going away was in dishonour, His coming again *has been* in glory" (361; italics mine). The past tense is significant; Jesus has already come again, so Warschauer seemed to think, in the spiritual sense, as Jesus was obviously quite wrong about the imminence of the kingdom anyway. But that does not seem to constitute an insurmountable barrier to the Warschauerian piety:

"*Who say ye that I am?*" is His challenge to every age; and every age anew returns the answer, laden with an ever deeper significance as generation follows generation, "*Thou art the Christ of God.*"

Thanks be to God for His unspeakable Gift. (361)

If Headlam is history in the service of faith, Warschauer is faith in spite of history. His book gained but modest approval in its own time, and, in fact, it was something of a novelty.[39] On the one hand it attained to the most radical criticism of the text — deferring but little to Bultmann in that regard — but this criticism was regularly deflected by the frequent pious exclamations and sermonizing. It was an exquisite, if also somewhat exaggerated, instance of British *Wissenschaft* marching safely under the banner of theological confession. Even the deference to Schweitzer in the not-quite-full absorption of the *konsequente Eschatologie* was, in the end, further muted by being redressed in the familiar old clothes of the liberal gospel of Fatherhood and brotherhood. We need not here think in terms of some kind of hypocrisy at work, for no doubt the confessions were seriously intended, and no doubt so was the scholarship.

American work on the historical Jesus went on very much unabated in the 1920s and if anything actually increased. It also went forward very much in the liberal vein, with little impact from Form Criticism, although there were some significant movements in a direction represented by the "Chicago School" and the sociohistorical method.

Americans seemed to produce a certain number of texts on the life of Jesus, intended for students, and therefore works without the attending scholarly apparatus, but at the same time works that reflected the current state of the scholarly discussion.[40] One example would be that of Edward Increase Bosworth, whose text on Jesus enjoyed several reprints and a life extending to 1935.[41] It was a typical presentation in most respects, a kind of liberal Jesus who had been modified to include some eschatological influence. Its stated purpose was to reproduce the religion of Jesus himself, in the fashion of good liberalism, or modernism, as understood on the American scene.

Edward Increase Bosworth

Bosworth described the basic sources (Mark and Q, with an oral tradition underlying them); Matthew and Luke provided supplementation and even John was

---

39. Reviews were mixed; see J. M. Lloyd-Thomas in *HibJ* 25 (1927): 655–66; *Times Literary Supplement* 26 (1927): 754; Lord Charnwood in *The Modern Churchman* 17 (1927–28): 132–38; *ExpTim* 38 (1926–27): 393. Most noted Warschauer's apparent reverence combined with serious criticism, with some puzzlement over how Warschauer managed to hold them together. Some wondered at his reading of Jesus' moods and intentions. The general inclination to disregard Warschauer probably also had something to do with his lack of standing in the academy, since he held no academic post. Still, Burkitt's provision of an introduction may be taken as some sign of the level of Warschauer's work.

40. It is almost a universal characteristic of lives of Jesus to be presented this way; Bultmann's kept to that pattern, as did that of Paul Wernle, and Dibelius as well. A presentation of Jesus sans the encumbrance of technical notes and the like seemed to be fashionable.

41. Edward Increase Bosworth, *The Life and Teaching of Jesus According to the First Three Gospels* (New York: Macmillan, 1924). Bosworth was New Testament Professor at Oberlin Graduate School of Theology.

occasionally appealed to. He characterized the background of Jesus' times, historically and socially, according to the better standards of the day, along with the usual depreciation of the scribes and Pharisees.

Apocalyptic eschatology was sketched, followed by some speculation about Jesus' youth and private years. The baptism by John is a given, wherein Jesus experienced a sense of messianic calling which, however, needed time to develop. Jesus began as a Galilean prophet and healer; he also kept his messiahship at first a secret. The kingdom is eschatological, and thought to be near, as seen in the defeat of the demons. Conflict with scribes and Pharisees arose early in Galilee (food laws, Sabbath, fasting). The scribes found Jesus politically dangerous. This clash terminated his work in Galilee, forcing a journey north. The difference between Jesus and the scribes was in the concept of God, with Jesus portraying God as the loving heavenly Father who allowed men to forgive, and who was not interested in the scribes' gloomy laws and requirements.

The miracle stories suffered rationalization. "Jesus, too, was so charged with the life of God that great tides of healthful psychic influence probably flowed out from his person to those who were in expectant spiritual touch with him" (134). Jairus's daughter did not really die.

Ethically, Jesus demanded the righteousness expected in the new age of the kingdom: a matter of the heart, expressed above all in the love commandment. Love demanded repentance and trust toward the heavenly Father.

Jesus demanded loyalty to his own person as the One chosen by God to embody the will of God. He did think of himself as Son of man, acting already and to come in the future as the eschatological ruler.

After Caesarea-Philippi Jesus began to speak of himself as Son of man in a messianic sense. He combined with it the idea of the suffering servant of Isaiah. The suffering was a new and disconcerting idea introduced by Jesus, although the specific predictions of suffering are probably not historical. What Jesus likely said was that he would die and then participate in the general resurrection soon to occur.

Bosworth's characterization of the kingdom in Jesus' concept was that

> the Kingdom was to be a world civilization in which honesty and friendliness in personal life and social institutions would be made universal and secure, a civilization in which all men as sons of God, the Heavenly Father, would work together in a powerful, true and faithful brotherhood at all the varied tasks to be set for them by the unfolding will of God. (244)

How would the kingdom come? Jesus thought it was imminently breaking in, and even if he did affirm the imminence, that does not preclude some further development. There are also some sayings that speak of the kingdom as already a present fact (the Beelzebul controversy). But Jesus' basal principles remained those of fatherhood and brotherhood and the eternality of humans.

Jesus entered Jerusalem, bringing on more conflicts with scribes and Pharisees and generating further conflicts with the Sadducees over his attack on the temple (an act of moral indignation). Jesus sided neither with revolutionaries nor priests, but he attacked the Jerusalem scribes further and bitterly. Then he gave private teaching of an apocalyptic nature, while refusing to speculate on the time of the End. He ate the last supper; Judas thought of Jesus as a "queer sentimentalist" (352) unworthy of running a world empire and conspired in his betrayal. It is impossible to decide whether the last supper was a Passover or not; Jesus performed some acts with bread and wine, the original meaning of which is uncertain, but it seems he did not intend it to be repeated. The "remembrance" theme is later, from Paul.

Jesus was arrested, charged with blasphemy, and tried. One who claimed to be Son of man was likely considered a blasphemer, though Bosworth reckoned that Jesus thought of himself at least initially as embodying the spirit of the Son of man, and only later acknowledged his claim openly. Pilate wanted to find a way to release Jesus, but could not risk offense at Rome for stirring up the Jewish authorities at Jerusalem. The execution followed; Jesus drank no vinegar because he had already said he would not drink of the wine until he drank it anew in the kingdom. He died rather quickly. Bosworth ended with a kind of moral theory of the atonement, with Jesus' death shaming us today into an "ever deeper resentment of the evil in our hearts" (391). As to the resurrection, Bosworth described it as some people claiming that Jesus, on his way from the underworld to the topmost heaven, had stopped on the earth for a while and made himself known to his disciples. The first appearances were to Peter; the resurrection was Jesus' assurance to his disciples that the messianic program was going forth. The appearances were relatively minor matters and what counted was that "the personality of Jesus was present with such force as decisively to convince his disciples that he was with them and would continue to work with them as the leader appointed by God to establish righteousness in the life of man on earth" (405).

The liberal leanings of this work are clear enough without a pointer. We can overlook the slightly amusing opinions, such as the claim that Jesus refused the drink on the cross because he had promised to drink no more wine until he drank anew in the kingdom. What bears notice is that the Jesus who served "modernism" was this liberal one, modified by the eschatological nature of his message. The eschatology has to be conceded, but at the same time it does not lie at the heart of the picture.

George A. Barton

A similarly targeted book but of somewhat more conservative bent was that of George A. Barton.[42] The synoptics are the prime sources, but John has reliable

---

42. George Barton, *Jesus of Nazareth: A Biography* (New York: Macmillan, 1928). Barton was professor of Semitic Languages in the University of Pennsylvania and professor of New Testament Literature and Language in the Divinity School of the Protestant Episcopal Church in Philadelphia; and sometime professor of Biblical Literature and Semitic Languages in Bryn Mawr College.

traditions. The gospels are early — Mark c. 39–41, Luke c. 58–60. A plethora of background information was given: land, sects, temple, synagogue, education. Miracles were troubling to Barton and, in fact, he rationalized them wherever possible. People at that time tended to ascribe miracles to all manner of important people; we may accept that Jesus was a healer, and that he influenced people by his personality. Spiritual truth is nevertheless independent of miracles. As to chronology, the birth was in 8 B.C.E., John's preaching began in 28 C.E., the baptism of Jesus was in the same year, the first Passover was in 29, and the second Passover and crucifixion in 30 C.E. Barton envisioned a ministry of two years or less, two Passovers, and a Perean period — all, of course, derived from John.

The birth stories have some value; it is not impossible that the birth occurred in a stable in Bethlehem. Barton ruminated quite a bit over the childhood of Jesus and what it must have been like. Here his knowledge of ancient Palestinian conditions was evident, but it was accompanied by quite a bit of speculating about the "boy Jesus" and what he must have observed. The "silent years" were a lot less silent after Barton was through with them.

In his baptism Jesus realized he was the messiah. The temptation story is historical, the one genuine autobiographical piece in the tradition. Jesus saw that his kingdom would be one of love, not force, and would rule by its attraction to people. There would be no military ambitions for Jesus, but rather serving and preaching to the poor and the lowly. He returned to the Jordan initially (John); he did not tell anyone about being the messiah — he used the term "Son of man," which was ambiguous, and which might be messianic or might just refer to a man. Jesus used it until he could lead the crowds to his more spiritual view of the kingdom.

Jesus healed insane people (demoniacs). He accommodated himself to the thought and language of people about him; he cured Peter's mother-in-law by his "wholesome personality, which radiated health, hope, courage, faith" (139). Then Jesus took a tour through Galilee; here the story of Cana and the wedding feast occurred. Jesus then must have made a trip to Jerusalem for the first Passover (John). Nothing has been preserved of this trip. On the way back there was controversy with Pharisees who often "permitted the dead hand of the past to torment and destroy the tender life of the present" (161).

Two sermons were given, Luke's Sermon on the Plain and Matthew's Sermon on the Mount. The commandment to love your enemies is strongly metaphorical; Jesus was not giving instructions to rulers of empires, but to a small band bent on a special mission. Parables were stories told to illustrate a truth (the sower means that great truths can grow in good soil). Here also more rationalizing from Barton occurred (Jesus psychically healed the Gadarene demoniac and caused the swineherd to panic; Jairus's daughter was in a state of suspended animation).

Jesus went to Jerusalem for the Feast of Tabernacles, fearing Herod who had just put John the Baptist to death. There he met with Nicodemus and emphasized the spiritual kingdom. It would have been unwise to return to Galilee at the end of the festival, so he went to Perea. Then he sent out the seventy and taught (good Samaritan) on the way. The parables of the mustard seed and leaven meant that the kingdom, starting from a few, will grow into something embracing all humanity. Then Jesus returned to Jerusalem, now convinced he would die there, for Herod was after him. He arrived at the Feast of Dedication and taught (John), returning thereafter to Perea again. Material from Luke belongs here (parable of the great feast). The seventy returned, reporting success, which brought the famous lines in Luke 10:21–22, Jesus uttering his confidence in his relationship to the Father.

Jesus went then to Bethany, where Lazarus was called from his comatose state. Jesus fled from Herod, who thought him John the Baptist. He went through Samaria (meeting the woman at the well), and on to Nazareth, where he was not warmly received. He then went into Phoenician territory and finally passed through Galilee to the Decapolis. Healings and the feeding stories followed. Then he went back to Capernaum, crossing the sea. He spoke of eating his flesh and drinking his blood, then left Capernaum and went to Caesarea-Philippi. Here he emphasized that the kingdom is one of love, service, and suffering — a view not understood by the disciples, who harbored nationalistic ambitions. After a short stay again in Capernaum Jesus then went to Jerusalem. The entrance was a demonstration by Galilean peasants, and the attack on the temple was directed against greedy merchants.

Judas was a businessman who used his managerial skills to try to maneuver Jesus into declaring his messiahship. He meant to trick the priests and use them for his own purposes. The last supper was a Passover; Lazarus, the beloved disciple, was there. Jesus now was conscious that his death would effect the salvation of the world. He delivered a discourse on the vine and the vineyard and also washed the disciples' feet. After his arrest the disciples fled; the temple police arrested Jesus. At his trial before the Sanhedrin he was accused of blasphemy for making messianic claims (he did not deny he was the Son of God). Before Pilate he was tried on political charges and condemned. Mary and the beloved disciple were present at the scene. Jesus uttered what sounded like a despairing cry, but "God sent him a comforting consciousness of a Father's presence, and sympathy, and love" (387).

The appearances are the attestation to the resurrection; there is no better attested fact in history. The book then ended with rapturing over Jesus' superiority to all other founders of religions (Buddha, Confucius, Muhammed).

It is a curious book. Critical knowledge is in abundant evidence, and there is even something to be said for the authenticity of Johannine traditions. Yet the final impression is of something Diatesseron-like, Johannine oranges and synoptic apples. And there appear to be no real criteria of authenticity, except what the modern world thinks about miracles.

Walter E. Bundy

In the same year as Barton's work there appeared another work on Jesus, this time by Walter E. Bundy.[43] Bundy was thoroughly conversant with German and French literature and had earlier produced a quite competent accounting of the contention over Jesus' sanity.[44]

"Jesus," Bundy said in his preface, "was God's Galilean," but went on to portray him as a modern liberal.[45] The aim of the book was to engage in a study of Jesus' own personal religious experience. Bundy also noted Bultmann's work on Jesus, which he said would be a "stimulating study" for those who could read German. The two books, however, would never have recognized one another, for they belonged to different eras. Bundy's book valued Jesus as a "religious genius" and set itself the task of presenting Jesus' own religious experience as a model worthy of emulation.

The sources do not allow us a full evaluation of Jesus' religion and he wrote nothing. We must hold to the synoptics only, which are not biographies. Jesus came from the ordinary folk; the Old Testament was his book, and he was influenced by apocalyptic, though not like Paul with his "typically Rabbinical exegesis with its strained sense, made meanings, and painful processes of proof and reasoning" (15). The heart of the Old Testament lay in the command to love the neighbor. Most influenced by the prophets, Jesus was himself "a prophetic personality" (31), although he deemphasized the national and political element.

John the Baptist was also a prophet who burst the "bands of Judaism because he is too great to be cramped within the narrow confines of Judaism's ceremonial practice and conventional conception of religion" (41). He baptized Jesus and greatly influenced him, though there are also differences. Thus the Old Testament and John are elements that contributed to the formation of a religious genius like Jesus. The "genuine Jewishness of Jesus" (53) is impressive, but Jesus also was Judaism's fulfillment. "Jesus is Israel's reason for existence; in him her historical task is accomplished" (54). As to his originality

> Jesus is not to be measured over against his past or present by an absolute originality but by the contribution that comes in his experience of religion.... The very weight of Jesus' religious convictions, the certainty with which he expresses them is something new in the religion of his day and people. It was this unique religious experience that brought him out beyond the confines of his people's past and present; it came by an irresistible inner necessity that operated at the very core of his being.... Jesus was positively unique ... the prince of humanity's prophets, the perfection of religious genius. (59–60)

Much of what Jesus believed was part of the property of everyone (heaven, hell, Satan, angels, judgment, future life), but these were secondary; Jesus' personal

---

43. Walter E. Bundy, *The Religion of Jesus* (Indianapolis: Bobbs-Merrill, 1928). Bundy was professor of English Bible in DePauw University.

44. See below, chap. 8, n. 83.

45. Bundy, *Religion of Jesus*, ix.

faith was in God and his kingdom. He experienced God as numinous and as Father — his distinctive achievement. From this experience he criticized the piety of his day (prayer, cult). The kingdom of God in substance was prophetic, in form it was eschatological or apocalyptic (though Weiss, Schweitzer, and Loisy give an extreme view). The kingdom is a supernatural order to supplant the present one and as such is apocalyptic, not a social scheme. It has elements of a future event, of growth and development, of something already present, and of being the highest value. Eschatology lies at the heart, and yet it is but secondary. "Eschatology belongs simply to the upper strata of his faith in God and His kingdom" (126). The essential part is Jesus' faith in God and the kingdom that God brings; the form of his expectation was secondary. The kingdom comes by supernatural intervention, but Jesus was its messenger, its champion, and called people to it.

A large section of the book was devoted to examining Jesus' religious consciousness. Everything Jesus said, did, and thought was permeated by religion. He quested for the divine will and struggled with himself and God. He performed personal acts of piety, though did not frequent the temple and its cult. His baptism was a religious act (though it is uncertain what it meant exactly). Prayer was of great significance, and Bundy went on at length about Jesus as a pray-er and the nature of his prayers. Jesus' religious demands centered in God; men are to be childlike (a lengthy discourse ensued on this subject, along with the difficulty that "modern men" have in grasping the demand). Here Bundy was evidently struggling with himself, affirming that the western world was not attuned to Jesus' own religious consciousness, but at the same time "there is nothing in the religion of Jesus that conflicts essentially with true culture and civilization" (249). In other words, understood properly, Jesus really supports the modern world. The future religion of the West will be the religion of Jesus himself, not the religion about Jesus, that "weird web of theology that has obscured the real Jesus from our sight" (260). But Jesus never said anything about faith in himself, only in the kingdom of God. Entrance into the kingdom was paramount and dependent on performing the will of God. This is the task:

> To believe that God is a living and loving Father, that all men are His children, that God has a kingdom, that it can and will come, and that soon, and to devote the whole of human life, personal and social, to preparation for its coming to the extent of exhausting life itself in the kingdom's service, is a difficult religious task. But just such is *the religious experience of Jesus,* and over against its richness and reality our modern Christian experience appears as woefully impoverished and unreal. (266; italics his)

Finally Bundy traced out this dichotomy between the religion of Jesus and the religion about Jesus. Christianity became a religion about Jesus; it had its origin in the resurrection faith. Organized religion was the work of Paul and others as a result of the Easter experiences. Jesus saw only the kingdom, not the church. But only the religious experience of Jesus himself will meet our need. And who

is this Jesus? Everyone must decide for himself; Bundy was equally ambiguous
about whether Jesus ever thought of himself as Son of man.

This book, like Bosworth's, manages to acknowledge the impact of the eschatological "discovery" about Jesus, without at the same time giving it any truly
formative influence. Jesus remained a Ritschlian at the core of his being, even
as he proclaimed an eschatological kingdom. Such a proclamation, however, is
poorly serviceable to the "modern world" of "modern men," and therefore has
to be discounted. Bundy's work did not show any impact whatever from the
movement of the dialectical theology in Europe, though clearly the name of Karl
Barth was well known in America by that time, as indeed also was the work of
Bultmann. It seems probable that theological liberalism lived on much longer in
America because it served better the social gospel, it seemed still more attuned
to the mood of postwar America, and it was more useful in the cultural struggle with fundamentalism, which itself was too fond already of promoting various
eschatological-apocalyptic theories. What advantage would there be in giving
the fundamentalists still more ammunition?

To conclude this sampling of American work on the historical Jesus in the
decade of the twenties, we must now look at some weightier figures: Benjamin W.
Bacon (1860–1932) and his former student, Shirley Jackson Case (1872–1947),
as well as Case's colleague at Chicago, Shailer Mathews (1863–1941).

Benjamin W. Bacon

Bacon's career in theological education in America was stimulated initially by
the need to implement the "higher criticism" in American studies, which at the
end of the nineteenth century still exercised minimal impact.[46] Bacon, himself
a graduate of Yale (undergraduate and divinity school), had spent some years in
the pastorate, but had also gained a familiarity with German criticism and had
published a number of works even before the offer of an appointment to the faculty at the Yale Divinity School. Behind him were generations of New England
Puritan family tradition, accompanied by congregational church liberty of expression, that made him an attractive candidate to facilitate the new criticism at
Yale, even though, in fact, Bacon lacked the terminal degree (Ph.D.) and never
actually received one. He also had strong language capabilities, having lived in
Germany for a while, and had traveled and studied there, making the acquaintance of most of the leading scholars of the day there as well as in England. His
studies originally were conducted on the Old Testament, but he turned soon to
the New Testament, to both Johannine and synoptic issues. His aim was at some
point to produce a life of Jesus, but like Sanday at Oxford he never did, though

---

46. In his essay at the end of his career Bacon strikes just this note and gives an account of his
movement onto the faculty at Yale for this particular reason. See his essay, "Enter the Higher Criticism," in *Contemporary American Theology: Theological Autobiographies*, ed. Vergilius Ferm (New York:
Round Table Press, 1932) 1:1–50. Cf. also the biographical sketch by Bacon's longtime colleague at
Yale, Frank Porter, in the *Dictionary of American Biography* (see biographical appendix).

the outline of such a work can be gained from his major studies on *The Story of Jesus and the Beginnings of the Church: A Valuation of the Synoptic Record for History and for Religion*,[47] and later his Shaffer lectures, *Jesus the Son of God*.[48] We will deal here with the first.

Bacon did not wish to set the gospel of Jesus over against the gospel about Jesus, but wished instead to see how the one came from the other. It would be a mistake, he said, to offer the "paternalistic theism of the Sermon on the Mount and the Lord's Prayer" (12, 16) over against the Pauline preaching of the cross. Religion is concerned with the relation between God and humanity, whereas liberal Christianity, by offering only the gospel of Jesus, really results in reformed Judaism. Christianity is a religion of redemption, for sinners and a corrupted world. On the other hand, fundamentalism is equally a mistake, offering the conflict with science, although the real foe of the biblicist is the historical critic. The criticism of the nineteenth century, based in F. C. Baur's work, gave us vindication of the major Pauline epistles; it also taught us that the gospel story is not from Paul, but is Peter's work and comes from his witness. Bacon argued for the authenticity of the Papias association of Mark with Peter at Rome. He also postulated a second source, not identical with Q, but primitive. It had some narrative as a structure for discourse material, rather like the Stoic diatribe, and is the best source for Jesus' teaching. This Second Source (S, as Bacon labeled it) was also used by Mark. Q is the non-Markan material common to Matthew and Luke; S is a larger document including some material from Mark. In a broad sense the witness of Peter has to be reconstructed out of these two most primitive documents, Mark and S. As to the Peter-Paul distinction, we need the Peter tradition, though we could be Christians if we had only the Pauline version.

The gospels are not merely history and require analysis. The best is S, then Mark. The Petrine tradition began with the call to discipleship and had no birth stories; Peter knew the family and that it claimed Davidic descent, but Mark is silent on everything prior to John's movement. Mark was not interested in what was not preachable; he was interested in telling the story of the Christ of God.

The Galilean and Judean ministries were separated by Caesarea-Philippi; Jesus

---

47. Benjamin W. Bacon, *The Story of Jesus and the Beginnings of the Church: A Valuation of the Synoptic Record for History and for Religion* (New York: Century, 1927). This was preceded by many years of works on Mark and Matthew and John, with intentions to produce similar ones on Luke and "S" (Bacon's theory of a Q-like, not identical, collection found primarily in Q, but also used by Mark). These works would have formed the basis of his "life." There was also the earlier *Jesus and Paul* (New York: Macmillan, 1921), which gave a capsule picture of Jesus' ministry, though the main interest lay in tracing a line of continuity from Jesus to Paul. Bacon also thought a "life" could be assembled from his various commentaries, but never did so himself.

48. Benjamin W. Bacon, *Jesus the Son of God* (New York: H. Holt, 1930), was the first Shaffer lecture. It summarized compactly Bacon's views respecting Mark as the work of the Apostle (Peter), "S" (Q+other sections) as the Catechist's gospel. It is interesting that Bacon wished to call this source a "gospel" at a time when it was regarded largely as an unfocused collection of sayings (Harnack). Bacon thought it contained an introduction only barely reproduced in Mark, and ended with the supper promising reunion in the kingdom. His views were developed more extensively in his *Studies in Matthew* (New York: H. Holt, 1938).

was in exile at the time, forced there by the conspiring of the Pharisees with Herod against him. His career began in Capernaum, taking up the unfinished work of John the Baptist, preaching the kingdom of God. Jesus was an exorciser, according to Mark, from the outset (synagogue at Capernaum), but also, Bacon said, Jesus raised up Peter's mother who was suffering from malarial fever, common along the shore of the Sea of Galilee. Bacon took these incidents seriously, claiming that "the very homeliness of the scenes at synagogue service and fisherman's home guarantees its historicity" (134) and as the "plain prose of a simple eyewitness" (136). The preface to Mark's story, the baptism and association with John, as well as the temptation, have been incorporated from S. Galilee ends in Mark with the feeding story and withdrawal, and the story is bracketed by another feeding, the last supper. Both are sacramental, deliberately, with similarities in John. The feeding story looks forward to the supper. Peter's confession rests on a genuine recollection, but the following transfiguration story is poetry. At Caesarea-Philippi Jesus did enunciate a doctrine of a Danielic Son of man, even though the disciples continued to hold to a national Son of David. The addition of the suffering servant probably was Peter's explanation of the tragedy of Jesus' death, though it roots in Jesus' own claim to Son of man status at Caesarea-Philippi (because of the predictions of suffering).

S ranks even higher than Mark. It pictures Jesus as servant-Son and teacher. The great discourses of the Sermon on the Mount come from S. Mark incorporated little, save only some parables of the kingdom and the "mystery" saying. As to Jesus' message

> Jesus' doctrine of the kingdom was new, distinctive, different. But it was not obscure. It was not hidden; it did not even contradict the old. It only glorified and transfigured it with the touch of One who could see God at work. It was teaching for the simplest of hearers by the greatest religious Teacher that ever lived. (215)

Jesus went to Jerusalem to restore Israel's mission as Jehovah's servant and witness. "Messiah" is not a title he would have chosen; he deemphasized it. He did not wish to be a nationalistic messiah, but (contra Wrede) neither did the resurrection faith first call forth the messianic faith. Jesus did have a nationalistic sense — the ideal to restore his nation. Otherwise the crucifixion as king of the Jews is incomprehensible. Yet Jesus was no fanatic; he suffered a "patriot's death" (226). Jesus' mission and the reason for taking up the role of messiah were to complete the work begun at his association with John the Baptist, of making a people ready by repentance for the coming of God (kingdom). He went to Jerusalem to make just this national appeal, at a time (Passover) of maximum impact. It was dangerous for him.

Mark's chronology of the last week requires correction from John; the supper was the day before Passover. It was a solemn farewell, a *Kiddush*, the meal of sanctification. Mark converted the occasion into a Passover. Jesus then sanctified the bread and wine as symbols of his body and blood, a dedication like that of

Jewish martyrs of old. Peter's story ends with Gethsemane and the arrest and denial. Thereafter all is hearsay.

For Jesus' teaching we have to take the S material; it is better reported in Luke than in Matthew, who wished to make Jesus a new Moses, the giver of a new Law, dividing his gospel into five sections in emulation of the Pentateuch. Unlike John the Baptist, who was a severe preacher of judgment, Jesus spoke of forgiveness and reconciliation, sought out sinners and publicans and the lost, and saw therein a present divine sovereignty through an inward working of the Spirit of God. There is no interim ethic; the ethic was not distinguished by the difference between now and then, but between inner and outer, temporal and spiritual. What about the Son of man title? Bacon played down the use of the title in an apocalyptic sense: it was stereotyped, having little to do with Jesus' own claims. Mostly the title seems to be a substitute for servant in S (the Son of man is to give his life as a ransom), whereas Mark mostly has the apocalyptic Son of man. Is it a question of either/or? No; Jesus did speak of this Danielic kingdom of the Son of man who would receive his kingdom at the judgment day. That theme can be seen even in Paul, without the use of the title. Mark mixes servant and Son of man. We cannot say that Jesus himself brought servant and Son of man together, nor can we say how literally Jesus meant the language about the Son of man coming on the clouds of heaven. It seems that he did believe in an immediate vindication.

Finally, Bacon sketched the arising of the church from the resurrection faith — also Peter's witness — analyzing the early confessions in Paul (1 Corinthians 15). He ended by characterizing the Christian faith as mediation of eternal life though the divine Spirit. That is its essence.

Bacon's work, unlike most liberal projects, did not attempt to elevate the historical Jesus at the expense of the Christ of the kerygma. It seems unnecessarily complicated by the S theory, a kind of *Ur-Q*, that was not easily disentangled from the broader sources. A more systematic effort on Bacon's part to construct a fully evolved picture of Jesus would no doubt have yielded something with a different shape; but probably it is fair to suggest that his outlook had equal amounts of English and American perspectives, along with mostly just vintage Bacon.

Shirley Jackson Case

Bacon's student, Shirley Jackson Case (1872–1947), came from Canada to the United States where, after some brief early teaching in secondary institutions (primarily in mathematics), he studied at Yale under Bacon and Frank Porter, and eventually arrived at the University of Chicago where he had a distinguished career for thirty years. Case was a prolific writer, publishing some sixteen books and innumerable articles and book reviews. He also edited the *American Journal of Theology* as well as its successor, the *Journal of Religion*. His postretirement years were spent largely at my own institution, Florida Southern College, where

Case wrote additional works, such as his most philosophical book, *The Christian Philosophy of History*, and continued his interest in the question of the historical Jesus and in his second major area of scholarly concern, church history.[49] He died in 1947.

Case was engaged in the development and application of the so-called socio-historical method, the primary characteristic associated with the Chicago School. It was, in fact, not something unknown under the sun, but in the first place a rigorous application of all forms of historical method in order to determine as fully as possible the social and cultural environment from which a movement, such as that of Jesus, sprang. All historical movements have *genetic* connections, that is, they evolve from other forms and can best be understood by studying this evolutionary process with as wide a net as can be cast. This emphasis on social setting is what gave Case's work its distinctive flavor. In fact, it was of such significance that it constituted for him the single most important criterion for the determination of authentic traditions in the inquiry into the origins of the Jesus movement. As Case put it in his 1927 book on Jesus:

> Every statement in the records is to be judged by the degree of its suitableness to the distinctive environment of Jesus, on the one hand, and to that of the framers of gospel tradition at one or another stage in the history of Christianity, on the other. When consistently applied, this test will prove our safest guide in recovering from the present gospel records dependable information regarding the life and teaching of the earthly Jesus.[50]

So it was not simply for Case a question of a *literary* decision, but of a *social* judgment, comparing social conditions in order to arrive at a decision as to what can be considered appropriate to the distinctive environment of Jesus or what is more fitting to the circumstances of the later church. That is undoubtedly why, though he was fully conversant with the more recent *Formgeschichte*, Case did not adopt its categories, for he evidently regarded it as another method of purely literary analysis.

Case's sympathies with what can be broadly called "liberalism" are evident in his optimistic purpose, which was "to depict Jesus as he actually appeared to the men of his own time in Palestine nineteen hundred years ago" (v). The previous attention to literary approaches was to be corrected by a "more than usual emphasis upon the social point of view" (vi), that is, the integration of Jesus within his own environment. And the introduction announced that it would seek the Jesus who lies behind the varying pictures given of him in the different gospels: "We of today would see Jesus, the real Jesus of history, exactly as he lived in Palestine among his contemporaries nineteen hundred years ago" (6).

---

49. Shirley Jackson Case, *The Christian Philosophy of History* (Chicago: University of Chicago Press, 1943).

50. Shirley Jackson Case, *Jesus: A New Biography* (Chicago: University of Chicago Press, 1927), 115. Case's lecture notes contain similar statements of some more detail and stem from earlier periods in his career.

Given Case's method, a great deal of prolegomena was necessary to establish the existing social conditions. He began with a consideration of ancient biographies, then characterized each of the gospels. Mark emphasizes Jesus' deeds, the imminence of the kingdom, while Matthew and Luke reproduce the essentials of Mark with additions (genealogies, birth stories). Q's interests are visible as well; it makes central the religion of Jesus, not the religion about Jesus. John was "primarily concerned to picture Jesus in the official role of founder of a new religion" (44–45). Canonicity does not guarantee historicity, nor does a claim to apostolic authorship or some special theory of inspiration. The apocryphal material could also contain something historical. There is no apostolic authorship of any gospel.

The gospels remain the primary sources. Each is an interpretation of the Jesus story and emerges from the life of a community. The customary high evaluation of Mark and Q, with M and L having little value at all and John omitted altogether, is not sufficient. Each of these had a prior history and has to be assessed on the basis of the social experience visible there. The gospels are as much a record of the community preserving the tradition as they are of the Jesus tradition about which they speak:

> Each gospel revealed the distinctive social experience of its particular writer and his immediate associates within one or another area of growing Christianity. While formally his work was a biography of Jesus, virtually it was also a treatise dealing with issues and interests of the author's own day. (106)

Each gospel was bound up with the "life-interests" of the different Christian bodies. So the problem of the life of Jesus is greatly complicated. However, Jesus also lived in a particular social environment. He must be integrated within his own time and place. This allows more reliable judgments about traditions; those that reflect Jesus' own environment need not be questioned. On the other hand, matters that reflect the later social setting of the community will be questioned. Of course the first disciples had the same setting as Jesus. Initially the tradition largely painted Jesus accurately, but as it moved into the wider world new situations required new interpretations and adaptation to a new social setting. So social experience is the most reliable test.

Conditions in Palestine were then characterized in some detail (geography, history from the Maccabean period down to the revolt of 66–70 c.e., as well as various sectarian groups). Populations in Judea and Galilee were estimated, along with descriptions of occupations and the like. They were heterogeneous societies, urban as well as agricultural, with centers of commerce and variegated social strata. Outside Jerusalem the most important city was Sepphoris, which had a wide range of commerce. Foreigners abounded in Palestine. Palestine was "virtually flooded with cultural importations from the Graeco-Roman world" (131) and bore evidences of extensive hellenization. Not everyone would have agreed on opposition to Rome; for example, Sepphoris did not support the revolution. Social institutions as well were well founded at the time of Jesus (temple, Sanhedrin, synagogue).

Case speculated concerning the probable home life of Jesus, though, of course, what he was interested in was sketching the social setting to which Jesus was exposed. We know nothing of the "silent years." The gospels have little to say; the birth stories reflect the social situation of the later church. The virgin birth was especially good material to present to the gentile world, just as the genealogy was appropriate to the Jewish, all to accredit or "officialize" Jesus. Bethlehem as the place of birth was part of the same process. Nazareth lacks any such officializing and must therefore be original.

The date of Jesus' birth is uncertain. We can only conclude that Jesus grew up in that period after the death of Herod in 4 B.C.E. We can suppose that Jesus was exposed to the same influences of any Jewish boy of that time: the importance of home, family, and village life. He had four brothers and at least two sisters; of these only James stood out, and he was said to be conservative and pious. Education would have occurred at home and in the synagogue. It is likely that Jesus knew and used Aramaic, not so likely Hebrew, and he may have picked up some Greek through contact with foreigners. He was not a formally trained scribe, but a carpenter, an artisan.

Nazareth's proximity to Sepphoris is more significant than has been allowed. It was an urban area where Jesus may have pursued his trade, for a "carpenter" was someone who labored at the building trade in general, not just a wood-worker. Jesus' unconventionality in associating with the outcasts of society may have come from exposure to all kinds of people in the urban environment of Sepphoris. Also that he did not ask people to separate themselves from society is different from many reformers, and may well be a consequence of his exposure to urban influences, that is, tested against his social environment Jesus appeared to be different at this point. Jesus may have been influenced by the opposition to the rebellion at Sepphoris, since he did not evidently see himself as a political revolutionary.

Jesus' baptism by John is factual (it was embarrassing to the Christian community), though John has been reinterpreted by the Christians to make him into a confessor to Jesus. John belonged in the apocalyptic tradition, advocating withdrawal from the activity of the time to the wilderness to prepare for the great Day of Judgment and to cultivate individual righteousness. Still the movement must have had social and political implications, even though John's mission evidently was to prepare people for the coming day of judgment.

John the reformer aroused the interest of Jesus, who was moved by the eschatological preaching of John and took up the role of prophet, as he likely would have so characterized himself. An arresting initial experience was characteristic of the prophet; the stories of Jesus' baptism and temptation preserve this recollection in Jesus' case. He must have had a sense of a task to perform and of being endowed by the Spirit, for such was characteristic of the prophet. This was the context for the temptation story, which has been reinterpreted by the evangelists in light of their own interests. Originally it had to do with how the unschooled artisan should proceed with his task.

Jesus broke with John's movement. Unlike John he chose not to stay in the wilderness, but to work in society as an itinerant prophet. A chronology of times and places is not possible, and the evangelists were not interested in a biography. It is probable that there was more activity in Judea than the synoptics allow (a prophet would surely think of Jerusalem), and more in Galilee than John allows. More than two years of public activity is not inconsistent with probability; death in the third year seems likely. Whether Jesus' death occurred on 14 or 15 Nisan is problematic, though the Johannine representation of 14 has the greater claim, likely in the year 29 of the present era.

Jesus chose twelve who helped to prepare for the kingdom. They were likely attracted to Jesus personally; they may have been attracted to the thought of rebellion, though Jesus did not preach that. It was dangerous in that time to be surrounded by so many enthusiastic followers; the entrance into Jerusalem would have aroused suspicions.

The picture of conflict in Jesus' ministry has been exaggerated from the later perspective of the Christian community. In fact, we need a more sympathetic understanding of Pharisaism and the scribes. It is doubtful that Jesus launched a deliberate attack on them, but his prophetic consciousness conflicted with them. The difference between him and them was personal and social. He was of the ordinary people and did not scrupulously keep the Law; he was an innovator, a nonconformist leading people astray.

Jesus must have known of the dangers to himself. He probably expected assassination, which is why he withdrew quietly to Gethsemane with three disciples who were also equipped with weapons for defense. Judas betrayed the location; Jesus was tried and condemned as a political insurrectionist. The story was colored by later Christian interests, but the fact remains. It is likely that Pilate would not have condemned Jesus — he was not a sufficient political threat — had the Sanhedrin offered objection. The record, however, has magnified the action of the Jews. Pilate acted freely and consistent with his own will, though the Sadducees were doubtless glad to be rid of a disturber of the peace and the Pharisees as well because Jesus, as an unlearned *Am ha-aretz*, was a menace to the correct observance of the religious rites.

Case then focused his concern on a discussion of the religion that Jesus himself lived. The Jesus of history is freely mixed with the Christ of faith, and the line is not easily drawn. Jesus was depicted as performing miracles, but the overlay with the miraculous does not accord well with the image of a prophet of reform in Israel. Jesus likely did think he could triumph over the demons and do exorcisms, but his work was primarily didactic, to teach.

What did he think of himself? He could have used the word "son," but without any special connotations. As to the Son of man, it would be difficult to imagine how Jesus would have thought of himself as such, since the Son of man was a figure already in heaven awaiting his revelation. How did Jesus imagine he would displace this figure and become the messianic ruler of the endtime? No, that thought was only comprehensible in light of the christological stimulus of the resurrection experiences. "Messianic self-interpretation had not concerned him," said Case. "The outstanding feature of Jesus' religion," he said, "was the prophet's characteristic awareness of the presence of God" (377, 378). Certainly it was all very supernatural; the demons were as real as God. Jesus was involved in the struggle of good and evil, impelled by the prophetic vocation. At the heart was his awareness of a relation to God the Father, the God of righteousness and love. Also at the center was his sense of service to his fellow-men, of self-giving, and a life of ethical and spiritual activity.

Jesus was not a rabbi (the title was not used anyway in his time), but certainly had a message. Here Case described the process of remembering that message in the early church and the difficulties of separating it out from the church's own message. The end result shows that Jesus' message was the kingdom of God and preparing people for it. God's rule would suddenly be established and the judgment would follow. Jesus issued a call to repentance; his chief task was to prepare people to enter the kingdom. The message was probably not political, though anyone speaking of the kingdom could hardly have entirely avoided the subject. Yet the available evidence suggests that Jesus "was no messianic revolutionist. . . . He was an eschatologist, not a messianist" (426–27). Only personal righteousness would count in the kingdom. Conformity to the will of God was central. God was the loving Father, but also the implacable Judge and Ruler. The present material world was to be renounced. Jesus was not ascetic, but people were to exemplify the life now which was to be expected in the new age. He demanded perfection, complete sacrifice, renunciation; his demands eventually led him to Golgotha.

Case's picture of Jesus was, like that of many of his contemporaries, drawn with the same liberal strokes modified by eschatological considerations. Yet it was also marked by some distinctive features: a severe approach to the text — Jesus was a prophet only, not the Son of man or messiah — that brings Case nearer to, say, Bultmann or Nathaniel Schmidt. And what might well have exercised a more creative influence was the sociohistorical method, but its impact seemed not to extend very far beyond the Chicago School or, for that matter, very far beyond Case's own time. Analyzing the reasons would take us past the scope of what can here be permitted; it seems likely that the method was not well enough defined and articulated to distinguish it from existing practices or what was already on the scene and would become dominant (*Formgeschichte*). Yet it contained a very valuable *emphasis*, which lay in giving special attention to the social setting, indeed in the insistence on the importance of that setting. On the face of it *Formgeschichte* promised the same thing, but in reality the attention to community seemed not to get much beyond a formal principle; Bultmann's work, for instance, confined itself still to issues of the literary text, which is undoubtedly how it seemed to Case, and therefore he did not find *Formgeschichte* to be an illuminating enterprise. Bultmann's Jesus also seemed to operate largely in a social vacuum.

Case also had his critics,[51] and it is true that the sociohistorical method as such left few disciples. But this much might be ventured: the insistence on the integration of Jesus within his social setting might not have made judgments concerning authenticity any easier, but it would likely have ensured that a more Jewish Jesus would have survived. There is in Case's work a notable lack of that urgent need in liberal lives generally, as we have frequently noticed, to discover a Jesus who has transcended Judaism or broken its framework, and all the rest. It might also be considered — though obviously what-might-have-beens are always suspect — that a more vigorous sociological approach would have entered upon the scene much sooner in the twentieth century. In this respect the true heirs of Shirley Jackson Case — at least methodologically — are not Ernst Käsemann and the New Questers, but the likes of Gerd Theissen, Richard Horsley, Dominic Crossan, and, antecedent to all, Howard Clark Kee.

Shailer Mathews

A contemporary and close personal friend of Case's was Shailer Mathews, who preceded Case both at Chicago and in the deanship of the Divinity School. Mathews was associated with the very beginnings of sociology in America and with the social gospel.[52] His work, *Jesus on Social Institutions*, while not a "life" in the usual sense, deserves some attention here as a formative work of the social gospel movement and representative of American works on Jesus.[53]

Jesus on Social Institutions was a thoroughgoing revision of — indeed, replacement for — Mathews's 1897 work that remained popular and in print and use for many years. The 1928 version was characterized by a greater attention to the eschatological element in Jesus' message, but many of the core components of the first book remained. In the original work Mathews had considered the eschatological aspect of Jesus' message, decided that there was a present emphasis that predominated, and defined the central proclamation of Jesus in this way: "By the kingdom of God Jesus meant *an ideal* (though progressively approximated) *social order in which the relation of men to God is that of sons, and* (therefore) *to*

---

51. Reviews were abundant; most significant among them were Henry J. Cadbury's in *JR* 8 (1928): 130–36, who noted that the sociohistorical method was not so new as its advocates seemed to think; and Burton Scott Easton's review in *ATR* (1927–28): 250–57, with criticism of Case's excessive space devoted to background, too little argumentation for his critical judgments.

52. Mathews founded the *Journal of Sociology* and his first work on *The Social Teaching of Jesus: An Essay in Christian Sociology* (New York: Macmillan, 1897) began as articles in the journal.

53. Shailer Mathews, *Jesus on Social Institutions* (New York: Macmillan, 1928). It was reprinted in the Lives of Jesus series, ed. Leander Keck (Philadelphia: Fortress Press, 1971), with introduction by Kenneth Cauthen. Ernest DeWitt Burton and Shailer Mathews also produced a long-running text on Jesus, *The Life of Christ*, University of Chicago Publications in Religious Education (Chicago: University of Chicago Press, 1900; 2d rev. ed., 1901; 3d rev. ed., 1927). It was more of a commentary on the synoptic texts (after the first edition, which included John also); the last edition, revised by Mathews after Burton's death, shows the impact of the eschatological interpretation.

each other, that of brothers" (italics his).[54] In the second work the eschatological interpretation came to greater prominence. We will here focus on that work.

Jesus' time was one of messianic movements and of revolution. Of apocalyptic writings Mathews said, "This apocalyptic literature was deeply religious, but in outlook it was political rather than theological...the code language of the revolutionary spirit" (24). And Jesus "taught men who were already committed to discontent with existing social conditions to have faith in the power of God to establish a new age. He was a leader of a band of hope" (28). Jesus joined John's revolutionary movement, but the "revolutionary spirit was not to be insurrectionary, but spiritual" (30). God's kingdom was gift, not to be taken by violence.

Jesus thought himself to be the messiah at his baptism and to prepare persons for the coming kingdom. He shared the hopes of his contemporaries for the coming kingdom, but modified them. "God was not an emperor but a father; the reign of God was not so much a kingdom as a triumph of the goodwill of God in human affairs" (34). In other words, Jesus taught that God was the loving Father and based his social revolution on that assumption. He differed from his contemporaries in that he expected the kingdom to come by love among brothers, not by force and violence. But he also adopted revolutionary techniques; he formed a group of the discontented. Jesus was an agitator, choosing the twelve and the seventy for purposes of propaganda. He put himself in a paradoxical position, organizing what looked like a political movement but refusing to use his following for violence. His emphasis was the good will of God, the benevolence of love. "He transformed the revolutionary spirit into a new moral attitude pregnant with social implications" (42).

Revolutions are begun by minorities with high expectations that they will be the beneficiaries of the revolution. "Men who have suffered injustice have always been ready to exact terrible payment from their oppressors. Revolutions are not made of rosewater" (44).

Jesus impressed people with cures and exorcisms, but his chief appeal was the call to repentance. He identified with the poor and oppressed, and had a prophet's fate. "The respectability of his own day killed him and the respectability of our day has appropriated him," as Mathews wryly observed (49).

Jesus elevated love as a social base. In contrast the church elevated Jesus' death as a sacrifice for sinners. Love is the universal law of the world; as Jesus set it forth it was "an urge to social coöperation in which the coöperating parties treat each other as persons" (55). Individual desires and needs are subordinated to the group. Jesus opposed acquisitiveness, vindictiveness, and claims to ecclesiastical exclusiveness or possession of true knowledge. He criticized the Pharisees and allied himself with the *Am ha-aretz.* He emphasized humanity's relationship to God through moral attitudes as opposed to the Pharisaic emphasis on law.

---

54. Mathews, *Social Teaching of Jesus*, 54.

He foresaw his prophetic fate as a consequence of his attacks on his opponents. Still, it remains true that Jesus was not seeking to establish the kingdom but to prepare people to enter it. He was not a social reformer: "To make Jesus a social reformer, much more a social legislator, is to misinterpret him. He dealt with attitudes of individuals rather than with programs of society" (62). Specific social teachings are products of the love ideal.

Jesus was not an ascetic, but was sensitive to matters of ordinary civility (dress, social behavior at meals), was democratic in spirit (he did not recognize the validity of class distinctions), a friend of all, a believer in the equality of love, not merit or ability, and a friend of the oppressed who also made duty to one another paramount. Religious trust was the foundation of his activity. As to family, Jesus taught monogamy, the sacredness of marriage, that it did not rank below asceticism, and that it was to be bound by love but also not above the kingdom. Jesus opposed divorce (though it is impossible to legislate on this basis). Regarding wealth, Jesus seemed to preach against it and to side with the poor. The church has done likewise, but not without irony: "The preaching of the church against wealth has been equaled only by its zeal to obtain it" (91). Jesus taught that wealth was to be based on brotherliness, on sharing what is gained for the good of all. He warned against acquisitiveness, but had sympathy for the poor.

Jesus was no socialist or communist. And one cannot take Jesus' words on wealth as a basis for operating an economic system. Jesus was a moralist, not an economist. The poor, with whom he sympathized, do not generate cultural systems. Said Mathews, "Unless progress from primitive savagery to our present civilization be regarded as degenerate, wealth must be recognized as one basis for such progress" (101). In other words, we cannot build a civilization on Jesus' words used as a blueprint for society. In fact, we have to eliminate from his teachings all those things that come from his eschatological expectation of the end of the world, such as giving away wealth, selling what you have and giving to the poor. "We must not treat his immediate relations with a discontented, oppressed, poverty-stricken people as something to be generalized into a universal ethical ideal. For there is no necessary virtue in poverty any more than there is necessarily evil in wealth" (102). Jesus neither championed *laissez faire* economics nor condemned it; he was not an economic philosopher, not a Karl Marx. He was concerned with the question of relationship to the Father, whether persons have done the will of the Father, whether they have loved all people, regardless of class, status, and the like.

As to the state, Jesus gave no political teaching, though was himself obedient and noninterfering toward the state. His kingdom was not of this world. Nor was he an anarchist, or anything else, such as a democrat, a monarchist, or a socialist. He recommended no particular form of government. Love was his message. And war? Certainly it is best to try to persuade nations to avoid war as an instrument of policy, but that is not to say that a Christian citizen cannot engage in a specific war. Everything depends on cases:

> The principle of neighborliness means the protection of victims of possible injustice
> just as truly as caring for their sufferings after they have been abused.... War must
> be shown to involve losses of human progress greater than the losses resulting from
> non-resistance. (115–16)

Jesus' teaching is an ideal; it is impossible to expect that it will be embodied in
social legislation. What is to be hoped for is a group that will embody in themselves and in all around them the ideal of Jesus. That is the idea of the church.
It must embody the ideals of the founder, even though it must use the methods
of modern science. The church has started many social welfare movements that
were subsequently taken over by state or governmental agencies. The church
should start more and encourage the basic altruism of society. "Men cannot
gather social figs from individual thistles" (131).

But the church is not just another social agency and cannot abandon its religious function. The main function of the church is to stand for the relation
between humankind and God and to ground all social activity in the love of
God. Members are those who really believe that the attitude of love can be
institutionalized in some way in society.

In concluding his work Mathews affirmed the monumental influence of Jesus
on western civilization. Even compared with other religious figures Jesus is
unique. "His personality is more potent, his life is more exemplary, and his death
is the center of the ritual and theology of a civilization that is transforming humanity" (148–49). His influence and his social gospel have three pillars: first, no
economic determinism or any mechanistic philosophy, but freedom under God,
to whom persons can pray, work, and hope; second, Jesus' ideal leads to a unified
personality in social relations — a good individual will be a good social citizen;
third, goodwill is a viable basis for a society, even if Christians differ on methods.

So spoke the speakers of the social gospel, looking to Jesus as the pioneer of
their faith, even though it was an eschatological Jesus who stood at the fountain-
head. Never mind; we can still find there the impetus that sweetens a scientific,
capitalistic world, making it more civilized. Such was, after all, the modernist
program and the same might well have been said of Schweitzer even, who was
also concerned for the future of civilization. Mathews was, in his own special
way, finding in Jesus the necessary inspiration to keep alive the flame in a world
confounded by its own incivility. That was not such a sorry purpose, and it carried the significant lesson that eschatological hopes need not conflict with social
values, and, indeed, necessarily give rise to them.

Meyer, Simkhovitch, and Schmidt

Two nonbiblical historians also contributed works on Jesus in this decade that
have often been referred to. One was the massive volume of the Berlin historian
Eduard Meyer, who set the Jesus story in a sweeping historical framework, even

though the actual presentation of Jesus was fairly brief and circumspect.[55] Jesus' world was Pharisaic, but he differed in his emphasis on the inner essence of the Law and opposed the tradition of the elders. He maintained a certain freedom even from the Law itself and set love at the center. His ethic was then nothing but a transposing of the categorical imperative into a practical commandment. Judaism was overcome from within. This provided the occasion of conflict.

Jesus proclaimed the kingdom of God; not many seemed to respond. He demanded a total self-giving to the will of God — not world denial or fleeing from the world, but world detachment. Jesus was not an ascetic, but was free from social constraints (spoke against riches and the like); he forgave sins and lived in the power of God the Father. He demanded faith as a condition of entering the kingdom of God. He held with the Pharisees on the hope of another world, eternal life, and hell for sinners. But he also interiorized the kingdom. He thought he was the messiah, though not the founder of a sect or a new religion. He rejected the popular ideas of the messiah and taught a religious individualism, setting aside national ideals. Not a Davidic son was he, but Son of man, world judge who would raise the holy ones from the dead. Thereby also he was Son of God, a sense that was rooted in his total commitment to the will of the Father and inner unity with God. Yet he also had no sense of elevating himself to deity. He kept his messiahship to himself.

Jesus must have known that a prophet's fate awaited him. Peter's confession was a critical point; with a group believing in him he now had to go to Jerusalem, to the center of Israel. He arrived right before Passover, agreeing to a messianic entrance that led to the beginning of a conflict that would end in his destruction. He must have known that an attempt to gain support by a public demonstration could not succeed and would only bring opposition from the Romans. His messianic claim allowed him to be presented before the people as a blasphemer and to the procurator as a rebel and usurper. Perhaps he hoped for a divine intervention at the last, but none came and he died crying out to God. He might have been shortly forgotten, but instead called to life a movement that indeed transformed Judaism and finally Rome itself. He, not Caesar, was looked to as the world judge.

Columbia University Professor Vladimir G. Simkhovitch contributed a slender volume, opposite in size from Meyer's work, and opposite also in its conception of Jesus.[56] Simkhovitch observed that when we come across a figure of history around whom so many have gathered, we have to ask what it was that was stirring the masses at the time. What was stirring the masses at the time of Jesus was the sociocultural fate of the Jewish people, their political destiny. This concern came to expression in many ways and especially in the form of messianic hopes. It is impossible that Jesus should not have been fully aware of this fact, for it was

---

55. Eduard Meyer, *Ursprung und Anfänge des Christentums*, 2 vols. (Stuttgart: J. G. Cotta, 1921). The presentation of Jesus is found in 2:420–62.
56. Vladimir G. Simkhovitch, *Toward the Understanding of Jesus* (New York: Macmillan, 1925).

about the survival of his own people, about "the problem of escape from certain annihilation" (28). Simkhovitch relied considerably on Josephus for reconstructing a picture of this struggle and also gave his own reading of certain gospel texts, including some from John, that tended to support his representation of a Jesus who shared the widespread concern for the fate of the nation at the hands of the Romans. But what separated Jesus was his advocacy of nonresistance, even of love for the enemy. The Pharisees, said Simkhovitch, could have overlooked Jesus' heresies, as they obviously did those of the Sadducees, but they could not forgive him the notion of submission to Rome. Jesus rejected the Zealot solution, as he did also the alternative of assimilation to Roman culture, and called for a spiritual revival. The kingdom of heaven was to be within us. Israel's only consolation was to be light to the nations, salvation to the world — accepted in humility. Such a program was inevitably to find vociferous and even violent rejection, and that was Jesus' fate.

So the two "secular" historians read Jesus about as differently as had any others. The association of Jesus more closely with the sociopolitical scene is decidedly more American; his disassociation therefrom is decidedly more German. Meyer raised up a Jesus more interested in separating from Judaism, Simkhovitch one more interested in saving it.

K. L. Schmidt, in addition to his stimulating study of the synoptic framework, also contributed an essay on Jesus in the 1929 edition of *Religion in Geschichte und Gegenwart*.[57] It gives some history of research and summarizes problems and possibilities in the life of Jesus. Nothing can be gained from the birth stories; Jesus proclaimed the kingdom, which was at the core *Herrschaft*, not *Reich*. It was an eschatological concept going back to the prophets and apocalyptists; it only would come by direct intervention from heaven, as gift from God the Father to his son Israel. Pharisees and Zealots held to a political view, but not Jesus and John the Baptist, though each fell victim to political factors. John was an old prophet of the End demanding repentance. Jesus agreed, but did not take over John's asceticism or his baptism. Rather, he preached salvation and repentance, grace and judgment. There was no political messiahship for Jesus, but he expected the Son of man on the clouds of heaven. The dead would be raised and judgment held. Unlike the apocalyptists, however, Jesus declined to paint a picture or conjure up signs. Non-Jews could participate, for the Jew as such had no special claim on God. But Jesus advocated no particular "-ism," whether individualism, humanitarianism, optimism, pessimism, nationalism, internationalism, monism, or dualism. As for the Law, he set scribe against scribe (divorce), and separated the essential from the unessential. There could be no halfway devotion to the will of God: either/or! Here also belonged the antitheses of the Sermon on the Mount.

As to Jesus' acts, he certainly healed and forgave sinners and practiced exorcism. The temple cleansing was an act that embodied the preaching of re-

---

57. *RGG* (1929): vol. J–Me, 110–51.

pentance. Likely also Jesus regarded himself as messiah (cf. Matt. 16:18, the "church" as the eschatological true Israel). Peter and the others are the true community of God that cannot be destroyed. Jesus then intended a messianic community. Peter's priority remains a puzzle parallel to the choice of Israel. Jesus' messianic position was the ground of his suffering and death; he was condemned by the Jewish authorities as a godless messianic aspirant and by Pilate as a dangerous pretender to the throne. Perhaps Jesus saw himself as Son of man, though it is not really a messianic title in Daniel.

Schmidt offered a form-critical Jesus, denuded of any particular historical framework of activity, not unlike Bultmann's Jesus, but with more openness to messianic claims and a degree of interest in community-founding. Unlike, say, a Shailer Mathews, he betrayed no real interest in establishing a socially relevant Jesus or of transforming the eschatological one into something more acceptable.

We began this survey of the twenties by noticing how destructive was the Great War; along the way were efforts at reconciliation among the combatant nations, with mid- and latter-decade conferences between German and English theologians and scholars. The results were published in 1930 in both German and English versions, and it is worth sampling this work as we wind down the decade.[58]

Adolf Deissmann's essay on "The Name Jesus" was a response to William Benjamin Smith's claim of a pre-Christian Jesus cult. Deissmann examined the inscriptional and other evidence, but found no reason to claim the existence of such a cult. Jesus as the name of a cult deity arose only as a Christian practice. Gerhard Kittel ("The Jesus of History") offered the thesis that the New Testament itself is predicated on the particularity of a contingent event of history and therefore concern for the historical Jesus in all its particularity is essential. Christianity assumes this burden. At the same time only faith can "see" the reality of what is thereby given, so both the historical Jesus and the Christ of faith are bound indissolubly together.

C. H. Dodd's essay on "Jesus as Teacher and Prophet" suggested some comparisons with the rabbis, showing similarity but also that Jesus departed from the rabbis in taking up an independent position toward the Law and tradition, sometimes setting them aside, and showing himself by rabbinic standards to be unorthodox. He also had characteristics of a prophet, including prophetic speech forms, visions and auditions, predictions, symbolic actions, emphasis on the ethical as opposed to the ceremonial, and a nonnationalistic eschatology. The kingdom of God was more prophetic than apocalyptic or rabbinic. He also demanded repentance. Personally also Jesus exhibited a pneumatic call and held to predestinarianism, with himself as the instrument of a mission to Israel. Yet he

---

58. G. K. A. Bell and D. Adolf Deissmann, *Mysterium Christi: Christological Studies by British and German Theologians* (London: Longmans, Green, 1930).

also went beyond the prophets; for him the time was no longer imminent, but actually fulfilled. That changed his teaching and his person.

Edwyn Hoskyns, in "Jesus, the Messiah," wished to find more christology in the historical Jesus than was customarily seen. He affirmed that Jesus was "unique," and observed the necessity nevertheless of Jesus' connection with the Old Testament.

It is a collection of worthy essays, and perhaps more important is simply its existence as a collaborative work. The decade seemed to promise something better in the area of historical Jesus studies, but it ended in economic mire, and the western world turned in a different direction that carried with it severe implications for theological-biblical inquiry. The fate of the historical Jesus in the march up to another western war of still greater scale must now engage our attention.

Chapter 5

JESUS BETWEEN WARS
The Thirties

The economic depression that followed on the collapse of the stock market, first in America then elsewhere, cast its gloom in every corner. "Hoovervilles" — those gatherings of the homeless in desperate, temporary structures — arose around the land of America, taking their name from a president whose policies could not cope with the circumstances; such communities of misery seemed to signify the destitution that descended on the whole western world. Fascism bred in some places, with longer term world malaise, while socialism of varying brands gained followers in England and the United States.

The socioeconomic devastation corresponded to a theological stillness in some quarters; in America the historical Jesus was muted, with little done on the subject in the way of new "lives" of Jesus. The Germans had already slipped into virtual silence, with not much more than the works of Rudolf Otto and Martin Dibelius to mention. The most substantial efforts emanated from England and France. At the same time all centers were being compelled to come to terms with Form Criticism.

The Impact of Form Criticism

At the close of the previous decade and the opening of the new one, both the English and Americans had begun to absorb the "new" criticism from Germany; the French seemed largely unimpressed. The Americans may have been a step ahead of the British in acknowledging Form Criticism, with early essays from Bultmann and Dibelius.[1] And Burton Scott Easton had undertaken an exten-

---

1. Rudolf Bultmann, "The New Approach to the Synoptic Problem," *JR* (1926): 337–62. Later was *Form Criticism: Two Essays on New Testament Research,* trans. Frederick C. Grant, Harper Torchbook (New York: Harper, 1962; orig. pub., n.p.: Willett, Clark, 1934). Dibelius also contributed "The Structure and Literary Character of the Gospels," *HTR* 20 (1927): 151–70. Also there was the contributed article by Ludwig Köhler, "The Meaning and Possibilities of Formgeschichte," *JR* 8 (1928): 603–15. (Köhler demonstrated already the existence of the so-called principle of coherence.) Probably the earliest — and sympathetic — respondent was Henry Cadbury, "Between Jesus and the Gospels," *HTR* 16 (1923): 81–92.

sive and well-informed evaluation of *Formgeschichte* in his *The Gospel Before the Gospels,* to which we can direct some attention.[2]

Easton agreed with Erich Fascher[3] that Form Criticism had some limited value, but that it cannot give the relative ages of the forms it identifies, nor can it contribute to the historical estimation of the contents of any story. The synoptic tradition is more attuned to genuine sayings than to the post-Easter circumstances of the church. For Easton, Bultmann and Wellhausen canonized the whole palestinian church by attributing to it an anonymous creativity, whereas in reality it was the teaching of Jesus that created the community. Easton preferred to find originality in such items as the baptism and the temptation, which went back to Jesus himself and were related by him to his disciples. The messianic consciousness of Jesus is also historical, rooting in a genuine expression at Caesarea-Philippi.

Of two leading descriptions in England, one by Vincent Taylor and the other by R. H. Lightfoot, Lightfoot's is the most inclined favorably toward Form Criticism.[4] Taylor assumed as sources Mark, Q, M, and L (the latter two may be only oral), and the validity of the Proto-Luke theory of B. H. Streeter. Some opinions: Dibelius is the pathfinder; Schmidt's rejection of the outline is questionable; Bultmann is Strauss redivivus, a "study in the cult of the conceivable."[5] Albertz's study of the synoptic controversy stories disagreed with Bultmann's skepticism and showed that the conflict stories existed prior to Mark. Taylor agreed with Fascher's critique that the form alone gives no ground for making historical judgments. Still, he said, Form Criticism has considerable value as a tool. It helps penetrate the period 30–50 C.E., to be an earwitness; it need not lead to skepticism.

Taylor described the various classifications or forms. Here he suggested his own title of pronouncement stories for paradigms or apophthegms. The terms are too loose generally, he said. Too much subjectivity enters; the study of forms moves beyond form to historical judgments. But what happened to eyewitnesses anyway? The disciples must have all vanished into heaven after the resurrection. Taylor then examined in some detail a number of instances of various forms of the tradition (pronouncement stories, sayings, parables, healings, miracles, pas-

---

2. Burton Scott Easton, *The Gospel Before the Gospels* (New York: Scribner's, 1928). Easton was Professor of the Literature and Interpretation of the New Testament, General Theological Seminary, New York.

3. Above, chap. 3, n. 12.

4. Taylor in *The Formation of the Gospel Tradition* (London: Macmillan, 1933; 2d ed., 1935; reprinted 1945, 1949, 1953); Lightfoot in *History and Interpretation in the Gospels* (New York: Harper, 1934). Taylor was Principal of Wesley College, Ferens Professor of New Testament Language and Literature, and also Examiner in Biblical Theology, London University; and Lightfoot was Dean Ireland's Professor of Exegesis in the University of Oxford and Examining Chaplain to the Archbishop of Canterbury. At about the same time was the essay by the Glasgow professor G. H. C. Macgregor, "Recent Gospel Criticism and Our Approach to the Life of Jesus," *ExpTim* 45 (1933–34): 198– 203, 283–86. He found Form Criticism too harsh in its judgments and expressed the fairly common opinion that the form is not a sure clue to historicity.

5. Taylor, *Formation of the Gospel Tradition*, 15.

sion narrative, stories) and set forth a theory of the emergence of the gospel tradition 30–50. There were short recollections, the passion story, and the meeting of practical needs, shaped by preaching. Eyewitnesses were still present. The resurrection appearances were primary, with also questions of ordinary life, rules, ethics, pronouncement stories, and miracles. So there was a self-contained story and sayings; groups of material dominate. From 50–60, material was gathered into groups, though it was not yet a narrative; topical collections and pronouncement stories were grouped, the sayings collections arose (Q). From 65 on, gospels were compiled; Proto-Luke was first, but it was never published separately — only after adding in Mark. The latter appeared 65–70 at Rome, then Matthew.

Lightfoot adopted the perspective of Form Criticism entirely, referring to Dibelius and Bultmann, with the latter regarded as deducing somewhat more radical conclusions than the former. Lightfoot analyzed Mark especially in terms of its newly seen character; it is not a biographical or historical work, though these are present, but a work with a doctrinal perspective: Jesus is the (secret) messiah. Wrede's view is the correct one; the secret attempts to explain why this messiah was so little accepted as such in his time.

Mark consists of small units of oral tradition, growing out of the life-setting of the church; preaching especially (Dibelius) was the justifying need, and paradigm was the historical unit. The passion narrative was the first connected whole story. Lightfoot discussed the perspectives of Mark and Matthew and Luke, offering many insights of a redaction-historical nature.

In the end the skepticism of Form Criticism infected Lightfoot. His conclusion:

> The form of the earthly no less than of the heavenly Christ is for the most part hidden from us. For all the inestimable value of the gospels, they yield us little more than a whisper of his voice; we trace in them but the outskirts of his ways.[6]

There were also capable reports on Form Criticism, if not as well known as those of Taylor and Lightfoot, provided by Floyd Filson and Alan Richardson, both in 1938.[7] Filson's work was aimed primarily at ministers and argued for the value of criticism. Its critique of Form Criticism was that it dismissed too quickly the connecting links, that there were still eyewitnesses, that the oral process of the

---

6. Lightfoot, *History and Interpretation in the Gospels*, 225. Lightfoot had a curious footnote (27 n. 1) on the origin of the symbol Q. He reported that his friend Armitage Robinson claimed credit for it, that he was lecturing in the 1890s on Mark at Cambridge and referred to Mark as P (for Peter, based on Peter's reminiscences). He then called the sayings source Q, simply because it came after P in the alphabet. His hearers, he said, carried the practice to Germany, where soon enough a better explanation was found (*Quelle*). Lightfoot then quoted F. C. Burkitt as attributing the first appearance of "Q" to Julius Wellhausen. An unlikely story, I would suppose, but it would illustrate how often events of historic magnitude originate in something quite mundane.

7. Filson in *Origins of the Gospels* (New York: Abingdon Press, 1938); Richardson in *The Gospels in the Making: An Introduction to the Recent Criticism of the Synoptic Gospels* (London: Student Christian Movement Press, 1938). Filson was Professor of New Testament Literature and History, Presbyterian Theological Seminary, Chicago, and Richardson was then Vicar of Cambo and Examining Chaplain to the Bishop of Newcastle.

gospels did not really resemble folklore, and that too much creative power was ascribed to the community. There was also an informed discussion of the state of synoptic studies, with reports on the then-current scholarly opinion.

Richardson also sought to write something of Form Criticism for a primarily nontechnical audience and to provide a brief accounting of Jesus' work and words. He described the synoptic problem, the dating and provenience of the three gospels, and the oral period underlying the gospels, along with notice of the evangelists' freedom in selecting and editing their material according to the needs of the community. Mark was analyzed as a work representing the preaching of the Roman church. Forms of the oral tradition behind it were examined, with the point — by now recognizable — that there are limits to the value of the classification process, that the content is not related to the form. Richardson referred to the poetic form of sayings and concluded that Jesus required his disciples to memorize them, like a rabbi.

Richardson then also offered a summary of the teaching of Jesus: the eschatological kingdom (sovereignty of God, a present-future reality, not political, not a social order, not built by men). Schweitzer's thesis is unacceptable; there was no kingdom in the near future and no interim ethic. Jesus reinterpreted the idea of the messiah, though it was the church who applied the Isaianic idea of the suffering servant. Jesus made the messiah the bearer of the messianic woes; the Son of man was to be a ransom, and would give his life to effect forgiveness.

The synoptics tell us what the earliest communities believed about Jesus. Faith and theology are intertwined in the gospels, yet an outline of Jesus' ministry is faithfully preserved. This tension between faith and history has to be allowed to stand. Christianity is a historical religion, and therefore criticism is necessary. It functions in the same way as did tradition for the ancient church (a criterion of genuineness, a check on error and heresy); therefore also faith is to be tested by criticism, even though faith is not dependent on criticism. Faith is response to the encounter with God; the Christ of faith cannot be proved or disproved by criticism.

So Form Criticism was being absorbed, but it was not merely being swallowed.[8] That British-American reticence to import things German without qualification remained firmly in place. At its core the issue was the question of historical judgments over authenticity and, in fact, it is a reasonable critique that identification of "forms" in itself leads to identification of originality. Form Criticism would have been better thought of as *Traditionsgeschichte*, for that is the task to which it set itself. To make that shift does not, however, as the critiquers seemed to think, argue for any higher degree of historical reliability in the transmitted tradition. To point out some holes in the theory or practice of Form Criticism is not at the same time to elevate the historical reliability of the text.

---

8. In some cases there was outright rejection; see W. Emery Barnes, *Gospel Criticism and Form Criticism* (Edinburgh: T. & T. Clark, 1936). Barnes directed his ire particularly at Dibelius and called the whole movement the *Geist der stets verneint*.

The German Context

While the Americans and British were scurrying to deal with the impact of Form Criticism, the Germans, on their part, would soon be occupied with issues of greater intensity: the church struggle prompted by the policies of the Third Reich, the whole "Jewish question," and the ideological debates with the so-called German Christians. This history is too complex to be entered upon here, but it surely contributed to a dampening down of all scientific work and in particular interest in the historical Jesus.[9] Tragic was the assent of more than a few theologians, not to mention pastors, to the program of the Nazis.[10]

Germany, however, continued to hold a grudging recognition as the center of innovative work in the field, evoking a sometimes wry comment among others. Some excerpts from a letter to Shirley Jackson Case from a former student, Stewart S. Cole, who was at the time on sabbatical leave in Marburg, will make the point:

> I have met two German scholars lately who have asked that I convey to you their cordial regards — Martin Dibelius of Heidelberg and Rudolf Bultmann of Marburg.... Both men, exponents of "Formgeschichte" in their New Testament studies, arrive at very different conclusions theologically. Bultmann, ultraradical in his treatment of the synoptics, saves the bible as *the* book of Christian revelation by his adoption of the Barthian dialectics. Dibelius believes he can find a few authentic sayings and acts of Jesus in the gospels which warrant him in believing that Jesus accepted himself as the messiah. His Christian faith uses these materials to make of Jesus the Christ of the "revealing" God. Is it not strange how these men pass from the logic of "historisimus," which is necessarily humanistic, to that of theistic affirmations, without any apparent sense of their unrelatedness? But, that is "German." A comparative study of German and American theological methods would be quite interesting.... Bultmann is probably the most discussed New Testament man in Germany today. He, as so many Germans, labors under the impression that other people have little or nothing to contribute to religious scholarship. I asked him if he had read your "biography of Jesus." He said he had never

---

9. There is a vast literature. An English-language account of the church struggle is that by Richard Gutteridge, *The German Evangelical Church and the Jews, 1879–1950* (New York: Harper, 1976). An interesting work at the time was the unusual trio Wilhelm Hauer, Karl Heim, and Karl Adam, *Germany's New Religion: The German Faith Movement,* trans. T. S. K. Scott-Craig and R. E. Davies (New York: Abingdon Press, 1937). A poignant witness to the events surrounding Karl Barth's dismissal on June 21, 1934, from his post for refusing to sign a loyalty oath specifically mentioning Hitler can be seen in his letter exchanges with Bultmann, in Bernd Jaspert, *Karl Barth — Rudolf Bultmann Letters 1922–1966,* trans. and ed. Geoffrey W. Bromiley (Grand Rapids, Mich.: Eerdmans, 1981), esp. 78–79. Bultmann, along with many others, had signed the oath; a common justification was found in the historic Lutheran doctrine of the two kingdoms (the state exercising its rightful claim, though implicit was the assumption that the Christian's conscience could not be compelled, just the point Barth was unwilling to concede only implicitly). The growing preoccupation with "the Jewish question" is attested in the *Bibliographisches Beiblatt der Theologischen Literaturzeitung,* which begins inauspiciously in a section covering 1933 with a few titles under the heading of *Die antisemitische Frage* and grew by the end of publication (1942) into a small mountain dealing with *Judenfrage. Die antisemitische Frage.*

10. E.g., Robert P. Ericksen, *Theologians under Hitler: Gerhard Kittel, Paul Althaus, and Emanuel Hirsch* (New Haven: Yale University Press, 1985).

heard of it, but would order the book at once and review it in one of the German journals.[11]

Cole went on to remark that, of all the American and English scholars, only the name of B. H. Streeter was regularly mentioned in Marburg classrooms. It would hardly be fair, however, to say that there was no interest on the part of German *Wissenschaft* in the theological situation in America and in England as well; in fact, to judge from the articles appearing around this time there was more interest than had previously been the case.[12]

Nevertheless, the decade of the thirties produced, in Germany, a limited interest in the historical Jesus, the most prominent being the work of Rudolf Otto, with some contributions also from Martin Dibelius.

Rudolf Otto

Otto was a *Religionsgeschichtler* and *Systematiker* at Marburg, better known previously for his work on *Das Heilige*, although he had many years earlier composed a "life" of Jesus that did not gain much attention.[13] His book, which was quickly translated into English,[14] called upon *religionsgeschichtliche* placement of Jesus and his movement and directed itself especially against Bultmann's emphasis on a Jesus with an individually oriented message about a future-only kingdom demanding decision. The book fell into two major parts: Book 1 took up the kingdom of God and Christ's preaching, book 2 the kingdom of God and the Son of man.

Concern for the uniqueness of Jesus was pervasive. The very first sentence of the book read: "Jesus was distinctive and unique, but without prejudice to

---

11. Cole was Professor of Religious Education at Crozer. The letter is handwritten and preserved in the archives at Florida Southern College. It bears the date of May 20, 1930. The list of Bultmann's works in *TRu*, n.f. 22 (1954): 3–20, gives no indication that Bultmann ever reviewed Case's book. On the other hand, Case had clearly read Bultmann's *Jesus*, for he had a personal copy that contains signs of his marginal markings. It is less clear whether Cole was being quite fair in his characterization of Bultmann.

12. See Heinz-Horst Schrey, "Die gegenwärtige Lage der amerikanischen Theologie," *TRu*, n.f. 10 (1938): 23–56. The article focuses on the social gospel and pragmatism, with some notices of "enthusiasm." Earlier was the piece by A. E. Burckhardt, "Moderne Richtungen im theologischen Denken Amerikas," *ZTK*, n.f. 8 (1927): 202–26; and the article of Alexander Purdy, "Das Neue Testament in der amerikanischen Theologie," *TRu*, n.f. 3 (1931): 367–85, giving an overview of NT studies. English literature was surveyed at the end of the decade by Walter Gutbrod, "Aus der neueren englischen Literatur zum Neuen Testament," *TRu*, n.f. 11 (1939): 263–77, continued in a second article in *TRu*, n.f. 12 (1940): 1–23. Kendrick Grobel's later article, "Amerikanische Literatur zum Neuen Testament seit 1938," *TRu*, n.f. (1948): 142–56, classified American work into various categories, resembling a rating system (original research, accounts of research, popular, and so on) for the benefit of its German readers. The *Theologische Rundschau* had been resurrected by Bultmann and Hans von Soden, who coedited it, so obviously Bultmann had a hand in publishing these articles.

13. Rudolf Otto, *Leben und Wirken Jesu nach historisch-kritischer auffassung* (Göttingen: Vandenhoeck and Ruprecht, 1902); English trans., *Life and Ministry of Jesus According to the Historical and Critical Method*, trans. H. J. Whitby (Chicago: Open Court Publishing, 1908). It largely traded on liberal themes; its emphasis on the present kingdom contained a germ of the later work. Schweitzer gave it a bare footnote (*Quest of the Historical Jesus*, 301 n. 2).

14. Otto, *Reich Gottes und Menschensohn*. Translation apparently in 1935; it appears to be the case that works more sympathetic to the receiving country are more rapidly translated.

his distinctive and unique character we may say that he belonged to a general class" (13). That class, as it evolves, was that Jesus was a charismatic evange- list, but first Otto investigated the background of the kingdom of God concept, locating it in Indo-European or Aryan or Iranian (Persian-Zoroastrian) escha- tological conceptions. Jesus' Galilean roots and irregular practices (associating with Samaritans and the like) also meant that Jesus was "not a Jew in the ortho- dox and one-sided sense" (18). His preaching depended on apocalyptic thought, such as is represented in Enoch, which itself was hardly orthodox or typical. The immediate background lay in Yahweh's *malkuth*, first conceived as heaven, then eschatologized as heaven coming to earth in the last days. As the world became more remote from God, demons and Satan appeared, signifying a sharp dualism, with apocalypticism the result. Yet Jesus was not an apocalyptist in the sense of indulging in fantastic world journeys. In interpreting his message we must also avoid modernisms — no "call to decision" based on an existence-philosophy.

Jesus' preaching spoke of a supramundane order, an eschatological, trans- formed order, denoting the end of all previous existence and accompanied by resurrection of the dead. This order calls to repentance (not decision); it has the character of an absolute demand — "genuine," not consistent eschatology — and it is a wondrous new creation, a miracle. *Basileia* is not to be translated "royal sovereignty," for the kingdom is not an organized community, a *polis* or *politeuma*. Rather, it is a "realm of royal sovereignty" (53), a realm that comes down from above. The Son of man, angels, thrones, and old figures like Abraham are also part of the picture. This inbreaking realm also has *dynamis*, wonderful power from above. It appeared in Jesus' charismatic activity and was opposed to Satan's activity. Jesus' mighty works were closely related to this inbreaking; so was his own person, which was that of the unrevealed Son of man, that is, he is part of the kingdom that was already breaking in. As proclamation of a new obedience (righteousness) it demands repentance, but the idea of a crisis is not part of it, for it is otherworldly and breaks off all things worldly. None of this is identi- cal with the usual Davidic messianic claims, though certainly it meant the end of every empire, including the Roman. We must remember that the figure who came with this announcement was nailed to the cross; Pilate would not have bothered with some Galilean itinerant rabbi asking for some immediate decision.

Jesus preached and worked more than two years. The time is fulfilled, he said — at hand, virtually present. There is in the message an irrational element in that Jesus also made ethical demands at the same time which presuppose no sense of eschatological urgency. Schweitzer called that an interim ethic and said it was a marvelous ethic, but failed to see how it could unite with an imminent eschatological message. That was, for Otto, part of the "Irrationality of the gen- uine and typically eschatological attitude" (62). He offered prior examples from Zoroaster, Muhammed, Francis, and Luther.

How was Jesus unique in relation to his environment? He differed from John in that John spoke of the coming judgment, Jesus of the coming kingdom, in- deed, that the kingdom has come already in the present. Jesus used ideas from apocalypticism, but "he ranged far beyond them by an idea which was entirely unique and peculiar to him, that the kingdom — supramundane, future, and belonging to a new era — penetrated from the future into the present, from its place in the beyond into this order, and was operative redemptively as a divine dynamis, an inbreaking realm of salvation" (72). It can be both future and present because it is a *mirum*, a miracle. John was also a gloomy preacher of repentance and practitioner of a magical water sacrament in preparation for the eschatological kingdom; Jesus practiced no baptism, and spoke a glad message of salvation now in a kingdom already present.

As to the sources for the message of Jesus, Otto followed the rather idiosyncratic theories of W. Bussmann[15] and developed the idea that there was a primal source before the synoptics, called the "St." (from *Stammschrift*, or parent-writing), the source of the three synoptics that they took over and enlarged, revised, and edited. Luke is later than Matthew or Mark, but used an older version of the St. than the other two. Matthew used a Galilean rescension, Mark a Roman one. Luke used the original. Matthew and Mark did not have an identical version before them.

The beelzebul scene shows a very old Aryan-Iranian tradition that the kingdom is the power that overcomes Satan's power. From this scene it can be seen that Jesus connected himself to the coming of the kingdom. He is the eschatological redeemer, the manifestation of the inbreaking power of the kingdom. This kingdom exercises its presence "forcefully," *biazetai* (Matt. 11:12). Yet also the kingdom comes "of itself" (Mark 4:3–8, 26–29, from St.), though the secrecy theory of the parables is later, not from St. Allegory is not original; a parable is an analogy in which the ordinary illuminates the spiritual. The seed parable represents growth, but only "of itself," with no human help. It is the kingdom now growing mysteriously, making its way into being, the kingdom of heaven on earth.

This kingdom is to be seen against the background of Jesus' anti-Pharisaic preaching; for example, Jesus said to receive the kingdom like a child, but childlike was totally contrary to the Pharisaic mind, for the childlike is intuitive and open, whereas the Pharisaic was calculating and contriving, using the Law to secure self-righteousness. The kingdom that comes of itself puts an end to Pharisaic salvation by righteousness. This new spirit of Jesus "threatened and eventually overcame the religious world of a rabbinic Judaism which was then developing." This new spirit, symbolized in the childlike attitude, was "aroused by Jesus, and moving in his way, swept through Judaism, threatening it with disintegration."[16] The mustard seed parable shows that the kingdom is the eschatological sphere of salvation, growing miraculously from tiny beginnings to marvelous endings. The net parable speaks of all kinds being caught up in the process (allegorized

---

15. Wilhelm Bussmann, *Synoptische Studien* (Halle: Buchhandlung des Waisenhauses, 1925–31). See below, chap. 8, 294.

16. Otto, *The Kingdom of God and the Son of Man*, trans. Floyd V. Filson and Bertam Lee Woolf (Grand Rapids, Mich.: Zondervan, n.d.), 121, 122.

by Matthew into a judgment-allegory). The treasure and pearl also speak of the accidental character of the kingdom, of an incalculable blessing. This emphasis on the kingdom as already present disappeared because it was displaced by the later church's christology; the experience of the Spirit replaced the experience of the kingdom, and the conception of the church displaced the mystery of the kingdom.

In the second part of the book Jesus was depicted as a prophet, but more than a prophet; he evoked a numinous nimbus about him. He confessed himself to be Son of man, though only after a certain point in his career (Caesarea-Philippi). He claimed the right to forgive sins and he knew himself to be the eschatological redeemer, combining Son of man with Servant of Yahweh and even also Wisdom. Otto then attempted to show through an extensive study of Enoch that Jesus came from that tradition and was profoundly influenced by it. In it Enoch is full of wisdom, is the judge of the endtime, the apocalyptic seer, Son of God, and finally the Son of man himself exalted to heaven:

> Long before Christ's appearance, a certain idea was fully developed in circles which had plainly been formed long before him and to which he himself plainly belonged. The idea was that a powerful preacher alike of righteousness, the coming judgment, and the blessed new age, a prophet of the eschatological Son of Man, would be transported at the end of his earthly career to God; that he would be exalted to become the one whom he had proclaimed, in the literal sense that he himself would become the very one whom he had proclaimed. (212–13)

So Jesus identified himself as this figure; powerfully influenced by apocalypticism, he was nevertheless not an apocalyptist in the sense that he did not engage in the usual speculations of apocalypticism, but saw himself as the eschatological suffering servant of Deutero-Isaiah.

There were two periods in Jesus' ministry — before and after Caesarea-Philippi — one when he did not speak of his messiahship and another in which he did, to his disciples. The Transfiguration followed (a historical element, perhaps, confirmation by vision of Peter's confession), then came the decision to go to Jerusalem, where Jesus was given eschatological acclaim (as the prophet of the eschatological kingdom); his attack on the temple aroused the suspicion of the authorities who delivered him to the political powers. His confession before the Sanhedrin is genuine (it could not have been invented, for it did not happen), though some Son of man sayings go back to an original "I," a fact obscured by later tradition. Jesus thought he would be exalted through his death to God and become the Son of man.

But the suffering messiah was the great new thing introduced by Christ and combined with the Son of man idea — an idea the disciples failed to grasp. The Son of man's suffering death would bring reconciled individuals into covenant with God, which also signified their belonging to the kingdom of God. Similarly, the last supper contained an eschatological act of the Son of man (though the supper was actually a chaburah meal). At the supper Jesus blessed the cup, gave the bread and uttered the saying about his body broken for "you," that is, his body broken in death. The rest was added later by the church as it converted the meal into a sacramental observance. The cup of blessing (*kos bel berakah*) promised the disciples a place in the kingdom and a share in his expiatory suffering, thus deepening the fellowship meal. The church extended that still further, emphasizing the original element of forgiveness that Jesus expected as a consequence of his redemptive suffering. There were still later developments, such as likening the cup to the blood of Jesus.

The last part of the work extended the understanding of Jesus as a charismatic evangelist. Jesus was a charismatic figure, as can be shown in his healings, his foretellings (seer), his exorcisms and prophecy; his impact was like that of a hagiographic figure (a "holy" man). There are examples in the history of religions (Islam, sufis). Otto cited the story of Jesus' walking on the sea; it is to be seen as an apparition, as the disciples' vision of Jesus as he also contemplated them in their danger and fear, thus "appearing" to be with them and comforting them. It was a psychic phenomenon not unknown elsewhere.

That Otto's work should be seen as moving "against skepticism" is certainly no accident,[17] for it not only found more in the Jesus tradition than Bultmann seemed to, but it also took a deliberately different tack, one implicitly and sometimes explicitly critical of Bultmann. Even if the peculiar source theory is bracketed out,[18] there remain affirmations not usually found at Marburg: the insistence on the kingdom as a reality beyond individual experience, as something already experienceable in the present, as having a cosmic, eschatological dimension that cannot be reduced to the decision of persons in a moment of crisis. All that resonated especially among English-language readers, as did the combination of suffering servant and Son of man attributed to Jesus. None of it, of course, registered with Bultmann, who continued to maintain his own understanding of kingdom as primarily *Gottesherrschaft*, as he had used it in his Jesus book, which faces every person with a crisis that summons to decision, a kingdom that cannot be said to be present, though it is so near as to determine the present. Nor could Bultmann accept the combination of suffering servant and Son of man as authentic to Jesus; as to the really new thing in Otto's presentation, the derivation of Jesus' understanding of himself from Enoch, that was a "complete illusion."[19]

In fact, the debate going on there was really moving on different levels. It seemed on the surface to be a historical debate about the message of Jesus and about what kind of figure Jesus actually was. At bottom it was about the application of the categories of existence to the entire presentation of Jesus in Bultmann

---

17. Heinrich Frick's characterization in his review, "Wider die Skepsis in der Leben-Jesu-Forschung: R. Otto's Jesus-Buch," *ZTK*, n.f. 16 (1935): 1–20. Frick found Otto's work compelling.

18. Bultmann rightly criticized Otto at this point in his own extensive review in *TRu*, n.f. 9 (1937): 1–35, though acknowledging nevertheless that the work should be evaluated on its other major points.

19. Ibid., 22.

and whether that process did not, in fact, produce a distortion in the picture of Jesus. In Otto's view it did, but, of course, for Bultmann some such "translation" of the message of Jesus becomes necessary in the "modern" world if anyone is to make sense of it and find it still useful. Otto emphasized that the kingdom was already breaking into the present, a marvelous entity (*Wunderding*). Understood this way, said Bultmann, it would be an illusion; it did not come, and Jesus' effect in the present would be not the *Wunderding* but an illusionary faith in the *Wunderding*.[20]

Nothing is ever exactly what it seems to be when it comes to theological debates; the actual issue was the hermeneutical one, but to attend to the arguments gives the impression of watching two parallel lines unfold.

Martin Dibelius

Martin Dibelius also contributed a modest volume on Jesus at the end of the decade.[21]

He began by raising the question of the relation between faith and history. In his work the two are separated, except that they may be combined in the same person [no doubt autobiographical]. But generally faith's assertions cannot be proved, though faith need not fear the work of historical science. The New Testament remains the humanly conditioned deposit of an event.

As to the sources, the non-Christian evidence provides little information. The gospels remain the best sources. They were not written by authors, but editors (here Dibelius reproduced essentially what he had written in the *Formgeschichte*). The two-document theory is presupposed. With respect to criteria of authenticity: Jesus spoke Aramaic, so his words were translated. That was a multiple process — it produced different versions; this strengthens the tradition. Further, Paul and others had a different thought world; thus where its evidence is lacking there is more confidence in the primitiveness of the tradition. And then occasionally there may be sayings taken over from the proverbial wisdom of Judaism; but the main thing is that we have to do with nongenuine sayings "only where the later circumstances, conditions, or problems of the already existing Church are clearly presupposed" (26).

A biography is not possible; there are only individual incidents, no reliable chronology, and there is a connected story only in the passion narrative. The "paradigms" are especially the repositories of the oldest traditions, since they served the preaching function of the community.

---

20. See ibid., 34–35.

21. Martin Dibelius, *Jesus*, Sammlung Göschen 1130 (Berlin: Walter de Gruyter, 1939). English trans. *Jesus*, trans. Charles B. Hedrick and Frederick C. Grant (Philadelphia: Westminster Press, 1949). References are to the English version. Worthy of mention also is Dibelius's *Gospel Criticism and Christology* (London: Ivor Nicholson and Watson, 1935), which insisted on the need for both gospel criticism and the christological confession of the church. See also his *The Message of Jesus*, trans. Frederick C. Grant (London: Nicholson and Watson, 1939). German original in 1935. It is a presentation of the relevant texts — paradigms, parables, tales, miracle stories, legends — offered in a new translation and accompanied by commentary.

As had come to be typical in a Jesus-presentation, Dibelius then characterized the background in Judaism — land and people. There was greater Greek influence in Galilee. (Here Dibelius noted a tendency to doubt Jesus' pure Jewish blood, which he rejected; "a doubt — nothing more," he said [42].) He spoke of Judaism as having greatly narrowed its conception of God in the hellenistic era: "The Lord of all peoples had become the party leader of the legalists; obedience to the ruler of history had become a finespun technique of piety" (43). Pharisees and scribes advanced that view. He described the parties or sects and general messianic hopes (Son of man conception).

John the Baptist inaugurated the movement. The question of chronology is difficult; Jesus probably died about 27–34, probably in 30 or 33. The Baptist appeared in 27–29. He was an eschatological preacher; Jesus' association with that movement is genuine, as was his baptism, though we do not know what it meant. It could not have been invented. It was likely a sign that the kingdom was drawing near, as was John's imprisonment. Jesus began a new movement, whose content was preaching of the kingdom, especially its nearness. It was an eschatological and messianic movement, without politics. Jesus went to Jerusalem to face the country with the ultimate verdict, the realization of the kingdom.

The kingdom of God is God's rule in the last days, his kingship. It embraces the whole cosmos, not some special territory. Nor is it something that grows, but it is brought about by God's power. It has drawn near, so that its signs can be seen. It is in the process of coming and has already been set in motion, but Dibelius stopped short of saying it was actually present. Jesus himself is the sign of the kingdom; the signs are among you, in your midst; they are Jesus and his deeds and message. So the exorcisms and healings — these "miracles" — are signs of the kingdom. Of course, Dibelius only admitted psychic healings and little else.

How did Jesus see himself? The evidence — the messianic entrance, the crucifixion, his action in the temple, the last supper — suggests a messianic self-evaluation. Jesus must have put forth a claim to be the Anointed, that is, that he would become God's future messiah and so knew himself to be the chosen One already when he entered the city. That gives credence to Peter's earlier confession. There was also available at that time the twofold notion of the Son of man as an exalted figure, but also as already concealed with God in heaven only to be revealed at the end of the ages. This provided a vehicle for Jesus to express his conviction of being the messiah-in-concealment now, and the glorious one to come in the future (as Son of man). The supper also suggests that possession of the rank of Son of man carried with it the thought of necessary suffering for Jesus, but that is somewhat of a supposition. Yet what remained decisive for Jesus was that he himself was the sign of the kingdom; his rank as messiah was to be hidden for a time in spite of his signs and deeds.

The teaching of Jesus is embodied significantly in the Sermon on the Mount, a collection of scattered sayings. Jesus gave no new law and remained within the framework of his people and their religion. Yet these ordinances of the old Jewish religion became for Jesus a means of disclosing the signs of the new, showing how people should behave in the face of the God who is coming. There was to be no more fasting, washing, meticulous sabbath observance; one must be ready for the kingdom. The kingdom alone is the goal, and it demands radical obedience. "Therefore all values, treasures, and goals belonging to the realm of politics, of civilization, of human society, sink out of sight" (110). Yet asceticism was no end in itself, even though Jesus expected total renunciation.

Yet Jesus differed from the legal religion in that now God's entering into the world calls into question the whole Jewish system of commandments and prohibitions. Humans stand now and always before God, which renders relative all other systems. Jesus' commands are not an interim ethic, even though they cannot be completely fulfilled before the time of the End, but only after the kingdom has come. There is thus a new existence to be lived now, characterized by faith, love, and prayer.

Jesus' message, said Dibelius, "kept within the frame of Judaism" (124). Yet Jesus' message, so radically proclaimed, devalued all other duties, such as ritual, legal, and nationalistic ones. He broke the sabbath, declined to fast, agreed in a duty to Caesar (but a greater to God), and his future expectation stood in sharpest contrast to the "system that is built on a give-and-take between God and men in the present" (125). Even the nation was not exempt; the Jews were like the guests invited to the banquet, but excused themselves (Luke 14:18). The message provoked hostility from the Jews: Jesus did not derive his teaching from the Bible, but spoke on his own authority. Such was heresy, even blasphemy. He also threw people out of the temple. The threat to the authorities led them to act against Jesus; probably John has the chronology right, with Passover on the Sabbath and Jesus' death the day before. We do not know about Judas's betrayal; probably he only betrayed Jesus' location. The Old Testament has contributed much to the story; the last words of Jesus are from Psalm 22. The last supper was not a Passover, but the founding of a new fellowship with its words about the bread and the cup, and in that sense it can be said that Jesus founded the church.

Jews did not have the right to carry out an execution then, so they had to turn Jesus over to Pilate; he was charged with being a political pretender and died as such.

And what of the Easter faith? The tomb stories are not the oldest tradition, but it can be said that "something happened" to the disciples after they fled. This "something" is the kernel of the Easter faith. It happened first to Peter. The disciples had to calculate that if Jesus were to come again as Son of man, he would have to be raised from the dead. So Dibelius seemed tempted by some such logical postulate, but did not evidently wish to derive the Easter faith from the Son of man expectation. He also mentioned that the last supper witnesses to an expectation on Jesus' part that he would drink anew in the kingdom, from which the disciples could have supposed that Jesus did not remain dead.

Was Jesus mistaken? If apocalyptic expectation is of the essence, we may have to say that Jesus was mistaken. But, in fact, it was not in the foreground for Jesus; what mattered was that Jesus proclaimed the radical claim of God and himself as the genuine sign of the kingdom. Whether this actuality exists is the question, and that remains a matter of faith, of decision. The meaning of the eschatology is that believers are in the world between the occurrence of the kingdom's coming (future) and its beginning in signs now, and therein lies the life of the Christian community. The history can be described to some degree and it is a responsibility of faith to do so as accurately as possible, but the recognition of the event and its actuality is the decision of faith or unfaith.

In any number of ways Dibelius was a little bit of the German version of the English scholar-theologian, practicing the most stringent kinds of criticism while also maintaining a visible degree of piety. He felt constrained to set forth his theological credentials as perhaps a prop against the right and necessity of criticism. In this respect he differed from Bultmann, who was content to allow his criticism to carry him wherever it would.

As to some particulars, Dibelius emphasized more Jesus as the "sign" of the kingdom, without going quite so far as to say that the kingdom was actually present. There was a greater willingness to make judgments about Jesus' own evaluation of himself, along with a Bultmann-like insistence on the decisional element in Jesus' demand. There was also still this ambiguous characterization of Judaism; Jesus came from Judaism, was a Jew, and remained within Judaism. Yet at the same time he went beyond it, differed from it, and even surpassed it in some sense. And that same Judaism continued to be set out in terms of an overbearing legalism against which Jesus protested and stirred up enemies who helped to do him in. Certainly Dibelius in this respect was no innovator, but did reproduce the conventional wisdom of the day.

In Great Britain

The English continued to press studies of the historical Jesus with a certain steadiness and, unlike their American counterparts, had more to show in the way of "lives" for the decade we are considering. A major work of T. W. Manson, while not a life of Jesus, deserves some consideration for its special perspective and methodology.[22]

T. W. Manson

The introduction set out the assumptions: presumed was the four-source theory of B. H. Streeter, with accompanying origins: Mark at Rome, Q at Antioch, M at Jerusalem, L at Caesarea. Mark was given preference as source as far as the

---

22. T. W. Manson, *The Teaching of Jesus: Studies of Its Form and Content* (Cambridge: University Press, 1931; 2d ed., 1935; pbk., 1963). There was a common practice then of treating the "life" of Jesus separately from the "teaching" of Jesus, but our purposes are better served by taking them together.

outline goes, with special importance devoted to Caesarea-Philippi (Peter's Confession, or "PC," as Manson abbreviated it); it is the "turning point" in the life of Jesus, marking the close of one period and the beginning of another. Manson further saw three delineateable streams of audiences with appropriate kinds of sayings addressed to each: those to hostile crowds, such as scribes and Pharisees (designated P, for polemical), those to larger groups of people (G, general), and those to the disciples (D, disciples). Manson conducted his research around these groups, noticing a difference in the nature of the words addressed to each both before and after Peter's Confession. Appendices summed up the research statistically, giving the words and phrases appropriate to each.

In a more extended discussion of the sources Manson accepted the Papias testimony about Mark as something like an objective account, or at least a dependable one ("Mk is a simple objective record of word and deed" [43]); Q likely comes from Papias's reference to the Logia; M is a very Jewish source from Palestine; while L is Luke's special material from Caesarea. Manson accepted Streeter's Proto-Luke theory,[23] compounded of Q+L, and later enlarged by infancy narratives plus insertions from Mark. Each of these sources was analyzed in terms of its proportions of P, G, and D material, and especially before and after Caesarea-Philippi, or before and after PC, to use Manson's terminology. Manson was of the opinion that M was to be used with caution, reflecting many tendencies and differences from Mark and Q; L was possibly derived from oral tradition but nevertheless contained very good material. The *Urmarkus* theory, said Manson, was discredited.

The teachings were originally in Aramaic and used poetic parallelism (Robert Lowth, C. F. Burney) and parables. The parable is to be understood as *mashal* (not as in Aristotle, comparison); it can be aphorism, byword, or popular wisdom. So a parable is "a literary creation in narrative form designed either to portray a type of character for warning or example or to embody a principle of God's governance of the world and men."[24] It intends to be understood and to communicate some religious insight or to stimulate the conscience. Examples of ethical ones would be the vineyard workers, pounds, and good Samaritan; some dealing with God's rule would be the mustard seed, leaven, and wheat and tares. The parable was not something to replace rational discourse, but was a mode of religious experience. The Markan saying that parables were meant to deceive was treated at length, with Manson appealing to the Targumic version of Isa. 6:9, and claiming that what Jesus meant was that everything comes to nondisciples in parables who see and hear but do not understand, for if they did they would repent and receive forgiveness. But Manson did appreciate the aesthetic quality of parables; they are works of art, word-pictures, embodying the ethical or something about the rule of God in the world.

The teaching of Jesus starts with the Fatherhood of God. That was not new

---

23. Below, chap. 8, 298.
24. Manson, *Teaching of Jesus*, 65.

with Jesus, but very much at the core for him. Manson noted that all cases of Father in Mark come after PC; he thought that the same could be inferred from Q (because it is that way in Luke who has the better order of Q). The same is true in L, but it is harder to say about M since most of M comes from the Sermon on the Mount, which has no particular order. There was great reserve on Jesus' part in speaking of God as Father; it was not a commonplace, but lay at the core of his religious experience. It was therefore too sacred to be uttered very much in public, though it was given to the disciples in private (Matt. 11:27=Luke 10:22, the relation of Son to Father; similarly in the Lord's Prayer).

As to God as king, Manson rejected both liberalism and thoroughgoing eschatology. The kingdom was not a social state produced either mechanically or evolutionarily. Manson analyzed his sources again, finding once more a division of pre- and post-PC. Before PC Jesus spoke of the kingdom coming, while afterwards he spoke of entering the kingdom. The same could be seen in the kinds of audiences: before PC words were addressed to G, afterwards to D. So in his later ministry Jesus began to speak of the kingdom as something to be entered. [Now and then Manson had to rid himself of problems and exceptions, such as Luke 7:28=Matt. 11:11, which is said to be likely out of place and belong in a later context.] All four sources (Mark, Q, M, L) support the same phenomenon, though M also had entrance sayings scattered all along. But M is not so good as the others. The significance of this difference is that Peter's Confession meant that now Jesus himself was to be recognized as the coming of the kingdom, that is, in his person is the kingdom coming now. Therefore the kingdom is a personal relation between king and subject: "The claim on God's part to rule, and the acknowledgment on man's part of the claim, together constitute the actual Kingdom: and Peter's Confession may fairly be regarded as just that acknowledgment that was needed to make the Kingdom *de jure* into a Kingdom *de facto*" (131). In this sense the kingdom is something spiritual and may be said to grow and develop, that is, extend its influence. Therefore also the kingdom appears in society, among people.

But there is also a further, final manifestation of the kingdom. There is no point in asking whether it is present or future; it is a personal relation, independent of temporal relations. It is the reign of God and it has these three components: an eternal fact, a manifestation in the present life of people, and a consummation still to come. Much of the rest of the book explicates these three points.

Manson traced the historical roots of the notion of God's sovereignty in the Old Testament, Judaism, and the rabbinic and apocalyptic material. The last is response to the theodicy problem: "Food for the fed-up" (150), built on dualism, the struggle of good and evil, God and Satan, derived from Persian influence, nationalistic but also later universal. There was nothing very original with Jesus here, but he experienced the sovereignty of God very intensely. The notion of God as king lay at the core of Jesus' life experience (just as fatherhood did; the two are the same). Jesus urged and preached decision, for or against God.

The end result is assured; God is sovereign, but men must decide. The kingship of God is also manifest in the world. Already in Israel God was king. Not all could accept God's rule, so a doctrine of the Remnant arose. Manson traced this idea through Elijah and Isaiah; it represented the individualizing of religion. It is also to be seen in Deuteronomy, and especially in Deutero-Isaiah as the servant who would be the community as saving Remnant and in Ezekiel as the restored people who enjoy salvation. There were two streams here, with Ezekiel representing the prototype of "strict Judaism" and Deutero-Isaiah that of "Evangelical Christianity" (181). Thereafter there is a saving Remnant or a saved Remnant, one leading to Pharisaism and the other to the apostolic message. So the kingdom of God is a remnant community, those who are God's people; in Pharisaism it is those who show their belongingness by their obedience to the Law. The kingdom now is a community acknowledging God as king; he would be their protector, guide, and legislator, and they would live in complete trust in and obedience to him.

Jesus accepted the kingdom in his own person; he was completely obedient, trusting in God. Again PC is decisive. The teaching goes in a new direction thereafter. The disciples are given more: the Son of man title is used, the kingdom is something entered. Before PC Jesus was seeking moral and religious insight, and getting the disciples to understand what was going on; he got it at Caesarea-Philippi and now expected confession to him as messiah. He then went to Jerusalem, not to compel anything by his death, but to deliver men from sin and make a final attack on Satan. Now also he spoke with more authority; for example, his use of "amen" was more pronounced after PC. He went to Jerusalem to make a religious revolution, to call men to belong to the kingdom, and to attack all institutions that inhibit that. That he went to die is correct, but the first and decisive battle was for the kingdom of the messiah and against the forces of evil. Thus Peter's Confession was the "watershed of the Gospel history" and it may be said that it "has changed the whole course of the world's history" (210).

What about the Son of man title? Jesus certainly used it. The analyzing of sources shows that most of the sayings fall after PC. Some may be eliminated as a periphrasis for "man," some are secondary (e.g., Matt. 13:37, 41), leaving two classes, the suffering sayings and the Parousia sayings. Manson argued that Son of man is the final term in a series of such, like Remnant, servant, the "I" of certain Psalms, and the Son of man from Daniel [he rejected Enoch as a source]. The Son of man is like the servant, an image for the ideal people of the kingdom, and restricted to Jesus himself as a result of his own ministry, which was to form the ideal people. Jesus himself embodied the people; he embodied the servant of Jehovah as Son of man. What Jesus thought was that he and his disciples would share that destiny as the collective Son of man, the saving Remnant. Unfortunately, the disciples failed. So at the end only Jesus was the Son of man and servant, the "incarnation of the Kingdom of God on earth" (235).

There was also an eschatological hope. The eschatological kingdom arises through the disparity between what is and what ought to be, given faith in a righteous God, and the nature of this hope depends upon the nature of the faith in God. Manson illustrated from the history of Israel. The difference between prophecy and apocalyptic, he said, was that in prophecy the destiny of Israel was a private matter between the nation and its God, whereas in apocalyptic the destiny of the nation was involved with the destiny of the whole world and the war between cosmic forces of good and evil. What about the teaching of Jesus? We cannot begin with Mark's apocalypse, for it contains community material; we begin with Q and the sayings about the coming Son of man (=Jesus and his body of believers, with the Parousia as the elevation of them to world power). That did not quite happen; Jesus became in himself alone the Son of man. He embodied the people, the Remnant; he became the Son of man–messiah. His coming will then be a drastic revolution, will bring judgment, with all persons judged by their attitude to Jesus as Son of man. It is probable that Jesus expected this Parousia to take place in the near future.

A final chapter summed up ethics and religion in Jesus. The teaching all goes together, so Manson thought. The morals explicate life in the kingdom. The conflicts with scribes are between the prophetic and the legal; the former was concerned with persons, the latter with acts. Jesus was concerned with changing persons inside, with individuals; his was not a plan of social reform. The Law was concerned with the nation as a whole; Jesus was concerned with the heart of the individual as the source of action. The Pharisees opposed him with all their might because of this difference. Jesus' teaching meant revolution, not reform. Manson's summary of the difference: "For Jesus good living is the spontaneous activity of a transformed character; for the Scribes and Pharisees it is obedience to a discipline imposed from without" (300). Or "For Judaism good conduct is a part of religion; for Jesus it is a product of religion" (305). The heart of it for Jesus was the twofold love commandment. Jesus also stressed repentance because of his insistence on the internal transformation. Forgiveness is necessary, as is also the practice of forgiving others.

It was a strange work in many ways. There were valuable insights into specific texts, and there was originality in the interpretation of such difficult subjects as the Son of man. There was a great confidence in the reliability of the gospel material, though not without criticism. There was nothing whatsoever about Form Criticism, and the whole structure falls apart if something like K. L. Schmidt's work be conceded, that is, that the Markan framework has only a literary value. Certainly Wrede got no notice from Manson. There was also a remarkable investment in the source analysis and "Audience Criticism," only in the latter instance for Manson the allusions to the audiences are historically accurate. In fact, there is a certain charm to the way in which Manson spun his web, if only so much of his work did not sound like fiction. It seems not yet to have occurred to him that everything on which he built up his case (before and after PC, audience references) is, at best, derived from Markan or Lukan or another's editorial labors.

Major-Manson-Wright

Another English work, in which Manson also participated, was issued in 1938 as the joint work of H. D. A. Major, T. W. Manson, and C. J. Wright.[25] It was not really a life of Jesus, but a kind of commentary on gospel texts [the Fourth Gospel was also included, but we exclude that section and thus also Wright's contribution in this review]. There are, however, some essays that focused on the issue of the life of Jesus and, especially, the methodology in pursuit of that quest. The work purported, in the introduction, to promote understanding of the gospels among the ordinary people — a serious ambition, given the substantial length of the work (958 pages); evidently it was meant to be a handbook to be kept and consulted as necessary.

The introduction, by Major, urged a study that is open to literary and historical criticism, but also "sensitive and reverent in the spheres of moral and spiritual truth." The four-source theory would be presupposed. Then Major raised questions about the historical validity of the gospels, giving the responses of various "schools," such as the Christ-myth theories, Form Criticism, Jesus-as-a-prophet school, and the eschatological school. The first was dismissed, the second more involved: Mark was in this view a bead-stringer, attaching units of oral tradition to a narrative string, but the string had no value. Major emphatically disagreed; Mark provides "a generally reliable guide" and while the gospels are mainly a church record, they also have *"a solid basis in historic fact"* (italics his). Shirley Jackson Case was cited as the prominent example of the Jesus-as-a-prophet school, with which Major disagreed, claiming instead that Jesus' ministry was messianic and that no other explanation fit the facts (why would the disciples be disillusioned over the death of a prophet?). The messianic secret is original. As to the eschatological school, Major was uncomfortable with a strictly or exclusively apocalyptic messiah (apocalyptic writings were "bright tracts for dark times"); not all apocalyptic sayings are authentic, and Jesus' Father-God cannot be the "avenging Deity of the apocalyptists." Jesus also filled the messianic belief with new meanings; he did not hold to "crude apocalyptic conceptions." And Jesus was a religious genius; to attribute borrowed apocalyptic ideas to him deprives him of his originality. This originality is to be understood not so much in the actual content of what Jesus said, but in the things he emphasized and the meanings he gave to old terms, as well as the new spirit he imparted (his personality evoked the spirit of faith, hope, and love). It is also, finally, not only critical knowledge of Jesus that matters, but the recognition of his impact on western civilization.[26] The work then moved into a commentary on incidents in Jesus' life, following largely Mark's outline, with references to Matthew and Luke. As examples, on the temptation: Jesus possessed a messianic consciousness, but did not proclaim it; he only gradually unveiled it. On the kingdom at

---

25. H. D. A. Major, T. W. Manson, and C. J. Wright, *The Mission and Message of Jesus: An Exposition of the Gospels in the Light of Modern Research* (New York: E. P. Dutton, 1938, 1946).

26. Ibid., xiv, xxii–xxv.

hand: the kingdom is not apocalyptic, but comes by individuals doing the will of God. "When the individual does that he enters into the Kingdom: the Kingdom has come in his heart" (38).

The second book, by T. W. Manson, dealt with the "Sayings of Jesus," though here Manson did not repeat his source and audience analysis. In fact, he sounded very much more like he had experienced a kind of conversion, attending more to the formation of the tradition in its oral stage. The words of Jesus, he said, were preserved orally because of pastoral needs in the church (training new converts and the like), though there was also a biographical interest (treasuring Jesus' words; like preserving a prophet's words) and a propaganda value (addressing persons in the larger society, as did Jewish and Stoic propagandists). Finally also the words of Jesus had value as response to Judaism, as the needs of the palestinian church to reply to its Jewish critics and to demonstrate that it was not a subversive or heretical movement. Of these motives, the first was the most powerful [here Manson sounded a little like Dibelius, except that he did not especially emphasize the preaching function].

Manson took Jesus to be something like a professional scribe, suggesting that he was seen by his opponents as an equal in his scholastic debates. Jesus spoke Aramaic, though he also knew and used Hebrew in his contests with the learned scribes. He wrote nothing; all came from oral tradition, with sometimes ordinary people remembering what he said and did, though mainly it was his own disciples who preserved his teaching. This oral recollection issued at first in small collections on various subjects, grouped by subject or catchword; then missionary needs led to larger groupings and translation into Greek (the Palestinian church formed larger groupings in its controversies, such as Q, M, and maybe L). Then finally came the gospels based on these collections (if Streeter's Proto-Luke theory is correct, then Q+L antedates Mark). The editorial methods of Matthew and Luke can be discerned by studying their treatment of Mark (Matthew conflates, while Luke selects).

The teaching falls into various forms: dialogue, pronouncement stories (Taylor), poetry, metaphor, simile, allegory, parable. The latter is the *mashal*, "nothing but an extended simile or metaphor" (325). There has to be an analogy between what is narrated and what the parable intends to explain. Usually there is only one point, but there may also be subsidiary ones. The allegory is a coded story; the story may have nothing to do with the lessons being taught. The parable is meant "to create trust in God and love to man by an appeal to conscience and insight, while the allegory is meant to convey information, stimulating interest by an appeal to the imagination" (327). Allegory probably comes not from Jesus but some later hand.

Manson offered some comments on the continuing value of Jesus' teaching, observing, contra Schweitzer, that the ethic was not interim; Jesus meant to give a direction, people acting so that their wills were harmonious with the will of God. The substance of this section was then taken up with commentary on the material in Q, M, and L.

Taken as a whole, the work looks a little like chastened liberalism. Form Criticism had had impact, but had not dislodged the idea that much could still be known about Jesus, that the sources remained basically sound. The apocalyptic Jesus had had his impact as well, but he seemed to be an unwelcome guest. Apocalypticism was something not devoutly to be wished — a deterioration, a decline from prophecy. It appears to have little coinage in the theological marketplace and accordingly had to be devalued. The interim ethic found the door closed altogether; a Jesus propounding that notion would have to be relegated to the dark closet of history, forever barred from entering the door of the modern world. And a nonmessianic Jesus would similarly be useless; he could not contain within himself *in nuce* the whole of Christian faith, and might well contradict it. That would be an abhorrence not lightly tolerated.

Such seem to be some of the issues underlying the presentation of Jesus in this work. Yet it would be unkind not to recognize also the seriousness of the scholarship and the depth of the learning. There is a huge fund of information and knowledge embodied in this collaborative book; that it was driven by an earnest piety does not diminish its force and impressiveness.

James MacKinnon

The Scotsman James MacKinnon produced his *The Historic Jesus* very much still along the lines of classical liberal lives as modified in the Scottish-English tradition.[27] "Historic" Jesus in the author's view referred to Jesus back then, with "Jesus of history" describing his continuing influence — much the opposite of the usual practice. Form Criticism, or *Traditionsgeschichte* as MacKinnon rightly called it (xii), would not be of much help in constructing the picture. It was too arbitrary and eliminated too much; instead a "cautious and judicial criticism" would be employed (xiii).

The virgin birth story is a legend and there are legendary features elsewhere in the birth stories, but some genuine elements survive (Anna, Simeon). The magi are legendary. Jesus was born 4–8 B.C.E. The background was sketched out: Galilee as affluent, a mixture of Judeans and Greeks, full of social and political unrest. The story of Jesus in Jerusalem at the age of 12 is historical. He had likely studied the Law and knew other literature like Enoch and the *Testament of the Twelve Patriarchs*. The parables are especially good windows onto his world and reflect a Jesus who was moved by nature and had the instinct of a poet. Galilee also fostered a more independent spirit toward conventional religion, though Jesus remained a Hebrew untouched by the Greeks. His religious views focused on God as Father and humanity's filial relation to him. He thought of himself as messiah, but not the nationalistic one. He was too "spiritually minded to concern himself with the crass politics of the time" (49) and was interested in the moral and spiritual. At the age of 26 he encountered the old prophet John the Baptist,

---

27. James MacKinnon, *The Historic Jesus* (London: Longmans, Green, 1931). MacKinnon was Regius Professor of Ecclesiastical History at the University of Edinburgh.

who also was not a political figure, but emphasized judgment, while Jesus came to speak of the Father-God. They only agreed on the idea of the coming new theocracy and the nonpolitical kingdom.

Jesus experienced his messianic call at his baptism, though it was an experience he kept to himself. The temptation shows his struggle over his vocation. He returned to Galilee and worked in the towns and villages for a time. Even though Mark's account is not ordered and had the purpose of serving mission preaching, of edification, we can still gain an outline of stages in the ministry from it (part of it comes from Peter). Jesus drew crowds in Galilee, but also suffered opposition from scribes and Pharisees as well as Herod, which forced him into a retreat. Caesarea-Philippi followed, the turning-point in his life. He foresaw his coming doom, but went on to Jerusalem anyway, to seal his mission through sacrifice and suffering.

The ministry lasted just over a year; Jesus appeared first as a prophet and only indirectly was messianic. The messiahship was veiled, for fear of misunderstanding. His mission aimed especially at the poor and the lowly. Jesus also healed as well as taught; he came not to overthrow Caesar, but to wage war on evil. He contested the formalism of the Pharisees. MacKinnon acknowledged the reshaping of Pharisaism going on among people like Montefiore, Herford, Friedländer, and Klausner,[28] but still found a contest over legalism. The predictions of the passion are genuine, though shaped by the later church. Jesus retained the apocalyptic sense of the kingdom, but thought that the kingdom in the ethical and spiritual sense was already being established. In the last days he assumed the role of the suffering messiah. The cleansing of the temple was the fateful event, along with his messianic claim. The assertion of his authority led the authorities to determine to kill him. His spiritual view of the kingdom ran contrary to that of the people. Jesus had no politics: "In this modern age of raging nationalism, which has periodically drenched the world in blood, it is not without a poignant interest that the greatest of religious teachers calmly ignored it."[29]

Jesus also claimed the title of Son of man, which he combined with suffering servant, an "absolutely original" fusion (195). Jesus still held to the apocalyptic expectation but emphasized the kingdom as ethical and spiritual. His ethics were not interim, but his expectation of a near Parousia was wrong and a relic of a bygone era, the husk in which he clothed his message. At the last supper Jesus spoke words of sacrifice and suffering, anticipating a new covenant, the kingdom, and continuing fellowship. The foot-washing from John is likely authentic, an enacted parable of service. The Johannine discourses are "well invented" if not genuine (234). Gethsemane reflects reality. The trial problems were dismissed, since the times, according to MacKinnon, were extraordinary and justified irregularities. Essentially both the Jews and Pilate played a role in Jesus' condemnation, though it was Pilate's sentence that was carried out. The

---

28. On the Jewish interpreters see chap. 7.
29. MacKinnon, *The Historic Jesus*, 184.

disciples' experience of appearances of Jesus after his death demonstrated the power of his personality.

MacKinnon accepted healings and tended to rationalize the nature miracles (walking on water was an optical illusion, people shared what they had at the feedings, Jairus's daughter was in a swoon, the widow's son at Nain was a case of suspended animation). Old Paulus would have recognized it all. As to originality, MacKinnon acknowledged the widespread parallels to Jesus' teaching in Judaism, but claimed that Jesus nevertheless stamped his own genius on it, especially in matters of religious prejudice, the challenge to legalism, the righteousness of the heart, the appeal to the outcast, and above all in his own distinctive religious experience. He was a "creative religious genius" (307). His messianic consciousness, however, did not mean he held a divine consciousness; he was capable of error. Yet even the resurrection faith "would hardly have been possible without the historic personality that underlay it" (380).

A. C. Bouquet

A. C. Bouquet produced a "new estimate" of Jesus in 1933,[30] though the new part seems to be an acknowledged modernist perspective, accompanied by an explicit refusal of Form Criticism. Aimed primarily at educated laity the book first traces the Old Testament and the prophetic background, then characterizes the time of Jesus (legalism, hair splitting and petty regulations, life as stiff and wooden).

Jesus was born at Bethlehem in 6 B.C.E. and died in 29 C.E. The Passover visit to Jerusalem at age 12 is true. Likely Jesus experienced hellenistic influences. His message was the kingdom of God, God's rule, kingdom, or commonwealth. After his death the movement spread; its success was due to the personality of the Founder. No biography is possible. John the Baptist was an apocalyptic prophet preparing for the "man" (Son of man). Jesus differed from him in that he proclaimed a spiritual, not a nationalistic commonwealth. Nor was he ascetic. He emphasized the concept of God as father, but also as holy love, not like a typical parent of "modern decadent civilization" (78). The kingdom as a commonwealth of souls also had a social dimension; it was already present in Jesus, who was the very embodiment of it. Jesus' kingdom was different from what Jews expected; it was not nationalistic, not a "Sinn Fein republic" (84). Jesus was a suffering servant, a pacifist king, not individualistic, for humankind is a social animal. He did not found the church, but it is the instrument for the establishment of the kingdom. Yet Jesus said little about obligations to the state and confined himself to relations to the neighbor. His activity was limited to Jews, but he enlarged the definition of neighbor.

Women were elevated by Jesus; they were equal to men, not to be considered merely creatures of sex.

---

30. A. C. Bouquet, *Jesus: A New Outline and Estimate* (Cambridge: Heffner, 1933). Bouquet was Stanton Lecturer in the Philosophy of Religion in the University of Cambridge.

Not much was new in Jesus' proclamation, yet people were struck by its novelty. Jesus took current teaching and put new fire into it. He thought of himself as the messenger of Malachi 3 and the Son of man of Daniel 7.

Was Jesus a failure? His "pathetic death" (103) might suggest that his life-theory was a failure, but his greatness precludes that. He experienced sonship to God and thought of himself as Son of man at the end, when also he offered his own life for his cause and he himself became part of his legacy.

His ministry lasted less than two years. Caesarea-Philippi was the turning point; afterward he went to Jerusalem. He came at the end of the line of prophets, confident that his message would be heard. At first he had success (entrance, temple-cleansing), then the crowd turned against him. He was compelled by circumstances to change his mind, no longer certain of success. He did not advocate armed rebellion and doubted the Davidic ancestry of the messiah. On Thursday evening he held a Chaburah, performed the Kiddush, and spoke some words; it was not a Passover. The trial and death followed with surprisingly little description from Bouquet. There "remained only one loyal Christian in the world, and He was apparently dead."[31] The expected return of Jesus originated not with him, but with the early disciples. No modern Christian has to be burdened with this traditional form of belief. Individuals may still hold to hope and expect judgment.

Miracles were a problem in retelling Jesus' story. Jesus did some things, had some physical powers, but he deemphasized them, and so should we. We have to allow for "deductions" from the record.[32] Appendices on various theological issues completed the book.

F. C. Burkitt

F. C. Burkitt never quite composed a full life of Jesus, but he did provide an "outline," as he called it, in 1932.[33] Burkitt maintained a strong confidence in the Markan record, seeing in it genuine reminiscences from Mark (who appeared in the garden as the fleeing naked youth), using Peter's memories also, and what he, Mark, had heard as a boy in Jerusalem.

The background to Jesus lies in apocalyptic thought, which Burkitt called the "Good Time Coming" (6). It was not necessarily connected to the idea of the messiah, who only ruled, when he did, after the new age had been inaugurated.

John the Baptist was a hermit emphasizing moral conduct, and he baptized Jesus. That was for Jesus a powerful religious experience that drove him into the wilderness. The result of his temptation was negative; his course was unclear, and only clarified after John's death. Then Jesus spoke of the kingdom, the Good Time Coming, and sent out disciples. This was the earlier stage of his activity.

---

31. Ibid., 110. This came as an odd statement from Bouquet after he had begun his book with Wellhausen's dictum that "Jesus was not a Christian — he was a Jew" (1).

32. This use of "deductions" was a polite English way of acknowledging critical judgments about the text. It can be seen as far back as William Sanday's usage.

33. F. C. Burkitt, *Jesus Christ: An Historical Outline* (London: Blackie and Son, 1932).

His teaching was "new" more in his manner than its content. The interim ethic is correct. So Jesus urged a passive attitude: no resistance, the happiness of the poor, no rebellion against Rome, giving to anyone who asks.

The kingdom is the rule of God the Father. Fatherhood had a special vividness for Jesus; he urged confidence in an affectionate Father. There was conflict with Pharisees, who saw religion as a code, whereas Jesus followed conscience, identified as the will of God. Jesus also was a healer, even if we allow for exaggeration. He was probably surprised by his own healings, as in Mark 1:21ff., where he commanded a deranged man to be silent. More healings followed.

Jesus expected the End, but it was delayed. His ministry was under two years, with the first year ending around Passover, followed by another year largely in retirement and ending with the journey to Jerusalem just before Passover.

Jesus' rift with the Pharisees rooted in historical reality; the Pharisees were too particular in their religion. Investigation of the Talmud shows that Jesus sometimes agreed with it and sometimes not, but in any case it is hard to know whether the Talmud accurately reflects pre-70 conditions. Yet there was undoubtedly a real hostility there.

The Markan parable theory stands; the mystery was that the kingdom was delayed and led to Jesus announcing later his suffering and then journeying to Jerusalem. John's inquiry to Jesus referred to Elijah. Jesus sent forth messengers — the disciples — who returned, but without the kingdom's coming. Thereafter Jesus withdrew for a time; here followed the feeding and storm stories. It was a period of nine months or so, including time outside Palestine. Afterwards Jesus had changed and determined to bring things to a crisis. So in his "retirement" period he came to a fuller knowledge of himself.

The "Son of man" is the messiah of supernatural character. The expression is Aramaic for "man" generally, or for a particular person obviously being referred to. There are sayings of this nature, but mostly the title refers to Daniel's or Enoch's "man." Jesus used it of the messiah-to-be; earlier he had told the disciples that they will not have gone through the cities of Israel before the Son of man has come (Matt. 10:23), but matters were different after Caesarea-Philippi and the title assumed a new value. Jesus went on to Jerusalem; his expectations and that of his disciples were different. They expected the kingdom to appear; Jesus likely did not exactly foresee his fate, yet even though he saw that his mission had little chance of success, he expected enough change for the prospect of longer term success. At least he had to risk failure and a violent death, else the new conditions could not happen. [Here Burkitt quoted Schweitzer on Jesus laying hold of the wheel of history.] Along the journey Jesus spoke of his death as a ransom; his death would be redemptive, hastening the new age. God called him to sacrifice everything for the kingdom. Here was something original with Jesus: his apocalyptic picture of the future included the reign of the Son of man, with himself as that Son of man, and especially new with him was his own life as a prologue, a life of service ending in death.

He entered Jerusalem amid shouts from his own disciples; he attacked the temple, threatening its destruction and rebuilding in three days. True worship needs little material support; Jesus put the focus on simplicity and the better intention, though he was not changing ritual or abolishing sacrifice. Nevertheless his act brought the authorities down on him. By Tuesday of the last week he had despaired of his hope; nothing had changed, but he did not advocate rebellion. He disappointed all elements: he was not the messiah and cast doubt on the Davidic ancestry of the messiah. The last supper shows that he had abandoned all hope for this life. The anointing by the woman was accepted "with grim humor" as "funeral care" (50). The chronological problem is conflicted, with Mark offering contradictory evidence. Mark 14:2 indicates the most likely scenario, that the last supper was not a Passover. [Here Burkitt was troubled as to how Peter could have been uncertain about the nature of the supper.] The story of the trial and arrest contains some genuine recollection (denials, Jesus' struggle — seen by a young Mark while the disciples slept), but the trial account is confused, and there were no followers present. It seems the Jewish authorities put a political coloring on Jesus in order to get the Roman government to agree to a death sentence. Jesus was passive and only assented to the idea of the Son of man coming on the clouds of heaven.

No disciples witnessed the crucifixion. Joseph's role is a puzzle. Was he a pious Jew like Tobit, burying corpses? As to the resurrection, it would be unscientific to write a life of Jesus and fail to consider it. Unlike other miracle stories the appearances had more than a transitory effect. They aroused the confidence that Jesus was still alive and speaking to the disciples. They occurred primarily at Jerusalem. Galilee never became Christian country.

Jesus fits no category, not sage, or teacher, or founder. He described himself as lighting a fire, and it still burns.

It is clear enough that Burkitt had imbibed deeply of the wine from Schweitzer's vineyard and, along with Warschauer, represented the perpetuation of Schweitzer's views in England. In this respect the customary accrediting of Jesus with an original combination of Son of man and suffering servant received a little different treatment, though was preserved in the works of Bouquet and MacKinnon and repeatedly elsewhere.[34] Burkitt's acceptance of the *Interimsethik* ran contrary to its almost universal rejection.

Jesus in France

We have heretofore had little occasion to notice French works, aside from Loisy, for no conspicuously significant degree of contribution emanated from that country, certainly nothing to compete with Renan. No doubt that was in part because the Protestant population of France was tiny and its scholarship similar, while Roman Catholic scholarship still labored under certain theological constraints

---

34. Vincent Taylor lent it normative expression about this time period with his *Jesus and His Sacrifice: A Study of the Passion-Sayings in the Gospels* (London: Macmillan, 1937, 1955).

that discouraged participation in the critical study of the life of Jesus, even though there was an abundance of Roman Catholic lives written in the period under consideration.[35] The major "lives" in this decade, however, came from two Frenchmen, Maurice Goguel and Ch. Guignebert,[36] both of whom had behind them a considerable body of work, some of which we will observe in another context.[37]

Maurice Goguel

The first part of Goguel's work (Prolegomena) was extensive, giving a history of research, and covering much of the territory already marched over more elo- quently by Schweitzer, with further reference to Renan and the French literature. The *formgeschichtliche Schule*, though "less original than it believes itself to be, and than it says it is," had concluded that the gospel framework was artificial and that the material in the gospels was simply produced to serve the life of the community.[38] The result was great skepticism about the possibility of composing a life of Jesus, and even the historicity of Jesus had come again under question in the person of P.-L. Couchoud.[39]

Goguel considered the sources (pagans, Pauline evidence, the synoptic prob- lem), characterizing each gospel with some redactional-critical remarks about the tendencies of each. Mark's plan is to be used with great caution, but there is valuable traditional material also in John. The apocryphal gospels cannot be used, the *Agrapha* only with care.

Goguel affirmed that the gospel tradition was by nature oral, but disagreed with Dibelius that anything like a *Biologie der Sage* could be constructed; there were only general facts, tendencies about this tradition, not laws. One should also be careful about claiming that the tradition was influenced by the cultus, which would be to explain one unknown by another. The only reliable method is to compare the narratives with one another and attempt to account for the differences in the texts. Form Criticism attempts a classification on the basis of types, which seems promising, but is in fact very arbitrary.

The tradition was preserved because of faith in the resurrection; the gos- pels were not produced until the Parousia hope began to wane and interest in the messianic element in Jesus' life was more emphasized. Thus a complex his- tory exists, but it is not impossible to reconstruct it. The form-critical school is

---

35. Some sampling is given below, chap. 8.

36. Goguel in *La Vie de Jésus* (Paris: Payot, 1932); English trans., *Jesus and the Origins of Christian- ity*, trans. Olive Wyon (New York: Macmillan, 1933). It was reprinted in 1960 as a Harper Torchbook in two volumes, with an introduction by C. Leslie Mitton. It is the latter that is used here. Earlier Goguel had provided an anticipation of his perspective in the essay, "The Problem of Jesus," *HTR* 23 (1930): 93–120. He sketched out the recent discussion, noticing the extreme scepticism, but thought it a passing stage. The study of Jesus should proceed from the teaching to the life, not vice-versa. Guignebert's work is referenced below, n. 44.

37. Below, chap. 8.

38. Goguel, *Jesus and the Origins of Christianity*, 58.

39. On Couchoud see below, chap. 8, 300–304.

right that the history has to be viewed from the perspective of the history of its tradition, but its approach is inadequate.

We do, however, need some criteria for distinguishing early from secondary elements in the tradition. We have to begin with an analysis of the different strata in the tradition, then estimate the value of that material. Goguel then laid down something like a criterion of dissimilarity, noting that whatever differs from the conceptions such as might be found in 1 Cor. 15:3–4, the creed of the earliest undifferentiated Christianity, would have to be seen as archaic tradition:

> Every time that we find, attributed to Jesus or recommended by him, an attitude which is contrary to that which is current in the very earliest form of the Church, there is room to suppose that we are in the presence of an historical fact.[40]

Thus the command to go nowhere among the Samaritans (Matt. 10:5) is authentic because it contradicts the church's practice; likewise the saying before the Sanhedrin (Mark 14:62) is authentic because it contains no reference to the resurrection. Sayings established this way may be used to establish others that are harmonious with these. Form also counts, that is, sayings of a certain form, Hebraic in character, such as parable and aphorisms, can be appealed to, though not absolutely. Having established the *facts* about Jesus, his sayings and deeds, one may then do the real work of the historian, which is to set things in their proper order and connection, to give psychological causes and the like, the work of a *life* of Jesus. This amounts to reproducing the state of mind of the figures of history; Jesus' career was driven by his thought and its development.[41]

This thought of Jesus is more accessible than his life. We must employ psychological conjecture and even intuition. We have to have something like the spirit of Jesus in order to understand Jesus.[42] It is also necessary to set that life in a wider context, namely, the ongoing history of the community, which Goguel promised to do in a subsequent volume.

Miracle is a special problem in itself. The criterion of credibility must apply; some things are no longer credible. Some come from the imagination of the narrators and some are by way of theological explanation (virgin birth, even the resurrection). No doubt Jesus did heal and cast out demons.

It is likely that Jesus died in the Passover of 28. The birth likely occurred sometime shortly before the death of Herod in March or April of 4 B.C.E. Goguel thought, largely on the basis of valid traditions in John, that the ministry of Jesus went as follows: at the end of the year 26 or the beginning of 27 Jesus went

40. Goguel, *Jesus and the Origins of Christianity*, 206.

41. Goguel's view here recalls the later English historian R. G. Collingwood, for whom the essence of historiography lay in rethinking the thoughts of historical agents. See *The Idea of History* (London: Oxford University Press, 1956).

42. Echoing Paul Wernle; cf. above, chap. 3, 90. Something similar was held by Bultmann in his notion of having a life-relation to the text as a presupposition of understanding (Dilthey). A clear instance was Bultmann's later essay, "Is Exegesis Without Presuppositions Possible?," in *Existence and Faith: Shorter Writings of Rudolf Bultmann*, trans. with an introduction by Schubert Ogden, Living Age Books (New York: Meridian, 1960).

to John the Baptist, left him in the spring of 27, and worked in Galilee until September. Then he left Galilee and went to Jerusalem, staying until December when he withdrew for a period of time away from Jerusalem; he then returned to Jerusalem on the eve of Passover in 28 and there met his end.

The birth stories have no value. We know of Jesus' family, his parents' names, and his sisters and brothers. The virgin birth is theological. Jesus spoke Aramaic, and it is doubtful he knew Greek or Hebrew — at best a little of the latter. It is true that the Judaism of his day was already partially hellenized, so some influence could be hypothesized. There was no noticeable influence from the Essenes.

Jesus began with John the Baptist. The baptism is certain, even though the accounts are not historical (they already presuppose Jesus' messiahship). Jesus baptized and preached just like John, then severed his connection because he had changed his views on the efficacy of baptism (as purification). Yet for him John was the forerunner of the messianic era. For his part John saw Jesus as an unfaithful disciple, even a "renegade."[43]

Jesus' teaching so fused form and content that it was "something quite unique" (282). Jesus made extensive use of images, pictures, and metaphors, as in the parable. Parable is a story that demonstrates a religious principle or truth by appealing to a similar principle in the material order, the life of the natural world, or human relations. It is not an allegory, as Jülicher showed, though Jülicher's solution was too rigid. There might be some allegorical element in a parable. The gospel theory that the parables were intended to mask something is false. As to style, Jesus was a poet; his words are marked by use of doublets, parallelism, antithesis, rhythm, and imagery.

The Galilean ministry consisted of two periods: at first success, with some hostility. Jesus gathered intimate disciples, and larger crowds who were not disciples flocked to him. There was also hostility from authorities over ritual law and sabbath observance. Capernaum was his headquarters. In the second part the opposition became more bitter; it emanated from Pharisees and also Herod the tetrarch. Capernaum was no longer his center; he went into remote and solitary places — the Decapolis, Caesarea Philippi, Tyre.

What was Jesus' thought then? He fell out of sympathy with John the Baptist; a new time needed something new. This was the germ of an idea that would eventually lead to the "abrogation of the religion of Israel" (311). Jesus proclaimed the kingdom: that was a new order meaning the end of the old. It was eschatological, but not apocalyptic. It signified the approaching End, but Jesus drew no pictures and did not engage in the speculations of the apocalypticists. For Jesus the kingdom was a fact in the moral order, the circumstance in which persons will be fully obedient to God. It would be established by God's will and power.

Jesus began to preach a new religion, even if he was not himself aware of it at

---

43. Goguel, *Jesus and the Origins of Christianity,* 279.

that time. He felt that he was a prophet at the outset, not the messiah. He was a messenger of God who was transformed into *the* messenger of God. He limited his activity to Jewish people, but it seems that in his last days he despaired of the nation and began to think that the whole religious economy of the Jews would be abolished. He never went into towns like Sepphoris or Tiberias; there is at best a germ of universalism in his actions and words.

The first disciples came from John's disciples; some renounced all to follow him in his demand for preaching the kingdom and preparing people for its coming. The group of the Twelve could go back to Jesus, though they may have been simply a special intimate group. There was opposition from Pharisees; Jesus did not admit the authority of the oral law and scandalized them. He also aroused the hostility of Herod Antipas, which was the cause of his removal from Galilee and his going to Jerusalem. At first Jesus was optimistic, expecting the kingdom soon and the messiah to appear. This new outburst of his movement caught Herod's attention and he decided to move against Jesus. Thereafter Jesus was a hunted man and made many rapid movements, staying nowhere very long. It is also probable that Jesus did not openly claim messiahship; the "secret" contains the truth (as does Wrede's interpretation) that Jesus was very reserved; likely Jesus thought he was the messiah-to-be at the establishment of the kingdom. He would not have shared the popular ideas associated with the messiah, and tried to discourage them. Therefore he also preferred the term "Son of man," which was of more recent origin and had a degree of elasticity.

Jesus fed the crowds messianic meals, just as the last supper evoked the messianic banquet, though the people thought of a political movement. Herod's hostility led to a decision: to evade Herod or fight. Jesus' refusal to become a king (John), or to use force and supernatural power, lost him the masses. What about the disciples? Here occurred the conversation at Caesarea Philippi, which has an analogue in John 6:66–69. Some disciples maintained undying loyalty; thereafter Jesus asked not only for loyalty to his message, but to his own person — an evolution in his thought from the earlier missionary journey. Here certain Son of man words about confessing Jesus show that he was linking himself to the Son of man, to the messiah. How did Jesus arrive at this? On moral grounds: the kingdom was a new moral order, as he proclaimed it, but not everyone accepted that. Yet Jesus found no sin in his own heart; he must have realized his moral superiority and concluded that he had a unique vocation. He was not merely one of the messengers, but the messenger, God's son and messenger. Here lay the beginning of his messianic consciousness.

At the same time Jesus must have realized that he would have to pass through a period of suffering and travail. The very specific sayings about suffering are theological, but something like Luke 27:25 is authentic. It was probably prompted by Jesus' meditation on being hunted by Herod. He likely did not face the possibility of his own death before the very end, but sufferings were in any case a part of God's design for the kingdom. It was this realization that also brought with it the acceptance of the title of Son of man. After his humiliation and rejection he would appear as the Son of man in glory: "Jesus did not believe that he was the Messiah *although* he had to suffer; he believed that he was the Messiah *because* he had to suffer. This is the great paradox, the great originality, of his Gospel" (392). He then went to Jerusalem, fleeing Herod's hostility. Later the church papered this over with other explanations (the "ransom").

He stayed in Jerusalem from September or October until the Feast of Dedication in December. Then he retired to Perea, remaining in contact with the disciples in Jerusalem, and returned at Passover. The synoptics have confused Jesus' return with his arrival, with the consequence that they have only a minimal stay in Jerusalem connected with Passover. At first Jesus made a strong impression on the crowds, as in Galilee; people saw him as a prophet. Yet Jerusalem was not really captured, and the hostility of the authorities was aroused; they were scandalized by his healings, his preaching, his welcoming of publicans and sinners, and his claims to authority. Then he said that the temple would be destroyed, forecasting the end of Judaism. That caused a rupture and led to accusations of blasphemy. Jesus left the city, but hoped that a messianic arrival would bring the people over to him. Did he intend to resume his teaching? Probably not, as the last supper shows. He knew that the end for him was at hand. The authorities put him before Pilate as the leader of a popular movement. Events thereafter moved swiftly.

On the date of the last supper and the death of Jesus, Goguel followed John (14 Nisan), though admitting that all is uncertain. Jesus died about the time of Passover. At the supper Jesus had a foreboding of betrayal by Judas. He took a cup of wine (in Luke's version), mentioned that he would not celebrate the Passover or drink any more wine, and expressed his confidence in being reunited with the disciples in the kingdom of God. He accepted voluntarily his suffering without necessarily knowing just how that would make possible the coming kingdom and his coming as the glorious messiah. The mention of the bread is an allusion also to his approaching death that he willingly accepted.

The passion narrative was originally a unit in itself. The trial story is driven by hostility toward Judaism and a desire to accommodate the Romans. There were two trials, but not three (Luke). The Jews may have taken the initiative in arresting Jesus, but the Roman cohort was also involved, so Jesus was arrested as an agitator, even though the Jewish authorities regarded him as a blasphemer. Pilate was led to arrest Jesus, but secured some statement beforehand from the Sanhedrin so that he could not later be accused of having shed the blood of an innocent man or risk having the people rise against him.

Jesus was obsessed with the dangers to him. He did foresee Peter's failure, though the details are unhistorical (historical was only Jesus' rebuke of Peter's presumption in claiming undying fidelity). The saying gave rise to the story of a threefold denial. Gethsemane is unhistorical literally, but "in an admirable allegory it expresses what took place in the soul of Jesus" (495). Judas's betrayal is historical, though it is unclear what Judas betrayed or why. At his arrest Jesus' friends tried to defend him. At his trial, his words about destroying the temple and his messianic declaration are both authentic. If they had been invented later they would have referred to the resurrection. Jesus believed that the old order was about to perish, and the new sanctuary would be constructed in the messianic age. Thus Jesus announced that he would destroy the temple and rebuild it, proclaimed himself as messiah, and said that he would return seated on the clouds of heaven. It was not blasphemous to claim to be messiah, but his words against the temple were. Actually, there was no trial before the Sanhedrin; Jesus was arrested by the Romans and taken before the Sanhedrin only because Pilate desired it. The insults to Jesus are probable. Luke's trial before Herod is unhistorical. His death among malefactors remains uncertain; the darkness is a legend. The cry of dereliction is authentic (the church never could believe that its master would feel deserted by God).

Goguel concluded his story with some reflection on the significance of Jesus' work and message. He emphasized the Jewish context of Jesus' teaching, though with some ambiguity. He said that Jesus' thought "does not actually contain any new element," then added that, although Jesus shared the views of Judaism about the revelation of God, he nevertheless "introduced ideas into this conception which made it wholly new" (553). The Old Testament was for him absolute, yet Jesus questioned it. He taught no passive or mechanical obedience, but acknowledged the conscience in everyone "which acts as a living ferment in the soul" (555). His difference from Judaism was something original and new; in the former it is the objectified Law that is expected, whereas for Jesus God has become interior, directly perceived by the soul. This was an entirely new conception of the revelation of God, while the theoretical idea of God remained undistinguished from Judaism. "The unique originality of Jesus consists in his sense of the presence of God, in that conscious and living communion with God in which he lives" (558). God is both absolutely transcendent and near, both Judge and Father.

In Judaism God's grace is divorced from his justice. For Jesus forgiveness gives communion with God, not that one must first become pure before having this communion. Jesus also brought forth a new idea of the kingdom of God. Jesus agreed that the kingdom would mean the restoration of God's sovereignty, now thwarted by the rule of sin and Satan. In his conception the kingdom was thoroughly eschatological (though not apocalyptic), nonpolitical, and not present. He differed from his contemporaries in that he saw the kingdom as the fulfillment of God's will, not God's power at the service of the Jewish people. Jesus' thought actually passed through three phases: he believed the Parousia was near at the point of sending out the disciples on their mission; shortly after he began to abandon that nearness, saying only that some then present would see the kingdom come; still later he claimed entire ignorance of the time of the kingdom, and became more and more opposed to the apocalyptic idea. Thus

> This leads us to think that this conception was merely the framework for the thought of Jesus provided by the surroundings in which he lived. He thought in

eschatological terms just as he spoke Aramaic, but that which is most intimate and essential in his thought may not be connected any more closely with eschatological thought than with the Aramaic tongue. (572)

Jesus used the Son of man title; there are analogies in Daniel and Enoch. He made a messianic impression and spoke of himself as connected with the Son of man. That can only mean that Jesus spoke of himself as the Son of man to come in the future, though it is a natural anticipation to think of himself as already acting as such in the present. It is not possible to know the precise moment at which Jesus began to feel himself to be messiah, or Son of man. Probably the ideas of suffering and the Son of man developed together. His consciousness of being Son of God probably also developed at the same time, though Son of God does not denote divinity. All men are sons, but there is with Jesus a special sense because he had no sense of sin.

Jesus taught no new morality; both he and Judaism taught obedience. But he conceived of obedience in a new way and demonstrated originality in that his ethic was spoken to those living in expectation of the kingdom. The beatitudes, for example, are future, and assert that poverty and hunger and the like are conditions of obtaining the supreme good, the kingdom. Jesus also gave positive commands, like the love commandment. It was not meant to be merely an ideal, though it has a heroic element. Jesus' originality lay not in the content, but how he linked it to a new religious conception and experience.

Jesus did not feel he was establishing a new religion and did not condemn the religion of the Jews. Yet he was faithful to "ideal Judaism," thereby detaching himself from "empirical Judaism" (588) and condemning it without himself feeling he was starting a new religion. The new religion, however, did grow out of Jesus' ministry, and developed further the impression that Jesus had left. Thus there was a continuity between Jesus and the church that came after him.

Goguel's work traveled its own path. Methodologically, comparing texts is necessary; not altogether discounting John or its underlying tradition is also an arguable alternative. The criteria of authenticity are appropriately thought out, if not modified. Yet the wide disparity between Goguel's views and others' illustrates the ongoing problem of attaining a standard that might produce an equally widespread agreement.

The psychologizing and probing around in Jesus' mind will also seem very much like unwarranted speculation and imposing more on these texts than they are able to bear. In this respect Goguel, though a master of his subject and the extant literature, resembled his liberal predecessors. He marked seemingly a time when much of western scholarship was attempting to come to terms with that heritage and to push beyond it, but his detachment from Form Criticism likely left him with no newer tools to do so.

Goguel also displayed a commonly held ambiguity about the Jewishness of Jesus and the originality or uniqueness of Jesus. Jesus was fully Jewish, but in virtually every significant way he went beyond Judaism. Goguel himself was not original in that stance, but he embodied the position in a particularly characteristic way.

Charles Guignebert

The work by Ch. (Charles) Guignebert, Professor of the History of Christianity at the Sorbonne, was a lengthy and rather prodigious piece of historical writing that claimed to give only a historical presentation and to be seeking after the truth.[44] Its judgments were generally severe.

Guignebert examined the sources, with all external ones dismissed (Tacitus, Josephus, and others), while in the New Testament only the synoptics were acceptable. His analysis traded on the distinction between Jesus and Christ: the church glorified Jesus and lost track of his authentic voice — christology superseded Jesus. Guignebert then cited the form critics who were basically correct, in his view: the gospels are essentially cult legends.

No historical life of Jesus is possible. There is a problem of even determining the authenticity of sayings. The most we can hope for is to have the gist of something Jesus said that did not conflict with the christology of the church. The best sources are Q and *Urmarkus*.

Form Criticism, however, is not as novel as its proponents seem to think, nor are its results always so convincing. "It has not revolutionized anything" (62), said Guignebert (with perhaps some excusable lack of foresight), but it has systematized methods that needed a stricter application. Already in hand was the understanding of the oral tradition; Form Criticism provided a systematized way of approaching it.

The myth-theories of Drews, Robertson, Smith, Jensen, Couchoud, and Kalthoff were all to be rejected. Paul represented an obstacle for all such theories; for Paul Jesus was God, but one who was a man. This transformation took place on hellenistic soil, where Jesus moved from messiah to savior. Christianity developed a Christ myth "at the expense of Jesus" (75), but it did not invent him.

Jesus was born in Galilee, but nothing much more can be said. Of the date we cannot say within fifteen years; the birth stories are merely hagiography. Joseph was maybe a carpenter; at least he was of lowly origins. All the birth information is mythological, and there is nothing from Jesus' childhood. We can surmise that Jesus had no education beyond what was necessary for an ordinary Jew. He probably spoke Aramaic, but it is unknown whether he also knew Hebrew or Greek. The latter is unlikely. He was influenced by Pharisaism, especially its messianic hope, but he was not a Pharisee. The messianic belief was likely a part of his upbringing. The story of Jesus in Jerusalem at the age of 12 is improbable.

---

44. Charles Guignebert, *Jesus*, L'évolution de l'humanité synthese collective 29 (Paris: La Renaissance du livre, 1933); English trans., *Jesus*, trans. S. H. Hooke, The History of Civilization (New York: Knopf, 1935). There is a clumsy reference system, with the notes referring to a numbered (Roman) bibliography at the end of the book.

Even the story of the baptism of Jesus by John is not closed to doubt; it could be merely a cultic story, a mythical account. John the Baptist was an eschatological prophet who stirred excitement among the *Am ha-aretz;* his baptism of Jesus seems probable, but we cannot say whether Jesus actually had some kind of vision or revelation at that time. The temptation is legendary. Of the separation of Jesus from John, nothing can be known; probably Jesus was John's disciple, but eventually differed from him and broke away.

As to Jesus' mental state, Guignebert dismissed the psychiatrists' efforts to analyze Jesus, but also offered the opinion that someone with Jesus' self-evaluation was not a normal person. On the other hand, prophets were not normal persons either. Jesus was certainly an enthusiast, but he was not unbalanced, nor was he an ascetic or gloomy person.

As to miracles, Jesus believed in them — he accepted such things as demonic possession — but he rejected them as proofs or authentications. The stories in the gospels resemble those elsewhere in the ancient world, and Jesus seems to have looked upon miracles much the same as his contemporaries.

The length of his ministry was a few months at best or, discounting his time in hiding or in flight, perhaps only a few weeks. He achieved success among the *anawim,* but also experienced some degree of failure. His message was not that attractive (repent, wait for the kingdom, possess no arms, be resigned to circumstances). There was conflict with the Pharisees, but much of that picture is artificial. He also had a number of disciples; a special group of the twelve is improbable, as is also their mission — more common hagiography, from a later period. As to Jesus' itinerary, Mark is on the whole reliable: five to six weeks in Galilee, where Jesus was hounded, moved around a lot, and finally fled to Jerusalem, his last hope, for Galilee had to be accounted a failure. The entrance into Jerusalem, however, is untrue — it would be impossible for an unknown *nabi* to make such a showing. It also is incomprehensible why the authorities did not immediately seize him.

Jesus' teaching came in isolated logia; the larger discourses were not likely spoken. The first disciples preserved his preaching of the near End, but they made larger collections only when they began to doubt the Parousia, that is, only after the separation from Judaism (about twenty-five to thirty years later). Jesus and the disciples clearly belonged in a Jewish context, and the largest changes in the tradition occurred in the hellenistic communities. There still remains, however, an early layer of tradition that is detectable, even if it is not extensive. This early layer comes from Jesus. The authentic material can be recognized by its location in a Galilean context, by sayings that are addressed to disciples and do not reflect any ecclesiastical organization or system. Comparative criticism is necessary, relying on what is simple and unsystematic, with a small number of ideas based on religious precepts that were already known. One should not exaggerate the specialness of Jesus' teaching: "It is as if people unconsciously attempted, as it were, to compensate for depriving him of his divine nature by attributing to him superhuman qualities" (245–46). Guignebert was, of course, alluding to the liberals (citing Holtzmann, Jülicher).

Jesus was a prophet of the eschatological kingdom and expected its near advent. This was the central idea in his message, expressed in an outpouring of speech in the form of aphorisms, striking sayings, and pithy dialogues. Parables were especially characteristic; they were comparisons used to set forth an idea. They were not allegories, which are fictions that do not mean what they say. A parable is meant to illuminate. Mark's hiding theory is absurd.

What did Jesus think of himself? Son? Son of God? Messiah? Son of man? Guignebert found nothing original in the first two; the latter two were not identical originally. Some Son of man sayings represented merely an original "I," others were messianic. Jesus could only have used Son of man in a nonmessianic sense. There is also little to support the claim that Jesus saw himself as the messiah. The passion predictions also have no originality, but reflect Jesus' own fate. Nor can there be seen any trace of a development in his messianic consciousness. He never gave himself out as the messiah, but only acknowledged being a prophet.

In regard to Judaism, Jesus never attempted to overthrow the Law. He assumed a prophetic liberty in interpreting the Law and bringing about its true fulfillment, but he did not intend to abolish it. He also set a religion of the heart over against ritual, but that, too, is only prophetic. He also commanded no sacraments (Baptism and the Eucharist are from later tradition). Yet Jesus was not like the rabbis — he was not characterized by formalism or pedantry. He also departed from his contemporaries at the point of his sympathy for "sinners," those who did not obey the Law (sinners are the *Am ha-aretz*). He was also not a universalist.

The apostles founded the church. Jesus did not envision an organization under Peter; Jesus was himself the herald of the kingdom, not the founder of an institution.

The concept of the kingdom has its roots in Judaism. It is not spiritual, but has in mind the kingdom on earth, a radical transformation of all things, the raising of the righteous dead. But it was not for Jesus national or political — it involved only individual persons. There was also nothing in Jesus' message of a present kingdom, though he expected the supernatural one imminently, with probably Jerusalem as its center. The conditions of its coming were repentance and doing the will of God (summarized in the love commandment).

For Jesus God was both Ruler and Father, as in Judaism generally. Jesus emphasized the fatherliness of God, as seen in the expression *Abba* and in the notices of Jesus' frequent praying.

Ethically, Jesus insisted on repentance; he had a sense of sin, of a conscience. He was not, however, merely a moral reformer; his ethics were an essential part of his proclamation of the kingdom. The ethics anticipate the future kingdom, which will liquidate humanity. In that sense the ethics do not foresee a lengthy future. Especially the law of love is central; it was not new, but Jesus gave it an absolute and binding character. He was not an ascetic, but there was in him some sense of overcoming the world. Nor was he a socialist, for he did not care about the poor or rich for their own sake. He did seem to renounce sexual relations; there would be none in the kingdom. He was not a feminist or family advocate and promoted no social, economic, or political morality. He cannot be said to have been concerned for culture. "It is the height of absurdity to use the teaching of Jesus to vindicate modern civilization" (387). In fact, Jesus had no ethics and no systematic code of morals. His originality in that regard lay only in his view that life had to be seen in the light of the kingdom, in his obsession with the kingdom, and the supremacy of the law of love.

We do not know Jesus' messianic expectations, but evidently he anticipated the End with its accompanying resurrection and judgment. The latter was individual, not nationalistic.

Jesus was close to Pharisaic Judaism in his outlook. The later tradition has read back into his story its own hostility toward the rabbis. Yet Jesus did differ in his closeness to the sinners and his greater stress on love. He crystallized the essence of Pharisaism and took up the prophet's freedom to interpret the Law.

The Easter faith made Jesus the messiah and gave rise to the church. The church was not the work of Jesus.

The last week of Jesus' ministry contains multiple problems, such as chronology, which are simply unresolvable. The last supper is overlaid with the sacramental practice of the church, and characterized by its parallels in the mystery religions. The only authentic element is the promise of eating again in the kingdom. The episode of Judas' betrayal is meaningless; it may be that Judas personified the Judaism that delivered Jesus to Pilate, but any factual basis for the story is unknown. There are abundant problems with the account of Jesus' trial as well. It was largely an artifice to lay responsibility on the Jews. It is probable that Jesus was arrested, judged, and condemned by the Roman procurator, probably as a messianic pretender. The crucifixion is historical, but the scene is not. We can only say that "he was arrested, tried, condemned and executed" (489).

No one knew the place of Jesus' burial. The disciples had no idea what happened to the body; it might more likely have been thrown into a pit for the executed than placed in a new tomb. The appearance tradition is the earliest and antedates the tomb stories, but it is primarily concerned "to establish apostolic authority and justify the existence of the church" (511).

The appearances were visions and were contagious. Peter was the first. Here Guignebert indulged in some psychologizing of his own about Peter's state of mind: Peter returned to Galilee surrounded by many memories of Jesus and saw Jesus, probably along the shore and "under conditions favorable to hallucinations" (522). Then contagion worked; from there the legend grew into stories about bodily ascension, an empty tomb, and so on. Prophecy helped, along with relevant scripture texts. The conclusion is that we do not know what happened to Jesus' body. Christianity, however, rests on the resurrection faith.

Jesus was mistaken about the End; he should simply have vanished from history like others before him. But the love of the disciples gave him life. Only in a broad sense can we say that he gave rise to the movement that followed him, though not as the result of his own direct intention.

Guignebert's portrayal represented a stringent criticism matching that of the form critics without the formal attachment to the method. His Jesus was shrunken and seemed to be a blood relation of the one sketched out by Loisy. As a telling from the perspective of a "pure" historian, Guignebert's work succeeded admirably; it ground no theological axe and seemingly had no investment in the telling other than the discovery of historical actuality. If that resulted in a picture that faith could only construe with difficulty for its own purposes, then so be it. In that sense the Frenchman's labors, while having no theological interest, nevertheless posed the decision for the faithful in a particularly pointed way: Is this Jesus about whom we know so little the one from God, or shall we look for another?

But if Guignebert's work wore the mantle of the ultraradical, Loisy's transferred it to himself. And if years earlier Tyrrell could say that "Loisy makes Lagrange almost safe,"[45] how much more so he might have felt about the Loisy of later times. Loisy provided no life of Jesus, but in his later works he set forth a capsule version of Jesus that we may take as normative for his final views.[46]

Alfred Loisy Revisited

According to Loisy, Jesus appeared in relation to John the Baptist, a prophet of the End and preacher of the kingdom of God ahead of Jesus. He was ascetic, though not an Essene. He preached regeneration. Not much else can be said about him due to the legendizing that went on.

There is no doubt as to the historicity of Jesus, though the birth stories are legendary. He was probably born somewhere around Capernaum. Nazareth is an attempt to explain the use of "Nazarean." Perhaps the latter was the name of a John-sect of which Jesus was once a member. The baptism of Jesus by John is a myth vindicating the institution of Christian baptism. Jesus was a wandering preacher, a prophet of the kingdom of God like John. He doubtless had a gift of healing, especially exorcism. He preached with some success in a small area and perhaps traveled some after Antipas pursued him. He recruited disciples, though the notices of swelling crowds are all exaggeration. He did little beyond Galilee; the Sermon on the Mount was never preached.

---

45. In a letter of Oct. 3, 1907 to von Hügel; see Maud Petre's *Von Hügel and Tyrrell*, 162.

46. Found in Loisy, *The Birth of the Christian Religion* and partially in *The Origins of the New Testament*. The first volume was published in 1930, the second in 1936. I use here the version of the two published together, *The Birth of the Christian Religion and The Origins of the New Testament*, trans. L. P. Jacks (New Hyde Park, N.Y.: University Books, 1962). Chap. 2 especially of *Birth of the Christian Religion* contains Loisy's summary.

The gospels were formed later out of catechetical interests. There was no need to transmit Jesus' teaching, for the kingdom was soon coming. So a body of teaching was built up for Jesus; one source was rabbinic, another hellenistic Judaism.

There was a man Jesus whose father was Joseph and mother was Mary and who also had brothers. The surest thing about him is the preaching of the near kingdom. There was no apocalyptic speculation or zealot violence. He expected the end of the age and the overthrow of Satan's rule and the final judgment. Everything is subject to the eschatological kingdom. So also it must be the case that Jesus expected a role for himself. Son of man perhaps? That was an idea of Chaldeo-Iranian origin, pre-Christian, but likely of no influence on Jesus himself. Rather, he presented himself as the envoy of God, not merely a prophet or sage or a moralist, and not the messiah, though he was proclaimed that way after his death.

It is unlikely that Jesus had been in Jerusalem as a preacher of the kingdom before his final journey. He probably preached a few months in Galilee at best; his reasons for going to Jerusalem are uncertain. Perhaps he was fleeing Antipas or was seeking a place for his message or even had lost his crowds in Galilee. More likely he held the hope of proclaiming his message at the very center of national life. The entrance story is improbable, as is the expulsion of the traders from the temple, and it is unlikely he would have been allowed to teach in the temple without interference. Either some kind of a riot or a popular movement aroused the interest of the procurator, though Jesus' affair seemed to be less urgent than that of a Theudas or the Egyptian.

Most everything revolving around the supper is mythical, following 1 Corinthians which was imposed on an earlier interpretation as a foretaste of happiness in the kingdom. Perhaps Jesus suggested such at daily meals with his disciples. The Gethsemane scene shows the great ordeal undergone by the Christ. None of the arrest scene is historical. Perhaps Jesus was arrested at night by sudden surprise, by the temple police or the Romans.

The trial is a liturgical dramatization. Said Loisy, "Let those who can find their way through this judicial phantasmagoria" (84). The one stable fact is the crucifixion, which was imposed on rebels, and on Jesus before Passover. Only Rome acted, not the Sanhedrin; Jesus' movement was considered subversive, as a threat to Rome, even though he did not himself advocate revolution. The trial has as its purpose to blame the Jews. The Barabbas tale is a fiction and Jesus' statements and actions bear only a christological value. The place of execution can be retained historically, but other items are either dramatic, ritualistic, theological, or symbolic. "Jesus was promptly condemned and promptly executed; he died in torment and, save for his executioners, there can hardly have been any to witness his agony" (87). Loisy added that the body was likely thrown into a ditch, perhaps the Akeldama field to which later tradition inaptly attached the name of Judas.

There is little in Bultmann, widely reputed to be *the* most skeptical of all, that exceeded or even equaled Loisy, and Loisy needed no appeals to Form Criticism. At the same time there is always a risk in stretching too far beyond the unspoken boundaries of a field of knowledge; such transgressions are rewarded less with universal disapproval than discreet avoidance. A similar fate very nearly befell Schweitzer, in that few of his own countrymen were willing to confront his issues. Loisy left no great following and perhaps some of it was due to a reach that exceeded a reasonable grasp.

American Work on the Historical Jesus

The Americans, as we said at the outset, had little to offer in the way of lives of Jesus, though work on smaller subjects went on apace.[47] A survey of the literature reveals a substantial decline from the previous decade. The work of Burton Scott Easton, while ostensibly an examination of the views of the gospels, contains a compact summary of the historical Jesus.[48]

Burton Scott Easton

Following an analysis of the formation of the synoptic tradition and the Judaic background, Easton examined Jesus' teaching. Jesus never violated any actual Old Testament law, yet he made distinctions in the Law. On divorce, for example, his view expressed God's will purely, while the Law only made the best of a corrupt condition of society. The Sabbath was transcended by human needs. The food laws held mostly hygienic value for Jesus. Jesus and Pharisees clashed over the application of the love commandment, the summary of the law. The rabbis taught obedience for obedience's sake; the summary to the rabbis meant only that love was the general intent of the whole law, but that did not invalidate specific laws. Easton then argued that Paul's later position could prevail because of Jesus' own earlier stance toward the law. He then also gave a basic argument for something like situation ethics, that is, love may require not following a precept of Jesus himself (for example, turning the other cheek).

Jesus was not a social gospeler; he preached a transcendental kingdom, which meant the end of all social order. So Jesus' task was to prepare for the kingdom; love may have social implications, but there is nothing directly from Jesus on that subject. His community was based on God and on imitation of God [Barthians, Easton said, would be horrified]. As to evil, Jesus held to moral dualism and never explained it. His notion of salvation separated him from Pharisaism, which said that fulfilling the law with substantial completeness was necessary,

---

47. See below, chap. 8.
48. Burton Scott Easton, *Christ in the Gospels* (New York: Scribner's, 1930).

though we are finally saved by mercy and love as demonstrated in achievement. Jesus affirmed pardon given by God, not first as a demand as in the Sermon on the Mount, but as grace of the God who goes out after the sinner. Salvation comes by accepting sonship to the Father who then enables the sons to be obedient.

The kingdom is the visible rule of God, eschatological and maybe apocalyptic (the latter defined only by "signs" that accompany the near kingdom); it is the end of history. The present sayings only mean that now the process has started, and is soon to come. We can say that "Jesus' apocalypticism has become something taken for granted" (164). What did Jesus think his role was? Messiah? The debate goes on. He was crucified as a royal pretender, for claiming to be "king." Did he claim to be Son of man? Yes, in the apocalyptic sense, the future ruling messiah.

Jesus' ethic was bound up with warnings about the impending judgment, but it was not an interim ethic. He must have had years of preparation before his baptism and his sense of call as messiah. The temptation is essentially true. In Galilee there was teaching about the fatherhood of God and the apocalyptic kingdom; there were healings, exorcisms, and conflict with scribes. The conflict is excessively darkened in the gospels' portrayal; yet Jesus and Pharisees were incompatible. Jesus discarded fasting.

The disciples were involved in the mission; Jesus gave them salvation — he brought them to God. There was a "double soteriology," one based on Jesus himself and the other on the future kingdom. A "wholly novel conception" (190), said Easton, Jesus giving salvation through himself. The kingdom was present, so was the messiah; the disciples realized Jesus' messiahship even before Caesarea-Philippi.

Jesus went to Jerusalem to deliver a message; he expected death, but could look beyond it for the final victory. Therefore he designated himself Son of man after Caesarea-Philippi (the passion predictions are *ex eventu*, but Luke 12:50 is genuine, referring to a baptism to be baptized with). Jesus staged his entrance grandly; the temple attack was also calculated, with all deliberate provocation. The chief priests decided he had to die. Jesus must have seen his death as of vital significance and expected to be reunited in the kingdom with the disciples. He warned them not to be arrested with him — hence the sword-word. Even their flight was justified.

A false claim to be a prophet was a capital offense; a claim to be a celestial being was blasphemy, but before Pilate the accusation was breach of the peace. The disciples were not totally unprepared and knew Jesus was going to the Father and would return as Son of man in glory. But their preaching went beyond that: he was resurrected and present through the Spirit. Their visions, of short duration, did not produce the Christian message, which already existed.

C. T. Craig

There is also the little volume by Clarence T. Craig,[49] which did not gain much attention, most likely because it was not prepared as a technical work. It was intended to offer a bridge between the scholar and the worker in religious education and to promote historical understanding of Jesus. It emphasized that current interest in Jesus lay not in the Christ of theology, but in the life and personality of Jesus.

A discussion of the sources began the work. Form Criticism has to be acknowledged, even if it has some arbitrariness and subjectivity about it. John may occasionally be preferred, though the synoptics are primary. "John is primarily an interpreter, not of what the eye saw, or the ear heard, but what entered into the heart of man" (34).

Jesus was a Jew, baptized by John, but he was no ascetic. He did not attack the Law, but appealed to the will of God. He had a prophetic conscience and valued human worth and personality. His God was the Father of forgiving love, but was not merely indulgent. A crisis was coming, the kingdom of God, the rule or sovereignty of God, and it entailed judgment. The powers of the messianic age were already being manifested. Its demands were the ethics, some of which were interim; the divorce saying was one. Jesus was also harsh on wealth. The modern world considers poverty a curse; Jesus thought wealth was.

Jesus was a teacher, but his secret was his personality. It was indeed the ground of the resurrection experiences. He projected the numinous and was conscious of a special mission. He did not think he was the Davidic messiah, but likely "did expect to be the coming heavenly 'Son of Man'" (54).

It is hard to know fully the role of the Pharisees in Jesus' fate. It was the Sadducees who took the final hand, driven by Jesus' action in cleansing the temple. He was a prophet who encroached on their business monopoly. Perhaps Judas betrayed the secret of his messiahship. It is also probable that Jesus saw opposition and death as a necessary prelude to the coming kingdom. His basis would not have been Isaiah 53, but the pattern of Maccabean martyrdom, with its vicarious suffering and death. The last supper was an enacted parable; Jesus' death was a gateway to the kingdom for the disciples. Only a few women were present to witness his death.

The resurrection transformed the disciples, though it remains impenetrable to the historian. There was no bodily resurrection for Paul. Thereafter Jesus was interpreted in many different ways.

Problems of the "life" of Jesus are the miracles (the disciples told such stories because they already had faith, not to gain it); legends (virgin birth, birth stories, which are truth of another sort); the gospel attitude toward the Jews (Jesus'

---

49. C. T. Craig, *Jesus in Our Teaching* (New York: Abingdon, 1931). Craig was then Professor of New Testament Language and Literature at Oberlin Graduate School of Theology, was later at Yale. See also the summary in his general introduction, *The Beginning of Christianity* (New York: Abingdon-Cokesbury, 1943).

critique was that of a prophet; he did not condemn a race); and God's providence (suffering and pain are a risk in a good world). The authority of Jesus still resides in Christian experience. Jesus still inspires by his personality, in "his infinite capacity to stir the enthusiasms of men, and enlist their loyalty to their noblest ideals" (92).

Walter Bell Denney

There is also the textbook by Walter Bell Denney,[50] Professor of Philosophy and Religion at Russell Sage College, but its themes are very familiar. A single quote from the foreword, setting out the nonapocalyptic perspective in the book, sums up its position:

> The present book dissents completely from this view [i.e., the apocalyptic one]. It holds that the mind of Jesus is most deeply and faithfully reflected in the "Teaching Source" [Q], and that the central idea of Jesus was that he was the Son of God, not in an apocalyptic, or even a Messianic, sense, but in the deep religious sense that he knew God as his Heavenly Father, and felt that the supreme end of life was to live in a manner worthy of such a Father. Since the ruling idea of apocalyptic teaching is that God is not a Forgiving Father, but an Unforgiving Avenger, we cannot believe that Jesus shared this current view; rather, he spent his life protesting against it. The apocalyptic ideas attributed to Jesus in the Gospels, are, we hold, read back into his real history by the early Christians, who were neither so simple nor so great as he was, and who were themselves ardent apocalyptists. (xiii)

The book then proceeded to portray Jesus faithfully according to this old liberal scheme, with Judaism bearing much of the brunt of the criticism and the foil against which this enlightened, modern-sounding Jesus played out his work and message. Jesus' goal was to bring his nation under his new conception of God and to save them from a fatal conflict with Rome (if only they abandoned their apocalyptic hunger for revenge and learned soon enough that the Romans were really their brothers). It did not work, of course, for Jesus stirred up too many opponents who finally secured his death at Jerusalem. Nevertheless, his message, which can be recovered by modern criticism, has hung on and provides for us a paradigm of practice in our own religious life. The book ended with effulgences over Jesus' impact on western civilization and his continuing importance in modern culture (labor relations and so on).

These three works demonstrate some loss of interest in the project of composing lives of Jesus in this decade. What survived shows still the shape of liberalism around the edges, as modified by the impact of the eschatological interpreta-

---

50. Walter Bell Denney, *The Career and Significance of Jesus* (New York: Thomas Nelson and Sons, 1934). Russell Sage College was named for a New York financier who amassed a fortune in the late nineteenth century and whose spouse, Margaret Olivia Slocum Sage, the inheritor of his fortune, established the college in Troy, New York, in 1916. Denney was a former student of Benjamin W. Bacon.

tion. But, in fact, the mood in American scholarship was more likely reflected in Henry Cadbury's monograph, *The Peril of Modernizing Jesus.*[51]

Henry J. Cadbury

Cadbury started from the observation of the frequent anachronizing of Jesus, as in the kingdom-as-fatherhood-and-brotherhood of liberalism or the picturing of Jesus as a laissez-faire capitalist. The early Christians also "modernized" Jesus in that they interpreted him into their own contexts; we still do that when we choose to ignore the element of miracle or the apocalyptic element in his ministry because it is not congenial to our modern mind. Modernization is likely inevitable, but ought to be resisted, and to do so requires a realization of our own prejudices and attention to the mentality of Jesus' own age. In fact, the best way to avoid modernization is to demonstrate Jesus' likeness to his environment, to his Jewishness. The gospels still reflect this Palestinian context: the *a fortiori* argument, parable, the practical and concrete ethic. This Jewishness argues for the historicity of the gospels.

Jesus was unmodern in certain of his views, such as his apocalypticism, his acceptance of demonic possession, his theism, and his belief in the devil and miracles. The social gospel has also claimed Jesus, but did Jesus have a social outlook at all? He did not pronounce on most social issues — divorce is an unfortunate exception — and his concern seemed to lie with individuals. He thought not of social interrelations, but of one individual at a time. He made no appeal to social motives; the parable of the good Samaritan focused not on the needy one but on the helper, the doer, the one who was merciful. Jesus cannot be made into a modern socialist or a communist or a capitalist or a militarist. "Jesus' concern is not so much the saving of society but a society of saviors" (116). In fact, Jesus' purpose is not really discernible. The attribution of purpose and planning is mostly modern. Jesus was more casual.

In most respects Jesus was a Jew, with little that could be considered new or original. He was religiously motivated and urged doing the will of God. He differed from Judaism in that he was more lenient on the definition of permitted healing on the sabbath. Yet there was in him no wholesale condemnation of the law, but a groping toward a more spiritual foundation away from the legalistic one. He was mystical and practiced prayer. He had visions and auditions (baptism, temptation); he was passive and urged submission to the will of God. Similarly it was so with his messiahship — not something he seized, but something that came to him from God. He took God for granted, assumed God, but he gave no new knowledge of God.

Both faith and history endure; history illustrates faith and faith interprets history.

---

51. Henry Cadbury, *The Peril of Modernizing Jesus* (New York: Macmillan, 1937). Cadbury was then Professor of Divinity at the Harvard Divinity School.

The book contained a capsule picture of Jesus, though its main intent was to issue a warning against reading into the historical Jesus all our own presuppositions, a point that Schweitzer as well as others (Tyrrell) had made much earlier, but which could not be made often enough. The prospect that it would be heeded seemed dim, for the record tends to indicate that too often the motivation for investigating the "problem" of Jesus shows itself in the results attained.

Theological Concerns

In fact, the question of the *meaning* of Jesus and the history connected with him always lay near the surface, especially in the Anglo-American tradition. Two English works that symbolize this concern bracketed the decade, and we may close this time period with reference to them.

The joint effort of Edwyn Hoskyns and Noel Davey enjoyed a lengthy life and represents a very able and conservative analysis of the Jesus-question.[52] Christianity has a theological interest in historical study of Jesus. "Inadequate or false reconstruction of the history of Jesus of Nazareth cuts at the heart of Christianity" and, accordingly, critical study of the New Testament is therefore "the prime activity of the Church" (10). But, of course, there are no assured results. In fact, there is a riddle: the relation between Jesus of Nazareth and the primitive church. We know the primitive church, less so Jesus of Nazareth, and what we do know gives results that are "very few, very surprising and very inconvenient" (13).

The book claimed to be written for the nonexpert, so it first gave a survey of various disciplines within New Testament studies — philology, textual criticism, and the like, then turned to more historical considerations. Taking 1 Peter's portrayal of Jesus as the innocent, crucified man, the authors asked whether this Old Testament context (Servant) was imposed on him or whether it arose from the actual, concrete life of Jesus. Mark also used the Old Testament often; did he impose it on Jesus or was there something in Jesus' own life and activity that compelled just that interpretation? If also we should look behind the synoptic tradition we find four blocks of primitive tradition (Mark, Q, M, L). If analysis can produce a unity of direction, a general agreement, then the tradition goes back to Jesus. If not, the editors have imposed their own views and setting, and the historian is at a loss for discovering the historical Jesus.

Matthew's and Luke's tendencies were investigated with the conclusion that they did not distort their Markan source, even while adding teaching material to it. There were insightful comments on the editorial work and perspectives of Matthew and Luke. Then Mark's christology was interrogated, Hoskyns and Davey finding that it originated in Jesus himself. "There is not the slightest

---

52. Edwyn Hoskyns and Noel Davey, *The Riddle of the New Testament* (London: Faber and Faber, 1931; 3d ed., 1947; reprinted 1949, 1952, 1957, 1964).

ground" (112) for thinking Mark was without justification for emphasizing Jesus as the humiliated Son of man, or that Mark saw the exorcisms as unique; even the spirits recognized Jesus.

So: the christology that runs through the record was not imposed by the evangelists, but was found in various strata of tradition as it came to the evangelists and controlled that tradition. The history of Jesus was already interpreted, but through the Old Testament, that is, Jesus himself interpreted it to fulfill his own purpose. For example, he died at Jerusalem because he had to as messiah. So Mark, Matthew, and Luke are all interpreting an event already interpreted for them. This christological Old Testament interpretation comes from Jesus himself.

This thesis was then tested by examining miracles, parables, and aphorisms. If christology is not there, then it must have come from the church and been imposed on the tradition.

The miracles in Mark are signs of the presence of the messiah and of his power, as seen in Old Testament prophecy. They witness to the advent of the kingdom; thus christology underlies the miracles. Are parables general illustrations or do they have a christological claim and a special history behind them? The authors provided some discussion of metaphor, simile, allegory, and parable, concluding that parables have some of both metaphor and allegory, or metaphor and simile, as in Jesus' parables, which are also rooted in an Old Testament background. Parables also hold this christological element, for they too speak of a divine event, a messianic event, now taking place, with human destiny dependent on one's attitude toward this event. So their understanding depends on recognition of this christological element — the recognition that Jesus is messiah. That is why parables in fact represent the mystery of the kingdom; only the inner circle of faith grasps them.

But perhaps in aphorisms we can find only Jesus the moral teacher. Comparison with rabbinic material shows little original in Jesus' sayings. But there are differences also, else why did the authorities oppose him to death? Here belong his acting with authority and a sense of urgency, the antitheses of the Sermon on the Mount, and his setting aside precepts of the law, such as sabbath observance and fasting. So Jesus cannot be fitted into contemporary Judaism; the law was fulfilled in following Jesus, in accepting his call to the kingdom and to salvation. The aphorisms then also are utterances of the messiah bringing the kingdom of God in which the law is fulfilled in humiliation, which is the condition for entering the kingdom. So the aphorisms belong with the parables and miracles; christology is found in all. We can therefore not detect at any level of the synoptic tradition an imposition of christology on a nonchristological history.

The conclusion was careful:

> This does not of course mean that the framework in which the evangelists have set the miracles, parables and aphorisms themselves, when isolated from the framework, are straight historical records. What it does mean is that both the framework and the miracles, parables and aphorisms set in it emerge from, lie upon, and rightly interpret, the general matter of the tradition. Rightly, as far as we are able to judge,

since the analysis of the gospels does not anywhere show the grain of the tradition running in a contrary direction. The material is everywhere Christological, although it remains, none the less, fragmentary and episodic. The three evangelists have done little more than arrange the tradition. (145)

An extension of the examination to John, Paul, and Hebrews issued in a similar result. The historical reality of Jesus was important for all of them. None created the theological history; they received it already that way, then interpreted it. The primitive Christian faith emerged from Jesus, and thus the historian is a slave of the theologian and the ordinary believer. "Nowhere in the New Testament are the writers imposing an interpretation upon a history. The history contains the purpose, and is indeed controlled by it" (172).

Jesus himself was moved by a single purpose that unified his life and work. He meant to work out in a human life complete obedience to God. The whole weight of the law and prophets had come upon him; that raised a conflict — with evil, as in the exorcisms and temptation — a conflict unto death and humiliation. He acted as the slave of God to bring about the new people of God. The power of the primitive church lay in its conviction that Jesus' own claim to his purpose was, in fact, the purpose of God. The resurrection is beyond the historian's grasp, but belongs to the history, for it was the ratification of Jesus' obedience and righteousness. Otherwise the resurrection is meaningless.

The authors finished by claiming to have solved the historical problem, but that still did not preclude the decision of faith, which cannot be the function of the New Testament critic. In Hoskyns and Davey's opinion the evidence itself has driven them to their conclusions.

C. H. Dodd also set out from the proposition that Christianity is a historical religion, fixed in a series of events as revelation of God.[53] Dodd referred to the recent emphasis on transcendence as a reaction to liberalism's desire to find the facts behind *Gemeindetheologie*, which could then be reinterpreted as we wish. There is no such thing as "facts" in that sense; all history is occurrence plus its interpretation. For Dodd the new emphasis on transcendence [Barthianism] was good, for it showed us again that the gospels were written for faith, were religious documents. Still, their character as history is not to be discounted, else Christianity would become Gnosticism. The New Testament speaks of the kerygma, about historical events, but also historical events that are simultaneously eschatological events. Similarly the figure of Christ is a historical figure, but also an eschatological one.

The early Christians took over messianic concepts, but not all of them (they rejected the nationalistic figure); they applied scripture, though the use of Servant is due to Jesus himself, the impact of history on traditional eschatology.

There is more to be learned from Paul than many have allowed, and even from Hebrews, the other epistles, and Acts. There are common themes of the

---

53. C. H. Dodd, *History and the Gospel* (New York: Scribner's, 1938). At the time Dodd was Norris-Hulse Professor of Divinity in the University of Cambridge.

kerygma. This kerygma had elements of proclamation and teaching embodied, for example, in Mark and Q. Thus also this historical tradition had been preserved in the framework of proclamation. Form Criticism shows that a primitive tradition lies at the base of the passion narrative; it underlies also other epistles and the kerygma. The value of Form Criticism is that it allows grouping by material and different strains of tradition, and comparison of these traditions and groupings. What emerges is the remarkable fact that each group gives a picture of the ministry of Jesus from a particular viewpoint, yet the same figure is being described.

Dodd aimed at recovering the oldest form of tradition, which is itself still permeated with messianic interpretation. He favored a method that started with the existence of the church, and compared all documents to arrive at the oldest tradition through observing the growth of the tradition. The oldest is the most primitive. We can hope to prove, Dodd said, that the church grew up around a central tradition that "yields a coherent picture of Jesus Christ, what He was, what He stood for, what He said, did and suffered" (110). The assumption is that either there were facts with an interpretation imposed upon them or the interpretation was imposed by facts as experienced at the time, in that context, and this interpretation had historical consequences.

After some examination of the historical background, Dodd made some observations about the Jesus of history. Jesus took no side, formed no party. He preached the kingdom of God and an ethical absolute. The latter was not interim, but intended for those who have experienced the end of the world and the coming kingdom. It is an ideal, but never really fulfillable. The ethical demands are the unattainable that we are obliged to attempt to attain. They also reveal to us our sinfulness and therefore also bring grace. Everything is oriented to this absolute, the kingdom of God. There is no mysticism or withdrawal from society in this ethic, like the Essenes. Dodd observed pungently that "if Jesus had joined the Essenes, He need never have been crucified" (129). But Jesus raised suspicions of the ruling class; his acts broke down the barriers of social balance in Judaism (conflict over the law). Jesus did not intend to contest Israel as the people of God; he saw himself as her messiah and limited his work to Israel. He performed two symbolic acts: the entrance into the city and the purifying of the temple. In one he offered himself as a leader to Israel and in the other he challenged the authority of the hierarchy. So Romans, Zealotism, and Pharisaism combined against Jesus. His crucifixion was the judgment of the kingdom of God on the world.

What of Israel? The last supper showed that the disciples were to be the nucleus of a new Israel; they would sit at table in the kingdom. He gave them the bread and cup, and they were members of the new Israel by partaking of his body and bread. This people of the new covenant only come into being after the death-resurrection of the messiah.

How is this fulfillment, as the New Testament says, of the history of Israel? Historically, some evolution happened; it is not a direct line. The Talmud is nearer. It is a long and complex process, marked by Israel's apostasies and prophets, a history intersected vertically by the Word of God. Likewise in the history of Jesus the kingdom of God impacts the world in judgment and mercy. Paul is the example. The fulfillment of Christ is not the end of a long development, but its concentration in one decisive moment of all that determined the preceding history. Thus it is an eschatological event.

The rise of the church was one fact as a result of the life, death, and resurrection of Jesus. Yet this eschatological expectation of the kingdom hardly made a ripple in the history of the world at first. Also the church resembled the world and could hardly realize its eschatological understanding empirically. It had a paradoxical character — a supernatural society, but also one of fallible persons. The church has been an instrument for both good and evil alike.

How are the sacred and secular history (*Heilsgeschichte*) related? In the end all history is sacred history, for it is in the mind of God. The Bible speaks thus through the myth of creation and judgment, and therefore sees history as a process of redemption, not merely as events in time. The church experiences this in sacrament and proclamation. Nevertheless, progress is not a proper category for the Christian grasp of history; rather, history is a process determined by the creative act of God vertically from above. The proclamation of the gospel creates a crisis, individual and social, from which comes a new creation. Thus is the coming of the kingdom of God. The meaning of history is seen in redemption and revelation. Only the kingdom of God can give meaning to history, for it is beyond history and yet comes within history. Only the eternal can subsume the temporal.

There are parallels between what Dodd was doing and the work of Hoskyns and Davey, though clearly the latter operated from a more conservative perspective. And in the attempt to locate the origin of the church's christology in Jesus himself, both followed a line already set forth earlier, much earlier actually,[54] one that would continue with considerable force in work yet to come.[55] The perception was widespread, and would come to expression in a somewhat different form and certainly out of a different cultural milieu, that there must be a line of continuity from Jesus to the early church, else the church's faith lacks a ground in history. This question, which figured so prominently in English theological reflection, soon enough would lead to something that would be called a "New Quest" of the historical Jesus. In fact, its driving force was an old question that had taken a somewhat different (German) form by the theological position assumed by Bultmann, and made more intense by the entire debate over demythologizing that flowed around the western world, especially after the Second World War. But among the English and the Scots, and less so among the Americans, the question had long taken form as a matter for theological discussion. And the

---

54. See, for example, James Denney, *Jesus and the Gospel: Christianity Justified in the Mind of Christ* (London: Hodder and Stoughton, 1908). The title sums up the content of the book very aptly.

55. See below, chap. 6, esp. the work of William Manson.

quintessential British answer seemed inevitably to found the church's faith in Jesus within the historical figure, even if only implicitly. Many could agree with the proposition that there is no layer of tradition within the New Testament that is not christological. But the question still haunts the whole arena of Jesus studies as to whether this at-bottom christology can be traced to Jesus himself and, even if it cannot, whether that really finally matters to Christian faith. Not everyone would agree that the only alternative would be a nonhistorical Jesus.

But time and circumstance would not permit a world conversation on that or any other issue. For the western world was preparing for itself another bath of blood and destruction. The decade of the twenties terminated in an economically darkened world; the decade of the thirties ended even more gravely, with Hitler's assault on land and life and even civilization itself. The causes that brought a highly civilized people to this end are beyond our telling, but we will try to observe their effects on the enterprise of the historical Jesus in the remaining decade of the first half-century.

Chapter 6

APOCALYPSE VISITED

The Forties

Theological scholarship suffered during the war, along with everything else. The expected national hostilities prevailed; the journals reflected again, as in the Great War, the conscription of academic pages for nationalistic purposes. Each side may as well have trotted out its previous writings.[1] The German journals *Theologische Literaturzeitung* and *Zeitschrift für die Neutestamentliche Wissenschaft* ceased publication in 1944;[2] Père Lagrange's *Revue biblique* went underground under the title *Vivre et Penser* (1941–44), and scholarly work shrank everywhere. The Germans had virtually nothing to show for the period, and were in any case preoccupied with the Dialectical Theology, but a degree of work continued in Great Britain as well as in America. There was little in the way of striking advance in the subject. It was a time of continuing to evaluate Form Criticism and its seemingly foreboding consequences, and of reiterating and further developing positions already staked out.

Issues and "Lives" in Great Britain

In fact, the British were conducting a debate among themselves as to the viability of further work on the historical Jesus, prompted by the infiltration of Form Criticism. A series of articles in the *Expository Times* displays the contours of this debate. R. H. Lightfoot provided an assessment of Form Criticism that sounded like a distillation of his earlier book on the subject, with some more positive evaluation of the potential benefits of Form Criticism.[3] The mere "whisper of his voice"[4] to which Lightfoot had alluded in his earlier work seemed to have grown at least into a low mumble, though still the main value of the new method is first the light it sheds on the life and faith of the primitive community. But that

---

1. In fact the *Hibbert Journal* did, reprinting Henri Bergson's 1915 piece, "Life and Matter at War," *HibJ* 38 (1939): 4–12.

2. *ZTK* did not publish after 1938 until 1949, but it is not clear whether that was related to the military situation.

3. R. H. Lightfoot, "Form Criticism and Gospel Study," *ExpTim* 53 (1941–42): 51–54. Lightfoot was giving an invited article in response to the more critical essay of F. J. Badcock, "Form Criticism," *ExpTim* 53 (1941–42): 16–20.

4. Above, 143.

may not be taken to mean that historical material is not present in the gospels; modification of the tradition occurs, but "there is no reason to think that it is present to a disconcerting degree, or to call in question the reliability of the record as a whole." Lightfoot declined to say whether Form Criticism would help us "draw nearer to the central Figure of the Gospels," though it will surely help to understand the shaping of traditions in the earliest period.[5]

In the same issue Vincent Taylor raised the question directly: Can a life of Jesus be written at all?[6] Taking off from the labors of Wrede, Schmidt, Bultmann, and non-Germans like Case, Goguel, and even Lagrange,[7] Taylor remarked that "Form Criticism has dried up the stream of Leben-Jesu-Research."[8] But Taylor, observing the greater British confidence in the reliability of the Markan record, faulted his contemporaries for not pushing their view further: "The universities of Great Britain are silent. No one apparently has the knowledge, imagination, and, above all, the courage to face failure in the attempt to re-tell the Story of Stories to a dying world. We discuss everything and construct nothing" (62).

Taylor then set out the problems inherent in constructing such a story (value of the sources, evaluation of miracles, obtaining a sequence of events); few things are absolute, but the effort must be continued, even in the face of probable failures. Above all, any adequate judgment of the Person of Christ will have to take into account a theology: "Without a dogmatic interest the writing of a Life of Christ is impossible" (64). Here Taylor would include some kind of doctrine of kenosis and of atonement, but not, evidently, in the simple sense that the historian's labor must be hedged in by theological assumptions, but rather that the humanness of Jesus is to be taken seriously and that — as with Schweitzer — Jesus himself thought dogmatically, especially concerning himself and his mission.

C. J. Cadoux also registered his dissent from the growing assumption that a life of Jesus could not be written.[9] Cadoux insisted that one should not bring theological presuppositions to the study of the life of Jesus, but at the same time felt a profound skepticism with regard to the value of Form Criticism — it itself

---

5. Lightfoot, "Form Criticism and Gospel Study," 53–54.

6. Vincent Taylor, "Is It Possible to Write a Life of Christ?: Some Aspects of the Modern Problem," *ExpTim* 53 (1941–42): 61–65.

7. In fairness to Lagrange, it should be said that he had rather sharp things to say about Form Criticism; see his review of Bultmann's *Die Geschichte der synoptischen Tradition* in *RB* 31 (1922): 287–92. He noted that not even Catholics rated the creativity of the community so highly. At the same time Lagrange himself declined to attempt a life of Jesus along classical Roman Catholic lines and confined himself mostly to writing commentaries on the gospels (see chap. 8 for some further attention to his work). Some years later Lagrange's successor, Pierre Benoit, would also take up the subject of Form Criticism, but without departing from Lagrange's critique. See "Réflexions sur la 'Formgeschichtliche Methode,'" *RB* 53 (1946): 481–512.

8. Taylor, "Is It Possible to Write a Life of Christ?," 61.

9. C. J. Cadoux, "Is It Possible to Write a Life of Christ?: A Second Answer," *ExpTim* 53 (1941–42): 175–77. Cadoux's own position was favorably endorsed a few years later by Roderic Dunkerley, "The Life of Jesus: A New Approach," *ExpTim* 57 (1945–46): 264–68. Cadoux's portrayal of a Jesus as the messiah concerned for the fate of Israel provided the basis of a coherent life of Jesus, according to Dunkerley.

displayed widely varying results of questionable value and brought us not much beyond the previous liberal positions, and, besides, was being used mainly to support "conservative and particularly Barthian views." Neither did Cadoux find the previous, warm reception given to Schweitzer among some English scholars commendable, since Schweitzer bequeathed to us "a deluded eschatological fanatic, historically far less real than the liberal Jesus and much further removed from the Christ of traditional faith" (177). And while certainly no biography of Jesus is possible, in the sense of a chronologically arranged picture, nevertheless the various episodes in the gospels can be grouped in clusters that will roughly correspond to the actual sequence of happenings. So it cannot be claimed that a life of Christ is impossible, even though it is surrounded with many problems.

T. W. Manson also offered his judgment that form-critical analysis ascribed too much to the church and its needs, that there remained a substantial body of reliable material going back to eyewitnesses in the case of narrative, and to Jesus himself in the case of teaching.[10] Nevertheless, what remains is a skeleton, not enough to write anything like a continuous account of the ministry, to say nothing of a life. The alternative is to engage in "padding," filling up pages with "background" and speculation, such as early in Christian beginnings produced apocryphal gospels; most current books — Bultmann, Dibelius — are very small works. Eduard Meyer's approach of setting Jesus in a very large historical context was commended. We are in better shape to do that than previously, with better and fairer evaluations of Pharisaism, for instance. We can set Jesus' ministry in its appropriate context, reading back and forth from Judaism to the early church; we can give a reasonable account of his public activity, of matters that brought him to his cross. But even to travel this far requires an exhaustive attention to every single pericope and its *Sitz im Leben*.

So British scholarship, as represented in these leading figures, approached the half-century rather far removed from the turn of the century. The welcome extended (and later withdrawn) by William Sanday to Schweitzer had worn quickly thin, though the eschatological interpretation lingered; liberalism also had spent much of its force, while Form Criticism, though entering by the front door, had not yet settled in as a permanent resident. Yesterday's certainties had become today's ambiguities. And yet there remained something for the historical Jesus critic to do; if optimism about the record was muted, it was not entirely silenced, and theological needs continued to exercise their demands. The British were not prepared to pretend that they were merely historians involved in inquiring into an interesting question. The issue of faith and history was never far off the agenda.

C. J. Cadoux

One of the most persistent writers about the historical Jesus was C. J. Cadoux. As indicated above, Cadoux never abandoned this question and produced two

10. T. W. Manson, "Is It Possible to Write a Life of Christ?," *ExpTim* 53 (1941–42): 248–51.

substantial works on Jesus in the decade of the forties. The first, likely published in 1941, assumed an iconoclastic stance toward many of the preceding
movements (Schweitzer: Jesus a deluded visionary; Form Criticism: wildly varying results; Barthian theology: no help at all for the historical Jesus).[11] Cadoux
himself affirmed the essential trustworthiness of the record, though certainly
took no uncritical position. Streeter's hypothesis on the synoptic problem was
accepted; no Johannine discourse material may be used; no agrapha; the little
apocalypse of Mark 13 is of doubtful authenticity. Jesus was influenced by eschatology, but that was secondary to more practical matters — Jesus was concerned
with helping real persons in concrete situations. Cadoux also assumed that Jesus
saw himself as messiah, did not initially expect suffering and death, and had a
deep interest in the relationship between Israel and Rome.

Theologically, Cadoux was convinced of the need to return to the historical
Jesus "as being the only means of conserving certain religious and ethical values which the traditional Christology (unintentionally, no doubt) threatens to
obscure" (19). Faith is not thereby threatened, for Jesus' saving power rests on
a different foundation.

As to the sources, Mark comes from Rome, based on Peter's recollections;
"M" is a collection of sayings and stories c. 55–60 at Jerusalem; "L" is by Luke
who also wrote the gospel; Matthew was not the apostle but a learned Jewish-
Christian, though his historical authority is "decidedly low" (22).

Jesus saw himself as both son in a special sense and also as messiah. "That
Jesus did actually claim to be both *the* Son of God and the Jewish Messiah is historically undeniable" (34). The baptism attests to his consciousness of sonship,
as does *Abba*; Jesus' emphasis on fatherhood likely has some connection with
his relationship with Joseph, though he seemed not to be close to his mother.
The emphasis on fatherhood was unprecedented in Judaism. Jesus also thought
of himself as a servant to his Father; he applied the Isaianic concept of the servant to himself. On this basis he exhibited love and compassion for others and
sought to bring them into the same filial intimacy with God as himself. Strikingly new was his portrayal of God as one who actively sought out sinners. Jesus
did not limit himself to individuals, however, but also focused on the corporate
and social.

Jesus' consciousness of sonship and servant, attained at his baptism, was
held as a secret at first, for he did not wish to be misunderstood. Also apocalyptic ideas, such as the concept of Son of Man, were secondary to his
son-consciousness. Jesus thought of himself as a lowly servant doing good, not
as a popular hero. The work of the kingdom consisted of exorcisms, healings,
and teachings. The kingdom was already present in these signs, especially exorcisms. Belief in such "discarnate beings" (65) is still not impossible. Jesus saw
himself as winning a victory over the devil — something likely based in his own

---

11. C. J. Cadoux, *The Historic Mission of Jesus: A Constructive Re-examination of the Eschatological
Teaching in the Synoptic Gospels* (New York: Harper, n.d. [1941?]).

experience of temptation. The beelzebul controversy (Luke 11:20 par.) especially demonstrates this point, and also indicates how the kingdom was seen by Jesus as already a present reality.

Jesus spoke and acted with authority, as a teacher and prophet; in contrast to the scribes he quoted no one and amazed people by his personality. He forgave sins or at least assured sinners of forgiveness, disregarded the Mosaic law of the Sabbath, and delegated further authority to his disciples.

His Davidic descent is problematic, but it is possible that the family knew itself to be such. The question of whether he used the title of Son of Man is admittedly complex, with no general agreement. Some uses seem to come from the church, but there are still examples that go back to Jesus. The term in Aramaic meant simply "man"; in Daniel this "man" was representative of Israel, and in Enoch he was the eschatological Judge. Jesus spoke of himself as the suffering-dying and coming Son of man; its prime meaning is found in Ezekiel and Daniel 7. The eschatological passages refer to Jesus himself as the saving Remnant of Israel with himself at its head. The Danielic figure was enriched by the servant passages of Deutero-Isaiah. This use, however, only appeared in the record after the scene at Caesarea-Philippi.

Jesus' use of the kingdom of God concept differed from the "often grotesque beliefs of the apocalyptic writers" (109). Kingdom was not a realm or domain, but kingship or sovereignty. It meant submission to God as king. At the same time God remains the Father; therefore entering the kingdom implies the attitude of a son, expressing filial love to God. As sovereignty the kingdom also implies a social entity, a society of human beings and therefore something that can grow.

What was new about Jesus was his *stress*, what he emphasized. He virtually deposed the Law and emphasized instead motive. There was about him no "pettifogging externalism" (117). The love commandment was supreme, but above all it was Jesus' own quality of personal life that was the original thing — his example, and the power and force of his own moral and spiritual qualities. The stress on motive was illustration of the way, the proper conduct of the kingdom. Thereby Jesus de-emphasized the external and set aside whatever conflicted with spiritual and moral interests. Some implications of a social nature of his emphasis included the divorce prohibition, love of enemies, and devaluation of property. He did not intend an interim ethic, even if he expected an early cataclysmic end; rather, his commands were based on insight into the will of God and inherent moral and spiritual values.

The kingdom exists where men yield obedience to God and therefore is present; it is especially present in Jesus himself, in his activity and work. As present it grows (sower, seed growing secretly, mustard, tares); it is also future, though not as the result of an evolutionary development, but as an inevitable climax to its growth and presence. Jesus shared Israel's national aspirations and its hope for a kingdom. He demonstrated veneration for Israel's institutions: the Law, the temple, Jerusalem, the scriptures, and he saw himself as Israel's messiah, limiting his work to Israel (even though Gentiles would be included in the kingdom). Israel was to be the ideal instrument for the salvation of the whole world. But as national messiah Jesus had to see the kingdom as earthly; he could not have ignored the political scene and the yearning of his people to be free. It would have been inappropriate otherwise for a prophet and someone who came forward as messiah. But the kingdom would not come by war or military means; Jesus instead sought an Israel to be the servant and friend of humankind, to reject vengeance on Rome, and become a moral and spiritual guide to the world.

As to the future kingdom Cadoux distinguished between an earlier and later time in Jesus' ministry. The earlier was a more joyful period, with Jesus anticipating acceptance of his message. Later, after experiencing rejection and hostility, he began speaking of his passion. The future kingdom would come to his own generation as fulfillment of its already-at-work presence and with human cooperation. Jesus spoke of both a coming kingdom and of life beyond death for individuals; the two fused in his view. So he held to notions of paradise as well as of Gehenna, the place of torment. There would be a resurrection and judgment; God is the Judge, the Son of man the witness. Jesus also used the imagery of a messianic banquet.

Jesus accepted his own death. He suffered opposition on many fronts (Pharisees, Sadducees, populace) that convinced him of his ultimate death unless he either fled or fought. Only after Caesarea-Philippi did he express his expectation (though the three predictions may have originally been only one). Yet also Jesus saw some service to come from his death that he described in sacrificial terms. That came from the idea of the suffering servant, who moves people to penitence by his suffering.

Cadoux rejected Schweitzer's theory that Jesus acted out of his own apocalyptic dogmatic assumptions; rather, Jesus acted in reaction to his enemies. Cadoux saw the opposition to Jesus from Pharisees as concentrated in his critique of the Law and of Pharisaism, from Sadducees based on his threat to good order, from the people generally who were not inclined to accept his universalism, but saw him as a flawed messiah who did not fulfill their nationalistic aspirations. It is probable that Jesus expected to be stoned.

The cry of dereliction at his death expressed his anguish; he thought his death would do what his life had not, that is, move sinful men to repentance.

Jesus foresaw the revolt against Rome and thought that it would necessarily follow from the rejection of himself and in particular his teaching on love of enemies [evidence cited from the woes over Galilean towns, the Galileans slain by Pilate, the lamentation over Jerusalem]. The crowd turned against Jesus for his advocacy of enemy love. War would be punishment for the rejection of Jesus, but only as a kind of "automatic" reflex of the operation of moral law.

As to the resurrection, the disciples experienced objective visions. The tomb stories lack strong evidence and probably flowed out of the visionary experiences. Nothing is known of what happened to the physical body; the three days probably simply meant a short interval, so resurrection and return likely collapsed together in Jesus' mind (hence the Parousia predictions are promise of return in the sense of resurrection). God would vindicate Jesus; he expected a brief period of absence in paradise before his return. The return as Son of man depends on Daniel and refers to his glorious coming at the head of the righteous community. During the short interval the disciples should preach of him, expect persecution and the like. Jesus founded a church in the sense of a community believing in him (Matthew 16 is not genuine), but there was no commanded baptism, and the practice of the Lord's Supper as a repeated rite likely did not originate with Jesus. The supper took place, but it was a foretaste of the messianic banquet and of Jesus' sacrificial death as service for others.

Cadoux also took up issues of criticism and faith. He was openly opposed to Barthianism; he rejected the claim that said it was wrong to attempt to get behind the faith-picture to a historical Jesus. The only condition is a humble reverence for truth. Cadoux claimed that his picture accurately represented the synoptic portrayal, less the editorial glosses and tendencies of the evangelists; this picture is not complete, but is nevertheless authoritative.

Regarding the ongoing relevance of Jesus' teaching, it must be acknowledged that Jesus certainly held to much that is irrelevant: the imminent End, judgment, demons. Cadoux would have nothing to do with Roman Catholic or fundamentalist positions, or the notion that Jesus was merely accommodating himself to the thought forms of his day. He also rejected the Ritschlian-liberal dismissal of the eschatological element and found himself attracted to the view that treats the "difficult" matters in Jesus' teaching — the eschatology, and such — as poetic and metaphorical, the oriental mind at work. They need a deliteralizing, though we cannot ignore the fact that Jesus likely meant some of it to be taken realistically. So we have to admit that Jesus was limited, that the eschatological teaching contains error; the prophecies were wrong. We should not be shocked that the Incarnate One took upon himself the beliefs of his age, nor does faith need to fear to investigate fully the life of one who was so great that his meaning cannot be exhausted. At the least his eschatology expressed the urgency of God's demand upon us. In any case, death awaits us all.

The posthumous 1948 work did not actually advance Cadoux's views in any significant way;[12] it seemed to be aimed at a more general, literate audience and, consistent with its title as a "life," sought to provide a more chronological account while also demonstrating a greater willingness to utilize Johannine material in that process.

After providing some standard background material and discussion of the sources, Cadoux entered onto the story of Jesus. The birth stories have little value; the virgin birth is untrue, and it probably arose out of Isa. 7:14. But likely Jesus was descended from David. He knew Aramaic and Hebrew and probably some Greek. He early experienced communion with God as his Father (the story

---

12. C. J. Cadoux, *The Life of Jesus,* Penguin Books (West Dayton, Middlesex: Northumberland Press, 1948). Cadoux died on August 4, 1947, just after finishing the book.

of Jesus at age 12 is historical) and contemplated his mission to heal human ills. There was a period of something over two years between his baptism and his death, so he started his activity in 28 C.E.

His baptism by John is certain and crucial; it meant his consecration as messiah. In it he was "consecrating himself afresh to the heavenly Father's service" (47). Probably also the idea of the messiah as servant entered at that point. Jesus became conscious of new power as messiah, as is seen in the story of the temptation.

Jesus then worked for a while in Galilee (including Cana), then went to Jerusalem for the Passover (from John), meeting Nicodemus. There were eight to nine months of baptizing activity in Judea, terminated by the arrest of John.

Jesus had a consciousness of being the "son" and carried on a mission of compassion in the role of suffering servant; he campaigned against Satan and the devils; he declined to make his messiahship public. He lived in the intensity of the fatherhood of God, which belonged with the proclamation of the kingdom of God; the Father is also the King and expects filial response as a condition of entering the kingdom. The new life of the kingdom was the subject of Jesus' ethics; it was not an interim ethic, but centered in the love commandment. That was not new with Jesus, who did not repudiate the Law, but its reach and content were new.

Jesus had a political concern; he sought to banish hostility between Israel and Rome, not through violence but through deeds of love. His urging of love of enemies brought him condemnation. Jesus expected acceptance of his message and his role as messiah, but was disappointed. The use of the Son of man title before and after Caesarea-Philippi reflects this state of affairs. Caesarea-Philippi is a critical scene for understanding Jesus' ministry. On this basis we can allocate different episodes in his activity, for otherwise placement of events is difficult. [Cadoux followed this principle and allocated various teachings — aphorisms, sayings, parables, and scenes — as he thought appropriate.] After Caesarea-Philippi and the Transfiguration Jesus set out for Jerusalem to attend the Festival of Booths (October of 29). Various contentions occurred there; he then left Jerusalem after Booths, and came again in December for Dedication, with time in Galilee in between [here were assigned various incidents]. The threat from Antipas sent him back to Jerusalem at Dedication, and in early 30 (January) he went to the transjordan [more teaching was located there]. He crossed the Jordan and went on to Jericho, to Bethany and the raising of Lazarus (though whatever happened there is not explainable). He then fled to Ephraim until Passover; from there he would come again to Jerusalem.

Cadoux repeated here his earlier thesis of a Jesus with a political concern, who aroused enmity from most elements in Judaism: the Pharisees, Sadducees, and even the populace, who did not accept his more universal outlook or his attempt to seek reconciliation with Rome. Jesus' refusal as messiah to strike at Rome or even to defend himself was a factor. He could have avoided his fate, but his morality would not let him. He found consolation in the servant poems, which suggested a vindication that would come after his efficacious death had moved people to repentance. This was later put into sacrificial language.

The last supper is best located in John. Jesus came to Jerusalem on Sunday, Nisan 9 (he would not have traveled the day before, the Sabbath); there was an evening meal and an anointing. On Monday occurred the messianic entrance, on Tuesday the temple attack. Cadoux assigned sayings and scenes to each day; the scene of the woman in adultery from John was located on Wednesday. At the supper on Thursday there was foot-washing along with a messianic feast; the symbolic act of the bread and cup, representing Jesus' body and blood, amounted to saying that the whole personality of Jesus was nourishment for his followers. Subsequent events (from Mark) followed: Gethsemane, the arrest and trial with accusation of blasphemy (an unworthy claim to be messiah). Political charges were laid before Pilate, leading to Jesus' crucifixion. The roles of Joseph of Arimathea and Nicodemus were accepted as historical. The tomb and appearance stories contain contradictions, but the appearance stories are older and more reliable.

An epilogue took up theological issues and addressed both fundamentalists and the more orthodox. Of the Dialectical Theology Cadoux said, "Gentlemen, this will not do" (211). We need the historical Jesus; the church has always appealed to him. Faith need not fear the consequences of historical inquiry.

Cadoux's work was in some respects that of a still-convinced liberal, but also there were differences along the lines of the acceptance of the eschatological element and the characteristically English melding together in the self-consciousness of Jesus the notions of Son of God–Son of man and servant of Yahweh. More distinctive in Cadoux's presentation was the emphasis on the politically aware Jesus, who wished to deliver his people from a forthcoming disastrous revolt against Rome, but was a singular failure in that respect. To be sure, Cadoux's Jesus was committed to a nonviolent approach, urging a universal love directed to all persons, even enemies, and for that suffered rejection from his own people.[13] But that perspective at least addresses one of the continuing puzzles of the "life" of Jesus: How did this seemingly peaceable, loving, kindly person — all those usual designations of Jesus — manage to get himself violently executed? The perpetual problem with the liberal Jesus, and many others not so liberal, was that it was impossible to understand his end, his death. Someone who simply went about preaching the fatherliness of God, that we are all his children, and that we are all to love each other, cannot possibly have been threatening enough to anyone to get himself killed. The liberal Jesus was not worth killing; he was too innocuous. At least Cadoux ventured far enough to bring that question into view, though he himself thought that Jesus did not foresee all the consequences of his own attitudes.

---

13. The same position was advanced earlier by the American historian Vladimir Simkhovitch (above, chap. 4, 137–38).

William Manson

A still more impressive work is that by the Scottish professor William Manson.[14] It offered a denser analysis of similar positions, and maintained its own perspective while carrying on a dialogue with Form Criticism as represented in Bultmann especially. The preface stated succinctly the difference from Form Criticism: the messianic ideas of Israel were the source of not only the church's ideas about Jesus, but of Jesus himself. And the background of Jesus himself was the prophetic religion of the Old Testament.

For Manson the starting point was the certain fact that before any proclamation of Jesus as divine revelation was the acknowledgment of him as messiah, as Son of man, and this confession had to originate in the mind of Jesus himself. The argument followed: there is no nonmessianic faith in the gospels (Apollos might have been an exception). Mason rejected Wilhelm Bousset's reconstruction (Jesus' personality impressed on the disciples his messiahship; disappointed by his death, they substituted the notion of the Son of man and expected his return in glory). But, said Manson, his death on the cross marked him as excommunicated from God (Deut. 21:23). Could the disciples have surmounted that with no authorization from Jesus himself, even convinced of the Easter event? Would even Easter have led to the further claim of Jesus returning on the clouds of heaven as Son of man? Could they have introduced the suffering servant figure into their messianic hopes, especially if Jesus had made no messianic claims?

Manson rejected R. Reitzenstein's theory of the myth of the Son-of-man incognito, the primal man who fell prey to the powers of darkness, but left behind a part of his heavenly being from which the soul of man comes. The myth appears in the Son of man of Daniel, a redeemer figure. This supposedly provided the disciples with the idea of Jesus' heavenly origin and necessary suffering. But Manson found nothing of it in the gospel record. Universal Son-of-man redemption theories are too nebulous to build on. We have to go back to Jesus himself. From him we learn the meaning of kingdom of God, Son of God, and Son of man.

The messianic consciousness of Jesus is not traceable to its beginnings, but likely came as the result of a process, toward the end of his career. An intense awareness of God drove Jesus to a more than prophetic vision of the nearness of the kingdom and his own sense of vocation.

Manson accepted Streeter's solution to the synoptic problem, noting that Matthew's and Luke's use of Mark gives a clue as to how the whole tradition was redacted; the same tendencies must have been at work earlier. As to Form Criticism generally, it fails to see that historicity is determined by substance, not form, and that individuals, not communities, create. Also the tradition was

---

14. William Manson, *Jesus the Messiah: The Synoptic Tradition of the Revelation of God in Christ: With Special Reference to Form-Criticism* (London: Hodder and Stoughton, 1943). Manson was Professor of Biblical Criticism at the University of Edinburgh.

more closely connected to historical events than Form Criticism assumes. So we see Jesus through church tradition, but the image remains visible. That is so especially where that tradition moves contrary to the interests of the church.

Manson then took up a lengthy inquiry into various elements in the ministry of Jesus. He appealed to Acts and Mark as pointing to a primary tradition of signs and mighty deeds of Jesus (with instructive insights into Markan theology, though he thought Mark was composed for a hellenistic world). Mark's pronouncement stories show already a messianic revelational quality, and the miracle stories bear witness to the same point; the miracles are not late, but a primary stratum testifying to the messianic activity of Jesus. Parables also are signs of the mystery of the kingdom.

Q attests to an early interest in Jesus' teaching. The primary interest originally was what was done through Jesus the Christ. So it is all the more remarkable that the teaching came along with the other picture. The incorporation of Q into Matthew and Luke was perhaps the single most important event in the history of Christian literature; it put teaching at the heart of the kerygma and related the message of the kingdom to organic ideals in human nature (humility, love, service). Here Manson seemed to be urging the point that the ethicizing of the gospel of the signs of Jesus as messiah was a watershed event in primitive church history, in that it correlated the messianic revelatory picture with instinctive human concerns.

How can we recognize genuine Jesus material? Sayings expressing a crisis are original. Thus many wisdom-logia can be seen this way; Manson agreed largely with Bultmann's statement of the criterion for recognition of Jesus material: call to repentance, a new spirit, a sense of eschatological intensity, something that poses the crisis of the kingdom. Mainly Manson wished to show that the teaching had inherent messianic significance; he cited examples from prophetic and apocalyptic sayings. Even the Johannine Q saying (Matt. 11:25–30 par.) was taken as genuine; the situation was Jesus' disclosure to the disciples of his messiahship and his claim to impart a saving knowledge.

The ethical teaching bears a similar messianic impression. Q already was an abstraction, rootless logia valued for their own sake and able to be applied in varied situations. So Q had an absolute character as well as its original crisis-of-the-kingdom character and reflected that in its integration into Matthew and Luke.

Manson briefly examined the Sermon on the Mount. The sequence of Q is best preserved in Luke. In Matthew the Q material functions as a definition of the Christian doctrine of righteousness. Thus also here is disclosed its absolute character as revelation of the truth in Jesus. The Sermon is the revelation of the Son of man and is set in the context of grace (blessings on the poor, and so on). Parallels between the beatitudes and Isaiah 61 show that Jesus' thought was impregnated with Old Testament prophetic ideals.

The ethic of love is absolute and above law. The Law in Judaism stood between humankind and God, as also in apocalypticism. The expectation of the near End tended toward a lack of repentance and sincerity, along with fantasy and self-congratulation. Jesus' ethic was, however, existential, demanding unconditional surrender to God. Love transcended the Law by becoming the norm, an absolute that is nevertheless unattainable. Parallels in other sources from antiquity lack the rigor of Jesus' demand.

The near approach of the kingdom means grace and also that righteousness is possible. Jesus based this on prophetic principles, especially in the picture of the servant as a sufferer for others (turn the other cheek, love your enemies). Jesus announced an ethic of crisis and called for a break with the existing world. Yet if the ethic is truly connected with the kingdom that is itself only partly present and not yet fully manifest, then it would seem that the ethic itself is only partially realizable, not absolutely. Yet Jesus' ethic is "organic" to life here (91), for Jesus intended first to bring us to knowledge of the will of God (which shames us, and so on); it is therefore relevant, but also the norm is relative to the situation even as an absolute (and thus also organic).

As to such commands as nonresistance, they may seem anarchic, but reveal what perfect trust in God really would mean. We cannot press such demands on the state so as to lead to disorder and defeat of the good. Therefore it would be "not Christian to press the Christian absolute ... upon orders of life which stand outside of the powers of the kingdom of God" (93). The Christian ethic does not set up a law, but creates a transforming tension in society.

The examination of the tradition as a whole discloses that "*there is no smallest unit of this tradition which is not instinct with christological significance*" (94; italics his). That is, we cannot get behind the tradition to a nonmessianic stratum. At the same time the tradition kept to history; it did not exploit the entire messianic deposit — the warrior, king, judge are absent — but there is a consistent servant-figure of Isaiah. A recollection of actual history has guided the use of the Old Testament.

The tradition acknowledges a christological reticence on Jesus' part. The Son of man sayings are equivocal; we do not know the origins of this consciousness, but its certainty is clear. There was a stage where the claim was only implicit, not overt, even though always Jesus' personality stood in the framework of the crisis posed by the signs and message of the kingdom. So, again, the messianic idea of early Christianity bears the impression of the impact of historical fact upon the traditional doctrine of the last things. Jesus had an extraordinary sense of mission brought out by the application of Israel's messianic hopes to him, by himself and his church.

This sense of mission is incontestable — the crisis at hand, the fulfillment of prophecy, something greater at work, the mighty works, a sense of authority, calling disciples. The tradition ascribes three main titles to Jesus to express his significance: Son of God, servant, and Son of man. All have the common pattern of exaltation and divine gift; all are invested with wisdom, righteousness, the Spirit of God, and all display the mission to be a light to the Gentiles. And so: "*Functions first attributed to the Davidic prince in the prophets and in the Psalms reappear in a form transfigured or infiltrated with suffering in the person of the Servant and finally are invested with every circumstance of apocalyptic glory and splendor in the figure of the supernatural Son of Man*" (99; italics his). So a single expectation for a redeemer underwent different historical phases; of these Son of man is most prominent and expressive for Jesus of his messianic role. It had to do with the transcendent kingdom, was most final and transcendent and inclusive, and went beyond the nationalistic hope.

Son of God was for Mark et al. equivalent to messiah, as also in Q. Did it come from Jesus? Yes; it rooted in his experience of God as Father, in his filial relation to God. That appears in the story of the baptism and Matt. 11:25ff par.

As to the idea of the servant, it is never spoken of directly by Jesus, but it informs his mission. It was probably absorbed by Jesus into the Son of man concept (the Son of man came to minister). Son of man is the subject, the servant is the predicate (Son of man is the leading term, the servant defines what he does).

Son of man is original with Jesus, though not every instance goes back to him; sometimes it was inserted by the church. Only Jesus used the term, which hints at its originality. Not all examples were references to himself; some were used "objectively," as he did of the kingdom: the Son of man is not yet here, but projects into the present (like the kingdom). There are three categories: (1) the Son of man coming in glory — these are authentic, as in Mark 14:62, where we cannot see the church at work (unfulfilled predictions); (2) suffering and rejection and exaltation — these cannot be found in the messianic expectation of Judaism; (3) the present activity of the Son of man — aside from those that come from the church (Mark 2:10, 28); the latter relate to the present life of the Son of man. Manson found the idea of the exaltation of the Son of man from a life of suffering to originate in the mind of Jesus himself; it was Jesus who achieved a synthesis of servant and Son of man. The Son of man becomes redeemer — man, friend, benefactor, and vicarious substitute for human beings. Part of the attraction of the title for Jesus was this identification with the poor, the sinful and ostracized. In any case, the Son of man in Daniel and Ezekiel was an ethical figure (he brought a transformed life); that is to be seen behind Matthew's parable of judgment (Matt. 25:31–46).

Manson took up questions related to Jesus' passion and death. Did the disciples flee, lose faith, and only later interpret Jesus' death with the help of scripture, or was there already an interpretation at hand? "In the one case the Church began with the uninterpreted fact of the death of Jesus and found a meaning for it in Scripture; in the other case it started from an accepted association between that death and our sins and found that nexus of ideas corroborated by Scripture" (124). The disciples were not so likely completely devastated by the crucifixion, as is often assumed.

The details of the passion predictions may have been supplied by history, but they are authentic at their core. Jesus himself spoke of his suffering and death as a ransom based on Isaiah 53. The background lies in the Old Testament, in

Enoch, and in 4 Maccabees (the value of the martyrs and the suffering of the righteous). In this context Manson observed that criticism cannot establish the authenticity of any word absolutely, but it can show that it is not impossible that Jesus held this or that idea or uttered some particular saying.

As to the accounts of the last supper, Manson ranked Mark's version earlier than Paul's. The Lukan form represents a separate tradition. John's chronology is to be preferred. But whether Mark or Paul, Jesus gave a new meaning to an old (probably Chaburah) meal. The use of the cup and bread points to the messianic kingdom and Jesus' own sacrificial offering. The Son of man is the Isaianic servant who brings salvation to his people and attains the glory of the Son of man. The covenant blood is blood applied in blessing to Israel, that is, Jesus' life as offering to God and available for persons.

An epilogue reasserted the origin of messianic hopes in Jesus himself. Also, Manson said, Jesus transcended apocalyptic dualism by bringing the salvation of God near again. Apocalypse in Judaism had put everything off to a distant future; Jesus brought that salvation into relationship with the world by bringing the present under the form and power of the world to come (the kingdom as already here at work).

Manson's work represents a highly sophisticated accounting of the Anglo-Scottish alternative reading of the historical Jesus. It was a response to the Wrede-Bultmann axis that ran through much of German approaches to the historical Jesus, and it poses the critical question: Did Christian faith originate in the mind of Jesus or only in the experience of his followers? The alternatives were starkly set, and there was little middle ground between them. Either Jesus held a messianic view of himself or he did not, though naturally we can also demur and say that we do not know. For the Anglo-Scottish mind the thought that Jesus himself did not hold the original christology is an intolerable one. The assumption appears to be that locating the christology in Jesus himself provides a greater authentication for faith, although that is a problematic proposition. What would it really prove if Jesus thought himself to be the messiah? Would faith be more comforted or its decision made easier? Besides, there is a double-edged sword here, as the issue of Jesus' sanity already had demonstrated.

Yet the position as enunciated by Manson so well cannot be merely dismissed with a wave of a theological hand. It is a powerful alternative, residing at bottom on the arguable notion that a nonmessianic tradition cannot be found in the (mainly synoptic) gospels. The earliest stratum already exhibits messianic faith.[15] And when a theologizing process clearly occurs, as in the application of scripture to the story of Jesus, that is not a case of applying for the first time an interpretation to uninterpreted events (if such things exist), but of understanding anew

---

15. It has to be added by way of clarification that Manson in particular was not always careful about whether he was reading at the level of the historical Jesus or of the evangelists or some other stage. These distinctions have to be scrupulously maintained if the fundamental thesis is to have convincing power.

or in renewed circumstances a set of events that came with their own interpretation. That is what Manson meant when he referred to history impressing itself on scripture, not the other way around.[16]

George S. Duncan

A final example of another, not dissimilar work is the book by George S. Duncan that appeared in 1947; it broke no new ground, but may be taken as marking the conclusion of the decade in the production of Anglo-Scottish work on the historical Jesus.[17]

The preface stated that the aim of the book was to get a perspective on viewing Jesus. No life or objectivity is possible, but a portrait within the faith of the church is the best. Duncan would seek for the main "peaks" in the story.

The author first sketched some research history — Strauss, liberalism generally. The latter has been dethroned. Jesus cannot be separated from his influence — the rise of the church — after him; nor can miracles be dismissed out of hand. Also the exclusivity of Mark and Q was denied, while John and Streeter's Proto-Luke theory were appealed to (Q+special L, inserted into Mark). Form Criticism is too skeptical; it does not allow enough for the impact of Jesus himself. If Bultmann is right, Christian faith is rooted in a myth. Yet Duncan found something valuable in Form Criticism: its use rightly led to the conclusion that there is no biography, and then showed us how the gospel tradition came to be and how it was shaped. Therefore it strengthened evidence for the historical value of the tradition. The quest can be renewed with hope and confidence.

Duncan placed the message of Jesus under the heading of the God-man concept. God is transcendent (some Persian dualism resides in the background) and present. Humankind, as in the Old Testament, is the most exalted being of creation made in the image of God. Jesus' aim was to establish the fatherly rule of God. This fatherhood was only for those in relationship to him. The kingdom of God is the rule of God; people place themselves under it. The time is always now. Jesus stood on ethical and spiritual principles; he was not an apocalyptist. The fatherhood of God and the kingdom of God amount to the same thing, the acknowledgment of God as Father and King. The kingdom begins with its establishment in the hearts of people. Jesus had an eschatology, if by eschatology is meant fulfillment. His expectation was happening already, not as the last in a string of events. Such a view carried ethical implications.

Many titles were given Jesus, and he claimed most of them: Son of God, Son of man, Messiah, Lord. The concept of messiah had many streams — Israel's

---

16. The same points had been made a dozen years before in the work of Hoskyns and Davey (above, chap. 5, 185–87).

17. George S. Duncan, *Jesus, Son of Man: Studies Contributory to a Modern Portrait* (London: Nisbet, 1947). Duncan was Principal of St. Mary's College and Regius Professor of Biblical Criticism, University of St. Andrews. The book was the Croall lectures (twenty-ninth) in Edinburgh for 1937; the war intervened and prevented publication until 1947, along with some expansions.

deliverer, Son of man, suffering servant. The usual prophetic expectation was that God himself would intervene, but there was no prophet-messiah. There was also no suffering messiah in Judaism. Here Duncan characterized the beliefs of various sects and parties and also the nature of popular religion; he ascribed the apocalyptic hope to ordinary people who despaired of conditions and hoped for divine intervention. Luke 1–2 show these hopes, the true religion of the pious Israelite, not legalism or apocalyptic frenzy.

John the Baptist was eschatological and ethical. True eschatology is ethical, in that it demands repentance. The coming One of John was Elijah, with himself as a servant — a prophetic, not apocalyptic view. As to Jesus and John, the Fourth Gospel provides insight; John saw the Spirit on Jesus and came to see him as the mighty One, and also as servant (proclaiming him Lamb, Son, and prophet like Moses or Elijah). The same can be seen in John's inquiry from prison about Jesus' messianic status. Are you the prophet? he asked. His faith in Jesus must have wavered in prison. The difference between Jesus and John was that Jesus had the Spirit. On this accounting, one can only imagine John's surprise when Jesus said he, John, was Elijah. Duncan skipped lightly over why Jesus might have come for a baptism of repentance.

Jesus did think of himself as Son of God, but it was not messianic. He had the experience — the revelation of his sonship — at his baptism. That made others his brothers, since all are also sons (though Jesus was in a unique sense). So Jesus' purpose was to gather a family of sons for the Father.

Did Jesus think he was messiah? While rejecting Wrede's thesis Duncan still conceded that Jesus made no open claims to messiahship. He did not refuse messiahship, but turned toward the idea of the Son of man. In his entrance into Jerusalem he wished to suggest the idea of the humble king, not messiah. The open acknowledgment of messiahship occurred only after Easter.

Jesus used the title "Son of man" of himself, but it did not come from Enoch. It was derived rather from Daniel, in that "Son of man" meant the true people of God. Duncan gave the three categories of Son of man sayings around which the discussion revolved: eschatological coming, suffering, and general-present; or Parousia, passion, and earthly life. There are no sayings linking judgment and suffering, as though Jesus thought first of his humiliation, then of his future vindication. Ezekiel supplied some details. The Son of man is then a prophet, the messenger of judgment and salvation who also embodied in his personal life the purposes of God for all humankind. His work was the creation of the true people of God, a new order of humanity. From Caesarea-Philippi on Jesus referred more narrowly to himself, his suffering and future glory. The suffering sayings come from Jesus, even if the church added some details. There was also a corporate implication, in that all in Jesus' fellowship share his fate.

Jesus saw himself as fulfilling the will of God in going to Jerusalem. He expected his death; it was a sacrifice, bridging the chasm of sin between humans and God. He was to bring home the lost, which he had done in his ministry anyway, extending the forgiveness of God and often speaking of such in his parables and enacting in his healings. This seeking of sinners was initiated by God the Father (here Jesus differed from others of his day) — a revolutionary notion that was opposed to the Pharisaic way and specifically challenged the sacrificial system.

In his future function as Son of man Jesus could have been referring to (1) his rising again, (2) his enthronement, or (3) his Parousia. But more likely he held a more spiritual conception. Some Parousia sayings are from the church; probably Jesus played that down in any case. The resurrection was for him a triumph over death (emergence from the tomb was not the point). What was important in his coming in judgment was actually his present lordship, but he did also use the picture-language of the future.

Mark 9:1 suggests an unfulfilled expectation. Some event short of the final consummation is in view, something like the beginnings of the new order following Jesus' death and resurrection. So the End is near because God has drawn near in redemption; it is at hand because the Spirit is present and operative. Thus the kingdom of God has come and will come, but that is not two comings, even though we should not eliminate the future.

Jesus also claimed to be Lord. It was a spiritual lordship, yet he also triumphed over the temple, the laws, and his opponents.

What about the final judgment? Matthew 25, which comes from Jesus, is not really about the judgment-scene itself, but the principles upon which the judgment occurs — feeding the hungry and so on. It has an ethical base that lifts it above apocalypticism.

Jesus called disciples, not merely as a rabbi or teacher might, but as a prophet would. He trained disciples for manifesting the kingdom here and now. His methods were teaching; parables were especially characteristic. They were not meant to confuse, but some failed to understand them. His ethics described the behavior of the disciples on a daily basis, as sons of the Father would act. They were not an interim ethic or even conditions of the kingdom, but as the kingdom was present already they were a call to live life in accordance with the time of fulfillment.

Did Jesus mean to found the Church? Certainly he intended a fellowship, behind which lies the history of Israel as community. The supper was simply the last of many, the bread a symbol of the unity of believers with Christ in fellowship, the blood a sharing in his death. We cannot say that Jesus founded the church; he found a community in ruins and set about reestablishing it — but it was a community, not an institution or organization.

The church's faith today resides in resurrection, the messiahship, Jesus' coming, and the Spirit. The apocalyptic hopes in the early church cannot simply be repeated. The early believers were already living in the time of the Spirit, the presence of God.

The last of the book was cognizant of the war and the need for the gospel to speak anew, but first found it helpful to go back and "see Jesus."

Bare outlines do not often do justice to a work, but the main themes are recognizable and even quite familiar. Duncan considered much in the tradition to be trustworthy — most of it, in fact — though also he had a high degree of critical awareness and carried on a dialogue with secondary literature. The by-now familiar position that ascribes to Jesus the consciousness of Son–Servant–Son of man was set forth, but just how Jesus managed to get all those together in his consciousness at the same time was left unexplained. There was also too much in the book that was "And yet" theology: Form Criticism is too radical, and yet it helps confirm the tradition; Jesus preached an eschatological kingdom, and yet the present element was what was important; he claimed to be Son of man, and yet his present rule was most significant; the End is near, and yet the real consummation has come already in the Spirit and the church. And so on. Some might see that as queasiness over perplexing issues, others as a failure of nerve. More charitably it is a cultural trait, a willingness to find something worthwhile in a variety of positions and a recognition of the relativity of all positions.

The Historical Jesus in American Circles

To cross the Atlantic to America is not, after all, to visit an alien planet; there is much that is shared from abroad, as it should be, but there remains also a distinctive flavor, as there is wherever we have traveled. The war doubtless created a degree of motionlessness; the breakdown of communications among scholarly communities forecloses the sharing of findings and resources. If there is a positive side to that situation, it is that such communities are compelled to develop their own distinctive traits. These traits can be seen in the modest amount of activity surrounding the question of the historical Jesus in America in the decade of the forties. In most respects what is to be observed is the strengthening and advancing of what had already come into place.

C. C. McCown

Such a work was the review of *Leben-Jesu-Forschung* by C. C. McCown, appearing in 1940.[18] It undertook to examine the "Quest" from a sociohistorical perspective; for example, Strauss's work ought to be seen in light of the post-Napoleonic period of malaise and retrogression and the conflict of the new currents engendered by the industrialism that coursed through Europe. Later, the Great War succeeded in doing what eschatology and *Interimsethik* could not: undermine the authority of Jesus. The eschatological Jesus was considered to be of no social relevance whatever. McCown, however, did not think that apocalypticism was socially irrelevant. He argued that apocalyptic movements have always had utopian views and were directed to the betterment of the world on

---

18. C. C. McCown, *The Search for the Real Jesus: A Century of Historical Study* (New York: Scribner's, 1940). McCown was Professor of New Testament Literature and Director of the Palestine Institute in the Pacific School of Religion. He had earlier produced a splendid accounting of the social gospel movement in *The Genesis of the Social Gospel: The Meaning of the Ideals of Jesus in the Light of their Antecedents* (New York: Knopf, 1929). He believed Jesus to have claimed the messiahship as an apocalyptic prophet.

behalf of the poor and oppressed. He observed that in the preaching of Jesus future and present were equally mingled, with the consequence that for Jesus the eschatology was not as consistent as Schweitzer thought. The eschatology did not therefore destroy the ethics; the latter was not interim. Much progress has been made in reconstructing the historical Jesus, in spite of problems. As to the ongoing relevance of Jesus' message and teaching:

> They must be translated and interpreted for other times and places and peoples. The expectation of the imminent kingdom, which he shared, was wrong. The social, economic, and political conditions he faced were very different from ours. Therefore the methods by which we may hope for the realization of God's will on earth will be very different from his. It is not, however, an unhistorical modernization to say that the ideal, nevertheless, remains the same. If any one today wishes to be a son of the Father in whom Jesus believed, he will exhibit the same unwavering faith in righteousness, the same absolute devotion, the same unlimited selflessness, and the same thoroughly revolutionary temper. No Christian can be satisfied with things as they are. (300)

It was a temperate, if still optimistic, assessment of human possibilities in the west, as moved still by the liberal vision of Jesus. It had no sympathy for the Barthian return to dogmatics.

David E. Adams

A work not commanding very much attention, but one deserving some mention, if only for its suggestive approach, is that of David E. Adams.[19] Like McCown he put himself in the liberal camp in a broad sense; his book aimed at redressing some of the difficulties the "modern man" has with the biblical material: problems presented by the text can be overcome when it is seen that they arise from not understanding the text in its own context. There is also the need to show how the forms of thought and expression therein were peculiar to another time and must be disentangled from that time and respoken in a more modern idiom.

The main thesis was that Jesus was presented in the gospels as a "Man of God," a type of figure depicted throughout the Old Testament (Abraham, Moses, prophets) and whose characteristics were given (fifteen of them). Adams then traced the depiction of Jesus throughout the synoptic record in a kind of minicommentary on the relevant texts (eliminating John from consideration). Along the way he indulged freely in considerations of authenticity, but without any formal discussion of the criteria. The primary consideration seemed to be the way in which the later church has impacted the tradition. Another, unspoken criterion was the old rational one of noncontradiction (the virgin birth contradicts the genealogy and so on). The author seemed *au courant* with the scholarship of the time, noting that no life or biography can be composed; only incidents are usable.

---

19. David Adams, *Man of God* (New York: Harper, 1941). Adams was Professor of the History and Literature of Religion at Mount Holyoke College.

The geography and chronology are editorial. The miraculous Jesus was rationalized away. The journey north and subsequent move to Jerusalem are the turning point (not Caesarea-Philippi, which reflects the later faith of the church). Adams was loath to pronounce on the extent of apocalypticism in Jesus. The modern social gospel is a good thing and does not depend on being found in Jesus' words anyway. The heart of his message was (again) the fatherhood of God. The trial has unhistorical elements (Pilate emphasizing Jesus' innocence); the resurrection was the experience of the continuing reality of Jesus with his disciples.

In summarizing the picture of Jesus that resulted from his critical analysis of the texts, Adams offered a Jesus who spoke and acted as a Jew, more like a prophet than messiah. He was baptized by John, struggled with himself, and tried the way of a teacher. He surprised himself by becoming a healer. His growing prominence disturbed the authorities, forcing the journey north and the decision to go to Jerusalem, though much is unclear because of the overlay of the later church. Things did not go well at Jerusalem. It is uncertain that he anticipated death, but certainly he came to a tragic end. His legacy was a sense of nearness to God, of a personal power, of a sense of his permanence, not ended by his death, and of the experience of salvation (freedom from a sense of sin, capacity to lead a moral life). This Jesus fits better modern needs.

Whether Adams's "Man of God" can actually be identified as a formal *typos* may be argued, but the location of Jesus within a strongly Judaic origin was in itself a worthwhile move. Apparently, so far as I can see, no one took up the man-of-God hypothesis, and probably it was simply too broadly defined to constitute a recognizable category; otherwise, the Jesus depicted was drawn largely from the liberal stream, was characteristic of American attention to the social gospel, and occasionally offered some insights worthy of consideration.

John Wick Bowman

John Wick Bowman wished to inquire into Jesus' intention.[20] The book was aimed at the intelligent layman and the minister; and although it claimed no originality, Walter Marshall Horton (Fairchild Professor of Theology at Oberlin College), who wrote a foreword to it, characterized it as a "revolutionary" book. Horton exaggerated.

The book examined the probable background to Jesus and found it in the messianic prophetic expectation (Joel), with its call to repentance and constitution of the Remnant in Israel, to which were added the further themes of forgiveness, the Spirit, the judgment, and the messiah as agent of salvation and judgment. The picture corresponds to the sermons in Acts (C. H. Dodd) and has to have a basis in truth. The same model is to be seen in the ministries of John the Baptist and Jesus.

---

20. John Wick Bowman, *The Intention of Jesus* (Philadelphia: Westminster Press, 1943). Bowman was Professor of New Testament Literature and Exegesis, Western Theological Seminary, Pittsburgh, Pa.

The baptism of Jesus is historical; it cannot be explained as a church addition. Why did Jesus come to John? He answered the call to repent, which amounted to accepting the new movement or not. His baptism showed his agreement with the new movement, as well as his ordination as messiah and suffering servant (combining Psalm 2 with Isa. 42:1). The subsequent temptation demonstrated a struggle with the notion of the suffering versus the glorious messiah; he would be the former.

Bowman examined various cultural contexts for the historical Jesus (hellenistic, apocalyptic, legalistic, Davidic king, prophetic heritage). The latter was to be preferred, with Jesus' connection to John the Baptist as central.[21] Various groups at the time were discussed: the ritualists were Sadducees who introduced hellenism; Jesus was not influenced by them (he did not even know Greek). The apocalyptists were characterized by extravagant visions; there is nothing of apocalypticism in Jesus. All Jesus' teaching is from the Old Testament and the prophetic literature in particular. The legalists were the Pharisees; they get more respect than in earlier scholarship, though certainly Jesus was not one of them. The prophetic tradition embraced the ethical messiah, not the Son of man of apocalypticism; it included universalism, the Remnant concept, and a nonnational, individual relationship to God.

Did Jesus see himself as messiah? Yes, the messiah of the Remnant. This was an original and creative element in his thought, though it stood in continuity with the old. For evidence Bowman pointed to the winsomeness of Jesus' teaching, its authority and wisdom. Compared with the rabbis Jesus emphasized the intention, the motive. Also his signs, his healings, went with his word. This integration of teaching and activity was "startlingly unique,"[22] along with a sense of continuity with the prophetic tradition.

Jesus did speak of himself as Son of man. Sometimes it was only a substitute for "I"; but it was also his self-designation as messiah, and the originality of Jesus lay in adding the note of humiliation, of suffering and death. That began first at his baptism and temptation, based on his insight that love lies at the heart of the universe. Love requires suffering.

Still, the Son of man title was but a shell for the kernel of his thought about himself. It was an apocalyptic title, in which the suffering became detached from the notion of the suffering servant and attached to another (Son of man). Son of man referred to the eventual exaltation of the messiah, to which Jesus added the idea of suffering, an utterly unique combination. The process was as follows: he became conscious at his baptism of his messiahship, of the need for lowliness and suffering (a love-driven insight); later he used the Son of man title because of its elasticity to express this combination of exaltation and suffering.

---

21. In considering the Judaic environment, Bowman made an interesting observation about Jesus' originality, about which he was otherwise very concerned. He noted that, if Jesus were so discontinuous with his environment, he would be also to the later church (44). The point bears on the issue of determining authenticity.

22. Bowman, *Intention of Jesus*, 115

The concept of Jesus' lordship actually has the strongest claim to originality. He called others to follow him, to be disciples. The basis of his lordship was his filial relation to the Father. He himself was the unique Son; his lordship also was seen in his ethical purity, his holiness.

What did Jesus intend? The social gospel said that he intended others to follow his teaching, but not only did his words matter, allegiance to his person was also critical. He chose twelve; he created a Chaburah (the last supper was a Chaburah meal). He aimed at setting up a definitive group in which the kingdom ethic would be realized (the church). It is the fellowship of those who shared the kingdom's experience. Bowman agreed with the social gospel emphasis on the kingdom of God as an ethical imperative in the present, but missed the note of redemption and of community embodied in the church. A relation to Jesus is necessary; he inaugurates the kingdom of God on earth. He intended to raise up a Remnant, the new Israel, and he could do so because he was messiah of the Remnant spoken of in the prophets. Said Bowman:

> Can anyone doubt that this Jesus of the Gospels — the Jesus who thought and served and lived and died as that One did — is the *real* Jesus? Can anyone deny that the marvelously unique Lord of the Christian faith produced that faith, and not the faith that Lord? (225; italics his)

Bowman's end-thesis was then to suggest that the picture of Jesus was unique at that time and in that context and that this uniqueness went back to Jesus himself.

There is much that is commendable here: the location of Jesus in a believable context (prophetic, Remnant), the connecting of Jesus to the church that followed him. The quest for the originality of Jesus, with which Bowman seemed much concerned, was certainly not novel; it arises especially where a more conventional christology is missing, but it also appears in even more conservative circles. The liberals sought the uniqueness of Jesus because they had no other ground for a continuing interest in him; the conservatives sought it because they already had a christological interest in him. Both tended to purchase his originality at the price of his Jewishness, the liberals by a distorted emphasis on Jesus' "transcending" or "overcoming" of his Judaic environment, the conservatives by an often frenetic devaluing of everything Jewish in order to have Jesus stand out all the more. So, paradoxically, groups at opposite ends of the spectrum often arrived at the same place, but for opposite reasons: liberals because they had no christology and conservatives because they had too much.

Bowman wished to hold the historical figure in the context of church and confession. Jesus was unequivocally for him a product of his Jewish environment (Old Testament prophetic, messianic Remnant), and his originality was to be sought in that context. That would seem to be an appropriate posing of the question, though at the same time some more careful consideration of the terminology would have been appropriate (originality, uniqueness, novelty).

E. C. Colwell

E. C. Colwell supplied, if not a life, at least an accounting of Jesus' teaching.[23] The book was intended primarily for a nontechnical audience, as indeed Colwell thought — quite rightly — the teaching of Jesus was as well.

Jesus' teaching, Colwell said, had an *extravagant* quality — it was popular and marched along the edges of exaggeration. We know some of his methods (parables, single-point illustrations), though there are "silences" in the tradition and much has been lost. Other things are not explained, but simply assumed (belief in one God, scripture, Israel as the covenant people).

Colwell also demonstrated an interest in the originality of Jesus, which some scholarly study had obscured. Study of the parallels from Judaism was one factor (but Jesus used old things in new ways); another was the impact of Form Criticism and its emphasis on the creative role of the community, while a third element had to do with an abandonment of objectivity and the growth of skepticism, of which the "crisis theology" was a manifestation. Colwell's former colleague at Chicago, Shirley Jackson Case, was cited critically as an instance of losing the individuality of Jesus. Case's work "illumines every aspect of Jesus' career that was duplicated by his contemporaries, but it dulls the things in which he was an individual. It shows us Jesus the Jew, but not Jesus."[24]

Some examples of Jesus' extravagance — and presumably his originality — were then examined. Characteristic was not the golden rule, but the command to love even the enemy (extravagant); his humility (he did not say who he was), his parables, the teaching of a love without frontiers. He also held to God's power; the kingdom of God has a future element that cannot be eliminated (Dodd was wrong). But there is no apocalypse in Jesus and no interim ethic. John the Baptist was a consistent eschatologist [Colwell putting John where Schweitzer put Jesus]. The kingdom was present, but not exclusively. The core of the teaching lay in Jesus' proclamation of God's will; the coming of the kingdom with the clouds of heaven is a vain hope. But there was a social dream, a dream of justice and righteousness. In some ununderstandable way Jesus saw his work related to that kingdom; his followers saw the same in different ways. Faith in Jesus had a pre-Easter basis; the resurrection gave it a new definition and made it missionary. But it began in the days of his flesh in his message of the God of grace and power.

---

23. E. C. Colwell, *An Approach to the Teaching of Jesus* (New York: Abingdon-Cokesbury Press, 1946). Colwell was then president of the University of Chicago (1945). There was also the earlier work by Harvey Branscomb, *The Teaching of Jesus: A Textbook for College and Individual Use* (New York: Abingdon-Cokesbury Press, 1941). It was largely standard liberalism, with some social gospel emphasis in Jesus' proclamation of the kingdom, though still a nonpolitical Jesus. The kingdom was eschatological, but the primary focus was on the present (God's rule in the human heart); apocalypticism was devalued, the ethic of Jesus elevated (love, rooted in the concept of God as Father). The originality of Jesus lay in what he omitted and reshaped from his Jewish tradition. Branscomb was Professor of New Testament at Duke University.

24. Colwell, *An Approach to the Teaching of Jesus*, 46–47.

It was a responsible book, but it offered little that was not already well known. It also demonstrated the continuing and widespread interest in the question of Jesus' originality, or uniqueness with respect to his environment. That was a question whose luster never seemed to dull.

F. C. Grant

A more powerful interpreter on the American scene was Frederick C. Grant, who had behind him by the decade of the forties already an impressive body of work, including an early, if textbook-type, life of Jesus.[25] He produced two volumes closely together; the first was *The Gospel of the Kingdom,* and the second *The Earliest Gospel.* The second is less directed to reconstruction of the ministry of Jesus, so we shall focus on the first.[26]

Grant was not pleased with the eschatologists, notably Schweitzer; they were, he said, guilty of a basic insincerity, of playing with ideas, guided by intuition. The Jesus they produced was based upon mere picking and choosing among synoptic texts. Besides, they opened the door to Barthianism [a kind of disease apparently], "with its monstrous interpretation of the Gospel, its Marcionite Unknown God of Force and terror, its purely transcendental Christ, its Kingdom completely 'not of this world.'" Ritschlianism was better than "this bizarre system, which undercuts all Christian motivation toward social righteousness, denies the fundamental postulate of the Gospel, viz. that the Kingdom is coming in this world, and opens upon a dark cloudland of impressive but vague and barbarous incomprehensible ideas set forth in completely arbitrary terminology."[27]

Here was surely no timorous slouching away from assessment of the Barthian theology.

Grant took up the thesis that the Jesus movement was much more widespread than the gospels allow us to see, that it had a social significance from its inception, that, in fact, Jesus spoke primarily of a kingdom coming on the earth. Jesus' background was the prophetic religion of the Old Testament, not apoca-

---

25. F. C. Grant, *The Life and Times of Jesus* (New York: Abingdon Press, 1921). It was aimed at a young audience and, while it demonstrated critical knowledge, was a more confessional work. The germ of his later portrayals can be seen in his quite fine examination of the socioeconomic conditions at the time of Jesus, in *The Economic Background of the Gospels* (New York: Russell and Russell, 1926). It saw overtaxation and loss of soil productivity as leading to a time of political and social tensions. Jesus was not a political revolutionary, however, but represented nevertheless the hopes of the *anawim* for a better time. Economics illuminates the eschatology; Jesus inaugurated a movement of spiritual and ethical reform that would have social and economic consequences, but was not himself a political or social reformer.

26. F. C. Grant, *The Gospel of the Kingdom* (New York: Macmillan, 1940); Grant, *The Earliest Gospel: Studies in the Evangelic Tradition at its Point of Crystallization in Writing* (New York: Abingdon Press, 1943). *The Earliest Gospel* examined the tradition from a largely form-critical perspective, especially looking at the construction of Mark. It made many valuable comments of a redaction-critical nature (Mark is a martyr's church, the outlook of a sect; the author shifted the focus from Jesus' message of the kingdom to the person of Jesus himself).

27. Grant, *Gospel of the Kingdom,* x.

lypticism; he held to the old vision of the theocratic society, though devoid of its nationalism.

Grant began with the allusions to Jesus in the writings of Tacitus, from whom he drew the inference that Christianity was regarded as a dangerous social move-ment; Tacitus assumed this movement was already in full swing at the time of the death of its founder. This agrees with a few hints in the gospels themselves, for example, Jesus was charged with being a disturber of the peace and executed as the leader of a potentially revolutionary force (cf. Luke 23:2, 4–5, 6–12).

Jesus expected, then, the kingdom on earth, in his lifetime. But still it was a *religious* expectation, one of *social* redemption. The kingdom would be the perfect realization of the divine sovereignty on earth. Its roots were much closer to the Old Testament prophets and to "normative" Judaism than to the apocalyptic writings with their "wild, feverish, bizarre dreams of deluded fanatics" (15). This social gospel is the most primitive, the oldest level of the tradition. It is what got Jesus into trouble.

Grant examined the nature of the tradition. Form Criticism helps us to un-ravel the story. We see the editorial work of the evangelists and can assume that something similar went on in the oral period. The only way to attain to the historical Jesus is to move through the layers of the tradition, putting them in their proper relationship. A genetic arrangement, if not chronological one, is necessary.[28]

Looking at what the process brings, then, we see a Jesus appearing after the death of John the Baptist with a message about the kingdom of God. John and Jesus were not associated in their preaching — not only are they too different, but prophets do not have associates. So Jesus started his ministry in Galilee after John's death (though he was a follower of John). Mark is essentially reliable here, supported by the speeches preserved in the early parts of Acts. John was an old prophet who expected one to come to be the messenger of Malachi — an angel, one from Yahweh who would sit in judgment, but not the messiah. Later inter-pretation viewed that expectation as Elijah and subsequently identified it with John himself. John then preached the coming judgment and demanded a baptism of repentance, but had no message of the kingdom of God (contra Matthew).

Jesus was a Galilean, though he had come to John in Judea and may have had Judean descent. The nativity stories have no value, but other references (Paul, Hebrews) strengthen the assumption of the genuineness of Jesus' Davidic ancestry. John appeared about 28–29 and spoke of this messenger and sealed people with baptism. Jesus went to hear and was baptized. We can assume that he went as an obedient son of the Torah, to do the will of God, taking John's baptism to be just that. The baptism is messianic in Mark, but for Jesus it was more likely a prophetic call. He did not likely consider himself the messiah, not

---

28. "Genetic" was a term popular in the sociohistorical school at Chicago, used often by Shirley Jackson Case, though, in fact, he may have gotten it already from his Yale teachers Benjamin W. Bacon and Frank Porter. It described the causal connection of historical events, the ancestry of historical entities.

even Mark's messiah incognito, surely not the king of Israel, or even some other transformed idea of the messiah, such as the Son of man–servant of Yahweh. To think of himself as Son of man would be to have an unsound mind; or to suppose that he mandated his own life in accordance with the scriptural picture of the servant is all too artificial. These come from the church, brought about by the impact of the resurrection faith. This identification, however, was not likely without at least some prior confidence in Jesus as being something more than a prophet and teacher; the idea of Jesus as bringer or bearer of the kingdom was the basis of their faith in him.

Nevertheless, Grant added, we cannot really categorize Jesus by titles; he remains unique. It is his spirit, not some title, which is the ground of faith in him.

The messiah was only one form of eschatological expectation. Son of man was another, and had been combined in various Jewish and non-Jewish circles (widespread primal man speculations) before Jesus' time. Some Christians were influenced by these, but not necessarily Jesus himself. The temptation story from Q is not an exception; it is really a story of the ordeal of the messiah and has no historical basis.

After John's execution Jesus set out teaching and healing. He performed exorcisms and saw them as signs of the arrival of the kingdom.

There is no order in Mark's story; incidents and material are arranged by subject. Mark's order is imposed on the tradition; for instance, Caesarea-Philippi represents Peter's transcendent faith, and the Transfiguration is a resurrection appearance or ecstatic experience. We can only speak about Jesus' work in Galilee generally, about a journey to the north, and about Jerusalem, but details or order elude us. The entrance scene at Jerusalem does not speak for a messianic ministry; it is entirely out of keeping with Jesus' nonpolitical conception of the kingdom. It may have been a prophetic, symbolic act, a protest against militant nationalism (riding the ass).

Grant then accounted for the last week, the passion, where (following Form Criticism) something more can be said about order. The various debates show Jesus protesting against aggressive materialism; he also threatened the temple. Judas's betrayal consisted of turning over Jesus to the authorities. The high priest and the Sanhedrin condemned him as a royal pretender and handed him over to Pilate as an insurrectionist. They were aided in their ability to do so by Jesus' silence.

The resurrection is the first chapter in the history of the church. Jesus emerged as Lord, and remains so for the Christian. Paul is the preeminent example, but even he presupposes knowledge of Jesus' life and teaching. Yet it was the palestinian church that preserved the picture of Jesus and it is non-Pauline. Even today, however, this gentile Christianity, Grant said, is our type of Christianity, rather than that of the Jewish church. (Gentile Christianity was derived from Jewish Christianity, but at an earlier stage than the gospels, that is, with Paul.)

Jewish Christianity had two centers, Galilee and Judea. Galilee was characterized by its expectation of the apocalyptic Son of man, Judea was more rooted in the Old Treatment and the expectation of a national messiah. How was Jesus understood in his message of the kingdom of God? Some further grasp of the political and social conditions prevailing in Palestine generally is necessary.

Grant then recited the customary political and social history extending from Alexander to the Roman conquest, to the final perishing of the Jewish dream of a theocracy under the Roman imperium. He appealed often and, of course, necessarily, to Josephus, whom he regarded as a good source, if also an apologist for Judaism. In Jesus' day the political and economic conditions were palpably bad. The ordinary people were poor; taxation likely approached 25 percent of income, maybe as high as 35–40 percent. Many were hungry and homeless, even in an apparently prosperous Galilee. Economic insecurity abounded. Leading Roman families might have lived in the grand style under Augustus, and other provinces may have enjoyed more prosperity, but not so Palestine. The Jewish populace was being driven to the economic wall. That was the context in which first John the Baptist appeared with a message of impending doom, and then Jesus with one of an impending kingdom.

Two ways were especially evident among the Jews: that of the fanatical patriots and the conservative status-keepers. There was also the strictly religious view: let God intervene and bring about his judgment; pray for the coming of God's reign and prepare for it by repentance and obedience to the Law. Do not appeal to force. This view stands behind the apocalyptic literature, but it is not representative of "normative" Judaism or of Judaism as a whole. It is too esoteric, though we should not minimize its presence then; probably it was suppressed after the destruction of 70 C.E. Still other alternatives can be seen in the Zadokite fragments of some Damascus group and also in the Essenes, an ascetic body with gnostic tendencies.[29] The only solution for the Jewish mind could not be ascetic withdrawal, but the ultimate triumph of a benevolent God and his reign. So there were apocalypticism and asceticism, but a third movement represented a revival of prophecy in the persons of John the Baptist and Jesus. One said, "Repent, the judgment is coming." The other said, "Repent, the kingdom of God is at hand."

Grant then developed the movement from an earthly kingdom to a purely transcendent one through the New Testament, in order to arrive back at the question of how Jesus himself thought of the kingdom. He looked at the death of Jesus as a clue. Jesus was put to death as the head of a movement regarded as dangerous to Roman as well as Jewish interests. Therefore his hope must have been fixed on an earthly kingdom that was later spiritualized. The reverse process would be incomprehensible and accordingly that very process seen in the New Testament witnesses to the originality of the earthly kingdom. Jesus' expectation was for a theocracy, a revival of ancient prophecy for God's rule. It is not accidental that the terminology of "kingdom" is so rare in the current literature and

---

29. Grant, of course, did not have the benefit of the Dead Sea Scrolls.

so abundant in the gospels. There is no room in this expectation for a messiah or himself as king; there can be no human intermediaries.

So the kingdom of God was earthly, in Palestine, though its influence would extend worldwide (many would come from east and west). Jesus' own emphasis was on the ethical conditions for entrance into the kingdom. His ethics and eschatology come from the prophets and the Psalms of the Old Testament, not from the apocalyptic literature. His conception is a purely religious one, that of the old theocracy, a nonviolent view. It was unaffected by the political and social turmoil, but was nevertheless subject to misinterpretation as revolution. Therefore it can be said that Jesus' idea was "purely religious, not political or economic or as setting forth a program for social reform."[30] Of course, religion embraced the whole of life and Jesus was a teacher of religion (the greatest ever, and so on). The idea of the theocracy was an old one, so there was no need to explain it; it was set over against the fanatics and the various parties. Thus there is also no actual distinction between "religious" and "political."

The teaching of Jesus was simply and purely religious. He was not a social reformer, not like a Greek sage, or the founder of a movement, or an apocalyptist. There may be elements of all these, but they cannot all be true, for they cancel each other. The Jesus we meet in our sources is already an interpreted Jesus, as in Mark, Q, L, M, and John. No interpretation is adequate and all attempts to classify him are insufficient: "He is the most interesting, the most attractive, the most intriguing figure, to say no more, that our world has ever known" (139). So there are many layers of interpretation, but the earliest is that of Jesus as prophet and religious teacher. The kingdom he proclaimed is God's rule and cannot be constructed by men, even if its signs are already astir, in the healings and exorcisms. It is not purely realized (contra Dodd), for it is not yet fulfilled. Prophets always foreshorten the future, such that time distinctions were not important. The beatitudes also show how the kingdom is both present possession and future reward.

How was such a teacher as Jesus put to death as a revolutionary? None of the interpretations of him as Son of man and Servant come from Jesus; it would have been impossible for him to see himself as some celestial figure — a form of "deluded fanaticism" (153) that cannot be reconciled with the religious mind in the main body of the tradition. His messiahship arose after the resurrection, as earlier noted; then it was carried back by the early church into his ministry. But Jesus never claimed to be the messiah; he was not a madman. As far as his combining the ideas of Son of man and servant, that, too, came from the church. It is not necessary to assume some personal claim on his part in order to account for his death at the hands of the Romans. There was before him the death of John the Baptist, and the antagonism of the scribes and the hierarchy is itself enough to account for his death. The charge of sedition was preposterous, but Jesus was executed as the leader of a movement thought to be dangerous.

---

30. Grant, *Gospel of the Kingdom*, 132.

It was misinterpretation of the movement as political that made the crucifixion inevitable; it was theocracy as a reality in this world that made it plausible. The enthusiasm of his followers aroused messianic expectations of him, although the variety of titles ascribed to him shows that Jesus himself chose none of them, otherwise what he had chosen would surely have prevailed.

The center of the movement became the resurrection. That shifted the focus: the ethics of the kingdom became the ethics of the Lord.

A final section took up further questions of the relationship of gospel and church, with some more devaluing of apocalypticism (the "circle of bizarre, unwholesome, antisocial ideas" [170]), and an interesting distinction between eschatological and apocalyptic. All Jewish religion is eschatological in that it hopes great things from God; apocalypticism was this "bizarre" business of dreams and visions that presumed to know details of the divine purpose. Nevertheless, the expectation of the kingdom was still relevant; the kingdom is always coming, now and in the future, even if in the present moment in the western world people are not very religious and are alienated from the church.

It was an impressive piece of work, representing a maturing American scholarship in full command of its sources and of the available literature. There was much that was recognizably liberal in Grant, but it was not unwashed. There remained a devotion to critical method along with some confidence about recovering the historical Jesus and the importance of doing so, without at the same time diminishing the traditional christological portrayal. The Jesus who emerged had some liberal lineage, but in a more characteristically American way: a prophet-like figure attempting to reestablish the ancient theocracy, with all its social implications. At this latter point, however, Grant seemed to indulge in some sleight of hand, affirming the social and earthy aspects of the kingdom in Jesus' message, but still claiming it as primarily a "religious" concept. At the same time he conceded the wider implications of "religious" in the time of Jesus, so perhaps the problem was merely semantic and may better have been attended to without recourse to the word "religious." But it was also this linguistic confusion that left some discontent with what would seem to be a forthright solution to the question of Jesus' crucifixion: he was killed as the head of a dangerous movement. But then we are told that the movement was interpreted politically, as a mistake. That seems to take back most everything. Why, in fact, was not the movement actually dangerous? Were not the authorities right in perceiving the Jesus movement as a threat?

Along with this unwillingness to push the implications of his own position Grant maintained a high degree of contempt for apocalypticism, though that attitude prevailed almost everywhere. There was evidently a fear that an apocalyptic Jesus could never be defended in the modern world; he would simply have to be dismissed as a madman. But certainly some things were easily overlooked here as well: the iconoclastic power of apocalyptic thought, the value of vivid symbolism, even if the symbols have lost their original weight. Further, it might be said that if Grant was correct that Jesus indeed expected an earthly kingdom, the old theocracy installed by God, then perhaps John the Apocalyptist, the maker of speculative pictures, actually got it right.

John Knox

Union Theological Seminary professor John Knox also published three volumes in the forties that bore on the question of the historical Jesus, though none was a "life" of Jesus.[31] Each contained some reflection deserving notice.

The first volume directed itself also to the question of Jesus' originality. No biography of Jesus is possible, but it matters much to the church whether its portrait of Jesus goes back to historical actuality. Knox thought that more could be said about Jesus than was possible two decades earlier, alluding to Form Criticism, but still we only see Jesus through the eyes of writers who did not know him directly. He was an ancient Jew, but we cannot miss his powerful personality. He cannot be adequately described in either Jewish or hellenistic terms, but he was a Jew "of vastly more than ordinary stature" (9). He belonged as much to his time as Shakespeare did to Elizabethan England, yet this fact no more explains Shakespeare than does Jesus' belonging to his time. In part it explains him, but falls short as well. There are also problems of authenticity in the text, but most everyone can agree on Jesus' originality in his ethics, though less in terms of its content than in the way he expressed it. The ideas are Jewish, but Jesus was original in a characteristic Jewish way. He had three foci: kingdom of God, will of God, and love of God. The kingdom was the reign of peace, justice, freedom, and righteousness. It would be done by God and soon. So much is settled about Jesus. Also settled was that Jesus expected the kingdom on earth as well as in the hearts of human beings, but was also influenced by the other worldliness of apocalypticism. Yet the kingdom was not only a future hope, but also a present fact. It is "the eternal kingship of God" (17).

As to the will of God, "God demands nothing short of moral perfection — that is, absolute emptying of self, absolute renunciation of selfish pride and desire, absolute love for all men" (18). Jesus was not concerned for the practicality of that demand, only its truthfulness. Yet he also affirmed God's love for the sinner. So his teaching was new in the way in which he put it, in its power. It was also marked by an extravagance and an ardor or warmth.

Knox had no problem identifying qualities of Jesus' greatness: a person of charm and winsomeness, a *man* intensely loved by others, a keen observer of the human scene, with a great capacity for love and one who especially cared for children. His anger was not incompatible with his love; perhaps it was only at the cross that he finally forgave even his own enemies.

Did he declare himself to be the messiah? That seems improbable and likely happened only first in the early church, even though it seems that he had some

---

31. John Knox, *The Man Christ Jesus* (1941); *Christ the Lord* (1945); *On the Meaning of Christ* (1947). I use here the collection of all three in a single volume, *Jesus: Lord and Christ* (New York: Harper, 1958).

notion of his own special relation to the kingdom, else his disciples could hardly have come to see him as messiah. But finally the historian discovers that the secret of Jesus eludes him.

Knox examined the work of Paul as clue to Jesus; we would have to suppose that Paul knew more than he relates, yet he saw the humanity of Jesus as the disclosure of the self-humiliation of God, based on a quality of the character of the remembered Jesus.

The second work focused primarily on the meaning of Jesus in the early church and argued that this meaning can only be found in the community that formed around Jesus. Secular scholarship cannot understand Jesus; the New Testament was created by the church and only the church can grasp it. Knox's themes were how Jesus was remembered, known as living, and interpreted. The "remembering" section recited much of the formation of the tradition, with some more emphasis on remembering because it was significant first, then because it served the preaching and teaching needs of the community. Later legendary additions crept in. The facts of Jesus' career are that he came from Nazareth, had brothers and sisters, was a carpenter, had a synagogue education, was of the pious lower middle class, was awakened by the preaching of John the Baptist, taught and healed in the villages of Galilee, and gathered disciples. His career was of months, maybe a year, then he went to Jerusalem where the temple attack or just charges by Jewish groups brought him to the attention of the Romans who executed him. Hostility from scribes and Pharisees earlier played some role. So Jesus was remembered as a teacher and prophet who spoke of the kingdom of God as the eternal sovereignty of God that is to be acknowledged by humans in the doing of his will, and that will be the perfect establishment of his rule in the age to come.

How did Jesus think of his own role? He did not expect a political messiah, though maybe a theocratic ruler. Son of man is a confused subject; it does not appear in early writings such as Paul's, suggesting that only Jesus used the term, and probability favors his use of it in the general sense of "man" and also eschatologically. However, it was likely the church that first identified Jesus with the heavenly Man, even though Jesus probably saw some connection between himself and the coming judgment and therefore also the role of the Son of man. Knox rejected Otto's thesis and the identification of Son of man and suffering servant in Jesus' own thought. The community also remembered his teaching; its most striking characteristic is its uncompromising character, its absoluteness. There is no casuistry in Jesus and no interim ethic either.

Knox had some rather surprising things to say about the resurrection. The resurrection was a fact, "a part of the concrete empirical meaning of Jesus, not the result of mere reflection upon that meaning. Beliefs were based upon the resurrection; it was not itself a belief. It was something given. It was a reality grasped in faith" (118). So Jesus as resurrected was as much a part of the church's faith as Jesus remembered, as much a reality. The "fact of Jesus" is more than the bare factuality of Jesus as a historical figure; it is Jesus as he was known and remembered in the community. Jesus cannot be possessed apart from the resurrection faith: "The early church's knowledge of the living Christ cannot be separated, except by the most arbitrary procedures, from its knowledge of the crucified Jesus. The same person who was remembered was known still" (126).

The final volume extended these reflections and furthered the thought that Jesus as remembered cannot be separated from the experience of Jesus as resurrected. In this context Knox found something peculiar about the concern for the question of authenticity, for even the words of the risen Christ are part of the total event of Jesus. In this sense the Gospel of John can be "true," though not in the context of Jesus' historical career. Yet also Knox wished to say that the quest for the historical Jesus was worthwhile and important. Faith always wants to know, but that desire should be seen in the total context of the church's awareness of Jesus.

Knox's questions and probings sounded a different note. The inclusion of the resurrection, especially as a "fact" of the remembered Jesus, the insistence on the connection between Jesus and the community that bears his tradition, but without abandoning the critical enterprise — all that was decidedly unusual. The "fact" of the resurrection would seem incongruent in the mouth of a historian, but Knox did not mean to speak of it as some kind of isolated "bare fact"; rather, it was factual in the sense that it was an essential component of the story of Jesus as remembered in the community. The further considerations as to Jesus' originality were marked by some measure of sober judgment as well: Jesus' specialness has to be sought within Judaism, not simply over against it.

Henry J. Cadbury

Henry J. Cadbury also reflected further, and a little more positively, on the historical Jesus, in comparison with the reservations he had sounded a decade earlier.[32]

Cadbury did not seek to produce a life of Jesus, but to inquire into Jesus' cast of mind, his way of thinking, and his personality. The question of his originality seemed significant for Cadbury. Jesus' ethics were taken as the center point of inquiry; they are not to be construed as interim or even affected by his apocalyptic experience of the near End.

Cadbury noticed many types of argument in the words of Jesus: the *a fortiori* one occurred regularly; it was a comparison, as in the simile or more extensively in the parable. It showed a certain mathematical logic in Jesus' mind, as did also his use of analogy. And Jesus assumed a consistency between the natural and spiritual worlds, such that the one could illuminate the other. Jesus taught proportionate responsibility, but also an excess of virtue (as Montefiore had said), a going beyond what was expected.

---

32. Henry J. Cadbury, *Jesus What Manner of Man* (New York: Macmillan, 1947). On Cadbury's earlier reservation, see above, chap. 5, 184–85.

Parables were typical of Judaism; Jesus was not unique nor did he have a superior parable technique. Some parables have a biological growth model (seed parable=progress by stages); they inculcate patience, for the future cannot be compelled. It is not a matter of slow development, but of order. Some parables, however, also emphasize the future and the judgment. The absentee master is a recurrent theme. For Jesus God could be absent; humans may have to live without him, indeed, normally they are expected to be on their own. The loving father theme may be so much wishful thinking; more accurate may be the demanding overlord.

Parables also contain the theme of excuse-making, which is part of their verisimilitude and shows Jesus' insight into human nature.

The originality or uniqueness of Jesus cannot be estimated satisfactorily, for we do not know the whole of the ancient world. But then how different could he have been? We are now more aware of his Jewishness than ever. The hostility toward him from the Jewish leaders is factual, but was his movement a novelty? The gospels tend to obscure matters and to make Jesus less revolutionary than he likely was.

One distinctive feature of Jesus is the urgency that the apocalyptic element lent to his message, particularly in comparison with the rabbis. Also Jesus was more independent with respect to the Law, although he did not break with it. The exorcisms also seem to suggest a certain novelty in the sanction for Jesus' teaching (Mark's "new teaching" provoked by the exorcism). But complete novelty in Jesus' day would not even have been an asset. "Independent and distinctive," yes, but novel, no: "In Jesus we shall look for what was distinguished if not distinctive, what was characteristic and *sui generis,* rather than for something that would seem to us or his contemporaries original or novel" (67). It is better, said Cadbury, to speak of Jesus as radical, intense, or extreme, or even independent, meaning by the latter loyalty to one's own judgment. "Crucifixion," Cadbury observed, "is not the penalty for originality but for independence" (77).

How did Jesus get this way? Form Criticism has taught us the impossibility of arranging things in any kind of order and therefore of making any deductions about development and the like. We can say that as a teacher Jesus was something of a midwife, kindling a cognitive process, stimulating insight, and urging a moral truth universally recognized. But in the end the authority of Jesus' words lay in the words themselves; they were self-recommending and given an urgency by his apocalyptic message of the coming kingdom of God.

Cadbury's short work was marked by uncommon common sense, and offered a little slice of insight onto the turn of Jesus' mind here and there. The comments on Jesus' originality were worthwhile, quite in contrast to the more widespread and sometimes uneasy attempts to find in Jesus the absolutely unparalleled speaker of all words. A real issue here has cropped up in this narrative periodically and will do so again, and it has to do with Jesus' Jewishness, with his distinctiveness in regard to his environment, and related questions. Here we can be content to observe the more sane characterization by Cadbury that Jesus was distinguished if not distinctive, that some things were *characteristic* as opposed to novel or original. In this respect both Knox and Cadbury, especially Cadbury, exhibited a sanity that was, if not original, at least characteristic.

Americans then, coming to the end of the decade, seemed more inclined to offer slices of the Jesus tradition than full-scale lives. Form Criticism had its impact, no doubt, but it did not entirely abrogate the enterprise. It is still possible to write about Jesus, even if a more circumscribed figure should appear.[33] And probably as well the war itself was a discouraging factor.

Sand, Scrolls, and Caves

History usually surprises us and often enough mystifies us, and it was preparing, in the forties, a surprise — two, actually — that would stir the world of biblical scholarship for years to come, and is still doing so. One was the less-celebrated discovery in 1945 of a cache of manuscripts near Nag Hammadi in Upper Egypt by some peasants looking for nitrates to fertilize their fields.[34] Two brothers, Muḥammed and Khalīfah ʿAlī, stumbled on a jar while digging around a boulder; Muḥammed cracked open the jar and papyrus fragments flew into the air. He took the find to his home in al-Qaṣr, the site of ancient Chenoboskia, where the early pioneer in monasticism, Pachomius, had lived. The manuscripts were given to the Coptic priest from al-Qaṣr for safekeeping, since Muḥammed's family was embroiled in a blood feud with another family and his home subject to search by the authorities. A brother of the priest's wife, recognizing the value of one of the manuscripts (Codex III), received permission to take it to Cairo where he showed it to a physician interested in the Coptic language. The physician, George Sobhi, notified the Department of Antiquities, who compensated the brother-in-law of the priest for it and placed it in the Cairo Museum. The date was October 4, 1946.

The remainder of the manuscripts had a checkered history thereafter. Muḥammed's widow burned part of them, thinking them worthless, while neighbors and others acquired the remainder for little or nothing and sold them off. Antiquities dealers became involved. Codex I was eventually offered for sale in New York and Ann Arbor in 1949 without any takers and ended up at the Jung

---

33. This seems much the mood of Morton S. Enslin's essay, "Light from the Quest," *HTR* 42 (1949): 19–33, in which the conditions for pursuing a quest are considered. The obtuseness of the disciples in Mark is a Markan creation; the disciples must have understood Jesus; he was not vague to his contemporaries. Enslin's earlier introduction, *Christian Beginnings* (New York: Harper, 1938), depicted a Jesus separated from John the Baptist — later Christian apologetics brought them together — and who appeared as a prophet of the kingdom of God, a future if imminent apocalyptic event. His movement was threatening enough as a disturber of the peace to assure his final fate in Jerusalem.

34. This account leans on the narration by James M. Robinson in his introduction to *The Nag Hammadi Library in English* (San Francisco: Harper, 1978; rev. ed., 1988).

Institute in Zurich, where it acquired the name of the "Jung Codex."[35] It later returned to the Cairo Museum. The remainder of the collection was subsequently acquired by the Department of Antiquities as well, and the whole now resides in the Cairo Museum.

Publication and translation have been slow, and nothing of any consequence appeared in the remainder of the time period we are discussing. Over a longer time it has become apparent that the documents are the remainder of a form of (Christian, incipient?) Gnosticism, whether associated with the Pachomian movement or not, and their value for the history and interaction of Christianity and Gnosticism is incalculable. Their utility in terms of the question of the historical Jesus revolves around the assessment and significance of a single document found in the collection, the *Gospel of Thomas*. Most of the literature surrounding this discussion has grown up in the period beyond our time frame, so we will reserve that for a later volume. But let us notice: Thomas opens the possibility, seriously for the first time, that a noncanonical work may embody some sayings of Jesus independent of the New Testament, an alternative stream — or perhaps a trickle — of Jesus material not hitherto available.[36] It does not seem likely that this material, even on a generous estimate, would contribute enough to affect significantly the picture of Jesus that can be reconstructed from the (primarily synoptic) gospels, so its value, in the end, should not be overblown. We remain still very much dependent on the data in the New Testament.[37]

The other discovery (1947), the Dead Sea Scrolls, has generated much more widespread attention and even controversy over the years, as publication and access to them have seemed slow, and the necessary work of assembling often tiny fragments into larger pieces has proceeded fitfully. The process has aroused suspicions of a scholarly and theological cover-up, with some supposing that the scrolls contain truly revolutionary matter that will unravel Christian faith. All such suppositions, on inspection, have rightly been proven to be nonsense, but the flames continue to be fanned. All the major works are freely available, even if the tinier fragments have still to be deciphered — a work that will likely go on for another generation.

---

35. So named because it was given by an American philanthropist (through the intermediary Gilles Quispel) in honor of the eminent depth psychologist C. G. Jung. Its most significant component was a copy of the Gospel of Truth, a gnostic-tending work long known to exist but hitherto unpossessed.

36. The Oxyrhynchus papyri found in 1897 and 1903 are now recognized to form a part of the same work. A standard accounting was H. G. E. White, *The Sayings of Jesus from Oxyrhynchus* (Cambridge: University Press, 1920). Other agrapha exist and there is, of course, a substantial body of other, noncanonical literature, but there is no defensible opinion that it contains any tradition of Jesus' words that is of substantive value. An earlier collection of apocryphal agrapha and other material was that by Roderic Dunkerley, *The Unwritten Gospel: Ana and Agrapha of Jesus* (London: George Allen and Unwin, 1925).

37. Even the estimate of the Jesus Seminar (see above, chap. 1, n. 39) does not accredit a large percentage of the logia in Thomas and among those given a "red" or "pink" rating most seem to be variations on known synoptic words as opposed to ones previously unknown.

The story of the discovery is widely known and need not be rehearsed here in any detail. Early participants in the story were not always sure of the origin of the discovery,[38] though it is agreed now that the initial discovery was made by three cousins of Ta âmireh bedouin, while grazing their flock of sheep and goats.[39] One of them, Muḥammed Khalil, was rummaging around among the caves of wadi Qumran (perhaps searching for a lost goat) and allegedly threw a rock into what is now known as Cave 1, striking what sounded like earthen jars. Another cousin, Muḥammed Ahmed el-Hamed (ed-Dîb), later slipped away from the others and into the cave, where he spied ten large jars, one of which contained some bundles of manuscripts. These were subsequently carried to Bethlehem, to a cobbler's shop, and were eventually acquired by the Syrian Archbishop Athanasius Yeshue Samuel of St. Mark's Monastery in the Old City of Jerusalem. The *Rule of the Community* (1QS), *Habakkuk Pesher* (1QpHab), *Genesis Apocryphon* (1QapGen),[40] and a copy of Isaiah were the first scrolls sold by the cobbler Kando (Khalil Eskander Shahin), who also obtained three more scrolls that wound up later in the possession of Eliezer L. Sukenik of Hebrew University (1QM, 1QH, 1QIsa[b]).[41] One of the many strange twists in the story was that the first set of scrolls traveled to America where the archbishop sought to sell them without success, only to have Yigael Yadin, Sukenik's son and outstanding scholar-archaeologist himself, arrange later to purchase them there for Israel. Sukenik himself had access to them at one point earlier and wanted to buy them, but saw them go away and lamented that they probably were forever lost to the Jewish people. He was wrong, but did not live to know that. Yet he also had the extraordinary experience of purchasing some of these scrolls on the very day the United Nations passed a resolution establishing the state of Israel.

Cave 1 was located through the efforts of Philippe Lippens, a Belgium officer serving as a UN observer, who took a profound interest in the story and enlisted the help of Roland de Vaux of the École Biblique and G. L. Harding, Chief In-

---

38. Millar Burrows, *The Dead Sea Scrolls* (New York: Viking Press, 1955). Burrows recounts his own participation in the evaluation and publication of the scrolls brought to the Syrian Archbishop, who subsequently sought the help of the American Oriental School of Research in evaluating the scrolls he had acquired.

39. The account follows the narrative of James H. Charlesworth in the exquisite production of the American Interfaith Institute, *The Dead Sea Scrolls: Rule of the Community*, ed. James H. Charlesworth with Henry W. L. Rietz (Philadelphia: American Interfaith Institute, 1996). Yigael Yadin's account of his and his father's participation is also helpfully recounted in James H. Charlesworth, ed., *The Message of the Scrolls*, Christian Origins Library (New York: Crossroad, 1992; originally published, New York: Grosset and Dunlap, 1962). Yadin's account was first published in 1957. The Burrows account is also helpful.

40. Burrows gave the name "Manual of Discipline" to the *Rule*, inspired, he said, by an analogy to the Methodist *Book of Discipline* (though he was not a Methodist); and the *Genesis Apocryphon* was referred to as the "Lamech Apocalypse," caused by John Trever's initial identification of the scroll as the lost apocryphal book of that name. 1QapGen had not been unrolled even at the time Burrows wrote his book.

41. Yadin's narrative, utilizing Sukenik's diary, reported that a Syrian Orthodox friend of Sukenik's had purchased the scrolls directly from the bedouins. He was probably referring to George Isaiah, who was contacted by Khalil Eskander.

spector of Antiquities for Jordan. Harding and de Vaux directed the excavation in February/March 1949, turning up still more scroll fragments along with pottery evidence. Unfortunately, they did not arrive before treasure hunters visited the cave in November/December of 1948. It was not until November/December of 1951 that a major exploration of the site at Qumran, hitherto thought of as a Roman fortress, was conducted by Harding and de Vaux. Cave 4, containing the greatest variety of texts, was not discovered until 1952.

The first discussions revolved around identification of the age and origin of the scrolls; after the publication of the major works from Cave 1, first by Sukenik (1948) of his scrolls, and later (1950) by Burrows of those held by the archbishop, who had agreed earlier to the photographing of them by John Trever and William H. Brownlee. The publication set off a widespread discussion — the scrolls seem to have been fated for controversy. Not everyone agreed as to the age and authenticity of the scrolls; Solomon Zeitlin, for example, of Dropsie College, dismissed them as late, even medieval; G. R. Driver of Oxford assigned them a date of 200–500 C.E. and complained of the way the discovery had been treated and the failure to bring the texts to the British Museum for proper evaluation. (Burrows reported that he had consulted with T. C. Skeat of the British Museum without result.) Others joined in the assessment of the paleographic evidence; from the start W. F. Albright unhesitatingly declared the scrolls he had seen — actually, the Trever-Brownlee photographs — to be authentic, giving them a date of about 100 B.C.E. In February of 1949 already a series appeared in *Theologische Literaturzeitung;* leading essayists were Paul Kahle and Otto Eissfeldt. Bo Reiche of Uppsala was one of the first to attempt to locate the historical setting of the scrolls, by efforts to identify the Righteous Teacher and the "wicked priest" (Onias, Jason). A significant impact came from the analyses of the Sorbonne scholar André Dupont-Sommer, who identified the Kittim as the Romans and the wicked priest as alternately Aristobulus II and Hyrcanus. He was also the first to suggest, publicly at least, that the scrolls were the possession of a group of Essenes. Kahle aligned himself with Dupont-Sommer on that question and also provided some stimulus for the effort to excavate the site at Qumran for its possible connection with the cave and the scrolls, which, of course, proved to be a correct intuition.[42] Dupont-Sommer stirred further controversy by his suggestion of many parallels between Jesus and the Teacher in the scrolls; the Roman Catholic scholar Joseph Bonsirven was moved to issue some response.[43]

A blizzard of writing, as well as controversy, has since continued to surround the scrolls, and no one can comprehend it all. It is still widely agreed, though contested here and there, that the library eventually recovered in a series of caves was the original possession of a group of Essenes. The first consequence of the discovery was then to cast considerable new light on a sect within Judaism at

---

42. Here I am following Burrows's account, including the various authors referred to.

43. André Dupont-Sommer, *The Jewish Sect of Qumran and the Essenes: New Studies on the Dead Sea Scrolls,* trans. R. D. Barnett (London: Valentine, Mitchel, 1954), and *The Essene Writings from Qumran,* trans. G. Vermes (Cleveland: World Publishing, 1962).

the time of Christianity, indeed prior to it and for some time thereafter contemporaneous with it. Then immediate issues arose for the Christian community as to what implications the scrolls carried for the illumination of Christian origins; this question remains on the agenda, though the fringe element that actually supposes itself able to find Jesus at Qumran carries no weight. The scrolls have been and continue to be an extremely valuable resource for understanding the nature of Judaism at that time; in fact, it would be more accurate to speak of "Judaisms" now.[44] And the scrolls have also supplied parallels of a striking nature for many aspects of the New Testament. There is no demonstrable direct relationship between Jesus of Nazareth and the Qumran community, even if one should allow that John the Baptist might well have been an Essene or was somehow associated with Essenism. Some Greek fragments of texts (7Q5) have inspired the claim that small pieces of the Gospel of Mark appeared at Qumran, but unanimity on this question scarcely exists either. If so, it would be an astonishing conclusion, for it would indicate some kind of direct relationship, but such has not been demonstrated to the satisfaction of the academy.[45]

It is evident that the Dead Sea Scrolls have been more influential in the twentieth century than they were in their own time. They were, after all, the work of a sectarian group, maybe even just that part of it that lived ascetically by the Dead Sea. Did that community and its literary output actually exercise any impact on the larger society?[46] A similar question could also be asked about the Jesus movement, and a similar answer given: perhaps neither had much immediate impact. But certainly the longer-term influence of the Christian movement far exceeded that of Essenism, though here there are other factors that have to be considered. In that respect the Jesus movement survived and exercised its influence through the success of the community bearing Jesus' name. To be sure, the intensive literary work at Qumran betrays a group conducting serious intellectual activity and therefore out of the ordinary; and the mere possession of such a library would seem to set the Essenes well aside from most social groups. But how far recognized were those facts? How far did the Essenes themselves extend their own understanding of their social world? Nothing instructive along those lines appears in either Philo or Josephus, who seem ignorant of any extensive Essene literary production.[47]

---

44. The phrase is Jacob Neusner's, in Jacob Neusner, William Scott Green, and Ernest S. Frerichs, eds., *Judaisms and Their Messiahs at the Turn of the Christian Era* (Cambridge: Cambridge University Press, 1987).

45. A compact and very sane assessment is given by Joseph A. Fitzmyer, in "The Dead Sea Scrolls and Christian Origins: General Methodological Considerations," in the series co-edited by James H. Charlesworth and myself, *The Dead Sea Scrolls and Christian Faith*, Faith and Scholarship Colloquies 5 (Harrisburg, Pa.: Trinity Press International, 1998), 1–19. Fitzmyer's essay outlines circumspectly the appropriate methodology in using the Scrolls.

46. I do not mean to lessen in any way the value of the scrolls for textual history, cultural understanding, or any other of the myriad contributions they have made to our grasp of Judaism and Christianity today.

47. Both Philo and Josephus know of Essene study of the law and ancient writings, but nothing specifically of an elaborate Essene library.

Interesting questions, perhaps also unresolvable. What matters is how the scrolls have revolutionized our grasp of Judaism prior to and contemporaneous with Christianity. They have also furthered and will continue to further our understanding of Christian origins, even if, as must be emphasized, they have nothing whatsoever to say about Jesus directly.[48] At some future date it may be possible to attain to a fair evaluation of the true import of the scrolls to their own time, aside from their obviously explosive effect in our time. The ultimate history of the scrolls — if ever such is written — will have at least two large chapters, and it will be interesting to see which has the greater share.

Meanwhile, the search for Jesus goes on.

---

48. A clear statement of the parallels and differences is set forth by James H. Charlesworth in "The Dead Sea Scrolls and the Historical Jesus," in *Jesus and the Dead Sea Scrolls,* ed. Charlesworth, Anchor Bible Reference Library (New York: Doubleday, 1992), 1–74.

Chapter 7

THE JEWISH QUEST FOR JESUS

Throughout the first half of the century a struggle went on for the Jewish soul of Jesus. This theme has been evident in the works already surveyed, but it is a subject of such interest and significance that it must now be investigated on its own. In fact, it has acquired already the status of a subdiscipline and has produced a number of works devoted to it exclusively. Credit for the pioneering effort in this time period must be extended to the Uppsala scholar Gösta Lindeskog, whose 1938 work was — and remains — the standard statement covering the material up to that point in time.[1] Lindeskog's account was scholarly, thorough, and reliable. I am pleased to acknowledge its help in rehearsal of this story.

Historical Background

We are concerned here with the encounter of Jewish scholarship with Jesus occurring in the first half of the twentieth century, but a longer history exists. The factors that made possible interest in Jesus in Judaism were emancipation, assimilation, and reform. By "emancipation" is meant the extension of full citizenship

---

1. Lindeskog's work is *Die Jesusfrage im neuzeitlichen Judentum: Ein Beitrag zur Geschichte der Leben-Jesu-Forschung,* Seminar zu Uppsala herausgegeben von *Anton Fridrichsen* (Leipzig: Alfred Lorentz; Uppsala: A. B. Lundequistska Bokhandeln, 1938). A second edition appeared in 1952, but was unavailable to me. Before Lindeskog there were a number of smaller surveys, such as Ernest R. Trattner, *As a Jew Sees Jesus* (New York: Scribner's, 1931); Thomas Walker, *Jewish Views of Jesus: An Introduction and an Appreciation* (London: George Allen and Unwin, 1931); Herbert Danby's earlier survey, *The Jew and Christianity: Some Phases, Ancient and Modern of the Jewish Attitude Towards Christianity* (London: Sheldon, 1927); and the work of the French Jesuit Joseph Bonsirven, *Les Juifs et Jésus: Attitudes nouvelles* (Paris: Gabriel Beauchesne et ses Fils, 1937). The latter is a popular rather than scientific work and comes at the subject from the perspective of Roman Catholic dogmatics (cf. Lindeskog, *Die Jesusfrage,* 6–7). The book by Jakob Jocz, *The Jewish People and Jesus Christ: A Study in the Relationship between the Jewish People and Jesus Christ* (London: SPCK, 1949), covers some of the same territory and is a quite learned piece of work; whoever has it and Lindeskog's book possesses all the essential history up to the middle of the twentieth century. Jocz's work is driven by his interest in the theological issue of Jesus' divinity as the barrier between Jews and Christians, but nevertheless contains a great deal of useful information. Jocz was himself a "Hebrew Christian." The same may generally be said about the more recent book by Donald Hagner, *The Jewish Reclamation of Jesus: The Analysis and Critique of Modern Study of Jesus,* Academie Books (Grand Rapids, Mich.: Zondervan, 1984); it updates the story into the 1980s and is very valuable, but also has an avowedly evangelical agenda, that is, Jewish scholarship's attempt to "reclaim" Jesus can only succeed at the cost of some "unfairness" of interpretation to the gospel writers. Lindeskog provided an introduction to the work, but did not find it impossible to maintain Jesus' Jewishness along with his uniqueness. There are extensive bibliographies in Lindeskog, Jocz, and Hagner.

rights to Jews in society, a move that varied in time from place to place, but was stimulated by the Enlightenment and its attention to human rights, as seen especially in the English Deists and in the American and French Revolutions. What followed was "assimilation," or entrance into European culture as participating citizens, in contrast to the cultural isolation that had previously and for centuries characterized a more ghettoized Jewish life. From these two streams also finally evolved the reform movement in Judaism, issuing in liberal Judaism, which was the ultimate source of attempts to rediscover Jesus. Moses Mendelssohn (1729–86) could be construed as the father of modern Jewish liberalism, in that he argued for a revelation of religion in human reason and for the relation of all religions. Influenced by Locke and friends with Lessing, Mendelssohn made it possible for European culture to come into Judaism. Though not the founder of the reform movement in Judaism, he was, by virtue of translation of certain scriptural texts into German, the "Germanizer of Judaism."[2]

Abraham Geiger (1810–74) was the creator of modern Jewish theology.[3] He wished to raise a scientific theology and to meld Judaism into European culture. He introduced biblical criticism and the scientific study of Judaism. As such he lay the ground for an independent Jewish investigation into New Testament history and in particular into the origins of Christianity. He founded the *Jüdische Zeitschrift für Wissenschaft und Leben* and published extensively on Pharisaism, Sadduceeism, and the cultural and historical conditions at the time of Christianity. He first grasped the now-obvious fact that a proper understanding of Christianity can only proceed upon careful inquiry into the Judaism contemporary with it. The gospels, for example, should not be used, as Christian scholars had been accustomed to using them, as sources for the understanding of Judaism.

The honor of founding Jewish research into the life of Jesus, however, is usually accorded the Frenchman Joseph Salvador (1779–1873).[4] He had a Catholic mother and a Jewish ancestry that the family claimed stretched back to the Maccabees. A leader of French Judaism, he attempted to combine the ideology of the French Revolution with the Enlightenment (Moses founded a republic, was a rationalist, and so on). In 1839 he published his *Jésus-Christ et sa doctrine.* Its significance is that for the first time in France an attempt was made at explaining the origins of Christianity by purely historical methods. Salvador was contemporary with Strauss, but his source criticism was not as radical as Strauss's. He came to the conclusion, to be found often in Jewish inquiry, that Jesus' ethical teaching was already resident in Judaism; further, that Christianity was a kind of compromise between Judaism and Hellenism.

The modern period of Jewish research began in the latter part of the nineteenth century; significant figures were to be found in every major country, such as Moriz Friedländer and Daniel Cwohlson (Germany), Joseph Klausner (Germany,

---

2. Lindeskog, *Die Jesusfrage,* 37. This and the following summaries are gathered largely from various locations in Lindeskog, with help from Jocz, *The Jewish People and Jesus Christ.*

3. Lindeskog, *Die Jesusfrage,* 102–3.

4. Ibid., 86; Jocz, *The Jewish People and Jesus Christ,* 130.

Israel), Kaufmann Kohler and J. Z. Lauterbach (America), and especially C. G. Montefiore and Israel Abrahams (England). There is universal agreement that Montefiore is probably the most significant of all figures,[5] and we can take him as programmatic, along with Klausner, who also exercised considerable influence.

C. G. Montefiore

Claude Goldsmid Montefiore was the child of two distinguished Jewish families, the Montefiores and the Goldsmids; his grandmother was a Rothschild.[6] He received a private education, learning Hebrew, Greek, and German, studying at London University and Oxford, where especially he was influenced by the liberal Christian views of Benjamin Jowett. He also studied at Berlin at the Hochschule für die Wissenschaft des Judentums, an institution created for Jewish studies when German universities declined to provide Jewish faculties as they did Protestant and Catholic ones. Montefiore's tutor was Solomon Schechter, who eventually returned to England with Montefiore.[7] The two later divided over the future of Judaism, with Schechter more a respecter of tradition, while Montefiore sought a reformulation of Judaism in the modern world and a rethinking of the relationship of Judaism to Christianity.

To take in hand Montefiore's The Synoptic Gospels is to come upon a novel experience: a Jewish commentary on Christian gospels.[8] It is also to discover that, in spite of Montefiore's own disclaimers as to his lack of credentials for such a task, the work exhibits a full dialogue with current Christian scholarship and is resplendent with insightful remarks. Although obviously a summary of a commentary is out of the question, the introduction contains a sizable body (147 pages) of material that distills much of Montefiore's positions, and they can also be gained from his other publications.[9] We can also consult certain pertinent sections of the commentary.

The object of study, said Montefiore, was to be the teaching of Jesus; while his

5. Lindeskog, Die Jesusfrage, 177, 325, and passim; Jocz, The Jewish People and Jesus Christ, 119.

6. Biographical data in Lucy Cohen, Some Recollections of Claude Goldsmid Montefiore, 1858–1938 (London: Faber and Faber, 1940), and the prolegomenon by Lou Silberman to the reprint of Montefiore's The Synoptic Gospels, 2 vols. (New York: KTAV, 1968). See biographical appendix for more.

7. Some of Schechter's English works include Aspects of Rabbinic Theology (New York: Macmillan, 1909; New York: Schocken Books, 1961); also Studies in Judaism (Philadelphia: Jewish Publication Society of America, 1896, 1908, 1924). These studies are essays originally independently published and of a great variety; the first volume contains Schechter's original descriptions of the contents of the Cairo Genizah where he found thousands of manuscripts and fragments, though at the time of his writing had not turned up the document now known as the Damascus Document.

8. Montefiore, The Synoptic Gospels (London: Macmillan, 1909; 2d ed., 1927. 2 vols; reissued with a prolegomenon by Lou H. Silberman, New York: KTAV Publishing House, 1968). I used the 1968 edition.

9. Especially useful are Montefiore's Some Elements of the Religious Teaching of Jesus According to the Synoptic Gospels (London: Macmillan, 1910) at about the time of the commentary, along with "The Significance of Jesus for His Own Age," HibJ 10 (1911–12): 766–79; and the later articles, "The Originality of Jesus," and "What a Jew Thinks about Jesus," both in the Hibbert Journal (HibJ) 28 [1929–30]: 98–111 and 33 [1934–35]: 511–20), respectively. Lindeskog's various discussions are also to be highly commended.

person cannot have the value for the Jew that it does for a Christian, his teaching may have abiding value. Jesus links up with the prophets and even goes beyond them in some ways. The worth of his teaching is not dependent on whether he actually said it all or not; it can be taken simply as a whole. "We can just speak of its aroma, its spirit, whether Jesus said everything which is ascribed to him or not."[10] Montefiore did not simply dismiss the question of authenticity, but he put it, we might say, into a Jewish perspective. What matters is the totality of the tradition associated by the community with Jesus. Likewise Montefiore noted that the truth of the stories about Jesus is not so important; we do not, for example, believe in miracles in the old way. They may be interesting stories, but they are not the most consequential element.

Montefiore entered upon a rather extended discussion of introductory issues associated with the synoptic gospels (deliberately excluding John, for the usual reasons given in liberal circles). Mark may be regarded as a genius, the great originator, though certainly he did not compose a biography. Everything was written for edification (here Montefiore quoted form critics like K. L. Schmidt, in the later edition); it is usually dated around 70 (though Montefiore expressed a preference for B. W. Bacon's proposal of c. 80) and contains much genuine history. There are written sources behind Mark; the separate stories are the most original material, the framework the least. Montefiore often carried on a dialogue with other commentators, with his good friend F. C. Burkitt at one pole and Bultmann at the other. For Montefiore the truth lay somewhere in between. But, again, the precise determination of historicity is not so important; more important is Jesus' messianic consciousness — almost taken for granted — and the nature of his disputes with the rabbis. If Montefiore operated with a criterion of authenticity, it would have been the extent to which Mark (and likewise Matthew and Luke) sought to show Jesus' moral superiority and have him excel in every contest. The gospels are generally to be regarded as *Tendenzschriften* plus some "naive folktales" (xxxv). Montefiore conceded that there is probably something to be said for the traditional connection with Peter as the source of the gospel — at least Mark is Peter's story as preached by Mark, though the final version is by an anonymous compiler. What is to be gotten from Mark is something of the last year or eighteen months of Jesus' career and some elements of his character and teaching.[11] Similar treatments were accorded Matthew and Luke.

Some further comments were offered on the issue of authenticity: Montefiore imagined the disciples treasuring up Jesus' words and repeating them after his death. We can assign the words from "M" and "L" to Jesus when they accord

---

10. Montefiore, *Synoptic Gospels*, xxvi.

11. It is worth a small aside to observe that Montefiore invoked all the grand names at the time — Wellhausen, Harnack, Bultmann, Dibelius, Schmidt, Burkitt, Streeter, Bacon, Bousset, Goguel, Loisy — and often cited the conflicting opinions rendered by each, such that they tended to negate one another. Yet never did Montefiore cite any with contempt, while calling it "intensely interesting" (lix) that, for example, Bultmann and Streeter could come to such widely differing results.

with his character as gathered from Mark and Q, but still it is the overall picture that matters to modern Judaism.

A treatment of the sects and groups ensued, noting that the Pharisees were the greater party to which most people adhered. The *Am ha-aretz* (or *Am ha-arec*, by Montefiore's transliteration) were mostly observant; they ought not to be identified with the sinners befriended by Jesus, who were the nonobservant. The *Am ha-aretz*, in fact, could even be wealthy, not the usual poor portrayed. And certainly Jesus must have been brought up in Pharisaic ways; his parents were probably Pharisees. And while there was also undoubtedly some legalism among the smaller and weaker rabbinic figures, that was not characteristic of Pharisaism generally. Apocalypticism influenced Jesus, but he nevertheless kept closer to the prophets than to the apocalyptists.

Judaism at Jesus' time was full of variety and even contradictions. Its universal monotheistic faith was bound together with the national cult. Jesus, however, was an individualist who showed no interest in either politics or national life; his focus was on the individual. As a prophetic figure he announced doom and judgment on both Jew and Gentile. Israel was not exempt, but Jesus directed his message primarily toward individuals. He was sent to the lost and moved among them. This was an original element with Jesus.

He spoke of a coming kingdom and the judgment that ushers in the kingdom. His prophetic ethics constituted the conditions of entry into the kingdom. As to the Law, Jesus certainly depreciated outward observances, but he did not overthrow the Law. He taught the love ethic and emphasized the inward. He was, however, not like Hillel, who remained a servant of the Law and never its judge. "The spirit is different" in Hillel and in Jesus.[12] Jesus announced the kingdom with authority and assurance; he combined motifs from Amos and Second Isaiah, doom and comfort at the same time. This also was an original element.

Jesus was a healer and provided some signs of his divine mission. He proclaimed the forgiveness of sins and called others to repentance. He was convinced evidently that he was the messiah, though such a claim would have been a source of conflict, as would also any claim to be "son" in a special sense. These claims were exaggerated after Jesus' death and provided a still greater source of conflict. His life came to be portrayed as a divine drama, played out with full messianic awareness on his part, with himself a deified figure who foresaw his own death and resurrection. Historically speaking, as observed, Jesus may have seen himself as Son of God, messianically and spiritually (Psalm 2), but the community later extended that greatly. Whatever conflicts Jesus may have actually had with the rabbis, he could have gone on with just his teaching "without coming to an evil end" (cxxviii). The life-and-death struggles only occurred, Montefiore seemed to say, when the Christians made such gigantic claims about Jesus himself. We should look for the greatest authenticity in the teaching tradition.

---

12. Montefiore, *Synoptic Gospels*, cxx.

A commentary is not a "life," and a life cannot be written. Nevertheless, some life-related observations can be made: Jesus was likely born in 4 B.C.E. and died in 30 C.E. He had one to one and one-half years of public activity, with a ministry of two parts: Galilee and Jerusalem. The main issue is how he died. There is also the problem of the messiahship. Probably he did not at first see himself as messiah, but only a prophet. Whether he claimed the Son of man title is difficult virtually beyond solution. There are also problems of responsibility for his death, and whether there was really anything special about his teaching.

The typical Christian idea that there was a distinction between the ordinary Jewish concept of the messiah (a warlike, nationalistic figure) and Jesus' own, more spiritual idea is a distortion. There was actually no single messianic idea then. It seems likely that Jesus did expect, either before his death in some kind of dénouement, or at his Parousia afterwards, that he would rule. He also believed in a judgment, in which apparently many would be lost and those left would be subjects of the messianic king. There is no indication that Jesus intended to found a new religion.

Like an old prophet Jesus had opposition. Said Montefiore: "His teaching is a revival of prophetic Judaism, and in some respects points forward to the liberal Judaism of to-day" (cxxxiv). There are parallels to just about everything in his teaching from Judaism. What is original about it is its spirit, its intensity, its enthusiasm, its fervor (cxxxv), as opposed to a novelty of content. On some matters Jesus stood in opposition to the rabbis, for example, Sabbath observance, divorce, clean and unclean. Both believed in the divinity of the Law, but Jesus' more prophetic attitude pushed him to violations of the Law. He did not equate the ceremonial with the ethical and consequently set up a tragic conflict.

The founding of a new religion would not have been possible for one who anticipated the end of the world. "He was, and meant to remain, a Jew . . . he continued the work of Amos, Hosea, and Isaiah. His Kingdom of God, from one point of view, was a reformed Judaism" (cxxvvi). And, Montefiore noted, this reformed Judaism and a Unitarian Christianity might find common ground, could both claim Jesus as one of their own.

The commentary moves along the lines of the expressed Jewish interest. Though the question of Jesus' messianic claims is interesting, in the final analysis it is secondary to the interest presented by his teaching, which does not depend upon the messianic question. Likewise the baptism of Jesus has no particular value for Jews, though it is a historic fact, probably even a turning point. For Mark Jesus became Son of God at his baptism, though that does not mean that he became conscious of a divine sonship. It is more difficult to support the idea that here also Jesus saw himself as the Isaianic servant. Assuming, as seems likely, that Jesus did see himself as messiah, what kind of messiah was he? Certainly more than the one of Isaiah 11 and also an apocalyptic figure, for he expected the final judgment and the kingdom of God. That affected his views (though it does not render his ethic interim); the righteousness expected of the kingdom was his ethic. Service was one part of the expectation; he laid that on himself as well, from which may have come the idea of himself as the suffering messiah. Then perhaps as well came the further idea of the Son of man role and his rule in the future kingdom, after his service now. This messianic thought likely came later in his ministry, not at the baptism, but as a result of his ministry.

The political question was refused by Jesus. He was only interested in individuals.

Some points of interpretation for Montefiore: Mark 1:15 describes a great world crisis at hand, the equivalent of the ancient prophetic Day of the Lord. The wicked must repent and prepare. But, said Montefiore, all this eschatological teaching is of less value for us. Jesus was mistaken about the End, but the eschatological expectation did evoke the teaching, which does abide. At the heart of it lies the attitude of inwardness, love of enemies, the value of the ceremonial, the childlike attitude, faith, service, seeking sinners and the outcasts. But all these things are detachable from the eschatological views.

"Kingdom of God" is also sometimes merely a synonym for "heaven," sometimes it stands for a present activity, a gradual process, and a spiritual fact in the hearts of persons, though mostly it refers to a future entity.

The trial of Jesus: the charge of blasphemy was based on Jesus' claim that *he* would destroy and rebuild the temple (358). The Sadducean priesthood, together with the Romans, was responsible for Jesus' death. The resurrection visions were not illusions, though they were purely subjective. Of course, even Jews believe in immortality, so a belief in immortality assumes that Jesus was also resurrected.

The attention to Matthew and Luke provided more opportunity for elucidation of these themes. The birth material was skipped over lightly; for obvious reasons Montefiore centered on the Sermon on the Mount, recognizing its origin largely in Q, and noting its character as a miscellaneous collection of teaching. It matters little whether all of it came from Jesus or not; it is no better or worse either way.

The kingdom of God is the rule or dominion of God, as with the rabbis. It is the new world after the judgment. Jesus also spoke of rewards and punishments, even though Protestants especially are uncomfortable about it. Yet Jesus had no such fears. The rabbis' teaching has been distorted; they also spoke of *Lishmah*, or acting out of a higher motive (love). The new thing in Jesus was that reward is the same for all, and service is a duty that does not get a reward. Both Jesus and the rabbis taught that reward follows as the consequence of an action, much like a law of God. Result inevitably follows from cause.

Jesus did not urge anyone to break the Law. He was not teaching a new religion or righteousness. The antitheses of the Sermon probably show some enlargement over their original shape, but the point was not to set Jesus' teaching against the Decalogue. It was to offer a deepening, a more inward interpretation of the Law, and that is thoroughly rabbinic. The rabbis also knew of the distinction between the spirit and the letter of the Law, and it is false to say that Judaism only was concerned with the external, or only with action and reward. The Law was never to the Jew a fearsome taskmaster.

Original with Jesus was the saying about divorce (Matthew incorporates a secondary exception). His attitude on divorce was untenable, but the apparent attack on the inferiority of women was "of the highest importance and value" (2:67). Currently, however, the proscription of divorce would constitute an impossible burden.

Did Jesus' eschatology influence his ethic? Retaliation was outlawed; was that because the kingdom was coming? Jesus had no public justice in view, only how the members of the community were to act toward one another. As to love of enemies, Jesus' greatness is shown in his unlimited love demand, but, noted Montefiore, few of his followers have been able to adhere to that demand. It is a demand rarely taken to include any but private enemies; even Jesus himself seemed not to practice otherwise. "If Jesus meant that Christians were to love non-Christians — his disciples, those who refused to admit his claims — it is singular how completely and persistently his commands have been disobeyed, and how flagrantly many Christians still obey them" (2:79).

It is a remarkable work. Merely to invest such a monumental effort in a substantial piece of Christian literature is itself a feat of no small dimension, an extension of a hand from one community to another. In Montefiore's time that was an act not fully reciprocated.

The matters that have, for perhaps obvious reasons, concerned Jewish scholars are present in Montefiore's work in repeated abundance: the attitude toward the Law, the depiction of the Pharisees and Jesus' disputes with them, responsibility for Jesus' condemnation and death. Conspicuous by their presence are a highly positive evaluation of the teaching of Jesus and even his historical character. Montefiore's later articles, alluded to earlier, on the originality of Jesus and Jewish opinion of Jesus repeat many of these thoughts in a more condensed fashion.[13] Original with Jesus was his association with sinners, his prophetic attitude toward the ceremonial and the Sabbath, the intensity of his use of Father-Son-children, his emphasis on service and losing life in order to gain it (the newness lies in its absoluteness). In some ways Jesus was off the rabbinic line: he had a touch of asceticism (antifamily, selling one's possessions, exalting poverty). In some other ways — nonresistance, love of the enemies — he went beyond the rabbis. On divorce he went beyond Shammai even and sought to put women on an equal footing with men. He also opposed a reciprocal ethic, though here the rabbinic parallels are very close.

Montefiore conceded a high degree of originality to Jesus. The beatitudes, for example, have parallels to individual parts, but the whole exhibits an intensity, a glow, a demand for unqualified absoluteness. Probably Jesus' originality in this context was bound to his eschatological vision, his heavenly expectation, whereas the rabbis were more earthy, more practical. There should be room for both, for the unqualified demand of Jesus and the more nuanced applications rendered by the rabbis.

13. Above, p. 232, n. 9.

But the difference between Jews and Christians remains very great, said Montefiore, even in spite of all efforts to appreciate Jesus. Orthodox Christianity maintained the perfection of Jesus on the basis of the Trinity; Jesus was, in effect, the Second Person of the Trinity walking about on the earth. The modern era has placed less emphasis on Jesus' divinity and found his excellence in his moral character and perfection. One problem with assessing the latter claim is simply the length of Jesus' ministry. Can so short a time justify so exalted a claim of character? Certainly Jesus was one of the prophets, but was he more than a prophet or more original than any of them? Is there enough in what is known of his ministry to call his life the noblest ever? A brief examination of the Markan picture does not yield a certainty; a figure is present there of great power, an absolutist, someone of tenderness, a lover of children, a one-sided person. But the greatest of all who ever lived? That is a more difficult step. There is too much one-sidedness, too much intolerance toward those who disagreed with him. And, aside from his (deliberate?) death, where are the incidents in his life that compel admiration of nobility, of courage, of sacrifice? Actually, his life up to the end was not so difficult; he had few needs and mostly someone else supplied them.

So a Unitarian, for example, can find still his Master in Jesus, but the Jew already has in the Old Testament most of what that Unitarian finds. The orthodox Christian can find everything in an idealized picture of the Christ, but the Jew can only look at the actual life of Jesus. Even more, the Jew simply cannot find God in a man; only God can be his master.

There is a tendency to regard Montefiore's work as epochmaking,[14] though some of his Jewish contemporaries would not have agreed. Gerald Friedländer, for instance, thought that Montefiore had gone too far.[15] Jesus was a failure as a messiah. The kingdom never came; his claim to give a new law disqualified him as a prophet. He was a teacher, but the beatitudes can be found in Isaiah and the Psalms. There is no higher or better morality in the Sermon on the Mount than is taught by the Pharisees. In short, Judaism has nothing to learn from Jesus.

Some later opinion, such as that of Lou Silberman, wanted to emphasize that Montefiore's commentary on the synoptic gospels contained a rich scholarship, but that it was a "very personal statement of a theological point of view," and that, in the end, it was a "party document, that party being a party of one. It gave rise to no followers, no school."[16] In fact, there is something *sui generis*

---

14. Lindeskog so characterizes it (*Die Jesusfrage*, 177).

15. Gerald Friedländer, *The Jewish Sources of the Sermon on the Mount* (London: George Routledge and Sons; New York: Bloch Publishing, 1911). Friedländer was listed as rabbi of the Western Synagogue in London. Also a more orthodox view would be represented by Paul Goodman, *The Synagogue and the Church* (London: George Routledge and Sons; New York: E. P. Dutton, 1908). Goodman emphasized the depreciation of the Pharisees and scribes, that the gospels were wrong about many other things; the moral teaching of Jesus was mostly Jewish and where it was not — nonresistance, for example — not even Christians practiced it anyway, while other things, such as his celibacy and poverty, were irrelevant; the resurrection was witnessed by Mary Magdalene, a demented woman. Goodman saw Jesus as nearer the Essenes.

16. Silberman's prolegomenon to Montefiore, *Synoptic Gospels*, 15.

about Montefiore's work; it is a monument erected as much to the man and his own vision of liberal Judaism as to the gospels themselves. No one should denigrate that vision; it was born of a liberal spirit whose actualization was then and even now only too rare.

Montefiore's longer-term significance can most likely be seen in his well-crafted statement of the boundaries within which Jewish investigation of the Jesus tradition ought to occur; many Jewish investigators would not agree with his own assessment of the contributions or the originality of Jesus, but the abiding issues were set forth with lucidity and power. At the same time we cannot fail to notice that Montefiore's Jesus sounds suspiciously like a reformed Jew, indeed, was characterized as such. So Montefiore constructed a Jesus who was a liberal Jew, following in the fashion of Harnack, who made him a liberal Christian. And George Tyrrell's lesson comes around again: the face staring back from the bottom of the Jesus-well is our own. Or said differently: we go in quest of Jesus only to find the one we need at a given time. Perhaps only such a Jesus could have supplied the dynamic necessary for a Jewish-Christian accommodation, which was a needful thing. Unfortunately, what came instead was something more horrendous, more unimaginably horrible. Whether the Quest of the historical Jesus had anything to do with that event is a much more difficult question of a greater magnitude.

Many of the concerns to which Montefiore so powerfully addressed himself were, and remain, items on the agenda of Jewish scholarship. Some of these same issues can also be seen arising in the most read and publicized *Leben Jesu* to emanate from Jewish circles, that of Joseph Klausner.[17]

Joseph Klausner

Klausner was born in Russia in 1874 and was a zealous supporter of Zionism. He studied at Heidelberg in 1897 in philosophy and Semitic languages, obtaining his doctorate there; he came to Palestine in 1920 and published extensively and worked for a Palestinian home for the Jewish people.

The introduction to his work claimed that the book aimed to solve the contradiction that Jesus, though a Jew, had followers who were predominantly Gentile. Why did Israel reject Jesus? The study of Jesus should disclose what was Jewish about him and what not. The goal was objective: to see Jesus in his own time and environment and to attempt to construct a picture of Jesus that had no religious aim.

First Klausner considered the Talmudic material about Jesus, coming to the conclusion that it held reliable statements about Jesus, such as that he practiced sorcery (performed miracles, healed), led Israel astray (stirred trouble), mocked the words of the Wise, expounded scripture like a Pharisee, was hanged (crucified) as a false teacher on Passover eve, and his disciples healed in his

---

17. Joseph Klausner, *Jesus of Nazareth: His Life, Times, and Teaching,* trans. Herbert Danby (New York: Macmillan, 1925); reprinted 1927 and reissued 1929.

name. Unworthy are the stories about his birth (the Pandera legend, a corruption of the virgin birth claim); more important, the stories show the attitude of the *Tannaim* toward Jesus, that he was a true Jew, that he had a share in the world to come, and he expounded scripture, but that he also aroused their ire by sometimes setting aside the Law. The *Tannaim* forbade their disciples to heal.

The *Tol'doth Jesu* is discredited as having been composed about the tenth century and possessing no historical value at all. It only shows the attitude of the Jews toward Jesus between the fifth and tenth centuries.

As to Josephus, some of the *Antiquities* passage comes from Josephus, in particular the parts about Jesus as a wise man, a doer of wonderful things, and a teacher whose followers persisted in their devotion to him even after Pilate had condemned him to the cross. The passage referring to the death of James is to be accepted as genuine. The scanty references in Tacitus, Suetonius, and Pliny the Younger are also accepted as genuine, if of little use.

Paul provides evidence for the existence of Jesus and the influence he exerted, but there is little of Jesus' own message or activity. Most everything in Paul is concentrated on his own message about the crucified and risen Lord and therefore provides little to the investigator.

In the early Fathers, Justin Martyr and Papias supply some tradition, but it is of slight value in terms of the sayings of Jesus, as are generally the *Agrapha* found scattered through the Fathers.

The apocryphal gospels have no historical value, but certain "uncanonical" ones do (Peter, Egyptians, Hebrews) — with sayings not found in the canonical gospels. There are also additions in certain manuscripts (Bezae).

The sum of all is to show that Jesus lived in the Roman occupation and was of unusual personality.

Klausner then provided a history of discussion of the life of Jesus and the sources, going back to the English Deists and coming down to his own time. It was a capsule version of the story told by Schweitzer and more, including Schweitzer, but gave the grandest accolades to Wellhausen, who concluded that Jesus was indeed no Christian, but a Jew: "Never before did such a statement escape the pen of a Christian scholar, and such a scholar, and such an enemy of Jews and Judaism, as was Wellhausen." His judgment about Harnack (*What Is Christianity?*) was less kind: "There, the historical Jew, Jesus, disappears totally: virtually every word he taught is made to be of permanent and universal humanitarian interest." Harnack's Jesus was a modernist, the Jesus of the "liberal and anti-Jewish Germany of the early twentieth century" (96).

When Klausner came to speak of Jewish scholarship's presentation of Jesus he could find few works — only three, and two of them before 1900, with the third in 1920 (H. G. Enelow's *A Jewish View of Jesus*). He might have noted therefore the rarity of a work like his own and doubtless was aware of the fact. He gave some reply to Bousset's work and took notice of Montefiore, noting some (G. Friedländer) who were opposed, and mentioned the contributions of

G. Klein, M. Friedländer, and the converted Jew Alfred Edersheim. Opposite to it was Daniel Chwolson's work.

On the gospels, John is a philosophical work from the middle of the second century, though it may have a few historical fragments. Of the synoptics, Mark is the oldest (66–68), possibly by one of Mark's disciples (Mark himself was a disciple of Peter). He drew on early Aramaic written sources. Next is Matthew, founded on Mark and an Aramaic or Hebrew collection of sayings and further oral traditions. It was composed near the end of the century by a disciple of Matthew for Jewish Christians. Last came Luke, a disciple of Paul and a physician, who had a Greek education and gave an orderly account of Jesus, at the beginning of the second century. There is a lack of order in all the gospels, making a life impossible; everything is arranged by writers whose chief goal was religious, not historical or biographical.

Klausner then described the period from the Roman conquest to the destruction of the temple, drawing heavily on Josephus, characterizing religious and intellectual conditions, education, the social status of women (high), and widely held concepts (God, the sense of holiness, angels, harmful spirits, beliefs in an afterlife, rewards and punishment, the messiah and the "pangs" of the messianic age). Of the different parties the Essenes were the nearest to Jesus. All sects originated in the Maccabean period; from the Hasidim came the Essenes, the Pharisees, and the Zealots (who only became powerful in the time of Herod); the Sadducees came from the priests of the pre-Maccabean Hellenists. The Zealots were extremist Pharisees, patriots. They were also called *sicarii*. Pharisees were the popular party; Jesus criticized them, and there is something to that, but we also find it among the *Tannaim*. The Pharisees did tend to give the same importance to laws dealing with the ceremonial and ritual as those dealing with fellow men. There is some resemblance between Jesus and Hillel.

Jesus was born in Nazareth, a town little referred to in the ancient sources. The Talmud mentions how uncouth were Galileans and that they did not know the Torah. The Bethlehem tradition is theological. Jesus' father was a carpenter, an artisan. Jesus thus came from a class of simple laborers. He had four brothers and two sisters who were likely married. Joseph died while Jesus was still young. Jesus may have been taught by Joseph, but also must have learned in the synagogue. He would have been influenced by the natural environment of Nazareth and its beauty. Galilee became a cauldron of unrest due to heavy taxation. The story of Jesus at the age of 12 accompanying his parents to Jerusalem has been fashioned by Luke. Otherwise there is nothing about his youth, but silence about early life was typical among Jews, who were only interested in a man after he had appeared on the stage of history.

In the same way there is nothing of the life of John the Baptist. Luke's narratives of his origins are legendary (maybe excepted are his father's and mother's names). Josephus and the gospel's narrative of John's death supplement one another, except the gospels have the error of making Herodias the wife of Philip.

John the Baptist was a prophet who thought of himself as Elijah, the forerunner of the messiah; he was also a Nazirite and ascetic. He resembled the Essenes, but there were differences — the Essenes were not political, and John did not live apart from society. He proclaimed repentance and baptized as preparation for the messiah. The baptism signified a new birth. He had such influence that his movement survived him.

Jesus' baptism by John was the most decisive event in his life. Klausner speculated: "Perhaps his very name 'Jesus' (Yeshua, Yashua, Yashu), 'he shall save,' may have moved this simple villager to believe that he was the redeemer, just as Shabbethai Avi was influenced by the fact that he was born on the 9th of Ab, the day when, according to a legend, the Messiah was to be born" (252). The dazzling light was the Shekinah, and the seeming voice the Bath Qol:

> Suddenly there flashed through Jesus' mind, like blinding lightning, the idea that *he* was the hoped-for Messiah. This was the voice which he heard within him and for which he had been prepared by his thirty years of rich, cloistered, inner life at Nazareth. His dream acquired its utmost realization at this great moment in his life, the solemn moment of his baptism. (252)

Jesus hid his idea, for it would have sounded foolish. Mark speaks of a time of solitude afterwards. Jesus meditated on three ways his messiahship would take: king-messiah, one mighty in Torah, or bestower of material welfare. He rejected all three; he would keep his silence for the time being and proclaim his gospel of the kingdom without identifying the messiah. Jesus was a worker of miracles, as the messiah was supposed to be, though also the *Tannaim* and some scribes and Pharisees were. But with Jesus the miracles possessed an equal place with the teaching.

Klausner considered but rejected Wrede's theory; the disciples could not have proclaimed the crucified one as messiah had he himself not made that claim (though he did not do so in the early stages). Jesus was called Rabbi or Rabboni by others; he called himself Son of man, that is, simple flesh and blood. It was a title that both disclosed and hid; to those who knew Daniel and Enoch it had special significance. Sometimes Son of man was merely a man; then again he could be like the prophet Ezekiel; still further he could be like that messiah-king who would possess the everlasting kingdom.

A scientific biography of Jesus is not possible. We have a beginning and an end, but it is hard to fix the points in between. Probably there was only a year of ministry that had certain landmarks. Jesus set out first to continue John's preaching of the kingdom and repentance. He began in Capernaum and made disciples there. He impressed his hearers, who saw him as one speaking with authority. Unlike the scribes he used parable and allegory instead of exposition of scripture. He was also notable for his healings, which were of primary importance for him, if not for the scribes. The miracles are susceptible of various explanations (poetic exaggeration, illusion, the power of suggestion, and the like). The secrecy element can be seen as a desire not to have too much publicity, for sometimes the "miracles" probably did not work.

Jesus enjoyed his greatest success early in Galilee; he consorted with sinners and tax collectors, friends of Matthew. He practiced no fasting, yet remained steadfast to the Torah and observed the ceremonial laws like a Pharisee. That alone explains why James and Peter argued against Paul for retaining these laws. He mostly attracted the *Am ha-aretz,* with some exceptions, including women. There are exaggerations in the record, as in the feeding of 5,000 and mention of cities he passed through. But on the whole this was Jesus' most successful period, lasting perhaps two to three months. But clouds gathered; Pharisees and scribes were displeased by his consorting with sinners and his lack of fasting. He also told a man his sins were forgiven, owing obviously to his sufferings (paralytic), since suffering atones for sin (*Berachoth* 5a). The Pharisees saw that as blasphemy. The disciples also were eating corn (or raw wheat) on the Sabbath; that was the first time Jesus said that the Sabbath was made for man, not man for the Sabbath, a perspective that agrees with the Pharisaic point of view, though no one would agree that it was permissible to pluck corn on the Sabbath. It also aroused Pharisaic indignation that Jesus healed on the Sabbath. In the Mishnah one cannot heal an illness that is not dangerous. Here the authorities began to be cool toward Jesus, as well as people who venerated the Pharisees. Even his family was influenced and tried to take him back home, causing an irrevocable rupture with his family. Afterward Jesus changed his strategy, teaching from the sea in boats or outside towns, so the authorities could not easily catch him. In an act of boldness he went to Nazareth, but found rejection there.

Jesus chose twelve — an authentic recollection — and promised that they would sit on thrones judging the twelve tribes of Israel, with himself to come as the Son of man on the clouds of heaven. Peter was chief of the disciples, Judas the betrayer who came from afar (Kerioth, south of Hebron). He sent out the apostles who also preached and healed. More conflict with Pharisees was generated when Jesus permitted foods forbidden in the Torah. That completed the breach between Jesus and the Pharisees.

Jesus was a very different figure from the tender, mild person depicted by Christians. He displayed anger toward Pharisees; he fled from them into the regions of Tyre and Sidon. He met a Canaanite woman, the only time he dealt with strangers. Jesus was an "utter Jew" (294) and sent to Jews alone. The episode is too harsh not to be true, and also was written at a time when the community included many non-Jews. Bitterness at the towns of Chorazin and Bethsaida shows his situation growing worse; no progress in his work encouraged bitterness. He passed through the Decapolis; the swine story may be unhistorical, as also would be the reference to the legion.

Jesus moved on to Caesarea-Philippi. Despair was setting in; he had lost the "old buoyancy" (299). Did his disciples still believe in him? The confession-scene followed. It betrays expansions by the other evangelists, and it may be that the words of Matt. 11:25 were then spoken. Jesus spoke of his sufferings; the pangs of the messianic age usually are not applied to the messiah himself, but Jesus had already faced opposition. No doubt he saw his suffering as occurring in Jerusalem; there could be no better place or time (Passover) for the revelation of the messiah. The prediction of three days of death, then resurrection, exceeds probability. In fact, Jesus feared death. To imagine the messiah being put to death was incomprehensible. Isaiah 53 had to do with the nation, not a human messiah. So Jesus actually told his disciples that he would go to Jerusalem and suffer much, but be victorious and be recognized by the crowds as messiah. Peter disliked that scenario and argued with Jesus, who in turn rebuked him. The following words about taking up the cross are a later addition; crucifixion was not Jewish. The Son of man saying about being ashamed of Jesus is genuine; the coming would not be distant, but was near. The Transfiguration has an element of historicity, but Peter's imagination led to seeing Moses and Elijah.

Jesus set out for Jerusalem; in Capernaum the disciples argued about who was the greatest and were given the promise of sitting on twelve thrones. It was a worldly, material ideal, very Jewish. Passing through Samaria produced some opposition; then came Jericho, where occurred the scene with Zacchaeus, whom Jesus had probably known beforehand. The blind man was the first to acclaim him as Son of David, a traditional messianic title. Jesus chose to enter the city as messiah, riding on an ass (therefore not as a conqueror). The event compelled attention; some thought him the messiah, others a prophet. Jesus publicly revealed himself before the crowds as messiah.

Jesus was determined to announce himself as messiah, to demand repentance, and to promise his coming on the clouds of heaven, with the "pangs" to follow. Then would occur the overthrow of Rome with Jesus and his disciples occupying twelve thrones and Jesus as the Son of man. It was not his intention, however, to arouse a revolt. To bring men to repentance he must do some great deed, something public and religious, but not political; the deed was the purification of the temple. Jesus overturned tables and drove out traders, allowing no traffic (the Mishnah forbids any shortcuts); he exercised force in a violent fashion. His deed enraged the priests who could not, however, act until evening, so Jesus and his disciples left, satisfied that they had done what they wanted to (gain the approval of the people and arouse popular indignation against the leaders).

Jesus alienated everybody, the people who were disappointed in him, even the Sadducees now with his affirmation of the resurrection. But he remained a true Pharisaic Jew to the end, as can be seen in his summary of the twofold command of love as the heart of the Law. Jesus' diatribe against Pharisees is not surprising, though it should be seen as a collection of isolated sayings like the Sermon on the Mount. Much of the criticism was deserved, but also there was too much generalization. The Pharisees and Sadducees alike must have resented his attitude toward the temple, since he predicted its destruction. The apocalypse that followed contains much that is later, though still of Jewish origin. Authentic is the warning that no one knows the eschatological time, so the disciples must be prepared.

Judas was disappointed in Jesus; he saw contradictions in Jesus' teachings and actions (he taught nonresistance, but practiced violence; there was no evidence of the coming messiah). Judas must have thought him a false messiah, for he saw no mighty deeds in Jerusalem, no act of deliverance. Judas was an educated, sensitive person, unlike the other, dull-witted disciples.

Jesus celebrated the Passover on 13 Nisan, Thursday, and the Seder, the Passover meal, on that night (14 Nisan), with its unleavened bread and bitter herbs, instead of on the night of 15 Nisan. They ate the Passover; they ate the unleavened bread and drank the first of the four cups. The bitter herbs brought to mind the pangs of the messianic age. They sang the *Hallel,* and Jesus may have said that he would not drink until he drank anew in the kingdom. Other sayings about his body and blood recall the sacramental rites of later Christians.

Jesus did not foresee his death, even though he knew that his enemies were after him and his disciples were disappointing him. In the garden he prayed (*Abba,* a diminutive of affection) while the disciples slept. It is all a very human and tragic story. Judas betrayed Jesus' location, though much of the story contains legendary accretion. Pharisees were not involved. Even the Talmud hated these priests and their henchmen, the police. They arrested Jesus amid some violence and resistance. The young man who fled away naked was John Mark, who later recorded the incident and had heard Jesus' prayer before falling asleep.

The Sadducees feared another messiah and the high priest ordered Jesus' arrest. There was first a preliminary examination, not a trial. An inquiry of any sort could not have been conducted on the night of Passover or the first day of Passover. We have therefore to follow John and suppose that Jesus was crucified on the eve of Passover. Luke is right that the Sanhedrin assembled the next morning first. Witnesses were called, the temple incident may have been mentioned. Did Jesus claim to be the Son of man? "It was impossible but that the soul and feelings of Jesus — a mystic, a dreamer and an enthusiast — should be stirred to their depths. There is no doubt that he returned a positive answer" (342). The claim led to a charge of blasphemy, of equating himself with the Son of man of Daniel and sitting on the right hand of God. But Jesus had done nothing worthy of death, in the eyes of Pharisees at least; he had not spoken the "Name" or led anyone else to worship of other gods.

The evangelists pile up the guilt on the Jews. But who was present and heard it all? Peter got close, but denied Jesus, though here again there is much legendizing (cock crowing). The prescription for blasphemy was stoning, followed by hanging on a tree (actually, a piece of wood in the ground with a jutting beam). The Jews had no power of death at that time, so they handed Jesus over hastily to Pilate with the charge that he had assumed the role of messiah. Pilate's behavior as described in the gospels is unhistorical; only the political mattered to Pilate. But the Jews are not guilty for the death of Jesus, though they continue to be blamed: "Yet these nineteen hundred years past the world has gone on avenging the blood of Jesus the Jew upon his countrymen, the Jews, who have already paid the penalty, and still go on paying the penalty in rivers and torrents of blood" (348).

Crucifixion came to Rome from Persia via Carthage. The prisoner bore the crossbeam and was nailed, feet and hands, to the upright. Death was very painful and usually long. Jesus was weak and evidently died quickly. The death scene has much of scripture in it, but the final cry is probably from Jesus, even if Psalm 22 is quoted. Much else that is narrated was meant to show fulfillment. The body was taken by Joseph and buried. Men stayed at a distance, but the women had no fear. So ends the story of Jesus, so begins the story of Christianity.

Christianity would not have been possible without the epilogue: What happened to the body of Jesus? Christianity was not founded on a deception, but it is likely that Joseph did not wish to leave the body in his own new family burial site, so he removed it and buried it in an unknown grave. The women were not obviously expecting anything when they came to the tomb to anoint the body; they saw a vision of angels, which Mary Magdalene, who was known for having been hysterical, reported. Afterward the disciples went to Galilee and began also to have visions of Jesus, with Peter the first. These visions are the basis of Christianity; they are not based on deception, either. Peter and the others were really convinced that they had seen Jesus, as Paul also claimed.

Jesus remained to the end a Jew. His teaching in the Sermon on the Mount shows this clearly. He did not throw out the Law, even the ceremonial law, but he did regard the latter as of less importance than the moral law. Other sayings formed additions to the Law, but did not annul it. It is hard otherwise to understand how James and Peter, and others, could maintain the Law, while Paul opposed it. Jesus did have some point of contention with Judaism, for example, Sabbath-keeping, healing, the food laws; he almost, but not quite, nullified the Law. It was left to Paul to carry that process to the extreme. Jesus lacked a national perspective, a political perspective; he saw nothing in the ceremonial laws of a national nature. In fact, Jesus contributed nothing to the culture; he gave no new culture, but sought to abolish such as his nation possessed. He set himself against scribes and Pharisees, for whom all religion was bound up with the whole life of the nation; he formed no opposition to Rome (pay to Caesar what is Caesar's), advocated no civil justice (resist not evil, swear not at all, share all with the poor, have no family life, practice no divorce), and possessed no economics (depend on God, do not worry about goods). Jesus is the most Jewish of Jews; he is exaggerated Judaism. He urged abolition of property, blessings on the poor, contrasted the rich man and Lazarus — all a tendency toward communism. Judaism could only see in Jesus a great dangerous phantasy. "Hence the strange sight: — Judaism brought forth Christianity in its first form (the teaching of Jesus), but it thrust aside its daughter when it saw that she would slay the mother with a deadly kiss" (376).

As to his idea of God, Jesus did not claim to be God or the Son of God. He spoke of God as his Father, *Abba* (also used in the Talmud). He emphasized excessively God as his Father because he thought of himself as messiah. He gave the impression of one man closer to God than any other. Judaism was not able to accept that. Another point of disagreement was that Jesus said that all alike were sinners, were objects of God's care. That undermines the justice of God.

In assessing Jesus' ethical teaching Klausner summed up the Sermon on the Mount and claimed that it contains nothing that was not paralleled in Judaism, giving extensive examples. Yet what Jesus did was to establish an ethical system connected with his concept of God, with no real concern for national life. But Judaism had a national-world outlook, unlike Jesus, who only had a religious-ethical outlook. So Jesus then annulled Judaism as a nation; he gave an ethic applicable to anyone anywhere, and therefore broke down the barrier of nationalism. This was destructive, in Klausner's view, and is the reason why his people, Israel, rejected him. Jesus was not an ascetic, but his teaching would not suffice for a national code. The ethics are severed from daily life. "Such has been the case with Christianity from the time of Constantine till the present day: the religion has stood for what is highest ethically and ideally, while the political and social life has remained the other extreme of barbarity and paganism" (393). And when in fact did Christians ever actually live by Jesus' words? So asked Klausner. Even he himself urged turning the other cheek, but then ran people out of the temple and other such things.

Jesus' teaching is to be understood in the light of messianism and the expectation of the kingdom. The End was near, the kingdom was already present — the messiah is already here — therefore, nothing is permanent, there can be nothing lasting in culture. Judgment is close; repent and get ready — that is the message. There is nothing there of value for a permanent culture or society. That is again why Judaism could not accept Jesus. Jesus remained a Jew, but his extremist views later allowed such persons as Paul to divinize him.

What was the secret of Jesus' attraction and influence? He was humble but also intense. He was one of the people and possessed a popular appeal, and he was also expert in scriptures, and had a kindness of heart coupled with a violence of passion. He was also a man of the world, and the parables especially illustrate that he had a sense of reality. Of course, he also believed in the supernatural — a mystic faith coupled with a practical sense. He had a great sense of authority and spoke in parables, proverbs, epigrams, and the like, all of which was attractive to ordinary folk. Here shines in fact a single, remarkable personality. The tragedy of his death added to his luster, but the resurrection legend made him divine and exalted every virtue.

What is Jesus to the Jew today? He is not divine, the Son of God, not the messiah, not a lawgiver, a prophet, not even a Pharisaic rabbi; he is instead *"a great teacher of morality and an artist in parable"* (414; italics his). He remains unparalleled in his morality and parables, even though his ethic is so unreal that it is unuseable.

So Klausner ended his encounter with the historical Jesus.

If Montefiore acculturated Jesus in order to find in him something like a liberal Jew, then Klausner historicized him in order to read him out of Judaism. In the end there is unrelieved ambiguity: Jesus was a Jew, so it is said over and over; but he was a highly irrelevant one, a parabler of great note, to be sure, but a teacher of a morality so elevated that it could not touch the real world and could not do service for any form of Judaism. Yet we must not fail to appreciate Klausner's achievement, either, any less than Montefiore's. Both were, in fact, unique themselves, without disciples. There is hardly a Jewish life of Jesus after Klausner; his work is also *sui generis*.[18] But his work, and that of Montefiore and many another Jewish scholar plowing in the field of New Testament studies, has had a salutary effect, a necessary effect. To the remainder of that story we need now to attend.

More Revaluings

At the turn of the twentieth century it was common to present the Judaism of Jesus' day in the darkest of colors. Wilhelm Bousset, for example, presented such a picture of Judaism (whose boundaries were shattered by Jesus) as to call forth a rebuke from his friend Ernst Troeltsch for his dreadful picture.[19] But much the same understanding of Judaism can be seen in portrayals from other lands and traditions of a more conservative bent, right on through the better part of the first half century (Stalker et al.). One obviously apologetic purpose of the Jewish scholars in investigating the gospels was to revalue this view and provide a more temperate, and historically accurate, portrayal of Judaism. In time a number of scholars from Christian communities began to share in that process of revaluation, so that a more moderate consensus began to emerge by the decade of the twenties.[20] An influential Jewish work that doubtless contributed to this movement was that of Israel Abrahams, *Studies in Pharisaism and the Gospels*, which

---

18. There was the work of Hugh J. Schonfield, *Jesus, a Biography* (London: Banner Books, 1939; reprint, 1948). It appealed not only to John, but to the Clementine Homilies, Tol'doth Jeshua, and the Gospel of Thomas. It is novelized, but not as fictionalized as the author's later *The Passover Plot* (New York: Bantam Books, 1967). Also among more fringe Jewish authors was Robert Eisler, *The Messiah Jesus and John the Baptist*, English edition by Alexander Haggerty Krappe (New York: Dial Press, 1931). Eisler claimed to throw light on Christian origins by examining bits and pieces of evidence from early Christianity's enemies — works not easily available owing to the exercise of censorship on the records by Christians. The main interest lay in Slavonic Josephus (Haliōsis), which contained a more extensive characterization of Jesus and his activity. Eisler evidently failed to convince much of anyone; cf. J. M. Creed, "The Slavonic Version of Josephus' History of the Jewish War," *HTR* 25 (1932): 277–319, who gives a description of the available manuscripts and the problems along with a rejection of Eisler's theory that the Slavonic text represents what Josephus originally wrote.

19. Troeltsch in Drescher, *Ernst Troeltsch*, 49. Bousset's work was *Jesu Predigt in ihrem Gegensatz zum Judentum: Ein religionsgeschichtlicher Vergleich* (Göttingen, 1892), reviewed by Schweitzer, *Quest*, 241–49. There was also the later work, *Die Religion des Judentums im neutestamentlichen Zeitalter* (Berlin, 1903; 3d ed., *Die Religion des Judentums im späthellenistischen Zeitalter*, ed. Hugo Gressmann, Handbuch zum Neuen Testament 21 [Tübingen, 1926]). Bousset utilized the works of hellenistic Judaism and, like Wellhausen, was not a Talmudist (Lindeskog, *Die Jesusfrage*, 138, 142). A similar assessment from another direction was given by George Foot Moore, "Christian Writers on Judaism," *HTR* 14 (1921): 197–254. The article contained a thumbnail sketch of writers across the centuries.

20. Actually, Shirley Jackson Case had noticed the phenomenon earlier; see his "The Rehabilitation of Pharisaism," *Biblical World* 41 (1913): 92–98, with still some reservations as to the differences from Jesus. A later assessment was D. W. Riddle, "Jesus in Modern Research," *JR* 17 (1937): 170–82, describing the shift toward a very Jewish Jesus.

we may take as epitomizing a Jewish answer to Christian representation of Jesus' environment.[21]

Israel Abrahams

Abrahams, Reader in Talmudics at Cambridge, was a close friend of Montefiore's and cofounder with him of the *Jewish Quarterly Review*. The two worked in close relationship not only with one another, but with other Christian scholars as well. Abrahams's work was originally intended as addenda to Montefiore's commentary, but various circumstances dictated its appearance separately, in two different volumes (1917 and 1924). These discrete essays were bound together by no particular theme, except only to provide some light from an expert in rabbinics on issues that have often marched darkly across the pages of many a book on the life of Jesus. The essays still repay reading many years later. Here we will only note some representatives of the work.

"The Greatest Commandment" shows that the combination of the twofold love commandment was already known in Pharisaism, contrary to Wellhausen who ascribed it uniquely to Jesus and was unaware of its presence in the *Testament of Issachar*. On John the Baptist, Abrahams argued that Josephus better preserved the reasons for John's baptism (for bodily purification corresponding to inward change), while the baptism for forgiveness of sins was a Christian interpolation. On publicans and sinners: the latter were immoral persons, dishonest or of depraved occupation. The rabbis warned against associating with people of low morals, but Pharisaism was always willing to take back a sinner, though left it to the initiative of the sinner, while maintaining God's readiness to do so. Jesus seemed to differ by taking the initiative, though the rabbis also taught concern for the wrongdoer and the straying, but the point was to retrieve them from their sin. On Caesar and paying taxes: the rabbis said to pay them, but there was no compulsion to do so when Caesar infringed on God's sphere. As to divorce, Deuteronomic divorce was actually a restriction on the husband's right to discard his wife at will and without ceremony. Jesus may have been promulgating an interim ethic (angels do not marry), but more likely he was giving a general rule for his own disciples. The Pharisees permitted divorce, with mutual consent; the male declaration was an act of the male releasing his wife so that she was free to remarry. Yet a woman's consent was not required for her husband to divorce her. Hillel's often quoted dictum that she could be divorced if she "spoiled" her husband's food was meant metaphorically, as standing for something else (indecent conduct). On adultery as a ground, "adultery" was defined for a woman as having intercourse with anyone other than her husband, but for the male it was intercourse with a married woman other than his wife.

Jesus learned parables in the synagogue; probably there was a large stock of popular parables floating around. Abrahams agreed with Fiebig that there was an

---

21. Israel Abrahams, *Studies in Pharisaism and the Gospels*, Library of Biblical Studies (New York: KTAV, 1967). The original was first published by Cambridge Press, the first series in 1917 and the second series in 1924. The reprint here used contains a prolegomenon by Morton S. Enslin.

original personality in Jesus' parables, but the same was true of the rabbis.[22] The rabbinic parables suffer by contrast with those in the gospels because the former are rough gems, lacking the polish provided by the evangelists for Jesus' parables. Parables were means of illustration and enforcement of lessons on providence and duty. A parable "may imply more than it says, and may leave behind it more puzzles than it solves." The parables of the New Testament are "inculcations of moral and religious truths, profound but not mysterious."[23]

The rabbis allowed some Sabbath relaxation; observance must be waived in order to save life. The primary principle was danger to life; that always overrode the Sabbath. Commenting on the David-showbread incident in Mark, Abrahams referred to the Midrash that says that imminent starvation would allow Sabbath violation. Yet there remained differences on what could done on the Sabbath. The Pharisees thought that no work that was not pressing or postponable ought to be done, but Jesus was more liberal, for example, healing on the Sabbath. (Circumcision was an exception, as rightly noted in John 7:22.) The Pharisees would relieve distress, but for Jesus any act of mercy was permitted.

The rabbis taught that God's forgiveness knew no limitations and required no mediator. Humankind attains it by repentance. "Man must pay: but God is a lenient creditor, and he himself provides the coin for the remission of the debt" (1:146). Furthermore, the rabbis were universalists, seeing divine mercy as extending even to Gentiles, even if sometimes the pressure of circumstances indicated differently. The expectation of human forgiveness was already present in the Old Testament; the rabbis made it a duty, for which God was the model.

As to the frequent charges of hypocrisy against the Pharisees, there is much in Matthew 23 that comes from a later time. As well, the Pharisees themselves greatly denounced hypocrisy and would have condemned it if found among themselves. On tithing, the Pharisees were scrupulous without neglecting the weightier matters of the Law, whether one appeals to Hillel, Aqiba, or Rab (Abba Arika).

The parable of the good Samaritan appears to be a midrash on Lev. 19:18. The point of the parable (following Montefiore) is that love knows no limits of race, that whoever needs me is my neighbor. This was also the insistence of the Pharisees. The appearance of the Samaritan is an artistic device, castigating one's own community by referring to an outsider. Perhaps the original reference was to priests, levites, and Israelites, for which there are rabbinic parallels. The paradox of the gospel treatment of the Pharisees is that it excludes them from the message of the grace that Jesus brought, which is itself a step back from Pharisaism. Priests and levites in the parable likely referred to Pharisaic leaders.

The New Testament's picture of persecutions against Christians, as interpreted by Harnack, for example, is wrong. Most action was defensive, warning

---

22. See below, chap. 8, 286–93.
23. Abrahams, *Studies in Pharisaism and the Gospels*, 1:106–7.

against the dangers of Christianity. Rarely were any charges initiated by Jews; in fact, Jews were usually treated as badly as Christians in pagan attacks.

The Lord's Prayer seems to speak of a conditional forgiveness — God's and humanity's — that has no parallel in Judaism. God's forgiveness is always un-conditional. Excessive length of prayer was also condemned by Pharisees. Jesus' words on this score were probably directed to pagans.

Looking at the trial narrative, Abrahams referred to the position of Herbert Danby on the point that the Mishnaic Sanhedrin was an idealized body pro-jected back into an earlier time, from post-70 into the time of Jesus.[24] Abrahams disagreed and inclined to the view advocated by A. Büchler that there were two courts, one political, the other religious; Jesus appeared before the latter.[25]

Such was the flavor of these essays — spirited, informed, judicious. If there remained something of an apologetic nature about them, that, too, was under-standable. There was, after all, a great deal of rectifying to be done. But the work of both Abrahams and Montefiore was marked by a distinguished lack of acerbity and an openness that was not always the case with their Christian counterparts.

The Christian Side

Scholars from within the Christian tradition who were sensitive to another per-spective were not lacking. One of the most conspicuous among them was the Englishman R. Travers Herford, whose major work, *The Pharisees*, acknowledged indebtedness to the prior work of J. Z. Lauterbach and Leo Baeck.[26] The book was basically a defense of the Pharisees and their misrepresentation in the New Testament, though at the same time Herford did not think that Jesus could be explained as simply a Pharisee himself (Jesus was *sui generis*).

The Pharisees did not endorse apocalyptic literature — excepting Daniel, which was seen as prophecy — for they did not countenance its political aspects. Pharisaism rejected Zealotism (which seems to be almost synonymous with apoc-alypticism for Herford), for it was nonpolitical. Everything could be accomplished under the Torah.

Jesus came into Pharisaism as a brief moment in the latter's long history; he was the most intense and powerful spiritual personality in history (not a theo-logical, but a historical judgment, according to Herford). He taught much that was Pharisaic; the difference lay in the impact of Jesus' own personality. He had an especially vivid consciousness of God, on which he rested his sense of au-thority, unlike the Pharisees who appealed to the Torah. This constituted the point of collision with them. Jesus repudiated the tradition of the elders; he de-nounced the halakah and drew Pharisaic condemnation. They saw him as an

---

24. Herbert Danby, "The Bearing of the Rabbinical Criminal Code on the Jewish Trial Narratives in the Gospels," *JTS* 21 (1920): 51–76.

25. On this issue see below, n. 34.

26. R. Travers Herford, *The Pharisees* (London: George Allen and Allen and Unwin, 1924).

enemy, even though his death was the work of the Sadducees. After the time of Jesus the church was universalized; Paul was the primary figure, and the church centered around the person of Jesus. Paul distorted Judaism, against which the Jews are right to protest. Rabbinism (=Pharisaism) and Christianity continue to coexist, irreconcilable, but both have a validity as determined by their life experience.

There were, of course, many others, as can also be seen in Lindeskog's description,[27] such as George Foot Moore, whose massive work on Judaism exercised a long lasting influence and was in many ways a counterforce to the focus on the apocalyptic literature that had been dominant since the turn of the century.[28] Moore's ascription of the status of "a normative type of Judaism" (3) to the rabbinic literature can be seen in retrospect as exaggerated, but then he had not the benefit of the Dead Sea Scrolls either. Other works appeared, such as the standard collection of Strack-Billerbeck, whatever its shortcomings, and made material available that was not previously accessible.[29] Similar was the work of Herbert Danby in England, and worthy contributions came also from W. O. E. Oesterley, and F. C. Burkitt, with sane judgments provided in the works of Gustav Dalman, who grew up a pious Moravian and was interested in the conversion of Jews on the personal side, but operated at the highest levels in his scholarship.[30]

So there began to occur in the early decades of the twentieth century a revaluation of Pharisaism, stimulated by inquiries among Jewish scholars,[31] though not exclusively; the immediate consequence was to draw Jesus closer to Pharisaism than before, that is to say, closer to his (rabbinic) Jewish roots. A more Jewish Jesus resulted, though still the whole issue of his individuality, his originality, or his uniqueness (to state the matter more starkly) became all the more pressing.

---

27. Especially chaps. 7, 8, but generally throughout.

28. George Foot Moore, *Judaism in the First Centuries of the Christian Era: The Age of the Tannaim*, 2 vols. (Cambridge: Harvard University Press, 1927).

29. Hermann L. Strack and Paul Billerbeck *Kommentar zum Neuen Testament aus Talmud und Midrasch* (Munich: C. H. Beck'sche Verlagsbuchhandlung, 1922–69).

30. *The Mishnah*, trans. with introduction and explanatory notes by Herbert Danby (London: Oxford University Press, 1933). Cf. the collection of material in W. O. E. Oesterley, *Judaism and Christianity*, vol. 1, *The Age of Transition* (New York: Macmillan, 1937); Herbert Lowe's essay on Pharisaism is useful, as is Oesterley's on apocalypticism. F. C. Burkitt, *Jewish and Christian Apocalypses* (London: H. Milford, 1914). Dalman's earlier works were described in Schweitzer (*Quest*, 275–81); cf. his *Jesus-Jeshua*, trans. Paul P. Levertoff (New York: Macmillan, 1929). His views were conservative; Jesus was Jewish, but Dalman also cared about the difference from Judaism. There is a great deal of information in his works. Dalman continued the earlier legacy of Franz Delitzsch, the founder of the Institutum Judaicum at Berlin. Also see *The Words of Jesus Considered in the Light of Post-Biblical Writings and the Aramaic Language*, authorized English version by D. M. Kay (Edinburgh: T. & T. Clark, 1902).

31. I should note here the extensive study of Louis Finkelstein, first offered as an article in the *HTR* ("The Pharisees: Their Origin and Their Philosophy," *HTR* 22 [1929]: 185–261), later amplified in *The Pharisees: The Sociological Background of Their Faith* (Philadelphia: Jewish Publication Society, 1938). Finkelstein advanced the sociological thesis that the Pharisees were an original urban group and the Sadducees came from the country.

Conclusion

Some summary, drawing again on Lindeskog's work, will conclude this survey.

The Jewishness of Jesus became a "self-evident presupposition, an axiom" of Jewish lives.[32] Jesus was a Galilean, which likely meant a greater degree of freedom from Halakah, a more prophet-like figure. Also his connection with John the Baptist was seen as certain and important. Here began his preaching activity; his baptism was the most significant event in his life, his consciousness of a divine calling, even a messianic calling. Then he had a period of activity as a preacher, a healer, and a wonder-worker. Unlike the Pharisees he was no reader of texts and acted more like a prophet. His healings also made a great impression. His public ministry was (as in liberalism generally) divided into two periods; he suffered rejection from the masses and went to Jerusalem where he was crucified as a rebel.

Jewish interest was concentrated on Jesus' teaching (as seen above in Montefiore). The tendency was to find nothing really new in Jesus' teaching and to play down anything original. Christology came from Paul, not Jesus, who was a strong monotheist. The idea of God as Father and the command of neighbor love might have been new in the pagan world, but not in Judaism. The kingdom of God was also Jewish. Neither did Jesus overthrow the Law. Even the Pharisees would have agreed that the Sabbath was made for humans, not humans for the Sabbath. But the principle of *nihil novi* prevailed for a long time among Jewish scholars; what separated Jesus was a degree of religious intensity and power. Jesus did not dream of founding a new religion, but of renewing and purifying the old. His excess may not be practical, but it is a grand vision. Thus his originality is to be found in his combinations and new formulations. In this sense he was a religious genius (Montefiore). The non-Jewish in him was his claim to a special relation to God above other humans. He said, "But I say unto you," while the prophet said, "Thus says the LORD." He was also an individualist, a non-nationalist, and an extreme eschatologist, that is, his kingdom was not of this world. In that respect Jesus was in error: there was no kingdom and no messiah. His ethic was unworldly, not practical; this focus on ethics was reductionistic and useless for culture.

Did Jesus see himself as messiah? Liberals generally devalued the messianic consciousness of Jesus; Wrede carried it further. Jewish research consistently saw Jesus as a messianic pretender; otherwise his career would be an insoluble puzzle (this view goes back to Salvador, but also can be seen in Geiger, Graetz, Montefiore, and Klausner). Some Jewish scholars saw him as only a reformer, a prophet. There were about as many different views on the concepts of Son of man, servant, and Son of God as can be found among scholars of Christian persuasion. But generally Jewish scholarship saw Jesus' expectation as disappointed and therefore of no further relevance. Only his work, his ethic, has any lasting

---

32. Lindeskog, *Die Jesusfrage,* 209. The summary description here given of Jewish "lives" is borrowed from Lindeskog, conveniently in chap. 10, but also generally throughout.

value. Here lies the major point of difference with Christianity, for whom Jesus as bearer of the Word and Doer as well is crucial.'

The trial and crucifixion of Jesus have always been a source of contention for Jewish scholarship, for obvious reasons (the denigration of Jews as Christ-killers and the like). As Lindeskog put it, "Their way through Christian lands has been an endless via dolorosa" (277). Salvador opened the discussion from the Jewish side, and others have contributed across the years. Philippson and others argued that it was the Romans alone who condemned Jesus;[33] Pilate's behavior in the gospels is unhistorical. While some concede that the priests had a role in the arrest of Jesus, most agree that the procurator was alone responsible for his crucifixion. Pilate, not the crowd, was really the bloodthirsty one. He condemned Jesus on political grounds, as king of the Jews. In any case Jesus was responsible for his own destiny; perhaps he sought death as a sacrificial offering to seal his life work, but, in any event, if the Christian dogma is true — Jesus died as redemption for humankind — then the Jews were only a tool in the hand of Providence.[34]

Paul is the incomprehensible one to Jewish scholarship. He postulated a divine being between humanity and God. Jesus awakened messianic hopes among his disciples, but otherwise he cannot be seen as the founder of Christianity. Jewish scholarship agreed with the *religionsgeschichtliche Schule* that Christianity was created after the death of Jesus as a syncretistic, complex entity. Its personal founder would more likely be Paul.

Jesus cannot have the significance for Judaism of being the messiah; he never met the conditions. He is really as irrelevant to liberal Judaism as to liberal Christianity; both have no pretense to a christology. Historical Judaism says that everything historical is relative; every event is unique, which by the law of development is soon out of date. Even if Jesus were considered the greatest man up to now, there is the possibility of a still greater yet to come. In any case that would not grant to anyone a privileged position before God, still less the position of mediator. Thus Jesus can have no relevance for Judaism; he is too bound to Christian dogma. He has been claimed by another religion, one often at odds with Judaism. Some modern Jews, like Montefiore, can claim Jesus' teaching for Judaism, but that is the assimilation tendency of liberal Judaism.

---

33. L. Philippson, *Haben die Juden Jesum wirklich gekreuzigt?* (Berlin, 1866); Lindeskog, *Die Jesus-frage,* 280–81. The American rabbi Emil Hirsch wrote often on this and related subjects; see his essays collected in *Twenty Discourses* (New York: Bloch Publishing, n.d.).

34. See also Solomon Zeitlin, *Who Crucified Jesus?* (New York: Harper, 1942). It was based on a series of previous articles titled "The Crucifixion of Jesus Re-examined," in *JQR* 31, n.s. (1940–41): 327–69, *JQR* 32, n.s. (1941–42): 175–89, 279–301. Like Büchler before him, Zeitlin argued for the existence of two Sanhedrins, one dealing with political and the other religious issues. This opinion was earlier denied by Danby, "Bearing of the Rabbinical Criminal Code," 51–76. Danby also referred to Büchler, *Das Synhedrium in Jerusalem* (Vienna, 1902). But Danby felt that the picture given in the Mishnah of the powers of the Sanhedrin was glorified, rendering questionable whether Jesus was ever tried by Jewish authorities. At best there might have been some preliminary investigation, but a trial before an all-powerful Sanhedrin was highly improbable.

Jewish research into Jesus is the child of emancipation, the Enlightenment, just as was the historical-critical research of Protestantism, while the former developed its own character. This Jewish research was moved by apologetics. To it we owe, according to Lindeskog, the clarification of what is genuinely Jewish in Jesus' thought and teaching. At the same time Jesus' personality and the origins of the church remain a puzzle for this Jewish scholarship and mark its limits as well as those of liberal Christianity.

Lindeskog summarized the main conclusions of Jewish research into Jesus as follows:

1. Jesus' roots lie in Pharisaism;

2. Jesus wished to be messiah, but his thought was an anomaly, not normal, a purely personal creation; and

3. Unrabbinic were Jesus' peculiar self-consciousness, the apocalyptic experience of the near kingdom of God; pushing the ethic to extremes; the denial of national interests; individualism; and the sovereign attitude toward the Law.

The Jewish contributions, according to Lindeskog, were an enriched picture of Pharisaic Judaism and investigations into palestinian Judaism. The high points were Montefiore and Klausner.

Interestingly, Form Criticism has not been of much concern to Jewish research. The attempt to separate the genuine from the inauthentic is insoluble and even strange. Remarking that the Jew would find that attitude inconceivable, Lindeskog further noted, "Ihm ist es selbstverständlich, dass die Schüler des grossen Rabbi Jeschua gespannt auf seine Worte actgaben, sie sich tief einprägten und sie später in der Gemeinde vortrugen und kommentierten."[35] Even if later additions crept in, that, too, is understandable, but does not compromise the substance of the tradition. This view, as Lindeskog rightly noted, is worthy of careful consideration.

The significance of Jewish research into the question of the historical Jesus lies beyond its immediate results and is to be sought in a larger cultural context and against a long background of divisiveness, hostility, and anger. Some of its grander figures, such as Montefiore, may have stretched beyond their contemporaries, but we should not diminish their importance thereby. There was a price to be paid for this stretching, as can be seen even in the more modest case of Stephen Wise, the liberal New York rabbi whose sermon asserting the historicity of Jesus led to a demand to surrender his position as chairman of the United Palestine Appeal in 1926 by conservative forces.[36] Saner judgments prevailed eventually, however, and Wise was restored to his chairmanship.

---

35. Lindeskog, Die Jesusfrage, 326.
36. Reported in the Literary Digest (January 1926): 30–31. Wise was an influential liberal Jew, a friend of presidents, and supporter of labor and social causes, who also wrote more widely; see his autobiography, Challenging Years: The Autobiography of Stephen Wise (New York: Putnam's Sons, 1949). His own discussion of the event mentioned here is found on 283–85.

Lindeskog ended his significant work lamenting the loss at the time of German Christian and Jewish collaboration in research; we may wonder whether this Jewish inquiry into the historical Jesus could have saved the situation, or, conversely, whether — to ask a more painful question — the bitter anti-Semitism of the Nazi period was in some degree a consequence of the previous, massive de-Judaizing of Jesus on the part of (generally Christian) scholars. Aside from the entirely frivolous contentions of a few, such as Houston Stewart Chamberlain or Walter Grundmann, that Jesus was Aryan,[37] a much harder issue would be to come to any judgment about the impact of the widely prevailing image of Jesus as virtually a non-Jew held in almost all western centers of learning at the beginning of the century and for some time into the century. Certainly anti-Semitism was no special possession of Germany, though its roots seemed to run deeper there,[38] and the countervailing forces provided by a C. G. Montefiore or an Israel Abrahams did not prevail in Germany.[39] But the question of demonstrating a link between historical Jesus portrayals and the subsequent Holocaust would require a monumental investigation of its own and is so amorphous that the probability of success would be minimal. My own suspicion, merely to venture an intuition, is that the treatment of Jesus in scholarship, and thereby in churches as well, had an indirect influence in preparing people to think of Jesus as disconnected from Judaism and therefore to separate the two in making moral evaluations. The same could, of course, be affirmed of places other than Germany. The instinct of Jewish scholarship to attempt to reclaim Jesus was then not merely an exercise in recovering its own history, but a movement of self-survival as well.

---

37. Chamberlain's claim that Jesus "had not a drop of genuinely Jewish blood in his veins" is found in *The Foundations of the Nineteenth Century*, trans. John Lees, 2 vols. (New York: John Lane, 1910; 5th printing, 1914), 1:211–12; Grundmann, in his *Jesus der Galiläer und das Judentum* (Leipzig: Verlag Georg Wigand, 1940; 2d ed., 1941), concluded that Jesus "auf Grund seiner seelischen Artung kein Jude gewesen sein kann." Most such arguments proceeded largely on the basis of the alleged non-Jewish character of Galilee and Jesus' contentions with Pharisaism. Chamberlain was actually an Englishman who had migrated to Germany. It was no less than Harnack who ascribed the origin of Christianity to Jesus, with "Judaizing" a kind of secondary development, although, in a different way, conservatives of all sorts had been doing the same thing for a very long time. A compact discussion, with reference to Q and Wellhausen's contrary assertion of Jesus as Jew, is found in the recent volume on the Hermeneia series by Hans Dieter Betz, *The Sermon on the Mount*, Hermeneia Critical and Historical Commentary on the Bible (Minneapolis: Fortress Press, 1995), esp. 32–44.

38. Gutteridge (above, chap. 5, n. 9) traced it back to Luther.

39. There were, of course, as we have observed, very able Jewish scholars in Germany, but the same kind of working relationships with Christian scholars that Montefiore represented seemed sorely absent.

Chapter 8

THEMES, TOPICS,
AND SMALLER MATTERS

To compose a life of Jesus is at the same time to come to a decision about a large number of individual topics — the ethics of Jesus, the Sermon on the Mount, whether Jesus claimed to be messiah, the concept of Son of man, and just a host of such issues. Each of these questions constitutes a worthwhile inquiry in itself and each comes trailing a substantial bibliography of its own. In fact, there is hardly a single verse in the whole of the gospels, especially the synoptics, that has not called forth a body of literature. To make a major survey of this literature would be altogether impossible, so here we can do little more than sample some of the most representative themes and the works they inspired.

At the opening of the twentieth century the debate over the degree and significance of eschatology was still in full swing, even as Schweitzer entered the discussion with what would prove to be so forceful a presentation that it would shape the issue for years to come. But others also were extensively involved in the conversation, such as E. C. Dewick, H. Latimer Jackson, R. H. Charles, Ernst von Dobschütz, and Luis Muirhead, to name but a few of the participants not so well recognized as a Schweitzer or a Johannes Weiss.

The Debate Over Eschatology

Dewick's *Primitive Christian Eschatology* carries its learned inquiry back into primitive animism and ancient Egyptian and Babylonian beliefs, coming forward into the Old Testament and expectations of personal immortality, the message of the prophets, and more cosmic eschatological hopes (the last judgment, the kingdom of God, the messiah).[1] In his survey, Dewick passed through the postexilic period, noting Persian influences and the onset of apocalyptic writing. The latter was seen as a child of prophecy, a product of historical crisis, arising to justify the ways of God to men. It is essentially pessimistic, not attaining the moral grandeur of prophecy. Its expectation of a near End was "founded on a pious fraud and ending in an irresponsible fancy" (55). Dewick then proceeded

---

1. E. C. Dewick, *Primitive Christian Eschatology* (Cambridge: University Press, 1912). Dewick was Tutor and Dean of St. Aidan's College, Birkenhead, and Teacher in Ecclesiastical History in the University of Liverpool.

through Maccabees, Daniel, Pharisaic thought, Psalms of Solomon, Enoch, and 4 Ezra before turning to Jesus' eschatology. Jesus spoke of the near kingdom, which embraced the eschatological judgment, and an ideal future, though it was not only transcendental and future but also present. There was likewise room for human activity, for growth in the kingdom, for moral behavior. The ethics, the demand for repentance, were to fulfill the conditions of the kingdom's coming. Jesus thought of himself as the messiah, probably from his baptism on, though he did not express it openly until after Caesarea-Philippi, claiming it explicitly at his trial. Jesus used the title "Son of man" ambiguously in public and openly to the disciples, designating himself as messiah in the eschatological sense. He also spoke of his coming sufferings, yet had no political interest. The balance of the work extended the discussion into the remainder of the New Testament and the early patristic writings.

Ernst von Dobschütz's *The Eschatology of the Gospels* seemed largely concerned to maintain the liberal Jesus over against the apparent onslaught of Schweitzer, whose Jesus was a "misguided enthusiast" and an "eccentric" who could hardly become a symbol for millions of Christians.[2] The expectation of the imminent End had not much influence on Jesus; it did not change his ethics, which cannot be considered merely interim. Eschatology was only the form, not the kernel, of Jesus' message. His real position lay in his unbroken communion with God, in contrast to Judaism where God was distant and remote. Jesus presented God as the Father and the kingdom as at hand, present already in his own person, as can be seen in the exorcisms. Yet the kingdom is still to come in glory; only now people are God's children. The kingdom was for Jesus primarily a moral estate in which there would be no opposition to the will of God; it could only be brought about by God. Jesus claimed the messiahship and expected the kingdom in his own generation. But also the kingdom is present already in inward experience and outward exorcism.

H. Latimer Jackson's *The Eschatology of Jesus* also characterized the kingdom as having both a future and a present element.[3] It is given by God, but human effort can hasten its coming. There are signs of its coming and humans must prepare for it through purity of heart. The kingdom comes to earth and brings the judgment. Jesus also has a role in that he is its herald, its prophet. Only slowly did his unique relation to God dawn on him; he was destined to be the messiah, the Son of man, and then would come as judge of the earth.

Jackson traced the eschatology through the Old Testament, apocalyptic literature, and Judaism. Jesus differed in that he included Gentiles, though also shared some ideas of his time. He had little interest in politics, but did see his suffering

---

2. Ernst von Dobschütz, *The Eschatology of the Gospels* (London: Hodder and Stoughton, 1910), 59. There was also his "The Eschatology of the Gospels," *The Expositor* 9 (1910): 97–113. Von Dobschütz was then Professor of New Testament Exegesis at the University of Strassburg, later at Halle.

3. H. Latimer Jackson, *The Eschatology of Jesus,* The Hulsean Lectures (London: Macmillan, 1913).

and death as necessary to his mission. The passion predictions go back to Jesus, even if they were later amplified. Jesus was not like an apocalyptic visionary or dreamer. His effect on civilization has been tremendous.

R. H. Charles worked extensively in the pseudepigraphical and apocryphal texts, providing the standard English reference for both literatures for many years to come.[4] His *Eschatology: The Doctrine of a Future Life in Israel, Judaism and Christianity* became a standard English statement for many years.[5] Charles understood eschatology broadly as the final condition of humanity and the world, and described early Hebrew, Jewish, and Christian eschatology. Old Testament eschatology was originally one of individual destiny and came from heathen sources, envisioning the survival of the *nephesh* in Sheol, but not an individual immortality. Eventually the monotheism of Yahwism annihilated Sheol and gave birth to individual immortality. That came under prophets like Jeremiah and Ezekiel with their proclamation of individual retribution.

An eschatology of the nation developed concurrently, out of the notion of the Day of Yahweh, the day of national blessedness. Under the prophets it became the hope for a regenerated kingdom, of a nation performing the divine will. The kingdom was the community ruled over by God in which his will is done. This article of Israelite faith passed through pre- and postexilic writings; the preexilic ones dealt with the fate of the nation, the postexilic with that of the individual, brought about by the destruction of the state. The eschatology of the exile also came to speak less about judgment and more about blessing brought in by the messianic kingdom (narrowly conceived in Ezekiel, more broadly in Deutero-Isaiah with its servant songs [=pious in Israel]). Deliverance by supernatural help, set forth in Ezekiel, would become a permanent element in apocalypticism, as seen in Daniel. And, finally, the hope of blessedness for the nation and the individual merged (Daniel, Isaiah apocalypse). A true synthesis developed which spoke of a resurrection of the righteous, a spiritual resurrection, in that it was founded on the individual's communion with God and restoration to that communion after death. This was an original Jewish inspiration. Its defect was that this restoration had to await the messianic kingdom; meanwhile, the individual resided in Sheol. Between Isaiah and Daniel a transformation occurred: resurrection was no longer the prerogative of the righteous Israelite, but of the good and bad in Israel.

Charles saw no need to revert to the Mazdean hypothesis (his terminology) to explain these developments. It may have helped shape the doctrine of resurrection in Daniel, but not that in Isaiah 27. There was also no real influence from Plato or Greek sources generally; Israel's ideas grew from her conception of Yahweh (monotheism).

---

4. R. H. Charles, *Apocrypha and Pseudepigrapha of the Old Testament in English*, 2 vols. (Oxford: Clarendon Press, 1913). Charles (1855–1931) at the time of these Jowett lectures was Professor of Biblical Greek at Trinity College, Dublin.

5. The Jowett Lectures, published in 1899, second edition 1913. I use the Schocken paperback reprint with an introduction by Wesley Buchanan (New York: Schocken Books, 1963).

The apocalyptic literature was the work of Chasids. Both "apocalyptic" and prophecy shared certain elements: visions, trance, allegory. But apocalyptic advanced beyond the Sheol of prophetism to the idea of a blessed future life, c. 100 B.C.E. This apocalyptic kingdom was not of this world, but would be heaven itself. Prophecy foresaw only Sheol as an end for individuals, though there are traces of apocalyptic in Ezekiel. Both were ethical, based on the righteousness of God. The major difference between the two lay in their scope; apocalyptic was timeless and universal. From the apocalyptic side Christianity was born, especially in Galilee where apocalyptic and not legalism prevailed. Pharisaism had then two sides: the legal and the apocalyptic. Both derived from the Law, which was of eternal validity in both. Christianity abandoned the legalistic side and thus apocalyptic Pharisaism became the parent of Christianity.

Charles characterized various apocalyptic works (Enoch, Daniel, *Sibyllines, Testament of the Twelve Patriarchs, Jubilees*) and assigned dates to each. He wished to show the development of the hope for personal immortality and its separation from the messianic kingdom, a true synthesis, as he put it, finally achieved by Christianity. Enoch 37–71 presented a renewed earth as the site of the messianic kingdom and a new heaven as well, along with a unique doctrine of the Son of man, which has to be taken as the source of the New Testament concept. The Christian transformation lay in the relation of all persons in the community to the messiah as head in the kingdom, with membership constituted by a personal relationship to him. This new synthesis was created out of the mass of heterogeneous ideas in Judaism. Charles acknowledged that some of the cruder details remain here and there in the New Testament.

The synoptic record shows a present kingdom as a part of Jesus' early ministry. The future kingdom would come by growth but also eschatologically, introduced by God himself. Jesus' experience of rejection led to the emphasis on the future kingdom and intervention by God (excluding the apocalypse of Mark 13). Jesus expected the kingdom soon and was wrong. He anticipated being the judge; only the righteous would attain the resurrection.

In the tradition of the minister-scholar at that time Luis Muirhead produced a knowledgeable book on *The Eschatology of Jesus* that sets out from Johannes Weiss's thesis while critiquing it as well, insisting that Weiss failed to attend to the present element in the kingdom-proclamation of Jesus.[6] The kingdom represents a glorious future, but also is on earth, a world empire, and embraces personal immortality. The apocalyptic imagery in Jesus' proclamation is dominated by the ethical element, though he did not say that the kingdom would come by human effort. In spite of these acknowledgments, the kingdom is defined as the "*sum of all the good things,* belonging to the *supernatural life of God's children,* and, primarily, powers of *holy truth and love* acting on the *human conscience and will*" (114; italics his).

---

6. Luis Muirhead, *The Eschatology of Jesus* (London: Andrew Melrose, 1904). Muirhead was minister of St. Luke's Church, Broughty Ferry.

Jesus is the bringer of the kingdom to earth and establishes it there. He is the messiah who effectuates the kingdom now through suffering and service and in the future brings it to consummation. He expected the present worldly order to collapse soon, but gave no time or date. There was nothing political about his expectation. He did oppose Pharisaism — dead legalism — and the temple — a dead system — but the collapse of Judaism would not equate to the coming of the kingdom. He saw his own death as releasing a power for the redemption of the world. He referred to himself as Son of man, in the third person, which was deliberately mysterious and suggestive, but not necessarily the messiah, which he only declared at Caesarea-Philippi. His messiahship came as a revelation to him, with the details to be acquired. First was baptism, then suffering. Jesus belonged to humanity, but had a destiny and a dignity beyond that, which was what Son of man expressed. It was a concept without a fixed meaning on which Jesus impressed his own mark. Daniel was a starting point, but further traces are seen in Enoch and 4 Ezra. What Jesus did was unite the majesty of Son of man with the suffering and service of his own life. Herein lies his originality.[7]

The Enigmatic Son of Man

One issue begets another, and related to the general subject of eschatology was the question of the Son of man, surely one of the most notorious of all problems. Schweitzer's facile claim that "the Son-of-Man problem is both historically solvable and has been solved" (*Quest*, 281) appears in retrospect as less than prophetic, to be kind about it, for few topics have gathered to themselves so much literature with so little result. Schweitzer to the contrary, this subject is probably just insoluable.[8] And yet it really does matter as to whether Jesus considered himself to be this figure in some sense. If this issue cannot be resolved, can a trustworthy picture of Jesus be attained? Other things can be more reasonably described, such as the ethics, but if the goal is to provide a picture inclusive of Jesus' own self-evaluation, then the goal is out of reach.

The meaning of ὁ υἱὸς τοῦ ἀνθρώπου in its Aramaic original was rehearsed rather thoroughly around the beginning of the century, as described by Schweitzer.[9] Little changed afterward. Some further works attempted to locate the source of the Son of man concept. H. J. Holtzmann's "retrograde book of an

---

7. A moderately critical work also at the same time that ought to be noticed was that of Edward William Winstanley, *Jesus and the Future* (Edinburgh: T. & T. Clark, 1913). Winstanley focused his attention on the synoptic texts; the kingdom was coming soon in a catastrophic way, not actually present, but potentially present. Jesus transformed the political and national elements through stress on the personal and ethical. He joined suffering with the Son of Man.

8. "Insoluable" here means the inability to construct a consensus in the field as to the authenticity and usage of any of the categories of Son of Man sayings in the gospels.

9. *Quest*, various discussions in chap. 17.

aging theologian" preferred to find it in Daniel,[10] while the Amsterdam professor Daniel Völter wished to find it in Ezekiel, tying it to Jesus' sense of prophetic
call as one sent to bring salvation.[11]

The *religionsgeschichtliche* investigations of Richard Reitzenstein, on the other
hand, looked to a widespread myth of a primal man with particular roots in
Iranian-gnostic thought, a being overcome by the powers of darkness, an event
that gave rise to the entrapment of human souls in the material world. This
primal "man" himself had to become redeemed before he could effect human
salvation; thus the redeemed redeemer appears in various incarnations, including
the Son of Man in Daniel and therefore also stands behind the idea of Jesus'
heavenly origin and suffering.[12] Yale scholar Karl Kraeling took up Reitzenstein's
hypothesis but, unlike Reitzenstein, did not think that Jesus used the term in a
redemptive sense — the redemptive features were syncretistic accretions to the
anthropos tradition.[13]

On the whole attention focused on the question of whether Jesus used the
title at all and, if so, in what sense. The familiar three categories (presently
active, suffering, future coming) had been recognized for a long time, and it
was around these types that the debate was conducted. Variations included the
idea that Jesus claimed one form or another at an early point in his ministry,
and shifted to something else later. For example, he first thought of himself as
Son of man to come in the kingdom, then later took up the notion of suffering
after having encountered severe hostility in his public ministry. The conservative Princeton scholar Geerhardus Vos was concerned to claim all types of Son

---

10. Holtzmann's own characterization in *Das messianische Bewusstein Jesu: Ein Beitrag zur Leben-
Jesu-Forschung* (Tübingen: J. C. B. Mohr [Paul Siebeck], 1907), 3. He was imagining how the book
might be received.

11. Daniel Völter, *Die Grundfrage des Lebens Jesu* (Stuttgart: A. Bonz Erben, 1936). Earlier was his
Das messianische Bewusstein Jesu (Strassburg: J. H. Ed. Heitz, 1907) that also disclaimed Holtzmann's
preference for Daniel.

12. Especially *Das iranische Erlösungsmysterium: Religionsgeschichtliche Untersuchungen* (Bonn:
A. Marcus and W. Weber's Verlag, 1924); earlier was the more general *Die hellenistischen Mysterienreligionen: Nach ihren Grundgedanken und Wirkungen* (Leipzig: Teubner, 1910; 3d ed., 1924); English
trans., *Hellenistic Mystery Religions: Their Basic Ideas and Significance*, trans. John E. Steeley, Pittsburgh Theological Monograph Series 15 (Pittsburgh: Pickwick Press, 1978), which focused especially
on hellenistic influence on Paul. Reitzenstein's friend Wilhelm Bousset had also postulated an origin
in apocalypticism without tracing it further back; he also held it likely that none of the Son of man
tradition originated with Jesus, but reflected the theology of the primitive community. See his classic
Kurios Christos, trans. John E. Steeley (Nashville: Abington, 1970). The later work of Erik Sjöberg
(*Der Menschensohn im Äthiopischen Henobuch* [Lund: C. W. K. Gleerup, 1946]) found that the Son
of man conception evolved from the idea of the *Urmensch*, but had come to differ radically in detail,
especially in the cosmogonic functions of the two (Son of man does not function as redeemer in the
present, only in the endtime; is not engaged in a struggle with the powers of darkness, the world was
not made from his body, he is not a redeemed redeemer except in the sense of leading the righteous
to redemption). Son of man was, in fact, a new formulation out of the *Urmensch* idea brought about
under the influence of Israel's developing messianism. See esp. chap. 9 in Sjöberg's work.

13. Karl Kraeling, *Anthropos and Son of Man: A Study in the Religious Syncretism of the Hellenistic
Orient* (New York: Columbia University Press, 1927). Kraeling was at the time Instructor at the
Lutheran Theological Seminary at Philadelphia, but later came to Yale.

of man sayings for Jesus and to deny all the theories of the liberals, and was less welcoming toward Schweitzer than he had been at first.[14] His evaluation of the texts left none seriously damaged and he ended expounding on the blood sacrifice of Jesus. George Barton, consistent with his earlier work (above, chap. 5), found still that Jesus possessed a "supernormal consciousness," that he thought of himself as messiah–Son of man, though it is interesting that Barton then felt it necessary to defend this Jesus against the suspicion of lunacy (his sanity was guaranteed by his ethical and spiritual qualities).[15]

Benjamin Bacon, however, in characteristically original fashion, found Jesus' consciousness to be rooted in wisdom, in an old messianism in which Israel was God's son, realized by the doing of God's will.[16] So: Son, but not Son of man, which was, excepting the ones as eponymous for "man" generally, not authentic. Later Bacon would modify his position, asserting that Jesus in his early ministry (before Caesarea-Philippi) spoke not directly of himself, but of the Son of man in an objective and impersonal way, a kind of veiled way, until the issue of his fate was forced. His victory would have to come, not as son of David, but as Son of man at the judgment.[17] Nathaniel Schmidt held his position that Jesus used none of the titles, that all arose later in the church.[18] Pierson Parker saw no messianic meaning to the title at all and thought that Jesus probably only meant it in the sense of prophetic leadership.[19]

Among the Scots and the English, J. Courtney James argued for the authenticity of all three: sometimes only "man" is intended, some were used prophetically by Jesus to indicate his mission, then others were used messianically for himself as representative of his people, then still others eschatologically for his future rule.[20] Vincent Taylor advanced the thesis that the Parousia sayings belonged to an earlier stage of the ministry and one that passed in Jesus' thought.[21] The suffering sayings came later and represented a reinterpretation in

---

14. Geerhardus Vos, *The Self-Disclosure of Jesus: The Modern Debate about the Messianic Consciousness* (New York: George H. Doran, 1926). We met Vos earlier (chap. 1) in discussing the reactions to Schweitzer. His book was reprinted in 1954 with some additions by his son James.

15. George A. Barton, "The Person of Christ in the Modern Literature Concerning His Life," *ATR* 13 (1931): 56–71. The essay found a widespread consensus that Jesus did consider himself to be the messiah. For Barton that demonstrated the fact that the church's faith resided in Jesus himself.

16. In Bacon's early article, "Jesus as Son of Man," *HTR* 3 (1910): 325–40.

17. Benjamin Bacon, "The 'Son of Man' in the Usage of Jesus," *JBL* 41 (1922): 143–82.

18. Schmidt first set forth his position in the article on "Son of Man" in the *Encyclopedia Biblica*, then in his volume reviewed above (chap. 2), again in "The Origins of Jewish Eschatology," *JBL* 31 (1922): 102–14, and repeated in "Recent Study of the Term 'Son of Man,'" *JBL* 45 (1926): 326–49. He also maintained his allegiance to the priority of Matthew. Carl Patton agreed with his basic thesis in "Did Jesus Call Himself the Son of Man?," *JR* 2 (1922): 501–11. Answer: No.

19. Pierson Parker, "The Meaning of 'Son of Man,'" *JBL* 60 (1941): 151–57.

20. J. Courtney James, "The Son of Man: Origin and Uses of the Title," *ExpTim* 36 (1924–25): 309–14.

21. Vincent Taylor, "The Son of Man Sayings Relating to the Parousia," *ExpTim* 58 (1946–47): 12–15.

terms of the suffering servant.[22] Probably the earlier ones were meant to express Son of man as a corporate figure. Bultmann, of course, accepted Wrede's reading of the messiahship (post-Easter) and, while some Son of man sayings only refer to "man" generally, only the future ones with their bothersome distinction between Jesus and Son of man belong to old tradition.[23]

It is all like wandering a pathway through a thicket of briars: a sideways movement and there is bleeding everywhere. Every possible combination and solution have been proposed and none has won the day. The prospects remain still rather bleak.

Kingdom of God

More agreement was reached on the question of the nature of the kingdom of God in Jesus' proclamation. Weiss and Schweitzer are generally given credit for forcing scholarship to acknowledge the critical significance of an eschatological understanding of the kingdom, though, in fact, the apprehension of eschatology was widespread. There remained some terminological confusion over the words "eschatology, eschatological," and "apocalypse, apocalyptic." Especially English language writing tended to misappropriate the word "apocalyptic," allowing it to function as a noun, undoubtedly due to influence from the German *Apokalyptik.* This practice continued right on through the first half century and even beyond. But more important, "apocalyptic" was seen as the specific activity of speculating about the other world, in often highly visionary and bizarre terms, and was regarded as a debased form of prophecy — something like prophecy fallen from grace. And therefore "apocalyptic" was a none-too-flattering term to apply to the proclamation of Jesus. Sometimes, however, the word seemed simply to mean "near expectation" and in that sense was freely applied to Jesus' preaching. Nevertheless a widespread consensus emerged for the better part of the half century that in some sense the kingdom was eschatological. The issues were whether the kingdom was present, future, or both, and what Jesus' relationship to the kingdom was.

The Englishman S. H. Hooke composed two studies on Jesus and the kingdom which are among a few such works demonstrating some special impact of

---

22. This thesis was also maintained widely; see early on James Drummond's rather good discussion in a pair of articles, "The Use and Meaning of the Phrase 'The Son of Man' in the Synoptic Gospels," pt. 1, *JTS* 2 (1901): 350–58; pt. 2, *JTS* 2 (1901): 539–71. See also the specialized study of H. G. Hatch, *The Messianic Consciousness of Jesus: An Investigation of Christological Data in the Synoptic Gospels* (London: SPCK, 1939). Hatch also held all categories of Son of Man sayings to be authentic.

23. Early in Bultmann's "Die Frage nach dem messianischen Bewusstein Jesu und das Petrus-Bekenntnis," *ZNW* (1920): 165–74. Peter's confession reflects his Easter vision. There was also agreement on the eschatological consciousness of Jesus in "Die Bedeutung der Eschatologie des Neuen Testaments," *ZTK* 27 (1917): 76–87, while seeing Jesus as coming closer to the prophetic model. But Jesus taught no interim ethic. Bultmann's positions were repeated variously across the years in his *History of the Synoptic Tradition* as well as in his *Theology of the New Testament* and *Jesus and the Word.*

Schweitzer. The first, *Christ and the Kingdom of God*, seems to organize its understanding around various crises in his career.[24] It asserts that Jesus expected the near End, Hooke taking Matt. 10:23 at face value. Jesus would be manifested as the messiah of an earthly kingdom meant for the poor and downtrodden. He awaited signs of the beginning of the tribulation and his own manifestation as Son of man. He experienced bitter disappointment at the return of the disciples from their mission, leading to a further decision that he must bear the yoke of the kingdom in himself. That marked the end of hope for a kingdom in Galilee and of a kingdom without his own death. It also marked the conclusion of the first stage in his ministry.

There followed a period of training of the disciples for the kingdom (here Hooke inserted the parables of Matthew 13), then a second crisis in Jesus' life at Caesarea-Philippi. Jesus saw a new assembly arising around him that would not be defeated by the powers of death. The future of the kingdom was assured, though it was not a nationalistic one. Isaiah 53 became part of Jesus' thought as he knew that the kingdom could not come without his death. A final period followed in which Jesus may have seen his death as a part of the tribulation, with his own resurrection to be the Parousia, the "moment which brings in the Kingdom" (94). The disciples did not understand, for they knew nothing of a dying messiah.

Jesus' entrance into the city and his attack on the temple rendered him a dangerous figure. The crowds thought of him as a prophet, maybe Elijah. The final crisis had begun. Jesus desired to eat the Passover with his disciples; he had a sense of the extreme nearness of the kingdom. It would be the end of all glorious and patriotic hopes, for the messiah would be executed as a criminal. In Gethsemane he faced the horror of going out like a criminal. His final death cry was not only despair (Psalm 22), but also vindication ("Father, into your hands…"). A final section of the work sums up the ongoing meaning of Jesus and his message.

Years later Hooke would take up the subject again with *The Kingdom of God in the Experience of Jesus*.[25] Two moments were defining for Jesus: his baptism and temptation, both of which he must have recounted to the disciples. The first brought a consciousness of sonship, with echoes of a servant; he took upon himself the yoke of the kingdom. The second demonstrated a consciousness of a messianic destiny. The Sermon on the Mount exhibits the righteousness required to enter the kingdom — not an interim ethic, but what the sons of the Father do. The powers of the kingdom are visible in Jesus' mighty deeds. The kingdom is already a reality, but Jesus announced the swift and certain rule of

---

24. S. H. Hooke, *Christ and the Kingdom of God* (New York: Association Press, 1917). Hooke was then at Jesus College, Oxford, and Victoria College, University of Toronto. The book was intended mainly as a study book, but nevertheless contained responsible insights.

25. S. H. Hooke, *The Kingdom of God in the Experience of Jesus*, Colet Library of Modern Christian Thought and Teaching 8 (London: Gerald Duckworth, 1949). Then Hooke was Professor Emeritus of Old Testament Studies in the University of London.

God and the defeat of Satan. Its coming would be an act of God. Jesus expected to be transformed into the Son of man on his throne at the coming of the kingdom, though at the outset of his ministry he anticipated the restoration of Israel under a Davidic messianic king. Matt. 10:23 shows that he anticipated the kingdom imminently. The return of the disciples from their mission brought disappointment; something further was required, for the message of repentance was not heard. The death of John the forerunner showed Jesus that he too must go the way of suffering, the way of the servant of Isaiah.

He put his decision to the disciples at Caesarea-Philippi and went to Jerusalem feeling that some great act must occur through him before the obstacles to the kingdom could be overcome. His views grew and developed as he saw the hand of the Father guiding his destiny. In coming to accept the death of the messiah he destroyed the eschatological conditions and thereby introduced the inwardness of the kingdom (forgiveness, the power to overcome obstacles between humanity and God). In the cross he experienced sin as separation from God; he became sin, in Paul's terms. In that moment God bridged the gap between himself and humanity, the kingdom came, Jesus was glorified and reigned from the tree. Thereafter the forgiveness of the kingdom was everywhere available. His resurrection was necessary for him to become the messiah in the kingdom.

These works have a curious combination of influence from Schweitzer, especially in the use of Matt. 10:23 and the notion that Jesus must somehow take upon himself the sufferings of the kingdom. But they also wander so far into conventional theology attributed to Jesus that they ultimately disqualify themselves as historical accounts. What remains is the view of the kingdom as eschatological, but also as present reality in some sense.

E. F. Scott, an American professor from Union Theological Seminary, also produced works on the kingdom, one of which at least survived over a period of time.[26] The 1911 volume traces out the concept of kingdom in the Old Testament and postexilic period and on into apocalypticism, then likewise tracks the idea of the messiah. Scott took the New Testament itself as source for popular feeling at the time of Jesus. The kingdom in Jesus' message was apocalyptic in form, but ethical interests predominated (moral preparation for the kingdom). The kingdom would come suddenly, though there are also indications of gradual growth. There is also already a present kingdom; at least the kingdom is so near that Jesus speaks of it as already here. It can be entered and possessed as by anticipation. Its signs are the miracles.

Unlike John the Baptist Jesus broke free of the Jewish conception of morality as outward obedience, emphasizing inwardness and internal assent to the will of God. Unique to Jesus was the demand to abandon everything and follow him.

---

26. E. F. Scott, *The Kingdom and the Messiah* (Edinburgh: T. & T. Clark, 1911). It was still being reprinted in 1929. There was also *The Kingdom of God in the New Testament* (New York: Macmillan, 1931).

The coming kingdom required a complete change. The eschatology provided the framework for the higher morality Jesus taught. The interim ethic is not valid. Neither did Jesus offer the kingdom as a reward, but reward was the natural outcome of service already begun. How did Jesus see the kingdom related to his work? Matt. 10:23 shows a sense of urgency, but the verse probably meant only that Jesus was attempting to stir the fervor of the people to such a faith that God would hasten the time of the kingdom. The powers of the kingdom were being manifested already through Jesus; the consciousness of being messiah was being gradually forced on him — not first at the baptism, but explicitly at Caesarea-Philippi. Then the notion of suffering was added. That Jesus enjoined secrecy means that the messiahship was still a problem for him. He came to a reinterpretation in terms of the servant, and he also shifted the focus to the ethical and religious. It is likely that Jesus did speak of himself as Son of man, identical with messiah. The title pointed to a mysterious future when Jesus would be the glorious messiah. So his messiahship paralleled the kingdom: both now and in the future. He was the messiah-king who would rule by dying. The abiding value of apocalypticism lies in its hope of a new age of righteousness.

The second volume carries forth many of the same themes, but with some more emphasis on the presentness of the kingdom in Jesus' activity. The nearness of the kingdom was motivation for Jesus' moral appeal; the later church has heightened the apocalyptic element in Jesus' message. He was not more apocalyptic than the rabbis. He saw the kingdom as both present and future. The kingdom is a moral and spiritual order; Jesus was concerned with the virtuous life, and wrapped his message in apocalyptic forms. He did not reduce religion to morality, but he also taught no interim ethic; the ethics lay at the heart of the kingdom. This kingdom also has a social aspect; it necessarily involves community, and Jesus could not but think of men always in their relations to other men. Jesus thought of himself as messiah, but not the nationalistic one. He was to be the instrument of the kingdom, to bring about life in harmony with God. This kingdom "far transcended the old Jewish conceptions" (133).

The balance of the work extended these thoughts through the rest of the New Testament. Again, what is visible, aside from the ongoing liberal themes and the special interests of Scott in ethics, was the emphasis on the present kingdom. Somehow it seemed necessary to moderate the apocalyptic picture by a more intense attention to a kingdom present and active.

It was C. H. Dodd who pushed the emphasis on the present kingdom to its furthest extent and argued that for Jesus the kingdom was *only* present, giving rise to the notion of "realized eschatology."[27] Actually, there seemed to be some slipping around there, with Dodd acknowledging a future kingdom while relegating it to some timeless future beyond history, and therefore also not countable as that kingdom to come on the earth. But that Dodd wished to lay the burden of Jesus' proclamation on a kingdom already present can hardly be doubted. The

---

27. C. H. Dodd, *The Parables of the Kingdom* (1935; rev. ed., New York: Scribner's, 1961).

kingdom has actually come; it is present in the ministry of Jesus himself. Key texts were Luke 11:20 (Matt. 12:28), Mark 1:14–15, Luke 17:20–21, and scenes like the Beelzebul controversy. Other texts not so congenial to Dodd were dealt with in somewhat strained fashion. Mark 9:1, for example, was taken to say, "until they have seen that the kingdom of God has come with power" (37). Other items were historical predictions, such as the doom of the temple. Jesus did think of himself as the Son of man, but that meant that the kingdom has come and Jesus as Son of man has come. Jesus did use some apocalyptic symbols to represent a reality beyond history; the Son of man has come and will come. What cannot be experienceable in history is committed to symbol and picture.

The emphasis on the kingdom as present was not new with Dodd, as we have seen, but he stood nearly alone in claiming it as the (virtually) sole thrust in Jesus' message. His proposal stirred dissenting responses. C. T. Craig sought to show that Dodd had misinterpreted key verses like Mark 1:15 and 9:1, then suggested Dodd was anachronizing Jesus in terms of Barthian theology (Dodd's use of "crisis" to portray the situation Jesus posed).[28] Craig insisted on the future rule that would replace the current world of misery and sin. Kenneth Clark focused his inquiry on an etymological study of the relevant terms ἐγγίζειν and φθάνειν.[29] His study convinced him that they must mean "to arrive, come near"; thus "the kingdom has reached you," but that does not exclude the future element.

But more than anyone W. G. Kümmel set forth the case for both a future and a present kingdom.[30] With characteristic thoroughness Kümmel examined exegetically all the relevant texts, while also carrying on a conversation with others, and came to the conclusion that both the presentness and the future must be maintained with equal vigor. Jesus spoke of a kingdom already manifesting itself to which people are expected to take up a stance; to do so is to take an attitude toward Jesus himself, who is also the one to exercise the function of judge in the future kingdom. What is now promised will find its fulfillment in the (near) future. According to Kümmel Jesus expected his own death, resurrection, and parousia, with a time interval between death-resurrection and parousia.

The eschatological message of Jesus was not apocalyptic instruction, to use Kümmel's own characterization; Mark 13 contains much that is inauthentic, though Jesus did undoubtedly connect the coming of the kingdom with cosmic upheavals — the eschatological destruction of the temple, for example. But Kümmel was unwilling to characterize the message of Jesus as apocalyp-

---

28. C. T. Craig, "Realized Eschatology," *JBL* 56 (1937): 17–26.

29. Kenneth Clark, "Realized Eschatology," *JBL* 59 (1940): 367–83.

30. W. G. Kümmel, *Promise and Fulfilment: The Eschatological Message of Jesus*, trans. Dorothea M. Barton, Studies in Biblical Theology 23 (London: SCM Press, 1957; 2d ed., 1961). The original German was *Verheißung und Erfüllung: Untersuchungen zur eschatologischen Verkündigung Jesu*, ATANT 6 (Basel: H. Majer, 1945). The English contained updated references to the secondary literature that was unavailable during the war.

tic, indeed, saw it as anti-apocalyptic. ("Apocalyptic" here evidently referred to endtime speculation, bizarre picturing, date calculation, and the like.)

In contrast to Dodd and Bultmann, Kümmel insisted on the futurity of the kingdom. He was willing to part with the *imminence*, but not the futurity, without which Jesus' message would be denuded of its authority. He recognized that Bultmann and Dodd were concerned with the contemporization of Jesus' message, or how to avoid being left with a word that had been deprived of weight by the failure of its predictions. The kingdom did not come, and 1,940 years is a long time. Bultmann had proposed the notion of demythologizing the New Testament or translating its mythological speech into the language of Heidegger's existentialist categories. Interpretation is necessary, but the reduction of the future language of the kingdom to the moment of individual decision was a journey into a place where Kümmel (and others as well) was unwilling to go.

Aside from Kümmel much of German-language work seemed directed to the issue of the dogmatic value of the eschatological interpretation of Jesus' kingdom-proclamation, especially in the 1920s and early 1930s. That interest stemmed no doubt from the influence of Schweitzer. What can be done with this apocalyptic Jesus who proclaimed an imminent eschatological kingdom? Bultmann's answer did not everywhere satisfy, though the Dialectical movement itself also stimulated efforts to address the question of the utility of the eschatology for a Christian dogmatic. Among these we can consider as example that of Heinz-Dietrich Wendland, though certainly others as well contributed to the dialogue.[31] Wendland's work proposes to grasp theologically the kingdom of God in Jesus' proclamation and in the primitive church, to use that as a basis for inquiring into the ground and nature of the church in the New

---

31. Heinz-Dieter Wendland, *Die Eschatologie des Reiches Gottes bei Jesus: Eine Studie über den Zusammenhang von Eschatologies, Ethik und Kirchenproblem* (Gütersloh: Bertelsmann, 1931). Wendland was then Privatdozent in Theology at Heidelberg. The work was his *Habilitationschrift.*

A summary of the research was given by the Swedish scholar Folke Holmström, *Das eschatologische Denken der Gegenwart*, Deutsche Ausgabe (Gütersloh: Bertelsmann, 1936), who divided the twentieth century into three periods: (1) *Zeitgeschichtliche Epoche* (History-of-religions School, nineteenth century, up to Weiss-Schweitzer; (2) *ungeschichtlich Epoche* (postwar period, theology of transcendence, of crisis, echoed in Form Criticism); (3) *Ansätze zu einer offenbarungsgeschichtlichen Synthese*, the contemporary period marked by a return to the indispensable value of eschatology for biblical Christianity (Althaus especially). Cf also Harald Diem, "Das eschatologische Problem in der gegenwärtigen Theologie," *TRu*, n.f. (1939): 228–47, giving an accounting of a number of these works. Schweitzer's own work was taken up and continued in the dogmatic arena by Martin Werner and his student Fritz Buri. See Werner's *The Formation of Christian Dogma*, trans. S. G. F. Brandon (London: A. & C. Black, 1957; pbk., Boston: Beacon Press, 1957). Werner set out from Schweitzer's *konsequente* eschatology to describe the origins of Christian dogma, from Jesus' apocalyptic expectation to the dogmatic changes consequent upon the failed Parousia. We could also notice here Paul Feine's *Jesus* (Gütersloh: Bertelsmann, 1930), which oriented itself to the theological value of Jesus' proclamation; and worthy of mention would be Oscar Cullmann, *Christ and Time: The Primitive Christian Conception of Time and History*, trans. Floyd V. Filson (Philadelphia: Westminster, 1950); Cullmann's apt comparison of Christian interim existence to that of "D-day," the time between invasion and final victory, gained much attention. His work was directed more to the whole New Testament than Jesus' proclamation. The essay by Amos Wilder (below, 277 n. 46) also took account of contemporary research.

Testament, then ask about the relation of eschatology and ethics. He noted influences from Bultmann, Paul Althaus, and Adolf Schlatter, while carrying on a dialogue with contemporaries like G. Gloege and Wilhelm Michaelis.[32] Systematic theology presupposes New Testament theology; the old dualism (Windisch, for example) between historical-critical and faith interpretations has to be overcome. The kingdom-message of Jesus has to seen in the light of its dogmatic consequences (christology, church, ethics).

Jesus' proclamation stems from his God-concept (*Gottesgedanke*), which he took from Judaism but also raised to a higher level. The coming kingdom of God is God's rule (*Gottesherrschaft*, following Bultmann), his unconditional royal activity through which he proves himself to be Lord. So kingdom is first a matter of majesty and authority and then an area of rule (*Reich*), the carrying forth and accomplishment of the divine Rule or Lordship over the world. So this *Gottesherrschaft* is the *königliche Handeln Gottes*, an event, a deed of God, in which God is grasped as Lord. "Gottes Herrschaft ist sein Handeln."[33] The kingdom is dynamic, active, but also it is eternal life, something entered. It is not doable by human beings, for it has the character of a gift. It speaks of God's activity in judgment and grace and therefore appears also as a demand for repentance alongside a message of salvation. All that is expressed in the image of the reign and of the fatherhood of God. The kingdom is also fulfillment, a rebirth, and thereby also universal, confronting individuals with decision (Bultmann), but also expressing without speculation the expectation of παλιγγενεσία, a new creation, and therefore intended not only for individuals but the whole cosmos.

Wendland also emphasized often the exclusion of any purely immanental, evolutionary, or humanistic understanding of the kingdom (Ritschlianism, for example). It cannot be constructed by persons and it is present only as the present is the time of decision, the eschatologically determined now, qualified by God-coming-to-us. The kingdom (as expressed in the beatitudes, Lord's Prayer) is not a present possession, but its promise is given now. The future determines the present, but the kingdom is not present as possession. It remains future; even the entering sayings refer to the kingdom's determining persons in the present and imposing the demand of an either/or and the new righteousness. Likewise the demon expulsions of Jesus express the effective power of the kingdom and the dynamic God-concept of Jesus that underlies that. The rule of God overpowers all other rules.

But the final solution to the question of the presentness of the kingdom has to be christological, for the presentness is to be connected with the bearer of the message of the kingdom (cf. Jesus' answer to John the Baptist). Here also

---

32. Gloege in *Reich Gottes und Kirche im Neuen Testament* (Gütersloh: Bertelsmann, 1929); Wilhelm Michaelis, *Täufer, Jesus, Urgemeinde: Die Predigt vom Reiche Gottes vor und nach Pfingsten* (Gütersloh: Bertelsmann, 1928). Michaelis especially wished to show that the proclamation of Jesus that has in view the situation before Easter-Pentecost can consequently only have validity for the church now in light of the Easter-Pentecost experience.

33. Wendland, *Die Eschatologie des Reiches Gottes bei Jesus*, 16.

may be found the line that leads from the kingdom-proclamation of Jesus to the Christ-proclamation of the church.

Jesus' ethic was also grounded in his God-concept. The only good is the holy will of God, just like the kingdom. Jesus' demand for repentance placed persons in the either/or situation: the kingdom or not, a new direction, the final chance to change. Jesus' attitude toward the world was thus conditioned by his eschatological expectation, but was not ascetic. The kingdom calls for human response as service and brotherhood. This ethical eschatology — and eschatological ethic — seems unreal to us because we have surrendered the idea of God behind it and also because we are now in a new situation (after Easter and Pentecost) that presupposes a new creative act of God. That is why our proclamation has to be seen in this new light. Nevertheless, the fact that the End has not come does not mean that God has abandoned his will toward fulfillment; to take that position would be to destroy the power of God and thus also amount to the destruction of faith itself. The same demand for repentance applies before and after Easter-Pentecost. The interim ethic remains true in that all of life is lived between creation and fulfillment, the life of faith and hope. But we cannot have recourse to the solution of liberalism, which severed the love-ethic of Jesus from his eschatology and thus presented Jesus to the modern conscience as a religious conscience to be chosen or not, for Jesus' ethic intends to make clear the unconditional will of God valid for all times. The absoluteness and eschatological character of the ethic are one and the same.

Related issues were treated by Wendland: Jesus' struggle against Pharisaism (he overcame it, gave reward a new content as gift of grace); love is obedience to God and neighbor, commanded just as repentance is commanded (repentance is decision for God, love of neighbor is decision for the neighbor); the command of Jesus is fulfillable in that it implies empowerment for acting (the context of the commandment is promise of salvation). So the ethic stands in inner relationship to the kingdom. It is moral demand stemming from the perfect, holy will of God for those who would enter the kingdom. In the actual kingdom itself (Schweitzer also said) there is no more ethic. In the present time the community after Easter and Pentecost is still driven by the commandment, the Sermon on the Mount, and the ethic of Jesus.

The notion of community or church also arises out of connection with Jesus' God-concept, just as the kingdom does. Ritschl recognized the *Königsherrschaft* of βασιλεία but emphasized its character as human activity and thus destroyed its eschatological nature; he was attempting to synthesize the humanistic-immanental concept of the kingdom of God of Rationalism with the God-thought of Jesus and the notion of a divine revelation in Christ, but produced a distortion in the synoptic picture as well as in the apostolic concept of community by losing the unconditionedness and power of God. Those who enter the kingdom are not citizens and do not form a kingdom by enacting the will of God in love; rather, the kingdom comes from the grace of God, as gift. It is not earned, but those who do the will of God enter it. The kingdom is not created by doing the will of God, but through the gift of the kingdom people can and do perform the will of God. However, the community now is in the midst of good and evil alike; only in the future is there perfect fulfillment.

Jesus' calling of disciples implied a community, which also arises out of the message of the coming kingdom, through Jesus' action as bearer of the kingdom, for the essence of the kingdom is one with the person who brings it. This discipleship shares in Jesus' suffering and eventuates in the community awaiting the kingdom. Peter has a special place of preference, based on his revelation at Caesarea-Philippi, but nevertheless it is Jesus who builds the church. The church-community is the actualization of the true Israel and the people of God, a community prepared for the End; it is only fulfilled at the parousia of the Son of man.

Christology and the kingdom cannot be separated; Jesus' person determines his word, his preaching. The message is thus not merely teaching, but fulfillment, the coming of the kingdom itself. Jesus' designation as Son of God and his miraculous deeds also belong to the kingdom, bound to his thought about God. The defeat of the demons, more able to be acknowledged in light of modern understandings that help overcome rationalism, gives us greater sensitivity to the New Testament at this point. Here also arise issues of death and evil, to which is addressed the New Testament concepts of the resurrection of the dead and the fulfillment of the End.

Wendland's book bears the marks of the postwar period in which it appeared, with a renewed vigor of interest in the question of eschatology and its pertinence to Christian faith. The hand of Barth seems to shadow the text, which perhaps also had been influenced by Paul Althaus. The effort to explicate the theological value in the message of Jesus and bring it into relationship to Christian dogma was an enterprise occurring over a period of some years and would find its finest expression in the masterful work of Jürgen Moltmann.[34]

On another side, the work of the Strasbourg professor Jean Héring disclaims any dogmatic interest, even while seeing the question of the eschatological message of Jesus in a larger philosophical context (the problem of evil).[35] Various answers appear to the question of evil: optimistic (the world is the work of a good creator-God); fatalistic (evil is retribution of the creator against humanity); and dualistic (eschatological, devil versus God). Jesus belongs in the latter category, but for him evil is not from God, as the healings show. Illness is a disfiguration of the good creation and thus it accompanies the announcement of the coming kingdom. Evil spirits are a kind of inevitable malady; demons are fallen angels.

Yet we cannot know how Jesus ultimately resolved the problem of evil in his mind. A solution would have to be consistent with his proclamation; there

---

34. Jürgen Moltmann, *Theology of Hope*, trans. James W. Leitch (New York: Harper, 1967).

35. Jean Héring, *La Royaume de Dieu et sa Venue* (1937; new rev. ed., Neuchatel: Delachaux et Niestlé, 1959).

could be no denial of the reality of evil, no Marcionism, and no perfectionism. Not evolution but redemption is the way. There are three questions about the kingdom in Jesus' proclamation:

1. Is it religious and moral, or does it imply a transformation of nature?

2. Is it present — actually — or only future?

3. Is it revolutionary or evolutionary?

It is not spiritual, but real and imminent — "au milieu de vous" (43; cf. Luke 17:21). It is future, but casts its shadow over the present and promises an eschatological transformation, even if we can also say that the kingdom realizes itself in the hearts of those who accept the preaching and repent.

Héring then undertook an analysis of various kinds of messianic and nonmessianic eschatologies, tracing the ideas through the Old Testament, the first generation of Taanaites, apocryphal and pseudepigraphical literature. He came to the conclusion that a heavenly messiah coming on the clouds was inconceivable in the Judaism of the first century, as was also the idea of a suffering messiah. He found the idea of the Son of man in the gospels to go back to old tradition, with its probable roots in Daniel and Enoch. The typical three types were discussed; (1) eschatological; (2) thanatological; (3) earthly life of Jesus prior to the passion. Jesus did believe in the coming of the "man," this mysterious being arriving miraculously, and he also said there was a soteriological agreement between his own ministry and the coming of the man, but he left open any identification of himself with the man in the future.[36] The second group of sayings bears no apparent relationship to the first (no eschatological text speaks of suffering and vice-versa), sounding like two sons of man who are mutually ignorant of one another. There is also a germ here of the church's later faith, but it is difficult to understand why the later community would choose the title "Son of man" for this purpose. Héring preferred to think that Jesus spoke in the passion sayings of himself, but not in the sense of the Danielic man — perhaps as a man or man in general who would have to suffer, which was then enlarged in the later community. The third group spoke only of man in general.

On the issue of Jesus' messianic consciousness, the primary texts are the scene at Caesarea-Philippi and the trial (Mark 16:62, 15:2–5). What cause of offense did Jesus give? Not blasphemy, but his identification of himself, a mortal, with a heavenly being seated at the right hand of God. The Sadducees would not have accepted the authority of Daniel anyway, much less Enoch. Before Pilate Jesus was more ambiguous. At Caesarea-Philippi Jesus refused any messianic royalty. It was the later church that messianized Jesus, as can be seen in Mark's portrayal.

---

36. Héring referred to Enoch 71:14, where ostensibly the Ancient of Days told Enoch that he, Enoch, was this Son of man (and thus Jesus also would similarly be acclaimed). Héring found some light in Rudolf Otto's allusion to the fravashi or celestial double of an incarnated soul awaiting its reunion in heaven. The explanation covers a multitude of problems.

(The entrance scene is apologetic; the demons' recognition of Jesus reflects only the thaumaturge imposing his control.) So Jesus himself operated on the margins of Judaism, speaking of a coming "man" with whom he would be identified; this Son of man would lead the kingdom into the visible world.

A second section of the work is devoted to examination of Pauline themes on the same subject.

The Ethics of Jesus

An issue that has followed this narrative all along is Jesus' ethics, and particularly how the ethics of the message relate to the eschatology. Schweitzer lamented the lack of any thorough study of Jesus' ethic, especially in light of the newer eschatological insight. He himself had already determined that anything other than a grasp of Jesus' ethic as interim necessarily would end in hopeless compromise (*Geschichte*, 594). But certainly few would agree with Schweitzer, and throughout the time period we are considering there was an almost obligatory denial of Schweitzer's theory of *Interimsethik*. Evidently few could stand the possibility that Jesus' ethical injunctions were not intended to provide permanent guidance.[37]

The strength of the social gospel in America produced there a sizable concern with ethical issues. The works of Francis Peabody and Walter Rauschenbusch were predicated largely on a liberal reading of the gospels, though Peabody even included John among his sources.[38] Independent studies of Jesus' ethics were not common. In 1904 C. A. Briggs — anticipating Schweitzer's comment — observed that the study of Jesus' ethics was an unexplored field and presented his own proposals.[39] Briggs succeeded in bringing the ethics into relation with the kingdom, but it was not an apocalyptic kingdom. The promises of the near kingdom were fulfilled at Pentecost. The kingdom is to be seen against the background of the Old Testament as the rule of God and becomes visible in doing the will of God. It is essentially ethical and is to be entered by repentance and moral change. The essence of Jesus' demand was love, godlike love. Jesus addressed his demands primarily to individuals, but nevertheless there are social implications. Jesus elevated family, sanctified labor by his participation in it, consecrated property by his use of it, but interfered with private property as needed. He said little about the state and recognized two spheres, one of the state and another of the kingdom. He was opposed by Pharisees, even though he did not abrogate the law. Yet he did relativize it and set love at the center.

37. An example of all these points converging would be E. F. Scott, "The Significance of Jesus for Modern Religion in View of His Eschatological Teaching," *AJT* (1914): 225–40.

38. Peabody in *Jesus Christ and the Social Question: An Examination of the Teaching of Jesus in Its Relation to Some of the Problems of Modern Social Life* (New York: Macmillan, 1900); Rauschenbusch in *Christianity and the Social Crisis* (New York: Macmillan, 1907); also his *A Theology for the Social Gospel*.

39. C. A. Briggs, *The Ethical Teaching of Jesus* (New York: Scribner's, 1904).

Henry Churchill King also ventured into the field in 1910.[40] He made some interesting observations with respect to use of the sources. How can we know what comes from Jesus? He referred to Schmiedel's "pillar passages," and to Burkitt's criterion of double-attested sayings,[41] calling them the "criteria of the exceptional and the recurring."[42] Where the two criteria agree, there should be no doubt as to originality. But the picture that emerged proved to be very much of a liberal stripe — a Jesus with an inward moral life of his own, teaching sacrifice and self-giving love, candid and open, convinced that life was serious and had meaning. King also drew some lessons from the two oldest sources, Mark and Q: the temptation story urges us to be worthy of the power we have, to found a spiritual kingdom, and change the self before outward circumstances. All that contrasts with the pettiness of the Pharisees. Jesus' revolutionary kingdom was the good news of the heavenly Father; his originality lay in the thoroughness with which he carried forth the theme of fatherhood, sonship, and so on. Examination of the special material in Matthew and Luke yielded much of the same, with a catalogue of similar virtues (inwardness, watchfulness, willingness to obey, sacrifice, love, mercy, forgiveness). The Sermon on the Mount — a single discourse going back to Jesus — shows still more of the same: the loving Father, brotherhood, the inner life, the unity of the ethical and the religious, a society based on love.

But no one exhibited a more concentrated preoccupation with the ethics question than E. F. Scott. His 1924 work on *The Ethical Teaching of Jesus* had a lengthy life and obviously had something to say to its time.[43] It generally plays in a liberal key, with some required sour notes from the eschatological symphony.

The book sets out from the proposition that the heart of religion is the character it produces and thus the ethic of Jesus is the constant element in Christianity. At the same time the ethic was inseparable from his religion. The synoptic gospels are the main source and harmonious enough to provide some confidence in their reliability. John is excluded. The sources of Jesus' ethic were Judaism and the Old Testament, though he did not merely repeat that; his own ethic showed an internal harmony and sprang also from his relation to God as Father. Trust in God was the principle of all goodness. Jesus' emphasis on the value of the individual was original with him, as was also the idea that the morality of an act depended on the thought or intention behind it. His own character gave reality to his ethic.

---

40. Henry Churchill King, *The Ethics of Jesus* (New York: Macmillan, 1910). King was President of Oberlin College. The book was the William Belden Noble Lectures for 1909 at Harvard. In the same year was Lyman Abbott's *The Ethical Teaching of Jesus* (Philadelphia: University of Pennsylvania Press, 1910). It also employed familiar liberal themes; the kingdom was not eschatological, but a new social order and depends on character. A special concern was how to deal with Jesus' excoriation of wealth.

41. Above chap. 2, n. 10.

42. King, *The Ethics of Jesus*, 15.

43. E. F. Scott, *The Ethical Teaching of Jesus* (New York: Macmillan, 1924; 2d ed., 1934). Reprinted eight times.

Jesus was not a systematic teacher and his ethical instructions arose from concrete situations. He gave no formal or legal code, but asserted principles. That is why he used parables, to enforce a principle. Neither did he break with the Law, even if he also made a breach with it inevitable. His fulfillment was finally dissolution, for he held that some things were more important than others (the decalogue versus the ritual laws), and even simplified the moral code by reducing it to the love commandment. Even more, he emphasized inwardness; the will is everything, not rules. Right action comes from the heart. Thus the real goal of his ethic was "moral autonomy" (36), the coinciding of human will with the divine on every occasion.

The basis of Jesus' ethic was religious — God as the Father of all, humans as his children, and the valuation of the human soul. There was nothing mystical about it; Jesus taught obedience and acts of justice and compassion. His ethic was not to be construed as interim; he was not giving some rules for the moment, but setting forth principles of the will of God as it always is. Apocalyptic was really foreign to Jesus' mind; it was pessimistic, whereas he was confident of God's rule over the world. Jesus "fell in with the traditional outlook on the future" (44), but really held to something else, as he did in his attitude to the Law. The message was in conflict with the form in which it came; ultimately Jesus shattered the apocalyptic scheme, even if he seemed to be unaware of this conflict in himself. Actually, the effect of the apocalyptic hope was only to intensify the moral demand. Still, he did see the kingdom as future and approaching. It would be God's doing and it would be miraculous. Renunciation was required, though Jesus was not ascetic. He emphasized spiritual things as foremost; there is no security in "things."

Jesus' teaching was also profoundly social and communal. His morality could be realized only in society; he put the focus on individuals and from them would come social obligation (love of neighbor, see others as children of God). He was not a social reformer in the modern sense; everything was religiously based. He also taught reward, but only for those who served freely, out of "uncalculating goodness" (64). He taught faith in God's providence, but also allowed prudence and foresight. As to nonresistance, another side pointed to punishment and anger (temple scene, attacks on Pharisees). What he forbade was retaliation, not use of force or acceptance of injustice. Yet also he demanded kindness to others, even the enemy, and expressed the futility of seeking revenge, which only makes two wrongs. He did not actually counsel nonresistance, but opposing evil with good. He had nothing really to say about the state — the Caesar word indicates that to benefit from the state is to owe it something (civic duty), but basically Jesus had a religious message. The kingdom of God implied a new order, suggesting that submission to the state was practical, since it would soon pass away. As to wealth and possessions, Jesus' attitude grew out of his apocalyptic view and consequently is not of permanent validity. Wealth was permitted so long as it was used for higher ends. He also gave a high place to the family, but subordinated it to the kingdom of God. Divorce was prohibited, but that was in a time when male power dominated women and consequently cannot be literally accepted any longer. Other virtues Jesus inculcated were humility, sincerity, fidelity, and courage, while he condemned pride, arrogance, and oppression.

Jesus sought character formation, and his originality lay in his own character, which was that of the kingdom. He lived now as though the kingdom were already here.[44]

Scott's work was popular at the time because it represented a widespread mood in America and it provided on behalf of "modernism" an accounting of a Jesus ethic with which "modern men" could live, or thought they could. The impossible elements could be dismissed as irrelevant apocalyptic parts, and all could be subsumed under the major heading of the love commandment.[45] There was, after all, some ground in the tradition of Jesus' words for that anyway.

It was Amos Wilder who reflected more substantially and creatively on the issue of the relation of the ethics to the eschatology.[46] Eschatology is myth, he said, symbolizing a truth, the coming future. It comes out of oppression, of hard times and the sway of evil; it requires a divine act of intervention. It was not merely a symbol to the ancient, though we do not need to be too literal; its imagery is like art: not consistent, but fantastic. It has become literalized, but it was really ethical and prophetic at its core. It did not encourage abandonment of the world to merely divine intervention, but led to an active effort "in sacrifice and martyrdom."[47] Its ethics are implied; the kingdom was a dramatization of values.

Jesus' view was almost not apocalyptic — there were no speculations and pictures. He spoke more like a poet; kingdom and Son of man underwent transformation, in that he related them to himself. The ethics were not interim, nor were they exclusively otherworldly.

In Jesus are found both historical and transcendental elements, for example, himself as both prophet and coming Son of man. The eschatology gives seriousness to the historical (present and future). Jesus' speech about the new world order lends ground and urgency to the present. When speaking directly of transcendence he has recourse to symbol (symbol is the nonself-conscious use of imaginative concepts).

---

44. Similarly in Scott's article, "The Originality of Jesus' Ethical Teaching," *JBL* 48 (1929): 109–15.

45. Similar ideas are found in Burton Scott Easton, "The Ethic of Jesus in the New Testament," *ATR* 14 (1932): 1–12. Easton sounded very much like a situation ethicist.

46. Amos Wilder, *Eschatology and Ethics in the Teaching of Jesus* (New York: Harper, 1939). A revised edition appeared in 1950 with added material, some of which was published first as an article, "The Eschatology of Jesus in Recent Criticism and Interpretation," *JR* 28 (1948): 177–85. The article reviewed such works as F. Holmström's *Das eschatologische Denken der Gegenwart*, itself surveying positions in the early part of the century. Wilder wished to hold still to the transcendental kingdom as socially relevant and to symbols of hope and future kingdom, especially as against Bultmann who had given up mythology and in so doing had no ground, in Wilder's view, for the social-historical value of Jesus' message. A further Conclusion was added also containing more reflections on the conditionedness of Jesus' ethics and its pertinence to the current scene. The perspective in Wilder's work was also indicated earlier in his article, "The Nature of Jewish Eschatology," *JBL* 50 (1931): 201–6.

47. Wilder, *Eschatology and Ethics in the Teaching of Jesus*, 18.

On the relation of eschatology and ethics, the issue is what gives sanction to the ethical demands of Jesus. The repentance theme has first to be considered. The coming kingdom gives sanction for repentance, but also announces God's grace as the reason for repentance. The kingdom is thus both promise and judgment; both are ethical sanctions. Repentance is offered as possibly hastening the coming of the kingdom.

Reward and penalties also appeared in Jesus' teaching as ethical sanction, but the ground lay in his gospel of the kingdom as free, as gift. The appeal then was to gratitude and imitation. The background lies in the prophetic message. On the negative side is the eschatological threat; it arises where Jesus had experienced rejection by Israel. Dominant is the last judgment and the nearness of the kingdom. Other sanctions are noneschatological and sapiential (common-sense appeal), but still are related to the kingdom as illustration from the current world.

Besides threat there is also promise of reward now or satisfaction in current life. But even these are eschatological in that the kingdom has already begun. The beatitudes are significant; they are hortatory and bespeak the ethics of grace. Here Jesus went beyond the rabbis; the reward is God himself (cf. laborers in the vineyard). Another set of sanctions includes the appeal to suppression of self-interest, but also to reason and conscience, to the heart, to the self-evidentness of the appeal itself, and to the ultimate discernment of the hearers. These are based on the nature of God himself (imitation); God's will is to be done simply because God is supremely good.

The prime sanction, however, lies in Jesus' experience of the majesty and glory of God. All power and rule belong to God and obedience is due him. That can be seen in the Lord's Prayer and the hallowing of the name, that "prophetic vision of God's sanctity and glory that animates everything in the evangelical proclamation" (146). This also lies behind the eschatological sanctions. Scripture is also a sanction, as is the example of Jesus himself.

In summary, the eschatological sanction is dominant, but its roots are in the essential sanction, the nature of God. The essential sanction appeals to the moral consciousness, scripture, and Jesus' own examples. "Apocalyptic" is symbolic, fiction, and cannot be the substance of a true sanction. God as sanction leads to retributive consequences, dramatized by Jesus in the picture of the last judgment. This is the fiction of the religious imagination.

Wilder disagreed with Bultmann, critiquing the latter's reduction of everything to the drastic moment of decision; that lacks a social context and also gives us a God of a forbidding nature to whom we can merely capitulate. It is also not possible to separate Jesus as eschatological prophet from Jesus as wisdom teacher.

How does the eschatological expectation affect the content of the ethics, especially given the presentness of the kingdom? The times of salvation mean that the old ways have been modified (the Law and the prophets were until John); but also this gives a new content to the law itself—Jesus "fulfilled and corrected the law" (179). Any particular statute may be overruled in light of the whole or of the need of man. For Jesus the purpose of the commandment was to "over-throw the law as law" (190). Here is the novelty of Jesus; his thought roots in the sense that the new age was present and brought the new ethic of the kingdom. The same can be seen in Jesus' attitude to sinners; the new time means the time of forgiveness. That also connects with Jesus' own consciousness of filial relation to God and to the present time of salvation. Thus also Jesus could speak with authority, and this sense of authority was responsible for his radical ethic and his break with the Judaism of his time.

This ethic is best described not as an interim ethic, but as ethics of the time of salvation or new covenant ethics. It represents the righteousness of those living in the days of the new covenant.

But did Jesus not give the ethics as conditions for entering the kingdom? Yes, but since eschatology is poetry or myth, that only formally determines the ethics; the judgment and so on are presentations of the future. The eschatology is but a mythopoetic expression of something more permanent.

As to content, the ethics virtually supersede the law. Jesus went beyond the scribes and even beyond the prophets and based his ethics on the nature of God, with its emphasis on the new forgiveness.

Ethics is also discipleship, whose radical nature is seen in the need to con-tend against the powers that oppose the kingdom in the short time before the kingdom comes. The kingdom is represented in Jesus' own person; it makes ex-traordinary claims in the time of crisis. These are the claims of discipleship: confessing Jesus as the prophet of the kingdom. So confession and ethics be-long together (e.g., take up your cross). Some of these were more characteristic of the later part of Jesus' ministry, when his enemies were more evident and the response of the people was less certain. They relate to particular circumstances (rich young ruler, for instance) and are special vocation. The drastic demands are conditioned by the situation of Jesus' own ministry (antifamily themes); they are not generally applicable, and are not interim either, but are occasional.

The last chapters of the work picture Jesus as bearer of the kingdom in his own person, especially in his passion, beginning from Galilee. His death would have some critical significance — the final means of the overthrow of the evil powers (the cup and baptism sayings).

Wilder's insight into the mythopoetic nature of eschatology is not unique, of course, but his appreciation of the eschatological-apocalyptic thought is rare. Bultmann, for example, considered eschatological-apocalyptic thought as mythical and sought to demythologize it, seeing it as an inappropriate (in moder-nity) objectification of God-talk, a projection in this-worldly terms of the other worldly. Wilder, on the other hand, sought to appreciate the symbolic value of such language as containing something powerful and important in faith com-munities. His stance was the intuitive appreciation of the poet, Bultmann's was more that of the scientist who would reduce mythology to manageable formu-las. Wilder also rejected Schweitzer's interim ethic theory, as almost everybody did, and grounded the ethic instead in the nature of God. At the same time he conceded that certain features of Jesus' ethical demand had to be considered as occasional and specific to the circumstance, if not interim. Wilder's is a view that represents a needed corrective to an overly egregious devaluation of the eschatological nature of Jesus' proclamation and the fear that its recognition will inevitably lead to a loss of authority in the contemporary world.

The Sermon on the Mount

Similar issues also arose in consideration of the Sermon on the Mount, a topic that was among the most popular for separate treatment. Even setting aside the issues driven by the needs of wartime, there was a variety of offerings in this area to which we may devote some modest attention.

Early in the century Benjamin W. Bacon offered a brief analysis.[48] The form of the Sermon was given in Matthew, a neolegalist who also saw Christianity as reformed Judaism. Separate sayings were joined together and the context altered. Yet Bacon wanted to maintain that there was an original discourse of Jesus with a single theme, namely, the new Torah of the righteousness of the kingdom of God. The discourse was older than either Matthew or Luke, even if it was not derivable from Jesus in quite this form.

Bacon adduced parallels from halachoth, but still found Jesus more in the mode of prophet. More appropriate to him was haggadah. The Sermon was addressed to disciples originally, consisted of varied discourses — on riches, prayer, and so on — with Luke supplying the better version usually. The "antitheses" are more original in Matthew. Bacon then provided his version of the original Sermon, along with critical commentary on individual sayings. Jesus gave a new Torah for the kingdom. The new went beyond the old Pharisaic expectation of reward for obedience. Everything in the Sermon is application of the one principle of love. That was Jesus' substitution of principle for rule.

Heinrich Weinel offered a short work of some popular quality, though certainly not without academic content.[49] The theme of the Sermon in Matthew is the righteousness that Jesus wished to put in place of that of the Pharisees. The Sermon has three parts relating to this righteousness: (1) 5:20–45, its essence; (2) 6:1–18, its practice; and (3) 6:10–33, its importance. Matthew is responsible for the structure, using material from the *Spruchquelle* and Psalms. The concept of righteousness is Matthew's, as is the collection itself. There was no actual sermon. Weinel then proceeded to an analysis of texts, attempting to locate the original form of sayings and finding four passages where differences between Luke and Matthew were significant (Beatitudes, Matt. 5:21–48, false prophets, Lord's Prayer). He reduced the beatitudes to their simplest form (Blessed are the poor,

48. Benjamin W. Bacon, *The Sermon on the Mount: Its Literary Structure and Didactic Purpose* (New York: Macmillan, 1902).

49. Heinrich Weinel, *Die Bergpredigt: Ihr Aufbau, ihr ursprünglicher Sinn und ihre Echtheit, ihre Stellung in der Religionsgeschichte und ihre Bedeutung für die Gegenwart* (Leipzig: B. G. Teubner, 1920).

blessed are the sorrowing, blessed are the hungering, blessed are the compassionate, blessed are the pure in heart, blessed are the peacemakers). And of the message he said, "The promise of the kingdom of God is also especially in the words of Jesus internal and at the same time external: it is a new world in which all tears are wiped away, all longing stilled, in which the peacemakers rule and the first shall be those who are servants of all others" (27).

On the other passages, Matthew likely found his "But I say unto you" in his source and expanded it; he also formed the words about the false prophets; the Lord's prayer is more original in Matthew, though Luke more accurately omits doing of the will and retains the (original) text to "Let your holy Spirit come upon us and purify us." [Here Weinel opted for a weaker textual tradition.] So the original prayer was: Father, holy be your name; your kingdom come; give us today our bread for tomorrow; and forgive us our debts (sins), as also we forgive our debtors; and lead us not into temptation.

Weinel then examined parallel material in Mark, the apocryphal tradition, the agrapha, the patristic literature, but found little of any real value. As to authenticity, we have to exclude what shows itself to be the evangelist's additions and what reflects the church's teaching and its interests.

Weinel disagreed with those who found the Sermon on the Mount to be merely paralleled everywhere in Judaism. The Sermon has to do with a new life, a new humankind; it intends a new attitude and a new heart. Jesus sharpened the old into something new (murder to anger, infidelity to lust, divorce to no divorce, perjury to nonswearing, hatred of enemy to love, purity more thorough-going). Purity and love are the main content of this ideal, this new humankind; especially love of the enemy is the definitive thing to be said about God and persons. This ideal sets forth an either/or: God or mammon, cut off the hand that offends. The good heart grounds the good deed, even though we must agree that Jesus also spoke of reward and punishment. As an ethical prophet Jesus grounded his demand in the will of God. Be like God, he said, whose sun shines on the just and the unjust.

The religion of the Sermon focuses first on God the Father. Like God one should love the enemy. This Father is also the Holy One who forgives freely, while also directing his holiness against "hypocrites." Jesus approached God in the way of the prophet, through revelation and prayer. He revealed the Father ("But I say to you"). The Lord's Prayer is the model. The kingdom is the new world, judgment and promise for the current world. It is eternal life, yet also hope for this world and its change. The poor become rich, the hungry satisfied, tears are wiped away. The kingdom comes as God wills, and he will reign over nature and history, illness and guilt, time and eternity.

Weinel's study then takes up parallel comparisons with other moral-ethical systems (Judaism, Talmud, Buddhism, Koran, Confucianism), but Weinel found nothing inspiring more nobility or redemption than the Sermon. A last section looks at the Sermon and the present, including Nietzsche, Schopenhauer, and Naumann and other socializers. Weinel found something to berate in his own generation: "It is the cancerous sore of our Christian faith that, instead of clearly and greatly demanding the whole and the pure, it has preferred to cringe in the corner and approve everything that the commonality of our public life has affirmed as necessary" (99). Some further comments on the economic, political, and legal life conclude the study.

Later came Martin Dibelius's Shaffer lectures at Yale for 1937.[50] Interest in the Sermon is seen in the light of the world situation, with the decline of Christianity as the force in western civilization. The Sermon gives no answers to issues of war and peace or social problems, though it remains at the heart of Christian ethics. We have to approach it with philology and historical questions. It is not a real sermon; discourses were added to different groups at various times. It is in Matthew's presentation the best example of Jesus' preaching. It was addressed to the Christian community, regardless of the literary setting.

The beatitudes describe Christian virtues, the antitheses express the new law of righteousness. Matthew and Luke betray a previous source — Q[51] — that contained an original source of Jesus' teaching. Here Dibelius provided a description of the evolution of the tradition and how it was formed, consistent with his earlier works. The Sermon shows Jesus as a teacher and preacher; it is not socratic dialogue. It is therefore a summary of sayings whose historical occasion is lost. It likely includes insertions of some inauthentic elements, to be determined by comparison of Matthew and Luke and observation of the editorial methods of each.

The result is a picture of a Jesus who proclaimed the will of God; his ethic was not interim, but represented God's will as valid now and for all time, but only fully in the eschatological kingdom. He proclaimed the will of God now in light of the coming kingdom. This was his "religious radicalism" (52). The command to love the enemies is most probably original; Jesus was speaking of private enemies, not national ones. Here he was urging the pure will of God. He spoke hyperbolically, but meant to be taken seriously. The beatitudes are more original in Luke than Matthew; they speak of the eschatological kingdom for the poor and downtrodden.

Jesus said to go beyond the Law (even though not all of Matt. 5:17–20 comes from Jesus). But insistence on the righteousness that exceeds that of the scribes is genuinely from Jesus. He wished to reveal the true will of God that was hidden in the Law. What was new in Jesus was the nearness of the kingdom, a new sense of urgency. That is to be seen also in the Lord's Prayer — coming of the kingdom, petition for bread, forgiveness. The difference between the old and the new is that the message of the kingdom demands total obedience. The old obedience is overcome by the new; now people live in dependence on the will of

---

50. Martin Dibelius, *The Sermon on the Mount* (New York: Scribner's, 1940).

51. Dibelius added the interesting comment that he learned from Paul Wernle that "Q" originated in a group at Göttingen (Wernle, Bousset, Weiss) who wanted a symbol without any special presuppositions and thus chose *Quelle* as opposed to any other (e.g., *Spruchquelle*) (27).

God and want to do it. Their conduct is not determined by the standard of the old law; the message of the kingdom transforms people and they now do more than the old law demanded.

Who then was this Jesus who spoke with such authority? Harnack's non-christological Jesus, who only spoke of the Father? No, but he was the "sign" of the kingdom, in his healings and his words. He was the warrant for the kingdom, its embodiment for his disciples. All that was so before Easter; afterwards, his words became a new law, the testament of Jesus. Some disciples doubtless felt he was messiah before Easter. The church after Jesus also proclaimed an eschatological expectation related to its preaching needs and practical conduct and altered the Sermon in light of its own new situation.

Dibelius also took up issues of the contemporary relevance of the Sermon. Full obedience is impossible now, he said. The Sermon is a sign, judging as well as blessing. The problems are compounded by the secularization of the world and the failure of the church to deal with issues. There are now, he noticed, socialistic tendencies not dependent on the churches. In fact, the world pays little attention to the Sermon on the Mount, regarding it as impractical. Dibelius saw no value in the dogmatic idea that the purpose of the Sermon was to teach us our sinfulness. His own preferred view was that Jesus proclaimed the will of God as a sign of the kingdom, but did not intend to give a full application in the world. Jesus' purpose was to transform people in preparation for the kingdom, and we have to uphold its standard even if we no longer expect the imminent end of the world. So Christians should live on their own responsibility before God; it is their task to do the signs of the kingdom, but there is no one solution.

The most thoroughgoing consideration of the Sermon was given by Hans Windisch.[52] Windisch was concerned to maintain a rigid separation between historical and theological exegesis. He seemed especially bothered by Bultmann's meshing of the two. His own intention was to give a historical view, then come to theological exegesis as a separate enterprise.

Matthew's context is thoroughly eschatological, the conditions for entering the kingdom. But the Sermon is also "religious legislation" as new Torah. Not imminence but demand of the absolute is what gives the Sermon its radicalism. Love of enemies is not eschatologically connected; God's perfection is the model. Likewise, retaliation is noneschatological; other words have to do with world-reversal and fulfilling the will of God. There are also wisdom sayings in which a reward at the end gives them an eschatological argument. Faith in providence and in the kingdom fuse. Eschatological are beatitudes and the kingdom sayings, the Lord's Prayer, storing up riches, judgment sayings, warnings of the judgment, and concluding parables. The Lord's Prayer is a "prayer formula for

---

52. Hans Windisch, *The Meaning of the Sermon on the Mount: A Contribution to the Historical Understanding of the Gospels and to the Problem of Their True Exegesis*, trans. S. MacLean Gilmour (Philadelphia: Westminster Press, 1951). First published as *Der Sinn der Bergpredigt* (Leipzig: J. C. Hinrich's Verlag, 1928; rev. ed., 1937).

an eschatological community" (39). There is then radicalized wisdom teaching and prophetic-eschatological proclamation. Both root in the idea of God held by Jesus.

Windisch then undertook an extended treatment of different approaches to the Sermon, from Kant and Herrmann to Bultmann, Dibelius, Carl Stange and Gerhard Kittel. He offered critiques of all; many interpreters assume that Jesus could not have taught something no longer acceptable in Marburg or Heidelberg. Windisch proposed to examine the Sermon on the hypothesis that it was meant to be taken seriously.

Matthew presents a Jesus as a new lawgiver who intended his explication of the will of God to be obeyed. The words of Jesus are admittance to the kingdom, enforced with a fearful judgment. Jesus himself did not intend to abrogate the Law; some sayings suggest a negation of parts of the Law, though others suggest legalism. On divorce: Jesus, said Windisch, had no idea of an unendurable marriage. He intended his laws to be obeyed, just as the "men of old" did. Even the command to love the enemy is not to be weakened. God is ultimately the model. Jesus radicalized an already (Deuteronomic) radical demand to love the neighbor.

Jesus' opposition to the scribes was not based on opposition to the Torah itself, but to scribal halakah and the importance of certain laws. He had no interest in something like the Pauline redemption from the Law; his redemption was the kingdom of God.

The Sermon is for the converted, directed to the true children of God. The proclamation of the kingdom provided the possibility of obedience, along with the consciousness of being a child of God. Unlike Paul neither Matthew nor Jesus cared about the notion of disobedient sinners, or about the impracticability of the demands of the Sermon.

The Sermon had no political reference at all; it has to do with the neighbor and the brother, but not with the citizen, government, or the employer: "Community, economic, and national organization, and the ethical relationships therein entailed, are not considered in the Sermon on the Mount or elsewhere in Jesus' ethical teaching, not evaluated and also not depreciated" (122).

As to Jesus' attitude toward Judaism in the Sermon, Matthew gives the Sermon a christological framework by depicting Jesus as messiah, as legislator of a new law, the future Judge and Lord, but not as a Pauline mediator and redeemer. The soteriology of the passion is not in the Sermon and is at odds with it; the Sermon is pre-Christian and pre-Pauline, "liberal Jewish-Christian" (130). It is also pre-Marcion, in that Matthew proclaimed the new law of Christ in place of the law of Moses. So the Sermon is best described as "anti-Jewish, anti-Mosaic Christian Judaism" (131). It supersedes Judaism; Matthew paradoxically seeks both to supersede and to fulfill Judaism, but the dominant side is fulfillment, not supersession in a Pauline sense. The isolated parallels to Jesus' antitheses in Judaism suggest that there was no intent to repudiate the whole of Judaism. Windisch said,

> It would be easier to speak of a "supersession" of Judaism to the extent that "Chris-
> tian" ideas, which also are to be discovered in Judaism, alone have validity in the
> Sermon on the Mount. This, however, involves the dissolution of Judaism, for the
> whole system of rabbinism has to fall away. (132)

This possibility, Windisch noted, was seen already in Hillel's version of the
Golden Rule, but could not occur within Judaism.

Rabbinic and Pharisaic Judaism are under attack in the Sermon. Jesus took
the idea of obedience from them, but did not agree to the rabbinic insistence
that the cultic and the ethico-religious were the same in value. He also singled
out other matters that were primary; this too was considered threatening and
led to the abolishment of the Torah. And as well he repudiated the oral law
where it seemed obstructive or pernicious — a sovereign attitude unacceptable
to the rabbis. And he addressed himself to the individual, isolating him from
his ethnic and national environment. So Jesus' teaching was meant as obedience
for individuals; community only arises as a consequence of that. In these factors are seen Jesus' radical understanding of the will of God. This radical stance
was not unique, but "its consistent application to all relationships of life, accompanied by a disregard of elementary necessities and of the claims of nation, of
family, and of spiritual and cultic authorities, was new and strange to the Jews."
These factors formed the ground of the rejection of Jesus. Especially his "personality," as embodied in his consciousness of mission and his freedom from the
tradition gathered around the Torah, constituted the basis of rejection. He can
be seen as rabbi, wisdom teacher, prophet, and messiah, but none quite does
him justice. His claim to authority was "sinister, strange, unlawful, and sacrile-
gious, and because of it he was rejected and condemned." Either he was greater
than the Torah-system or not; others decided he was not. "Jesus did not reform
such Judaism [rabbinic]. He destroyed it." If we understand Judaism as more
than rabbinic, then he remained within it. Actually, he was a unique person
who combined prophet, wisdom teacher, and scribe, and was thus a new type
of messianic figure and prophet. The result is paradoxical; Jesus stands within
the Israelite-Jewish tradition, but has grown away from rabbinic Judaism. "Jesus
proclaims a purified prophetism." The Sermon on the Mount is predominantly
anti-Jewish in the same way that the Talmud is anti-Christian (148–50).

Windisch saw the cross casting a shadow across the Sermon, for it represented
the verdict that Sadducean and Pharisaic Judaism had to reach about Jesus. Such
a person's claim — undermining Torah, repudiating halakah — was false and
blasphemous, and he would be crucified "as a deceiver and as a danger to his
people" (152). In a footnote Windisch added that perhaps Jesus was handed
over to Pilate as a pseudo-messiah, a rebel and heretic combined.

Windisch's final section undertook some theological exegesis, an enterprise
with its own rights and responsibilities, but different from historical exegesis. He
praised Barth for contributing to the rights of theological exegesis, while still
lamenting the reading of modern theological ideas back into the text, which

he saw occurring in Bultmann, Dibelius, Lohmyer, and even Barth as well. He addressed himself to some long-standing issues, such as the practicability of the Sermon. Can its injunctions really be obeyed? One could take a Pauline solution and set the Sermon in a context of redemption by grace without which the demands appear as unbearable, but that also depreciates the Sermon as well as the entire gospel of Jesus, neither of which is dependent on the death of Christ. Jesus' gospel speaks of becoming children of God the Father, with this fellowship expressing itself in service to one's fellow human beings.

It is also legitimate to introduce the Spirit into the Sermon, even though that was not present originally, for only through the Spirit can we gain the grace of obedience. The cross can also be introduced, for it was the Sermon that brought Jesus to his cross.

But also we do not need to regard the imperatives of the Sermon as literally fulfillable claims. There are too many values and claims upon us in family, state, and civilization. Jesus' injunctions are expressions of values to be fulfilled in other ways. If someone strikes you, you seek redress at law, while trying not to be revengeful. In war pacifism is probably a preferred response, but there are allowable differences.

The Sermon is not hostile to civilization, but it gives no duties because of such an order. It is eschatological and individualistic, not social, but social and humane laws are in keeping with its spirit. On that ground there is some bifurcation between personal and social responsibility, and we should attempt to develop a Christian morality for social and political matters. Thus Windisch found himself close to Herrmann and Dibelius, but was not willing to concede that those views were Jesus' own views or intentions. In short, theological exegesis has the right to critique and go beyond the Sermon if necessary.

Windisch's work reflects his customary commitment to depth and thoroughness. His insistence on a vigorous separation between historical and theological exegesis was perhaps a bequest from his strongly liberal roots; it was already under some fire from the dialectical theology and would come even more strongly into contention with the later "New Hermeneutic," which wished to do the opposite (move directly from text to sermon). It would seem odd to claim that Jesus intended to be taken seriously, then assert also the right to set that intention aside in the name of theological necessity. That produces a fierce tension in the text, not to mention the interpreter, but it has to be conceded that herein reside complex issues of scriptural authority, as well as of the application of critical methods to the study of the text. The exploration of these issues stands outside our field of play, but their presence as a player has to be recognized.

Parables

The parables of Jesus also produced a number of special studies. Adolf Jülicher's massive tome continued to prevail as the standard in the field to which everyone was accountable, even though there were dissenters on some points.[53] Some early works took exception to Jülicher's restriction of a parable's meaning to a single point,[54] while others found his understanding of parable by referring to Aristotle's rhetoric to be misleading and insisted that the Jewish parallels were the most relevant.[55] But largely in the English-language tradition there continued a steady, if unspectacular, trickle of works on the parables.[56] H. B. Swete's work was published years after the lectures that inspired it (1907) and offered very little of value.[57] Jülicher's one point was retained, but his rejection of the Markan secrecy theory as secondary was declined by Swete. The kingdom was seen as sovereignty, not an area, but also purely spiritual and ethical. The kingdom is within, the chief point of the parables. So, for example, the parable of the sower teaches that those to whom the word comes are responsible for its failure to effect its purpose. The work of Willard Robinson contained some more reflection on the meaning of parable.[58] Its background is the *mashal*, the point of which is to make a comparison. It is not an allegory, which is a "metaphor in an advanced stage." Simile should be taken literally, metaphor not. When the disciples are urged to be wise as serpents and harmless as doves, that is simile; when the Pharisees are said to devour widows' houses, that is metaphor. Parable is a simile; it makes a comparison, whereas allegory departs from nature and reality. Parable holds on to verisimilitude and probability. So parables are similes, even narrative similes, rather than metaphors or extended allegories.

---

53. Adolf Jülicher, *Die Gleichnisreden Jesu*, 2d ed. (Tübingen: J. C. B. Mohr [Paul Siebeck], 1910). There is no English version, but a very short article by Jülicher on "parables" appeared in the *Encyclopedia Biblica*.

54. The original review by William Sanday, "A New Work on the Parables," in *JTS* 1 (1900): 161–80, recognized Jülicher's work as likely to persuade those who take the scientific approach seriously, but thought Jülicher overused the one-point idea. He also found the book too long by two-thirds; a shorter one, he said, would likely become a classic and find a welcome translation into English. Unfortunately, it only became longer.

55. Ch. A. Bugge, *Die Haupt-Parabeln Jesu* (Giessen: J. Richer'sche Verlagsbuchhandlung [Alfred Töpelmann], 1903). Also Paul Fiebig, *Die Gleichnisreden Jesu im Lichte der rabbinischen Gleichnisse des neutestamentlichen Zeitalters* (Tübingen: J. C. B. Mohr [Paul Siebeck], 1912); the later published book of W. O. E. Oesterley, *The Gospel Parables in the Light of Their Jewish Background* (New York: Macmillan, 1936), was actually based on lectures originally given in 1915–19, with updated material. Bugge critiqued Jülicher's exclusive appeal to Aristotle and also wished to examine the theological import of the parables; Fiebig extended Bugge's inquiry while also claiming the originality of Jesus' parables compared to the rabbinic; and Oesterley continued to accept allegorical interpretation (as did Fiebig), illuminating details from the rabbinic material, but not much more.

56. The earlier work by G. Campbell Morgan, *The Parables of the Kingdom* (New York: Fleming H. Revell, 1907), did not abandon the allegorical interpretation, though recognized parable as a laying of one thing alongside another. He also observed the eschatological nature of parables; they were meant for the time between the ages to solicit human response. The work by Laurence E. Browne, *The Parables of the Gospels in the Light of Modern Criticism* (Cambridge: University Press, 1913), had some interesting things to observe about allegory, metaphor, and simile (allegory is a string of metaphors with no relationship between the elements compared; simile intends to explain higher concepts by means of lower ones). Browne carried on a dialogue with Jülicher, frequently disagreeing. Browne was Lecturer at St. Augustines College, Canterbury.

57. H. B. Swete, *The Parables of the Kingdom* (London: Macmillan, 1920).

58. Willard Robinson, *The Parables of Jesus in Their Relation to His Ministry* (Chicago: University of Chicago Press, 1928).

Similes aim to convince; parables have but one point and intend to arouse action. The main subject of Jesus' parables was the kingdom of God, the spiritual communion of souls. The synoptic context of the parables generally preserves the original occasion.

A substantive work was that of the Glasgow professor A. T. Cadoux.[59] He characterized parable as a work of art used in conflict. Jesus was its master. Mark's theory of parables as hiding something was to be rejected. In the course of writing down the parables the church lost their original meaning; they have to be seen in their original context insofar as it can be reconstructed.

Because parable is an art, form is a standard of authenticity. So, for example, the form of Luke's version of the wicked husbandmen is more original, as reflecting a Q version, and speaks to the issue of Jesus' authority. Jesus said to the authorities that by plotting to kill him they acknowledge that his authority is higher than theirs.

On allegory and parable, Cadoux referred to Bultmann's statement that parable keeps nearer to experience and causes us to transfer judgment. Allegory is representative, whereas parable evokes a judgment in one field and applies it to another. There may be more than one point of contact between two fields or realities. The parable gets its power from its connection with a unique, concrete situation, whereas allegory gives figurative expression to general propositions. Jülicher insisted on only a single point of comparison, which makes a parable platitudinous, but a parable has to be an organic whole, with each part vital to the whole. Its natural point connects to its immediate occasion:

> We should therefore expect the parables to find their application in the concrete conditions of Jesus' work, in his endeavour to win acceptance for a conception of the Kingdom of God that was new and likely to be distasteful to his people, in the controversies in which his work and his ways involved him, in the vindication of his ways to his followers and others, and generally in any aspects of his endeavour or truth that could not well be put into immediate speech. (56)

So parables are to be seen in their concrete setting, "not as pictorial renderings of accepted truths, but as moments in the creative reaction of Jesus upon the life around him. They take us into the brunt of his warfare" (59).

On form as a key to determining authenticity, Cadoux engaged in analyses of the different versions, seeking the better story. Luke's version of the Great Supper is more original, though the third excuse is unlikely and there was probably only one recruiting. The "artistic rights" (72) of the parable have to be observed, that is, what departs from the form of a parable, its fundamental characteristics.

Cadoux also included many short metaphors under the heading of parables (such as salt saying, mustard seed, city on a hill), and sought to classify parables into various types: conflict, vindication, crisis and opportunity, future, duty and personality, God and man. He then discussed each of these types with detailed

---

59. A. T. Cadoux, *The Parables of Jesus: Their Art and Use* (London: James Clarke, n.d.). Apparently published in 1930, with an American edition in 1931.

illustration. Conflict: the prodigal son answers self-righteous Pharisees; the un-just steward figure was originally condemned and represented the high priests who bargained away their spiritual trust to accompany Rome and secure them-selves in power. Vindication: the woman with oil and the man with two creditors who forgave both represent a vindication of Jesus' conduct; the sower vindicates Jesus' appeal to universalism as opposed to Jewish exclusivism, and as well his ap-peal to reason and conscience against authority and precedent. Crisis: the seed harvest asserts that the kingdom is at hand and suddenly calls for humans to cooperate and do their part. Future: the unjust judge says that God will vin-dicate his elect; the Son of man (taking the comparison to lightning lighting up the sky) expresses the same. Duty and personality: in the rich fool the mes-sage is about valuing things above persons. God and man: the debtor forgiven much, the Pharisee and the publican, and the unprofitable servant saying all issue a defense of Jesus' emphasis on God as Father and persons as children; the alternative is ownership, in which people are then moved by the idea of merit.

C. H. Dodd's influence on parable study has been long acknowledged, and we earlier cast a glance at his classic study in connection with the notion of "realized eschatology."[60] We will look here at his actual work on the parables.

The parables, said Dodd, are Jesus' "most characteristic element"; there is nothing that sounds "a clearer ring of authenticity" (1). The parable is pictorial, a concretizing of truth, a metaphor or simile that leaves "the mind in sufficient doubt about its precise application to tease it into active thought" (5). Para-ble has a single point of comparison, has believability, and is characterized by "dramatic realism" (9). Unlike the gloomy pessimists who wrote the apocalypses Jesus saw nature as possessing or unfolding divinity. The apocalyptists, being of a scholastic mind, only give us allegories.

Like Cadoux Dodd saw the parables as argumentative, forcing the hearer to make a judgment about a situation presented to him. Jülicher was right about allegory, but inadequate on moral generalizations as the point of parables. We have to locate the parable in the concrete setting of Jesus' life; the evangelists may or may not be a reliable guide to that end.

As set out previously, Dodd then undertook an examination of the kingdom in Jesus' preaching, finding the notion of "realized eschatology" to be dominant. He then set about locating parables from this perspective in the concrete situa-tions of Jesus' ministry. For example, the parables of the treasure in a field and of the pearl of great price say to the hearer: You can possess the kingdom now; throw caution to the winds and follow me. He disagreed with Jülicher that the parable of the wicked husbandmen was a construct of the later church, a pure allegory. It actually represented real conditions at the time in Galilee, though the ending may be inauthentic and the story has been manipulated (the number of servants should be reduced to three, followed by the son). The "son" in the story is required by the logic of the narrative, which must climax in an outrageous act.

---

60. Above, 267–68.

There is also no allusion to the manner of the son's death. So the parable goes back to Jesus as judgment over Israel for her rebellion and assault upon himself as successor to the prophets.

Dodd then explored the history of the church after Jesus' death, showing its tendency to reinterpret the sayings of Jesus in order to give them permanent significance and to turn sayings referring to a crisis of the past into a crisis of the future. Homiletical and eschatological motives were at work, and in these the original setting often became obscured. The salt saying was applied in different ways by the evangelists, but for Jesus it probably meant a comparison with Israel who has wasted itself and is spoiled. The talents spoke under the metaphor of an unprofitable servant of the pious Jew who renders the religion of Israel barren. The evangelists added paranetic and eschatological connotations. Parables of crisis underwent transformations; the faithful and unfaithful servants parable has in view for the church the delayed Parousia, but for Jesus it pilloried the religious leaders of the Jews as God's unfaithful servants. The ten virgins spoke of the crisis presented by the present kingdom.

There were parables of growth: sower, tares, mustard seed, secretly growing seed. The latter spoke of Jesus himself standing at the harvest and putting in the sickle. The sower asserted that in spite of all failures the harvest is now ready and abundant. The tares answered objections: the presence of too many sinners cannot nevertheless delay the kingdom, which is itself a process of sifting and judgment. Mustard seed is not a contrast between small and great, but growth up to a point where the tree can shelter birds; so it says that the time is here when the blessings of the kingdom are available for all (the tree symbolizes a great empire). So growth means a period of growth for which the harvest is here now.

The end of the work addressed itself to the question of theological relevance in the church. Jesus did think of himself as Son of man, but Dodd understood that to mean that the kingdom has come and Jesus as the Son of man has come. Yet also Dodd here reasserted the use of apocalyptic symbols on Jesus' part to represent a transcendent, eternal order, not experienceable in history. Jesus also spoke about his suffering and undergoing a crisis, as would his disciples, especially as he neared Jerusalem.

An informed work is that of B. T. D. Smith.[61] His study stood in Dodd's shadow and consequently did not receive very significant recognition, but it contains some valuable insights.

He began also by examining the meanings behind "parable," citing the Hebrew *mashal*, which was a comparison of most any sort ("to be like") and was applied to proverbs, riddles, and analogies. There was also *hidah* or riddle, indirect speech or even enigma, while *mashal* could be used for allegory (Ezekiel) and parable for apocalyptic prediction (Enoch). Compared to Greek, Hebrew suffered a paucity of terms for such a variety of speech.

---

61. B. T. D. Smith, *The Parables of the Synoptic Gospels: A Critical Study* (Cambridge: University Press, 1937). Smith was Fellow and Tutor of Sidney Sussex College, Cambridge.

The synoptics contain similes and metaphors, and, like Jülicher, Smith appealed to Aristotle for some distinctions. Simile is a comparison formally expressed; metaphor transfers the designation of one to the other. Similitude depicts in detail familiar scenes and relationships; parable denotes narrative illustrations. Thus "All we like sheep have gone astray" is a simile, while "Hear, O you shepherd of Israel" is a metaphor. In the one we are *like* sheep; in the other we *are* sheep. Similitude and parable shade off into one another.

Four of the synoptic parables are really example stories (Pharisee and publican, Dives-Lazarus, rich fool, good Samaritan). They teach directly, not by analogy, and are not therefore figurative.

Allegory does not set one thing beside another, but substitutes one thing for another. Allegory is not a metaphor, but symbol is its characteristic; it is "a description in code" (21). Unlike simile or metaphor it need not be lifelike. There are two allegories in the synoptic gospels: the wicked husbandmen and Matthew's version of the unwilling guests. They lack verisimilitude, that is, the husbandmen beat the servants to death, yet the owner — unbelievably — kept sending more of them, including finally his own son.[62]

Smith classified the parabolic material by form: proverbs, aphorism, and parables. Parable and simile obey the laws of popular storytelling, of which two rules are visible in the parables: the rule of repetition and the rule of three (repeated elements, three times — three kinds of soil, three excuses, three visits of the vineyard owner to the marketplace).[63] Parallelism also is widespread; introductions are often formulary. Smith believed that no original settings of the parables are preserved in their context; he noted editorial work and applications that had been added. The parables were collected for purposes of Christian instruction, and some may have been created by Christian teachers or borrowed from Jewish sources. The greater part of them, however, are genuine and contain lifelikeness and genuine people, along with an element of the unexpected. It is these parables with their humor, irony, and knowledge of human character that are most representative of Jesus of Nazareth.

There are rabbinic parallels to the parables, but the immediate background of the parables is the pious poor of Galilee. The message differs from the apocalyptic hope of the kingdom and also from the rabbis in its lack of nationalism.

---

62. Dodd had noticed that in the wicked tenants a genuine situation was reflected (absentee landlords opposed by Galilean peasantry), and that the narrative required an "outrageous" act. If Dodd is correct, then the parable may actually have intended to disavow revolutionaries who hid their greed behind patriotic motives. The killing of the son would then mean: There is nothing these bandits will not do for their ends! But Smith's point would apply verisimilitude to the issue of authenticity: Is the father's behavior believable? For example, in the parable of the Prodigal Son the father's action in fêting the prodigal is extraordinary, but if he had stood idly by while the elder son killed his younger brother in a fit of jealousy then the story would have been destroyed. The killing of the son in the Wicked Tenants seems to have a logic that appeals more powerfully to one who stands under the light of the Easter gospel.

63. Smith referred to Dibelius in *Formgeschichte des Evangeliums*, in turn citing an Axel Olrik, Epische Gesetze der Volksdichtung, in *Zeitschrift für deutscher Altertum* (1909): 1ff.

Jesus expected the rule of God soon and suddenly (though Dodd's realized eschatology is unacceptable). Jesus blessed the poor and the pious and set himself in opposition to Pharisees; their obedience was not from the heart.

Smith's work then concentrated on the interpretation of individual parables, of which we have to content ourselves with brief notice. The problematic dishonest steward was addressed to the unconverted, said Smith, and urged them to leave no stone unturned to be ready for the kingdom. The other applications were secondary. To his earlier judgment about the wicked husbandmen (tenants) he added the further point that the story violates the "rule of three," and that the story should have ended with the killing of the servant.

Joachim Jeremias was heir to these works on the parables and wove many of these threads into his own garment, with compelling result and the construction of a work that would become a standard in the field.[64]

Jeremias acknowledged the continuing validity of Jülicher's advance in the elimination of allegory from the parables of Jesus, though recognizing that Jülicher's reduction of the parables to a single point of universal validity was an inadequate understanding of their nature. He credited Dodd with the "breakthrough" that sought to locate the parables in Jesus' own historical context and thus to cast new light on their original meaning.[65] His own project then intended to carry forth Dodd's work and to seek the original *Sitz im Leben Jesu* lying behind the parables. To that end he set forth a series of interpretive principles and illustrated them from the text. The principles are effectively a characterization of the history of the tradition of the transmission of the parables. Only in this way can the original *Sitz im Leben Jesu* be reconstructed so as to "hear again his authentic voice."[66]

These principles involve recognition of how the parables underwent interpretation and sometimes transformation as a result of (1) translation from Aramaic into Greek; (2) representational changes (historical, geographical details); (3) embellishment (such as increasing numbers); (4) attachment of Old Testament and folklore themes; (5) change of audience (crowds or opponents originally changed to the later church, and so on); (6) shift from the eschatological to the hortatory (unjust steward, for example); (7) impact of the church's setting (delay of the Parousia, as an instance, as in the ten virgins); (8) allegorization; (9) collection and conflation (gathering of parables by subject, pairing

---

64. Joachim Jeremias, *The Parables of the Kingdom*, trans. S. H. Hooke (New York: Scribner's, 1963). The original German was *Die Gleichnisse Jesu* (Zurich: Zwingli-Verlag, 1947). Also underrated were the works by the Americans Albert E. Barnett, *Understanding the Parables of Our Lord* (Nashville: Cokesbury, 1940); and, surprisingly, that by the parish minister Charles W. F. Smith, *The Jesus of the Parables* (Philadelphia: Westminster Press, 1948). Barnett came from the Chicago School and emphasized the social context of the parables. Smith connected them with Jesus' controversial activity; the parables led Jesus to his cross.

65. Jeremias gave Cadoux credit for anticipating Dodd; he thought Smith should have attended more to the theological meaning of the parables. He also agreed with Cadoux and Dodd that the parables were used as weapons of warfare, as Jesus' response to his critics and skeptics.

66. Jeremias, *The Parables of the Kingdom*, 22.

by theme); and (10) provision of a secondary setting in the gospels — redactional framework, introductory formulae, generalizing conclusions. Each of these was illustrated profusely from the material.

Jeremias then set forth the message found in the parables under a number of different headings. He also found everywhere an implied christology. Jesus proclaimed the kingdom as imminent, as good news to the poor and outcasts [Jeremias oddly seemed to equate "poor" with "sinners and publicans"]. The kingdom presents a crisis demanding a response on the part of the hearer; this response is also a response to Jesus himself, who speaks and acts as God's representative. There is also assurance of the presence and promise of the kingdom, and judgment too for those who do not respond to it. The last hour has struck; for some it is already too late. Jeremias evinced a rather conservative reading of much of the gospel story in general, with Jesus' public activity divided at Caesarea-Philippi by Peter's confession and thereafter driven by disclosure of his coming passion, which will be followed by his ultimate triumph and installation as the glorified Son of man.

Jeremias's work encapsulated the best of parable research at that time.[67] Its possession of immense historical detail and vigorous pressing of the quest for the actual *Sitz im Leben Jesu* are impressive and often very compelling. Sometimes the material seems squeezed beyond a reasonable bound. By way of brief illustration we can return to that most puzzling of parables, the wicked husbandmen (or tenants). Jeremias agreed largely with Dodd's location of the historical setting and claimed also that the parable thereby displayed verisimilitude as a genuine parable of Jesus. He then found that the parable was originally intended to be Jesus' vindication of his message to the poor: the vineyard will be taken away (from the leaders in Israel) and given to "others" (who must be the poor). The killing of the son greatly intensifies the gravity of the rejection of Jesus' message. Jeremias noted that the tenants must have assumed that the appearance of the son meant that the owner was dead and therefore their killing of him as sole heir would classify the property legally as ownerless property that they could then claim (Jeremias citing evidence to justify the practice).

But a number of subtle steps is required to arrive at this point: the assumption that the tenants saw the son as (sole) heir, that the father-owner was dead, that the "others" refers to the poor. It sounds too much, in fact, like a studied effort to make some sense of a text that otherwise does not make very much sense and requires some importation of imaginative material to do so. Nevertheless, the effort reflected in Jeremias and his predecessors to reach back to the original setting of the parables was highly constructive and productive of new perspectives on the force and nature of parable as Jesus used it.

---

67. See, for example, F. C. Grant's highly favorable review in *ATR* 30 (1948): 118–21. Grant reported that Jeremias had agreed to the modification of his (Dodd's) position suggested by Ernst Haenchen of *sich realisierenden Eschatologie.*

Synoptic Problems

The issues with which Schweitzer concluded his work were the John-synoptic contention, natural-supernatural interpretation, and eschatological and non-eschatological understanding of Jesus. The first two he declared solved, while the third lay before scholarship as the last great battleground of *Leben-Jesu-Forschung*. He himself, of course, had the proper key for the resolution of the third. And, in fact, there was truth to his characterization: the synoptics remain the prime source, though the contention over the extent of Johannine usage persisted; few other than fundamentalists or, in a different way, Roman Catholics declined to adopt critical methods. And while the synoptic problem was widely considered to have been solved in the theory of Markan priority and adoption of the Q hypothesis, there remained vestigial discussion of the source issues.[68] Primarily, though not exclusively, it was the English who pursued the matter, and the three major documents representative of their quest were Vincent Stanton's *The Gospels as Historical Documents*, William Sanday's seminar on the question, whose results were published as *Studies in the Synoptic Problem*, and B. H. Streeter's classic, *The Four Gospels: A Study of Origins*.[69] Some variation on the commonly accepted theories was attempted by the Americans Ernest DeWitt Burton and Edgar J. Goodspeed, who wished to maintain Matthew's and Luke's use of Mark, but divided Q essentially into two parts, a G and a P, or more specifically Pl (Luke's version) and Pm (Matthew's version).[70] There was also other specifically Matthean and Lukan material, oral or written. And there was also the theory of the German Wilhelm Bussmann, who held a variant theory of the underlying synoptic sources, but failed to convince many.[71] Bussmann supposed a parent document back of all three synoptics; Luke's version was shorter than Mark's, Matthew's the same as Mark's, but Mark preserved the best structure of the original. This original Bussmann called G (*Geschichtsquelle*). Luke used it in its original form, Matthew used it in an enlarged form as expanded by a Galilean Christian. Mark was produced by a Roman Christian who used the same form of G seen in Matthew, and there were other written sources, but the basic one was G.[72]

---

68. The Mark-Q theory was specifically rejected by the Pontifical Biblical Commission in 1912.

69. Part 2 of Stanton's work was *The Synoptic Gospels* (Cambridge: Cambridge University Press, 1909). The third part dealt with the Gospel of John. Stanton was Professor of Divinity at Cambridge University. William Sanday, ed., *Studies in the Synoptic Problem* (Oxford: Clarendon Press, 1911); B. H. Streeter, *The Four Gospels: A Study of Origins* (London: Macmillan, 1924; 4th rev. printing, 1930).

70. Ernest DeWitt Burton and Edgar J. Goodspeed, *A Harmony of the Synoptic Gospels in Greek* (Chicago: University of Chicago Press, 1920; 2d ed., 1947). Earlier was Burton's *Some Principles of Literary Criticism and Their Application to the Synoptic Problem* (Chicago: University of Chicago Press, 1904).

71. Bussmann, *Synoptische Studien*. Rudolf Otto's source work owed something to Bussmann; above, p. 148 n. 15.

72. For this bare summary I am indebted to Filson, *Origins of the Gospels*. It is difficult to find many who seem actually to have read Bussmann.

Stanton's work encompassed the whole of the synoptic problem as well as other works then contemporary, such as the better-known ones of Wellhausen and Harnack.[73] Stanton summarized the accepted results at the time: the similarities between Matthew and Luke presuppose Greek sources, not translations from Hebrew or Aramaic; those relations cannot be explained on the basis of oral tradition; the third gospel is not dependent on the first or vice-versa for their common contents; a record nearly identical to our Mark was largely used in the composition of Matthew and Luke;[74] and Matthew and Luke had another document, largely of discourses and sayings, that they combined with Mark. Stanton gave the arguments for Markan priority as well (Matthew and Luke only begin to agree after the birth narratives; most of Mark is found in Matthew and Luke and is the source of the common outline; mostly Matthew and Luke, when they omit Markan material, do not omit the same material; when either Matthew or Luke differs from Mark's sequence the other adheres to it; the agreement of Matthew and Luke with Mark is very high, and their agreement with each other against Mark is very low). The Gospel of Mark also has behind it a developmental history; Luke used a version that conformed virtually to the original Markan gospel, while Matthew's conforms closely to our surviving Mark. Stanton postulated these different Marks from an analysis of Luke's "omissions."

Stanton seemed to prefer to refer to the material common to Matthew and Luke as the "Logian document," but also deferred to the use coming into practice then of designating it as "Q." He saw it as arising out of the catechetical and missionary needs of the church. At first the Aramaic-speaking community needed primarily a record of teaching, whereas the Greek-speaking converts would require more of an account of Jesus. From the latter arose the Gospel of Mark. As the gentile converts required more, the logical course would have been a translation of the Logian document. Stanton saw the differences between Matthew's and Luke's use of Q as arising from the availability of two different translations. Luke inserted his translation into Mark largely in two blocks and thus has better preserved the original order, whereas Matthew arranged his according to topics and subject matter. Nevertheless, Stanton inclined to the traditional (Papias) statement that a discourse by Matthew lay behind the Logia-source and was best preserved in the Gospel of Matthew. Luke, on the other hand, used a differently expanded version of Q. So, according to Stanton's reconstructions, both Q and Mark existed in different versions when incorporated into the work of Matthew and Luke. Stanton also gave some quite fine commentary on the redactional work of the evangelists; his was altogether a splendid

---

73. Harnack's reconstruction of Q was *The Sayings of Jesus: The Second Source of St. Matthew and St. Luke,* trans. J. R. Wilkinson, New Testament Studies 2. Crown Theological Library 23 (London: Williams and Norgate, 1908). Wellhausen's work was his *Einleitung in die drei ersten Evangelium* (Berlin: Reimer, 1905).

74. It is interesting that Stanton here credited the earliest theory of Markan priority and utilization by the other two to G. C. Storr, *Über den Zweck der evangelischen Geschichte Johannes* [1786] (Stanton, *Gospels as Historical Documents,* 31–32), who was barely mentioned by Schweitzer.

accounting of the issues and some original solutions to the problems, even if those solutions did not quite carry the day.

The Sanday volume contains essays by members of the synoptic question symposium (John Hawkins, N. P. Williams, W. C. Allen, B. H. Streeter, and J. Vernon Bartlet, with Sanday providing an introduction). The essays were actually a diverse collection of material on the synoptic gospels, including the underlying languages as well as the source question, with some attention to theological perspectives of the evangelists. Both Hawkins and Streeter presented their reconstructions of Q in conversation with those of Harnack and Wellhausen. Streeter also contributed an essay on apocalyptic eschatology, arguing that there was a tendency in the early church toward putting ever more apocalyptic sayings in Jesus' mouth, while Jesus' own tendency was in the opposite direction, toward emphasizing the present, gradual kingdom and its internal aspects. Allen's essay on "The Aramaic Background of the Gospels" suggested that Mark wrote in Greek based on an Aramaic oral tradition. The Gospel of Matthew used a document consisting of discourses by the apostle Matthew, either in Greek or an original Aramaic. Luke was also acquainted with some of its contents. He examined a number of Aramaisms to support his contention.

N. P. Williams examined W. Wendling's three-strata hypothesis of Mark: M^1 the historian, M^2 the poet, and M^3 the evangelist or theologian. For Williams the issue was how to weigh Mark's authority; only a single tradition is available if Mark was used by Matthew and Luke. Was Mark Petrine and primary or barely Petrine and following a lengthy development of church tradition? This Wendling hypothesis, said Williams, was the original *Urmarkus* theory, that is, an M^1 or gospel drawn up first, and poetized by M^2 (who loved nature, and so on). This interpolated Mark was used by Luke, then M^3 got hold of it and gave it its present shape. He was the final redactor, adding about one-third to one-half of it. It was he who did the theological work, producing the messianic secret, the atonement, and the Pauline doctrine of the church. Williams argued for the historicity of Mark's presentation and disagreed with the redactional work.

Streeter's Proto-Luke theory may have owed something to Bartlet, whose essay on "The Sources of St. Luke's Gospel" proposed a two-document theory of Luke: Q was used by Luke in an independent form (QL), which was found already in Luke's special source (S), while Q included the Logia. So the special material in Luke was S+QL. That also would explain the minor agreements of Matthew and Luke against Mark as due to their use of Q in different versions.

The American Carl Patton offered a detailed analysis of the problem, with a very able grasp of the issues, while carrying on a conversation with the leading essayists.[75] Patton prescinded from the *Urmarkus* theory and saw other grounds for accounting for the minor agreements of Matthew and Luke against Mark (Matthew and Luke had different copies of Mark, fortuitous change, assimi-

---

75. Carl S. Patton, *Sources of the Synoptic Gospels*, University of Michigan Studies: Humanistic Series 5 (New York: Macmillan, 1915).

lation). But Patton regarded his greatest contribution to the question as the hypothesis of two rescensions of Q (Q^{Matt} and Q^{Lk}). He assumed that Matthew and Luke had Greek translations of Q which rested on different copies of an Aramaic original. Q was always growing, aided by oral tradition, so it circulated in different forms. First Patton worked up the material of Q as represented in Matthew and Luke together, then attempted to set forth the rescensions each used. The total content of Q is the sum of all three. "Q" initially referred to the material where identity or near-identity left no question, or where minor variation was clearly the work of one or the other (Matthew or Luke). There were also about fifty verses that Mark used from Q. Matthew and Luke used rescensions later than Mark's. Q^{Matt} and Q^{Lk} then represented translation variants based on two different Aramaic texts.

Streeter's later work (*The Four Gospels*) saw Proto-Luke as midway between Q and Mark — Luke sans Markan material or Q or infancy narratives. Streeter was impressed by Luke's "disuse" of Mark (the Lukan "omissions"), which he saw as less a case of interpretation than of having an existing framework into which Markan material was interpolated. So Luke had a larger document, Q+L, a complete gospel larger than Mark, which was the major source. Where it diverged from Mark, he chose it. Proto-Luke then is Q+L; it contained five sections and several smaller passages were derived from it. It may have been Luke himself who first combined Q+L. It should be dated as contemporary with Mark. Streeter found the ground for assigning it to Luke in a comparison of its material with other Lukan works (Luke, Acts).

Streeter also offered the classic arguments for the priority of Mark: agreement of word and order, Matthew often supporting Mark where Luke diverges and vice-versa. The minor agreements do not need recourse to an *Urmarkus* theory for explanation; they are due to parallel versions of Q; corruption of the manuscripts due to assimilation of Matthew-Luke parallel material; or coincidental improvements of style. Possibly Sanday was correct that the text of Mark used by Matthew and Luke had been subjected to slight stylistic revision. Q can only be reconstructed tentatively; overlap with Mark represents independent tradition.

Streeter's source analyses, along with some extended study of text families and their origins, led him to his four-document hypothesis: Mark, the old Roman gospel; M, a Jerusalem source; L, from Caesarea; Q, originally in Aramaic, perhaps provided by Matthew for Galilean Christians (thus from Antioch). Matthew's priority in the canon is accounted for by its representation of the gospels of Rome, Jerusalem, and Antioch.

A section on John characterized John as a mystical prophet, closer to Philo and Plato than the Old Testament. John walked somewhere between the Gnostics and the apocalyptists, ordering his work according to the logos-become-flesh doctrine in which factual matter had significance as parable. Streeter thought that John knew and used Mark and Luke. Its author was a disciple of the apostle John and probably the "Elder" of the epistles; the Beloved Disciple was the apostle idealized.

Although Streeter's Proto-Luke theory never quite persuaded large numbers of his colleagues,[76] his main work was nevertheless influential and can fairly be said to be the standard statement on the problem at the time. The two-source theory never quite yielded to the four-source theory, but Streeter's effort doubtless represented both the climax and the conclusion to source analysis for some time.[77] Preoccupation with the nature of oral tradition pushed source analysis into the background by disclosing its limitations and opening up the possibility of getting beyond written sources.

What was not yet possible was a more intense focus on the theological perspective of the evangelists themselves, or Redaction Criticism, as it came later to be known. That there was already a significant understanding of the gospel writers as something more than mere editors and as having a theological point of view should by now be evident from the works we have surveyed. The movement beyond source criticism was clearly taken in Form Criticism, which was, as it were, a step back in time. The effort to come to a more precise understanding of the evangelists as creative writers would not flower for some years yet, but there were obvious antecedents. One of the most immediate ones that we may notice in concluding this survey was a work by the Harvard professor James Hardy Ropes.[78]

Ropes proposed to view the gospel writers as *authors*, not merely as paste-and-scissors editors piecing together already existing documents. Mark was not a biography, to be sure, but at least a "theological pamphlet" that wanted to explain how Jesus' career ended in a criminal's death. The author did so by showing the issue that brought Jesus, innocent though he was, to the cross, and by demonstrating that Jesus' death was the divine way to a glorious future messiahship. Matthew was a kind of handbook, a record of the words and deeds of the founder of the church. Matthew was more historical, a "man of distinguished literary ability."[79] The gospel was written for the edification of believers; the author loved structure and uniformity. Matthew differed from Mark, not telling a tragic story of conflict, but focusing on the practical activity of the messiah. Luke was a man of greater literary culture, but of less originality or "force of intellect" than Mark or Matthew (59). He had biographical intentions; the speeches of Acts were drawn up as a good historian then would do. Probably the "we" of

---

76. A version was accepted by Vincent Taylor, *Behind the Third Gospel* (Oxford: Clarendon Press, 1926).

77. That remains true even though there were and always have been advocates of the Griesbach hypothesis. The minor agreements of Matthew and Luke over against Mark remain a problem for the prevailing theory.

78. James Hardy Ropes, *The Synoptic Gospels* (Cambridge: Harvard University Press, 1934; New York: Oxford University Press, 1960). Ropes died in 1933 and the book was published posthumously. Credit as a pioneer in this direction also properly belongs to Henry J. Cadbury, *The Making of Luke-Acts* (New York: Macmillan, 1927).

79. Ropes, *Synoptic Gospels*, 10, 41. This elevation of Matthew was actually unusual then, with most writers considering Matthew to be a kind of Jewish scribe of decided tendentious qualities.

Acts links up with the preface to indicate the presence of the author himself as source. Ropes accepted the tradition that Luke, a companion of Paul's, wrote the gospel. It was the first real attempt at a biography, the life of a divine hero. It was governed more by "artistic feeling" (72) than theological thought. The author did not portray Paul's thought very well. His main idea about Jesus was that he brought salvation for both Gentiles and Jews.

Ropes was not entirely comfortable with the Q hypothesis and leaned toward the idea of Luke drawing on Matthew. He recognized that oral tradition lay behind the sources, but did not expect much solid results from Form Criticism.

There was surely an abundance of other subtopics that filled the journals and book binderies in the first half century; a survey would require several more volumes. There were presentations of the general historical, political, and cultural background; Schürer continued as a major source, though others also contributed.[80] Chronology sometimes evoked special studies, while other topics like miracles gained some attention.[81] A few sought to determine the Aramaic original underlying Jesus' words, while still others, like C. F. Burney, thought they could recover the poetic shape of Jesus' sayings.[82] Encyclopedia and dictionaries still continued to flourish, and the *Theologische Wörterbuch zum Neuen Testament* edited by Gerhard Kittel would gestate for yet many more years, with numbers of worthwhile semantic studies.

---

80. Emil Schürer, *A History of the Jewish People in the Time of Jesus Christ*, trans. John MacPherson, Sophia Taylor, and Peter Christie (Edinburgh: T. & T. Clark, 1886–90); a new English version has been revised and edited by Geza Vermes and Fergus Miller (Edinburgh: T. & T. Clark, 1973). Shailer Mathews, *A History of New Testament Times in Palestine 175 B.C.–A.D. 70* (New York: Macmillan, 1906; new and rev. ed., *New Testament Times in Palestine* (New York: Macmillan, 1933); Ch. Guignebert, *The Jewish World in the Time of Jesus* (New York: University Books, 1959; original French, 1935); Joseph Bonsirven, *Palestinian Judaism in the Time of Jesus Christ*, trans. William Wolf (New York: Holt, Rinehart and Winston, 1964; French in 1950); Gustav Dalman, *Sacred Sites and Ways: Studies in the Topography of the Gospels*, trans. Paul P. Levertoff (New York: Macmillan, 1935); Joachim Jeremias, *Jerusalem in the Time of Jesus: An Investigation into Economic and Social Conditions During the New Testament Period*, trans. F. H. Cave and C. H. Cave (Philadelphia: Fortress Press, 1969); Adolf Deissmann, *Light from the Ancient East*, trans. Lionel R. M. Strachan (New York: George H. Doran, 1927); Camden M. Cobern, *The New Archaeological Discoveries and Their Bearing upon the New Testament and upon the Life and Times of the Primitive Church* (New York: Funk and Wagnalls, 1917); William F. Albright, *From the Stone Age to Christianity* (Baltimore: Johns Hopkins Press, 1940; Garden City, N.Y.: Doubleday, 1957).

81. For works on chronology, see A. T. Olmstead, "The Chronology of Jesus' Life," *ATR* 24 (1942): 1–26; Olmstead was an orientalist who argued for the superiority of Johannine chronology and a birth date of 20 B.C.E. Also much earlier was Leonhard Fendt, *Die Dauer der öffentlichen Wirksamkeit Jesu* (Munich: J. J. Lentner, 1906); argued for a ministry of about a year, with public activity commencing before a passover and death occurring also at the time of the next one. Works on miracles include Karl Beth, *The Miracles of Jesus* (New York: Eaton and Manis, 1907); Alan Richardson, *The Miracle Stories of the Gospels* (London: SCM Press, 1941); C. H. Dodd, "Miracles in the Gospels," *ExpTim* 44 (1932–33): 504–9.

82. Matthew Black, *An Aramaic Approach to the Gospels and Acts* (Oxford: Clarendon Press, 1946; 3d rev. ed., 1963). Much of a similar effort found in Dalman's *Jesus-Jeschua*. C. F. Burney, *The Poetry of Our Lord: An Examination of the Formal Elements of Hebrew Poetry in the Discourse of Jesus Christ* (Oxford: Clarendon Press, 1925).

The Return of the Nonhistorical Jesus

But now to modulate into a slightly different key we can recall that, of the other of Schweitzer's issues around the turn of the century, the question of Jesus' sanity recurred infrequently,[83] but one that never quite seemed to go away was the question of the historicity of Jesus. Arthur Drews continued, in fact, to stir the waters, constructing what looked like a career around the question. His *Christ Myth* was reissued a number of times, and he offered further publications as well. Hans Windisch also reported on the subject again immediately upon the restoration of the journal *Theologische Rundschau*.[84] There were also more minor contributions, such as that of the Danish *littérateur* George Brandes, who had the bad taste to compare the Jesus story to the William Tell legend.[85] But the major refreshing of the issue emanated from France in the person of the genial physician-turned-man-of-letters Paul-Louis Couchoud. The French had participated little in the previous debate,[86] but this time the discussion was almost entirely a French affair.[87] There were publications elsewhere, of course; some of those appearing in the *Hibbert Journal* were nevertheless all by Frenchmen, with Loisy providing a detailed analysis of Couchoud's work, so much so that it could virtually be reconstructed from the critique alone.[88] Maurice Goguel also took a significant role as reporter and combatant.[89] For his part Couchoud tended to

---

83. The best accounting is that by Walter Bundy, *The Psychic Health of Jesus* (New York: Macmillan, 1922). It covered much of Schweitzer's ground and carried the discussion forward. Bundy identified the issue as a problem in "pathography," that is, pathological analysis based on biography. He recognized the liberal roots of the problem and ended about where Schweitzer did: Jesus was not abnormal in his own context.

84. Arthur Drews, *Hat Jesus Gelebt?* (Verlag freie Religion in Mainz, 1928); Drews, *Die Leugnung der Geschichtlichkeit Jesu in Vergangenheit und Gegenwart* (Karlsruhe: G. Braun, 1926); Drews, *Das Markus Evangelium als Zeugnis gegen die Geschichtlichkeit Jesu* (Jena: E. Diederichs, 1921). Windisch in "Das Problem der Geschichtlichkeit Jesu: Die Außerchristlichen Zeugnisse," *TRu*, n.f. 1 (1929): 266–88; and also "Das Problem der Geschichtlichkeit Jesu: Die Christusmythe," *TRu*, n.f. 2 (1930): 207–52.

85. Georg Brandes, *Jesus: A Myth*, trans from the Danish by Edwin Björkman (London: Brentano's, n.d.). Paul was the founder of Christianity; Jesus was Yahweh himself merged out of messianic hopes of Isaiah's servant, the persecuted man of Psalms, and the Wisdom of Solomon. The study by Henry Frank, *Jesus: A Modern Study* (New York: Greenberg, 1930), trades on the Jesus-Paul dichotomy, attributing Christianity to Paul without denying Jesus' historicity entirely (he came from an Essene cult to which John also belonged); H. G. Wood, *Did Christ Really Live?* (New York: Macmillan, 1938), gives a capsule history of the debate and offers a defense of Jesus' historicity.

86. Ch. Guignebert's *Le Problème de Jésus* (Paris: Ernest Flammarion, 1914) was, as far as I can see, the major contribution.

87. Another was Edouard Dujardin, *Ancient History of the God Jesus*, abridged English version by A. Brodie Sanders (London: Watts, 1938).

88. Loisy, "Was Jesus an Historical Person?," *HibJ* 36 (1937–38): 380–94, 509–29; Couchoud's response in "The Historicity of Jesus," *HibJ* 37 (1938–39): 193–214. Couchoud hardly noticed the severe wounds inflicted on him by Loisy.

89. Maurice Goguel in *Jesus the Nazarene Myth or History?*, trans. Frederick Stephens (New York: D. Appleton, 1926). Couchoud's work was the "dream of a poet rather than the work of an historian" (v); see also Goguel's article, "Recent French Discussion of the Historical Existence of Jesus Christ," *HTR* 19 (1926): 115–42.

give a nonresponsive response to all his critics — rather like the Markan Jesus reclining peacefully in a boat beset everywhere by storms.

Couchoud's work came forth piecemeal at first, appearing initially in issues of the *Mercure de France,* and subsequently Couchoud set forth his fuller theory in separate volumes.[90] He displayed no animus toward Christianity, even in fact expressed repeated appreciation for it. But he was convinced, like John Robertson before him, to whom he dedicated his major work (*The Creation of Christ*), that a myth existed before the fact of Christianity. The first essay (in *The Enigma of Jesus*) contained an introduction by J. G. Frazer, who did not subscribe to the theory of the mythical Jesus, but gave Couchoud credit for his dispassionate analysis.

Couchoud first dismissed the external evidence (Josephus, Talmud, Tacitus, Suetonius), then examined the New Testament. He noted that Paul had nothing of the historical Jesus and, since Mark is the source of the other two (and John is pure theology), then it becomes a question of Mark [shades of Bruno Bauer]. Mark is not a historical text, but a kind of commentary on biblical texts and recollections on which Christianity has been built up, a sort of midrash on Psalms, Isaiah, and Pauline theology. It came from Rome about the time of Domitian. Jesus may have lived, but it is only a possibility.

Couchoud turned then to the origins of Christianity, remarking on Renan and Loisy, and taking the latter as the model of a modern critic whom he admired greatly, and from whom he had learned much. He summed up what could be known about Loisy's Jesus, which was not much. Like Theudas and others Jesus was a messianic agitator. Couchoud wondered whether this was enough to kindle Christianity. Was he a real figure?[91]

Turning to Paul, Couchoud said that here we meet a Jew affirming the deity of Jesus alongside that of Yahweh. This alone makes Jesus' existence impossible. How can a man be made into the equal of Yahweh? No, Paul preached monotheism, but in another form, as Jesus the Savior. His Jesus was not a historical figure; he was a heavenly figure, crucified in heaven, a mystical event brought about by powers above. Jesus was the result of a new exegesis of old biblical texts. The ideas came from the prophets, the servant-concept, and the notion of the righteous man. This figure, born of scripture, "appeared" to various people. Jesus was thus a god becoming a man.

So Jesus was solely a spiritual reality. It was Mark who materialized him, a

---

90. First on March 1, 1923, was "L'énigma de Jésus"; English trans., *The Enigma of Jesus,* trans. Winifred Whale (London: Watts, 1924); then on March 1, 1924, was "Le Mystère de Jésus"; both were collected as *Le Mystère de Jésus* (Paris: F. Rieder et Cie, 1926). His major work was Couchoud, *Jésus: Le Dieu Fait Homme* (Paris: Les Editions Rieder, 1937); English trans., *The Creation of Christ: An Outline of the Beginnings of Christianity,* 2 vols., trans. C. Bradlaugh Bonner (London: Watts, 1939). Couchoud's reply to Loisy was attached to this work as an appendix. The volume in 1944, *Histoire de Jésus* (Paris: Presses Universitaires de France, 1944), appears to be a reprint of this main work under a different title.

91. It is evident that Loisy's anxiety to refute Couchoud arose in part from Couchoud's appeal to Loisy; Couchoud evidently regarded his own position as simply a logical extension of Loisy's.

legendizing of Paul's mystical gospel. The gospels are therefore a second stage of the Christian mystery. But Jesus remains still as the "highest aspiration of human souls beneath the western sky" (105).

The major work on *The Creation of Christ* extended the line of inquiry further. Couchoud traced first the messianic idea — Son of man in Daniel and Enoch (a combination of the Danielic and Isaianic servant). Enoch was the core of Christianity; seventy years before Christ there were Christians, just not by name. It was a band of readers, hoping for the heavenly man.

Basically Christianity came out of the work of John the Baptist, who preached the coming of the heavenly man and baptism. New names were found for the man: Lord, Christ, Jesus. The latter derived from a tortured exegesis of Exod. 23:20–21 (LXX), along with Num. 13:16, so that the name upon the messenger was Joshua (=Jesus).[92] So a picture grew up of the Son of man–Servant=Joshua=Jesus who suffered an expiatory death. His death among the wicked suggested other visions, that is, death for sins and resurrection on the third day (Hosea), apparitions to Peter, James, Paul, and John. Thus a new movement started. Couchoud provided a sketch of its history.

So Christianity was a schismatic movement of Baptist followers; both went their independent ways. Prophets in the church spread the message about the eschatological coming of the Son of man. The community divided into Jewish and gentile Christians. Especially Paul put on Christianity its special stamp. His legacy was a message of a crucified God (from the reading of the Psalms, esp. Psalm 22), a scandalous message. It was a projection onto the divine plane of Paul's own tortured life. Paul had a mystic union with the crucified One, initiated by baptism.

Revelation was the work of John the apostle, the last of the original witnesses to the resurrected One; he depicts the victory of the sacrificial lamb. The book is pre-70, after 64, around 65. John abominated the mysticism of Paul; a struggle ensued. Who would prevail, John's God-hero (and those he represented — Peter, James, the Twelve, the Five Hundred) or Paul's crucified God? Paul and John had incompatible Christs, but the future belonged to Paul.

The period 70–120 is obscure; Christianity had four centers: Rome, Alexandria, Antioch, and Ephesus. From Antioch came Matthew and the Didache; from Alexander Gnosticism; Rome was still Jewish-Christian; Ephesus was the home of John. The prophets were all gone, but the organization grew, with *episcopoi* and the like. The community needed to present a picture of Jesus, as can be seen in Hebrews, where Jesus is the eternal sacrifice in a real body of flesh and blood. Jesus suffered in the flesh, but not yet on earth.

Enter Marcion the religious genius. He set out to restore the Pauline gospel. He collected the letters and likely authored the life of Paul at the core of Acts. (Marcion was a sea captain, seen in Acts.) The father of Paul's Christ, who broke

---

92. Couchoud actually borrowed here from some speculations of Justin Martyr on the Exodus passage, finding the name Jesus there.

the Law, could have nothing to do with the Hebrew God Yahweh; thus Marcion rejected the Old Testament. Jesus' sacrifice was to redeem humankind from the creator God; the true God is limitless love. So Marcion started a church that went beyond Paul; it was ascetic and had no prophets, but women were included. It was episcopal, with Marcion at the head.

Marcion needed to show that the Christian claim of a Jesus who appeared had no relation to Jewish scriptures, but was something new, a terrestrial fact. Crucifixion was therefore a terrestrial fact, and therefore a story arose. Some, like Pliny and Tacitus, picked it up and connected it with Pontius Pilate. Marcion accepted this pagan idea; from this assertion of crucifixion as event the whole life could then be assembled using previous prophecies, revelation of sayings, texts, and so on. This happened at first around 128–129 in the mind of Marcion; he chose 28–29 for the crucifixion, and finished the story in 132. This Marcionite tale is embodied in the Gospel of Luke (Couchoud gave it as appendix 1 of his book). It contained disconnected pericopes, parables, and prophecies, with no chronological order (only in the passion narrative).

Mark was a poor imitation of Marcion's gospel, prepared at Rome and reflecting already separation from the Jews and influenced by Paulinism. It was first seen c. 140 in Asia Minor. Matthew was a Christian scribe who completed Mark's gospel — a revised edition of Mark — in the light of Marcion's, arranging it into five parts, like the law of Moses, and provided a prologue and epilogue (birth, passion); it was written in Aramaic (Papias). Matthew was Jewish, possessed a rabbinical mind, and produced a Christian Pentateuch for the Aramean churches, to get converts from Jews. It was approved at Rome as an antidote to Marcion, though it originated in Syria.

The Johannine letters were aimed at Marcion; he was the antichrist. They were composed by the same author as wrote the gospel (though before it). The gospel presented Jesus as God who trod the earth, giving life now to believers. It was written at Ephesus and used Mark and Marcion's gospel. Allusions to Bar-Cocheba (16:2 et al.) give a date after 135. Thus all the gospels were to be dated around 134–135. Marcion was anathema to the Johannine author. Luke was the work of Clement at Rome, an anti-Marcionite tract with the Holy Spirit as the central character.

Jesus thus formed eventually conquered the western world and shaped its civilization. This Jesus is in reality "no more than man's own heart, aware of itself mysteriously in the agony of its infinite feebleness and in the exaltation of its measureless strength."[93]

Appendix 1 provided the gospel of Marcion. Its text was most strongly preserved in Codex D (Bezae) in its version of Luke.[94]

---

93. Couchoud, *Creation of Christ*, 2:315.

94. That Couchoud did not disdain the role of prophet himself (if also a poor one) is indicated by his further notion that the idea of Jesus, which has now had so long an evolution, would by 1940 have passed out of history into the realm of "collective mental images." (Cited by Goguel in the article referenced above, n. 89; reference is on p. 127 of the article.) This concept of *représentations*

Couchoud's is a work that condemns itself; the "tortured exegesis" by which the name Jesus was derived from biblical texts is that of Couchoud himself. At bottom he sought a more spiritual conception of Christianity, one unfettered by the messy mix-up with history; that is a thought that his hero Marcion would have approved, but one that the church in its wisdom long ago disavowed.

Roman Catholic Lives of Jesus

It may seem strange to classify Roman Catholic "lives" of Jesus as a special topic; while that would be inappropriate anymore, a different circumstance prevailed in the first half of the century. There was a common resemblance among such lives that was not accidental; they were constrained by the dictates of dogma and the opinions of the Pontifical Biblical Commission. Even so, their authors were often highly learned figures quite familiar with the latest rumblings among their Protestant compatriots, and it is worthwhile to notice some of their labors. We can pass on the less technical of these,[95] and look to the scholars. The best of them were without question those by Léonce de Grandmaison, Jules Lebreton, and Père Lagrange, though the latter's by its own definition was not a "life."

Léonce de Grandmaison's two-volume *Jesus Christ: His Person, His Message, His Credentials* appeared posthumously; it was the climax of his life's work, having been completed in January of 1927, with the author's death ensuing in June of the same year before publication.[96]

The first volume expends considerable space on discussion of the sources; most of those beyond the limits of the canon were dismissed: Josephus has no direct value, the rabbis relate odious fables, pagan writers possess some important facts; there are a few agrapha, but mainly the canon of the New Testament applies. Paul (thirteen letters, fourteen if Hebrews is included) was not an eyewitness, but saw the risen Lord and was not indifferent to the human life of Jesus. The text of the gospels is reliable.

As to methods, Grandmaison mentioned German works such as those of Schmidt, Albertz, Bertam, Dibelius, and Bultmann, and even acknowledged

---

collectives emanates from sociological circles (Durkheim) and designates an idea-image shared by a group. Couchoud's thesis was that the historical Jesus arose from a community with a collective concept of a Jesus-god. Now the historical Jesus would presumably suffer a reverse fate. This sociological conception was employed also by members of the *Annales* school, in particular Marc Bloch, one of the founders. The school was concerned to write history thematically and culturally, not simply politically-chronologically. The school took its name from its organ, *Annales d'histoire économique et sociale* (1929). An English account is that by Peter Burke, *The French Historical Revolution: The Annales School* (Stanford: Stanford University Press, 1990).

95. Popular ones were Rev. Father Didon's *Jesus Christ*, 2 vols. (London: Kegan Paul, Trench, Trübner, 1906), in the early part of the century, and A. J. Maas, *The Life of Jesus Christ According to the Gospel History*, 8th ed. (St. Louis: B. Herder, 1927). First printed in 1890. Both were basically harmonizations using all four gospels.

96. Léonce de Grandmaison, *Jesus Christ: His Person, His Message, His Credentials*, 2 vols, trans. Dom Basil Whelan (New York: Sheed and Ward, 1935).

some influence, but largely negatively, it would seem.[97] The gospels are not anonymous community creations; the word of Jesus was sacred and set the standard from the beginning. The order of events in the gospels is largely historical. The gospels themselves are a new type of literature, a fusion of the teaching of Jesus with his person; they are "less apologies than epiphanies" (53). They are of Jewish origin, their material first passed on orally; repetitions and polishings may account for their similarities. Grandmaison described each synoptic gospel in turn, giving church tradition about their origins, but with some insight into their particularity (Matthew is Jewish and pre-70, Mark's account is loose chronologically). Grandmaison assumed the "synoptic fact," that is, the agreements of all, from which it can be deduced that there was first an oral transmission followed by bits of writing. A comparison gives a prototype: Luke depends on Mark but also shows the same material as in Matthew. Matthew depends on Mark for order, but otherwise has its own priority. Mark's frame goes back to Peter, but Matthew is earlier. He was the arranger, following Papias, of the words of Jesus. Thus Grandmaison opted for a dependence of Luke on Matthew (rather than the Q hypothesis, which was proscribed anyway). Though Matthew is dependent on Mark for the framework, it still itself goes back to an early Jewish-Christian community, Matthew filling Mark's Petrine framework with more (Petrine) material.

The historical value of the synoptics is very high, reflecting the original and authentic voice of Jesus. The burden lies on the denier of authenticity. The synoptics portray a pre-70 Galilean Judaism. They also reflect a doctrinal stage prior to the decades of 50–60, as comparison with Paul shows. As to John, there are varying opinions and church traditions, but its apostolic origin remains untouched (John was also the Beloved Disciple). There is no problem with the unity of John, aside from some obvious disorder in the text. It is a spiritual gospel, but means to impart historical value. Grandmaison referred to the accuracy of its topographical details and saw its author as a Palestinian. So: the gospel is by John the apostle, who was first a follower of John the Baptist, then of Jesus; the gospel can be used as supplement or complement to the other gospels.

Grandmaison generally set aside Form Criticism, seeing in it too much ascription of creativity to the community. He found there some influence from Durkheim, while himself offering nevertheless some interesting and valid comments on the preservation of oral material, its forms and rhythms. The differences in the gospels might be seen as rhythmic variations.

The political and social history was characterized briefly, with description of the various parties in Judaism. There was expressed some appreciation for Pharisees, notwithstanding their "formalism" of the Law and "complacent casuistry" (274–75). On the intellectual setting, apocalypse was used by Jesus; it was symbolic, spoke of the End, was anonymous, and arose out of crisis. Its idea of the

---

97. Ibid., 42 n. 2.

kingdom of God had its origin in the covenant, in Yahweh's rule, and spoke of the new day coming that would bring justice and the great Assize.

The second volume takes up the ministry of Jesus. John the Baptist contributed the recognition of Jesus as God's well-beloved Son. Some disciples of Jesus came from John; the baptism was the official sanction of Jesus as the Elect One. The temptation was related by Jesus and is history.

Jesus was believed to be the son of Joseph and to have brothers and sisters (actually "cousins and near relatives," as the Aramaic would allow to be included under that terminology; Jesus had no uterine brothers). Jesus did not openly claim the messiahship, which would have been dangerous and misunderstood [though here Grandmaison denigrated Wrede and Bultmann]; he had to include the role of suffering. Jesus exercised first the role of prophet, but chose the name of Son of man. The background to that title lies in Daniel (messiah), is in 4 Ezra, even more so Enoch, and also in Ezekiel as the lowly man. So it was a title of enigma, a *mashal* of sorts, which can be seen in Jesus' usage. Hiding is appropriate, for not all saw Jesus favorably; his "friends" rejected him. [Here Grandmaison has Mary show up among those "relatives" in Mark because of her sensitivity to Jesus' suffering.][98]

Jesus' explained the parables to the disciples, the insiders.

Jesus taught the fatherhood of God; it has parallels in paganism and in Israel. God requires service, a filial relation, and exercises his providence. Francis of Assisi is the best commentary on the realism of Jesus' words. The beatitudes are found in two forms in Matthew and Luke and no doubt were uttered by Jesus in still other versions.

The kingdom of God is God's union with humankind that has begun already and leads to eternal life. It has both individual and social dimensions; it grows now and is also the spiritual Jerusalem. Peter is the guardian of the city gates; here and now it is the church. In John Jesus is the kingdom. Jesus also taught the love commandment, which may be difficult but not impossible to follow.

Jesus presented himself as master of the Law, even while also being faithful to it and taking liberty with it. He gave it its original design. His authority was expressed in his teaching, healing, and forgiving. As son to the Father he was also messiah. The scene at Caesarea-Philippi is genuine, especially in Matthew. To consider oneself Son of the Blessed was blasphemy and ground for condemnation. But Jesus knew himself to be the messiah. He was either what he said he was or he was a "pitiable visionary" (191). There was no development in his thought, either; the time of his public ministry was too short.

Grandmaison examined the religion of Jesus. He was a son to his Father; he prayed often and did the will of the Father, even unto death. He was not a mystic or penitent, yet he was a real man, but with no moral evil in him. He did not

---

98. Ibid., 33 n. 2.

repent and his relations with men were tender and authoritative. He accepted sinners, a scandalous practice defended in the parables of the prodigal son and the shepherd who leaves the ninety-nine and seeks the one. Yet also Jesus spoke as a prophet in harsh tones; that is the true idea of the kingdom, vehemence and tenderness combined.

Jesus' thought was semitic, couched in the language of wisdom, apocalyptic, parables, and aphorisms; his originality lay in how he transformed these forms. Also his deeds reflected his tranquility, his equanimity. His inner life offered "the most beautiful picture of the pure fulness of the divine Being that it has ever been men's privilege to behold" (236).

Looking at the "problem" of Jesus Grandmaison set forth an extensive history of critical views about Jesus, from the ancient pagans (Celsus) on through the Renaissance and the eighteenth-century rationalists (Voltaire, Bolingbroke, Reimarus, the liberals, Schleiermacher, Strauss, Renan, Nietzsche, Tyrrell, Loisy, Sabatier, and Couchoud). It was a learned survey, though in the end all were seen as driven simply by their presuppositions of a rationalist nature. Grandmaison himself inquired about the "mystery" of Jesus and argued for something transcendent in the historical Jesus. He offered a learned account of a variety of christologies, from Sanday to Seeberg to Herrmann, only to reject them all, while maintaining the Chalcedonian formula.

A series of notes on miscellaneous subjects ended the work (texts like Matt. 11:25 par., the Lord's Supper, the sanity of Jesus, Freud's notion of religion as a product of the libido, expressing social suppression of the sexual instinct in the form of myths, dreams, and legends, Jesus as an ecstatic, the value of the tradition about Apollonius of Tyana).

It was a work of learning and prodigious effort. Grandmaison knew his way around the theological maze of liberal Protestant thought, yet those works were paraded before the reader only to be dismissed. There really was no dialogue going on there; it was a one-sided conversation. In the end, for all the erudition evidenced in this work the reader inevitably would know what lay on the next page even before reaching it, especially so if one already knew the pronouncements of the Pontifical Biblical Commission.

By his own admission Père Lagrange's work on Jesus was not an attempt to do a "life," but rather to allow the gospels to speak as the only kind of life that can be written.[99] There are differences among the gospels, but in fact two manuscripts with slight differences witness independently to the same event. Still the problems of constructing a chronological account have led to foregoing a "life." Following his own earlier synopsis Lagrange sought to show that Luke's order and John's chronology were the best basis for a life, while Mark was the best representative of Petrine catechesis, Luke the best historian, and Matthew the better narrator of Jesus' discourses.

---

99. M.-J. Lagrange, *The Gospel of Jesus Christ,* 2 vols., trans. members of the English Dominican Province (Westminster, Md.: Newman Bookshop, 1938).

The work is a running commentary on the gospels, in actuality a sturdy defense of the veracity of the gospels' narrative. Peter's oral telling determined the shape of the gospel, from the baptism to the ascension, and in between Peter would relate the most significant events and utterances. Matthew the tax collector was known before as Levi and reinterpreted this story showing Jesus as the expected messiah. He wrote in Aramaic. At Rome Mark wrote down Peter's memories, his catechesis or oral teaching. Luke, though not an original disciple, took over Matthew's work, incorporating most of it into his own while improving some on the order. Matthew had been already translated by Greek-speaking disciples — at least its discourses — into Greek. Maybe Luke only possessed the discourse, but however that may have been, Matthew's order had little influence on Luke. The latter knew more of the ministry of Jesus in Judea than Mark. John knew all three of the other gospels, but wrote independently and gave the same material infrequently and according to his own reminiscence. He was more precise about times and places and provided more knowledge of such things.

The translator of Matthew was not slavish, sometimes giving the substance and was probably influenced by Mark. Mark and Greek Matthew were to be dated before 70; Mark and Aramaic Matthew much earlier. Luke, who used Mark, wrote his gospel before Acts that he finished in 67, the year of Paul's martyrdom, maybe even earlier.

Following these views of the origins of the gospels, the remainder of the book carries on a commentary on texts and issues. In fact, it looked very much like the pages of the *Revue biblique,* containing a vast amount of historical, archaeological, and topographical data, but rarely touching the text critically. There was, to borrow from an American folk song, never a "discouraging word" on Lagrange's range. There was also some fancy exegetical footwork, noticeable particularly where the elements of Catholic dogma were involved. Mary's reply to the Annunciation by Gabriel means: "I desire not to know a man." Probably also Joseph was of the same mind as Mary, so marrying him was no violation of her intent [two celibates joining in marriage].

Matthew's structured genealogy probably means he did not to intend to give a complete genealogy. Perhaps Luke's differences indicate that he was following a collateral line. The star suggests something like Halley's comet.

Jesus spoke Aramaic, though also he knew Greek and Hebrew.

The Gospel of John figures in the narrative. On the wedding at Cana: Jesus' comment to Mary really expresses honor — there is no need for them to intervene in the matter. The temple cleansing comes early; the placement elsewhere by the synoptics is of no significance. What matters is what Jesus did, not when. On Mark 3:21, it is general relatives who show up out of kindness to take charge of Jesus. The brothers are part of these general relatives.

The parables are comparisons, while allegories are a series of metaphors, each representing some further reality. Sometimes the two are mingled in Jesus. We should not tie Jesus down to the subtleties of Greek rhetoric. The parables primarily speak of the kingdom of God, which is the family of those called to perfection and who practice Jesus' words. It is a new order of things; it goes on, evolves, and finally terminates in a judgment and a separation.

Miracles happened as described.

In Mark 6:3 the underlying semitic terms could include cousins or more distant relations. James is a special problem. He is the same as Paul's brother of the Lord, but in reality is the brother of Joses, whose mother was also that Mary mentioned in Mark 15:40.

And so on. The commentary runs on, with often impressive display of learning and command of details, but also with the familiar emasculation of an intellect wedded to an unrelenting mistress.

The work of Jules Lebreton was also the climax of the author's work, he said;[100] its purpose was expressed by John 17:34, "Now this is eternal life: That they may know thee, the only true God, and Jesus Christ, whom thou has sent." It was a large book (460 pages, English) of two volumes, but essentially it was a commentary on texts from all four gospels, arranged according to the author's chronological scheme.

In the introduction Lebreton accepted all church tradition about the authors of the gospels (Mark was Peter's voice, John by the apostle, and so on) and saw the gospels as collective remembering by the apostles plus Mary and family members (infancy narratives). He granted that both Roman Catholic dogma and Form Criticism recognized oral tradition, but for the former the gospels are historical records witnessing to Christ, while for the latter it is the church that has created Jesus as messiah and Son of God. But he conceded that the gospels are driven by predominantly religious interests; the story they tell is one of salvation. Thus they emphasize the passion narrative. Each writer also emphasized different aspects of Jesus' ministry, so we have to make distinctions about the placement of material and the order of events (the temple-cleansing would be placed at the beginning, following John). But there are also problems of locating incidents and teaching and no chronological biography is possible.

Lebreton then set forth the chronological data available, with a degree of dancing through the problems (date of birth, length of the ministry), and concluded that the birth must have been 7 B.C.E., death on 14 Nisan 30 C.E., with a ministry of two or just above two years. In spite of the problems of establishing chronology, Lebreton found it possible to integrate material from all four gospels and arrive at a rather well-defined scheme, as follows:

> In January A.D. 28, Jesus was baptized and retired into the desert: in March He returned to the Jordan, visited Cana and Capharnaum; went up to Jerusalem for the Passover, drove the traffickers out of the Temple, and preached throughout Judea. In May, John the Baptist was thrown into prison, and our Lord went to Nazareth and Capharnaum by way of Samaria. In June came the incidents of the

---

100. Jules Lebreton, *The Life and Teaching of Jesus Christ Our Lord* (New York: Macmillan, 1950); original French edition *La Vie et L'Enseignement de Jésus Christ notre Seigneur* (Paris: Gabriel Beauchesne, 1934.) Lebreton was Professor at L'Institut Catholique, Paris.

disciples plucking the ears of corn, of the calling of the Apostles and the Sermon on the Mount. In November, we have the parable of the Sower; in December, Jesus stilled the tempest and went to Nazareth for the second time. In February, A.D. 19, occurred the sending of the Apostles; in March, the death of John the Baptist; in April, the Feeding of the Five Thousand, shortly before Passover; in June, Jesus went to Jerusalem for Pentecost and cured the paralytic; then, crossing Phenice and Decapolis, He fed the Four Thousand and went to Caesarea Philippi; at the end of August the Transfiguration took place. In October, Jesus was at Jerusalem for the Feast of Tabernacles, where He cured the man born blind; in December, He was there again for the Feast of the Dedication. In March, A.D. 30, He raised Lazarus, retired to Ephrem and returned to Jerusalem by Jericho. In April, at Passover, He was put to death (introduction, xxx–xxxi).

Lebreton then set about going through this scheme while dealing with the textual material. His analysis was accompanied by a sense of piety and devotion. The birth story "varies greatly" between the two sources (1), he noted, and said that we should not be surprised, but never really explained why we should not be surprised or what the variation meant. Instead he spoke about how natural it was for the evangelists to emphasize the central facts of salvation and to treat the birth as a kind of prologue to that, and only when people became curious could the birth information have been gleaned from Mary and the circle around her.[101] An analysis of the Johannine Prologue on the Logos was undertaken as the appropriate commentary on the birth narratives. Lebreton also found that Luke's narrative came from Mary and Matthew's from Joseph. Of the birth event itself he said, "Mary was not, like other mothers, exhausted by the birth of her child, and could face the first cares of motherhood alone." Of Jesus in his childhood we learn that "from the beginning He showed Himself fully conscious of who He was and of the line of action He must take."[102]

Of Jesus' relations we were advised that Mary had no children; the brothers of Jesus mentioned in the narrative are not half-brothers or children of Joseph, though Lebreton hedged a bit as to exactly whose children they were (sisters unknown, James and Joseph probably from some other Mary [Matt. 27:5; Mark 15:40]).

John the Baptist was the Precursor. His whole preaching centered on the coming of Christ. Jesus' own baptism was an act of humility and sanctified baptism. The temptation was related by Jesus himself to the disciples. He was aware of his messiahship, but it was a gentle and humble one. The Gospel of John fills in much of the relationship between Jesus and John. The first miracle was at Cana; Jesus' seemingly rude words to Mary were simply a declining of her request.

---

101. This obvious dodge inspires unanswerable questions: Why then did not the interrogators ask Mary some further questions, especially about those silent years? What kind of child was Jesus? Did he eat his soup and do his household chores? Or was he a dreamer who languished by the fields and flocks?

102. Lebreton, *Life and Teaching of Jesus Christ Our Lord*, 17, 27.

On the kingdom of God: Jehovah is the king of Israel and the world, but many refuse the kingship. The messiah's function is to inaugurate it now, to begin now, in the hearts of people and later to enforce it through judgment. It is a kingdom of justice and sanctity.

The Pharisees were mortal enemies of Jesus; all the synoptic controversy scenes are historical. After the healing of the paralytic the Pharisees began plotting Jesus' death. He came to free people from the terrible burdens laid on them by the Pharisees. He also chose thirteen of his own apostles and made Peter the head of the Apostolic College. Lebreton furnished characterizations of the apostles as tradition allowed.

The Sermon on the Mount (same sermon as in Luke) was an actual discourse, if only the leading points. The differences on, say, the beatitudes suggest two different preservations in the church of a single sermon. The beatitudes put forth the idea of the Christian life. The function of the Law was to prepare for the kingdom of God, to be a kind of teacher. Thus the Law was not to be abrogated, so Jesus said, until it had fulfilled its work.

In his parables Jesus introduced a new method, speaking one way publicly and another privately. To the Jews who were blind to the truth he spoke one way, knowing they would not understand, but in order to drive them to him, asking him for interpretations, as an act of grace. To the apostles he gave the truth, for they must pass it on. The allegorical treatments are original. The mustard seed and leaven show the growth of the kingdom.

Lebreton described the Judean ministry in meticulous detail, with large doses of Johannine material. There was no hint of a dichotomy in the way in which the Johannine Jesus and the synoptic Jesus spoke. Lebreton did find some "embarrassments" in the accounts of the Last Supper, but was ultimately undeterred by them. He opted for Nisan 14, yet wanted to hold the supper as also a passover meal. Perhaps Jesus anticipated the passover, celebrating early (also sacrificing the lamb early, on his own authority), though that could only be speculative. There was no problem imagining the foot-washing occurring at the same time. All those embarrassing cups at the supper (counting the western text of Luke) were reconciled by making Luke's first mention of them one of the paschal cups. The ransom idea prevailed in the Eucharist.

No protest was raised against anything in the trial narratives. The Sanhedrin acted illegally; Pilate acted reluctantly. The tomb events were followed by a narration of all the appearances.

Lebreton's work was certainly the least able of the three here described, as is likely evident from the summary. Reading it was a little like sitting through an overlong film, with all the doors locked. If frivolous prayers could gain a hearing, the reader would doubtless shout skyward for a merciful end.

There is a sadness about these works of Roman Catholics; a critical spirit was struggling to emerge in and from them, but could not do so. Nevertheless they preserved in that particular tradition a devotion to prodigious study and to a biblical scholarship as it was there understood. In time these pioneers would find a just succession, if too late for the likes of a Loisy or a Tyrrell. But such is the fate of those who go first down unfamiliar paths.

But now we must move on to new soil and an end ourselves, to see how Jesus appeared in public eyes and how he was managed in the hands of the sometimes barely competent and the untutored. It is an experience worthy of a lingering moment.

Chapter 9

JESUS AS PUBLIC ICON
Popularizing

Popularizing is often denigrated, especially in the academy. But, in fact, it is difficult to do well; at its best it communicates the results of serious scholarship to a literate public. At the least it requires a confident command of the field and a capacity to translate technical matters into something comprehensible to the ordinary reader. The Jesus story has always seemed to be a special target for popularizers, among whom are both the pious and those who fancy they have some knowledge worthy of public communication. There is, in fact, a considerable mountain of such works, and only the merest sample can here be examined. I have sought to present some examples from various cultures and times across the fifty years of this survey to indicate the variety and dimension of this literature. I have also set aside strictly fictional works,[1] and kept to the primary consideration that a work aim at a popular audience, whether composed by a scholar or not.

It is striking just how many of these works emanate from a generally liberal source; their authors are often moved by a desire to share some truth they feel they have come upon and need to express. They may wish to liberate their audience from a captive ignorance, or they may wish to liberate Jesus from his admirers in the church and so conceal an underlying anti-institutional motive. A few were composed in counterreaction to liberalism, wishing only to exalt Jesus in some sense. The expert who comes upon these works has the experience

---

1. One of the more enduring was Charles Sheldon's *In His Steps* (1896; New York: Grosset and Dunlap, 1935). A product of the social gospel movement, it recited the story of a congregation moved by a young man urging members always to consider "What would Jesus do?" before acting. Sheldon's work was widely published and reprinted over a lengthy time, though not until 1935 did a publisher agree to provide Sheldon some financial profit from his own work; it had first been printed in a local newspaper that failed to secure the appropriate copyright and so allowed the work to pass into the public domain. A new movement of young people inspired by Sheldon's book has recently begun circulating bracelets with the initials "W.W.J.D." on them. The movement has in turn generated a new book by the same title (*What Would Jesus Do?*) by Garrett Sheldon, great-grandson of Charles.

There are also works as widely diverse as Sholem Asch, *The Nazarene,* trans. Maurice Samuel (New York: Putnam's, 1939); or the Russian Dmitri Merezhkovsky, *Jesus Manifest,* trans. Edward Gellibrand (London: Jonathan Cape, 1935), and *Jesus the Unknown,* trans. H. Chrouschoff Matheson (New York: Scribner's, 1934), though the latter two more resemble mystical meditations on the Jesus story.

of seeing what has happened to his or her children; it is sometimes a painful business, but it is invariably interesting.

Otto Borchert

Among the earliest works was that of the German pastor Otto Borchert, whose book, *Goldgrund des Lebensbildes Jesu*, was sixteen years getting to press, but became widely read, though it appeared in English translation only in 1933.[2] The English title, *The Originality of Jesus*, better reflected the actual content of the work, which was a piece of conservative apologetics aimed at demonstrating the uniqueness of Jesus as portrayed in the gospel record. The author was a former businessman who had studied at Leipzig, Halle, and Wittenberg, and claimed to have had quite negative experiences in his education, especially in encountering Strauss, and wished to elaborate a different view. His basic thesis was that the community did not transform Jesus; rather, it was awestruck by him even when that portrayal ran counter to its own interests. So Borchert wished to show this element of "offense" in Jesus as the surest sign of the authenticity of the picture. It was a gigantic commentary on the principle of dissimilarity, though Borchert would not have recognized that characterization.

Jesus did not fulfill the messianic expectations and caused offense. He made himself divine and asked too much, attacking the temple, but also made himself too lowly, recommending taxes to Caesar, not opposing his arresters, and acting like a pitiful king. In other ways he was offensive: he was poor, a carpenter, from Nazareth — a nothing place — and associated with Samaritans. And not least was his scandalous death.

Jesus was not a great sage in the Greek sense; he was not Aristotle's noble-minded man. He also refused to return insult for insult and loved his enemies. Nor could he be Plato's philosopher-king. He also seemed to lack courage, fleeing from Herod, struggling in Gethsemane, and breaking down on the cross — unlike Socrates, who died a willing death. He did not even treat his mother well. None of that could have been invented by an admiring group of Gentiles or Jews. His disciples were offended at him; even after Easter they still clung to Judaism and the Law. Judas especially, but John the Baptist as well, was offended by him.

More modern people are no different, whether Frederick the Great or Nietzsche. Both the strong and the weak rebel against him. Jesus' humility, the company he kept, and his love of enemies are equally unacceptable.

The picture of Jesus was often changed to soften the offense. Among the hellenists the apocryphal gospels show that Jesus was invested with god-like features, especially in the stories of his childhood and his passion. The Germans

---

2. Otto Borchert, *Goldgrund des Lebensbildes Jesu: Eine apologetische Studie* (Braunschweig: Hellmuth Wollermann, 1900); English trans. *The Originality of Jesus*, trans. L. M. Stalker (New York: Macmillan, 1933). Borchert was pastor and inspector of schools, Westerhausen, Hanover. More biographical data are generally available on all authors in this chapter in the biographical appendix (Borchert excepted).

produced the Heliand, where Christ was portrayed as a rich and powerful German king, for its author could not stand the offense of the lowly Christ. Roman influence lives on in the Roman Catholic Church, which transformed him into the head of an institution emulating the model of empire. In the pope Jesus became a ruler; lowliness and service vanished, and in the place of poverty appeared pomp and wealth.

The offense Jesus gives is rooted in the actuality of his history. Certainly there are some problems of exaggeration, but we have only the picture given in the gospels on which to rely. Returning to the historical Jesus is futile; the search for some historical Jesus behind the gospels is unsettling to laymen and hopeless anyway, for no agreement among the scholars exists. We therefore should accept the gospel picture *en bloc:* "This likeness in its entirety is credible to us. The general impression is genuine" (123).

Sometimes miracles are also a stumbling block to the modern person. It is pointless to argue the issue of possibility; miracles were *necessary* in order to focus attention on Jesus and cover up the offense (as example, the resurrection overcame the scandal of the cross).

Jesus' claims also caused offense, especially his discourses about his status as divine Son and his origins with God. [Here Borchert appealed, as he often did, to the Gospel of John.]

But there is also another side to the picture of Jesus. If he gave offense, he also demonstrated his glory.

The image of Jesus set forth by Borchert pictured a unique life, but the gospel records escaped Borchert's hand critically unscathed; the supposed variations among them actually support historicity, for they amount to independent confirmation. The Gospel of John was composed by John the apostle, an eyewitness, who saw more deeply in his old age into the glory of Jesus and spoke with greater freedom than the other writers.

Citing such texts as Jesus' escape from the crowd at Nazareth, his attack on the temple, the power of his gaze, and the fact he never seemed to be ill, Borchert concluded that Jesus was physically impressive, robust even, had great power of endurance, and was never out of control. He also had "soul-gifts," such as courage — he knew how to die — but also beautiful anger, tenderness, kindliness, and a womanly feeling for others. He was open but enjoyed solitude, was mild but heroic, simple yet wise; he knew himself the judge of the world but remained meek and lowly.

He had a ready wit, was a great speaker, a poet, a marvelous conversationalist, and possessed a superb sense of realism and naturalism. He was a great thinker, and saw that natural law prevailed in the spiritual world as well. [Borchert derived that from Jesus' use of analogies from nature.] There is originality in his joining the twofold commandments of love of God and neighbor, in the Lord's Prayer, in his use of psychology and pedagogy, and in his stirring of social reform.

Even more impressive was his knowledge of God. He saw himself as a son to the Father, as in a natural relationship. His proclamation of God as Father whose nature is love was new and unheard of, for in Judaism God was distant and unapproachable.

Jesus had a rich prayer life. He drew inspiration from the scripture, but also realized he was its goal and end, and he refashioned it as necessary. He respected the legal ordinances of his time, but also saw no temple in the future and criticized Sabbath practice, fasting, and the like. Love was the one requirement. He revalued all values: the last are first, servants are above all, all neighbors are to be loved. He was moved only by love extended even to the enemy. And finally he offered his life for a hostile world.

Jesus elevated women and children, putting women on a level of equality with men. He had no aversion to the rich, even though he found them hard soil to cultivate and attacked their severity. He was also the friend of sinners and the humble, the nonobservant. He acted out of pity, out of the joy over finding the lost. He condemned sin with mercy; his love was earnest.

Jesus used the gifts of the world. He was called a wine bibber; he rejoiced in life and delighted in the beauties of nature. He never had a sense of world-weariness; he was innocent of the world in that way because he also knew himself to be its lord. He never married, for he was already living according to the laws of the kingdom; marriage was impossible for him, but not for others. He did not deny the duties of the world, but acted with restraint. No culture was an end in itself; humans were made for God, and culture for humanity.

Jesus is superior to Buddha and all the others. He had a consciousness of being Son in a unique sense, of having no beginning. He was also the messiah, yet not a revolutionary, a supernatural messiah, but a suffering servant–messiah. As Son of man he was human but also hidden messiah, for his kingdom was not the kingdom of traditional hopes. He spoke with authority, uttering the "Amen" at the beginning, prefacing his words with "I say unto you." He forgave sins, sent out disciples, and bestowed authority on his church. He was to be the judge of the world, with himself as the standard of judgment. The resurrection and ascension demonstrated his lordship over the world.

A sense of relief ensues upon closing the book. Although there are interesting points — some still being made, such as the use of "Amen," the sufficiency of the gospels' picture of Jesus for faith — and there is a cleverness about stealing the principle of nonconformity for apologetic purposes, yet in the end the book defeats itself in its own intent. The reader is lost in the overwhelming "glory" side of the picture, and the final impression is that of an uncritical work that leads not where its author wished, but to a discomforting discontent with a Jesus about whom everything can be said.

Alfred W. Martin

Americans seemed especially caught up in the effort to represent Jesus before the public, and an instance of a liberal work (1913) addressed to the public was that of Alfred W. Martin, *The Life of Jesus in the Light of the Higher Criticism.*[3] The book provided a spirited defense of the higher criticism and was rather well informed about its history and its procedures. Martin's main point was that criticism liberates, even as it necessarily destroys some things along the way. The life of Jesus served as illustration.

The birth stories have no value as history: "They are not histories of fact, but symbols of the quality of his person" (69). The virgin birth was added later. Jesus was probably born at Nazareth in 4 B.C.E. Nothing reliable about his childhood has survived. His education was probably at home and in the synagogue. He must have met many different kinds of people in Galilee.

Jesus began his work with John the Baptist and was conscious of a messianic calling. The temptation story is fanciful, though it may have a historical core in that Jesus retired for meditation. Jesus as a healer has multiple attestation and is based in actual history. He used a psychic approach; the healings are all understandable on that ground and nothing contradicts modern medicine. Other miracles are more bothersome, and can be interpreted symbolically, allegorically, or as parables. Noting the years of oral tradition that underlie the gospels, Martin observed that "we are justified in questioning only their competency, not their honesty, and the more startling the story they tell, the greater the amount of evidence required for us to believe it" (132). Then people believed that the miracles attested the divinity of Jesus; today we believe that the spiritual greatness of Jesus gave rise to the miracles.

Jesus shared the eschatology of his time, even though his interest was in the spiritual. He expected an apocalyptic kingdom and a judgment. We cannot modernize Jesus. We have, for example, to agree to his attack on the Pharisees, ugly as it sounds. And the socialist who finds socialism in Jesus distorts the record; Jesus was an eschatologist who anticipated the near End.

> He came not to readjust social conditions, not to attempt a reorganization of society on untried economic principles. He came solely to refine men's lives, to quicken in each individual the sense of his divine origin and the infinite possibilities for moral progress inhering in each, even in the very lowest. (175–76)

Jesus opposed Pharisees, hurling harsh accusations against them (Sabbath-keeping, purity laws). Hardness of Pharisaic opposition was a factor in his decision to go to Jerusalem, though still only a remote and indirect cause of crucifixion. Was his entrance into Jerusalem messianic? If so, that would mean he had abandoned the ethical and spiritual concept of messiahship in favor of the political one. He is pictured as the latter, but that was not his own view. The temple cleansing is true, an "act of heroic imprudence" (190), for it aggravated the Sadducees, who took him to Pilate and denounced him as a rebel. The grounds of accusation are not clear; the trial was illegal, and Pilate behaved

3. Alfred W. Martin, *The Life of Jesus in the Light of the Higher Criticism* (New York: D. Appleton, 1913). Martin was a leader of the Society for Ethical Culture, New York City.

cravenly. Jesus' death was the consequence of hostility from Pharisees and Sadducees, along with collusion from Pilate. Jesus died for his cause, which was to bring men from their sins and to establish moral living. His cry from the cross was but a momentary misgiving.

As to the resurrection, the evidence from the gospels is contradictory and varying, not sufficient to compel us to believe in a physical resurrection. There is Paul's mention only of appearances, but these earlier statements were displaced by the tomb stories. "Resurrection" at the time of Jesus and Paul meant a rising from Sheol, the Paradise section, and being made ready for the messianic End. So Jesus arose from Sheol and went to heaven, the "first fruits" to do so. From there he will return for the messianic kingdom. The real fact of this resurrection was the "resurrection" of the disciples from despondency and despair.

The appearances belong to the area of psychical research. "The day of controversy over a stupendous miracle of which the accounts are hopelessly contradictory has passed, and inquiry henceforth can concern only the appearances of Jesus to his disciples and to Paul" (245). At bottom the spiritual grandeur and personality of Jesus gave rise to the conviction that he could not still be in Sheol, but must have arisen to heaven. "For Jesus lived so grandly and so gloriously as to have made his disciples certain of his immortality and of the deathlessness of his cause" (249).

Jesus was no creator of a church, but Paul was. Jesus exhibited the religion of Judaism at its best: a religion of love, peace, mercy, and justice, only now universalized by Jesus. The movement after his death was concerned to promote him as the coming messiah soon to return to earth to inaugurate his kingdom. That was not his own view. So Jesus was not the founder of Christianity, Paul was. And Paul was a neurotic, nervous person capable of strange visions. Haunted by the death of Stephen and the message of Jesus that recalled the suffering servant of Isaiah, Paul came to the thought that perhaps the Nazarenes were right. In these circumstances the vision occurred. During a period of meditation and retirement he acquired new views of the crucifixion and resurrection. Jesus' death was an expiation; his resurrection was from death; the Law took on new value. Paul was thus the real founder of Christianity.

The liberal gospel is here evidenced in all its themes and was in fact stated with a clarity and vigor that mirrored almost exactly the ethos at the time. If it also condescended to the text here and there, and to Paul as well, then that, too, was a remarkably accurate rendering of a widely held view.

Bouck White

Contemporary with Martin was Bouck White, who was also familiar with the panoply of Jesus research, but was primarily interested in promoting a socialist perspective. White's book, *The Call of the Carpenter*, was published originally in 1911; it is marked by a significant degree of literacy in writing, is sometimes amusing, and sometimes rises to elegant levels. It also epitomizes his socialist position, for which he paid up personally (to borrow from Camus) a significant price, spending some time in prison for disturbing the peace and burning the flag.[4]

The world-context for his work was set out at the beginning; he saw a rising tide of democracy along with a decline in the church. The workers of the world are against the church because it is the possession of the propertied class. But the proletarian rejection does not include Jesus, who still commands loyalty.

The society into which Jesus came was characterized thus: "The Roman Empire was a world-wide confederation of aristocracies for the perpetuation of human servitude.... Economic exploitation was the end in view, the organizing purpose throughout" (7). Jesus' mother, Mary, was a patriotic soul aiming to "upheave" an empire; Joseph was a good man, a proletarian, who was stirred by Caesar's tax. Jesus was nourished not only on Mary's milk, but her revolutionary spirit as well. Jesus was a "working class agitator" (38). James (brother) and John (Baptist) and Jesus all came from the same root, Mary, the cause of their social conscience.[5]

The parables likewise spoke of social destitution; the poor, farmers, ordinary householders, widows, debtors and creditors inhabit their world. John the Baptist also denounced social evil, but he had no program. After baptism at John's hands Jesus began to announce something new: "Get a new mind; for the Restoration is at hand."[6]

The kingdom is the kingdom of self-respect, a proclamation to all the world to unite the proletarian masses against the capitalist oppressor. It is virtually the same as announcing that democracy is at hand. Its purpose is to give rulership and dignity to the common people. Economics is its primary interest.

The Pharisees had contempt for the masses, promoting class hatred. They were bitter enemies of Jesus. Jerusalem was really their center, while Galilee was the home of the proletariat.

As to Jesus' miracles, the nature ones are not susceptible of demonstration. Others were the consequence of Jesus exercising his personality on recipients, radiating from laws in the "cortex and medulla" (100). But still these are incidental; sickness arose from the social diseases of the masses. Jesus was "a cunning physician" who "practised in the school of hygiene" (102).

---

4. Bouck White, *The Call of the Carpenter* (Garden City, N.Y.: Doubleday, 1914). The 1914 date appears to be a reprint, with the original issued in 1911. White was Head Resident of Trinity House, New York, 1908–13, until dismissed for his socialism. He had also earlier published *The Book of Daniel Drew* (New York: Doubleday, 1910; reprint, Larchmont, N.Y.: American Research Council, 1965), which was not flattering to Drew and was given a hostile reception from Drew's family who attempted to have the book suppressed. Drew was one of those nineteenth-century capitalist barons who made (and finally lost) a fortune in steamship and rail travel and on Wall Street through hard-nosed economic maneuvers. His gift of $250,000 to his own Methodist Church founded Drew Theological Seminary in 1867. Drew's revivalistic religion seemed to be no barrier to his business practices. For more on White see the biographical appendix.

5. White inferred most of this from the Lukan hymns at Jesus' birth (the establishment of the rule, elevation of the poor and lowly).

6. White, *Call of the Carpenter*, 67.

Jesus' message was directed to the outcasts, the lost, and the socially disinherited. The Sermon on the Mount was addressed to laborers to weld them together (no fighting among yourselves, and so on); the purpose was to increase their militance against their oppressors. Such is not opposite to the proclamation of love, for true love cannot abide the despoilers of humanity. "Jesus sought to breed a type of man that would look oppression in the face and wring its neck" (107). The beatitudes (more original in Luke) express this movement toward the poor and destitute. The meek are the terrible meek, those who have subordinated personal need for the group and the common cause.

Jesus' enemies were those at Jerusalem, authorities like Herodians, Sadducees, and Pharisees; the latter were the churchgoers of the day, who also were politically quietistic and sought to maintain the caste system. Jesus was one of the "dregs" of society and he associated with the dregs.

Jesus was also humorous. He was like a child who never grew up. "A genius is one who is a child at forty," said White (123). As to politics, Jesus was sneaky. The saying about rendering to Caesar what is Caesar's had in view the Jewish folklore that no nation can be conquered until it accepts the coinage of the conqueror. So Jesus' saying meant: render back to the Romans everything that belonged to them and banish them from the land — an embargo on their coinage, nonparticipation with Rome.

On economics, everyone gets a chance in the New Order. The parable of the laborers in the vineyard speaks of living up to a contract. There is no flat equality, but there is equality of opportunity. Luke's version of the synoptic apocalypse pictures the social earthquake that Jerusalem's oppressors were about to feel.

Opposition was inevitable. Jesus trained missionaries against the time of his own passing. He assumed also the title of "Christ" and thereby became a divine man to his followers. In Jerusalem he mounted an attack on the temple — a popular, social protest that made Jesus the hero of the city. The temple was basically a financial institution providing lucrative positions for the priests, who were themselves traders, financiers, property owners, and colluders with Rome. Jesus was not rejected by his nation, but his invective against the leaders led them to capture him at night, away from the people.

The last supper recapitulated the Exodus, that event of liberation under Moses, who had unfortunately become "embalmed" into the orthodoxy of the present "as is done in every age," observed White. "Your true conservative is he who worships a dead radical" (170). So Jesus actually bid his disciples to celebrate him as a memorial of a Moses-like liberation. The gospel accounts (especially John) picture Jesus as a kind of poser, an actor who knows all in advance and plays his part well, who in effect committed suicide. But in fact Jesus fought against death. Judas was not a Galilean and therefore could be bribed by Caiaphas. When Jesus went out of the city to escape possible assassins it was too late; Judas had given him away.

The trial took place before the masses had awakened and learned of his fate. A procurator like Pilate was generally a "slave driver over an entire province"

(170). But his wife was more sympathetic; many women were attracted to Jesus and they above all needed a deliverer (their position in society put them among the oppressed). Pilate, however, capitulated to the "temple set," even knowing that "an uncomfortable half-hour is awaiting him in the house as soon as she gets the news" (181). Rome put Jesus to death with the help of a few Romanized renegades among the privileged class of Jews.

Crucifixion was intended for slaves and used deliberately to intimidate, some-times for very small reasons. "A crucifixion every so often was good policy on the part of a large slave owner" (185). Jesus' message of self-respect ran counter to a system based on human degradation. Joseph of Arimathea's role is to be accred-ited because, though a rich man, he understood that wealth did not supersede human rights. "Bad Friday" was the greatest of crimes, with long consequences for many. Mary and John were present at the crucifixion.

As to resurrection, "Jesus dead was more alive than Jesus living" (199), how-ever one explains things. The disciples fled, that is, they ran to the city to rally the crowds. The people seem to have gathered in the afternoon and rioted; the temple veil was torn and the whole city shaken. The followers subsequently grew rapidly (Acts), and the movement began to spread beyond the bounds of Judea.

White continued his story with some not-so-flattering reconstruction of the post-Easter period, involving Paul's influence. The revolution did not come; Rome annexed Christianity. The whole thing was started by Paul, who rein-terpreted the movement to make it acceptable to Rome. Paul was a hellenist, a Pharisee, and a Roman, certainly not a Galilean. In fact, he had opposition from the Galilean wing (Galilean democracy opposed Pauline Roman imperialism). An imperial church grew, with Jesus as a new imperator. This amounted to a "Pharisaic assumption of superiority over the Galilean disciples" (231). Paul suf-fered persecution, but at the hands of the Jews, not Rome. He actually preached passivity to the proletariat and condemned personal, not social sin. Paul also ignored Mary, with the attitude typical of a hard Roman whose ideal was subju-gation. Rome finally killed him — like Cicero — when it had used him fully. It accorded him a nice citizen's death (beheading).

Other philosophers took up the Romanizing of Jesus and metamorphosed him into a cult of submissiveness. Constantine was its ratifier. Christianity then came onto the side of the privileged. Grafted onto Jesus' original simplicity was a doc-trine of monarchism and metaphysics. The church then became a partner in oppression.

The problem of the church today is not its lack of evangelism, but centrally, its doctrine of the Trinity, from which flows a "benign paternalism."[7] Ritschlian-ism rejected the Trinity and substituted the fatherly God. But the universe is not fatherly; nature is indifferent. Yet democracy sees the world as an ongoing fight, and we can draw comfort from Jesus the worker as our Companion.

---

7. Ibid., 279. The irony here should not escape the reader; White was head of Trinity House.

The Trinity also leads to despotism. The Christian's entanglement with theism was fatal, providing a bias toward an aristocratic structure. Theism puts at the top of the universe a God who created, forms, owns, and runs everything. It is boss-ism on a cosmic scale, and it leads to subservience on earth. So Fatherhood has to be transformed into "elder brotherhood" (290), for fatherhood is the expression of the patrician class, the *pater.*

The historical Jesus is still the charter of the church.

White's work commands some respect, if not for the kingdom of self-respect, for which he should have known better; yet he did know his way around critical and historical issues, even if they were submerged under the socialist umbrella. But, after all, he was not the first to enlist Jesus in his cause, and there is something avant garde about his thought, as still there are those not yet willing to forgive the church for having taken in Constantine, or, perhaps better, having been taken in by Constantine. The picture of Jesus that he constructed remains a powerful, if exaggerated, witness to just how little of the — maybe original — peasant Jesus has survived in the record.

Calvin Weiss Laufer

It would be hard to imagine a starker contrast between two graduates of the same institution (Union Theological Seminary) than Calvin Weiss Laufer and Bouck White. Though himself a noted hymnologist Laufer lacked White's sophistication and his biblical work largely contented itself with declaiming on Jesus' greatness and glory, so much so that it takes the prize as the purest exemplar of what I call — tongue firmly in cheek — a "gee-whiz-Jesus" book. This inclination to exalt Jesus as the founder and promoter of western civilization was widespread in the early part of the century and even lingered all along the way to mid-century. Laufer's book was *The Incomparable Christ.*[8]

According to Laufer, "There is more of Christ in the world to-day than in any previous period of history." And "modern culture has a Christian trend because Christ rules within it toward that end" (7).

The constant theme was the greatness of Jesus, how the world and humankind were drawn to him. The work was thoroughly sermonic and little critical, even though it suggested otherwise. Bousset was occasionally quoted, but without attribution, as was also "John Weiss" (e.g., 50). But then Laufer appealed to the Gospel of John to discuss what Jesus thought of himself. A slightly judicious reader would know that he or she was not in the domain of the critic.

The first chapter, bearing the title of the book itself, very much represents the whole. Laufer began, "His towering genius and uniqueness, incomparable worth and philanthropy, defy analysis and description" (14), but that did not deter him from giving them. On and on the panegyrics went. Some samples:

---

8. Calvin Weiss Laufer, *The Incomparable Christ* (New York: Abingdon, 1914). See the bibliographical appendix for more.

"He is the molding energy of modern civilization, so diffusive and pervasive, so efficacious and ubiquitous, that we cannot but feel the pulse of his incomparable life surging underneath" (25). Well underneath apparently, as in the same year of Laufer's book the Great War began, the war to end all wars. Followers of the incomparable Christ set about gassing and otherwise killing one another.

Jesus thought he was in communion with God (John). He thought he was necessary to man (more John). He knew himself to be the messiah. He is guide and teacher, the very life of humankind, the supreme example of manhood and womanhood. The Incarnation elevates our nature; we are all sons of God. It gives us kinship to Jesus and means that God is with us in all important relations (birth, marriage, death).

Jesus is the key to God's character. God knows us, has compassion on us, watches over us, and brings us salvation. Laufer declined any particular theory of atonement, refusing to "wander in the jungle of theology, philosophy, and metaphysics" (97), indeed, any jungle resembling thought. Focus instead, he said, on the results of the atonement. God and the sinful world are brought together; God identifies with the world and exposes its sin through the cross. Jesus elevated children; they should receive proper treatment in the family. He also had a special concern for the castaway; here again is seen Jesus' greatness. "Others might consign them to the scrapheap of the world's dumpage; but not he" (129). Jesus cared about them because he saw their possibilities. "The lost prodigal may yet become the favored son of the fold." The world is awakening to "the value of the world's dumpage" (131). Laufer illustrated with the example of people making money from running garbage operations. Society is obligated to act because most castaways got that way because of earlier misfortunes. Love seeks the lost.

Jesus' spiritual supremacy is clear; he is the greatest. We see greatness in ourselves, but how much more in Jesus. But [a dark thought entered] what about all those grim events in the world? We need them to teach us. The storm beat on the disciples so they could learn something; San Francisco needs to learn from the earthquake that gold is not everything; God lies behind the cloud; the eagle fouls the nest so that the young may leave and fulfill their destiny.

The cross is the spiritual magnet of the world. Everywhere the cross, once the symbol of torture and shame, now draws men to Jesus, because it is the expression of love. Jesus could have used his power to avoid the cross, but went straight to it. Tragedy makes love more real.

Jesus enriches life; "Civilization is a commentary on Jesus Christ" (215), so much has he influenced everything. He has taught us that God is our father: "This is what Jesus said, as he thought of the mystery of life, pondered its gigantic forces, and felt the compulsion of its laws: 'My children, when these thoughts arise, say, "Father"'" (219). Jesus makes us feel at home in the world — the universe, our home, given by the Father to his children. He also points us to our immortality.

So ended the book in hymnic praise. The naively pious reader doubtless sighed with pleasure; the critical reader sighed otherwise.

Mary Austin

A more eloquent work appeared in the following year. By the *littérateur* and feminist Mary Austin, it was titled *The Man Jesus: Being a Brief Account of the Life and Teaching of the Prophet of Nazareth.*[9] It was composed with literary skill and betrayed its acquaintance with the critical questions of a generally liberal position.

Called at his baptism, Jesus underwent the temptation in which he refused the traditional role of the messiah. He practiced healing and preached the kingdom. He borrowed the title "Son of man" from Enoch, but by it he meant himself as merged in his corporate or social being. In that sense he claimed to forgive sins, that is, persons forgiving one another. The kingdom message had variations and new themes. Jesus meant to teach the relation of God and humankind, and one person to another (brotherhood). He did not at first see himself as messiah, only from Caesarea-Philippi onward. His ministry was that of a prophet. He set himself against the formalism of the Pharisees and scribes.

Mark supplied the outline. The geography and chronology were taken seriously by Austin, with the narrative material seen as essentially reliable. Some examples: after narrating the Markan account of the walking on the sea, Austin said, "So Mark sets down what he recalled of what Peter told him" (92). Yet also a critical attitude was taken: "We believe the miracles of healing because we have known of cures being accomplished in our own day, and we do not believe in walking on the water, because it isn't done among our acquaintances" (93). On the other hand the Transfiguration received this treatment:

> While Jesus was wrapt from himself did a white flash of his burning spirit strike across to them? Such things are possible. Or was it the alpen glow, that most transcendent of all the visible manifestations of God, flooding down from Hermon, touching all things with its divine transfiguration? (105)

A degree of romanticizing appeared:

> Art has done too much for this man, to paint him forever tried, scourged, forever a-dying. He was not only a man of the small towns, but of the hills, the open road. He is seen at his best here, striding a little ahead of his companions, bronzed, hardy, the turban off to catch the mountain coolness, the long hair blown backward from the rapt countenance, and over him a higher heaven than had yet lifted upon man. (100)

And, as well, Jesus represented more advanced views on women:

> Here, too, must have been established [final journey] that acceptance of women in the Father, so unequivocal that all Paul's prejudice could not afterward controvert it; he admitted them to argument, he permitted them to sit in privileged places. It does not appear that he anywhere expressed himself as opposed to any of the

---

9. Mary Austin, *The Man Jesus: Being a Brief Account of the Life and Teaching of the Prophet of Nazareth* (New York: Harper, 1915). A revised version was printed as *A Small Town Man* (New York: Harper, 1925).

current notions of sex inferiority; rather to conduct himself as if he had not known such distinctions to exist. . . . Themselves in bondage to the habit of their upbringing, the women of his following probably took less than he would have allowed them; it is not recorded that he ever refused any one of them what she asked. He included them, good and bad, in that democracy of the spirit which established a minimum value for every soul of both sexes and all classes. (129–30)

There was some slipping around the issue of the resurrection, Austin speaking about Jesus' appearances as though he just revived. She observed that the body was in good condition, the wounds were not necessarily fatal, the spear is mentioned only in John (a late gospel, second century) and that blood flowed from the wound, and blood does not flow from a dead body. Besides, Jesus was hale and hardy and so could have revived in the tomb, even though we cannot say for sure. She went on to describe Jesus' subsequent meeting with his disciples, and said:

He expected to come again after death to effect the reorganization of society on Messianic lines, but there is no evidence that his own reappearance in the frame and fashion in which he had first preached was either anticipated or understood by him. He believed that he had been dead and was alive again.

At some point he parted from the disciples and they interpreted it as an ascension (Acts).

A last part spoke of the ongoing relevance of the kingdom that Jesus preached: a kingdom of brotherhood, of communion with God, and of a society governed by such. A kingdom "up to us" (201), that is, whether we will give service or not. A particular political program is not important:

He believed in man and in God the Father, friend of the soul of man. He believed in the future, but he believed also in Here and Now. He believed that the ills of this world are curable while we are in the world by no other means than the spirit of Truth and Brotherliness working its lawful occasions among men. . . . For Christianity is not a system of theology, but a way of life in which the validity of your relation to God is witnessed in your relation to your neighbor. (212, 214)

It is a literate work, has some critical material in the mix, and possesses a "relevance" without posturing. Other works more technical could not lay claim to much more.

The decade of the twenties produced a still greater abundance of popular books, whose variety can be seen in works that range from the literary figures, Rollin Lynde Hartt and Robert Keable, on through the Italian Giovanni Papini, to the American businessman Bruce Barton and the Englishman J. Middleton Murry.[10] We will look at each in chronological turn.

---

10. Even so there are necessarily many omissions, such as the widely popular book by Robert Bird, *Jesus, the Carpenter of Nazareth* (New York: Scribner's, 1891); it was reprinted often in the 1920s. It was primarily a child's book and marked by the peculiar use of Elizabethan English.

Rollin Lynde Hartt

The book by Rollin Lynde Hartt, *The Man Himself,* clearly traded on liberal im-
pulses.[11] The author said he had been reading the Bible and came upon a strange
figure at the end:

> Toward the end, a sublime figure emerges — a figure so incomparably majes-
> tic that not even the admixtures of legend and metaphysics in his legend —
> no, nor the theological addenda contributed by primitive and naïvely incautious
> propagandists — can hide his greatness. (vi)

Hartt spoke of a young rabbi who saw himself as the messiah, who had first to
fill the role of suffering servant, and then would come on the clouds of heaven
as the Son of man. The church has pasted him over with other credentials,
covering up "the supreme religious genius of all time" (7).

His mission was to warn of the impending end and to infuse a new spirituality
into his time and people. The Jews were caught up in legalism and literalism.
Jesus claimed to be a prophet, though there is no prophetic call story; there were
also no politics and Jesus was no patriot — the end was too near anyway. For
the same reason he wrote nothing, thus exposing himself to legend-making and
god-making.

He did practice healing (psychotherapy). He required faith and used suggestion. His miracles were employed for persuasive purposes, but they were all
according to natural law.

Jesus never married, and family did not interest him. The reason again was
the imminent end. He did not forbid marriage, but was harsh about divorce. He
was mistaken about his second coming and the near end.

Jesus was not a socialist and he had impractical ideas about property. He was
against laying up treasure and wealth, and had no discernible interest in labor
or the slave question. He was no economist or sociologist. The kingdom could
have meant different things — the company of his followers, something within
oneself, or the messianic rule. The nearness of the kingdom was why Jesus had
no concern for economics, why he was pacifistic. We do not know that he was
opposed to war; he actually said nothing on the subject and was even ambivalent
about violence. The world would only be reformed at the end, at the coming of
the kingdom.

Jesus was no supporter of women's rights and offered nothing on the alcohol
question. His was a provincial mind; he accepted the concepts of Satan, angels, demons, and reincarnation (John=Elijah). The virgin birth came from later
theologians, who also gave us the idea of Jesus as the pre-existent Logos. It was
easy to be deified in that time, but Jesus himself never claimed to be a god and
instead acknowledged his humanness. He thought he was Son of God, but only
as a human messiah.

---

11. Rollin Lynde Hartt, *The Man Himself* (Garden City, N.Y.: Doubleday, 1923). Hartt had been
educated at Andover Newton Theological Seminary, but spent most of his career as a writer.

Nicea produced the trinity, which cannot be found in the New Testament, much less in Jesus himself. Jesus did speak of the Spirit, by which he meant the life of God in the soul of persons, a divine indwelling. The modern view of the natural world can identify with this, for now we know that all matter is alive, of the same substance. Truth is one. God is god of things visible and invisible. Hartt credited Jesus with this insight, which showed "how great he was" (102).

Jesus taught the new birth, a revolutionary idea. It expressed newness of life, unlike the old ways, of which Hartt wrote:

> Jehovah, a magnified business man, was a bargainer. Provide him with the smell of burning meat, worship him in accordance with an exceedingly high-church ritual, and obey ten thousand taboos, some of which were moral, and he would give you long life, perennial health, prosperity in your ranching ventures, success in your quarrels, and a place in the sun for your country at the expense of the rightful inhabitants, on whom he had no pity. Disobey, and all manner of calamities would befall you. (105)

The Fatherhood of God was supremely grasped by Jesus, indeed, he was the first to do so, as the Jews combined with it other ideas of God's wrath, his anger, and so on. Jesus proclaimed God as purely love. Jesus taught eternal damnation, but since he expected it to occur soon with himself as judge, we can ignore that. We should focus instead on Fatherhood and on the thought that at bottom all is Spirit or love. We can forgive Jesus his mistakes and thank him for his achievements. He was the first truly to grasp human nature also; he saw men as sons of God.

He was a great teacher, popular with people. He spoke parables and aphorisms. He was a mystic, but not a dreamer. He could also be assertive, as in the temple cleansing, demanding the new righteousness. Jesus was himself a lawyer, but he was angered by the substitution of propriety for principle, by fussy legalism. He also attacked law itself and emphasized righteousness of motive. He substituted the love commandment for the whole law. He also attacked the Pharisees, even as he loved his enemies. There is no inconsistency there, for love is not liking, as is seen in the parable of the Good Samaritan.

Some say Jesus was an unrealistic dreamer. His maxims about wealth and money are irrelevant to economics, and even destructive. So, said Hartt, ignore them. They are part of the expectation of the End. "He intended those maxims about property for Galilean yokels and villagers of the First Century, A.D., and for them alone" (172).

Jesus neither fashioned nor contemplated a new social order. He was concerned with reconstructing the individual. He had nothing to say about labor and capital. His end-expectation was the reason, though it is true that reconstructing individuals leads to reconstructing nations.

Jesus did believe in immortality and no doubt envisioned a literal heaven above. Belief in the three-story universe was common then, Hartt said, but we have outgrown it now. Jesus also believed in Hell, a physical reality for the wicked, from which there was no escape. He likely got his idea of himself as judge from John the Baptist, whom he regarded as Elijah (who was also his cousin). As for us moderns we may "content ourselves by recognizing that he [John] was unworthy to unloose the latchet of the Nazarene's shoes and quite mistaken about hell" (211).

Jesus' death as a sacrifice for the sins of all did not come from Jesus himself. This theological plan of salvation is morally abhorrent; yet Jesus did think of dying for his own idea, of obedience to his vision. He then planned his own death, and goaded the Jewish authorities into turning him over to Pilate. He martyred himself. He used violence in the temple attack for effect. His death was tragic and futile.

Jesus' body was buried in an unmarked grave where no disciples could know of it. Bodily resurrection tales arose, Jesus became legendized, and a movement started. Reports of seeing him led to the tales, and soon a new world religion began.

Jesus envisioned no world mission, but Paul did. He saw the universality of the religion and implemented it. He was a "bad theologian — few have been worse" (248) and today people who are rejecting Christianity are actually rejecting Paul's gospel, not Jesus'.

What would Jesus think if he could visit a modern church? He would be astounded to find no synagogues, but a new religion opposed to Judaism and worshiping him and praying in his name; he would be equally amazed to find a new organization (bishops and more), with sacraments of communion and baptism. We can imagine that he would approve only if it all led to greater obedience.

We can still today cling to God as ever present in humanity, in the universe, and as embodied love for his children, with ourselves as his sons. Doubt gives rise to genuine faith and allows "the man himself" to appear.

The liberal perspective is here given a voice, a voice with a harsher edge in the dismissal of so much in the name of mythology and legend. At the same time Schweitzer's eschatological Jesus rules and tends to render all else irrelevant. A certain condescension in the name of modernism prevails over the text, while, paradoxically, Jesus himself — cleaned up and shorn of his first-century ignorance — is reclaimed as the ethical hero of that same modernism.

Giovanni Papini

The Italian man of letters Giovanni Papini produced his *Storia de Christo* in 1921, with the English translation in 1923.[12] The latter went through twenty-one printings by 1925 and lived a lengthy literary life. The author's introduction says that he aimed to write something literate, something cultural, neither pious

---

12. Giovanni Papini, *Life of Christ*, trans. Dorothy Canfield Fisher (New York: Harcourt, Brace, 1923). Papini was born in 1881, was mostly self-educated, and went through a passionate atheism before returning to his Catholic faith, having discovered that only through religion could sanity be given to the world.

nor scholarly, for "the pious writers are unable to lead men to Christ, and the 'historians' lose Him in controversy" (9). So he meant to compose something by a layperson for laypersons that would appeal to those outside the faith.

Papini took as sources all the gospels, plus some of the Logia and *Agrapha*, some apocryphal texts carefully used, and he acknowledged nine to ten (nameless) modern works.

The birth stories are all literally true; Papini described in voluptuous phrases the appearance of the magi, the shepherds, the conditions of the stable, Herod's perfidy, and all the rest. He managed some speculation over Jesus' boyhood and youth, his work in the carpenter's shop, and his learning to think of God as his Father — the new and innovative idea of Jesus. The background in the Old Testament was sketched, starting with that innocent couple in the garden of paradise and continuing on up to the (then-) current conditions of Jewry. With more than a whiff of anti-Semitism, Papini spoke of this people who still rule over nations with money and its Bible, "while the progeny of those god-killers has become the most infamous but the most sacred of all the peoples" (46).

Jesus went to John the Baptist to fulfill the prophecy about the precursor of the messiah, not to purify himself. He afterwards fought off Satan; he refused Satan's offer of the kingdoms of the world, for his kingdom was not to be of this world, but was rather "in us" (68). After John's death he began his own preaching of the kingdom. Its time is always at hand; it was described so: "Most men are beasts. It is Christ's will that these beasts become saints. This is the simple and ever-living meaning of the Kingdom of God, and the kingdom of Heaven" (73). Nicodemus served as illustration (the new birth, the transformation of the soul).

Jesus preached in Capernaum and Nazareth. Papini pictured effusively all those showing up at the synagogue to hear him: property owners, peasants, fishermen, the poor. Especially the poor heard the good news.

The Sermon on the Mount was examined meticulously. The beatitudes describe the citizens of the kingdom; the values of the world are reversed (though just being poor, as in the first beatitude, is not enough to guarantee the kingdom). The antitheses were directed to the source of action; Jesus emphasized the intention, feeling; imagining adultery is the first step in committing it. He also repudiated the old law of retaliation and ordered nonresistance to evil. It is a repugnant command that few have actually ever followed, but it is the way of Jesus. Even if one is at the point of death "if he does not love his slayer, he has no right to call himself a Christian" (111).

The love commandment was not new — Papini cited parallels from Confucius to Philo and beyond — but only Jesus extended it to include even the enemy. "This is the greatest and the most original of Jesus' conceptions" (121). Love is the means for transforming men from beasts into saints. The Lord's Prayer was examined in similar detail, but with no hint of its eschatological import.

Jesus did miracles reluctantly. He was not unique as a miracle worker, for others also healed and did "miracles." On the resuscitations from the dead: Jesus never claimed to awaken the dead, only to awaken persons (referring to their being asleep). Death was only a sleep, deeper than usual sleep, aroused by love. As to events like the wine-to-water wedding at Cana, Papini denigrated the rationalists as "Voltairian vermin" (143) who missed the real transformation produced by Spirit over matter and the message that a new epoch was beginning. The fig-tree cursing is a gloss on the Lukan barren fig-tree story. The bread and fish miracle happened twice.

The parables of the king's son's wedding and the banquet are two different parables. Other parables (seed) were explained by Jesus to the disciples. The lesson of the prodigal son is the greater rejoicing in heaven over one repentant sinner than the safety of the ninety-nine. The samaritan speaks of the neighbor as the one who suffers and needs help.

Jesus made disciples or, better, he suffered the burden of them. "Before being tormented by his enemies, He gave himself over to be tormented by his friends" (177). They deserted him, failed to understand him, one betrayed him. Peter was called the rock, but that referred as much to the hardness of his head as to his firmness of faith. Yet he was the first to recognize Jesus as the Christ and this primacy cannot be canceled.

Jesus was a poor man of infinite riches. Wealth is a terrible master; voluntary poverty gives the only true wealth. The rich can enter the kingdom when they have made themselves voluntarily poor. On taxes, Jesus said to give back to Caesar what belongs to him, that is, his coin which he has minted. Marriage is a "concession to human nature and to the propagation of life," while celibacy is a "grace, a reward of the victory of the spirit over the body" (211). Jesus was celibate because he gave all for the love of all. Jesus denied his family, but did not mean to deny Mary, only to say that now he belonged no more to the little family at Nazareth, but to the larger human family.

Women loved Jesus, and he loved them without touching them. He accepted them in a way that was quite different from their treatment in that time. The disciples did not always understand (the samaritan woman story); they did not realize that the church would yet make a woman the link between the Son and the sons. The story of the woman caught in adultery is historical; other women were prominent in Jesus' ministry (Mary, Mary Magdalene, Martha, the woman wiping his feet with tears).

Caesarea-Philippi founded the church, based on Peter's faith. The passion predictions are all true. Three times already "they" tried to kill Jesus (Nazareth, first temple cleansing, Feast of Dedication). He came the last time to Jerusalem, entering on an ass, a symbol of strength in antiquity. Jesus asserted his claim to be the Christ, in effect a declaration of war. The first assault was on the temple; Jesus went to destroy it and its values (gospel against the Torah, love against the letter). The house of God had become the house of Mammon. The priests had a lucrative business there, as well as the traders and business leaders. Jesus offended them all and attacked the scribes and Pharisees as well. The latter were denounced as "hypocrites," who knew "all the words save one, the word of Life" (257).

The discourse on the Last Things was a second Sermon on the Mount. All the predictions are factual: Jesus spoke of the end of the Jewish kingdom and the end of the old world; his reappearance meant the start of the new kingdom.

Jesus offended all the powerful in Jerusalem — priests, vendors, bankers, merchants, anyone profiting from the temple activities. He had already been at risk for some time. Herod's threats earlier may have sent him north to Caesarea Philippi. At Jerusalem the priests, scribes, and Pharisees laid traps for him, and the uneasy crowd surrounded him with spies. "The wolves of the Altar and of business arranged a meeting of the Sanhedrin to reconcile law with assassination" (278). Judas solved the problem of when and where to act. His reasons remain hidden in the mystery of redemption.

Jesus washed the disciples' feet at the last supper, which was also a Passover meal. [Papini discreetly passed over chronological problems.] Jesus is present — a real presence — in every particle of the bread; his blood obliterated the old covenant and changed wine into blood, for all humanity.

Papini discoursed at length on what the cup was that Jesus asked to pass in Gethsemane. Perhaps, he said, it was the wrongs of others done and yet to come — Jesus would spare his followers that pain. Everything else followed: arrest, appearance before Annas, Caiaphas, and Pilate. All the gospels were melded together.

The trial was merely a ratification of the murderous intent in the hearts of the priests. Jesus was condemned as a blasphemer and a false prophet. Papini described in rancorous detail the abusing of Jesus.

Papini rehearsed Pilate's history, with scenes from the Gospel of John, and speculated on Claudia Procula's interests (Pilate's wife, the name from the Gospel of Nicodemus), then recounted Herod's involvement. Barabbas was a rabbinic student, as his name shows (Bar-rabban, son of the Master) and a Zealot, an assassin. He went free while Jesus was condemned.

The drama played out. Jesus was taken to the site of crucifixion, stripped naked, and three nails (for strength) driven into each palm. His feet, soles forced up against the beam, were nailed to the wood. Abuse followed, along with the exchange with the thieves. Water and blood flowed from Jesus' side. Joseph and Nicodemus came to recover the body; they struggled to draw out the nails, then laid the body on Mary's knees before carrying it to the tomb. The women cleansed and washed the body; it was perfumed by Nicodemus, then wrapped in linens (all in the darkness after sunset).

Papini described all the appearances in imaginative detail, with no hint of any problems in the text, right down to the ascension. Jesus is still with us and "every day we raise our weary and mortal eyes to that same Heaven from which He will descend in the terrible splendor of His glory" (408).

So ends the book. The temptation arose, after the pattern of weary scribes as recorded in their colophons, to praise God. It is an extremely verbose work. Papini never used one word where three would do. His was the work of one impassioned by a newly refound faith rescued from a wasted previous life; and he clearly had read quite a lot of history and wrote with a poetic flair that must have enthused his readers then, though, for my taste, it is often strained and stretched for effect. The translator, Dorothy Canfield Fisher, noted with some apology that she had excised some material from the text as unnecessary for the intended audience. It is unfortunate for the work that her impulse did not lead her farther along that path. More specifically unfortunate was that a kindlier editor did not tone down the anti-Semitisms.

Bruce Barton

A work of a quite different sensibility was that of Bruce Barton, *The Man Nobody Knows: A Discovery of the Real Jesus*.[13] Barton was the son of a dirt-poor (or so Barton represented) Tennessee preacher and he rose to considerable heights of wealth and fame through his business acumen in advertising and in his literary activities on the side.[14] His Jesus book sold in the thousands of copies and even inspired a film — a four-reeler no less — that found a wide reception in churches. What lay behind such an appeal?

Certainly there was a unique line of approach to Jesus. What Barton "discovered" was that Jesus himself was simply the greatest businessman and formulated all the basic rules of successful business and advertising. A more American Jesus could hardly be imagined.

The author explained how as a little boy he was sick of hearing about loving a meek and mild Jesus, a sissified Jesus, and that only years later did he revisit the gospels and there discover this amazing physical figure who was so successful that he had built a grand organization on a worldwide scale from a handful (twelve) of nobodies. It was this Jesus that Barton wished to present to the world.

His purpose, Barton said, was not to provide a biography, but to paint a picture, for which he would wander freely through the gospel material, using incidents as appropriate. So he imagined a Jesus at 30 feeling himself outgrowing Nazareth, like many another great man; hearing from businessmen about John, he went to him and had a fulfilling moment, only to be trailed thereafter by doubts, from which he would eventually emerge a winner. "The youth who had been a carpenter stayed in the wilderness, a man came out."[15] What were his

---

13. Bruce Barton, *The Man Nobody Knows: A Discovery of the Real Jesus* (Indianapolis: Bobbs-Merrill, 1925; copyright Crowell Publishing, 1924). See biographical appendix.

14. The book here considered was Barton's most famous, but not the first time he had plunged into the Jesus arena. See his *A Young Man's Jesus* (Boston: Pilgrim Press, 1914). It claimed that the time had come "for those of us who are this side of thirty-five to unite and take back our Jesus" (ix). The book intended to recover a muscular, real-man Jesus, as opposed to the effeminate, soft, unhappy, martyred Jesus. Ironically, Barton emphasized a Jesus who defended the poor, while his later work had a Jesus who was a model for the businessman.

15. Barton, *The Man Nobody Knows*, 18.

qualities of success? He had a personal magnetism, a sense of self-assurance, a capacity to pick the right men, and to see their abilities in a way they could not themselves. And then he had the patience to train his men. So marvelous was Jesus' executive methods that only "a few decades later the proud Emperor himself bowed his head to the teachings of this Nazareth carpenter, transmitted through common men" (31).

Barton expatiated on Jesus' physical prowess, using the temple scene as his model. Jesus ran off the extortioners and greedy merchants, after which he "stood flushed and panting, the little whip still in his hands"; and "as his right arm rose and fell, striking its blows with that little whip, the sleeve dropped back to reveal muscles hard as iron," and "no flabby priest or money-changer cared to try conclusions with that arm" (36–37). But the strong Jesus has been hidden away in the centuries of artwork and representations of him as a sacrificial lamb willing to die. He must have been a "real" man, a healthy, outdoor man, otherwise he could hardly have been such a successful healer to whom women were also attracted. And was he not a man of personal courage who faced his opponents without fear or faltering? Even at his arrest he was calm and ready for his arresters.

Yet Jesus also was more: a man who laughed and was full of joy. The sacrificial lamb of theology scarcely represents him. The gospels tell a different story: a wedding at Cana, his sociability with all kinds and classes, accusations of excessive eating and drinking. And even though he may have anticipated an imminent end, he soon fell away from that, and other, more optimistic notes entered his life and work. Jesus enjoyed and had a sense of humor, as in the story of the crippled man at the pool (John), whom Jesus healed with perhaps a chuckle as he imagined this old man, complainer for thirty-eight years, now having to explain and defend himself, even go to work for a living. Jesus' God was a loving Father, a "great Companion, a wonderful Friend, a kindly indulgent, joy-loving Father" (86). This portrayal of God as the Father of all humankind was truly revolutionary.

Jesus sent forth his missionaries to represent this idea to the world. How did he manage that? He had an affection for people that caught their attention; he knew how to interest people in what he wished to say. To a salesman that would be "putting yourself in step with your prospect" (104). According to Barton "Jesus taught all this without ever teaching it. Every one of his conversations, every contact between his mind and others, is worthy of the attentive study of any sales manager" (106). He knew just how to meet an objection in advance or to ask the piercing question without being argumentative. Or to exercise the highest leadership that summons men's energies to meet obstacles rather than gain rewards. The blood of the martyrs was indeed the seed of the church. Or as Barton preferred: "The great Idea prevailed" (123).

Jesus was the great advertiser; he knew how to master public attention. Barton imagined the stories of Jesus healing the paralytic, or the calling of Matthew, and other such acts of healing as front-page news, in effect setting tongues a-wagging everywhere. His service, not his preaching, was his advertisement. He went into the marketplace, and the contemporary marketplace is the newspaper and the magazine, where Jesus would surely speak if he were here today. The parables show how Jesus exemplified the principles of advertising: "Always a picture in the very first sentence; crisp, graphic language and a message so clear that even the dullest can not escape it" (143). Condensed, simple language, with sincerity and repetition of the theme — no one knew these principles better than Jesus.

Jesus was the founder of modern business. Did not he say, at the age of 12, in defending his conduct at Jerusalem, that he must be about his father's *business?* His business was life itself, but how did he conduct it? He emphasized service, which is what any smart company does in its advertising; he said you have to lose your life in order to find it, and anyone who loses himself in his work, without thought of making his fortune, will find the truth of that, too. Jesus succeeded that way, restoring people's self-respect, abolishing formalism in religion, and bringing a new concept of the fatherhood of God and the brotherhood of man. The greatest success lies in allowing one's work to become an instrument of a larger service to fellow men and women.

With such success principles in practice, how then did Jesus turn out? Here Barton did not fare so well, reconciling the successful Jesus with the one who got himself killed. Jesus' first return to little Nazareth was met by cynicism; then his brothers abandoned him (John), his family thought ill of him, John the Baptist doubted him, the people generally murmured against him, and even some of his disciples went away. It seemed he had had his day, and went to Jerusalem amid dwindling influence — a suicidal move, for the authorities there, too, had heard of his lost popularity. Arguments raged and he returned to Galilee (John's chronology). For a brief time crowds came again, but his ridicule of Pharisees and the like turned many away yet again. His little group of friends was still awaiting something visionary as he carried them once more to Jerusalem. It all ended badly. At the supper he remained unbowed, proclaiming that he had overcome the world. He had no desire to die and struggled in the garden, finally making his peace with his fate. At the end his disciples utterly deserted him while soldiers busied themselves casting lots for his garments. Yet let no one still think of him as weak and merely willing to die. "There have been leaders who could call forth enthusiasm when their fortunes ran high. But he, when his enemies had done their worst, so bore himself that a crucified felon looked into his dying eyes and saluted him as king" (219). So, presumably, Jesus won a kind of victory through his unsurpassable courage, a much less grander hero than Schweitzer's hero who was nevertheless of equal strangeness in the modern world.

So went the man nobody knows; better perhaps to retitle the work, "The Man Nobody Ought to Know." Its facile assimilation of Jesus into the current business climate was certainly a tour de force, but of a kind such that nobody would recognize the man of the book as the man of Nazareth.

J. Middleton Murry

J. Middleton Murry was another *littérateur* who produced his book, *Jesus, Man of Genius*, in 1926.[16] He was, he said, presenting a Jesus in whom he could believe, a man of genius; he did not then believe in him as a supernatural being. He has read the criticisms, but they do not agree with one another, so he set forth his own view.

John the Baptist preached a baptism for the forgiveness of sins; Jesus thought he was a sinner and went to John. (Before John all is legend in the gospels.) At his baptism Jesus knew he was a son, but was like all sons of God. The good news of the kingdom signified a time of love, not wrath; all men are sons and love is coming. All will know themselves as sons and God as Father.

On miracles: Jesus did none; he rejected them at the temptation. He did do healings, which are not the same thing as miracles. The latter are prodigies, or strange events compelling faith. The king of the kingdom is the Father; Jesus taught no interim ethic, but emphasized how to become a son. The Son of man was not Jesus, but the one to establish the kingdom.

Simon, called the Rock, was the source of Mark's Gospel; the account of him is ironic, since he was hardly rock-like. The secret of the kingdom about which Jesus spoke was the rebirth of the soul, while the kingdom was the family of reborn sons. It is the kingdom now and also not yet. There was to be a future consummation with Jesus as the forerunner. Yet maybe he thought he might be the one; he struggled with himself.

Threats from Pharisees and Herod sent him on his journey north. But the kingdom did not come.

Who was Jesus to himself? God's only son, though at first only a son, but he found no brothers, so he must be the only son. He must be the messiah, the Son of man. After Caesarea-Philippi he became the messiah-to-be; he had to put off flesh and blood to become the Son of man. Jesus probably expected to be miraculously changed, but he died without that happening. He would go from earthly prophet to heavenly messiah. All that had to occur at Jerusalem; he could count on death there from the Pharisees. After the Transfiguration Jesus was changed; he became a man of sorrows on his way to his death in Jerusalem. Caesarea-Philippi was therefore the big division; the teaching also changed afterward.

The kingdom of God had two aspects: the future eschatological rule and individuals now achieving the kingdom within themselves — the condition of wholeness and rebirth (knowledge of God as Father, one's self as son and doing the will of God). Jesus' ethics flowed out of that concept. Thus Jesus transformed the expectation of the kingdom with his inner-kingdom concept. After Caesarea-Philippi Jesus spoke differently; he was now judge and messiah-Savior who would

---

16. J. Middleton Murray, *Jesus, Man of Genius* (New York: Harper, 1926). It was reissued subsequently in 1934 and 1948 as *The Life of Jesus* (London: Jonathan Cape, 1948).

force the kingdom upon them, whereas before he was only the teacher of wisdom. So he went to Jerusalem to be the sacrificial lamb; he predicted his own death. His purpose was to die as the suffering messiah.

Judas's betrayal served Jesus' own purposes; there must have been an arrangement between them. The passion predictions, in their present form, are after the fact. Jesus did not think that he would die on the cross, much less have a bodily resurrection; he thought that at the last moment before death he would be taken up into another order of existence, then would come as judge. It did not happen.

Jesus determined his entrance into the city; he seemed a prophet to the crowd, but was messiah to himself. The temple attack, like the cursing of the fig tree, came out of exasperation and anger; he threatened priests and Pharisees. Conflicts over his authority occurred. The prediction of the overthrow of the temple hinted at the approaching kingdom. Jesus died on 14 Nisan, having predetermined his end; the last supper was an earnest of the kingdom, not a Passover. Jesus gave bread and wine as symbols; Judas betrayed his location. On the crucifixion: since the disciples fled, Simon of Cyrene must have provided the details. Jesus died quickly.

The appearance stories show that the truth of the resurrection was that Jesus had gone into a spiritual body (Paul). Peter's experience was of an objective presence, as was Paul's.

It is a mixed book, with some independent critical positions as announced, but also much that was borrowed from standard liberalism. It is hard to see why this particular Jesus was such a genius, when he seemed more to be a failed messiah.

Emile Ludwig

The decade of the twenties also produced two works by Jewish writers that deserve notice. One was that of the German Emil Ludwig, whose work, *The Son of Man: The Story of Jesus,* proposed to portray the "inner life of the prophet," since the key to him was to be found in his "human heart."[17] It was an imaginative reconstruction, based on much sound historical information, but also employing novelistic scenes and descriptions. For example, in the characterization of the setting in Jerusalem with which the book opens, Ludwig portrayed Pontius Pilate fuming over his inability to have Caesar's image on the coinage. People in Judaism were everywhere expecting a deliverer, a messiah, and Daniel was their favorite text. Among those imagined was Jesus the boy, lying out in the freedom and openness of nature, thinking his own independent thoughts.

John the Baptist appeared; he was like an Essene, though not one, and he struggled with himself over his mission. Jesus must have been awakened by news

---

17. Emil Ludwig, *The Son of Man: The Story of Jesus,* trans. Eden and Cedar Paul (Garden City, N.Y.: Garden City Publishing Co., 1928), xiv, xv. The original German was *Der Menschensohn, Geschichte eines Propheten* (Berlin: Ernst Rowohlt Verlag, 1928).

of his activity. Officials came from Jerusalem to question John as to who and what he was. Then came Jesus to be baptized at John's hands; the visionary experience terrified Jesus and he went to the wilderness to figure it out. Upon his return he met a crowd fleeing, telling him John had been arrested. Jesus saw that as a sign to take up his own message, so he went home and began formulating some plans.

He went first to Cana, where already his brothers and his mother had gone to a wedding. He felt his prophetic power and asked himself, when the wine was dissipated, whether he would "surely be strong enough to turn water into wine?" (109). He was, but Ludwig's verdict over the event left more questions: "Once more they stare at Jesus, who has been strong enough, through the wall, to make the cook out there believe what, from within, Jesus has willed him to believe."[18] The "miracle" apparently lay in persuading the cook into belief. What the guests thought was left unsaid.

Jesus began to preach at Capernaum, proclaiming the kingdom of God, speaking the parables of the fish and net, and attracting fishermen and others. Similarly, he returned to Cana, curing a demoniac in the synagogue by willing him to believe that his demon had left him. At Capernaum he stayed with Peter, healing his mother-in-law. At this point in his work he kept himself away from Jerusalem, as well as other cities like Sepphoris and Tiberias. His message — God is the Father and all are brothers — was intended for simple souls. His ethical teaching emphasized the inner intent and was actually more rigorous than the Law, especially where secret sins were concerned.

Ludwig often provided a context for sayings; for example, he imagined Jesus seeing a couple in the synagogue and, knowing that they were having an adulterous relationship, uttered the saying about the adultery of the heart.

Women followed Jesus; they understood better his talk of love. Jesus remained celibate, but did not impose that as a rule.

People saw Jesus as a prophet, as he did himself. He had no messianic role in mind, at least early in his activity, and made no messianic claims. The title "Son of man" was used to describe his lowliness, as in Ezekiel. Jesus largely led a life "out of touch with the main interests of his day and nation" (143). Yet he also managed to stir hostility from Pharisees over such issues as Sabbath practice and his eating with sinners. Among the latter would have been Mary Magdalene, who once came into a house where Jesus was a guest and kissed his feet.

In prison John pondered the news about Jesus, wondering who he really was, and finally sent messengers. Jesus' response pointed to his miracles as authentication of his work, though by that point he was in fact growing tired of them. But by calling John Elijah he implied that he himself was the messiah.

He returned for a time to Nazareth, where he experienced rejection and thereafter expected a longer period of suffering. Dark shadows fell across his path

---

18. Ibid., 110. Ludwig seemed not to notice why a Jesus who had recently declined to turn stones into bread would have to wonder at his ability to transform water into wine.

and his flight began. The hostility got the better of him and, driven through the Decapolis, he took on thoughts of royalty, supposing himself to be no longer the Son of man but the Son of God. The stress robbed him of his charm: the people of Gadara dreaded his presence there after he had driven one or two swine into the sea.

Returning from the Decapolis to Galilee, he was pursued by Pharisees. He told them that the kingdom was "within you," the essence of his message. But more confrontations followed, over plucking grain on the Sabbath, unclean foods, and so on. Jesus charged the Pharisees with hypocrisy; there was an open breach between them. People did not see him as the messiah, but called him Son of man, as he had referred to himself. He raised Jairus's daughter and upbraided the cities of Chorazin, Bethsaida, and Capernaum.

The death of John forced Jesus to flee to Caesarea-Philippi. There Peter acknowledged Jesus as messiah, which Jesus accepted gladly, for it confirmed his inner thoughts about himself. But now the messiah had to go to Jerusalem and deliver his message there. He could expect to be put to death there.

The Transfiguration occurred in a dream of Peter's. Afterward Jesus began to magnify his role, which was to be greater than Abraham's or Solomon's. He cherished the hope of a resurrection followed by the judgment; he saw himself presiding over the judgment and ruling forever. So the gentle carpenter who preached love had now come to grander aspirations, under the stress of opposition and hostility. He became a threat to the theocracy, to the state. He had declared himself to be the "bread of life" who had come down from heaven. Everything was reported to the Council at Jerusalem and to Herod, but Jesus went on anyway.

At his entrance the crowd of Galileans grew to thousands. Jesus felt terror and kept his silence. He reluctantly mounted an ass as "they" had asked him to do. It was a messianic act, though he was himself assailed by doubt. He went on to the temple, where he was dumbfounded by its commerce. Overpowered by rage he overturned tables and chased out the moneychangers. He sat on the temple steps, exhausted, as little children came around him singing hosanna. He was restored and left for Bethany for the night and then returned to the city.

Controversies followed. Ludwig included many stray words in this context and imagined people laughing at the crackpot from Galilee who now argued on the steps of the very temple where the day before he had run off the traders and was now undisturbed by them.

Pharisees and Sadducees colluded against Jesus. More controversy ensued, over payment of taxes to Caesar, resurrection, the woman caught in adultery. Salome, the mother of James and John, asked for a high position for her sons in the kingdom, and the next day all the disciples were wrangling over who was the greatest. Only Judas was silent, wondering what Jesus was doing to attain power. At supper in Bethany Jesus spoke of famines and earthquakes and of himself as messiah at the judgment. A woman appeared with ointment to anoint Jesus, provoking Judas's protest at its waste. Judas was frustrated that the rule had not been established; he covered his real ambition by convincing himself that he could force Jesus to his goal. After all, he knew his way around Jerusalem and Judea, whence he had come.

The Passover was celebrated; Jesus spoke over each of the four cups, the lamb and unleavened bread were eaten. Judas's betrayal was forecast and at the end Jesus took still more bread and compared it to his body, while the wine of the fourth cup was said to be his blood. Jesus and the disciples left, looking for a hiding place. He slipped into the hedge surrounding an olive orchard. Afraid, he prayed to live but felt "like a hunted beast when the hounds are close at hand" (279). He found no solace in the sleeping disciples; doubts assailed him. Had he taken the wrong path? He thought of the life that might have been: "The refuge of women's tender affection, gentle hands to stroke his hair, soft lips to kiss his feet, loving-kindness to cherish him in his daily doings ... to watch the growing-up of children, the little children whom he loved" (280).

Then arose the clamor of weapons. The temple guard, led by Judas, along with servants of the high priest, went to Bethany looking for him; then, not finding him, returned and located his hiding place. Judas identified Jesus in the darkness with a kiss. The disciples fled.

Annas, together with about one-third of the Council, met twice, once in the evening and once in the morning. Witnesses were summoned who referred to Jesus' threat against the temple. Annas forced a messianic admission from Jesus and he was charged with blasphemy. Peter denied knowing Jesus. The Great Council in the morning ratified the decision of the Small Council. Jesus was taken to Pilate and tried as a traitor against Rome. Then he sent Jesus to Herod, who saw him as merely a fool and mocked him, then returned him to Pilate. After the release of Barabbas Jesus was abused and condemned as king of the Jews to loud acclaim of the priests and the rabble.

Ludwig described the crucifixion from Jesus' perspective. Nails, one per hand and one through both feet, were affixed, with support by a seat. On seeing the nails Jesus was overwhelmed by horror and fainted. He later awakened to find himself on the cross. Few people were there; most were celebrating Passover. Jesus promised one of the two thieves dying with him that he would be also in paradise with Jesus, showing that Jesus still clung to some hope of deliverance. He cried out in the words of Psalm 22 and was given a numbing drink, which he took, before uttering a loud cry and dying.

A stranger and the women took down the body and carried it unanointed to the tomb. No more work could be done before the Sabbath had passed. The next evening they came but found the tomb empty and the body missing. Many rumors abounded. "But the women, who love him, believe that in waking dreams they have seen the risen Jesus in the flesh" (315).

Ludwig's book reflects the romanticizing biographies typical of the time; it runs perilously close to the lines of Schweitzer's fictional lives, constructing imaginary internal conflicts and thoughts of Jesus and others. It has some literary merits and some sense of historical insight, but these are often overextended and the overall impression remains of someone who wished to be the German Renan.[19]

Henri Barbusse

Henri Barbusse was the other Jewish — and French — writer of note, whose book *Jesus* also played with imagination and fiction in the life of Jesus.[20] Barbusse volunteered for the war in 1914 at age 41 and was driven by the experience to become an active antiwar Communist. He was a significant literary figure who also opposed fascism and died in 1935 in Moscow, but was buried in Paris. His book said in the usual dedicatory space that he had come to love Jesus and would defend him against all critics, but the Jesus whom he loved seemed to be largely a cipher for his own values. The author, according to his introductory note, set himself the task of addressing his own tormented age, drawing a parallel between his time and that of Jesus. Barbusse mentioned that a subsequent volume would document the sources underlying his picture.[21]

The narrative has a strongly poetic character; the language is often eloquent and striking in its vividness. The story is told from Jesus' own perspective, in the first person. It begins with Jesus seeing his own village, his family, John the Baptist, his own growing up. Later he felt the pulse of revolution rising, seeing that "we are made do something just," to bring about justice.[22] Going to Jerusalem he saw that the burning of sacrificial flesh was little, while at the same time he confounded Israel's philosophers with his questions.

Jesus grown had a lover, according to Barbusse — not Mary Magdalene, but another who was nameless (Mary was a prostitute). Afterwards she and Jesus both felt ashamed. Another time there was a Priscilla, who herself, though, loved Jehiel, a friend of Jesus', and the two ran off together, angering Jesus. He later found them clasped together upon falling off a cliff onto stones, where he bound up their wounds and resolved his love for Priscilla. The experience allowed Jesus to feel with others the pain of loss and more sympathy for the poor and oppressed. He learned that all men's destiny is "to suffer the evil deeds of those above them" (71). The revolution will come, but it will come from earth to heaven, not the other way around. The first who lead the way will be accursed. Such would be Jesus, for they are the lovers of people everywhere.

Nicodemus appeared and was told of being born again, the new world created within which liberates from death. A certain Hilkiah came with him and was the one cured by Jesus of paralysis. He did not really know he was the cause

---

19. The Jesus who mentally speculated on his life that never was calls to mind the later work of the Greek Nicos Kazantzakis, *The Last Temptation of Christ*, trans. P. A. Bien (New York: Simon and Schuster, 1960), the filmed version of which stirred considerable controversy.

20. Henri Barbusse, *Jesus*, trans. Solon Librescot (New York: Macmaulay, 1927). Biographical data are from the introduction by Brian Rhys to Barbusse's *Under Fire*, trans. W. Fitzwater Wray (London: J. M. Dent; New York: E. P. Dutton, 1926). More in the biographical appendix.

21. To be titled *In the Footsteps of Jesus the Just*. It never appeared.

22. Barbusse, *Jesus*, 38.

of his own cure (his faith). "Grant your own prayers," said Jesus (89). It was similarly with the stilling of the storm; Jesus gave the disciples courage and they thought he was "a magician of God" (92). Discourses on the messiah show that the messiah is the spirit and the spirit is within us, as is the kingdom of heaven.

Judas was a small soul: "When I meet Judas, it is like running into a tree," said Jesus. Of the woman taken in adultery and his actions Jesus said, "Mercy is the sister of justice" (102, 103).

John the Baptist was a wild prophet. He was arrested and Jesus went to visit his habitation in the wilderness. In John's hut he found cryptic messages written in a dirt mound that served as a table. The messages were left untranslated.

The Sermon on the Mount spoke of doing unto others and how every person is like every other person. That is the sum of earthly justice. The poor and the simple were especially the objects of Jesus' teaching.

Afterward Jesus and Simon and Paul spoke together; the latter two then went off to preach Jesus' word. Jesus meditated at length on the problem of evil in the world, but had no answer.

A meeting with the Samaritan woman elicited the truth that God is within us; to project a God outside is to create an idol. He exists only within us, like the dead that we have loved. We make his image and credit him with our creations and our sins and errors as well. In Nietzschean-sounding terms, Barbusse saw a revolution arising, in which we humans would reattain our divine status on the corpse of God, and people would re-emerge "from the original sin of obedience" (134). Thus Jesus became the deliverer from an oppressive deity. When John Zebedee then asked about the new spirit within, he was told that everything comes from ourselves — our grasp of the truth, of justice, and of planning a new community of men. There is nothing more. The kingdom of heaven is within us and the one who knows his own self finds the kingdom. Whoever has seen himself has seen God and we are all brothers without a father. Our work begins with the poor and humble and blind and with dealing with injustice.

Jesus set about producing a community of the spirit and the poor and women. The latter have been enslaved, but woman is to be the equal of man.

Jesus betrayed anxieties about his mission and accomplishments. He imagined — like Ludwig's Jesus — having had a regular home, a wife and children. But he nevertheless returned to his mission.

Jews spoke of a national kingdom to Jesus. He instigated their revolt, said Simon the Zealot, but Jesus declined to be their king, for they sought revenge, not justice. Jesus' kingdom is within.

Jesus met Paul on the road to Damascus, Paul who erected a church and a faith on Jesus. But Jesus wanted none of it; he taught abolishment of dogma and ritual and any idea of immortality. But Paul persisted and argued to make of Jesus a dying-rising messiah, replete with sacrament and a doctrine of immortality. But, Jesus replied, it was the serpent who promised immortality, while God ordered people to return to the dust of the earth. Of this Paul Jesus said, "From afar, he seemed like a prophet of Israel, but when you approached him the odor of

Greek calculation rose from his garments." Paul was "of the race of builders . . . an immense Pharisee" (177, 179).

Jesus saw an apocalypse of the future, scribes fabricating books on the basis of prophecies, as did the scribes of the past, as did Paul. These councils and pontiffs and the like make of Jesus a mediator, and the poor and disinherited of the earth will give their life to the doctrine. Those who suffer will love the sufferer, but it is ultimately the rich who will support it and turn to oppression of the poor.

Jesus contemplated his death as a sacrifice before the world, to wring a victory from defeat. He attacked the temple and the people cheered. He spoke to the city and said, "Cast off your chains, whoever will" (196). He disclaimed having ever said, "Turn the other cheek." He preached against the rich and mighty. Barbusse imagined John Zacharias (John the Baptist) released and in the crowd agreeing and proclaiming Jesus as the Lamb who redeems the sins of the world. This revolution would be built on a prior one in their minds, the revolution of the spirit. Force is not excluded, if it is invoked on the side of right.

At the last supper Jesus discoursed on love and understanding (the latter precedes the former). The Spirit or Comforter he left them was the spirit of justice.

Jesus thought of his death and of life and its beauty. There is no rising from the grave for man. Jesus found his mother at her daily work and she complained that he had overstepped himself, that he was not content to be an honest carpenter, that he was a communist. Jesus had no answer and, reminded of Ashtoreth, said simply, "The goddess Mary" (221).

Jesus came to his disciples in a barn in the garden; they slept and he wept. Mary Magdalene came and spoke to him, telling him that he grasped the suffering and misery of men and had urged them to believe in themselves and to remake life in their own image and thus find salvation.

At his trial Jesus was convicted of being a conspirator against the state. Crucifixion was painful, his blood flowed; but still he could see the people and called to "the damned of the earth" (234) to rise up against the princes of the earth.

The book ends with a petition for Jesus to come to the aid of all who are sowing the seed of revolution in the soul of humanity.

It is obvious to even the superficial reader that this boldly imaginative work — bold enough to give offense still to some — is more and less than a historical portrait: more, for it moves in another world, an ideological one for which Jesus stands as symbol; and less, for it bears small resemblance to any historical actuality of Jesus. Its Jesus is woven out of the fabric of ancient Gnosticism and modern socialism. The final judgment is perhaps still that offered by Shirley Jackson Case seventy years ago: "The present book is an attempt — as literature, a brilliant attempt — to modernize Jesus in the interests of a particular type of human quest made acute by conditions in the post-war Europe of to-day."[23]

---

23. *New York Herald Tribune Books* 7 (January 8, 1928): 3.

François Mauriac

Still another Frenchman who labored over the life of Jesus was the noted *savant* and author François Mauriac, whose *Life of Jesus* passed through two editions and enjoyed a wide readership.[24] To take up the work of a noted literary artist is to hope for some special insight, but the expectation is mostly disappointed, for the work is governed by a rigid submission to Roman Catholic dogma that precludes any critical appropriation of the story. There is, to be sure, some striking phrasing, but the story told was openly that of Jesus who was God. To that end all four gospels were used without discrimination. Mauriac observed that he had earlier in life avidly read Loisy, but had come to conclude that the Christ living in the Church, in the saints, and in each of us was the foundation of faith, safe from the onslaughts of criticism. The book was not intended for scholars and, even though Mauriac admired the works of Lagrange, de Grandmaison, and Lebreton, he had chosen not to follow their example.

In fact, the book was a kind of commentary on movable texts, with the Gospel of John enjoying a noticeable presence. It is virtually impossible to give a sense of its best qualities, which reside in the extended comment on scenes and texts.

Jesus grew up at Nazareth; the brothers were really cousins. Mary must have wondered whether the promise at his birth was going to be kept, given the advanced age (30) to which Jesus had come before launching his public work. For his part Jesus treated her with some distance; he had all eternity to glorify her.

The miracle at Cana anticipated the Eucharist. Jesus worked at Capernaum and afterward went to Jerusalem where he attacked the temple. He also spoke of the kingdom of God, which is tantamount to salvation. His encounter with the Samaritan woman spoke of the value of all souls and of all races to the Father in heaven. Jesus also struggled with Pharisees, they accusing him of blasphemy (forgiving sins, claiming deity, violating the Sabbath). Secret meetings were held in Jerusalem to plot against Jesus. Judas, instrumental in the betrayal, was eager for profit and power. He was insincere and craven, taking and leaving what he wished of Jesus' words.

The teaching contained little that was absolutely new, but it was articulated with authority and an accent that was new. The Sermon on the Mount (taken as an actual sermon) asserted that acts committed in the heart are already consummated. Here Jesus overturned the Pharisaic scheme of justice. He urged love of the enemy and no revenge. Was Jesus mad? Yes, a state of madness is required to follow his way, but it is a madness that comes from love and is not frightening to one who has God as Father.

A respite followed the delivery of the Sermon. Jesus met a centurion — unusual, but "during those three years the Infinite Being became the neighbor of soldiers, of publicans, and of courtesans" (69). The woman with tears wiping Jesus' feet was the same who anointed him for burial, maybe Mary Magdalene,

---

24. François Mauriac, *Life of Jesus*, trans. Julie Kernan (New York: David McKay, 1937). Original French in 1936.

but the identification does not finally matter, for Mary is incarnate sin meeting incarnate purity. She was possessed and became the symbol of redemption from total defilement.[25]

Parables are stories and speak of the mystery of the kingdom. Some were understood, some not at all. This failure to grasp the mystery of the kingdom is itself a mystery, "the words of a God who chooses, who separates, who prefers one soul to another — because he is love" (86).

Jesus visited Jerusalem again; controversy drove him from the city. The feeding stories occurred, followed by his walking on the sea. After Caesarea-Philippi he returned to Jerusalem, and there defended the woman taken in adultery. His writing on the ground was his way of not looking at her. "Nothing human was foreign to the Nazarene," said Mauriac, "but because he was God he knew what no man may know: the unconquerable weakness of the woman, that crawling and cringing creature that she becomes at certain hours, before certain beings" (139). He seemed to have in view the Genesis story.

Healing the man born blind followed, and thereafter also more Johannine discourse material and the parable of the good Samaritan. More miscellaneous sayings were placed in Jerusalem. Jesus was harsh on the doctors of the law and the Pharisees, but he turned sympathetically to the poor and humble. Love, he taught, superseded justice. The great enemy was mammon, and even the poor would deserve condemnation should they choose to live in regret of not having riches. Judas especially hated this attitude in Jesus.

The kingdom had already come in a sense; it is interior, in us. That is equivalent to rebirth, the renewal of each person into a new person.

Marriage permits no divorce and no sex beyond its bounds.

Lazarus was literally raised, flesh and all, from the tomb. But also he was no longer merely ephemeral and therefore different from before.

The final entrance of Jesus into the city of Jerusalem stirred devotion from Judas and crowds. A final supper showed the disciples that now they would be nourished by Jesus forever. The meal was a Passover, but Mauriac noted no problems. The trial followed a Johannine scheme; all blame was laid on the priests and scribes. At his crucifixion the spear produced a flow of blood; the wild beasts lurked nearby.

The appearances were proofs of the resurrection, but each meeting with the risen One recalled something in ourselves — we who are dead and have need of life. The Ascension was no departure, for "already he was lying in ambush at the turn of the road which went from Jerusalem to Damascus, watching for Saul, his beloved persecutor. Thenceforth in the destiny of every man there was to be this God who lies in wait" (245).

It was a work that likely would stir those who did not need stirring, and its

---

25. This characterization of Mary led Mauriac to discourse at length on the evils of lust, as though prostitution were about *her* lust.

picture was purely that of the orthodox Christ of Catholic faith. Its literacy could not save it as history; it was a terrible work, well written.[26]

Robert Keable

Robert Keable was an English literary figure, whose book, *The Great Galilean,* was inspired by what Keable regarded as reactionary and illiberal people at the 1927 World Conference on Faith and Order at Lausanne.[27] Presumably he would correct such illiberalism; a discovery of the facts about the earthly life of Jesus would bring a revolution. He could be the one to bring about the revolution.

The book ventilated opinions about the historical Jesus and his bearing on the current scene in church and society. Only at the end was an ordered account of the historical Jesus briefly submitted.

Discussion of the sources disclosed knowledge of standard positions: prefer the synoptics over John, utilize Mark and Q. No biography is possible. The gospels were written to supply a knowledge of Jesus that had been only poorly understood (Paul, for example, gives little or no information about Jesus). The gospels were written after it was supposed that the world was not coming to a speedy end. Paulinism actually prevailed at the time, and the traditional Christ has ever since held sway. This Jesus was fashioned by the western mind and had a million contributors. He is the inevitable source of our civilization, but he never existed. Yet we cannot do without him, for he is still the object of our devotion, even though he is not the historical Jesus, about whom little can be known. So:

> The minister of religion has to remember that it is with the worship of the traditional Christ that he is mainly concerned. We did not set him in the ministry that he should be a professor or a kind of policeman. We set him there that he might be a minister or a servant of men. He can serve us best in our need by holding up before us the traditional Jesus, in all his beauty and nobility, whom we tend to forget. (45)

Nevertheless, Keable's concern was with this scanty historical figure. Jesus was an ignorant man who had no science, no special knowledge of God. He was said to bequeath to the world the idea of the Fatherhood of God. This idea makes no sense (in light of pervasive misery), but Jesus had common sense, as can be seen in his answer to the question about payment of taxes to Caesar, about the resurrection, and so on. Yet no one really pays attention to things like "love your enemies"; no one ever said to love the Germans in the Great War, and one curate (known to Keable) who asked people to pray for the German widows and dying men was driven from his curacy.

---

26. The review by M.-J. Lagrange was, as might be expected, kinder; he thanked Mauriac for bringing the God-man of dogma to a cultivated public (*RB* 45 [1936]: 321–45).

27. Robert Keable, *The Great Galilean* (Boston: Little, Brown, 1929). Keable was an English clergyman turned author.

Jesus took a different attitude toward sin. The Old Testament speaks of bloody atonement, and similar notions are to be seen in John, Paul, and the early church, but not the historical Jesus: "The sins which Christ denounced were social and of the spirit, and the sins that Paul denounces are theological and of the body" (76–77). Jesus found sinners and tax collectors more likable than the religious; there was no more need of propitiating an angry god. The church's concerns and sins today were not Christ's.

Jesus was a "spiritual genius." The church early on developed a sad attitude toward sex and marriage, while it elevated celibacy. Jesus met all types of people, "but a pair of human lovers would seem never to have come his way." Was he never in love? "If sex was a secondary thing to him, he would have been a nincompoop if he had not been aware that it was a primary thing in most men's lives" (94–95). Jesus must have advocated free love, that is, love is the most primary thing, above all ecclesiastical rules and regulations. On divorce, he meant that if love is lacking it is as though adultery had been committed.

The church made Calvary the important mount, not the Sermon on the Mount. Paul muddled things. Paul put forth the notion of the sacrificial death and coming of the future ruler — a pure fantasy. On the other hand, Jesus was also "impractical." He would disband armies and regenerate the heart. Our own political and social experiments are failures (capitalism, militarism). Nations are not likely to try the way of Jesus, but individuals could, and the world would be vastly different. There would be no enforced bad marriages and no prohibition; there would be money for science and medical research, food for the hungry, and workers with no more worries.

The heavenly Father was at the core for Jesus, while he was the servant of men. Ministers today preside at a sacrificial altar and make themselves judges. Organized religion is a failure. Keable ridiculed preaching, giving the example of a rationalist sermon he had just heard on Jesus' walking on the sea, explaining how the water was shallow, reedy, and sudden winds could give rise to misunderstanding. The disciples thought Jesus was walking on the sea, but he was only in the shallows; they thought they had suddenly arrived at the land to which they were going. Keable imagined a young boy — possibly himself — sitting on a pine bench in a mission hall, hearing the story and marveling in it, finding comfort in it, but hardly in the version he had just heard. Said Keable, "No profound story, however true, of a paddling Jesus and of a collection of panic-stricken fishermen who did not know the difference between marshy ground and solid earth could have had any such effect" (148). But the ministry today fails to live the story of the traditional Jesus and has deprived us of the historical one.

Worship is dying out — a deplorable fact. We need symbols, such as sacraments, only not those representing a bloody sacrifice for sin. But we can still remember the sacrifice of Jesus for his experiment.

An appendix contains a capsule reconstruction of the life of Jesus. He was born in the normal way in Nazareth. He was a genius in religion and the spiritual life. He taught that riches were to be found in a spiritual kingdom within. He taught and practiced a relationship to a spiritual Power he called his Father — very original. Jesus was a good Jew, though he set aside matters such as the Old Testament idea of an angry Jehovah.

He began by a baptism under John, seeing himself as God's son. The temptation followed, Jesus struggling with the issue of what kind of messiah he would be. He taught extensively, as can be seen in Q. He made disciples, including women, though the latter have been suppressed, the tradition listing only the twelve. He had gifts of healing, casting out demons (cured people), and curing others, though the reports have been exaggerated. At one point he probably fled the crowds, who wanted to make him king-messiah, and maybe also he fled from Herod. He knew his spiritual gospel would stir up opposition. The kingdom would grow like the mustard seed, but also come like the lightning — a contradiction Jesus left unresolved. There was conflict over the death of the messiah in his own mind. He went up to Jerusalem, tempted by the crowd at his entrance to be their kind of messiah. Judas thought he would force Jesus to make up his mind, but Jesus still clung to the spiritual kingdom, expecting perhaps a vindication that never came.

It is not surprising that apparition stories of Jesus happened after his death. It would be surprising if such a story had not been told about Jesus. Paul was the one who spread the tradition.

An epilogue, bearing the date of 1927, describes the sun rising above the mountains on Tahiti. In poetically cast language it ends with Keable turning toward his house, seeing Ilonk — his companion — and saying, "Christ is risen," she replying, "'He is risen indeed,' for she is Orthodox." And the book ends, "Alleluia!" (212).

The ending was deceptive, for Keable was no orthodox himself. And yet he was not merely a conventional iconoclast, for he understood the value of tradition and of symbolic projections of meaning in communal life. His affirmation of the resurrection at the end looks more like a blending of Christianity with nature-enthusiasm, of identification of the renewal of the earth with resurrection. Or perhaps it was again the symbolic weight of resurrection that attracted the author. Or perhaps, like Jesus, he meant to leave it parabolically open for the reader to reach his or her own conclusions. In any case, anyone who could find in Jesus advocacy of free love could find his values wherever he needed to.

Conrad Noel

The most fascinating figure to compose a life of Jesus in the decade of the thirties was undoubtedly the English Anglican priest Conrad Noel. His work lies somewhere on the boundaries of the merely popular and the learned. Like White before him, Noel had a rather specific cause to promote — socialism —

and enlisted Jesus for that purpose. The work appeared in 1937 as *The Life of Jesus.*[28]

Noel's own life was at least as interesting as his life of Jesus.[29] Born in 1869 he advocated socialism the whole of his adult life and sponsored often unpopular causes. Lenin was one of his heroes, though events in Russia gave him some problems. But for Noel politics was social justice and that was for him also the essence of the gospel. His activism in support of socialistic and workers' causes often had him embroiled in controversy. He died in 1942.

From an introductory note to his autobiography by the noted theologian and Archbishop of Canterbury William Temple comes a story about Noel that epitomizes his position. At a conference on Christian politics, economics, and citizenship, a certain speaker was characterizing the kingdom of God as the reign of God in the individual heart, whereupon Noel jumped up and hurried to the speaker's platform to offer a single utterance: "They shall come from the east and west and shall sit down with Abraham, Isaac, and Jacob in the reign of God in the individual heart."[30] The kingdom was not to be mistaken for a warm feeling inside.

In his Jesus book Noel gave first a picture of a Roman empire driven by greed and gain, surviving on slavery and oppression of the poor. He pictured a depraved upper class, rich and extravagant. Rome was a capitalistic empire based on exploitation of slaves, its colonies, peasants, and commercial wars. The Jews were — some — rich and powerful in the empire; these had abandoned the hope of a better world, but that hope was alive among the poor and lowly, of whom Jesus was one.

Jesus preached the kingdom, a kingdom of social justice and righteousness, a classless commonwealth. Noel first traced the origins of this idea through its Old Testament ancestry, observing motifs such as Moses the revolutionary, the land as the Lord's (not individual's), prohibition of usury, the prophetic attack on idolatry which was also an attack on its vices (Baalism was commercial and supported private property). The prophetic movement was one of social protest. In fact, the whole history of Israel was combed for evidence of the wealthy-proletarian struggle, right down to Jesus' day.

Apocalyptic was social and political. The apocalyptists were in revolt; the upper level class was looking to a heavenly reward. The apocalyptists were not reformers, but looked to a total transformation. The kingdom of God would be a New Age, brought about by God through his messenger.

---

28. Conrad Noel, *The Life of Jesus* (London: J. M. Dent, 1937). Also of value is his *Jesus the Heretic* (London: J. M. Dent, 1939), which offered the idea that the real heretics were those who condemned Jesus; he tried to recall Israel to its true prophetic roots (a kingdom of justice and righteousness). Interestingly, Noel proposed the trinity as the basis of the New World Order (kingdom); it models the infinite variety in harmony of that new order.

29. His autobiography is *Conrad Noel: An Autobiography,* ed. with foreword by Sidney Dark (London: Dent, 1945). The autobiography was put together posthumously.

30. Ibid., xi.

Personalities are important. Jesus was original; he put his own spirit into the old material. "Pietists" were an enemy [to Noel especially]. They were concerned only about the soul and were otherworldly; the kingdom, however, was a patriot hope.

Some romanticizing went on in Noel's version: Mary taught little Jesus the basic lessons of freedom (the Magnificat, a revolutionary song). On education: the Jews were the best educated of all; little boys had scrolls on which to practice writing. Jesus' sense of justice grew as he grew and as he heard about Herod's oppressive practices, as well as those of Rome.

Jesus did not marry, as might have been expected, but his mission would not permit it.

There was a Redemptionist Group (as can be seen in Simeon) that looked for national redemption. John the Baptist appeared as a prophet of such a group; his eschatological message proclaimed a new era arising from the ruins of the existing system. Jesus' baptism showed that he was allying himself with the movement. The temptation reflected a benevolent rule coming, to be achieved by being a servant, not by political craftiness. The disciples were of the working class and some were followers of the Baptist.

Jesus went to the Passover (John), where he assaulted the temple; he expelled the traders who extorted from the poor. He also then met Nicodemus. Later, when he left, he passed through Samaria and met the Samaritan woman; the story depicts a universal theme of the inclusion of all. Jesus subsequently returned to Jerusalem, where a healing violated the Sabbath. Then he traveled to Galilee where his campaign opened. He called Levi, or Matthew, author of the gospel. The Sermon on the Mount is the description of the new commonwealth. Among the beatitudes, the poor in spirit refer to peasants alive to Jesus' message; the meek are the alert and generous, the righteousness spoken of is none other than justice; being persecuted for righteousness' sake means becoming martyrs for justice.

The Lord's Prayer authorized the legitimacy of food (bread), but also the need for forgiveness (debts). The kingdom prayed for was the commonwealth of "spiritual buoyancy and material plenty."[31] Loans should bear no interest.

At the Nazareth synagogue a new order of society was announced. The tour in Galilee, Noel surmised, was financed by Mary Magdalene, a prostitute, the woman who washed Jesus' feet with her tears, and Joanna, a "bourgeois" woman.[32] But Jesus' followers were mostly workers.

Certain of Jesus' parables — mustard seed and leaven — speak not of slow growth or evolution, but of immediate revolution. Their point is not slowness, but surprising immediacy.

---

31. Noel, Life of Jesus, 346.
32. We can hardly imagine the offense created by this picture of Jesus living (partly) off the earnings of a prostitute.

Miracles are not to be ruled out a priori, though some things do not seem so miraculous anymore.

Jesus sent out the disciples. Matt. 10:23 refers either to the success of the mission or the first harvest after the resurrection and ascension (but not what Schweitzer thought). Jesus withdrew, followed by the feeding event, a sacramental meal, and a foretaste of the new world with abundance for all people. The subsequent reference in Mark 9:1 to the kingdom's coming "with power" referred to the postresurrection period and the new community.

The nation must repent before the new order; in the time of the new world order tyrannies will disappear. Then there will be a time "to cast out the oppressor within their gates" (412).

Noel referred often to the Lazarus-Dives story. It is about riches gotten at the expense of the poor. The sayings about the rich not inheriting the kingdom were especially appealing to Noel as indicators of the heart of Jesus' message. He also interpreted Luke 17:21 as describing the kingdom "among you," which Noel took to mean "among you before you know it" (444). By prohibiting divorce Jesus championed women's rights.

The entrance into Jerusalem had political implications. The temple attack again was directed toward the greed of the priests and others profiteering on the trade.

On some controversy scenes, Noel emphasized the political: Give back to Caesar what according to your custom and usage belongs to Caesar, and to God what is God's. Paying taxes is unimportant in light of the new world order. The anti-Pharisaic, anti-Sadducean polemic suggested to Noel that these were the powerful authorities; he had little sympathy with the efforts of Herford and Abrahams to draw a more compassionate picture.

Judas was a nationalist revolutionary; he was disgusted with Jesus and betrayed Jesus' hiding place.

The Last Supper was a Passover; Jesus also washed feet at the meal. At his trials Jesus was framed; he was accused of blasphemy, but a charge of treason was put before Pilate. Then Jesus said his kingdom was not of this world, meaning that he did not intend to set up a rival to Rome (an exploiting imperial kingdom). Did Jesus come to die? A substitutionary doctrine of atonement should be rejected; there is also no predestination to hell. The death of Jesus was a gathering up of all martyrdoms into a unique act of sacrifice.

The tomb stories vary; the earthquake frightened the guards and rolled back the stone. Mary and the Beloved Disciple and Peter were all present. Jesus rose body and soul and spirit. Noel appealed to science, with the analogy of the atoms rearranging themselves: a healthy body cannot be destroyed, but its central energy holds and is transformed. The ascension is symbolic language. Jesus withdrew into central Energy in and above the universe.

An epilogue recounts the joy of the resurrection; thereafter the revolutionary zeal died down and the church capitulated under Constantine. Noel spoke highly of the Russian revolution, though faulted it for its atheism.

Various appendices complete this rather lengthy book, with some criticism of the myth-theorists and various other groups (fundamentalists, pacifists), and Form Criticism, of which Noel held a low opinion.

In the end Noel's work is really not very critical, employing every gospel to construct its story. It is not even a well-written book, marred by rambling, verbose descriptions. The socialist interpretation has some ground in the text, though as the central, overriding theme it fails to convince. A strong point for Noel was that the apocalyptic interpretation was recognized and given an appropriate value as iconoclastic protest. The eschatological-apocalyptic voice is that of the oppressed expressing its hopes for a better world. It is a hope that can give rise to activism in the world, and need not, according to the common liberal critique, issue in an attitude of withdrawal and indifference. But Noel's work finally can best be seen as the expression of his own life commitment; it was himself that he authenticated in his story of Jesus. He was not the only one.

Albert Field Gilmore

Quite a different "life" was that of Albert Field Gilmore, whose work, *Who Was This Nazarene?: A Challenging and Definitive Biography of the Master,* went through ten printings in five years.[33] Its announced thesis was that "Jesus was not God, but that as the Son of God he became the great Teacher and demonstrator of divine Power, because he was able to overcome material law through his understanding of spiritual Law, the Law which governs God's Kingdom" (ix). If that sounds suspiciously like a New Age perspective, that is so because it surely was, only it was nineteenth-century New Ageism ("New Thought") as enunciated by Mary Baker Eddy, the founder of Christian Science. The Jesus Gilmore claimed to recover was the "Way-Shower," the Christ to humanity, leading to that new consciousness that is the kingdom of heaven.

The teaching Gilmore thought he found in the gospels was summarized thus: Jesus became conscious of being the Christ, the Truth within, the Comforter, and of grasping spiritual law so thoroughly that he became this Way-Shower, to deliver all persons from sin and sickness, misery and poverty, and even from "belief in death itself as a real and inevitable experience" (2). He triumphed over all material law and taught his disciples how to do the same.

After a cursory examination of the evidence for the historicity of Jesus and the background to the rise of Christianity, Gilmore embarked on a discussion of the gospels. Mostly the information given was standard, but a special affection for John became evident throughout (it was written by the apostle at an advanced age in Ephesus; he had Paul and the synoptics before him). It supplements but does not contradict the synoptics.

---

33. Alfred Field Gilmore, *Who Was This Nazarene? A Challenging and Definitive Biography of the Master* (New York: Prentice-Hall, 1940). Gilmore was a journalist and a frequent author. More in the biographical appendix.

The birth was 5–6 B.C.E.; Mary was so illumined that she "rose above the human law of generation." In Jesus the Christ idea, the "divine emanation" was expressed in a human life (31). His youth is largely unknown, but he was well educated and likely traveled to Sepphoris and often to Jerusalem.

John the Baptist, his cousin, was a prophet to whom Jesus came for baptism and there saw himself as Son of God. He saw John as the messenger, but he, John, had mental states preventing his entrance into the kingdom of heaven. The temptation showed Jesus refusing the tempter's effort to convince him that life was materially conceived. Jesus rejected the carnal mind and conquered what everyone must in order to gain "mental ascendancy over the conditions attendant upon material existence" (52).

Jesus preached in the synagogue at Nazareth, meeting hostility to his new ideas, then went to Cana where he broke the material laws at a wedding by making wine. He worked at Capernaum, saw himself as messiah who had come to establish the new state of consciousness. He repudiated family, showing his utter break with human ties and his spiritual status. "Jesus had indeed launched his barque upon the limitless sea of spiritual endeavor whose farthest shore was the infinite Unseen, where the real man eternally abides" (63).

His preaching and teaching centered about "a transformed state of consciousness" (65), which was the kingdom of heaven; the works of healing were its demonstration. The Sermon on the Mount points the way to this new state. It teaches that a child of God is perfect, sinless, and immune to evil; only the mortal is subject to the destroyer. The material view of humanity is false. Only realizing so can the neighbor, who is really lovely, be loved. Prayer functions to bring into consciousness the realization of sonship and brotherhood and Fatherhood. Jesus commended fasting as "withdrawing from the belief of life in matter and of a material universe" (73). The parable of the builder on sand/rock contrasts the mind set on the mortal and fleshly with that set on the eternal Christ.

A second appearance at Cana resulted in the healing of a nobleman's son and showed the truth of the triumph of spirit over matter. All along was opposition from those who failed to grasp Jesus' message. The miracles accredit him as Lord and Way-Shower. Paul later truly grasped Jesus and understood also that material law was "based upon the belief of the carnal mind that life, intelligence, and substance inhere in matter" (86).

Among Jesus' healings was restoration of the dead. Life is deathless: "Man, God's creature, was never born into matter and in consequence never dies out of matter. This understanding restored to the sense of material existence those who believed they had died" (87). Events such as walking on water were direct nullifications of the law of gravity.

A parable was a short allegory to communicate spiritual truth. The wheat and weeds: spiritual truth mixes in the mind with the carnal, expelling it. Treasure and pearl: give all for the new state of consciousness.

Eternal life (John) is turning away from the material. It is also the "resurrection experience" (108), like that of Jesus himself, who so lost all sense of materiality that he transcended his own body and thus "resurrected" himself. Lazarus is another example. When Jesus said that Lazarus was dead, he was only using ordinary language, for he did not believe in the reality of death. That cannot be an experience of a truly spiritual person. The calling forth of Lazarus showed that Jesus relieved him of his sense of death.

Jesus taught the Fatherhood of God, who is the Source of all, Infinite Mind. The kingdom is purified consciousness; it is here, always present. Jesus trained disciples to perpetuate his teaching. He did not direct himself to society, but to individuals who, in their transformed existence, would then transform society. Jesus was not political and did not see himself as a ruling king. At his entrance into Jerusalem he wept over the city, for he realized it was mired in materiality and sin. He attacked the false worship and formalism of the temple and provoked the authorities. When he spoke about the coming Son of man, he was referring to the Comforter, who is the Christ ever-present.

Gilmore seemed to dismiss the sacraments in his discussion of the last supper; the spiritual person has no need of material symbols. Jesus was speaking of his constant communion with God.

Gilmore seemed to assume a real crucifixion and death, but effectively canceled them because Jesus was in complete control of his physical body. His body was only an objectification of materiality; his real self was never crucified and never died. His consciousness, which never could be destroyed, revived the body and it came forth from the tomb. His spiritual selfhood appeared to the disciples; the "resurrection" was simply the crowning event of many such events brought about by Jesus' spiritual consciousness. The ascension means that the spiritual Jesus, the Christ, gave up his material body forever. It was an inevitable conclusion to his life.

A final section enlarges on the long-term impact of the Christ idea and the resurrection, from the first disciples to Paul and forward.

The book had a pretense to learning, but mainly only referred to C. F. Kent's *The Life and Teaching of Jesus*.[34] In fact, it operated from a thoroughly Christian Science perspective: the emphasis on "consciousness" — a favored term in cult-like movements of all sorts — the denial of the reality of materiality, the understanding of existence purely idealistically, the affirmation of mental acts of healing, the abrogation of death's reality. Jesus, in fact, was a Christian Scientist. There is hardly any of it that an ancient gnostic would not recognize and applaud.

Harry Emerson Fosdick

To be taken more seriously was the work by the noted liberal minister at Riverside Church in New York, Harry Emerson Fosdick, titled *The Man from Nazareth:*

---

34. Above, chap. 3, n. 19.

As His Contemporaries Saw Him.[35] The book did not purport to be a "life" of Jesus (though it covered much the same territory), but its special take on the text was to see Jesus through the eyes of his contemporaries (crowds, Pharisees, and others).

Fosdick first disposed of the myth-theory, then examined Form Criticism. The latter made too much of the creativity of the community; Paul offered more historical information than was usually conceded. There are problems in the (synoptic) gospels, but the differences actually attest to the effort to write a real story. Standard items of dating and place of origin of the gospels were assumed.

The "crowds" saw Jesus as a Jew, a common person, one like themselves, nearer to the Pharisees than other groups. But he had a distinctive personality; his parables, for example, were not new in form, but his were nevertheless "breathtaking" (49) in originality. He was an artist in parable. The people also liked his attacks on other Pharisees. Miracles were an attraction, though Jesus himself was more ambiguous about them and downplayed their importance. So crowds saw Jesus as a wonder-worker, a teacher, a prophet, a friend, a powerful personality, maybe even as messiah.

The Pharisees, of whom Fosdick gave a fairly temperate account (recognizing recent revaluations of them), were nevertheless as a party opposed to Jesus, even if some were attracted to him. He was busy undoing their work, minimizing the ceremonial and threatening the distinctive culture of Judaism. The Pharisees put everything on the same level, ceremonial and ethical demand alike. There were counter-currents (Hillel), but still Pharisees were legalists. Jesus was a reformer and, while he hoped for an ultimate divine intervention (kingdom of God), he also attacked the evils of greed, prejudice, unfairness to women, and legalism. Apocalyptic hopes were "a stimulus to energetic action" (86). The main cause of difference between Jesus and the Pharisees was that Jesus thought of saving individuals and the Pharisees of preserving a culture (i.e., from heathenism or assimilation). For Jesus the imposition of rules to assure that goal only led to external conformity, whereas people must be internally transformed. Thus Pharisaism was critiqued as hypocrisy and outward conformity.

The self-complacent (like the elder brother, the rich who loved wealth, Simon the Pharisee) found Jesus a perfectionist; he blamed them for being satisfied with their own righteousness. He also saw the Pharisees as morally self-satisfied, even though the Pharisees, for their part, did not see the fulfillment of the Law as a burden, but rather as their glory. Jesus did teach love of the enemy, understood as the attempt to break the cycle of hate for hate, violence for violence. "Do not resist one who is evil" comes out, according to Fosdick, as an injunction not to resist evil with evil.

Jesus fought the idea of merit and reward. His demand was for excess good-

---

35. Harry Emerson Fosdick, *The Man from Nazareth: As His Contemporaries Saw Him* (New York: Harper, 1949). Consult the biographical appendix.

ness. There was a certain exuberance about Jesus, always going beyond the expected.

The religious and moral outcasts were attracted to Jesus, he to them. The *Am ha-aretz* were the nonpracticing Jews, though they were not exclusively lower class. Jesus believed in the redeemability of sinners and pictured God acting according to that belief. Women and children, by their status in society, virtually belonged in the same category. It was, in fact, unusual that so many women are mentioned in the record as in the company of this rabbi. Jesus treated them as he did men and called for redress of injustices done them.

Jesus' sayings and actions toward family are troublesome. "Hating" father and mother really means that the supreme sacrifice for the kingdom is willingness to give up family, which actually is a high exaltation of the family. [Here Fosdick outparadoxed Jesus.] Jesus' statements are problematic for those who hold to the belief in the virgin birth.

The first disciples felt Jesus' friendship and saw something new and prophetic in him. They thought of him as the messiah; whether he thought of himself as such is unknown. The disciples first thought of him as a prophet, then saw his unique relationship to God and moved to the thought of him as son — not divine — and finally as messiah. The latter carried a variety of meanings, however, though at least for the disciples it must have meant that he was God's agent, the instrument of salvation in Israel and in ushering in the kingdom. It is probable also that they came to see him as servant, as likely Jesus himself did as sacrificial Savior. This idea was combined finally with that of Son of man, though it was not until after the experience of resurrection that the latter was fully developed.

Militant nationalists might have seen Jesus as a national leader; he was tempted by that, but the militants turned against him. He cleansed the temple, but it was an act of religious reform. He sought no violent insurrection, but saw a bleak future for Israel and the destruction of Jerusalem. Perhaps he saw his people's rejection of him as rejection of their own salvation. His ethic of love of enemies was not compatible with the nationalists. It is paradoxical that Jesus the nonmilitant one died as an insurrectionist. He enraged the rulers in Jerusalem (attacked the temple); the people were with him, for they also resented the graft, but he was finally condemned as a political offender. "So the great pacifist was crucified as a criminal insurrectionist" (213).

Palestine at the time was widely hellenized; Greek was understood all around in Galilee and in Jerusalem as well. Diaspora Jews were influenced by Greco-Roman culture, and it is probable that Jesus was exposed to hellenistic Jews. The latter were more liberal and accommodating to culture and it would have been these for whom Jesus was more attractive. Was Jesus himself a universalist? He may have limited his first preaching to Israel, but it is unimaginable that he did not see the "lost sheep of the house of Israel" in many parts of the world. He did not command the universal mission as in Matthew 28, but showed an interest in Gentiles and they did also in him. He had before him the prophetic tradition of ethical monotheism and he cared for people regardless of who they were. Every soul was of infinite value in the sight of God. The kingdom also expressed his universalism: the kingdom is the sovereignty of God that all could enter now, though also it would be finally consummated. It was open to all on the basis of their ethical and spiritual attainment.

An epilogue asserts that it is the personality of Jesus that impressed the first disciples and still attracts people. We can still find the answer in him to the profoundest spiritual needs.

Fosdick's work moved beyond amateurism; he knew the issues and the dialogue about the historical Jesus, and he was able to set them forth in quite readable and attractive ways. The liberal lines remain visible in the presentation, if modified by the eschatological "discovery" that had also impressed itself onto the mainstream of New Testament scholarship.

Edgar J. Goodspeed

A final work to consider is that of the New Testament scholar at Chicago, Edgar J. Goodspeed, whose *A Life of Jesus* also reflected his own upbringing in a generally liberal environment (see the biographical appendix). He recognized that no biography of Jesus was possible, and also suggested that an emotionless presentation would not be effective.

A discussion of the gospels introduces this life: John was at Ephesus and was influenced by the letters of Paul; Mark was based on what John Mark remembered of Peter's Aramaic preaching; Matthew gives a picture of Jesus the Teacher, Luke's history appeared about 90 c.e. An oral period stands back of all. There is little help from literary works in Judaism, not much either from the Romans.

Jesus was born in 4 b.c.e., a descendant of David, in Bethlehem, in the time of Herod the Great. He attended synagogue as a boy and went at age 12 to Jerusalem. He derived the idea of God as his Father from his study of the prophets and the Psalms. Otherwise, there is a period of twenty years' silence in his life. We can infer that he had a religious life, though also there must have been some family divisions (James), from which came some dissatisfaction with the religion at home and in Nazareth.

John the Baptist appeared in 28–29; people saw him as an Elijah, the messenger before the Day of the Lord. He criticized the religious leaders and demanded baptism. Jesus, his cousin, came to him, was his disciple. At his baptism a great sense of vocation came over him, filling him with the Spirit. He later described the experience to his disciples, just as also he must have related the story of the Temptation.

He preached around the Sea of Galilee, proclaiming the kingdom of God as good news (unlike John, preacher of judgment); he did not claim to be messiah. He experienced rejection at home and worked the shores of Galilee, announcing the beginning of the reign of God. He called disciples at Capernaum and spent time with Simon, perhaps relating for the first time his baptismal experience with his choice as God's Beloved. He also spoke and cured a demoniac in the synagogue on the Sabbath. [He cured the man's delusion, as Goodspeed put it.] Jesus became known chiefly as a healer and a wonder-worker. He began his work at the end of 28 and it lasted about six months.

The Markan outline prevailed. Jesus and the disciples went about Galilee, contending with Pharisees and their masses of external minutiae — their "petty regulations" (62). Jesus went to the common people and the outcasts with a message of God's love and care for them as His children. He clashed with the Pharisees over his forgiveness of sins, association with sinners and tax collectors, fasting, and Sabbath practice. He made mortal enemies: "The shadow of the cross already falls across the gospel story" (71).

The Sermon on the Mount spoke of how to act in the kingdom of heaven on earth. While Pharisaism had been recently reappraised, noted Goodspeed, it nevertheless remained a "calculating religion" that was "based on agreement" between two parties (82). But Jesus emphasized attitude; he demanded the perfect, beyond the realm of Judaism.

Conflict with family and teaching followed. A parable is a fiction applied to moral instruction. The seed-sowing parable delivers a warning to consider what kind of seed a person will be. Parables appealed to the familiar to deliver a deep message with a religious direction.

Goodspeed engaged in some rationalizing of miracles, even a little outright denial. On the demoniac and the swine story, Goodspeed suggested that the man was controlled by multiple personalities and that Jesus "humored him" (92). The animals panicked at the scene and rushed into the sea. At Nazareth the synagogue people tried to toss him off the cliff, but "with his awe-inspiring mien, he strode through the midst of them and was gone" (99). Of the feeding story, Jesus' example of sharing moved everyone to do likewise. On the sea-walking, the disciples were frightened by this ghostlike figure "as though walking on the sea" and they "screamed with fear" (106). But we have to understand that demons, ghosts, and phantoms were part of the disciples' common world.

John the Baptist played Elijah to Jesus' role as suffering servant. More clashes with the Pharisees (food laws, washing) led to Jesus' fleeing through Tyre and Sidon and later arriving at Caesarea-Philippi. There Jesus reinterpreted the title of "messiah," introducing the notion of suffering. He also spoke of the harsh conditions of discipleship and of the End that was soon to come. He shared the apocalyptic views of his contemporaries about the coming judgment and the End. He recognized that the kingdom was already here, but also that there would be a future triumph of God. "Son of man" can mean either merely a man or the messianic agent.

Jesus meant to go to Jerusalem; he did not wish to die in Galilee, but would face his enemies in Jerusalem. At Passover he would offer himself as messiah and take the consequences; or, as Goodspeed put it, offer them their "messianic destiny, the moral and religious leadership of mankind" (134).

Along the way to Jerusalem Jesus taught and sent out more disciples, passing through Samaria and recounting famous parables, such as the prodigal son and the good Samaritan. He hoped to stir a popular backing and set up the kingdom — not a political one, but one in the hearts and lives of people. Jesus became changed and absorbed as he traveled, but the disciples were expecting a glorious triumph (sitting on thrones). Jesus made secret arrangements for celebrating the Passover and dramatized his entrance into the city. He assumed the role of messiah. At the temple he attacked the prerogatives of the priesthood, seeking a decision and defending the position of the poor and exploited. Pharisees now cooperated with Sadducees to rid themselves of Jesus. He spoke harshly now of Pharisees who had hedged the Law about with frivolous detail and made it inaccessible to ordinary people. Religion was an "aristocratic privilege" (183).

At the last supper Jesus took leave of his disciples and instructed them to repeat the meal as a memorial to him, perpetuating his work and memory. He also meant to weld the disciples into a new covenant community — in effect, to found the church. The meal was originally a Passover observance, with four cups of wine and all the rest.

We should not, however, blame the Jewish people for what happened to Jesus. The priests were behind it. Blasphemy was alleged against Jesus, which the governor could take to mean that Jesus wished to be king. So Jesus was condemned and died with a cry of disillusionment and despair, maybe out of delirium. Only women were present at the end, which was no peaceful death for Jesus. Joseph buried him as an act of piety, as was practiced in Judaism.

The ending to Mark's story has been lost, but has been preserved in Matthew who scrupulously follows Mark up to that point and therefore it can be assumed that he has kept Mark's material intact. So there was a meeting in Galilee; the story describes this amazing phenomenon that speaks of Jesus as a continuing spiritual presence with his disciples. The explication of that theme is the gospel of John.

Goodspeed was clearly in command of his material and had the capacity to communicate at the popular level, even though his work makes some demands on an uninformed audience. The Jesus presented is still in the mold of his liberal predecessors — a nonmiracle-working figure contending with Pharisaic opponents — but with also some conversion to the eschatological faith.

On the whole these works are not such contemptible performances as they might seem; they address themselves to the ongoing issue of the relevance of Jesus and to truthfulness in his name. And if in their endeavor to speak to those concerns they sometimes abandon too far the connection with history, then let it be so. The earliest church also ran that risk and some of its partisans did likewise, flirting with a nonhistorical figure at the center. The desire to elevate Jesus always carries with it the danger of losing him.

If there is one overwhelming impression from these popular works, it is that their variety matches and even exceeds that produced by their more scholarly counterparts. And yet we need not dismiss them on that ground, either, for they demonstrate something of the seductive power of the image of Jesus. The western world never wearies of retelling Jesus' story and finds a thousand ways to do it. Is that because there still burns a resilient faith in even an increasingly secularized society? Or is it merely testimony to the fascination of a figure so enigmatic that no single explanation ever suffices? Perhaps the "genius" of Jesus, about which so many have essayed to compose, is itself this capacity to inspire seemingly endless visions, so that finally the quest for the historical Jesus presents itself as the perpetual quest for human authenticity.

Meso-Logue

BACK AND FORTH

We began this journey by observing differences of scholarly style, of traditions rooted in national and cultural identities. There is almost an identifiable German historical Jesus, an English one, an American one, and so on. Almost, but not quite, and direct correlations do not seem to exist. But in general terms, a liberal German version would tend to be nonpolitical and stand out from his environment, a unique phenomenon even though parallels abound. The English (often Scottish as well) would actually come closer to a common paradigm, almost as though there lay deep in the bowels of the Bodleian library an *Ur-Leben-Jesu* to which everyone had access, and it pictured a Jesus who posed himself as the suffering servant–Son of man messiah, aware of it at his baptism and foreseeing his fate in Jerusalem. The American Jesus borrowed much from his German counterparts, but with a greater focus on the social implications of his message. So certainly one of Schweitzer's original lessons keeps coming around, and it reminds us of the propensity to find in Jesus that which we need to find and to paint him in the colors of our own time and culture. In this sense the deniers of Jesus' historicity were right: there is no historical Jesus, not because he did not exist, but because he is available only in pluriform ways.

At the same time we should not overlook the existence of some consensuses. There is a universal commitment to a critical method, and while a grand struggle went on to arrive at this point, by midcentury hardly anyone would have contested it. Even in Roman Catholic circles the dam had burst and the flood was coming. On specific issues, there was widespread agreement that Jesus had in fact been baptized by John — Loisy is an exception — though not everyone agreed on its meaning. Furthermore, the relationship between Jesus and John remained something of a puzzle; Jesus associated with John, but declined his apocalyptic message, so it was widely thought. Some kind of a break has to be assumed, though the text is less than specific on that point.

Certainly also the eschatological nature of Jesus' preaching was everywhere conceded. Schweitzer's work — and Weiss before him — had its impact, though the debate over present and future aspects of the message continued unabated for some time and tended finally toward an agreement on some degree of both. There also remained a fundamental suspicion of apocalypticism and frequent efforts to disassociate Jesus from it. Apocalypticism was regarded as largely a retreat from the world, or, even worse, the rantings of maniacs. Little effort was extended toward seeing how an apocalyptic worldview could also be associated with a pronounced social concern (with some exceptions, as seen in Shailer Mathews and C. C. McCown). The American medievalist Richard Landes suggests a slightly different possibility: that apocalyptic movements inevitably create social change by their *failed* expectations.[1] That is, such groups transgress social boundaries in the light of their expectation of a coming transformed world — what F. C. Burkitt aptly called the Good Time Coming. The new world is at hand: everyone will be equal, there will be justice for all, and so on. When the expectation fails, as inevitably it must, such groups are left with a whole new set of social attitudes that have to be assimilated and are usually also spread around. So Shailer Mathews's characterization of the apocalypses as the code language of revolution has much to commend it,[2] provided that we allow the language to become eventful in social ways. Most of the liberal voices in our study were not so willing. Even further, how apocalyptic, speculative pictures of the future, which are surely the work of an educated scribal class, can be integrated sociologically with a peasant or lower social group is an issue that had not occurred to anyone to raise.

There was also a virtually unanimous agreement — a negative point — that Schweitzer's *Interimsethik* was untenable and an inappropriate reading of Jesus' ethical teaching (Burkitt was an exception). Here again the ground of the ethic, however, left room for debate. Amos Wilder's emphasis on the aesthetic and symbolic dimension in the eschatological message of Jesus had hardly any parallels among his contemporaries, and deserved more exploration than it received. Bousset had spoken of the symbolic significance of the historical Jesus in general, but in a quite different context (historicity of Jesus).

Another smaller point gathering near universal agreement was that Jesus was a healer, especially that he healed and exorcized. Just how much of the healing tradition should be accredited was not agreed to, although the other side of the miracle coin, the nature miracles, scared away most everybody. Not much had changed on that question since the older days of rationalism.

There was also the obvious fact of Jesus' death by crucifixion, though there remained plenty of room for disagreement over the reason for Jesus' condemnation and death. The recognition was clearly growing, however, that the Jewish authorities, not to mention the people, had been unjustly blamed and that the Romans must assume responsibility. Part of the problem lay in the fact that hardly anyone was willing to concede any political significance — a consensus

---

1. As cited in Stephen Jay Gould's *Questioning the Millennium* (New York: Harmony Books, 1997), 61–62, without specific attribution. There are scattered remarks in Richard Landes' *Relics, Apocalypse, and the Deceits of History: Ademar of Chabannes, 989–1034,* Harvard Historical Studies 117 (Cambridge: Harvard University Press, 1995), esp. 287ff., with reference to *les terreurs de l'an mil,* so called by some, surrounding the end of the first millennium and especially the work of the monk Ademar, the chief focus of the book. There are references also to a larger body of studies on apocalypticism, e.g., 288 n. 3.

2. Mathews, *New Testament Times in Palestine,* 238.

in itself — to Jesus' death. A dilemma seemed to reside in the tradition: a non-political, nonviolent Jesus who suffered a political, violent death. The customary explanations were that it was all somehow a mistake, that the Jewish authorities swayed Pilate to carry out their nefarious wills, or that Jesus' movement was misinterpreted politically. A few, like C. J. Cadoux or F. C. Grant, sought a closer link between Jesus' activity and his political death.

In fact, there is something hauntingly dissonant about the death of Jesus. If we think of other such deaths, something like Socrates comes to mind, but the differences are also profound. Socrates died surrounded by his disciples; Jesus' deserted him. Both were disavowed by public authorities, but the manner of Socrates' death was honorable, while Jesus could not look forward to being honorably gathered to his ancestors; in fact, by the law (Deut. 21:23; Gal. 3:13) he was cut off, accursed by God. A modern parallel might be suggested by the assassination of Martin Luther King Jr., but while both events were public, only Jesus' was an act of the state. In each case the social context differs. Perhaps we have not yet taken sufficient account of that social context.[3] If Jesus were crucified merely as a messianic aspirant, he might well have been regarded as a hero in some quarters, but there is no hint of such an evaluation. The actual course of events will no doubt forever remain a mystery, barring the discovery of some official archives, but the best reconstructions will need to pay attention to the social impact of Jesus' movement in order to find an adequate ground for his death. It will hardly do anymore merely to describe a Jesus who spoke only to individuals about their private lives and urged everyone to love everyone else. The predominant opinion that Jesus displayed no special concern with *politics* as such has something to commend it, if by that we mean that he apparently (if the record is reliable) did not explicitly focus on the political issues of the day; but that ought not to exclude consideration of the larger *social* ramifications of the movement to which he gave birth.[4]

The Jewishness of Jesus also came to be taken as axiomatic by the middle of the century, concurrent with more sober evaluations of Pharisaism in particular and Judaism generally. Much of that was due to the impact of Jewish scholarship and its attention to the historical Jesus. How this Jewish Jesus came to be lost has been alluded to all along the way, but some further backward glancing is appropriate at this midpoint.

The core issue was the originality or uniqueness of Jesus. This became an issue particularly in the liberal school early on in the century. *Religionsgeschicht-*

---

3. Shirley Jackson Case saw the death as social conflict, the *Am ha-aretz* of whom Jesus was one arraigned against the forces of scribism. An interesting study would be to collect the scenes of public executions from antiquity to determine whether parallels exist and what was their social context.

4. Political here has in view the Roman occupation and its implications and not only inner-Jewish affairs, which were certainly political insofar as religion and politics were inseparable. It can be further noted, as many have, that the immediate cause of Jesus' arrest was his attack on the temple. That speaks to the issue of his own intention, for if he had intended a purely political act aimed at Rome, he might well have attempted to overrun the Antonia or at least direct some symbolic gesture toward it. But that kingdom of God itself is a political metaphor can hardly be contested.

liche investigations disclosed a Jesus whose message — the center for liberalism — had many parallels, such that it seemed that Jesus had nothing original to say. The liberals had also compounded the predicament because they no longer held to any christology and were thereby driven to seek other reasons for maintaining an interest in Jesus. The position of liberalism subjected it to criticism from the left in the form of the denial of Jesus' historicity, and from the right from those who said it had abandoned Christian faith altogether. One maneuver was to emphasize Jesus' marvelous contributions to western civilization and his importance for its maintenance; this temptation especially found embodiment in popular portrayals of Jesus, though it was not at all lacking in scholarly ones. It foundered, and still does, on the unpleasant fact that there is little in Jesus that lends itself to such a treatment, as Klausner had pointed out. Civilization needs law; Jesus seemed to take a somewhat sovereign attitude toward it. Society prizes wealth; Jesus, as C. T. Craig observed, spurned it. Even today Jesus is invoked as defender of family values; actually, he spoke harshly of the ties that bind, apparently practiced celibacy, never married, and distanced himself from the family that attempted to put him away.[5] Some may have considered that he came under the Deuteronomic stricture against a rebellious son who was to be stoned as a glutton and a drunkard (Deut. 21:20; Matt. 11:19=Luke 7:34). He prohibited divorce, urged love of enemies, and forbade revenge — all matters that few have ever willingly subscribed to. The world generally also bows to the powerful; Jesus sought out the poor and outcasts. He left no art, no music, and no literary works, though he did create some incredible poetic parables. But it is hardly possible to take his message as a whole and erect a civilization on it. His influence cannot be gauged apart from the community that arose after him persuaded of his resurrection.

It is also probably impossible to know just exactly what influence Jesus had on his own time. Was it a truly revolutionary movement attended by thousands? Undoubtedly it assumed a threatening shape, else it would not have ended so badly. Would it have been permanent without the subsequent Easter faith?[6] That seems retrospectively highly unlikely, and consequently the attempt to erect a faith severed from christological underpinnings is probably futile.[7] Whether such a faith should be called Christian faith is yet another question.

---

5. I assume the authenticity of those relevant Markan scenes; it could be argued that they merely serve Mark's basic suffering-disciple theme, which they do, but that does not necessarily rule them out. The sayings about children and the kingdom form no exception, for there it is a matter of the naive openness of children that counts in the kingdom, not of a special affection being manifested for children in themselves (though naturally there is no reason to imagine that Jesus disliked children).

6. How and why the earliest title given him was ὁ χριστός remains pertinent, if also puzzling, especially for a criticism that thinks Jesus himself made no messianic claims.

7. I have suggested elsewhere that it is possible to think of the total picture of Jesus, the historical Jesus, as a kind of parable that can inform existence in various ways, but I did not propose to set it over against the Easter faith of the community. See the essay "Jesus as Parable," in *Earthing Christologies: From Jesus Parables to Jesus the Parable*, ed. James H. Charlesworth and Walter P. Weaver, Faith and Scholarship Colloquies (Valley Forge, Pa.: Trinity Press International, 1995), 19–45.

Here also those recurring questions about the "relevance" of Jesus for the "modern" world, especially so characteristic for English and American writers, come into play. Not only the ethic of Jesus, but his apparent trust in a benevolent providence clanged harshly in modern ears. Such trust would seem rationally indefensible, given the force and nature of indeterminate evil events in the world. But it can also be asked: Was Jesus himself so totally unaware of the difficulties wrapped in his proclamation? I would think not, and there are hints to that effect in his recognition of the rain falling equally on the just and the unjust, and in such sayings as are collected in Luke 13:1–5, warning about the fate of Galileans whose blood Pilate mixed with their sacrifices and of the nameless eighteen upon whom the tower of Siloam had chanced to crash. Here was a good opportunity to say something about the relevance of his posture, but Jesus declined to do so and contented himself with advancing another lesson about repentance, presumably in anticipation of the kingdom. Perhaps Bultmann spoke the appropriate word on this point: In Jesus' view God is not obliged to provide an explanation to human beings of their course in life. Certainly Jesus did not offer any such explanation, but just as certainly he was familiar with the randomness of life and its apparent inconsistency with the notion of a benevolent fatherly God overseeing even the plummeting sparrows. Faith in such a God stands on no empirical ground, but Jesus stood there nevertheless. This nevertheless seems characteristic of him, and it can only be assented to in the context of a faith-decision.

But to come back: the categories of "original" or "unique" will remain problematic, if only because we do not and hardly can possess all the variables in Jesus' environment, or anybody else's, in order to make such a judgment, as already Henry Cadbury recognized. "Unique" was important to those who had lost the customary ground for interest in Jesus, that is, those with no christology, if not only for them.[8] This same concern was implicated in the establishment of the criteria of authenticity. In order to demonstrate the uniqueness of Jesus, it had to be shown that there was an irreducible minimum of genuine material that could then be seen as Jesus' novel contribution. At first the criteria of authenticity were limited to multiple attestation and difference from the theology of the community after Jesus. At the same time, as can be seen in Weinel (1911), there was this emphasis on the special position of Jesus, how he transcended his environment, broke the framework of his Judaic context, and so on. In his consideration of the logia Bultmann moved the discussion a step further when he proposed that, in order to attain this irreducible minimum, all that was from wisdom, folklore, rabbinic, and apocalyptic literature should be discounted. Bultmann had no particular agenda so far as I can see except to reach a bottom layer of tradition, but the effect was to contribute to a picture of a Jesus who merely transcended his Jewish setting. The quest for the uniqueness of Jesus issued fi-

8. As noted earlier (above, 212), this focus was not the exclusive preserve of the liberals, as conservative scholars as well were given to elevating Jesus and searching for his uniqueness, though each was moved by a different reason.

nally in a scarcely Jewish Jesus. There were mitigating movements elsewhere, as can be seen in the sociohistorical emphasis of the so-called Chicago School, more particularly in the work of Shirley Jackson Case. Its insistence was precisely the opposite: to set Jesus within his own social environment. But that movement proved to be a Pauline ἔκτρωμα, born out of its time.

A more circumspect method has emerged certainly since the period covered by this study, with the development and application of sociological and cultural-anthropological models. It remains legitimate to ask about the *distinctiveness* of Jesus, or what was *characteristic* of Jesus, as can be asked about any historical figure, *within* his social context. To press the question still further and ask about the *uniqueness* of Jesus is to mount a higher level challenge and one that seems impossible to respond to adequately, and perhaps even one that arouses the suspicion of being simply an enterprise of apologetics.[9]

Is the historical Jesus necessary? So some ask. Probably he is not, but he is inevitable. Historical Jesus, by definition the Jesus reconstructed by historical study, is — to produce a seeming truism — the only access today to the *historical* figure. In earlier times the church still maintained the *necessity* of Jesus as a genuine figure of history, else its own confessional position would have been endangered and exposed to some form of Gnosticism. To suppose, as Troeltsch did, that the historicity of Jesus as the head of the cultic community is necessary and therefore the labors of the scholars and professors are also necessary for faith, is to discount centuries of the faithful who had no access to a historical Jesus. There are still today millions who do not know of any historical Jesus; part of the interest of the dialectical movement was to insure that ordinary believers were not delivered irretrievably into the hands of the specialists. That remains an authentic concern.

Others might be content with the story itself, with symbol and myth, similar to Bousset's symbolic Jesus.[10] There is much to be said for that. Religious groups create discourse communities within which they speak knowingly to one another a shared language that informs their communal existence. It is not often asked, within those communities, whether the discourse refers back to something provable in history. If it should be shown that it does not, that might well destroy the community or at least precipitate a crisis within it. Schweitzer could calmly contemplate the possibility that Christian faith might have to get along with a nonhistorical Jesus, and he expressed his wish for the creation of a metaphysics

---

9. Surely it can be argued that Jesus is unique in his impact on western history and so on, but the question again is whether that impact can be measured apart from the community that came after him proclaiming his resurrection from the dead and his installation into the office of eschatological Redeemer.

10. A pertinent early article was by K. C. Anderson, "The Collapse of Liberal Christianity," *HibJ* 8 (1909–10): 301–20, who argued the truth of story whether provable or not; poetry is the finest form of truth, and myth is the unconscious poetry of the human heart uttering truths too subtle for the mind to grasp. (316). Anderson was contending for the orthodox picture, even if it cannot be shown to be connected to the historical figure. Benjamin W. Bacon dissented in a succeeding article, "The Mythical Collapse of Historical Christianity," *HibJ* 9 (1910–11): 731–53.

that would undergird the enterprise of Christian faith. His wrath was aimed at those who had tied the knot so tightly with the shifting fortunes of history. But some might find it plausible and possible to live with a meaningful story, knowing that most humans do so anyway on a daily basis. That does not preclude wishing to know as much as can be known about the source of the story, but at least it delivers the conscience from a troubled anxiety over the rootage of the story in demonstrable history. It also says nothing about the value of one story over another, but in the end those are matters of decision or at least of belonging already within a given faith community.[11]

One of the difficulties — and there is more than one — to be faced when attempting to lodge Christian faith exclusively in the historical Jesus is that some of the most demanding issues in life cannot be adequately addressed. Faith is reduced to ethical guidance, with perhaps some authority attributable to Jesus' eschatological hope, even though his apparent anticipation of the imminent kingdom was disappointed. But certain elements are missing that are represented only in the kerygmatic message after Easter: a salvation already effective and present and a sacramental community worshiping and serving in Jesus' name. Already this gap in the liberal vision was seen and urged against liberalism in the early part of the century,[12] and it remains a contentious point for anyone wishing to locate Christian faith in the historical Jesus.

So it is a wondrous if sometimes fitful journey through the landscape of *Leben-Jesu-Forschung*. There are manifold figures residing there, both among the authors and the Jesuses as well. But some are noticeably absent, among them *women* authors. Here and there are whispers of women participants, shadow-figures around the edges: an Ada Weinel, anonymous members of Sanday's synoptic problem seminar, a Mary Austin, a Mary Lyman, and there are male authors who rose to advocate on behalf of women. There is also a handful of books about Jesus and women, even one written by a woman.[13] But predominantly women appeared

---

11. My point here is not that provable history in general is unimportant, but that, with regard to the special story of Jesus, that part of it that can be demonstrated seems to most Christians the least significant, while the most significant is that part of it that is the least demonstrable.

12. For example, the urgings of the orthodox Scottish theologian Hugh R. Mackintosh, "The Liberal Conception of Jesus in Its Strength and Weakness," *AJT* 16 (1912): 410–25, esp. 422–23. He was not unsympathetic to the quest of the historical Jesus.

13. Johannes Leipoldt, *Jesus und die Frauen* (Leipzig: Quelle und Meyer, 1921); Madeline Southard, *The Attitude of Jesus toward Women* (New York: George H. Doran, 1927). Both traced the position of women in ancient cultures and found Jesus ahead of all in his treatment of women as equals of men. The work by Peter Ketter, *Christ and Womankind,* trans. Isabel McHugh (Westminster, Md.: Newman Press, 1951[German original, 1935]), is a Roman Catholic defense of traditional roles of women: Mary is the model of femininity. Leipoldt's sympathies apparently gravitated later to *Nationale Socialismus*, though the bio in *NDBb 14* (see biographical appendix) took no notice of his involvement; yet even as early as 1923 he composed a monograph questioning the Jewishness of Jesus (*War Jesus Jude?* [Leipzig: A. Deichert, 1923]). On Mary Lyman, see the biographical appendix and her little study book on Jesus in the annotated bibliography. There was also in America the Columbia University professor in religious education, Adelaide Teague Case (1887–1948), who was also the first woman to serve on the faculty of the Episcopal Theological Seminary in Cambridge,

mainly as authors of children's books, or books of a generally edifying nature, or ones having some bearing on religious education.[14] How impoverished by that circumstance studies of the historical Jesus have been can only be regretted. A different world lay ahead, though some years ahead.

That world would be for a short time one still shaped by the creative energies emanating from the German side but over a longer period would begin to shift its center to America. Even at the conclusion of the war this thought entered the conversation of the American academy, in an address by the president of the Society of Biblical Literature and Exegesis for 1945, Morton Scott Enslin.[15] He saw opportunity for American leadership in the field of biblical scholarship in the current international scene in which Germany and England were in little condition to make any substantial contribution for an unknown time; too many in Germany had prostituted themselves to the national cause, too many in England were long in the habit of ignoring the Americans. The opportunity was there, but Enslin expressed grave doubts as to whether the Americans were quite up to the challenge, what with ministerial students more interested in warm hearts than impassioned intellects, and tired liberals feigning devotion to Barthian dialectics. It was not an optimistic assessment, though probably one item that, in fact, did push America forward was a fortuitous early participation in the uncovering and publication of the Dead Sea Scrolls.

An aging Shirley Jackson Case, on the other hand, was preparing a new volume on *The Personal Religion of Jesus,* as a kind of response to the Barthian movement or, as he put it, "to revive historical interest in Jesus of Nazareth."[16] Case and most American-English liberals never quite made their peace with Barthianism. It seems unlikely that a new liberal version of the historical Jesus would have stanched the dialectical movement, whose time had come, but such a work anticipated at least the new Quest, as it came to be called, in its effort to return to the question of the historical Jesus. So there was a state of flux at the time; newer forces were making their way more widely into the western world and still crossing swords with the old guard.

Massachusetts. Her volume, *As Modern Writers See Jesus: A Descriptive Bibliography of Books About Jesus* (Boston: Pilgrim Press, 1927), gave a thumbnail sketch of a variety of material on Jesus, from then current lives (Klausner, Bosworth, Headlam, and so on) to poetry and plays about Jesus. (See further *NotAW* 1:301–2, and Sydney Temple, ed., *Peace Is Possible: Essays Dedicated to the Memory of Adelaide T. Case* [Deep River, Conn.: New Era Press, 1949].)

14. Bibliography of children's works in Warren Kissinger, *The Lives of Jesus: A History and Bibliography* (New York: Garland Publishing, 1985).

15. "The Future of Biblical Studies," *JBL* 65 (1946): 1–12.

16. The remains are found in the archives at Florida Southern. The quote is from a proposed preface in his own handwriting, and there is unfinished material from his work on the book. Case's health problems and his death in 1947 precluded any further development of the idea. The first chapter was published as "The Lure of Christology," in *JR* 25 (1945): 157–67. The otherwise perceptive work by William Hynes, *Shirley Jackson Case and the Chicago School: The Socio-Historical Method,* Biblical Scholarship in North America 5 (Chico, Calif.: Scholars Press, 1981), doubted the existence of such a book (25) on the evidence then available, but the material supporting it has since been uncovered.

I would not by any means wish to end by demeaning that old guard. There have been occasions all along the way when the movement broadly known as liberalism has seemingly been chastised. In fact, liberalism left an amazing legacy; it gave us much and we are not really done with its heritage. It gave us a developed critical methodology, posed the great issues of faith and culture, and sought a path that would allow Christian faith to exist in a world that was increasingly hostile or indifferent to such faith. Even Bultmann must be seen as still largely following its way in his desire to find an appropriate hermeneutic with which to present the Christian proclamation. Barth's rejection was more decidedly complete, and while Barth surely ranks as the greatest dogmatic theologian of the twentieth century, the task he set himself is not one that appeals to everyone.

But enough: a tale worth telling remains before us. The direction taken in the ensuing three decades is the story that awaits.

BIOGRAPHICAL APPENDIX

Sources found are listed parenthetically after each name; those sources actually consulted are given in bold abbreviated form, according to the table set forth below. A single or special source used is listed as appropriate, without abbreviations. The list of names does not include every figure mentioned and biographical data are meager or difficult to locate in some instances. Some are included whose role in the narrative was minor, but who might otherwise be of a wider interest. Others whose general biographies were included in the narrative may not be repeated here.

Sources and Abbreviations

AAR	American Academy of Religion
Alli	*Allibone: A Critical Dictionary of English Literature*
AlliSUP	*Allibone: A Critical Dictionary of English Literature (Supplement)*
AmAu&B	*American Authors and Books*
AmBi	*American Biographies*
AmLY	*The American Literary Yearbook*
AnCL	*Anthology of Children's Literature*
AmWomWr	*American Women Writers*
ApCAB	*Appleton's Cyclopedia of American Biography*
Au&Wr	*The Author's and Writer's Who's Who*
AuBYP	*Authors of Books for Young People*
BdD	*The Bibliophile Dictionary*
BiD&SB	*Biographical Dictionary and Synopsis of Books*
BiDrAC	*Biographical Directory of the American Congress*
BiDAmM	*Biographical Dictionary of American Music*
BiDSA	*Biographical Dictionary of Southern Authors*
CasWL	*Cassell's Encyclopedia of World Literature*
CathA	*Catholic Authors*
ChPo	*Childhood in Poetry*
CIDMEL	*Columbia Dictionary of Modern European Literature*
CnDAL	*Concise Dictionary of American Literature*
ConAmA	*Contemporary American Authors*
ConAmL	*Contemporary American Literature*

ConAu	*Contemporary Authors*
ConAuNRS	*Contemporary Authors*, New Revision series
ConAuP	*Contemporary Authors*, Permanent series (2 vols.)
ConAuR	*Contemporary Authors*, first Revision series
CurBio	*Current Biography*
CyAL	*Cyclopedia of American Literature*
CyWA	*Cyclopedia of World Authors*
DcAmAu	*Dictionary of American Authors*
DcAmB	*Dictionary of American Biography*
DcAmReB	*Dictionary of American Religious Biography*
DcBF	*Dictionnaire de Biographie Française*
DcEnL	*Dictionary of English Literature*
DcLEL	*A Dictionary of Literature in the English Language*
DcNAA	*A Dictionary of North American Authors*
DcNB	*Dictionary of National Biography*
Drake	*Drake: Dictionary of American Biography*
DrASP	*Directory of American Scholars*, vol. 4, *Philosophy, Religion, and Law*
EncAB	*Encyclopedia of American Biography*
EncTR	*Encyclopedia of the Third Reich*
EncWL	*Encyclopedia of World Literature in the Twentieth Century*
EvEuW	*Everyman's Dictionary of European Writers*
EvLB	*Everyman's Dictionary of Literary Biography, English and American*
Ferm	Virgilius Ferm, ed., *Contemporary American Theology: Theological Autobiographies* (New York: Round Table Press, 1932), vol. I.
ICC	*International Critical Commentary*
IndAu	*Indiana Authors and Their Books*
IntAu&W	*International Authors and Writers Who's Who*
IntWW	*The International Who's Who*
InWom	*Index to Women*
JBL	*Journal of Biblical Literature*
Kep	Appendix to Thomas Kepler, ed., *Contemporary Thinking About Jesus: an Anthology* (New York and Nashville: Abingdon-Cokesbury, 1944)
Kml	Biographical Appendix in W. G. Kümmel, *The New Testament: the History of the Investigation of Its Problems*, trans. S. McLean Gilmour and Howard C. Kee (Nashville: Abingdon, 1972)
LibW	*Liberty's Women*
LinLib L	*The Lincoln Library of Language Arts*
LinLib S	*The Lincoln Library of Social Studies*
LongCTC	*Longman Companion to Twentieth Century Literature*

ModFrL	*Modern French Literature*
McGEWB	*The McGraw-Hill Encyclopedia of World Biography*
NatCAB	*The National Cyclopedia of American Biography*
NDBb	*Neue Deutsche Biographie (Bayerischen Akademie der Wissenschaften)*
NDNC	*Nouveau Dictionnaire National des Contemporains*
NotAW	*Notable American Women*
NewC	*The New Century Handbook of English Literature*
NotNAT	*Notable Names in the American Theatre*
NYT	*New York Times*
OhAu&B	*Ohio Authors and Books*
OxAm	*The Oxford Companion to American Literature*
OxFr	*The Oxford Companion to French Literature*
OxGer	*The Oxford Companion to German Literature*
PenEur	*The Penguin Companion to European Literature*
P-M Hanbk	Dean G. Peerman and Martin E. Marty, eds., A *Handbook of Christian Theologians* (New York: World, 1965)
PoIre	*The Poets of Ireland*
REn	*The Reader's Encyclopedia*
REnAL	*The Reader's Encyclopedia of American Literature*
RGG	*Religion in Geschichte und Gegenwart*
S	Supplement
SBLE	*Society of Biblical Literature and Exegesis*
Str&VC	*Story and Verse for Children*
TwCA	*Twentieth Century Authors*
TwCBDA	*The Twentieth Century Biographical Dictionary of Notable Americans*
TwCW	*Twentieth Century Writing*
WebAB	*Webster's American Biographies*
Wei?	*Wer Ist's?*
WeW	*Wer ist Wer*
WhAm	*Who Was Who in America*
WhGB	*Who Was Who (Great Britain)*
WhE&EA	*Who Was Who among English and European Authors*
WhLit	*Who Was Who in Literature*
WhNAA	*Who Was Who among North American Authors*
Who	*Who's Who*
WhoAm	*Who's Who in America*
WhoAmP	*Who's Who in American Politics*
WhoF	*Who's Who in France* (English title, contents in French)

WhoLA	*Who's Who among Living Authors of Older Nations*
WhoWorJ	*Who's Who in World Jewry*
WhoRel	*Who's Who in Religion*
WomWWA	*Woman's Who's Who of America*
WorAu	*World Authors*
WhoWor	*Who's Who in the World*
WrDr	*The Writer's Directory*

Note: Generally, page numbers are omitted since virtually all sources are arranged alphabetically. An exception is *NatCAB,* in which case the page number follows the colon after volume number (e.g., 23:133). *Who's Who* volumes are referenced by years, except *Who Was* volumes, which are referenced by volume number.

*Indicates an unconfirmed date and refers to the last reference in the sources.

Contemporary Authors in the original series (above, without further designation) was issued in vols. 1, 2, 3, and 4, and then 5–8 through 97–100. Thereafter it was issued in single volumes, 101–168. A revision series was also issued, comprising most of the original series and some further information; it was also in the form of several volumes to a single book, with four volumes each through 97–100. The New Revision series is issued in single volumes. Two separate volumes were issued as the Permanent series.

Biographies

1. **Abbott, Lyman** (1835–1922). Congregational minister, journalist, lawyer, advocate of liberal theological positions. Educated New York University (B.A.), studied law independently and practiced for six years (1853–59), then took up theological studies. Served parishes in Indiana during the Civil War, encouraging reconciliation, then moved to New York to become corresponding secretary of the American Union Commission and pastor of the New England Congregational Church. Wrote for *Harper's* magazine and later published works such as *The Life and Literature of the Ancient Hebrews* and *The Theology of an Evolutionist,* seeking sympathetic alliance between theology and evolution. He was allied with Henry Ward Beecher as editor of the *Christian Union* and later succeeded Beecher at Plymouth Church, Brooklyn. Supported Theodore Roosevelt and the Progressive Party, as well as the early entry of America in the Great War. (*Alli; AlliSUP; AmAu&B; AmLY; ApCAB; BdD; Bid&SB; CyAL; DcAmAu;* **DcAmB; DcAmReB;** *DcEnL; DcNAA; Drake; LinLib L, LinLib S; McGEWB; NatCAB; OxAm; REn; REnAL; TwCA; TwCA S; TwCBDA; WebAB; WhAm 1; WhoAmP.*)

2. **Abrahams, Israel** (1858–1925). Abrahams was educated at Jews' College, London, and University College, London; he held an M.A. from London and Cambridge, a Lit.D. from Western Pennsylvania, and a D.D. from Hebrew Union College, Cincinnati. Author and lecturer, Abrahams was Reader in Talmudics and Rabbinic Literature at Cambridge, formerly Senior Tutor at Jews' College, London. Coedited the *Jewish Quarterly Review* with C. G. Montefiore and contributed frequent articles. Other publications included his *Studies in Pharisaism and the Gospels,* as well as *Aspects of Judaism, Jewish Life in the Middle Ages,*

Annotated Hebrew Prayer Book, Essays on the Future of Palestine. He enjoyed photography as a recreation. (**McGEWB; WhGB** 4; *WhoWorJ* 1972.)

3. **Adams, David** (1891–1952). Clergyman and educator, son of a Congregational clergyman and Greek scholar. Educated at Phillips Academy, graduated B.A. at Dartmouth (1913), and B.D. at Union Theological Seminary (1916). Served pastorates in Massachusetts and Ohio before coming to Mount Holyoke College, where he headed the Department of Religion and Philosophy from 1932 to the end of his life. He sought to integrate modern psychology and historical criticism into his teaching of religion. He wrote two books and many articles and also published short stories for adults and children, the most notable of which was "Truth is Stranger" in the *Atlantic* (Aug. 1926). Member of Phi Beta Kappa, Society of Biblical Literature and Exegesis. Married with three children, enjoyed mountain climbing and gardening. (**NatCAB** 39:396.)

4. **Allen, W[illoughby] C[harles]** (1867–1953). Was Principal of Egerton Hall, Manchester, and Lecturer in Theology and Hebrew at Exeter College, Oxford. Educated at Exeter College, with first class honors in theology (1890) and Oriental studies (1892). Winner of many prizes in his academic training, he published the commentary on Matthew in the *ICC*, Mark in *Oxford Church Biblical Commentary, The Christian Hope* (with L. W. Grensted), *Introduction to the Books of the New Testament,* and made contributions to the *Encyclopedia Biblica* and to *Hastings' Dictionary of the Bible*. (**Who** 1953.)

5. **Austin, Mary Hunter** (1868–1934). Graduated B.S. from Blackburn University with a deep interest in the influence of physical environment on plants and human cultural patterns. Taught school, married Stafford Wallace Hunter; the birth of a mentally retarded child and unsuccessful marriage were reflected in her early writings. She set herself to championing women's rights; in 1908, thinking herself fatally ill, she went to Italy and studied prayer and mysticism with the Blue Nuns, from which came a book, *Christ in Italy.* Time in London and Paris produced a Fabian intellectualism. Much of her views were enshrined in her play, *The Arrow Maker* (1911) and the novel *A Woman of Genius* (1922). Her views were generally liberal and moderately socialistic, with influence from John Reed and Walter Lippmann. She settled in Santa Fe, New Mexico, in 1924, supporting Native American rights and fashioning a philosophy that blended Native American, Spanish, and American cultures. She published 32 volumes and some 200 articles. Her autobiography was *Earth Horizon* (1932); she was cremated following her death and her ashes eventually lodged in a rock crevice at the summit of Mount Picacho near Santa Fe. (*AmAu&B; AmBi; AmLY; AmWomWr; AnCL; CnDAL; ConAmA; ConAmL; DcAmAu; DcAmB S1; DcLEL; DcNAA; InWom; LibW; NotAW; OxAm; REnAL; Str&VC; TwCA; TwCA S; WebAB; WhAm* 1; *WhNAA; WomWWA* 1914.)

6. **Bacon, Benjamin Wisner** (1860–1932). Congregational clergyman, writer, and professor, Bacon was one of the leading scholars of his day. His family came from New England colonial stock. He was educated in New Haven and partly also in Europe (Gymnasium in Coburg, Germany, and the Collège de Genève, Switzerland), graduating from Yale with an A.B. in 1881 and B.D. in 1884. Some violin skills helped him work his way through his theological studies. He served pastorates in Old Lyme, Connecticut, and in Oswego, New York, before being appointed Buckingham Professor of New Testament Criticism and Interpretation at Yale. He served a year as director of the American School of Oriental Study in Jerusalem and gained permission later for the Yale excavations at Gerasa in

1928. His publications were extensive, with commentaries on Mark (1925) and Matthew (1930), extensive work on John (1910, 1918, 1933 [the last posthumously]), and his Shaffer lectures, *Jesus the Son of God* (1930). He was a leading figure in the acceptance and use of the "higher criticism" on the American scene. (**DcAmB S1;** DcNAA; **Ferm; Kep;** NatCAB 23; WhAm 1; DcAmAu.)

7. **Baeck, Leo** (1873–1956). Born in Prussia and died in London, Baeck was a prominent rabbi in Oppeln, Düsseldorf, and Berlin and lectured at the Hochschule für die Wissenschaft des Judentums in Berlin. He sought an accommodation with German culture, as is seen in his main work, *Das Wesen des Judentums* (1905), and during the Hitler period declined to leave Germany, refusing asylum in America. He was imprisoned at Theresienstadt in 1943 (Czechoslovakia), but was one of only 700 survivors out of 50,000 persons sent there. He was remembered for the comfort he provided the inmates. After the war he resumed his leadership in the Jewish community and also served as visiting professor at Hebrew Union College in Cincinnati. Other writings included *The Pharisees and Other Essays* (1947) and *This People Israel: The Meaning of Jewish Existence* (1955). The Leo Baeck Institute was founded in 1954, with branches in London and New York, and serves Baeck's original vision. (**ConAu** 115; **EncTR.**)

8. **Baldensperger, Wilhelm** (1856–1936). Studied at Strassburg (Lic. Theol.), Göttingen, and Paris. Served pastoral appointment in Alsace and as instructor in Strassburg and became Professor of New Testament in Giessen from 1892 until World War I. During the war he lectured at Lausanne in Switzerland and returned to Strassburg afterward. He wrote widely on apocalypticism and the significance of apologetics in primitive Christianity. Some of his writings were *Die Selbstbewußtein Jesu im Lichte der messianischen Hoffnung* (1903) and *L'influence du dilettantisme artistique sur la moral et la réligion* (1890). (**Kml; Wei? 1914.**)

9. **Barbusse, Henri** (1874–1935). A child of a French father and English mother, Barbusse spent his early years in England, but was educated at the Collège Rollin in Paris and worked as a journalist, becoming an editor of the magazine *Je Sais Tout* by 1910 under the tutelage of the Jewish writer Catulle Mendès and in time his son-in-law. Barbusse's life was transformed by the Great War; he served in some of the heaviest fighting, though was never wounded, and was cited three times for bravery. He was discharged for illness. His best-known work was *Le Feu* (*Under Fire*), a stirring antiwar protest against inhumanity and injustice. After the Russian revolution Barbusse took up the Communist cause and for the remainder of his days wrote and acted in support of it. He died in Russia where he had gone as a delegate to the seventh Congress of the Third International, having contracted pneumonia. (*CasWL; CIDMEL; CyWA; EncWL; EvEuW; LinLib L, LinLib S; LongCTC; ModFrL; NewC; OxFr; PenEur; REn;* **TwCA;** *TwCA S; TwCW; WhE&EA; WhoLA;* **introduction** to *Under Fire.*)

10. **Bartlet, Vernon** (1863–1940). Educated at Highgate School and Exeter College, Oxford (M.A.), Bartlet studied at Mansfield College under A. M. Fairbairn, assuming the position of senior tutor in residence and winning various honors along the way. He retired as Professor of Church History in Mansfield College, Oxford. His publications included contributions to journals such as *JTS* and encyclopedia (*Hastings Dictionary, Britannica, Peake's*) and books that included the Century Bible commentary on Acts, *Christ and Civ-*

ilization (1910), the essay in *Studies in the Synoptic Problem* (1910), and coeditorship of a variety of other works. (**WhGB** 3; *WhoLA.*)

11. **Barton, Bruce Fairchild** (1886–1967). Advertising executive, author, and U.S. congressman, Barton was the son of a Tennessee circuit-riding minister, though often exaggerated his youthful poverty. Barton went to Berea College in Kentucky, but transferred to Amherst and graduated in 1907 with a Phi Beta Kappa key, working as an editor of a religious newspaper in Montana at first, then moving to New York and becoming assistant sales manager at *Collier's* magazine. After the war he formed an advertising agency that eventually merged with another company to comprise one of the largest agencies in the country. His client list included such firms as General Electric, General Motors, Dunlop Tires, and Lever Brothers. He created the character Betty Crocker, the archetypical housewife. Some disaffection with his own success led him into politics and he ran successfully for Congress in 1936 as a Republican opposed to Roosevelt and represented Manhattan's affluent silk-stocking district. A losing campaign for the Senate in 1940 ended his political career and he returned to his advertising business until his retirement in 1961. (*AmAu&B*; *BiDrAC*; *CurBio* 61–67; **DcAmB S8;** *EncAB*; *OhAu&B*; *WebAB*; *WhAm* 4; *WhAmP*; *WhNAA.*)

12. **Barton, George Aaron** (1859–1942). Born in Canada of devout Quakers, Barton attended Oakwood Seminary (a Quaker school in Poughkeepsie, N.Y.), becoming a Quaker minister in 1879. He went on to Haverford College (A.B., 1882), taught briefly at the Friends School in Providence, R.I., then studied at Harvard, receiving his Ph.D. in 1891. He then went to Bryn Mawr College where he stayed for 30 years before coming to the University of Pennsylvania as Professor of Semitic Languages and the History of Religion. He served as director of the American School of Oriental Research in Baghdad from 1921 to 1934, having also held that same title for the School in Jerusalem earlier. He also taught at the Divinity School of the Protestant Episcopal Church in Philadelphia and through the influence of James Montgomery joined the Episcopal Church. His strong feelings about German actions in World War I led him to renounce Quaker pacifism. His publications and influence were substantial; the textbook *Archaeology and the Bible* (1916) was a standard for many years, as was his *A Sketch of Semitic Origins* (1902), later replaced by *Semitic and Hamitic Origins* (1934). He also produced the *ICC* commentary on Ecclesiastes (1908) and was a leading expert in cuneiform epigraphy of the Sumerian and Akkadian eras. (*AmAu&B*; **DcAmB S3;** *DcNAA*; *WhAm* 2; *WhNAA.*)

13. **Bennett, W[illiam] H[enry]** (1855–1920). Bennett was educated at the Philological School, City of London School, Lancashire Independent College, Owens College (M.A.), London, and St. John's College, Cambridge, with a first class in the Theological Tripos. He was lecturer in Hebrew at Firth College, Sheffield (1887–88), Professor of Old Testament Exegesis, New and Hackney Colleges (1891–1913), and Principal of Lancashire College, Manchester, from 1913 on. His publications included extensive contributions to the *Expositor's Bible*, the *Century Bible*, and *Hastings' Bible Dictionary*. (**Who** 1921.)

14. **Beveridge, John** (1857–1943). Educated at Glasgow (M.A., B.D.), Beveridge was minister in various Scottish appointments (Stow, Midlothian, Wolverhampton, and Dundee) before spending many years at Gartmore, Perthshire. He took up the study of Norway and received the Centenary Medal of Oslo University in 1911 and was a Knight of St. Olaf (1938). His various publications included translations of Norwegian works into English,

as well as compositions of his own (*The Olaf Sagas* [1914] and *The Norse King Sagas* [1930]). His wide range of interests also included his own native Scotland, as seen in his presidency of the Scottish Esperanto Federation and the Scottish Beekeepers' Association. He was one of the translators of the New Testament into Esperanto (an artificial language invented by a Polish physician in 1887). (**WhGB** IV.)

15. **Bosworth, Edward Increase** (1861–1927). Bosworth studied at Oberlin College but graduated from Yale (1883), then from Oberlin Theological Seminary (1886). He served a year's pastorate, and returned to Oberlin as Professor of English Bible and subsequently Professor of New Testament Language and Literature (1892). He later became dean of the seminary and acting president of the college in 1918–19. Foreign study also marked his academic career (Leipzig [1890–91]; Athens [1891–92]; lectured in Japan [1907], Turkey [1911], and Athens [1927]). Together with Henry Churchill King (see below) Bosworth exerted a profound influence on the life of Oberlin and through it the religious life of his day. His *The Life and Teaching of Jesus* was preceded by a number of studies on Jesus, Acts, and Romans. (**DcAmB;** DcNAA; OhAu&B; WhAm 1.)

16. **Bowman, John Wick** (1894–1986). Educated at Wooster College (A.B., 1916), Princeton University (A.M., 1919), Princeton Theological Seminary (B.D., 1920), and Southern Baptist Theological Seminary (Ph.D., 1930), with postdoctoral studies at Zurich, Bowman was a Presbyterian clergyman who held positions at United Theological College, Saharanpur, India, Western Theological Seminary, and particularly San Francisco Theological Seminary, where he was Robert Dollar Professor of New Testament (1944–61). He also was a Fulbright lecturer at St. Andrews, Scotland, and in Tokyo, Japan, and lectured widely in seminaries in the United States and elsewhere. His publication career spanned a lengthy time; *The Intention of Jesus* (1943) was followed by extensive studies in Revelation, Matthew, Hebrews, James, Peter, and more work on Jesus' teaching (1963) and the historical Jesus (*Which Jesus?* [1970]), as well as contributions to various journals and encyclopedia. (*AmAu&B*; **ConAuR 1–4; ConAuNRS 6; WhoAm** 1978–79; WhAm 10.)

17. **Bousset, Wilhelm** (1865–1920). Studied at Erlangen (1884–85), Leipzig (1885–86), and Göttingen (D. Theol. 1889), becoming privatdozent at the latter in 1889, then associate professor (1896) and professor in 1916. He was a founding force in the *religionsgeschichtliche Schule,* and contributed works on Judaism and early Christianity, in addition to works in textual criticism and patristics. Some of his writings were *Jesu Predigt in ihrem Gegensatz zum Judentum* (1902); *Textkritische Studien zum Neuen Testament* (1894); *Die Offenbarung Johannes* (1896, 1906), *Was Wissen wir von Jesus?* (1906), Commentaries on 2 Corinthians and Galatians (1906), and *Kurios Christos* (1913; English trans., 1970). (**Kml; Wei**? 1914; **Giessener Gelehrte** *in der ersten Hälfte des 20. Jahrhunderts,* ed. Hans Georg Gundel, Peter Moraw and Volker Press, Veröffentlichungen der Historischen Kommission für Hessen 35 [Marburg: N. G. Elwert, 1982].)

18. **Briggs, Charles Augustus** (1841–1913). Studied at the University of Virginia (1857–60), Union Theological Seminary (1861–63), and Berlin (1866–69), and served as Presbyterian minister in Roselle, N.J. (1870–74) before becoming Professor of Hebrew and Cognate Languages at Union (1874–91), then Professor of Biblical Theology (1891–1904), and finally Professor of Theological Encyclopedia and Symbolics (1904–13). His inaugural lecture of 1891 led to charges of heresy that were initially dismissed, but on appeal of the prosecution committee a trial was held in December of 1892, following which

Briggs was exonerated. An appeal to the General Assembly, however, was upheld and Briggs suspended from the ministry. The seminary retained him anyway and severed its relationship to the assembly. Briggs later turned to the Episcopal Church. The issues had to do with his theological adherence to the Westminster Confession and his unqualified support of historical criticism. His scholarship was of the highest level and his publications included contributions to the *ICC* and the standard Hebrew Lexicon, as well as *The Messiah of the Apostles* (1895), and *A History of the Study of Theology,* 2 vols. (1916). (*AlliSUP; AmAu&B; AmBi; ApCAB; BiD&SB; DcAmAu;* **DcAmB; DcAmReB;** *DcNAA;* **NatCAB** 7:318–19; *TwCBDA; WhAm* 1; *WhNAA.*)

19. **Bultmann, Rudolf Karl** (1884–1976). Son of a clergyman whose grandfather was also a missionary in Africa, Bultmann had two brothers and a sister; one brother was lost in World War I and the other died in a concentration camp in World War II. After excelling in the Oldenburg Gymnasium Bultmann went to Tübingen, then to Berlin, studying with Harnack and Gunkel, and then obtained his qualifying exam and taught at the Oldenburg Gymnasium (1906). He entered Marburg and studied under Johannes Weiss, Adolf Jülicher, Wilhelm Herrmann, and Wilhelm Heitmüller. His degree came in 1910; he was privatdozent at Marburg, then went to Breslau in 1916 and in 1920–21 to Giessen, only to return to Marburg in 1921, where he spent the remainder of his career (retired 1951). Influences on his life were his training in the liberal school, his association with Martin Heidegger, and also the theological position generally known as the Dialectical Theology. Bultmann's impact on the twentieth century has been immeasurable, with his pioneering work in *Formgeschichte,* the issue of myth in the New Testament, and the hermeneutical issues surrounding the interpretation of the New Testament in the "modern" world. His publications are too extensive for any listing and encompass virtually every area of prominent study in the New Testament (synoptics, historical Jesus, John, Paul, theology of the New Testament). Most of his major works have been translated into English and various other languages. ("**Autobiographical Reflections**" in *Existence and Faith;* **CurBio** 1972, 1976; **Kml;** *LinLib L; IntWW* 1974–76; *ConAuR* 5–8; *IntAu&W* 1977; **Kep;** *McGEWB; OxGer;* **P-M Hanbk;** *WhoWor* 1974; *WorAu.*)

20. **Bundy, Walter Ernest** (1889–1961). Graduated A.B. from DePauw University (1912) and twice from Boston University School of Theology (S.T.B., 1915; Ph.D., 1921). Also studied at Basel, 1916–17. He was involved in the war as vice-consul, Military Intelligence (Basel), 1917–19, and a member of the American Peace Mission to Vienna, Austria, in 1919. He became Professor of English Bible at DePauw University in 1919 and continued until his retirement in 1955. His works included *The Psychic Health of Jesus* (1922), *The Religion of Jesus* (1928), *Our Recovery of Jesus* (1929), and *Jesus and the First Three Gospels* (1955). (**Archives,** DePauw University; **IndAu;** *WhAm* 8.)

21. **Burkitt, Francis Crawford** (1864–1935). Born of a well-to-do merchant father, Burkitt never had to worry over financial sustenance and gave himself completely to his studies. He attended Harrow in 1878 and entered Trinity College, Cambridge, in 1883, graduating a scholar in 1886, first in mathematics, but soon turned his attention to the study of Hebrew. He finished in 1888, but not until 1903 did he hold academic office, a lectureship in paleography previously held by Rendel Harris. He became Norrisian Professor of Divinity in 1905 and combined that later with the Hulsean professorship in 1934. Burkitt began studying Syriac and helped transcribe the Sinaitic Syriac palimpsest discovered by Agnew Lewis, publishing an edition of the Old Syriac gospels. His notable contributions

came in his role as a "modernist" who accepted the tools of criticism and also introduced and sponsored the new eschatological interpretations of Johannes Weiss and Albert
Schweitzer. Later, however, he would decline the *formgeschichtliche* method and cling to
the value of the Markan record and the historical core at the heart of Christian origins. Burkitt also had a wide variety of other interests, writing on Francis of Assisi, the
Eucharist, Manicheanism, and Gnosticism. He was a preeminent scholar of wide learning, fairness of mind, with friends and colleagues across religious and confessional lines.
(DcNB; JTS 36 [1935]: 225–54; Kep; *WhE&EA; WhLit; WhoLA.)*

22. **Burrows, Millar** (1889–1980). Educated at Cornell University (B.A., 1912), Union
    Theological Seminary (M.Div., 1915), and Yale University (Ph.D., 1925), Burrows was
    a Presbyterian minister who pastored churches in rural Texas (1915–19) before entering
    academia at Tusculum College, Greenville, Tennessee. He then went to Brown University
    as assistant professor (1925–29), becoming Professor of Biblical Literature and History of
    Religions in 1932, and arrived at Yale as Professor of Biblical Theology (1934–58). He was
    director of the American School of Oriental Research in Jerusalem, 1931–32 and 1947–
    48, the latter when the Dead Sea Scrolls started to become available. He contributed a
    number of works on the scrolls (*The Dead Sea Scrolls* [1955], *More Light on the Dead Sea
    Scrolls* [1958]) as well as other subjects (*What Mean These Stones?* [1941], *Jesus in the
    First Three Gospels* [1977]), and numerous articles to professional journals. The *Manual
    of Discipline*, as Burrows called the Rule of the Community, was first published under his
    editorship. (*Au&Wr* 1971; *IntAu&Wr; CurBio* 1956; **ConAu** 81–84, 97–100; *OhAu&B;
    Who* 1974; **WhoAm** 1975–76; *WhoRel* 1975–77; *WrDr* 1976–80.)

23. **Burton, Ernest DeWitt** (1856–1925). Born in Granville, Ohio, the son of a Baptist
    minister, Burton was educated at Griswold College in Davenport, Iowa, and Denison
    University (1876), then entered Rochester Theological Seminary, graduating in 1882. He
    remained for a year there teaching Greek, was ordained Baptist minister in 1883, and be-
    came Professor of New Testament Interpretation at Newton. In 1887 he studied for a year
    at Leipzig and in 1894 at Berlin. Two years before (1892) he had accepted the position
    of head of the Department of New Testament and Early Christian Literature at the newly
    founded University of Chicago and its Divinity School. He continued in that post until
    elected president of the university in 1923, in which he served until his death, making
    significant contributions to the enlarging of the university's financial and academic goals.
    He also served a time as director of libraries of the university and editor of *Biblical World*
    and *American Journal of Theology*. His publications in his field were numerous; most no-
    table were his *Syntax of Moods and Tenses in New Testament Greek* (1893), *Harmony of the
    Synoptic Gospels* (1904), *Principles of Literary Criticism and Their Application to the Synoptic
    Problem* (1904), and his commentary on Galatians in the *ICC* (1920). (*AmBi; DcAmAu;*
    DcAmB; *OhAu&B;* **NatCAB** 29:22–23; *WhAm* 1).

24. **Cadbury, Henry Joel** (1883–1974). Educated at Haverford College (1903) and Harvard
    (M.A., 1904; Ph.D., 1914), Cadbury served as professor at all ranks at Haverford (1910–
    19), then at Andover Seminary (1919–26), at Bryn Mawr College (1926–34), and Hollis
    Professor of Divinity and Dexter Lecturer on Biblical Literature at Harvard (1934–54).
    He also served as lecturer at the Quaker School of Graduate Study, Wallingford, Penn-
    sylvania from 1954 to 1972. Earlier he directed the Andover-Harvard Theological library
    (1938–54). He published extensively by article and book; among the best-known were
    National Ideals in the Old Testament (1920), *The Making of Luke-Acts* (1927), *The Peril of*

Modernizing Jesus (1937), *Jesus: What Manner of Man* (1947; 2d ed., 1958). Cadbury's interests extended beyond scholarly production; he was a pacifist in the Quaker tradition and was one of the founding agents behind the American Friends Service Committee, which raised millions for privation and suffering in needy countries. Cadbury's advocacy of peace and criticism of anti-German fervor resulted in dismissal from Haverford in 1918, but as chairman of the AFSC in 1947 he accepted the Nobel Peace Prize. (*AmAu&B*; **ConAu; DcAmReB; WhoAm** 1932–33; *WhAm* 6; *WhNAA*.)

25. **Cadoux, A. T.** (1874–1948). Educated in Smyrna, Croydon, Cape of Good Hope, London, and held the B.A. and D.D. degrees. Publications included *Essays in Christian Thinking, Jesus and Civil Government; The Parables of Jesus: Their Art and Use,* and *A New Orthodoxy of Jesus and Personality.* (**WhE&EA.**)

26. **Cadoux, Cecil John** (1883–1947). Born in Smyrna, Turkey, of a merchant father and his wife, Cadoux was educated at Stamford House School; St. Dunstan's College, Catford; Strand School, King's College, London; and Mansfield College, Oxford. He served as Isherwood Fellow and Lecturer in Hebrew at Mansfield College (1914–19); Professor of New Testament Criticism, Exegesis, and Theology, and of Christian Sociology, Yorkshire United Independent College in Bradford (1919–33); from then to his death he was Mackennal Professor of Church History and Vice-Principal, Mansfield College, Oxford. His publications extended from *The Christian Attitude to War* (1919) to *The Early Church and the World* (1925), *The Case for Evangelical Modernism* (1938), and the two works on Jesus, *The Historic Mission of Jesus* (1941) and *The Life of Jesus* (1947). (**Kep** 1; *New York Times*, Aug. 18, 1947, 17; **WhGB** 4; **WhE&EA.**)

27. **Case, Shirley Jackson** (1872–1947). Born and raised in Canada (Hatfield Point), Case studied at Acadia University, Nova Scotia (A.B., 1893; M.A., 1896) and taught mathematics (St. Martin's Seminary, New Brunswick; Horton Collegiate Academy at Acadia) and mathematics and Greek (New Hampshire Literary Institute) before entering Yale Divinity School, where he graduated with honors (B.D., Ph.D.) and went on to the Cobb Divinity School, Bates College (1906–8). From there he was invited to the faculty at the University of Chicago Divinity School, where he spent the remainder of his major academic career, serving as Professor of New Testament Interpretation, Professor of Early Church History, chairman of the Church History Department, and finally united the two interests as Professor of the History of Early Christianity. He served also as dean of the Divinity School (1933–38) when he retired and afterward lectured a year at Bexley Hall of the Episcopal Theological Seminary and became Professor of Religion and Dean of the Florida School of Religion at Florida Southern College, remaining there until his death. His career was distinguished by outstanding contributions in both church history and New Testament studies and in administration. He published sixteen books and numerous articles and, along with Shailer Mathews, was the moving force behind the sociohistorical method, which came to be the distinguishing characteristic of the "Chicago School." Case was a "modernist" whose liberal roots lay in his membership in the Free Baptist Christian Church, and he was a primary campaigner in the fundamentalist wars especially in the decade of the twenties. Among his works were *The Evolution of Early Christianity* (1914), *The Social Origins of Christianity* (1923), *Jesus, a New Biography* (1927), *Jesus Through the Centuries* (1931), and *The Christian Philosophy of History* (1943). (*AmAu&B*; **DcAmB S4; DcAmReB;** *DcNAA*; **Kep; NatCAB** 36:152–53; *WhAm* 2; *WhNAA*; **archives,** Florida Southern College.)

28. **Charles, R[obert] H[enry]** (1855–1931). Priest of the Church of England and Archdeacon at Westminster, Charles was educated at Belfast Academy and Queen's College, Belfast, graduating B.A. (1877) and M.A. (1880) with honors. A spiritual crisis sent him to Trinity College, Dublin, to seek ordination. He spent time in Germany and Switzerland and took ordination in 1883–84 and served curacies so assiduously that his health was impaired and rest was required. He traveled to Germany for a year, at which time he began the serious study of the apocalyptic literature. He returned and settled at Oxford where extensive publication followed, beginning with his translation of the book of Enoch (1893) and leading to the commentaries (*ICC*) on Revelation (1920) and Daniel (1929). Further critical editions of apocryphal and pseudepigraphical texts followed, culminating in the standard English work *The Apocrypha and Pseudepigrapha of the Old Testament in English* (2 vols.). Charles brought together his reflections in his Jowett lectures of 1898–99 and his later *Religious Development between the Old and the New Testaments.* Charles remained unsurpassed as an authority in the apocryphal and pseudepigraphical literature. (*AlliSUP*; **DcNB; WhE&EA;** *WhLit.*)

29. **Clark, Kenneth Willis** (1898–1979). Clark studied at Yale (A.B., 1924), Colgate Rochester Divinity School (B.D., 1927), and University of Chicago (Ph.D., 1931). Clark was ordained in the Northern Baptist Convention (1926), but later joined the Methodist Church. After service as a pastor in New York State, he came to the Duke University Divinity School, first as instructor in New Testament (1931–37), and advanced to professor (1945). His expertise lay in textual criticism primarily, and he served variously as director of the microfilm expedition to the Greek Patriarchal Library, general editor of the expedition to St. Catherine's monastery, and on the International Greek New Testament Project. His publications included *A Descriptive Catalogue of Greek New Testament Manuscripts in America* (1937), *Checklist of Manuscripts in St. Catherine's Monastery* (1952), *The Gentile Bias and Other Essays* (1979), as well as contributions to the *Interpreter's Bible, Interpreter's Dictionary of the Bible,* and *Peake's Commentary.* (**WhoAm** 1978–79.)

30. **Colwell, E[rnest] C[adman]** (1901–74). A Methodist minister, Colwell was educated at Emory University (Ph.B., 1923), Emory's Candler School of Theology (B.D., 1927), and the University of Chicago (Ph.D., 1930). His academic career began at Emory (1924–30) as instructor, and he later returned to become dean of faculties and vice-president (1951–57), then went to Chicago, working his way through various levels of professor to becoming president of the university (1945–51). He also served as president of the Southern California School of Theology at Claremont (1957–68), as Distinguished Professor of New Testament (1968–71), and from 1969 to 1974 was Visiting Professor of Greek at Stetson University in Deland, Florida. Along the way he served a wide range of positions in higher education and received honorary degrees from a variety of distinguished universities. His contributions lay especially in textual criticism and philology, though extended also to works on John (*John Defends the Gospel* [1936], *The Gospel of the Spirit* [1953]) as well as Jesus (*An Approach to the Teaching of Jesus* [1947], *Jesus and the Gospel* [1963], and *Jesus and the Historian* [1968]). (*AmAu&B;* **ConAuNRS 4;** *IntWW;* **Kep;** *WhAm* 6; **Who** 1974–75)

31. **Couchoud, Paul-Louis** (1879–1959). Attended the École normale supérieure in philosophy (1898) and later studied medicine at Paris, composing his doctoral thesis on *L'asthénie primitive* (1911). A grant enabled him to travel to China and Japan, from which came translations of works in Japanese and the book *Sages et poètes d'Asie* (1916). His in-

terests focused on the origins of religion and his activity and publication in that area grew extensively. *L'énigma de Jésus* (1923) was followed by *Le douloureux débat*. *Les prêtres et le mariage* (1927), *Le problème de Jésus et les origines du christianisme* (1932), *Jésus le Dieu fait homme* (1937), *Le Dieu Jésus* (1951), and still others. His wide interests are seen in his editing of the memoirs of Robert de Montesquiou (1923), Pascal's *Discours de la condition de l'homme* (1947), and various journals, such as the *Revue des sciences psychologiques*. Couchoud was also close friend of Anatole France and the sculptor Bourdelle. (**DcBF 9.**)

32. **Craig, C[larence] T[ucker]** (1895–1953). Educated at Morningside College, Iowa (A.B., 1915) and Boston University (S.T.B., 1919; Ph.D., 1924), Craig also received an M.A. from Yale (1946), and pursued graduate study at Harvard (1919–20), Basel (1920), and Berlin (1921–22). He taught at the Anglo-Chinese College in Foochow, China (1915–16) and served various pastorates in the Methodist Episcopal Church in Massachusetts, Indiana, Cincinnati, and Brooklyn before going to Oberlin Graduate School of Theology (1928–46), Yale Divinity School (1946–49), and Drew Theological Seminary (1949–53), where he served as dean. In addition to publications in various learned journals, Craig wrote *Jesus in Our Teaching* (1931), *The Christian's Personal Religion* (1925), *The Study of the New Testament* (1939), and *The Beginning of Christianity* (1943), as well as other books, and provided an introduction to the Revised Standard Version of the Bible (1946). (**Kep;** *OhAu&B;* **WhAm 3.**)

33. **Dalman, Gustav** (1855–1941). Born at Niesky, Dalman attended the gymnasium of the Brethren Community there. He studied theology at Gnadenfeld and, following a period as a teacher for the Brethren, became instructor at the theological seminary at Gnadenfeld, followed by an appointment as teacher at the Institutum Delitschianum (1887), and privatdozent (1891) at Leipzig. He then became director of the German Evangelical Institute for the Study of Antiquity in the Holy Land at Jerusalem (1902–14). He was Professor of Old Testament in Greifswald in 1925 and from then on director of the Gustav-Dalman Institute for the Study of Palestine. His extensive publications demonstrated his linguistic skills in Aramaic and his mastery of the archaeological and topographical character of Palestine, among them *Grammatik des Jüdisch-palästinischen Aramäisch* (1894), *Jesus-Jeshua* (1929; English trans., 1929); *Orte und Wege Jesu* (1919; English trans., *Sacred Sites and Ways: Studies in the Topography of the Gospels* [1935]), *Worte Jesu* (1898; English trans., *The Words of Jesus* [1902]). (**Kml; WhE&EA.**)

34. **Danby, Herbert** (1889–1953). Danby was educated at Church Middle Class School, Leeds, and Keble College, Oxford, where he won many prizes and attained also his M.A. (1914) and D.D. (1923). He was ordained deacon in 1913 and priest in 1914, thereafter serving as curate of Waddesdon, Bucks (1913–14), subwarden of St. Deninol's Library, Hawarden (1914–19), librarian, St. George's Cathedral, Jerusalem (1921–36), Grinfield Lecturer on the Septuagint (1939–43), also serving as Examining Chaplain to the Bishop of Jerusalem (1928–36) and dean of the Palestine Board of Higher Studies (1923–36). In 1936 he became Regius Professor of Hebrew, Oxford, and Canon of Christ Church. His expertise in Hebrew was manifested especially in his translations of the Mishnah (1933), *An English and Modern Hebrew Dictionary* (1939), and Joseph Klausner's *Jesus of Nazareth* (1925). Other works were published in books and journals. He enjoyed golf and music. (**WhGB 5;** *WhLit.*)

35. **Davison, W[illiam] T[heophilus]** (1846–1935). Educated at Kingswood School (London, M.A.), Davison was engaged in pastoral work in the Methodist Church (1868–81), then became Professor of Biblical Literature, Richmond (1881–91), then Professor of Theology, Handsworth College (1891–1904), and then returned to Richmond as Professor of Theology (1905–20). He served as president of the Wesleyan Methodist Conference (1901). His publications included *The Christian Conscience, The Word in the Heart, The Praises of Israel, Wisdom Literature of the Old Testament, The Christian Interpretation of Life,* and *The Living Word in a Changing World.* (**WhGB** 3.)

36. **Dewick, E. C.** (1884–1958). Dewick studied at St. John's College, Cambridge (B.A., 1906; M.A., 1909; B.D., 1938; D.D., 1950), was awarded many prizes (Septuagint, Hulsean); served curacies at St. Peter's, Norbiton, Kingston-on-Thames, as tutor, dean, vice-principal, and principal of St. Aidan's College, Birkenhead (1911–19), and also Teacher in Ecclesiastical History at Liverpool University (1911–19). Dewick was also involved heavily in the mission field, teaching and administering in various colleges and universities in Ceylon and especially India (Calcutta, Agra, and Nagpur). He lectured widely (Cambridge, Oxford, St. Andrews, Strasbourg, and many others) and served positions such as External Examiner, Oxford, Durham, and Examining Chaplain in various places. His other publications included *Christ's Message in Times of Crisis* (1916), *The Indwelling God* (1938), *The Gospel and Other Faiths* (1948), and *The Christian Attitude to Other Religions* (1953). (**WhGB** 5; **WhE&EA.**)

37. **Dibelius, Martin** (1883–1947). Educated at the Universities of Neuchatel, Leipzig, Tübingen, and Berlin (1901–5); a period of teaching in public and private schools (1908–14) followed, along with the position of privatdozent at Berlin (1910–15), followed by appointment at Heidelberg (1915 on). His works included various commentaries, studies in the gospels, Paul, Acts, and primitive Christian history. Among his writings were *Die urchristliche Überlieferung von Johannes dem Täufer* (1911), *Die Formgeschichte des Evangeliums* (1919; English trans., *From Tradition to Gospel* [1934]), *Die Botschaft von Jesus Christus* (1925; English trans., *The Message of Jesus Christ* [1939]), various commentaries, and *The Sermon on the Mount* (1940). (*IntWW* 1948; (**Kep; Kml; Wei?** 1928.)

38. **Dobschütz, Ernst von** (1870–1934). In 1893 Dobschütz became privatdozent in New Testament and associate professor at Jena (1898), then professor at Strassburg (1904), Breslau (1910), and finally Halle (1913), his birthplace. He wrote extensively in the areas of exegesis, primitive Christianity, textual criticism, and the study of legends. (**Kml.**)

39. **Dodd, Charles Harold** (1884–1973). Tutored in his father's school at Wrexham, Dodd went in 1902 to University College, Oxford, achieving a first in honor moderations (1904) and *literae humaniores* (1906) and in 1906 was elected a senior demy of Magdalen College, Oxford, but soon entered the ministry of the Congregational Church (ordained 1912). After three years of pastoral work he went to Oxford to succeed James Moffatt at Mansfield College. From 1915 to 1930 he pursued a distinctive scholarly career at Oxford, publishing some 20 books, among them *The Meaning of Paul for Today* (1920) and *The Authority of the Bible* (1928). In 1930 he moved to Manchester to succeed A. S. Peake as the Rylands Professor of Biblical Criticism and Exegesis. There followed more publication, such as *The Parables of the Kingdom* (1935), the commentary on Romans in the Moffatt series, *The Bible and the Greeks* (1935), and *The Apostolic Preaching and its Development* (1936). In 1935 Dodd followed F. C. Burkitt as the Norris-Hulse Professor of

Divinity at Cambridge, becoming the first non-Anglican since the Restoration to hold a position at either of the major universities. In his latter period he took up the investigation of the Fourth Gospel, with the two major works, *The Interpretation of the Fourth Gospel* (1953) and *Historical Tradition in the Fourth Gospel* (1963), and also in his retirement, *The Founder of Christianity* (1970). He also oversaw the inauguration and completion of *The New English Bible* and at age 86 presented it to the Queen Mother. (**Kep; Kml; DcNB.**)

40. **Drummond, James** (1835–1918). Graduated Trinity College, Dublin (1855) and, influenced by the life of the American William Ellery Channing, Drummond sought the ministry, training at Manchester New College, London. He served a single pastorate, then went to Manchester as lecturer in biblical and historical theology. When the school moved to Oxford, he went with it, retiring in 1906 but remaining at Oxford until his death. A Unitarian, Drummond prized the freedom of thought he experienced in that denomination; some of his views were atypical: miracle accounts were to be judged purely factually, but Drummond also concluded in favor of the Johannine authorship of the Fourth Gospel — at least in origin, for he also felt the gospel was unhistorical in its account of Jesus' ministry. Jesus was Lord and Savior in the sense of being the highest revelation from God and moral leader of the human race. A liberal on social and political issues, Drummond worked for peace, temperance, and women's suffrage. Some of his books were *The Jewish Messiah* (1877), *Philo-Judaeus* (1888), *The Character and Authorship of the Fourth Gospel* (1904), and *Studies in Christian Doctrine* (1908). (**DcNB.**)

41. **Duncan, George Simpson** (1884–1965). Studied at Edinburgh, Trinity College Cambridge, St. Andrews University, Marburg, Jena, and Heidelberg, holding the M.A. and B.D. from Edinburgh and M.A. from Trinity College. Ordained a Scottish Church minister he served as its moderator in 1949, was Professor of Biblical Criticism (1919–54) and principal (1940–54) of St. Mary's College in the University of St. Andrews, and vice-chancellor at the university (1952–53). He held honorary degrees from Glasgow, Edinburgh, and St. Andrews. In addition to *Jesus, Son of Man* (1948), his writings included *St. Paul's Ephesian Ministry* (1929) and the commentary on Galatians in the Moffatt New Testament Commentary (1934). (**WhGB** 6.)

42. **Dupont-Sommer, André** (1900–?*). Dupont-Sommer received his doctorate from the Sorbonne, was secretary, Collège de France (1934–40), Director of Studies, School of Higher Studies (1938), professor, University of Paris (1945–63), president of the Institute of Semitic Studies, University of Paris (1952–), professor, Collège de France (1963–71), and held memberships in scholarly and scientific organizations around the world. His works included *Le Quatrième Livre des Machabées* (1939), *La doctrine gnostique de la lettre "waw"* (1946), and extensive works on the Dead Sea Scrolls, among them *Nouveaux Aperçus sur les manuscrits de la mer Morte* (1953; English trans., *The Jewish Sect of Qumran and the Essenes* [1954]), and *Les écrits esséniens découverts près de la mer Morte* (1959; English trans., *The Essene Writings from Qumran*, 1962). (**IntAu&Wr; IntWW; NDNC** 3:316; ***Who** 1983.)

43. **Easton, Burton Scott** (1877–1950). Easton's ancestors stretched back to an immigrant from England in the seventeenth century; his father was a philologist and Professor of English and Comparative Philology at the University of Pennsylvania. Having studied at Göttingen (1894), Easton graduated from Pennsylvania (B.S., 1898; Ph.D., 1901) and Philadelphia Divinity School (later Divinity School of the Episcopal Church in Phila-

delphia) in 1905 (Th.D. in 1910), and became a deacon and priest in the Protestant Episcopal Church. He first taught mathematics in Iowa in 1898–99 and at Pennsylvania (1901–5), then went to Nashotah House (Wisconsin) as Professor of New Testament and in 1911 transferred to Western Theological Seminary, Chicago (later Seabury-Western). In 1919 he came to the General Theological Seminary in New York as Professor of Literature and Interpretation of the New Testament; he retired in 1946. He also was acting librarian (1924–46) and sub-dean (1940–48). Easton was responsible for developing the religion tables in the Dewey Decimal system. He also cofounded the Graduate School of Theology at the University of the South and lectured there in 1937–40. He was also one of the founders and original editor of the *Anglican Theological Review*. A frequent contributor to journals, Easton wrote on a variety of subjects in addition to *The Gospel before the Gospels* (1928) and *Christ in the Gospels* (1930), including commentaries on Luke (1926), Paul (1919) and Acts (1936). (**NatCAB** 38:347–38; *WhNAA; WhAm* 2.)

44. **Enslin, Morton Scott** (1897–1980). Educated at Harvard (A.B., 1919; Th.D., 1924), and Newton Theological Institution (B.D., 1922), Enslin was Professor of New Testament at Crozer Theological Seminary (1924–54), Lecturer in Patristics at the University of Pennsylvania (1925–54), Craig Professor of Biblical Languages and Literature at St. Lawrence University Theological School (1955–65), Visiting Lecturer and Chairman of the Department of History of Religion at Bryn Mawr College (1965–68), and Professor of Early Christian History at Dropsie University (1968–). He held a Phi Beta Kappa key and served in the U.S. Navy in World War I. His writings included *The Ethics of Paul* (1930), *Christian Beginnings* (1938), *The Prophet from Nazareth* (1961), and *From Jesus to Christianity* (1964). (*Au&Wr* 71; **ConAuR** 17–20, 134; *DrASP* 1974, 1978; *IntAu&Wr* 1976; **WhoAm** 1974–78; *WhoRel* 1975–77.)

45. **Filson, Floyd** (1896–1980). An ordained Presbyterian minister, Filson received his A.B. degree from Park College (1918), his B.D. from McCormick Theological Seminary (1922), and the Th.D. from Basel University (1930). His academic career was entirely at McCormick Theological Seminary, beginning as Instructor in Greek (1923–30), Professor of New Testament Literature and Exegesis (1930–34), Professor of New Testament Literature and History (1934–67), and included also a period as dean (1954–67) and acting president (1956). He served in the military in 1918–19 (second lieutenant, artillery) and took leadership positions in a variety of professional organizations (SBLE, AAR). His publications, in addition to *Origins of the Gospels* (1938), were extensive; examples would be *One Lord, One Faith* (1943), *Jesus Christ the Risen Lord* (1956), *A Commentary on the Gospel According to St. Matthew* (1960), *Three Crucial Decades: Studies in the Book of Acts* (1963), and *The Gospel According to John* (1963). And, in addition, he was translator or cotranslator of a number of important foreign works, such as Rudolf Otto's *The Kingdom of God and the Son of Man* (1938) and Oscar Cullmann's *Christ and Time* (1950), as well as coeditor with G. Ernest Wright of *The Westminster Historical Atlas to the Bible* (1945; rev. 1956). (**ConAu** 61–64; **Kep; WhoAm** 1976–77.)

46. **Foakes-Jackson, Frederick John** (1855–1941). Educated at Eton and Trinity College, Cambridge (B.A. 1879; M.A., 1882; B.D., 1903; D.D., 1905), Foakes-Jackson was Lecturer and Dean of Jesus College, Cambridge (1882–1916) and Briggs Graduate Professor of Christian Institutions, Union Theological Seminary, New York (1916–34). His most famous work was in collaboration with Kirsopp Lake, *The Beginnings of Christianity*, but many other publications were issued across the years, such as the *History of the Chris-*

tian Church (1891, 1923), *Biblical History of the Hebrews* (1903, 1924), *St. Paul, the Man and the Apostle* (1926), *Peter, Prince of Apostles* (1927), and *Society in England, 1750–1850* (1916). (*AmAu&B;* **WhE&EA; WhGB** 4; *WhoLit.*)

47. **Fosdick, Harry Emerson** (1878–1969). The leading liberal voice among clergymen in his day, Fosdick was educated at Colgate University (B.A., 1900), Colgate Seminary (1900–1901), Union Theological Seminary (B.D., 1904), and Columbia University (M.A., 1908). He held part-time positions at Union (1908–15) while also serving as the minister of First Baptist Church in Montclair, New Jersey. He then became Professor of Practical Theology at Union (1915–34), after which he went to Park Avenue Baptist Church. Under Fosdick's leadership the church agreed to build a new edifice in a less wealthy neighborhood; the result was Riverside Church in the Morningside Heights section of New York City. Fosdick remained there until his retirement in 1946 and thereafter also continued to write, lecture, and preach widely, most often in support of social and ecumenical causes. His was the most conspicuous voice for liberalism, especially in the controversies with fundamentalism. His sermon of 1921, "Shall the Fundamentalists Win?" aroused great opposition, with William Jennings Bryan at its head, demanding Fosdick's removal, but without success. He resigned voluntarily in 1925, but his influence continued on a national scale. His writings were numerous, from *The Modern Use of the Bible* (1924) to *A Guide to Understanding the Bible* (1938) and the autobiographical *The Living of These Days* (1956). (*AmAu&B; ApCAB* 10; *AuBYP; BiDAmM; ConAuR* 25–28; *CurBio* 40–69; *DcAmB;* **DcAmReB;** *LinLib L, LinLib S; McGEWB;* **NatCAB** 55:13–14; *REnAL.*)

48. **Gilbert, George Holley** (1854–1930). Gilbert received the A.B. and D.D. from Dartmouth (1878, 1894), a B.D. from Union Theological Seminary (1883), and a Ph.D. from the University of Leipzig (1885). Gilbert was an ordained Congregational minister, appointed Acting Professor of New Testament Literature (1886–87) and professor (1887–1901) at the Chicago Theological Seminary. He authored many books, such as *The Poetry of Job* (1888), *The Student's Life of Jesus* (1899), *The Student's Life of Paul* (1899), *The Revelation of Jesus* (1900), *The First Interpreters of Jesus* (1901), *A Commentary on Acts* (1908), *Jesus* (1912), and *Jesus and His Bible* (1926). (**WhoAm** 1928–29; *DcAmAu; DcNAA; WhNAA.*)

49. **Gilmore, Alfred Field** (1868–1943). Primarily an educator, author, and editor, Gilmore was educated at Bates College in Lewiston, Maine (A.B., 1892; M.A., 1895) and did graduate work at Harvard. After some early years as principal and superintendent of various schools in Maine, Gilmore worked for the American Book Company (Maine and New York City) and later engaged in the lumber business. In 1908 he became a Christian Scientist and was widely involved in the activities of that church, editing its various publications and serving on the editorial council of the *Christian Science Monitor.* He attended the Massachusetts Metaphysical College in 1922 and received the C.S.B. degree and became a teacher and practitioner. He also was a naturalist, especially interested in ornithology, and traveled around the world studying and lecturing on natural history. He wrote a number of books on birds in addition to works on Christian Science. He held a Phi Beta Kappa key, an honorary degree from Bates College, and was once a member of the Maine legislature (1900–1902). (**NatCAB** 39:390–91.)

50. **Glover, T[errot] R[eaveley]** (1869–1943). Classical scholar, historian, and prolific writer, Glover was the son of a Baptist minister and maintained his involvement in that church

all his life. His education was St. John's College, Cambridge (admitted 1888), where he won various prizes in classics before advancing to a fellowship in 1892. In 1896 he went to Queen's University in Kingston, Ontario, as a professor of Latin and in 1901 returned to Cambridge. In 1911 he was appointed university lecturer and remained there the rest of his life. Some of his classical works included *Life and Letters in the Fourth Century* (1901), *Studies in Virgil* (1904), *The Conflict of Religions in the Early Roman Empire* (1909), *Herodotus* (1924), *Democracy in the Ancient World* (1927), and *Greek Byways* (1927). He was a serious student of the classics, but with a sense of the whimsical. "I modestly claimed," he once said, "to understand irrelevance." His interests extended to larger realms of literature, and he had an unusual ability to communicate at a popular level. He also retained his interest in all things Canadian from his early experience there. He also lectured in the United States and was the recipient of six honorary degrees. (**DcNB.**)

51. **Goguel, Maurice** (1880–1955). Goguel was born and died at Paris, his family of Lutheran origin with a number of pastors among his ancestors. He studied at the Protestant Faculty at the University of Paris (Th.D., 1905; Lit.D., 1920 [Docteur ès lettres, 1910]), at Berlin and Marburg, and taught at the Free Faculty of Protestant Theology after the Separation as *chargé de cours* and then as Professor of the Exegesis of the New Testament. Later he served as dean of that institution. Still later (1927) he assumed the position formerly occupied by Alfred Loisy and in a decade succeeded Ch. Guignebert at the Sorbonne. His works included *Introduction au Nouveau Testament*, 5 vols. (1922–26); *Jésus de Nazareth, mythe ou histoire?* (1925; English trans., *Jesus the Nazarene Myth or History?* [1926]), *Jésus et les origines du Christianisme*, 3 vols. vol. 1 was *La Vie de Jésus* (1932; English trans., *The Life of Jesus* [1933], reprinted as *Jesus and the Origins of Christianity* [Harper Torchbook, 1960]). Goguel was a not-quite-satisfied liberal who felt that his faith nevertheless demanded a rigorous scientific method in his work. He was an *officier de la légion d'Honneur* and also held honorary degrees from Glasgow, Lausanne, St. Andrews, and Uppsala. (**DcBF; Kml; WhoF.**)

52. **Goodspeed, Edgar Johnson** (1871–1962). Educated at Denison University (A.B., 1890), Yale University, and the University of Chicago (D.B., 1897; Ph.D., 1898), with studies at the University of Berlin, Goodspeed took a position with the University of Chicago as instructor in biblical and patristic Greek in 1902, advanced to professor in 1915, chairman of the New Testament Department (1923–37), and Distinguished Service Professor (1933–37) when he retired. Early work in patristics and, along with Grenfell and Hunt, in translating papyri from Egypt, led ultimately to production of *New Testament: An American Translation* (1923). In addition, Goodspeed wrote prolifically on other subjects. Among his books were *The Story of the New Testament* (1916), *The Formation of the New Testament* (1926), *An Introduction to the New Testament* (1937), *History of Early Christian Literature* (1946), *Paul* (1947), and *Jesus* (1950). (*AmAu&B; AmLY; LinLib L, LinLib S; Kep;* **Nat-CAB** 52:481–82; *REnAL; TwCA S;* **WebAB; WhAm** 4; *WhNAA;* his autobiography is *As I Remember* [New York: Harper, 1953].)

53. **Grandmaison, Léonce Loyzeau de** (1868–1927). A Jesuit priest, Grandmaison studied at the Jesuit collège Ste-Croix and in 1886 joined his brother at the Compagnie réfugié à Slough (England). After three years of philosophy at Jersey and two of a professoriat at Mans, he returned to England for four years of theological study and was ordained priest in 1898. His time at various places occurred in the midst of the "modernist" crisis, which received denunciation from Grandmaison, with disapproval of Harnack, Loisy, Sabatier,

Le Roy, and Tyrrell. He came to Paris in 1908 as supérieur de las Maison des Écrivains dispersés and editor of the review *Études*. His encouragement and use of younger and more open contributors brought charges of being too progressive from some quarters, leading to the founding of *Recherches de science religieuse* for more technical work. He also became the moving force in the apostolic community of St.-François-Xavier and practiced the Ignatian spirituality until his death. But his life was transformed by the Great War, with the loss of a brother and many colleagues and other relatives. After the war he was relieved of editorship of *Études*, though retained *Recherches* and had a part in the founding of *Nouvelles religieuses*. He had the plan to compose a life of Jesus since an article of 1912 in *Dictionnaire apologétique* and retired to Jersey in 1926 to do so. The posthumous volume followed, as well as other works (*Le Dogma chrétien*, 1928; 3 vols. of *Écrits spirituels*, 1933–35). (**DcBF.**)

54. **Grant, F[rederick] C[lifton]** (1891–1974). Educated at Lawrence College (1907–9), Nashotah House (1909–11), General Theological Seminary (B.D., 1913), and Western Seminary (later Seabury-Western; S.T.M. and Th.D., 1916, 1922), Grant was ordained priest in the Protestant Episcopal Church. He served pastoral, professorial, and administrative appointments as rector, Trinity Church, Chicago (1921–24); dean, Bexley Hall Divinity School (1924–26); librarian and Professor of Systematic Theology, Berkeley Divinity School (1926–27); president, Western (Seabury-Western) Seminary (1927–38), and Professor of Biblical Theology, Union Theological Seminary, New York (1938–59). His publication career was extensive, from *The Life and Times of Jesus* (1921), *The Economic Background of the Gospels* (1926), *The Growth of the Gospels* (1933), *The Earliest Gospel* (1941), on to *Hellenistic Religions* (1953), and *The Vatican Council* (1966). He also served as a translator of works of German scholarship (Bultmann, Dibelius, Weiss), and was an editor of the *Anglican Theological Review*. Grant was noted as a person of exacting scholarship combined with serious faith commitments. (*AmAu&B*; **ConAuNRS** 47; **DcAmReB; Kep; WhE&EA;** *WhAm* 6; *WhNAA.*)

55. **Guignebert, Charles-Alfred-Honoré** (1867–1939). Of modest origins — his father was a cooper who died six months after Guignebert's birth — Guignebert was raised by his grandmother up to the age of 7. His mother remarried, this time to a professor of history; Guignebert was sent to the grammar school at Versailles and secondary school at Janson-de-Sailly. Following undergraduate study he hesitated among philosophy, history, music, and theater. Further studies led to the doctorate in liberal arts (1901) and a primary interest in the origins of Christianity. He approached the subject in the spirit of Renan, viewing Jesus as a simple Jewish prophet who had been transformed by hellenistic and neo-platonic influences into a mystical savior. His academic posts were successively professor at the Lycée d'Évreux (1894–96), also of Pau (1896–98) and Toulouse (1898–1905), and finally the Lycée Voltaire at Paris (1905–6) when the publication of a work on the history of primitive Christianity led to an appointment at the Sorbonne. In April 1919 he became *professeur adjoint* and *professeur titulaire* (1919–37). His works besides the major one on Jesus (1933) ranged from *Modernisme et tradition catholique en France* (1908) to *Le problème de Jésus* (1914), *La vie cachée de Jésus* (1921), *Le problème religieux dans la France d'aujourd'hui* (1922), and *Le Christ* (1943). (**DcBF; Kep.**)

56. **Hartt, Rollin Lynde** (1869–1946). Educated at Williams College (A.B., 1892) and Andover Theological Seminary (1896), Hartt was ordained in the Congregational Church and served pastorates in Montana and Massachusetts before traveling across America

and working as a journalist, writing for newspapers and magazines (*Boston Transcript, Chicago Tribune, Literary Digest, Atlantic Monthly*), though also he had studied Art at Paris in 1911–12. His articles included daily pieces in the *New York Tribune* under the heading, "As I Was Saying." His books included *The People at Play, Ruth of the Dolphin; Understanding the French; Confessions of a Clergyman;* and *The Man Himself.* (*AmAu&B;* **WhoAm** 1922–23; **WhAm** 2.)

57. **Hawkins, John Caesar** (1837–1929). Educated at Harrow and Oriel College, Oxford, with various prizes and distinctions, Hawkins served as vicar of St. Paul's, Chatham (1863–64), and Westcott, Surrey (1864–66), as rector of St. Albans (1866–68) and of Chelmsford (1878–80), and Select Preacher at Oxford (1899). His most significant publications included *Horae Synopticae: Contributions to the Study of the Synoptic Problem* (1899) and his essays in *Studies in the Synoptic Problem* (1911). (**Who** 1910; foreword by F. F. Bruce, in Hawkins, *Horae Synopticae* [reprint, Grand Rapids, Mich.: Baker Book House, 1968].)

58. **Headlam, A[rthur] C[ayley]** (1862–1947). Son of an Anglican priest, Headlam went to Winchester (1876) and New College, Oxford (1883–85), and was ordained priest in 1889. He traveled in the Near East with the eminent W. M. Ramsay and in 1895 with William Sanday produced the *ICC* commentary on the letter to the Romans. From 1896 he was rector at Welwyn, Hertfordshire, until 1903 when he became principal of King's College, London. He was a vigorous and somewhat combative administrator and had a tumultuous ten years at King's College, though not without achievement, and in 1918 became Regius Professor of Divinity at Oxford. Yet he had already won a strong reputation for an enlightened conservative scholarship along with a talent for administration, and in 1923 was consecrated as bishop of Gloucester. He resigned his see in 1945 and enjoyed his books, his coin collecting, and his garden. Among his other works (than *The Life and Teaching of Jesus the Christ*) was *The Fourth Gospel as History* (1948). (**DcNB.**)

59. **Heitmüller, Wilhelm** (1869–1926). Heitmüller studied at Greifswald, Marburg, Leipzig, and Göttingen, receiving his doctorate from the latter where also he became privatdozent in 1902. He went to Marburg in 1908, to Bonn in 1920, and Tübingen in 1924. His works included *Im Namen Jesu: Eine Sprach-und religionsgeschichtliche Untersuchung zum Neuen Testament* (1903), *Taufe und Abendmahl bei Paulus* (1903), *Johannesevangelium (Schriften des Neuen Testaments)* (1907); *Jesus* (1913), and he contributed to various journals as well as cofounding with Wilhelm Bousset the *Theologische Rundschau.* (**Kml; Wei?** 1914.)

60. **Hill, William Bancroft** (1857–1945). Educated at Phillips Exeter Academy and Harvard (B.A., 1879), Hill also studied at Columbia Law School (1880–81), Baltimore Law School (1881–81), and Union Theological Seminary (1883–86). He practiced law in 1882, then became a professor of philosophy at Park College in Maryland. In 1886 he was ordained in the Reformed Church and served pastorates from 1886 to 1902. In part of that time he was lecturer on the Bible at Vassar College, and was Professor of Biblical Literature there (1902–22) when he retired. He was a guest lecturer at various other institutions, such as Union Theological Seminary, and visited the Far East, Japan, Egypt, and Palestine. From 1921 to 1941 he was chairman of the Board of Trustees of the American University in Cairo. He also served as president of the general synod of the Reformed Church, worked with the YMCA, and was a trustee of Fukien Christian University in China. Among his various writings were *Guide to the Lives of Christ* (1905), *Introduction to the Life of Christ*

(1911), *Life of Christ* (1917), *Mountain Peaks in the Life of Our Lord* (1925), and *The Resurrection of Jesus Christ* (1930). He received numerous awards and honorary degrees. (*AmAu&B; AmLY; DcNAA;* **NatCAB** 34:212; *WhAm* 2.)

61. **Hooke, S[amuel] H[enry]** (1874–1968). Hooke had to abandon the course of his education early in life to help support his family after his father, an evangelist for the Plymouth Brethren, died. He returned at age 33 to Jesus College, Oxford, where he also joined the Church of England and set out upon an academic career as scholar and teacher, both of which he accomplished with zeal and honor. In 1931 he became Professor of Oriental Languages and Literature at Victoria College, Toronto, exercising a powerful influence over his students, such that he was encouraged by more conservative parents to resign. In 1926 he returned to London to study Babylonian, Assyrian, Hittite, and Egyptian texts from which his chief fame came, having been appointed Samuel Davidson Chair of Old Testament Studies at London. He retired in 1942, but continued to lecture around the world and write as well. He is best known for sponsoring the so-called Myth and Ritual School, a collection of scholars advocating the recurrence of patterns in the various ancient religions. Hooke was a person of deep religious sensibility who reveled in the joys of life, composing poetry and consuming good wine. He edited the *Palestine Exploration Quarterly* for 23 years and the two best-known essays of the myth-ritualists, *Myth and Ritual* (1933) and *The Labyrinth* (1935). (**DcNB.**)

62. **Hoskyns, Edwin Clement** (1884–1937). Educated at Haileybury, Jesus College, Cambridge, the University of Berlin, and Well Theological College, he was ordained in 1908 and appointed in 1912 warden of Stephenson Hall in the University of Sheffield. In 1915 he entered the war as chaplain, returning to Corpus Christi College, Cambridge, in 1919, where he served as dean of the chapel, as librarian and president. He was also canon theologian of Liverpool Cathedral (1932–35). He had made the acquaintance of Schweitzer and studied under Harnack at Berlin and been influenced by Loisy. He operated theologically from the perspective that the person of Jesus must be interpreted in light of the faith of the primitive church. His most important work was that with his pupil, Francis Noel Davey, *The Riddle of the New Testament* (1931), but he also composed *Cambridge Sermons* (1938, posthumously), *Essays Catholic and Critical* (1926), and an unfinished commentary on the Fourth Gospel, edited by Davey (1940). (**DcNB;** *WhE&EA.*)

63. **Hügel, Friedrich von** (1852–1925). A baron of the Holy Roman Empire, von Hügel was the son of an Austrian diplomat whose mother converted to Roman Catholicism from Presbyterianism. Von Hügel himself was raised Catholic, though for a time was tutored by a German Lutheran tutor. A spiritual crisis beset him when in 1870 an attack of typhus damaged his hearing permanently — a crisis from which he recovered with the help of a Dutch Dominican (Raymond Hocking) in Vienna. Other influences on him came from exposure to Jesuits. After marrying an English woman von Hügel took up residence in England and in 1914 was naturalized as a British subject. He studied widely, learning the new biblical criticism and defending it before a Roman Catholic congress at Freiburg in 1897 and later (1906) in a pamphlet coauthored with C. A. Briggs. He also cultivated friends among Protestant scholars as well as modernists like Loisy and, especially, George Tyrrell. His writings were largely in the area of philosophy of religion and mysticism, embracing works such as *Mystical Element of Religion as Studied in St. Catherine of Genoa and Her Friends* (1908), *Eternal Life: A Study of Its Implications and Applications,* and his posthumous Gifford lectures, *The Reality of God* (1931). (**DcNB.**)

64. **Jackson, H[enry] Latimer** (1851–1926). Educated in Germany and at Christ's College, Cambridge, Jackson was ordained to the curacy of St. Neots, Hunts, then rector of St. James, Sydney, and Fellow and Lecturer of St. Paul's College, University of Sydney (receiving also an M.A. there). He became Hulsean Lecturer at Cambridge (1912), Select Preacher (1906 and 1920), Lecturer in Modern and Medieval Dutch Literature (1918), and Lady Margaret Preacher (1919). He also occupied the rectorship of Little Canfield from 1911 on. His publications, besides *The Eschatology of Jesus* (1913), included *The Fourth Gospel and Some Recent German Criticism* (1906), *The Problem of the Fourth Gospel* (1918), and *A Manual of the Dutch Language* (1921). (**WhGB** 2.)

65. **Jeremias, Joachim** (1900–1979). Earned the Ph.D. at Leipzig (1922) and the Licentiate in 1923. He was privatdozent, 1925–28, at Leipzig, at the University of Berlin as professor (1928–29), the University of Greifswald as Professor of New Testament (1929–35), and the University of Göttingen (1935 on). Honorary degrees have come from Leipzig, St. Andrews, Uppsala, and Oxford. Jeremias's writings have been extensive; including *Jerusalem zur Zeit Jesu* (1923; 3d ed., 1962; English trans., *Jerusalem in the Time of Jesus* [1969, 3d ed., 1975]); *Die Abendmahlsworte Jesu* (1935; 4th ed., 1967; English trans., *The Eucharistic Words of Jesus* [1955; 3d ed., 1966]); *Die Gleichnisse Jesu* (1947; 8th ed., 1970; English trans., *The Parables of Jesus* [1954, 3d ed., 1972]); *Unbekannte Jesusworte* (1948; 3d ed., 1963; English trans., *Unknown Words of Jesus* [1957; rev. ed., 1964]); studies on Timothy, Titus and Hebrews, Abba, and *Neutestamentliche Theologie,* vol. 1, *Die Verkündigung Jesu* (1971; English trans., *New Testament Theology 1: The Proclamation of Jesus* [1971]). A world-class scholar, Jeremias has had influence especially in the study of the Last Supper and parables. (**ConAuNRS** 11; **WeW** 1974–75; ZNW 70 [1979]: 139–40.)

66. **Jülicher, Adolf** (1857–1938). Jülicher began his studies (1875) at Berlin with exposure to historical methodology that estranged him from his more pietistic Lutheran father, and came under teachers like Pfleiderer, Weizsäcker, Holtzmann, and Wellhausen. He received his licentiate in theology in 1886; during the period 1880–82 he had served pastoral duties that allowed him time for his qualifying thesis, the first study on parables (1886). Three semesters as privatdozent followed, and Jülicher thereafter went to Marburg as Professor of Church History and New Testament, where he remained until his retirement in 1923. In addition to his well-known work on parables and his *Introduction to the New Testament* (German original, *Einleitung in das Neue Testament,* 1894 and various editions; English trans., 1904), Jülicher wrote extensively in church history and New Testament in lexica articles and journals as well as books. (**Kml; Hans-Josef Klauck, "Adolf Jülicher — Leben, Werk und Wirkung,"** in *Historische Kritik in der Theologie: Beiträge zu ihrer Geschichte,* ed. Georg Schwaiger, Studien zur Theologie und Geistesgeschichte des Neunzehnten Jahrhunderts 32 [Göttingen: Vandenhoeck and Ruprecht, 1980], 99–150 [complete bibliography]).

67. **Keable, Robert** (1887–1927). An English novelist, Keable was the son of an evangelical minister and was educated at Magdalene College, Oxford, where he graduated with first-class honors in the History Tripos. He converted to the Anglican Church, became ordained in 1911, and after a year of curacy went to Africa as a missionary. In 1914 he was rector at Basutoland and in 1917–18 was chaplain with the South African forces in France. His misfortunes with ecclesiastical authorities caused him to resign from the church and he expressed his disdain in a novel, *Simon Called Peter,* which sold widely, was made into a film, and made the author independently wealthy. Other of his works did not

enjoy the same success, though *Peradventure: Or, The Silence of God* (1923) found some audience. His last work was *The Great Galilean* (1929), issued posthumously. Poor health sent him to Tahiti, where he died prematurely at age 40 of Bright's disease (nephritis). He was unmarried. (*EvLB; LongCTC;* **NewC;** *REn;* **TwCA;** *WhLit.*)

68. **Kent, C(harles) F(oster)** (1867–1925). From Palmyra, New York, Kent went to school at Palmyra Union Classical School and entered the Sheffield Scientific School in New Haven, but transferred to Yale College, graduating in 1889. He set out to study law, but was inspired by William R. Harper to pursue biblical studies. In 1891 he graduated Ph.D. from Yale in Semitic languages and philosophy. Following a year at Berlin and several months in Palestine and the Near East he taught at the University of Chicago (1882–95), followed by a year at Breslau, then went to Brown University (1898–1901) before returning to Yale as Woolsey Professor of Biblical Literature, W. R. Harper's chair, which Kent held until his death. He founded the National Council on Religion in Higher Education whose purpose was to facilitate training of persons for positions of teaching religion, and produced a series of 35 books on biblical subjects, among them *The Student's Old Testament*, 6 vols. (1904–27), *The Historical Bible*, 6 vols. (1908–16), and *The Shorter Bible*, 2 vols. (1918–21), in addition to his *The Life and Teachings of Jesus According to the Earliest Records* (1913), and the long-popular *A History of the Hebrew Commonwealth* (with Albert Edward Bailey, 1920). (*AmAu&B; AmLY;* **DcAmB S2;** *DcNAA;* **NatCAB** 24:28; *REnAL;* **TwCBDA;** *WhAm* 1.)

69. **King, Henry Churchill** (1858–1934). King began his studies at Hillsdale College (Michigan), transferring to Oberlin and graduating there A.B. (1879) and B.D. (1882) from the Oberlin Theological Seminary. After a year studying philosophy at Harvard (A.M., 1883), he returned to Oberlin as a professor of mathematics and (in 1891) of philosophy. He studied at Berlin in 1893–94, influenced by Hermann Loetze's philosophy and Albrecht Ritschl's theology. In 1897 he became Professor of Theology and Philosophy, dean of the College in 1901, and president in 1902, a position he held until 1927. He served a wide variety of offices in higher education, at the YMCA, and was in frequent demand as a lecturer and speaker. His publications included *Reconstruction in Theology* (1901), *Theology and the Social Consciousness* (1902), *The Ethics of Jesus* (1910), and *Fundamental Questions* (1917). His theological position may be characterized as liberal evangelicalism. (*AmAu&B; AmBi; AmLY; DcAmAu;* **DcAmB S1;** *DcNAA;* **NatCAB** 13:296; *OhAu&B;* **TwCBDA;** *WhAm* 1; *WhNAA.*)

70. **Knox, John** (1900–1990). Educated at Randolph-Macon College (A.B., 1919), Emory University (B.D., 1925), and the University of Chicago (Ph.D., 1935), Knox was ordained a Methodist minister and served pastorates in the Baltimore Conference, was professor at Emory (1924–27) and minister at Fisk University (1929–36), managing editor of *Christendom* (1936–38), and on the editorial staff of *Christian Century*, then went to Hartford Theological Seminary (1938–39), the University of Chicago (1939–42), and to Union Theological Seminary as Baldwin Professor of Sacred Literature (1943–66). He was ordained into the Episcopal Church in 1962 and upon retirement from Union went to Episcopal Theological Seminary Southwest (1966–71). A popular lecturer and writer, Knox left a large legacy of publication. Some of the better known works were *The Man Jesus Christ* (1941), *Christ the Lord* (1945), *On the Meaning of Christ* (1947), *Chapters in a Life of Paul* (1950), *Criticism and Faith* (1952), *The Ethic of Jesus in the Teaching of the Church* (1961), and *The Limits of Unbelief* (1971). He also edited the *Journal of Religion,*

was an associate editor of the *Interpreter's Bible*, to which he contributed a commentary on Romans. (*AmAu&B; Au&Wr* 1971; **ConAuR** 13–16, 132; **WhoAm** 1978; *WrDr* 1976.)

71. **Kohler, Kaufmann** (1843–1926). Born in Fürth (Bavaria), Germany, Kohler was educated at Munich, Berlin, and Leipzig (1865–69) and received the Ph.D. from Erlangen in 1868. He was called to Beth El Congregation in Detroit, then to Sinai Congregation in Chicago, and arrived in 1879 at Temple Beth El in New York City. After 23 years he became president of Hebrew Union College at Cincinnati (1903) and remained there until his retirement in 1922. He was a vigorous advocate for Reform Judaism, helping to organize the reform conference held at Pittsburgh in 1885, which adopted a set of principles for reform Judaism. He was also an active participant in the earlier 1869 Philadelphia Rabbinical Reform Conference. He held that the traditional faith had to evolve as conditions changed, and contributed profoundly toward that end through lecture, article, and book, with over 300 entries in the *Jewish Encyclopedia* alone. (**DcAmReB; NatCAB** 13:396.)

72. **Köhler, Ludwig** (1880–1956). After military service in Freiburg Köhler went to Zürich where he studied theology and oriental languages. Most influenced by P. W. Schmiedel, he received his Ph.D. (1908) with a study of the Greek and Hebrew text of Jeremiah 1–9, while also serving pastorates. In 1908 he was called as Professor of Old Testament to Zürich and in 1915 relinquished all pastoral work in order to concentrate on his scientific studies. He attained *Ordinarius* (professor) status in 1923 in both Old Testament and in practical theology. His main interest lay in Old Testament, where he gained his greatest reputation. He spent a year as guest lecturer at Chicago Theological Seminary and was called as rector of Zürich University (1930–32). His most significant work was his *Lexicon in Veteris Testamenti Libros* (1953; 3d ed. 1967–74, German and English), intended to be a revision of Gesenius-Buhl, but in fact a new work standing on its own. Other works included a study of Deutero-Isaiah and an Old Testament theology (1936; 4th ed., 1966). (**NDBb** 12.)

73. **Kraeling, Carl** (1897–1966). Attended Columbia University (A.B., 1918; Ph.D., 1927) and Lutheran Theological Seminary, Philadelphia (B.D., 1926), with further studies at the University of Pennsylvania (1919–21) and Union Theological Seminary (1922–23), and the doctorate at Heidelberg (1935). Ordained to the Lutheran ministry (1920), Kraeling was instructor and assistant professor at Lutheran Theological Seminary (1920–29), then assistant and associate professor at the Divinity School, Yale University (1929–41), and Buckingham Professor of New Testament Criticism and Interpretation (1941–50), where also he chaired the department of Near Eastern Languages and Literature (1947–1950). He then went to the University of Chicago as professor of Oriental Archaeology and Director of the Oriental Institute (1950–60; emeritus 1962). In addition to his *Anthropos and Son of Man* (1937), Kraeling also produced works such as *John the Baptist* (1951), and *Excavations at Dura-Europas VIII, The Synagogue* (1956). (**WhoAm** IV.)

74. **Kümmel, W. G.** (1905–?*). Kümmel received his doctorate in theology at Heidelberg (1928), became Professor of New Testament at Zürich (1932–51), Mainz (1951–52), and Marburg (1952–73), from where he retired. His publications are manifold and distinguished, such as his *Introduction to the New Testament* (1966; rev. ed. 1975), *Das Neue Testament: Geschichte der Erforschung seiner Probleme* (1958; English trans. *The New Testament: History of the Investigation of Its Problems* [1974]), and as noticed in the text,

Verheißung und Erfüllung (1945; 3d ed., 1956; English trans., *Promise and Fulfillment* [1957; 2d ed., 1961]). (*WeW* 1976–77; *WhoWor* 1976; *ZNW* 86 [1995]: 3–4.)

75. **Lagrange, M[arie]-J[oseph]** (1855–1938). Trained as a lawyer, Lagrange became a Dominican in 1879 and went into Spanish exile and was ordained priest in 1883. He continued his work in Toulouse and Vienna and in 1890 founded the Jerusalem L'École Pratique d'études bibliques, and also edited the *Révue Biblique* and contributed seven volumes to the *Études Bibliques* set of commentaries. He was also the author of various other works, essays and books, as well as extensive reviews of other works. (**Kml.**)

76. **Lake, Kirsopp** (1872–1946). Born at Southampton, England, Lake was educated at Lincoln College, Oxford (B.A., 1895; M.A., 1897); poor health forced him from a career in politics into the less physically strenuous one of a clergyman. Ordained deacon in 1895 and priest in 1896, he served curacies until 1904, one in Oxford where also he worked in the Bodleian Library cataloguing manuscripts. He wrote some works in that period, such as *The Text of the New Testament*, which enjoyed a wide usage for a lengthy period of time. He also edited a number of texts, including *Codex I of the Gospels and Its Allies* (1902), later known as "family 1" of the "Lake Group" of manuscripts. In 1904 he took a position at Leiden University, composed more books, and worked especially in the Greco-Roman background to the New Testament. In 1913 he came to the United States to deliver the Lowell lectures and teach a year at Episcopal Theological School in Cambridge; while there he accepted an appointment to the Harvard Divinity School, where he stayed until 1932, resigning his chair to enter into the History Department at Harvard. Among the most enduring of his works was the editing of the series *The Beginnings of Christianity* (1902–33), along with F. J. Foakes-Jackson. Along with his student, whom he subsequently married (second marriage), Sylva New, he also edited *Six Collations of New Testament Manuscripts* (1932) and issued ten volumes of facsimiles entitled *Dated Greek Minuscule Manuscripts to the Year 1200* (1934–39). (*AmAu&B*; **DcAmB S4;** *DcNAA; WhAm* 2.)

77. **Laufer, Calvin Weiss** (1874–1938). Laufer graduated A.B. at Franklin and Marshall College (1897) and Union Theological Seminary (1900), and did missionary work in the slums of New York City while in seminary, served pastorates thereafter (Long Island, 1900–1905; West Hoboken, N.J., 1905–14), and represented the Presbyterian Church (1914–24) in its publications and Sunday school work. Thereafter he was primarily a hymnologist, developing graded hymnals and himself composing hymns, and editing hymnbooks designed primarily for children and youth. His books included *Keynotes of Optimism* (1911), *The Incomparable Christ* (1914), and *The Bible–Story and Content* (1924). He was assistant editor of the official hymnal of the Presbyterian Church in the USA (1933). Personally he was described as a broad-minded, tolerant, and optimistic individual. (**NatCAB** 29:149–50.)

78. **Lauterbach, J[acob] Z[allel]** (1873–1942). Born in Austria, studied in Israel with education at Berlin and Göttingen (Ph.D., 1902), Lauterbach came to the United States in 1903 and was naturalized in 1909. He became Professor of Talmud at Hebrew Union College in 1911 and spent his career there. He contributed many articles to the *Jewish Encyclopedia*, the *Jewish Quarterly Review*, and wrote books such as *The Ethics of the Halakah* (1913), *The Sadducees and Pharisees* (1913), *Midrash and Mishnah* (1916), *An Introduction to the Talmud* (1925), *The Pharisees and Their Teachings* (1930), and *A Critical Edition of*

the Mekilta with an English Translation (1933). He was a significant figure in the Jewish Reform movement and in the revaluation of Pharisaism going on in the first part of the twentieth century. (**WhAm** 2; **WhNAA.**)

79. **Lebreton, Jules Marie** (1873–1956). Born in Tours, Lebreton earned the degree of Docteur ès lettres and became Professor of the History of Christian Origins at the Faculty of Catholic Theology, Paris. His publications included *La Vie Chrétienne au Premier Siècle* (1927), *La Vie et L'enseignement de Jésus Christ* (2 vols. [1934]; English trans., *Life and Teaching of Jesus Christ* [1931; rev. ed., 1948, 1960]), *Le Dieu Vivant* (n.d.), and editing the journals *Études* and *Recherches de Science Religieuse*. He also provided a work on *Le Père Léonce de Grandmaison* (1932). (**WhE&EA.**)

80. **Leipoldt, Johannes** (1880–1965). Leipoldt began his academic work in 1889 in Berlin and Leipzig in theology and Oriental studies and was awarded the Ph.D. with his monograph on "Schenute, der Begründer der national ägyptischen Kirche." In 1905 he qualified in church history and theology with a *Habilitationschrift* on *Didymus der Blinde von Alexandria*. His teaching followed as privatdozent in Leipzig and Hall, then in 1909 he became associate professor for New Testament at Kiel, and five years later went to the newly founded University of Münster and in 1916 succeeded his teacher Georg Heinrici in the Chair of New Testament at Leipzig. He retired in 1959. Leipoldt had expertise in languages, archaeology, coptic, rabbinics, New Testament, and early church history. He was one of the first to translate the Nag Hammadi text Gospel of Thomas and provide a commentary on it. He also worked extensively in the Oriental-hellenistic mystery cults. Much of his study was directed at establishing the peculiar element in Jesus' message, such that Leipoldt found already in Jesus a separation of Christianity from Judaism, without which Christianity could not, in his view, have become a world religion. (**NDBb** 14.)

81. **Lightfoot, R[obert] H[enry]** (1883–1953). Educated at Eaton, Worcester College, Oxford, Bishop's Hostel, Farnham, with first class theological honors (1907) and various other prizes and honors, Lightfoot served a curacy of Haslemere (1909–12), as bursar, vice-principal, and principal of Wells Theological College (1912–19), Examining Chaplain to the Archbishop of Centerbury (1913–53), Fellow and Chaplain of Lincoln College, Oxford (1919–21), and was Ireland Professor of Exegesis of Holy Scripture, Oxford (1934–49), when he retired. In addition to *History and Interpretation in the Gospels* (1935), Lightfoot wrote *Locality and Doctrine in the Gospels* (1938) and *The Gospel Message of Mark* (1950). (**Kep; WhGB** 5.)

82. **Lowrie, Walter** (1868–1959). Lowrie attended Princeton University, Princeton Theological Seminary, Greifswald, and Berlin, and the American Academy at Rome. His publications, besides his translations, included *Jesus According to St. Mark* (1928), *The Short Story of Jesus* (1943), and *Art in the Early Church* (1947). (**WhAm** 5; **WhE&EA;** *AmAu&B; AmLY; DcAmAu; WhNAA.*)

83. **Ludwig, Emil** (1881–1948). Born with Jewish descent surnamed Cohn, his professor (Breslau) father gave him the name Ludwig to offset the difficulties of possessing an obviously Jewish name. Ludwig attended Breslau and Heidelberg (Jur.Dr.), intending to become a lawyer, but never practiced. He was a writer from age 25 on, with some forays into plays and poems and some time in journalism, but predominantly Ludwig was remembered for his biographies, especially the dramatized type of biography then popular in Europe. He composed biographies in this style on Goethe, Napoleon, Bismarck, Lincoln,

Cleopatra, and offered interview-portraits of well-known figures (Roosevelt, portraits of Hitler, Mussolini, Stalin). His writings suffered condemnation from Nazi critics in the thirties and were burned, with Ludwig himself declared an enemy of the state. He had been a Swiss citizen since 1932, however, and came to the United States in 1940, but finished his life in his home at Ascona, Switzerland, at the age of 67. Many of his works are available in English translation. (**EncTR; EvEuW;** LinLib L, LinLib S; LongCTC; NotNAT B; OxGer; **TwCA, TwCA S;** WhLit; WhoAm 2; WhoLA.)

84. **Lyman, Mary Ely** (1887–1975). Lyman graduated at Mount Holyoke (1911), and taught school in Connecticut for two years before returning to Mount Holyoke as general secretary of the YWCA, where teaching Bible classes stimulated her interest in further study. She enrolled at Union Theological Seminary (N.Y.), receiving her B.D. in 1919, but as the only woman in the class she was not permitted to attend the commencement luncheon and sat with the faculty wives during the commencement, even though she was the ranking scholar in her class. She won a fellowship to study at Cambridge (1919–20), but the university declined to grant a theological degree to a woman or even to issue her a transcript certifying to her study. Only letters from her individual instructors were available when she applied to the University of Chicago Ph.D. program, to which she was admitted and attained her degree in 1924. A successful marriage to Eugene Lyman, professor at Union, was accompanied by teaching at Barnard College and Union. After her husband's retirement the couple moved to Virginia, where she taught and was dean at Sweet Briar College, and, following Eugene's death, she returned to Union as Professor of English Bible and Dean of Women Students, who were by then becoming more numerous. Various other positions followed her own retirement from Union in 1955, including Scripps College in Claremont, California, where she died of a stroke. Her writings included *Paul the Conqueror* (1919), *The Fourth Gospel and the Life of To-day* (1931), *The Christian Epic* (1936), *Jesus* (1937), and *Death and the Christian Answer* (1960). (**NotAW: The Modern Period**, 435–37; **New York Times**, Jan. 11, 1975, 32.)

85. **Machen, John Gresham** (1881–1937). Graduating from Johns Hopkins University (1901) followed by a further year there in study of the classics, Machen then went to Princeton Theological Seminary (B.D., 1905) and simultaneously (M.A., 1904) Princeton University. Study thereafter for a year in Marburg and Göttingen brought him briefly under the influence of Wilhelm Herrmann, only to become convinced that the dismantling of that theology was necessary for the survival of Christianity. Machen returned to serve at Princeton Seminary as instructor in the New Testament (1906–14) and Assistant Professor of New Testament Literature and Exegesis (1914–29). Ordination and some work with the YMCA in the war years were followed by a return to Princeton, where Machen became a staunch conservative, fundamentalist advocate in the controversies of the twenties. His book *Christianity and Liberalism* (1923) epitomized his position. The reorganization of Princeton in 1929 along more moderate lines led Machen to withdraw and to found Westminster Theological Seminary in Philadelphia, where he taught until his death in 1937. His own Presbytery suspended him in 1935 as a schismatic, leading him to help organize the Presbyterian Church of America. Probably his most enduring publication was his *New Testament Greek for Beginners* (1923), still in use. (**DcAmB S2;** DcNAA; **DcAmReB;** WebAB; WhAm 1; WhNAA.)

86. **Mackinnon, James** (1860–1945). Educated at Edinburgh, Bonn, and Heidelberg (M.A. Ph.D., D.D., D. Theol., LL.D.), Mackinnon was Lecturer in History in Queen Margaret

College, University of Glasgow, also Examiner in History, University of Edinburgh, Lecturer in History, University of St. Andrews (1896–1908), and Professor of Ecclesiastical History, Edinburgh (1908–30). His publications included *Culture in Early Scotland* (1892), *A History of Modern Liberty* (1906–8), *Luther and the Reformation*, 4 vols. (1925–30), *The Historic Jesus* (1931), and *The Gospel in the Early Church* (1933). (**Kep; Who** 1945.)

87. **Major, H[enry] D[ewesbury] A[lves]** (1871–1961). Born in Plymouth, as a child Major migrated to New Zealand where he graduated from Auckland University (B.A., 1895), was ordained deacon in 1895 and priest in 1896, thereafter serving curacies and also receiving his M.A. (1896) in natural sciences. He left for England in 1902 determined to learn criticism, entered Exeter College, Oxford, and studied with William Sanday, S. R. Driver, and W. C. Allen. In 1905 he took first class honors in theology and went to Ripon Clergy College in 1906. A tour of the Holy Land ensued, after which Major cast his lot entirely with the modernist movement and became its vigorous advocate. He edited the *Modern Churchman* most of his remaining years and managed annual Conferences of Modern Churchmen. Ripon was reopened after a closing during the war years at Oxford, with Major as principal, though he suffered from some efforts to arraign him on heresy charges. His response was *Resurrection of Relics* (1922), causing some conservatives to name him the "Anti-Christ of Oxford." In 1929 he was appointed vicar of Merton by Exeter College, Oxford. In 1933 the college was moved again, three miles from Oxford. In World War II most of its buildings were used as a hospital, but Major managed to keep it going through the war and beyond. Other of his works were *English Modernism: Its Origin, Methods, Aims* (1927), and *The Church and the Twentieth Century* (1936). (**DcNB; Kep.**)

88. **Manson, William** (1882–1958). Educated at the High School and University of Glasgow, took first class at Oxford (1908), studied theology at the United Free Church College (later Trinity College), Glasgow, and was ordained in 1911. Served charges (1911–14) and became Professor of New Testament Language and Literature, Knox College, Toronto (1919–25), and Professor of New Testament, New College, Edinburgh (1925), and in Edinburgh University (1935), and Professor of Biblical Criticism in the University of Edinburgh (1946–52). Active as lecturer and in ecumenical circles, Manson published across the years, with such books as *Christ's View of the Kingdom of God* (1918), *The Incarnate Glory: An Expository Study of St. John's Gospel* (1923), *The Gospel of Luke* (Moffatt Commentary, 1930), *Jesus the Messiah* (1943), and *The Epistle to the Hebrews* (1951). (**WhGB** 5.)

89. **Manson, T[homas] W[alter]** (1893–1958). Educated by his educator-father and at Glasgow University (M.A., 1917), Manson served in the artillery in World War I and was wounded in France. He returned to school in 1919 and prepared for ministry in the Presbyterian Church of England at Westminster College, Cambridge, while also enrolling in Christ's College, gaining a first class in Hebrew and Aramaic in 1923. Ordination followed, along with appointments in churches. While at Falstone, Northumberland, he produced his first book, *The Teaching of Jesus* (1931), which earned him recognition as a New Testament scholar. In 1932 he succeeded C. H. Dodd as Yates Chair in New Testament Greek at Mansfield, and later (1936) followed Dodd again as Rylands Professor of Biblical Criticism, where he remained until his death. He earned many honors and lectured widely and wrote influential, if not frequent, books and articles. Some others were *The Church's Ministry* (1948), and *The Servant-Messiah* (1953). He was also a popular teacher and preacher. (**DcNB.**)

90. **Martin, A[lfred] W[ilhelm]** (1862–1932). Martin was born in Cologne, Germany, but went to Montreal, Canada, as a youth and graduated from McGill University (A.B., 1882). He then received his S.T.B. and A.M. from Harvard (1885, 1886) and was ordained a Unitarian minister in 1888, serving churches in Massachusetts and in Tacoma, Washington. At the latter his powerful sermon on the future church to be erected on common ethical ideals prompted his church to disassociate from the Unitarians and become the First Free Church of Tacoma. A movement spread to a second group in Seattle, also headed by Martin. In 1907 he came to New York at the invitation of Felix Adler of the Society for Ethical Culture and remained associated with that group until his death. His great interest was in comparative religions, and he held the hope that the religion of the future would be a merger of all faiths, and he labored to that end. His books reflect his views, in such titles as *Great Religious Teachers of the East* (1911), *Life of Jesus in the Light of Higher Criticism* (1913), *Psychic Tendencies of Today* (1918), *A Critique of Christian Science* (1922), and *Comparative Religion and the Religion of the Future* (1925). (*AmLY; DcNAA;* **NatCAB** 23:138; *WhAm* 1; *WhNAA*.)

91. **Mathews, Shailer** (1863–1941). Received his undergraduate education at Colby College (A.B., 1884), and his theological degree from Newton Theological Institution (1887), but did not seek ordination and went instead into teaching, first at Colby as a professor of rhetoric, then of history and political economy (1889). He then took a year's leave to go to Berlin University, studying history, from which came his first book, *Select Mediaeval Documents* (1892). He returned to Colby, manifesting an interest in the new field of sociology under influence of his friend Albion W. Small. In 1894 he was invited to the University of Chicago to become Professor of New Testament History and Interpretation. In 1906 he became Professor of Historical and Comparative Theology, dean of the Divinity School in 1908, and remained so until his retirement in 1933. He was a leader in the sociohistorical interpretation of the New Testament and early Christian history and a modernist in the broad sense, supporting the social gospel movement. He maintained his commitment to his Baptist church tradition, even though he departed from traditional orthodox ways and beliefs. His twin interests appear in his presidency of the Federal Council of Churches (1912–16) and his role in founding the Northern Baptist Convention. Besides his *The Social Teaching of Jesus*, Mathews wrote many other books, among them *The Faith of Modernism* (1924), *The Atonement and the Social Process* (1930), and *Christianity and Social Process* (1933). (*AmAu&B;* **DcAmB S3; DcAmReB;** *DcNAA; LinLib L, LinLib S; NatCAB* 11; *TwCBDA; WhAm* 2; *WhNAA;* **introduction** by Kenneth Cauthen to *Jesus on Social Institutions*, Lives of Jesus [Philadelphia: Fortress Press, 1971].)

92. **Mauriac, François** (1885–1970). The French poet, playwright, and novelist was born of a middle-class family of landlord-farmers, his father dying when Mauriac was only 20 months old. His mother raised her children in the strictest Catholic fashion, François attending Catholic schools that provided severe discipline of life and routine. Nevertheless he began writing his poems and diary and making literary acquaintances. He attended briefly the École de Chartres in Paris (1906), but withdrew to pursue his literary activity, publishing his poems in 1909. Their reception assured him of his vocation as writer; he turned to the novel and also founded *Les Cahiers*, a magazine for Catholic literature. During World War I he worked as a hospital assistant, but contracted malaria and returned from Salonica. After the war he began to publish extensively; *The Kiss of the Leper* (1922) secured for him renown, and a number of splendid novels followed, such as *Le*

Fleuve de Feu (1923), *Genitrix* (1924), *The Desert of Love* (1925), and *Thérèse* (1927). A "conversion" in 1928–29 led to the emergence of the truly "Catholic" artist, after which Mauriac even returned Thérèse in *La Fin de la Nuit* (1935) to suffer for her earlier sins. But Mauriac's talents were nevertheless widely recognized; in 1932 he was elected president of the Société des Gens de Lettres and in 1933 to the French Academy. In World War II he aided the underground resistance writing under the pseudonym Forez; he won the Nobel prize for literature in 1952 and continued publication of fiction, poetry, and even work in film. (**ConAuP 2; TwCA.**)

93. **McCown, C[hester] C[harlton]** (1877–1958). Educated at Illinois Wesleyan, DePauw University (B.A., 1898), Garrett Biblical Institute (B.D., 1902), and the University of Chicago (Ph.D., 1914), McCown also studied at Heidelberg and Berlin. He was Professor of Biblical Literature at Wesley College (1909–12), Professor of New Testament Literature (1914–47), and dean (1928–36, 1945–46) of the Pacific School of Religion. He was also director of the Palestinian Archaeological Institute (1936–37), a fellow at the American School of Oriental Research, Jerusalem (1920–21; director, 1929–31; acting director and professor, 1935–36), and a joint director of the Yale–American School expedition at Jerash (Gerasa) in 1930–31. Besides various articles his books include *The Search for the Real Jesus* (1940), *The Ladder of Progress in Palestine* (1943), and *Tellen-Nasbeh Excavations* (1947). (**Kep; WhAm 5; WhNAA.**)

94. **Meyer, Eduard** (1855–1930). Schooling for Meyer was begun in a liberal arts environment at home and in the Johanneum Gymnasium he attended, where he acquired not only knowledge of classical languages and literature, as well as modern ones, but also access to Hebrew and Arabic. The director of the school also mediated to him the world-historical approach of B. G. Niebuhr even as he undertook further studies at Bonn (1872) and chiefly in Leipzig (1875) with the Egyptologist G. Ebers. Anthropological and religious-historical studies also marked his research interests, and he undertook the *Habilitation* in Ancient History in 1879 at Leipzig. An offer to produce a work on the history of antiquity set the tone of his career: the *Geschichte des Altertums* (beginning 1884 with *Geschichte des Orients bis zur Begründung des Perserreiches*) displayed Meyer as a historian of universal history. Later volumes in his universal *Geschichte* followed across the years. He was called to Breslau in 1885, moved to Halle in 1889, and to Berlin in 1902, where he remained until retirement (1923); he died in 1930 of a stroke. In the war years Meyer pursued nationalistic goals, supporting the unlimited U-boat campaign and seeing German's enemies as engaged in a cultural war against the fatherland. He served as rector of Berlin University, 1919–20. (**NDBb.**)

95. **Montefiore, C[laude] Joseph G[oldsmid]** (1858–1938). Educated privately and at Balliol, Oxford, Montefiore obtained a first class in *literae humaniores* (1881) and the following year studied at the Anstalt für Wissenschaft des Judentums, where he met Solomon Schechter, who was his tutor and returned to England with him. Jowett and Schechter were the two most significant influences on Montefiore in his early years. His family endowments allowed him the time and he possessed the ability to further freely his ambitions in the area of liberal Judaism and its cause. He helped maintain the Cambridge chair in rabbinics, coedited the *Jewish Quarterly Review* with Israel Abrahams, and produced a life-long stream of work of serious quality that represented the single most important contribution to Jewish-Christian dialogue and especially the recovery of the Jewishness of Jesus. Some of his works were *Liberal Judaism* (1903), *The Synoptic Gos-*

pels, 2 vols. (1909; 2d ed., 1927), *Some Elements of the Religious Teaching of Jesus* (1910), *Outlines of Liberal Judaism* (1912; 2d ed., 1923), *Judaism and St. Paul* (1914), *Rabbinic Literature and Gospel Teachings* (1930), and *A Rabbinic Anthology* (1930). He served also as president of the Liberal Jewish synagogue in London and president of the University College of Southampton (1915–34). (**DcNB;** Lucy Cohen, *Some Recollections of Claude Goldsmid Montefiore, 1858–1938* [1940]; **Kep; Kml.**)

96. **Montgomery, James Alan** (1866–1949). Took his undergraduate studies at the University of Pennsylvania (B.A., 1887) and theological work at the Philadelphia Divinity School (Episcopal, 1890), spent two years as fellow at Greifswald and Berlin, and returned to a curacy in New York City. Ordained priest in 1893, he became rector of St. Paul's in Philadelphia; in 1899 he became rector of the Church of the Epiphany in Germantown and simultaneously instructor in Old Testament at the Philadelphia Divinity School. He pursued his studies at the University of Pennsylvania, earning the Ph.D. in 1904 and thereafter devoted his career to teaching and research. He also taught at the University of Pennsylvania, beginning in 1909 and continuing to 1935. His most famous student was W. F. Albright, but Montgomery himself also published a number of important works, among them two commentaries in the ICC series, on Daniel and Kings (the latter posthumously). He also served a variety of positions in the academy, including director of the American Schools of Oriental Research and edited various journals (*JBL, BASOR*). (**DcAmB S4; WhAm 5.**)

97. **Moore, G[eorge] F[oot]** (1851–1931). Son of a Presbyterian minister, Moore was educated at Yale (1872) and Union Theological Seminary (1877), with studies in Germany (1885, 1909–10) between and after. After serving pastorates he came to Andover Theological Seminary as Professor of Old Testament (1883), and in 1902 was Professor of the History of Religion at Harvard, where he remained until his retirement in 1928. Twenty years at Andover established his reputation as an eminent scholar, with contributions to journals and the commentary on Judges in the ICC (1895). At Harvard he continued a career of distinguished work, with books like *The Literature of the Old Testament* (1913), *History of Religions*, 2 vols. (1913–19), and *Judaism in the First Centuries of the Christian Era: The Age of the Tannaim*, 3 vols. (1927–30). He was also a founder of the *Harvard Theological Review* and served as its editor (1908–14, 1921–31), as well as holding prominent positions in academic organizations. His reputation among Jewish scholars was such that he held a number of honorary degrees from Jewish institutions of higher learning (Hebrew Union College, Jewish Theological Seminary). His command of his field was unsurpassed. (*AmAu&B; AmBi;* **DcAmB;** *DcNAA;* **NatCAB** 42:459; *OhA&B; REnAL; TwCBDA; WhAm* 1.)

98. **Morgan, G[eorge] Campbell** (1863–1945). An English Congregational minister educated privately and at Douglas School, Cheltenham, with a D.D. from Chicago, Morgan published various books, such as *The Crises of Christ* (1904), *The Teaching of Christ* (1913), *Living Messages of Books of the Bible* (1912), and *The Acts of the Apostles*, and edited the *Westminster Bible Record* and the *Westminster Pulpit*. (*DcAmAu;* **NewC; WhE&EA.**)

99. **Murry, J[ohn] Middleton** (1889–1957). Of poor parents, Murry attended Christ's Hospital and Brasenose College, Oxford, through scholarships, earning his first class in honour moderations (1910) and second in *literae humaniores* (1912). He worked for a time for the *Westminster Gazette* and the *Times Literary Supplement*, worked in the War Office, and was

editor of the *Athenaeum* from 1919 until its merger with *Nation*, when he resigned and in 1923 founded the *Adelphi*, which he held until 1948. His critical work gained him a wide reputation and he was a noted figure in the postwar generation that included the likes of T. S. Eliot, Aldous Huxley, and D. H. Lawrence, with whom he had stormy and close relations. He wrote works such as *Dostoevsky* (1916) and other studies of Keats, Shakespeare, and D. H. Lawrence. His *Love, Freedom and Society* (1957) was based on a comparative study of Albert Schweitzer and D. H. Lawrence. He was married four times, having suffered through early deaths of his wives and unhappy relations. (**DcNB**.)

100. **Otto, Rudolf** (1869–1937). Educated at the Universities of Erlangen and Göttingen (D. Theol., D. Phil.), and began his academic career as a privatdozent at Göttingen in 1897, Otto was Associate Professor of Systematic Theology at Göttingen in 1904, professor at Breslau in 1914 and at Marburg in 1917–29. His chief interests were in dogmatics and the history of religions. His best known work was *Das Heilige* (1917; English trans., *The Idea of the Holy* [1923]), though also there appeared *India's Religion of Grace and Christianity Compared* (1930), *Philosophy of Religion* (1931), and *Mysticism* (1932). (**Kep; Kml; P-M Hanbk; RGG**^{3}.)

101. **Papini, Giovanni** (1881–1956). Author and essayist, Papini was educated at the University of Florence and in 1903–20 had a career as critic and editor of various reviews. In that time he was an atheist and anarchist and composed witty and unrelentingly icono-clastic essays toward mysticism and other forms of obscurantism, as he saw it. In 1920 he was "converted" to the Catholicism in which he had been reared and his writing assumed a quite different shape. He became the advocate of religion and a supporter of fascism. In 1933 he won the Mussolini Prize and in 1935 became Professor of Italian Literature at Bologne. He also associated himself with the futurism of Marinetti, who himself became involved in fascism. Besides his *Life of Christ* Papini wrote numerous articles and books, a number of which were translated into English (*Twilight of the Philosophies* [1906], *The Tragic of Everyday* [1906], *A Finished Man* [1913], *Bread and Wine* [1926], *St. Augustine* [1929], *Gog* [1930], *Laborers in the Vineyard* [1929]). (**WhE&EA**; *CathA* 1930; *EncWL*; *EvEuW*; *LongCTC*; *REn*; **TwCA; TwCW**; *WhoLA*.)

102. **Patton, Carl Safford** (1866–1939). Educated at Oberlin (A.B., 1888), Andover Theological Seminary (1892), and the University of Michigan (Ph.D., 1913), Patton was ordained in the Congregational Church and served pastorates in Maine, Michigan, Ohio, and California (1892–1926, 1929–33). He also was Professor of Homiletics and Practical Theology, Chicago Theological Seminary (1926–29), and held a similar post at the Pacific School of Religion (1933 on). In addition to his *Sources of the Synoptic Gospels* (1913), he wrote *Religion in the Thought of Today* (1924), *The Use of the Bible in Preaching* (1936), and *The Preparation and Delivery of Sermons* (1938). (**WhE&EA; WhAm** 1.)

103. **Peabody, Francis Greenwood** (1847–1936). Peabody attended Harvard College (A.B., 1869) and the Harvard Divinity School (A.M., S.T.B., 1872) and studied at Halle (1872–73). He taught briefly at Antioch College (Ohio), served a Unitarian parish in Cambridge, then entered the faculty at Harvard as lecturer on ethics and homiletics, in 1881 was appointed Parkman Professor of Theology and in 1886 Plummer Professor of Christian Morals. He developed what was likely the first course on Christian social ethics in an American theological seminary. In 1906 he became chair of a newly founded department of social ethics. Peabody was a founding force in the social gospel movement, though

mostly his views were of an optimistic as opposed to angrily critical nature, tending toward support of moderate social activities and programs. The main Christian hope was establishment of the kingdom of God on earth. His classic works *Jesus Christ and the Social Question* (1900) and *Jesus Christ and the Christian Character* (1905) still bear reading and disclose his positions well, though he produced many other works as well. (*AmAu&B; DcAmAu;* **DcAmB S2;** *DcAmReB; DcNAA; TwCBDA; WhAm 1; WhNAA.*)

104. **Rauschenbusch, Walter** (1861–1918). A pioneer in the social gospel movement in America, Rauschenbusch was educated at Rochester (B.A., 1884), Rochester Seminary (1886), with further study at Berlin, Kiel, and Marburg (1891–92). His service as minister of the Second German Baptist Church in New York (1886–87) exposed him to conditions of social deprivation and aroused his social conscience. He returned to Rochester on the faculty as Professor of New Testament Interpretation (1897–1902) and Professor of Church History (1902–18). He combined a deep evangelical fervor with social action, though based on the generally liberal proposition that the kingdom of God, even if divine in origin, was nevertheless capable of realization through human activity on earth. His more famous writings were *Christianity and the Social Crisis* (1907), *Christianizing the Social Order* (1912), *The Social Principle of Jesus* (1916), and *A Theology for the Social Gospel* (1917). (*AmAu&B;* **DcAmReB; DcAmB;** *EncAB;* McGEWB; **NatCAB** 19:193; *OxAm; REnAL; WebAB; WhAm 1.*)

105. **Reitzenstein, Richard** (1861–1931). Reitzenstein studied theology and classical philology and became privatdozent at Breslau in Classical Philology (1888), associate professor in Rostock (1889), professor at Giessen (1892), Strassburg (1893), Freiburg (1911), and Göttingen (1914). An exponent of *Religionsgeschichte* his many works revolved around Latin poets and hellenistic religions, especially Iranian mythology and its relationship to late antiquity mysticism. Some of his works were *Poimandres* (1904), *Die hellenistischen Mysterienreligionen* (1910, 1927; English trans., *Hellenistic Mystery Religions: Their Basic Ideas and Significance* [1978]), and *Das iranische Erlösungsmysterium* (1921). (**Kml; RGG**^{3})

106. **Robertson, A[rchibald] T[homas]** (1863–1934). His Virginia plantation-owning father impoverished by the Civil War, Robertson and his family came to North Carolina where the young man was instructed by a Baptist minister and then attended Wake Forest College, where he graduated with A.B. and A.M. (1885) and Th.M. from Southern Baptist Theological Seminary in 1888. He began teaching in New Testament at the latter institution and rose to Professor of New Testament Interpretation. He was a superb linguist and his greatest monument was the gigantic volume on *A Grammar of the Greek New Testament in the Light of Historical Research* (1914, 1931), in the preparation of which he spent six months in the Bodleian and British Museum libraries. A popular lecturer and preacher, Robertson also served in a variety of churches and published extensively across the years. Besides *Epochs in the Life of Jesus* (1908), there were other "epochs-books" on Paul (1909), Peter (1933), and John (1935), as well as his widely used *A New Short Grammar of the Greek New Testament* (1931, with William Hershey Davis), *The Pharisees and Jesus* (1920), and *Luke the Historian in the Light of Research* (1920). (*AmAu&B; AmLY; BiDSA; DcNAA;* **NatCAB** 25:402–3; *WhAm 1; WhNAA.*)

107. **Ropes, James Hardy** (1866–1933). Son of a minister-father who was librarian at Andover Theological Seminary, Ropes was himself educated at Harvard College (A.B., 1889) and Andover (1898), and studied further at Kiel, Halle, and Berlin. He was ordained in the

Congregational Church in 1901. He became a faculty member at Harvard first in 1895 as an instructor and rose to become Bussey Professor of New Testament Criticism and Interpretation (1903–10), then Hollis Professor of Divinity (1910–33). He directed the extension services of the university (1910–22) also and maintained an abiding interest in and relationship to (trustee, president of trustees) Radcliffe, Phillips Academy (where he graduated), and Andover Seminary. His most notable work was *The Text of Acts* (1926), but there were also books from *Die Sprüche Jesu die in den Kanonischen Evangelien night überliefert sind* (1896), to *Commentary on the Epistle of St. James* (1915), and *The Singular Problem of the Epistle to the Galatians* (1929). (*AmLY;* **DcAmB;** *DcNAA;* **NatCAB** 25:250–51; *WhAm* 1; *WhNAA.*)

108. **Sanday, William** (1843–1920). Sanday went to Oxford as a commoner of Balliol College, but gained a scholarship at Corpus Christi College in 1863, where he obtained first class in classical moderations and in *literae humaniores* and was elected Fellow of Trinity College. Following ordination as priest he served various parishes until he was invited to Oxford as Dean Ireland Professor of the Exegesis of Holy Scripture, then became Lady Margaret Professor of Divinity and Canon of Christ Church (1895–1919). He constructed an evolutionary plan for his life's work, moving from the "lower" to the "higher" criticism, the culmination of which was to be a life of Jesus, which never actually appeared. Early works were *The Authorship and Historical Character of the Fourth Gospel* (1872), *Portions of the Gospels according to St. Mark and St. Matthew from the Bobbio MS* (1886), with interruption for the ICC commentary on Romans with A. C. Headlam (1895), followed by studies pertaining to Jesus, *Outlines of the Life of Christ* (1905, from the *Hastings' Dictionary of the Bible), Life of Christ in Recent Research* (1907), and *Christologies Ancient and Modern* (1910). Sanday was important as a mediator of German perspectives to England–even though he worked tirelessly as a pamphleteer during the war–and had a large influence in bringing critical study into British circles. (**DcNB.**)

109. **Schechter, Solomon** (1847–1915). Educated through rabbinic and secular studies at Vienna (1875–79) and talmudic and secular studies at Berlin (1879–82), Schechter was Lecturer in Talmudics at Cambridge (1890–92), Reader in Rabbinics at Cambridge (1899–1902), Professor of Hebrew, University College, London (1899–1902), and president, Jewish Theological Seminary, New York (1902–15). An advocate of critical study of Judaism, Schechter came to England at the request of C. G. Montefiore in 1882 and published essays there, but achieved international recognition through the discovery of manuscripts and fragments in a Genizah at Cairo. The collection was given to Cambridge and supplied further illumination of Jewish views in antiquity. Schechter's acceptance of the presidency of the Jewish Theological Seminary resulted in a more vigorous institution there, embracing his own combination of adherence to rigorous scholarship combined with a conservative devotion to tradition. (**DcAmReB;** biography by Norman Bentwich, *Solomon Schechter: A Biography* [Philadelphia: Jewish Publication Society of America, 1938].)

110. **Schmidt, Nathaniel** (1862–1939). Born in Sweden, his father a fur trader and religious liberal, Schmidt studied at Stockholm for two years (1882–84) before coming to America to Colgate University (then Madison University), where he received his A.M. in 1887. He returned to Sweden, was married, but quickly returned to the United States to the ministry of the Swedish Baptist Church in New York. In 1888 he was offered a professorship at Colgate and taught there eight years, except for study at Berlin in 1890. In 1896

he became Professor of Semitic Languages and Oriental History at Cornell University. He spent 1904–5 in Palestine at what would become the American School of Oriental Research exploring the Negeb and Kadesh Barnea. At the same time he finished the book, *The Prophet of Nazareth* (1905). A succession of other works in journals and encyclopedia followed across the years. *The Coming Religion* (1930) epitomized his liberal views that the ideal religion of the future would be free of dogmas and creeds, would be focused on the ethical and scientific, and would find new forms of organization and fellowship. (*WhLit; DcAmAu; DcAmB S2; DcNAA; WhAm* 1.)

111. **Schmidt, K[arl] L[udwig]** (1891–1956). Schmidt studied theology and classical philology at Marburg and Berlin, obtaining his licentiate in theology (1913), then becoming assistant in the New Testament seminar at Berlin (1913–21), while also serving in the war (1915–16) and as a *Stadtvikar* in Berlin (1917–18). He then became privatdozent in New Testament at Berlin (1918–21), went to Giessen as professor (1921), similarly at Jena (1925), and Bonn (1929), where he was dismissed from his position. He then became a pastor in Switzerland and Professor of New Testament at Basel in 1935. Besides his well-known *Der Rahmen der Geschichte Jesu* (1921), he composed many works in Form Criticism, lexicography, and New Testament theology. (**Kml; Wei?** 1928.)

112. **Schmiedel, Paul Wilhelm** (1851–1935). Born near Dresden, Germany, Schmiedel studied at the Universities of Leipzig (1871–74) and Jena (Lic. Theol. 1878), with D. Theol. (hon. causa) from Strassburg (1892) and Ph.D. (hon. causa) from Zürich (1921). He was privatdozent at Jena (1878–90) and *Extraordinarius* (associate professor) (1890–93), then Professor of Theology at Zürich (1893–1923) and published extensively; among his writings were *Handkommentar zum Neuen Testament II: 1, Briefe an die Thessalonicher und die Korinther* (1890); *Die Person Jesu im Streite der Meinungen der Gegenwart* (1906; English trans., *Jesus in Modern Criticism* [1907]); *Evangelium, Briefe und Offenbarung des Johannes nach ihrer Entstehung und Bedeutung* (1906; English trans., *The Johannine Writings* [1908]); and *Ist die Bibel Gottes Wort?* (1927). (**WhE&EA; WhGB** 3.)

113. **Schonfield, Hugh J[oseph]** (1901–88). Born in London, Schonfield studied at St. Paul's School, the University of Glasgow, and King's College, University of London. He worked as a journalist, author, editor, and translator. His works included *The Lost "Book of the Nativity of John:" A Study in Messianic Folklore and Christian Origins* (1929), *The History of Jewish Christianity from the First to the Twentieth Century* (1936), *Jesus, a Biography* (1939), *The Jew of Tarsus: An Unorthodox Portrait of Paul* (1946), and *A Popular Dictionary of Judaism* (1962). He also edited *Letters to Frederick Tennyson* (1930), *Jesus Christ Nineteen Centuries After* (1933), and other nonreligious works. He translated the *Old Hebrew Text of St. Matthew's Gospel* (1927), and the Yeshu Toldot in *According to the Hebrews* (1937). His most controversial work was the 1965 *The Passover Plot: New Light on the History of Jesus*, offering the thesis that Jesus arranged his own drugging before crucifixion and did not actually die. Still later Schonfield used the pen name Hegesippus and authored more books on Christianity (*Those Incredible Christians* [1968], *The Pentecost Revolution* [1974]). (*Au&Wr* 1971; **ConAuR** 9–12 and 124; *IntAu&W* 1976–77; *WhE&EA.*)

114. **Scott, E[rnest] F[indlay]** (1868–1954). Born in Towlaw, County Durham, England, Scott received the B.A. from Balliol, Oxford (1892), the M.A. from Glasgow (1888), studied at the Theological College of the United Presbyterian Church at Edinburgh, and received a D.D. from St. Andrews (1909) and LL.D. from Queen's University, Ontario

(1920). He served as minister of Prestwick United Free Church, Scotland (1895–1908), then Professor of New Testament Literature, Queen's University, Canada (1908–19), and Union Theological Seminary (1919–38). His works were numerous, from *The Fourth Gospel* (1906), *The Beginning of the Church* (1914), *The Ethical Teaching of Jesus* (1924), *The Kingdom of God* (1931), and on to *The Crisis in the Life of Jesus* (1952) and *I Believe in the Holy Spirit* (1953). (**Ferm; Kep; WhAm** 3.)

115. **Selbie, W[illiam] B[oothby]** (1862–1944). Selbie attended Brasenose and Mansfield Colleges, Oxford, received M.A. from Trinity Hall, Cambridge (1904), and hon. D.D. from Glasgow (1911) and Oxford (1921). He became Lecturer in Hebrew and Old Testament at Mansfield College, Oxford (1889–90), served as minister of Highgate Congregational Church in London (1890–92), Emmanuel Congregational Church, Cambridge (1902–9), Lecturer in Pastoral Theology at Cheshunt College, Cambridge (1907–9), and principal of Mansfield College, Oxford (1909–32). Besides *The Life and Teaching of Jesus Christ* (1908), his books include *Aspects of Christ* (1909), *The Servant of God and Other Sermons* (1911), *Life of Andrew Martin* (1914), the *Christian Ethics in the Individual, the Family, and the State* (1929), *The Fatherhood of God* (1936), and *The Validity of Christian Belief* (1939). (**WhE&EA; WhGB** 4.)

116. **Simkhovitch, Vladimir Gregorievitch** (1874–1959). Born in Russia, Simkhovitch earned his Ph.D. at Halle in 1898 and became Professor of Economic History at Columbia in 1904. His writings included *Marxism versus Socialism* (1913), *Toward the Understanding of Jesus and Other Historical Essays* (1921), and various essays in English, German, and Russian on economic subjects. (**WhAm** 3.)

117. **Stalker, James** (1848–1927). Educated at Edinburgh, Halle, Berlin, and New College, Edinburgh, holding the M.A. and D.D., he was Professor of Church History in the United Free Church College, Aberdeen in 1902, following years of pastoral work since 1874. His works included *The Life of Jesus Christ* (1880; rev. ed., 1909), *The Life of St. Paul* (1880), *Imago Christi* (1889), *The Trial and Death of Jesus* (1894), *The Ethic of Jesus According to the Synoptic Gospels* (1909), *Christian Psychology* (1914). (**WhGB** 1.)

118. **Stanton, V[incent] H[enry]** (1846–1924). Born in Victoria, Hong Kong, where his father was Colonial Chaplain of Victoria, Stanton went to Trinity College, Cambridge (Minor scholar, 1866; Major scholar, 1868; B.A., 1870; M.A., 1873; B.D., 1890; D.D., 1891), in which time he also was Junior and Senior Dean, Tutor, Divinity Lecturer, and Select Preacher. He became Ely Professor of Divinity and Canon of Ely (1889–1916) and Regius Professor of Divinity (1916–22). His writings included *The Jewish and the Christian Messiah: A Study in the Earliest History of Christianity* (1887), *The Place of Authority in Matters of Religious Belief* (1891), *The Gospels as Historical Documents* (pt. 1, 1903; pt. 2, 1909; pt. 3, 1920), and various articles in dictionaries and encyclopedia. (**WhGB** 2.)

119. **Streeter, B[urnett] H[illman]** (1874–1937). Educated at King's College School in London and Oxford at Queen's College, Streeter then became fellow, dean, praelector, chaplain, and provost. Except for the posts of fellow and dean of Pembroke College (1899–1905) his entire career was spent at Oxford. He earned a first class in classical moderations (1895), *literae humaniores* (1897), and theology (1898). He also held the Dean Ireland's Professorship of Exegesis (1932–22). He was interested in a variety of fields, especially philosophy of religion, but his most enduring work was in New Testament. He was also known for his care for his students and for student life generally, and

was often a speaker at student and other conferences with humanitarian concerns. While returning from a conference of the Oxford Group in Switzerland his plane crashed in a fog near Basel, killing him and his wife (1937). Besides his *The Four Gospels* (1924), Streeter wrote *Reality: A New Correlation of Science and Religion* (1926), *The Chained Library* (1932), and *The Buddha and the Christ* (1932). (**DcNB.**)

120. **Taylor, Vincent** (1887–1968). Educated at the Divinity School of the University of London (B.D. Ph.D., D.D.) Taylor entered the Wesleyan ministry, serving pastoral charges for a number of years before becoming Principal and Ferens Professor of New Testament Language and Literature of Wesley College, Headingley, Leeds (1930–53) until retirement in 1954. He also held various Examiner roles (London, Wales) and visiting lectureships (Cambridge, Drew [USA]) and received the Burkitt medal in Biblical Studies from the British Academy. His publications were extensive over a lengthy period of time, from *The Historical Evidence for the Virgin Birth* (1920), *Behind the Third Gospel* (1926), *The Gospels: A Short Introduction* (1930), *Jesus and His Sacrifice* (1937), and on to *The Gospel According to St. Mark* (commentary, 1952), *The Life and Ministry of Jesus* (1954), and *The Text of the New Testament* (1969). (**Kep; WhGB 6.**)

121. **Thompson, J[ames] M[atthew]** (1878–1956). Educated at Christ Church, Oxford, a Fellow of Magdalen (1904–38), Thompson was Dean of Divinity (1906–15), temporary Master at Eton College (1917–19), University Lecturer in Modern French History (1931–39) and Lecturer in History (1942–45). His publications included *Jesus According to St. Mark* (1909), *The Synoptic Gospels* (1910), *Miracles in the New Testament* (1911), *Through Facts to Faith* (1912), *The French Revolution* (1943), *Napoleon Bonaparte* (1952), and *Robespierre and the French Revolution* (1972; c. 1952) (**Who** 1956.)

122. **Troeltsch, Ernst** (1865–1923). Studied at Erlangen, Berlin, and Göttingen, receiving his licentiate in theology (1888), then becoming privatdozent at Göttingen in 1891, associate professor at Bonn (1892), professor at Heidelberg (1894–1914), and at Berlin (1915–23). Some of his widely known works were *Die Absolutheit des Christentums und die Religionsgeschichte* (1902; English trans., *The Absoluteness of Christianity and the History of Religions* [1971]), and *Die Soziallehren der christlichen Kirchen und Gruppen* (1912; English trans., *The Social Teaching of the Christian Churches* [1931]). (**Wei?** 1914; **Drescher**, *Ernst Troeltsch: His Life and Work* [1993].)

123. **Tyrrell, George** (1861–1909). Born in Dublin, Tyrrell seemed always of a rebellious temperament. He joined the Roman Catholic Church in 1879 at age 18 and shortly thereafter became a postulant for admission to the Society of Jesus, taking vows in 1882. An early Thomist, he took the theological course and was consecrated priest in 1891. Various times of mission work and lecturing followed and in 1896 he arrived at London where he produced works of an orthodox nature. His views began to change, however, and publication of an article questioning the orthodox view of hell led to his removal to the Mission House at Richmond, Yorkshire. Further works followed, some pseudonymous, when a private letter he had written containing disavowals of conservative Catholic positions attained wide circulation and some publication, leading to his dismissal from the Jesuits. Unable to obtain episcopal recognition Tyrrell resided in Storrington, Sussex, and continued to publish, but his responses to the papal denunciations of modernism issued in his receiving a minor excommunication, with his case reserved to Rome. He had barely finished *Christianity at the Crossroads* (1909) when he was debilitated by Bright's disease

(nephritis) and died in 1909. He was deprived of burial in Catholic ground and lies in the parish cemetery at Storrington. (**DcNB;** *NewC; PoIre;* **TwCA;** Maude Petre, *Autobiography and Life of George Tyrrell.*)

124. **Vos, Geerhardus** (1862–1949). Born in Heerenveen in the Netherlands, Vos finished gymnasium in Amsterdam, then studied at the theological school of the Holland Christian Reformed Church in Grand Rapids, Michigan (1881–83), then at Princeton Theological Seminary (1883–85), Berlin (1885–86), and went to Strassburg (1886–88), receiving his Ph.D. there in 1888. He was ordained a Presbyterian minister in 1894, became professor at the Holland Christian Reformed School (1888–93), then went to Princeton as Professor of Biblical Theology (1893–1932). Among his writings were *The Mosaic Origin of the Pentateuchal Codes* (1886), *The Teaching of Jesus Concerning the Kingdom of God and the Church* (1903), *Grace and Glory* (1922), *The Self-Disclosure of Jesus* (1926), *The Pauline Eschatology* (1930), and *Old and New Testament Biblical Theology* (1948). He also composed some works in Dutch. (**WhAm** 3.)

125. **Warschauer (Warshaw), Joseph** (1869–?*). Warschauer was born in Poland and educated at Oxford (M.A.), University College (London), and the University of Jena (Ph.D.). He came to England as a boy and became a naturalized citizen in 1898. A Congregationalist, he served the Oakfield Road Church, Clifton (1899–1905), Anerley Congregational Church (1905–10), Horton Lane Congregational Church, Bradford (1910–15), Stephenson Street Congregational Church, North Shields (1915–23), but also worked as a journalist, editing *Health and Efficiency* and contributing theological works to journals. His other books included *The Coming of Christ* (1903), *Anti-Nunquam* (1904), *The Problem of the Fourth Gospel* (1904), *The New Evangel* (1907), *Jesus: Seven Questions* (1908), *Jesus or Christ* (1909), *What Is the Bible* (1911), *The Way of Understanding* (1913), and *The Historical Christ* (1927). (**WhE&EA;** **Who* 1943.)

126. **Weinel, Heinrich** (1874–1936). Received his doctorate and licentiate from Giessen in the same year (1898), became privatdozent at Berlin (1899), privatdozent and Inspector of Evangelical-Theological Institutes in Bonn (1900), Associate Professor of New Testament (1904) and professor (1907) at Jena. He became Chair of Systematic Theology in 1935. His prolific writings covered a broad range of issues, as seen in his works such as *Die Bildersprache Jesu* (1900), *Die Nichtkirchlichen und die frei Theologie* (1903), *Paulus* (1904, 1915), *Ist das "liberale" Jesusbild widerlegt?* (1910), *Religion in der Volkshochschule* (1919), and *Die deutsche-evangelische Kirche* (1933). Weinel campaigned most of his life for a "free" Christianity, as seen in his participation in the World Congress for Free Christianity and Religious Progress (1910; see prologue) and support of the "German faith movement" as a component in a united German church. (**Kml;** **RGG**^{3}; **Wei?** 1928.)

127. **Wendland, Heinz-Dietrich** (1900–?*). Graduated (Ph.D.) and habilitated (1929) at Heidelberg, where also he taught in 1929–68, with a time at Kiel (1937) and Münster (1955, Rektor 1964–65). At his retirement he held the position of Professor of Christianity and Society. His writings, besides *Eschatologie des Reiches Gottes bei Jesus* (1931), included *Die Kirche in der modernen Gesellschaft* (1958; 2d ed.), *Botschaft an den soziale Welt* (1959), *Der Begriff "Christlich-sozial"* (1962), *Einführung in die Sozialethik* (1963), and *Ethik des Neuen Testaments* (2d ed., 1975). (***WeW** 1979.)

128. **Wendte, Charles William** (1844–1931). Of immigrant German parentage, Wendte studied in Boston public schools and at the gymnasium in Verden, Hanover, and worked at

various occupations (customs in San Francisco, banking in Nevada) before turning to the ministry and entering Meadville Theological School and Harvard Divinity School (1869). He became a Unitarian minister in Chicago, Cincinnati, Rhode Island, Oakland, Los Angeles, before returning to Boston to the Theodore Parker Memorial Church in Boston (1901–5). He also undertook, beginning in 1901, the general secretaryship of the International Council of Liberal Religious Thinkers and Workers and also secretary of the foreign relations arm of the American Unitarian Association, while also serving as minister of the First Parish, Brighton, Massachusetts Church. His greatest labors were devoted to the success of a series of ecumenical and interreligious meetings, of which there were six, the fifth in Berlin and the sixth in Paris. He also served as editor for the publication of the proceedings. In addition, he published *Thomas Starr, King, Patriot and Preacher* (1921), *The Transfiguration of Life* (1930), as well as hymnals, and his autobiography, *The Wider Fellowship*, 2 vols. (1927). (*ChPo*; **DcAmB**; NatCAB 14; *OhA&B*; WhAm 1.)

129. **Wernle, Paul** (1872–1939). Studied at Göttingen under the influence of the *religions-geschichtliche Schule*, became privatdozent in New Testament at Basel, then Professor of Church History and the History of Dogma. His early works were in New Testament, with such publications as *Der Christ und die Sünde bei Paulus* (1897), *Die synoptische Frage* (1899), *Die Anfänge unserer Religion* (1904), and *Die Quellen des Lebens Jesu* (1904; English trans., *Sources of our Knowledge of the Life of Jesus* [1905]). His later works had to do with church history and dogma. (**Kml; Wei?** 1914.)

130. **White, (Charles) Bouck** (1874–1951). A graduate of Harvard (A.B., 1896) and Union Theological Seminary (B.D., 1902), White was ordained a Congregational minister in 1904 and served parishes in Clayton, New York (1904–7), Lewis Avenue Church, Brooklyn (1907–8), and was Head Resident, Trinity House, New York City (1908–13), when he was dismissed from his post for his espousal of socialism. He then founded a church called the Church of the Revolution and engaged in extensive activity promoting the causes of socialism, some of which (desecrating the flag, disturbing a church service) landed him in prison as an agitator. He also traveled extensively during the war to study the subject of the war and workers. Later he was removed from the Socialist Party and spent his latter years making pottery. His books included *The Book of Daniel Drew* (1910), *The Call of the Carpenter* (1911), *The Mixing* (1913), *The Immorality of Being Rich* (1914), *A Message to the World* (1914), *Letters from Prison* (1915), *The Carpenter and the Rich Man* (1914), and *The Free City* (1919). (**AmLY; WhoAm** 14–15; **WhAm** 5; articles in *New York Times*, 1903, 1910–17, 1919, 1937, 1951.)

131. **Wilder, Amos Niven** (1895–1993). Wilder's education began at Oberlin (1913–15), followed by service in the war (1916–19), with receipt of the Croix de Guerre. Wilder then attended Yale (B.A., 1920; B.D., 1924; Ph.D., 1933), with graduate study at Mansfield College, Oxford, and Harvard. After being ordained a Congregational minister (1926) and having served a pastorate (1925–28), Wilder then taught at Hamilton College (1930–33), Andover-Newton Theological School (1933–43), Chicago Theological Seminary (1943–54), and Harvard (1954–56), becoming Hollis Professor of Divinity (1956–63). He was the older brother of Thornton Wilder, novelist and playwright. His own commitment to the interrelation of literature and theology issued in works such as *Battle-Retrospect and Other Poems* (1923), *Arachne* (1928), *Spiritual Aspects of the New Poetry* (1940), *The Healing of the Waters* (1943), *Modern Poetry and the Christian Tradition: A Study in the Relation of Christianity to Culture* (1952), *Theology and Modern Literature* (1958), *The Lan-*

guage of the Gospel: Early Christian Rhetoric (1964; 1971), *Kerygma, Eschatology, and Social Ethics* (1966), *Grace Confounding* (1972), *Theopoetic: Theology and the Religious Imagination* (1976), and *Jesus' Parables and the War of Myths: Essays on Imagination in the Scripture* (1982). (*AmAu&B;* **ConAu** 141, **ConAuNRS** 47; *DrASP* 1974; **Kep;** *WhE&EA;* **WhoAm** 1978–79.)

132. **Williams, N[orman] P[owell]** (1883–1943). Elected a scholar of Christ Church, Oxford (1902), Williams took a first class in moderations (1904) and *literae humaniores* (1906) and held a fellowship at Magdalen College (1906–9), in which time he visited Strasbourg and Berlin, making the acquaintance of Schweitzer and Harnack. He was ordained deacon in 1908 and priest in 1909. He was known as an excellent preacher, lecturer, and tutor; his Bampton lectures for 1924, *The Ideas of the Fall and of Original Sin*, led to the D.D. degree and election as Lady Margaret Professor of Divinity with a canonry of Christ Church. Much of his energy was devoted to ecclesiastical matters and issues, but some of his works were *Form and Content in the Christian Tradition* (1916, with William Sanday), *Our Case as Against Rome* (1918), *The Grace of God* (1930), and editorship of *Northern Catholicism* (1933). (**DcNB;** *WhE&EA.*)

133. **Windisch, Hans** (1881–1935). Windisch studied at Leipzig, Marburg, and Berlin, and became privatdozent at Leipzig in 1908, professor at Leiden (1914), at Kiel (1929), and Halle (1935), where he died suddenly following a lecture. He was of the *religionsgeschichtliche Schule* and wrote extensively in that area and in the history of dogma and the primitive church. His Leiden period especially gave him liberty during the war to conduct research and writing, and his reports on research activity were noted for their thoroughness and universality. Among his many works were commentaries on the Catholic Epistles, Hebrews, and Barnabas (1911, 1913, 1920, Lietzmann's *Handbuch zum Neuen Testament*), 2 Corinthians (Meyer, 1924), and *Johannes und die Synoptiker* (1926). (**Erik Beijer,** "Hans Windisch und seine Bedeutung für die neutestamentliche Wissenschaft," *ZNW* 48 [1957]: 22–49; **Kml; Wei?** 1928.)

134. **Wright, C[harles] J[ames]** (1888–?*). Educated at Richmond College, London University (B.D., Ph.D.), Wright was a Wesleyan minister and Chair of Systematic Theology and Philosophy of Religion, Didsbury and Hartley Victoria, Manchester; and Lecturer, History of Doctrine, Manchester University. In 1944 he entered the Church of England. His publications included *Miracle in History and in Modern Thought* (1930), *The Meaning and Message of the Fourth Gospel* (1933), *The Eternal Kingdom* (1942), *Modern Issues in Religious Thought* (1937), and numerous contributions to journals. (***WhE&EA.**)

135. **Yadin, Yigael** (1917–84). Born in Jerusalem, son of Eleazar Sukenik (Yadin changed his name), Yadin was educated at Hebrew University (M.A., 1946; Ph.D., 1955), Yadin was a national figure in Israel, serving as chief of operations for the Jewish defense corps (Haganah) in the war of independence and afterwards as chief of staff of the Israeli defense forces until 1952, when he resigned in disagreement over Ben-Gurion's defense budget and turned his attention to archaeology entirely. He became a professor at Hebrew University and also served politically in the Knesset. His archaeological expeditions included Megiddo, Hazor, Dead Sea caves, and Masada. Extensive writings included *New Light on the Dead Sea Scrolls* (1954), *The Scroll of the War of the Sons of Light Against the Sons of Darkness* (1962), *Genesis Apocryphon: A Scroll from the Wilderness of Judea, Israel* (1958),

Aspects of the Dead Sea Scrolls (1958), and various publication reports on his expeditions. (**ConAu** 113; **ConAuNRS** 6.)

136. **Zeitlin, Solomon** (1888[?]-1976). Born in Russia, but educated at Dropsie University in Philadelphia (Ph.D., 1917), Zeitlin spent his career at that institution as a professor of history and rabbinics. Among his many writings were *Josephus on Jesus* (1931), *The History of the Jewish Commonwealth* (1933), *Maimonides: A Biography* (1935; 2d ed., 1955), *Who Crucified Jesus?* (1942; 4th ed., 1964), *The Dead Sea Scrolls and Modern Scholarship* (1965), *The Rise and Fall of the Judean State: A Political, Social, and Religious History of the Second Commonwealth* (vol. 1, 1962; vol. 2, 1967; vol. 3, 1977). Zeitlin was noted for his rigorous insistence that the Dead Sea Scrolls were of medieval origin and therefore of no value for the biblical time period. (**ConAu** 77–80.)

SELECT BIBLIOGRAPHY

Works Cited

Books

Abbott, Lyman. *The Ethical Teaching of Jesus*. Philadelphia: University of Pennsylvania Press, 1910.

Abrahams, Israel. *Studies in Pharisaism and the Gospels*. Cambridge: Cambridge Press, 1st ser., 1917; 2d ser., 1924. Reprint, Library of Biblical Studies, New York: KTAV, 1967.

Adams, David. *Man of God*. New York: Harper, 1941.

Albertz, Martin. *Die syntoptischen Streitgespräche: Ein Beitrag zur Formengeschichte des Urchristentums*. Berlin: Trowitzsch, 1921.

Albright, William F. *From the Stone Age to Christianity*. Baltimore: Johns Hopkins Press, 1940. Paperback, Garden City, N.Y.: Doubleday, 1957.

Asch, Sholem. *The Nazarene*. Trans. Maurice Samuel. New York: G. P. Putnam's Sons, 1939.

Austin, Mary. *The Man Jesus: Being a Brief Account of the Life and Teaching of the Prophet of Nazareth*. New York: Harper, 1915. Rev. ed., *A Small Town Man*. New York: Harper, 1925.

Bacon, Benjamin W. *Jesus and Paul*. New York: Macmillan, 1921.

———. *Jesus the Son of God*. New York: H. Holt, 1930.

———. *The Sermon on the Mount: Its Literary Structure and Didactic Purpose*. New York: Macmillan, 1902.

———. *The Story of Jesus and the Beginnings of the Church: A Valuation of the Synoptic Record for History and for Religion*. New York: Century, 1927.

Bähr, Hans Walter ed. *Albert Schweitzer: Letters 1905–1965*. Trans. Joachim Neugroschel. New York: Macmillan, 1992.

Barbusse, Henri. *Jesus*. Trans. Solon Librescot. New York: Macmaulay, 1927.

———. *Under Fire*. Trans. W. Fitzwater Wray with an introduction by Brian Rhys. London: J. M. Dent; New York: E. P. Dutton, 1926.

Barmann, Lawrence F., ed. *The Letters of Baron Friedrich von Hügel and Professor Norman Kemp Smith*. New York: Fordham University Press, 1981.

Barnes, W. Emery. *Gospel Criticism and Form Criticism*. Edinburgh: T. & T. Clark, 1936.

Barnett, Albert E. *Understanding the Parables of Our Lord*. Nashville: Cokesbury, 1940.

Barton, Bruce. *The Man Nobody Knows: A Discovery of the Real Jesus*. Indianapolis: Bobbs-Merrill, 1925.

———. *A Young Man's Jesus*. Boston: Pilgrim Press, 1914.

Barton, George. *Jesus of Nazareth: A Biography*. New York: Macmillan, 1928.

Bartsch, Hans Werner, ed. *Kerygma and Myth: A Theological Debate*. 2 vols. Trans. Reginald H. Fuller. Harper Torchbooks. New York: Harper and Brothers, 1961.

Bell, G. K. A., ed. *The War and the Kingdom of God*. London: Longmans, Green, 1915.

Bell, G. K. A., and D. Adolf Deissmann. *Mysterium Christi: Christological Studies by British and German Theologians.* London: Longmans, Green, 1930.

Bennett, W. H. *The Life of Christ According to St. Mark.* London: Hodder and Stoughton, 1907.

Bertram, Georg. *Die Leidensgeschichte Jesu und der Christuskult: Eine formgeschichtliche Untersuchung.* FRLANT. Göttingen: Vandenhoeck and Ruprecht, 1922.

Beth, Karl. *The Miracles of Jesus.* New York: Eaton and Manis, 1907.

Betz, Hans Dieter. *The Sermon on the Mount.* Hermeneia — A Critical and Historical Commentary on the Bible. Minneapolis: Fortress Press, 1995.

Bird, Robert. *Jesus, the Carpenter of Nazareth.* New York: Scribner's, 1891.

Black, Matthew. *An Aramaic Approach to the Gospels and Acts.* Oxford: Clarendon Press, 1946; 3d rev. ed., 1963.

Bonsirven, Joseph. *Les Juifs et Jésus: Attitudes nouvelles.* Paris: Gabriel Beauchesne et ses Fils, 1937.

———. *Palestinian Judaism in the Time of Jesus Christ.* Trans. William Wolf. New York: Holt, Rinehart and Winston, 1964.

Borchert, Otto. *The Originality of Jesus.* Trans. L. M. Stalker. New York: Macmillan, 1933. Translation of *Goldgrund des Lebensbildes Jesu: Eine apologetische Studie.* Braunschweig: Hellmuth Wollermann, 1900.

Bornkamm, Günther. *Jesus of Nazareth.* Trans. James M. Robinson with Irene and Fraser McLuskey. New York: Harper, 1960.

Bosworth, Edward Increase. *The Life and Teaching of Jesus According to the First Three Gospels.* New York: Macmillan, 1924.

Bouquet, A. C. *Jesus: A New Outline and Estimate.* Cambridge: Heffner, 1933.

Bowman, John Wick. *The Intention of Jesus.* Philadelphia: Westminster Press, 1943.

Brabazon, James. *Albert Schweitzer: A Biography.* New York: G. P. Putnam's Sons, 1975.

Brandes, Georg. *Jesus: A Myth.* Trans. from the Danish by Edwin Björkman. London: Brentano's, n.d.

Branscomb, Harvey. *The Teaching of Jesus: A Textbook for College and Individual Use.* New York: Abingdon-Cokesbury Press, 1941.

Briggs, C. A. *The Ethical Teaching of Jesus.* New York: Scribner's, 1904.

———. *New Light on the Life of Jesus.* New York: Scribner's, 1904.

Browne, Laurence E. *The Parables of the Gospels in the Light of Modern Criticism.* Cambridge: University Press, 1913.

Bugge, Ch. A. *Die Haupt-Parabeln Jesu.* Giessen: J. Richer'sche Verlagsbuchhandlung (Alfred Töpelmann), 1903.

Bullock, Alan, ed. *The Twentieth Century: A Promethean Age.* New York: McGraw-Hill, 1971.

Bultmann, Rudolf. *Form Criticism: Two Essays on New Testament Research.* Trans. Frederick C. Grant. Harper Torchbook. New York: Harper, 1962; orig. pub., n.p.: Willett, Clark, 1934.

———. *History of the Synoptic Tradition.* Rev. ed. Trans. John Marsh. Oxford: Basil Blackwell, 1963. Translation of *Die Geschichte der synoptischen Tradition.* FRLANT. Göttingen: Vandenhoeck and Ruprecht, 1921.

———. *Jesus and the Word.* Trans. Louise Pettibone Smith and Erminie Huntress Lantero. New York: Scribner's, 1934. Translation of *Jesus.* Berlin: Deutsche Bibliothek, 1926.

————. *Theology of the New Testament.* 2 vols. Trans. Kendrick Grobel. New York: Scribner's, 1951. Translation of *Theologie des Neuen Testaments.* Tübingen: J. C. B. Mohr (Paul Siebeck), 1948.

Bundy, Walter E. *The Psychic Health of Jesus.* New York: Macmillan, 1922.

————. *The Religion of Jesus.* Indianapolis: Bobbs-Merrill, 1928.

Burke, Peter. *The French Historical Revolution: The Annales School.* Stanford: Stanford University Press, 1990.

Burkitt, F. C. *The Earliest Sources for the Life of Jesus.* New and rev. ed. London: Constable and Company, 1922.

————. *The Gospel History and Its Transmission.* Edinburgh: T. & T. Clark, 1906.

————. *Jesus Christ: An Historical Outline.* London: Blackie and Son, 1932.

————. *Jewish and Christian Apocalypses.* London: H. Milford, 1914.

Burney, C. F. *The Poetry of Our Lord: An Examination of the Formal Elements of Hebrew Poetry in the Discourse of Jesus Christ.* Oxford: Clarendon Press, 1925.

Burrows, Miller. *The Dead Sea Scrolls.* New York: Viking Press, 1955.

Burton, Ernest DeWitt. *Some Principles of Literary Criticism and Their Application to the Synoptic Problem.* Chicago: University of Chicago Press, 1904.

Burton, Ernest DeWitt, and Edgar J. Goodspeed. *A Harmony of the Synoptic Gospels in Greek.* Chicago: University of Chicago Press, 1920; 2d ed., 1947.

Burton, Ernest DeWitt, and Shailer Mathews. *The Life of Christ.* University of Chicago Publications in Religious Education. Chicago: University of Chicago Press, 1900; 2d rev. ed., 1901; 3d rev. ed., 1927.

Bussmann, Wilhelm. *Synoptische Studien.* Halle: Buchhandlung des Waisenhauses, 1925–31.

Cadbury, Henry. *Jesus What Manner of Man.* New York: Macmillan, 1947.

————. *The Making of Luke-Acts.* New York: Macmillan, 1927.

————. *The Peril of Modernizing Jesus.* New York: Macmillan, 1937.

Cadoux, A. T. *The Parables of Jesus: Their Art and Use.* London: James Clarke, n.d.

Cadoux, C. J. *The Historic Mission of Jesus: A Constructive Re-examination of the Eschatological Teaching in the Synoptic Gospels.* New York: Harper, n.d. [1941?].

————. *The Life of Jesus.* Penguin Books. West Dayton, Middlesex: Northumberland Press, 1948.

Case, Shirley Jackson. *The Historicity of Jesus: A Criticism of the Contention that Jesus Never Lived, a Statement of the Evidence for His Existence, an Estimate of His Relation to Christianity.* Chicago: University of Chicago Press, 1912.

————. *Jesus: A New Biography.* Chicago: University of Chicago Press, 1927.

Chamberlain, Houston Stewart. *The Foundations of the Nineteenth Century.* Trans. John Lees. 2 vols. New York: John Lane, 1910; 5th printing, 1914.

Charles, R. H. *Apocrypha and Pseudepigrapha of the Old Testament in English.* 2 vols. Oxford: Clarendon Press, 1913.

————. *Eschatology: The Doctrine of a Future Life in Israel, Judaism, and Christianity.* London: A. & C. Black, 1899; 2d ed., 1913. Reprint, with an introduction by Wesley Buchanan, New York: Schocken Books, 1963.

Charlesworth, James H., ed., with Henry W. L. Rietz. *The Dead Sea Scrolls: Rule of the Community.* Philadelphia: American Interfaith Institute, 1996.

Charlesworth, James H., and Walter P. Weaver, eds. *Earthing Christologies: From Jesus' Parables to Jesus the Parable.* Faith and Scholarship Colloquies. Valley Forge, Pa.: Trinity Press International, 1995.

————, ed. *The Message of the Scrolls.* Christian Origins Library. New York: Crossroad, 1992. Orig. pub., New York: Grosset and Dunlap, 1962.

Clark, Henry. *The Ethical Mysticism of Albert Schweitzer.* Boston: Beacon Press, 1962.

Cobern, Camden M. *The New Archaeological Discoveries and Their Bearing upon the New Testament and upon the Life and Times of the Primitive Church.* New York: Funk and Wagnalls, 1917.

Cohen, Lucy. *Some Recollections of Claude Goldsmid Montefiore, 1858–1938.* London: Faber and Faber, 1940.

Collingwood, R. G. *The Idea of History.* London: Oxford University Press, 1956.

Colwell, E. C. *An Approach to the Teaching of Jesus.* New York: Abingdon-Cokesbury Press, 1946.

Conybeare, F. C. *The Historical Christ.* London: Watts, 1914.

Couchoud, Paul-Louis. *The Creation of Christ: An Outline of the Beginnings of Christianity.* 2 vols. Trans. C. Bradlaugh Bonner. London: Watts, 1939. Translation of *Jésus: Le Dieu Fait Homme.* Paris: Les Editions Rieder, 1937. Reprint, *Histoire de Jésus.* Paris: Presses Universitaires de France, 1944.

————. *The Enigma of Jesus.* Trans. Winifred Whale. London: Watts, 1924.

————. *Le Mystère de Jésus.* Paris: F. Rieder et Cie, Éditeurs, 1926.

Cox, C. B., and A. E. Dyson, eds. *The Twentieth Century Mind: History, Ideas, and Literature in Britain.* 2 vols. London: Oxford University Press, 1972.

Craig, C. T. *The Beginning of Christianity.* New York: Abingdon-Cokesbury Press, 1943.

————. *Jesus in Our Teaching.* New York: Abingdon, 1931.

Cullmann, Oscar. *Christ and Time: The Primitive Christian Conception of Time and History.* Trans. Floyd V. Filson. Philadelphia: Westminster, 1950.

Dalman, Gustav. *Jesus-Jeshua.* Trans. Paul P. Levertoff. New York: Macmillan, 1929.

————. *Sacred Sites and Ways: Studies in the Topography of the Gospels.* Trans. Paul P. Levertoff. New York: Macmillan, 1935.

————. *The Words of Jesus Considered in the Light of Post-Biblical Writings and the Aramaic Language.* Authorized English version by D. M. Kay. Edinburgh: T. & T. Clark, 1902.

Danby, Herbert. *The Jew and Christianity: Some Phases, Ancient and Modern of the Jewish Attitude Towards Christianity.* London: Sheldon, 1927.

de Grandmaison, Léonce. *Jesus Christ: His Person, His Message, His Credentials.* 2 vols. Trans. Dom Basil Whelan. New York: Sheed and Ward, 1935.

Deissmann, Adolf. *Light from the Ancient East.* Trans. Lionel R. M. Strachan. New York: George H. Doran, 1927.

Denney, James. *Jesus and the Gospel: Christianity Justified in the Mind of Christ.* London: Hodder and Stoughton, 1908.

Denney, Walter Bell. *The Career and Significance of Jesus.* New York: Thomas Nelson and Sons, 1934.

Dewick, E. C. *Primitive Christian Eschatology.* Cambridge: University Press, 1912.

Dibelius, Martin. *From Tradition to Gospel.* Trans. Bertram Lee Woolf in collaboration with the author. New York: Scribner's, [1935]. Translation of *Die Formgeschichte der Evangeliums.* Tübingen: J. C. B. Mohr (Paul Siebeck), 1919.

————. *Geschichte der urchristlichen Literatur.* Sammlung Göschen I: Evangelien und Apokalypten. Berlin: Walter de Gruyter, 1926.

————. *Gospel Criticism and Christology.* London: Ivor Nicholson and Watson, 1935.

———. *Jesus.* Trans. Charles B. Hedrick and Frederick C. Grant. Philadelphia: Westminster Press, 1949. Translation of *Jesus.* Sammlung Göschen 1130. Berlin: Walter de Gruyter, 1939.

———. *The Message of Jesus.* Trans. Frederick C. Grant. London: Nicholson and Watson, 1939.

———. *The Sermon on the Mount.* New York: Scribner's, 1940.

Didon, Rev. Father. *Jesus Christ.* 2 vols. London: Kegan Paul, Trench, Trübner, 1906.

Dobschütz, Ernst von. *The Eschatology of the Gospels.* London: Hodder and Stoughton, 1910.

Dodd, C. H. *History and the Gospel.* New York: Scribner's, 1938.

———. *The Parables of the Kingdom.* Rev. ed. New York: Scribner's, 1961.

Drescher, Hans-Georg. *Ernst Troeltsch: His Life and Work.* Trans. John Bowden. Minneapolis: Fortress Press, 1993.

Drews, Arthur. *The Christ Myth.* Trans. C. Delisle Burns. London: T. Fisher Unwin, 1910. Reprint, New York: Prometheus Books, 1998.

———. *Hat Jesus Gelebt?* Mainz: Verlag freie Religion in Mainz, 1928.

———. *Die Leugnung der Geschichtlichkeit Jesus in Vergangenheit und Gegenwart.* Karlsruhe: G. Braun, 1926.

———. *Das Markus Evangelium als Zeugnis gegen die Geschichtlichkeit Jesus.* Jena: E. Diederichs, 1921.

Dujardin, Edouard. *Ancient History of the God Jesus.* Abridged English version by A. Brodie Sanders. London: Watts, 1938.

Duncan, George S. *Jesus, Son of Man: Studies Contributory to a Modern Portrait.* London: Nisbet, 1947.

Dupont-Sommer, André. *The Essene Writings from Qumran.* Trans. G. Vermes. Cleveland: World Publishing, 1962.

———. *The Jewish Sect of Qumran and the Essenes: New Studies on the Dead Sea Scrolls.* Trans. R. D. Barnett. London: Valentine, Mitchel, 1954.

Easton, Burton Scott. *Christ in the Gospels.* New York: Scribner's, 1930.

———. *The Gospel Before the Gospels.* New York: Scribner's, 1928.

Edersheim, Alfred. *The Life and Times of Jesus the Messiah.* 8th rev. ed. New York: Longmans, Green, 1904.

Eisler, Robert. *The Messiah Jesus and John the Baptist.* English edition by Alexander Haggerty Krappe. New York: Dial Press, 1931.

Enslin, Morton Scott. *Christian Beginnings.* New York: Harper, 1938.

Ericksen, Robert P. *Theologians under Hitler: Gerhard Kittel, Paul Althaus, and Emanuel Hirsch.* New Haven: Yale University Press, 1985.

Fairbairn, A. M. *Studies in the Life of Christ.* 14th ed. London: Hodder and Stoughton, 1907.

Farrar, Frederick. *The Life of Christ.* New York: E. P. Dutton, 1874.

Fascher, Erich. *Die formgeschichtliche Methode: Eine Darstellung und Kritik, Zugleich ein Beitrag zur Geschichte des synoptischen Problems.* Giessen: Alfred Töpelmann, 1924.

Fendt, Leonhard. *Die Dauer der öffentlichen Wirksamkeit Jesu.* Munich: J. J. Lentner, 1906.

Fiebig, Paul. *Die Gleichnisreden Jesu im Lichte der rabbinischen Gleichnisse des neutestamentlichen Zeitalters.* Tübingen: J. C. B. Mohr (Paul Siebeck), 1912.

Filson, Floyd. *Origins of the Gospels.* New York: Abingdon Press, 1938.

Finkelstein, Louis. *The Pharisees: The Sociological Background of Their Faith.* Philadelphia: Jewish Publication Society, 1938.

Foakes-Jackson, F. J., ed. *The Faith and the War.* London: Macmillan, 1915.

Fosdick, Harry Emerson. *The Man from Nazareth: As His Contemporaries Saw Him.* New York: Harper, 1949.

Frank, Henry. *Jesus: A Modern Study.* New York: Greenberg, 1930.

Friedländer, Gerald. *The Jewish Sources of the Sermon on the Mount.* London: George Routledge and Sons; New York: Bloch Publishing, 1911.

Frenssen, Gustav. *Holy Land.* Trans. M. L. Hamilton. Boston: D. Estes, 1906.

————. *Gustav Frenssen, Village Sermons by a Novelist.* Trans. with an account of the author and his work by T. F. Kinloch. New York: D. Appleton, 1924.

Gilbert, George Holley. *Jesus.* New York: Macmillan, 1912.

————. *The Revelation of Jesus.* New York: Macmillan, 1899.

————. *The Student's Life of Jesus.* New York: Macmillan, 1896; 3d ed., 1902.

Gilmore, Alfred Field. *Who Was This Nazarene? A Challenging and Definitive Biography of the Master.* New York: Prentice-Hall, 1940.

Giran, Etienne. *Jesus of Nazareth: An Historical and Critical Survey of His Life and Teaching.* Trans. E. L. H. Thomas. London: The Sunday School Association, 1907.

Gloege, G. *Reich Gottes und Kirche im Neuen Testament.* Gütersloh: Bertelsmann, 1929.

Glover, T. R. *The Jesus of History.* London: Student Christian Movement, 1917.

Goodspeed, Edgar J. *A Life of Jesus.* New York: Harper, 1950.

Goguel, Maurice. *Jesus the Nazarene Myth or History?* Trans. Frederick Stephens. New York: D. Appleton, 1926.

————. *La Vie de Jésus.* Paris: Payot, 1932. English trans., *Jesus and the Origins of Christianity.* 2 vols. Trans. Olive Wyon. New York: Macmillan, 1933. Reprint, Harper Torchbook with introduction by C. Leslie Mitton. New York: Harper, 1960.

Goodman, Paul. *The Synagogue and the Church.* London: George Routledge and Sons; New York: E. P. Dutton, 1908.

Gould, Stephen Jay. *Questioning the Millennium.* New York: Harmony Books, 1997.

Grant, F. C. *The Earliest Gospel: Studies in the Evangelic Tradition at Its Point of Crystallization in Writing.* New York: Abingdon Press, 1943.

————. *The Economic Background of the Gospels.* New York: Russell and Russell, 1926.

————. *The Gospel of the Kingdom.* New York: Macmillan, 1940.

————. *The Life and Times of Jesus.* New York: Abingdon Press, 1921.

Grundmann, Walter. *Jesus der Galiläer und das Judentum.* Leipzig: Verlag Georg Wigand, 1940; 2d ed., 1941.

Guignebert, Charles. *Jesus.* Trans. S. H. Hooke. The History of Civilization. New York: Knopf, 1935. Translation of *Jesus.* L'évolution de l'humanité synthese collective 29. Paris: La Renaissance du livre, 1933.

————. *The Jewish World in the Time of Jesus.* New York: University Books, 1959.

————. *Le Problème de Jésus.* Paris: Ernest Flammarion, 1914.

Gutteridge, Richard. *The German Evangelical Church and the Jews, 1879–1950.* New York: Harper, 1976.

Hagner, Donald. *The Jewish Reclamation of Jesus: The Analysis and Critique of Modern Study of Jesus.* Academie Books. Grand Rapids, Mich.: Zondervan, 1984.

Harnack, Adolf von. *The Sayings of Jesus: The Second Source of St. Matthew and St. Luke.* Trans. J. R. Wilkinson. New Testament Studies 2. Crown Theological Library 23. London: Williams and Norgate, 1908.

———. *What Is Christianity?* Trans. Thomas Bailey Saunders. New York: Putnam's, 1903. Reprinted with introduction by Rudolf Bultmann. Fortress Texts in Modern Theology. Philadelphia: Fortress Press, 1986.

Hartt, Robin Lynde. *The Man Himself.* Garden City, N.Y.: Doubleday, 1923.

Hat Jesus gelebt? Berlin: Verlag des Deutschen Monistenbundes, 1910.

Hatch, H. G. *The Messianic Consciousness of Jesus: An Investigation of Christological Data in the Synoptic Gospels.* London: SPCK, 1939.

Hauer, Wilhelm, Karl Heim, and Karl Adam. *Germany's New Religion: The German Faith Movement.* Trans. T. S. K. Scott-Craig and R. E. Davies. New York: Abingdon Press, 1937.

Headlam, A. C. *The Life and Teaching of Jesus the Christ.* London: John Murray, 1923.

Heitmüller, Wilhelm. *Jesus.* Tübingen: J. C. B. Mohr (Paul Siebeck), 1913.

Herford, R. Travers. *The Pharisees.* London: George Allen and Allen and Unwin, 1924.

Héring, Jean. *La Royaume de Dieu et sa Venue.* New, rev. ed. Neuchatel: Delachaux et Niestlé, 1959.

Hill, William Bancroft. *Introduction to the Life of Christ.* New York: Scribner's, 1911.

Hillis, Newell Dwight. *The Influence of Christ in Modern Life.* New York: Hodder and Stoughton, 1900.

Holmström, Folke. *Das eschatologische Denken der Gegenwart.* Deutsche Ausgabe. Gütersloh: Bertelsmann, 1936.

Holtzmann, H. J. *Das messianische Bewusstein Jesu: ein Beitrag zur Leben-Jesu-Forschung.* Tübingen: J. C. B. Mohr (Paul Siebeck), 1907.

Holtzmann, Oskar. *The Life of Jesus.* Trans. J. T. Bealby and Maurice A. Canney. London: Adam and Charles Black, 1904.

Hoskyns, Edwin, and Noel Davey. *The Riddle of the New Testament.* London: Faber and Faber, 1931; 3d edition, 1947; reprinted 1949, 1952, 1957, 1964.

Hooke, S. H. *Christ and the Kingdom of God.* New York: Association Press, 1917.

———. *The Kingdom of God in the Experience of Jesus.* Colet Library of Modern Christian Thought and Teaching 8. London: Gerald Duckworth, 1949.

Hynes, William. *Shirley Jackson Case and the Chicago School: The Socio-Historical Method.* Biblical Scholarship in North America 5. Chico, Calif.: Scholars Press, 1981.

Jackson, H. Latimer. *The Eschatology of Jesus.* London: Macmillan, 1913.

Jaspert, Bernd. *Karl Barth — Rudolf Bultmann Letters 1922–1966.* Trans. and ed. Geoffrey W. Bromiley. Grand Rapids, Mich.: Eerdmans, 1981.

Jeremias, Joachim. *Jerusalem in the Time of Jesus: An Investigation into Economic and Social Conditions During the New Testament Period.* Trans. F. H. and C. H. Cave. Philadelphia: Fortress Press, 1969.

———. *The Parables of the Kingdom.* Trans. S. H. Hooke. New York: Scribner's, 1963. Translation of *Die Gleichnisse Jesu.* Zurich: Zwingli-Verlag, 1947.

Jesus Seminar. *The Five Gospels: The Search for the Authentic Words of Jesus.* New translation and commentary by Robert W. Funk, Roy W. Hoover, and the Jesus Seminar. A Polebridge Press Book. New York: Macmillan, 1993.

Jocz, Jacob. *The Jewish People and Jesus Christ: A Study in the Relationship between the Jewish People and Jesus Christ.* London: SPCK, 1949.

Jülicher, Adolf. *Die Gleichnisreden Jesu.* 2d ed. Tübingen: J. C. B. Mohr (Paul Siebeck), 1910.

———. *An Introduction to the New Testament.* Trans. Janet Penrose Ward. London: Smith, Elder, 1904.

———. *Neue Linien in der Kritik der evangelischen Überlieferung.* Giessen: Alfred Töpelmann, 1906.

Kähler, Martin. *The So-Called Historical Jesus and the Historic Biblical Christ.* Trans. and ed. with introduction by Carl E. Braaten. Seminar Editions. Philadelphia: Fortress Press, 1962.

Kazantzakis, Nicos. *The Last Temptation of Christ.* Trans. P. A. Bien. New York: Simon and Schuster, 1960.

Keable, Robert. *The Great Galilean.* Boston: Little, Brown, 1929.

Kee, Howard C., et al. *Christianity: A Social and Cultural History.* New York: Macmillan, 1991.

Kent, Charles Foster. *The Life and Teachings of Jesus According to the Earliest Records.* New York: Scribner's, 1913.

Ketter, Peter. *Christ and Womankind.* Trans. Isabel McHugh. Westminster, Md.: Newman Press, 1951.

King, Henry Churchill. *The Ethics of Jesus.* New York: Macmillan, 1910.

Klausner, Joseph. *Jesus of Nazareth: His Life, Times, and Teaching.* Trans. Herbert Danby. New York: Macmillan, 1925; reprinted 1927 and reissued 1929.

Knox, John. *Jesus: Lord and Christ.* New York: Harper, 1958.

Köhler, Ludwig. *Das Formgeschichtliche Problem des Neuen Testaments.* Tübingen: J. C. B. Mohr (Paul Siebeck), 1927.

Köhler, F. *Jesus.* Berlin: Union Deutsche Verlagsgesellschaft, 1928.

Kraeling, Karl. *Anthropos and Son of Man: A Study in the Religious Syncretism of the Hellenistic Orient.* New York: Columbia University Press, 1927.

Kümmel, W. G. *Promise and Fulfilment: The Eschatological Message of Jesus.* Trans. Dorothea M. Barton. Studies in Biblical Theology 23. London: SCM Press, 1957; 2d ed., 1961. Translation of *Verheißung und Erfüllung: Untersuchungen zur eschatologischen Verkündigung Jesu.* ATANT 6. Basel: H. Majer, 1945.

Lagrange, M.-J. *The Gospel of Jesus Christ.* 2 vols. Trans. members of the English Dominican Province. Westminster, Md.: Newman Bookshop, 1938.

Landes, Richard. *Relics, Apocalypse, and the Deceits of History: Ademar of Chabannes, 989–1034.* Harvard Historical Studies 117. Cambridge: Harvard University Press, 1995.

Laufer, Calvin Weiss. *The Incomparable Christ.* New York: Abingdon Press, 1914.

Lebreton, Jules. *The Life and Teaching of Jesus Christ Our Lord.* New York: Macmillan, 1950. Original French edition, *La Vie et L'Enseignement de Jésus Christ notre Seigneur.* Paris: Gabriel Beauchesne, 1934.

Leipoldt, Johannes. *Jesus und die Frauen.* Leipzig: Quelle und Meyer, 1921.

Lightfoot, R. H. *History and Interpretation in the Gospels.* New York: Harper, 1934.

Lilley, A. Leslie. *Modernism: A Record and Review.* London: Pitman and Sons, 1908.

Lindeskog, Gösta. *Die Jesusfrage im neuzeitlichen Judentum: Ein Beitrag zur Geschichte der Leben-Jesu-Forschung.* Seminar zu Uppsala herausgegeben von *Anton Fridrichsen.* Leipzig: Alfred Lorentz; Uppsala: A. B. Lundequistska Bokhandeln, 1938.

Loofs, Friederich. *What Is the Truth about Jesus Christ?: Problems of Christology.* Edinburgh: T. & T. Clark, 1913.

Loisy, Alfred. *The Birth of the Christian Religion and The Origins of the New Testament.* Trans. L. P. Jacks. New Hyde Park, N.Y.: University Books, 1962.

———. *Les Évangiles synoptiques.* 2 vols. Ceffonds, Près Montier-en-du [Haute-Marne]: Author, 1907–8.

———. *The Gospel and the Church.* Trans. L. P. Jacks with a new introduction by R. Joseph Hoffmann. Buffalo, N.Y.: Prometheus Books, 1988.

———. *Memoires pour servir à l'histoire de notre temps.* 3 vols. Paris: Emile Nourry, 1930–31.

———. *My Duel with the Vatican: The Autobiography of a Catholic Modernist.* Trans. Richard Wilson Boynton. New York: E. P. Dutton, 1924.

Ludwig, Emil. *The Son of Man: The Story of Jesus.* Trans. Eden and Cedar Paul. Garden City, N.Y.: Garden City Publishing, 1928. Original German *Der Menschensohn, Geschichte eines Propheten.* Berlin: Ernst Rowohlt Verlag, 1928.

Maas, A. J. *The Life of Jesus Christ According to the Gospel History.* 8th ed. St. Louis: B. Herder, 1927.

MacKinnon, James. *The Historic Jesus.* London: Longmans, Green, 1931.

Major, H. D. A., T. W. Manson, and C. J. Wright. *The Mission and Message of Jesus: An Exposition of the Gospels in the Light of Modern Research.* New York: E. P. Dutton, 1938, 1946.

Manson, T. W. *The Teaching of Jesus: Studies of Its Form and Content.* Cambridge: University Press, 1931; 2d ed., 1935; pbk., 1963.

Manson, William. *Jesus the Messiah: The Synoptic Tradition of the Revelation of God in Christ: With Special Reference to Form-Criticism.* London: Hodder and Stoughton, 1943.

Martin, Alfred W. *The Life of Jesus in the Light of the Higher Criticism.* New York: D. Appleton, 1913.

Mathews, Shailer. *A History of New Testament Times in Palestine, 175 B.C.–A.D. 70.* New York: Macmillan, 1906. New and revised ed., *New Testament Times in Palestine.* New York: Macmillan, 1933.

———. *Jesus on Social Institutions.* New York: Macmillan, 1928. Reprint, ed. Leander Keck, with introduction by Kenneth Cauthen. Lives of Jesus. Philadelphia: Fortress Press, 1971.

———. *The Messianic Hope in the New Testament.* Chicago: University of Chicago Press, 1905.

Maurenbrecher, Max. *Von Nazareth nach Golgotha: Untersuchungen über die weltgeschichtlichen Zusammenhänge des Urchristentums.* Berlin: Schöneberg, 1909.

Mauriac, François. *Life of Jesus.* Trans. Julie Kernan. New York: David McKay, 1937.

McCown, C. C. *The Genesis of the Social Gospel: The Meaning of the Ideals of Jesus in the Light of Their Antecedents.* New York: Knopf, 1929.

———. *The Search for the Real Jesus: A Century of Historical Study.* New York: Scribner's, 1940.

Merezhkovsky, Dmitri. *Jesus Manifest.* Trans. Edward Gellibrand. London: Jonathan Cape, 1935.

———. *Jesus the Unknown.* Trans. H. Chrouschoff Matheson. New York: Scribner's, 1934.

Meyer, Eduard. *Ursprung und Anfänge des Christentums.* 2 vols. Stuttgart: J. G. Cotta, 1921.

Michaelis, Wilhelm. *Täufer, Jesus, Urgemeinde: Die Predigt vom Reiche Gottes vor und nach Pfingsten.* Gütersloh: Bertelsmann, 1928.

The Mishnah. Translated with introduction and explanatory notes by Herbert Danby. London: Oxford University Press, 1933.

Moltmann, Jürgen. *Theology of Hope.* Trans. James W. Leitch. New York: Harper, 1967.

Montefiore, C. G. *Some Elements of the Religious Teaching of Jesus According to the Synoptic Gospels.* London: Macmillan, 1910.

———. *The Synoptic Gospels.* 2 vols. London: Macmillan, 1909; 2d ed., 1927. Reissued with a prolegomenon by Lou H. Silberman. New York: KTAV, 1968.

Moore, George Foot. *Judaism in the First Centuries of the Christian Era: The Age of the Tannaim.* 2 vols. Cambridge: Harvard University Press, 1927.

Morgan, G. Campbell. *The Parables of the Kingdom.* New York: Fleming H. Revell, 1907.

Muirhead, Luis. *The Eschatology of Jesus.* London: Andrew Melrose, 1904.

Murphy, Richard, ed. *Lagrange and Biblical Renewal.* Aquinas Institute Studies No. 1. Chicago: Priory Press, 1966.

Murphy-O'Connor, Jerome. *The École Biblique and the New Testament: A Century of Scholarship (1890–1990).* Göttingen: Vandenhoeck and Ruprecht, 1990.

Murry, J. Middleton. *Jesus, Man of Genius.* New York: Harper, 1926. Reissued as *The Life of Jesus.* London: Jonathan Cape, 1934, 1948.

Neusner, Jacob, William Scott Green, and Ernest S. Frerichs, eds. *Judaisms and Their Messiahs at the Turn of the Christian Era.* Cambridge: Cambridge University Press, 1987.

Noel, Conrad. *Conrad Noel: An Autobiography.* Edited with a foreword by Sidney Dark. London: Dent, 1945.

———. *Jesus the Heretic.* London: J. M. Dent, 1939.

———. *The Life of Jesus.* London: J. M. Dent, 1937.

Oesterley, W. O. E. *The Gospel Parables in the Light of Their Jewish Background.* New York: Macmillan, 1936.

———. *Judaism and Christianity.* Vol. 1, *The Age of Transition.* New York: Macmillan, 1937.

Otto, Rudolf. *The Kingdom of God and the Son of Man.* Trans. Floyd V. Filson and Bertam Lee Woolf. Grand Rapids, Mich.: Zondervan, n.d. Translation of *Reich Gottes und Menschensohn: Ein religionsgeschichtlicher Versuch.* Munich: Beck, 1933.

———. *Life and Ministry of Jesus According to the Historical and Critical Method.* Trans. H. J. Whitby. Chicago: Open Court Publishing, 1908. Translation of *Leben und Wirken Jesu nach historisch-kritischer auffassung.* Göttingen: Vandenhoeck and Ruprecht, 1902.

Pals, Daniel L. *The Victorian "Lives" of Jesus.* Trinity University Monograph Series in Religion 7. San Antonio: Trinity University Press, 1982.

Papini, Giovanni. *Life of Christ.* Trans. Dorothy Canfield Fisher. New York: Harcourt, Brace, 1923.

Patton, Carl S. *Sources of the Synoptic Gospels.* University of Michigan Studies: Humanistic Series 5. New York: Macmillan, 1915.

Peabody, Francis. *Jesus Christ and the Social Question: An Examination of the Teaching of Jesus in Its Relation to Some of the Problems of Modern Social Life.* New York: Macmillan, 1900.

Perrin, Norman. *Rediscovering the Teaching of Jesus.* New York: Harper, 1967.

Petre, Maude. *Alfred Loisy: His Religious Significance.* Cambridge: University Press, 1944.

———. *Autobiography and Life of George Tyrrell.* London: E. Arnold, 1912.

———. *Modernism, Its Failure and Its Fruits.* London: T. C. and A. C. Jack, 1918.

———. *My Way of Faith.* London: Dent, 1937.

———. *Von Hügel and Tyrrell: The Story of a Friendship.* New York: E. P. Dutton, 1927.

Rauschenbusch, Walter. *Christianity and the Social Crisis.* New York: Macmillan, 1907.

———. *A Theology for the Social Gospel.* New York: Macmillan, 1917.

Reitzenstein, Richard. *Das iranische Erlösungsmysterium: Religionsgeschichtliche Untersuchungen.* Bonn: A. Marcus and W. Weber's Verlag, 1924.

———. *Hellenistic Mystery Religions: Their Basic Ideas and Significance.* Trans. John E. Steeley. Pittsburgh Theological Monograph Series 15. Pittsburgh: Pickwick Press, 1978. Translation of *Die hellenistischen Mysterienreligionen: Nach ihren Grundgedanken und Wirkungen.* 3d ed. Leipzig: Teubner, 1924.

Renan, Ernest. *Life of Jesus.* New York: Howard Wilford Bell, 1904.

Rhees, Rush. *The Life of Jesus of Nazareth: A Study.* New York: Scribner's, 1900.

Richardson, Alan. *The Gospels in the Making: An Introduction to the Recent Criticism of the Synoptic Gospels.* London: Student Christian Movement Press, 1938.

———. *The Miracle Stories of the Gospels.* London: SCM Press, 1941.

Robertson, A. T. *Epochs in the Life of Jesus: A Study of Development and Struggle in the Messiah's Work.* New York: Scribner's, 1907.

Robertson, John M. *Christianity and Mythology.* London: Watts, 1900; 2d ed., 1910.

———. *The Historical Jesus: A Survey of Positions.* London: Watts, 1916.

———. *Pagan Christs: Studies in Comparative Hierology.* London: Watts, 1903; 2d ed., 1911.

Robinson, James M., General Editor. *The Nag Hammadi Library in English.* San Francisco: Harper, 1978; rev. ed., 1988.

Robinson, Willard. *The Parables of Jesus in Their Relation to His Ministry.* Chicago: University of Chicago Press, 1928.

Ropes, James Hardy. *The Synoptic Gospels.* Cambridge: Harvard University Press, 1934; Oxford University Press, 1960.

Rupp, George. *Culture-Protestantism: German Liberal Theology at the Turn of the Twentieth Century.* American Academy of Religion Studies in Religion 15. Atlanta: Scholars Press, 1977.

Sanday, William. *The Life of Christ in Recent Research.* New York: Oxford University Press, 1907.

———, ed. *Studies in the Synoptic Problem.* Oxford: Clarendon Press, 1911.

Saunders, Ernest W. *Searching the Scriptures: A History of the Society of Biblical Literature, 1880–1980.* Biblical Scholarship in North America 8. Chico, Calif.: Scholars Press, 1982.

Schechter, Solomon. *Aspects of Rabbinic Theology.* New York: Macmillan, 1909; New York: Schocken Books, 1961.

———. *Studies in Judaism.* 3 ser. Philadelphia: Jewish Publication Society of America, 1896, 1908, 1924.

Schmidt, K. L. *Der Rahmen der Geschichte Jesu: Literarkritische Untersuchungen Ältesten Jesusüberlieferung.* Berlin: Trowitzsch and Sohn, 1919.

Schmidt, Nathaniel. *The Prophet of Nazareth.* New York: Macmillan, 1905.

Schmiedel, Paul. *Jesus in Modern Criticism: A Lecture.* Trans. Maurice A. Canney. London: Adam and Charles Black, 1907.

Schonfield, Hugh J. *Jesus, a Biography.* London: Banner Books, 1939, 1948.

———. *The Passover Plot.* New York: Bantam Books, 1967.

Schürer, Emil. *A History of the Jewish People in the Time of Jesus Christ.* Trans. John Mac-Pherson, Sophia Taylor, and Peter Christie. Edinburgh: T. & T. Clark, 1886–90. Revised English version by Geza Vermes and Fergus Miller. Edinburgh: T. & T. Clark, 1973.

Schweitzer, Albert. *The Mystery of the Kingdom of God: The Secret of Jesus' Messiahship and Passion.* Translated with introduction by Walter Lowrie. New York: Dodd, Mead, 1914. Translation of *Das Messianitäts-und Leidensgeheimnis: Ein Skizze des Lebens Jesu.* Tübingen: J. C. B. Mohr, 1901.

———. *Geschichte der Leben-Jesu-Forschung.* Tübingen: J. C. B. Mohr (Paul Siebeck), 1913.

———. *Out of My Life and Thought: An Autobiography.* Trans. C. T. Campion. New York: Henry Holt, 1933. Translation of *Aus meinem Leben und Denken.* Hamburg: R. Meiner Verlag, 1931.

———. *The Psychiatric Study of Jesus.* Trans. with introduction by Charles R. Joy. Boston: Beacon Press, 1948. Translation of *Die psychiatrische Beurteilung Jesu.* Tübingen: J. C. B. Mohr, 1913.

———. *The Quest of the Historical Jesus: A Critical Study of Its Progress from Reimarus to Wrede.* Trans. W. Montgomery. London: Adam and Charles Black, 1910. Translation of *Von Reimarus zu Wrede: Eine Geschichte der Leben Jesu Forschung.* Tübingen: J. C. B. Mohr, 1906.

Scott, E. F. *The Ethical Teaching of Jesus.* New York: Macmillan, 1924; 2d ed., 1934.

———. *The Kingdom and the Messiah.* Edinburgh: T. & T. Clark, 1911.

———. *The Kingdom of God in the New Testament.* New York: Macmillan, 1931.

Seaver, George. *Albert Schweitzer: The Man and His Mind.* New York: Harper, 1947.

Selbie, W. B. *The Life and Teaching of Jesus Christ.* Century Bible Handbooks. New York: Hodder and Stoughton, 1908.

Selden, William K. *Princeton Theological Seminary: A Narrative History, 1812–1992.* Princeton: Princeton University Press, 1992.

Seeley, John R. *Ecce Homo: A Survey of the Life and Work of Christ.* Boston: Roberts Brothers, 1866.

Sheldon, Charles. *In His Steps.* 1896; New York: Grosset and Dunlap, 1935.

Simkhovitch, Vladimir. *Toward the Understanding of Jesus.* New York: Macmillan, 1925.

Sjöberg, Erik. *Der Menschensohn im Äthiopischen Henobuch.* Lund: C. W. K. Gleerup, 1946.

Smith, B. T. D. *The Parables of the Synoptic Gospels: A Critical Study.* Cambridge: University Press, 1937.

Smith, Charles W. F. *The Jesus of the Parables.* Philadelphia: Westminster Press, 1948.

Smith, David. *The Days of His Flesh: The Earthly Life of Our Lord and Saviour Jesus Christ.* 8th edition; New York: George H. Doran, n.d.

———. *The Historic Jesus.* London: Hodder and Stoughton, 1912.

Smith, William Benjamin. *The Birth of the Gospel: A Study of the Origin and Purport of the Primitive Allegory of the Jesus.* Ed. Addison Gulick. New York: Philosophical Library, 1957.

————. *Ecce Deus: Studies of Primitive Christianity.* Chicago: Open Court Publishing, 1912.

————. *Der vorchristliche Jesus: Vorstudien zur Entstehungsgeschichte des Urchristentums.* Jena: Verlagt bei Eugen Diederichs, 1906; 2d ed., 1911.

Southard, Madeline. *The Attitude of Jesus toward Women.* New York: George H. Doran, 1927.

Stalker, James. *The Life of Jesus Christ.* New York: Fleming H. Revell, 1880, 1891; new and rev. ed., 1909.

Stanton, Vincent Henry. *The Gospels as Historical Documents. Part 2, The Synoptic Gospels.* Cambridge: Cambridge University Press, 1909.

Strack, Hermann L., and Paul Billerbeck. *Kommentar zum Neuen Testament aus Talmud und Midrasch.* Munich: C. H. Beck'sche Verlagsbuchhandlung, 1922–69.

Streeter, B. H. *The Four Gospels: A Study of Origins.* London: Macmillan, 1924; 4th rev. ed., 1930.

Swete, H. B. *The Parables of the Kingdom.* London: Macmillan, 1920.

Taylor, Vincent. *Behind the Third Gospel.* Oxford: Clarendon Press, 1926.

————. *The Formation of the Gospel Tradition.* London: Macmillan, 1933; 2d ed., 1935; reprinted 1945, 1949, 1953.

————. *Jesus and His Sacrifice: A Study of the Passion-Sayings in the Gospels.* London: Macmillan, 1937, 1955.

Thompson, J. M. *Jesus According to S. Mark.* 2d ed. New York: E. P. Dutton, 1910.

This Fabulous Century, 1900–1910. By the editors of *Time-Life.* New York: Time-Life Books, 1969.

Thorburn, T. J. *The Mythical Interpretation of the Gospels: Critical Studies in the Historic Narratives.* Bross Library 7. New York: Scribner's, 1916.

Trattner, Ernest R. *As a Jew Sees Jesus.* New York: Scribner's, 1931.

Troeltsch, Ernst. "The Significance of the Historical Existence of Jesus for Faith." In *Ernst Troeltsch: Writings on Theology and Religion.* Trans. and ed. by Robert Morgan and Michael Pye. Louisville: Westminster/John Knox Press, 1977. Translation of *Die Bedeutung der Geschichtlichkeit Jesu für den Glauben.* Tübingen: J. C. B. Mohr (Paul Siebeck), 1911.

Tyrrell, George. *Christianity at the Crossroads.* London: Longmans, Green, 1909. Introduction by Maude Petre. Reissued with a foreword by A. R. Vidler. London: George Allen and Unwin, 1963.

Völter, Daniel. *Die Grundfrage des Lebens Jesu.* Stuttgart: A. Bonz' Erben, 1936.

————. *Das messianische Bewusstein Jesu.* Strassburg: J. H. Ed. Heitz, 1907.

Vos, Geerhardus. *The Self-Disclosure of Jesus: The Modern Debate about the Messianic Consciousness.* New York: George H. Doran, 1926.

Walker, Thomas. *Jewish Views of Jesus: An Introduction and an Appreciation.* London: George Allen and Unwin, 1931.

Warschauer, J. *The Historical Christ.* London: T. Fisher Unwin, 1927.

————. *Jesus or Christ?.* London: James Clark, 1909.

Weinel, Heinrich. *Die Bergpredigt: Ihr Aufbau, ihr ursprünglicher Sinn und ihre Echtheit, ihre Stellung in der Religionsgeschichte und ihre Bedeutung für die Gegenwart.* Leipzig: B. G. Teubner, 1920.

————. *Biblische Theologie des Neuen Testaments: Die Religion Jesu und des Urchristentums; Grundriss der theologischen Wissenschaften.* Dritter Teil, Zweiter Band. Tübingen: J. C. B. Mohr (Paul Siebeck), 1911; 3d ed., 1921.

Wellhausen, Julius. *Einleitung in die drei ersten Evangelium.* Berlin: Reimer, 1905.

Wendland, Heinz-Dieter. *Die Eschatologie des Reiches Gottes bei Jesus: Eine Studie über den Zusammenhang von Eschatologies, Ethik und Kirchenproblem.* Gütersloh: Bertelsmann, 1931.

Weiss, Johannes. *Jesus von Nazareth Mythus oder Geschichte? Eine Auseinandersetzung mit Karlhoff, Drews, Jensen.* Tübingen: J. C. B Mohr (Paul Siebeck), 1910.

————. *Jesus' Proclamation of the Kingdom of God.* Trans. Richard Hyde Hiers and David Larrimore Holland, with a preface by Rudolf Bultmann. Lives of Jesus. Philadelphia: Fortress Press, 1971. Translation of *Die Predigt Jesu vom Reiche Gottes.* Göttingen: Vandenhoeck and Ruprecht, 1892. 2d ed., 1900; 3d ed., 1964, ed. Ferdinand Hahn.

Wendte, Charles W., ed. *Fifth International Congress of Free Christianity and Religious Progress.* London: Williams and Norgate, 1911.

Wernle, Paul. *Jesus.* Tübingen: J. C. B. Mohr (Paul Siebeck), 1916; Feldausgabe, 1917.

————. *Die Reichsgotteshoffnung in den Ältesten Christlichen Dokumenten und bei Jesus.* Tübingen: J. C. B. Mohr, 1903.

————. *Sources of Our Knowledge of the Life of Jesus.* Trans. Edward Lummis. London: Philip Green, 1905.

Werner, Martin. *The Formation of Christian Dogma.* Trans. S. G. F. Brandon. London: A. & C. Black, 1957. Pbk., Boston: Beacon Press, 1957.

White, Bouck. *The Book of Daniel Drew.* New York: Doubleday, 1910. Reprint, Larchmont, N.Y.: American Research Council, 1965.

————. *The Call of the Carpenter.* Garden City, N.Y.: Doubleday, 1914.

White, H. G. E. *The Sayings of Jesus from Oxyrhynchus.* Cambridge: University Press, 1920.

Wilder, Amos. *Eschatology and Ethics in the Teaching of Jesus.* New York: Harper, 1939.

Windisch, Hans. *The Meaning of the Sermon on the Mount: A Contribution to the Historical Understanding of the Gospels and to the Problem of Their True Exegesis.* Trans. S. MacLean Gilmour. Philadelphia: Westminster Press, 1951. Translation of *Der Sinn der Bergpredigt.* Leipzig: J. C. Hinrich's Verlag, 1928; rev. ed., 1937.

Winstanley, Edward William. *Jesus and the Future.* Edinburgh: T. & T. Clark, 1913.

Wise, Stephen. *Challenging Years: The Autobiography of Stephen Wise.* New York: Putnam's, 1949.

Wood, H. G. *Did Christ Really Live?* New York: Macmillan, 1938.

Zeitlin, Solomon. *Who Crucified Jesus?* New York: Harper, 1942.

Articles and Pamphlets

Anderson, K. C. "The Collapse of Liberal Christianity." *HibJ* 8 (1909–10): 301–20.

Badcock, F. J. "Form Criticism." *ExpTim* 53 (1941–42): 16–20.

Bacon, Benjamin W. "Jesus as Son of Man." *HTR* 3 (1910): 325–40.

————. "The Mythical Collapse of Historical Christianity." *HibJ* 9 (1910–11): 731–53.

————. "The 'Son of Man' in the Usage of Jesus." *JBL* 41 (1922): 143–82.

————. "A Turning Point in Synoptic Criticism," *HTR* 1 (1908): 48–69.

Bang, J. P. "The Root of the Matter." *HibJ* 15 (1917): 1–17.

Barton, George A. "The Person of Christ in the Modern Literature Concerning His Life." *ATR* 13 (1931): 56–71.

Benoit, Pierre. "Réflexions sur la 'Formgeschichtliche Methode.'" *RB* 53 (1946): 481–512.

Bergson, Henri. "Life and Matter at War." *HibJ* 38 (1939): 4–12.

Beveridge, J. "'Against the Stream.'" *JTS* 5 (1903): 1–21.

Bousset, Wilhelm. "The Significance of the Personality of Jesus for Belief." Williams and Norgate, London, 1911. Also found in *Fifth International Congress of Free Christianity and Religious Progress*, ed. Charles Wendte. London: Williams and Norgate, 1911, 208–21.

Brown, Alexander. "How Does It Stand with the Bible?" *LQR* (1900): 71–82.

Bultmann, Rudolf. "Autobiographical Reflections." In *Existence and Faith: Shorter Writings of Rudolf Bultmann*, trans. with introduction by Schubert Ogden. Living Age Books. New York: Meridian Books, 1960.

———. "Die Bedeutung der Eschatologie des Neuen Testaments." *ZTK* 27 (1917): 76–87.

———. "Die Frage nach dem messianischen Bewusstein Jesu und das Petrus-Bekenntnis." *ZNW* (1920): 165–74.

———. "Is Exegesis Without Presuppositions Possible?" In *Existence and Faith: Shorter Writings of Rudolf Bultmann*, trans. with introduction by Schubert Ogden. Living Age Books. New York: Meridian, 1960.

———. "The New Approach to the Synoptic Problem." *JR* (1926): 335–62.

———. "The Significance of the Historical Jesus for the Theology of Paul." In *Faith and Understanding*, ed. Robert W. Funk, trans. Louise Pettibone Smith, 1:220–46. New York: Harper, 1966.

———. "The Primitive Christian Kerygma and the Historical Jesus." In *The Historical Jesus and the Kerygmatic Christ*, ed. and trans. Carl E. Braaten and Roy A. Harrisville, 15–52. New York: Abingdon Press, 1964.

Bultmann, Rudolf, and Karl Kundsin. *Form Criticism: Two Essays on New Testament Research*. Trans. Frederick C. Grant. Harper Torchbook. New York: Willett, Clark, 1934; Harper, 1962.

Burkitt, F. C. "The Eschatological Idea in the Gospel." In *Cambridge Biblical Essays*, ed. H. B. Swete. London: Macmillan, 1909.

Cadbury, Henry. "Between Jesus and the Gospels." *HTR* 16 (1923): 81–92.

Cadoux, C. J. "Is It Possible to Write a Life of Christ? A Second Answer." *ExpTim* 53 (1941–42): 175–77.

Case, Shirley Jackson. "The Historicity of Jesus." *AJT* 15 (1911): 20–42.

———. "Is Jesus a Historical Character?" *AJT* 15 (1911): 205–27.

———. "Jesus' Historicity: A Statement of the Problem." *AJT* 15 (1911): 265–68.

———. "The Rehabilitation of Pharisaism." *Biblical World* 41 (1913): 92–98.

Charlesworth, James H. "The Dead Sea Scrolls and the Historical Jesus." In *Jesus and the Dead Sea Scrolls*, ed. Charlesworth, 1–74. Anchor Bible Reference Library. New York: Doubleday, 1992.

Clark, Kenneth. "Realized Eschatology." *JBL* 59 (1940): 367–83.

Couchoud, Paul-Louis. "The Historicity of Jesus." *HibJ* 37 (1938–39): 193–214.

Craig, C. T. "Realized Eschatology." *JBL* 56 (1937): 17–26.

Crocker, Joseph. "American's Bondage to the German Spirit." *HibJ* 13 (1915): 801–14.

Danby, Herbert. "The Bearing of the Rabbinical Criminal Code on the Jewish Trial Narratives in the Gospels." *JTS* 21 (1920): 51–76.

Davison, W. T. "The Progress of Biblical Criticism." *LQR* (1900): 1–24.

Dibelius, Martin. "The Structure and Literary Character of the Gospels." *HTR* 20 (1927): 151–70.

Diem, Harald. "Das eschatologische Problem in der gegenwärtigen Theologie." *TRu*, n.f. (1939): 228–47.

Dodd, C. H. "The Framework of the Gospel Narrative." *ExpTim* 43 (1931–32): 396–400.

———. "Miracles in the Gospels." *ExpTim* 44 (1932–33): 504–9.

von Dobschütz, Ernst. "The Eschatology of the Gospels." *The Expositor* 9 (1910): 97–113.

Drummond, James. "The Use and Meaning of the Phrase 'The Son of Man' in the Synoptic Gospels." Pt. 1, *JTS* 2 (1901): 350–58; pt. 2, *JTS* 2 (1901): 539–71.

Dungan, David. "Albert Schweitzer's Disillusionment with the Historical Reconstruction of the Life of Jesus." *PSTJ* 29 (Spring 1976): 27–48.

Dunkerley, Roderic. "The Life of Jesus: A New Approach." *ExpTim* 57 (1945–46): 264–68.

Easton, Burton Scott. "The Ethic of Jesus in the New Testament." *ATR* 14 (1932): 1–12.

Enslin, Morton Scott. "The Future of Biblical Studies." *JBL* 65 (1946): 1–12.

———. "Light from the Quest." *HTR* 42 (1949): 19–33.

Epstein, M. "Some Recent German War Literature." *HibJ* 14 (1916): 15–29.

Ferguson, A. S. "More German Sermons." *HibJ* 15 (1917): 18–24.

Finkelstein, Louis. "The Pharisees: Their Origin and Their Philosophy." *HTR* 22 (1929): 185–261.

Fitzmyer, Joseph A. "The Dead Sea Scrolls and Christian Origins: General Methodological Considerations." In *The Dead Sea Scrolls and Christian Faith*, ed. James H. Charlesworth and Walter P. Weaver, 1–19. Faith and Scholarship Colloquies 5. Harrisburg, Pa.: Trinity Press International, 1998.

Goguel, Maurice. "The Problem of Jesus." *HTR* 23 (1930): 93–120.

———. "Recent French Discussion of the Historical Existence of Jesus Christ." *HTR* 19 (1926): 115–42.

Hastings, James, ed. *A Dictionary of the Bible*. Edinburgh: T. & T. Clark, 1899.

von Hügel, Friederich. "Father Tyrrell: Some Memorials of the Last Twelve Years of His Life." *HibJ* 8 (1909–10): 233–52.

James, J. Courtney. "The Son of Man: Origin and Uses of the Title." *ExpTim* 36 (1924–25): 309–14.

Jülicher, Adolf. "Parables." In *Encyclopedia Biblica*, ed. T. K. Cheyne. London: A. and C. Black, 1899.

Käsemann, Ernst. "The Problem of the Historical Jesus." In *Essays on New Testament Themes*, trans. W. J. Montague. Studies in Biblical Theology 41. Naperville, Ill.: Alec R. Allenson, 1964.

Kennedy, H. A. A. "The Life of Jesus in the Light of Recent Discussions." *AJT* 11 (1907): 150–57.

Köhler, Ludwig. "The Meaning and Possibilities of Formgeschichte." *JR* 8 (1928): 603–15.

Lake, Kirsopp. "Albert Schweitzer's Influence in Holland and England." In *The Albert Schweitzer Jubilee Book*, ed. A. A. Roback with J. S. Bixler and George Sarton,

427–39. Westport, Conn.: Greenwood Press, 1970. Originally published by Sci-Art Publishers in Cambridge, Massachusetts, 1945.

Lempp, Richard. "Church and Religion in Germany." *HTR* 14 (1921): 30–52.

———. "Present Religious Conditions in Germany." *HTR* 3 (1910): 85–124.

Lightfoot, R. H. "Form Criticism and Gospel Study." *ExpTim* 53 (1941–42): 51–54.

Loisy, Alfred. "Was Jesus an Historical Person?" *HibJ* 36 (1937–38): 380–94, 509–29.

———. "Remarques sur le volume 'Jésus ou le Christ.'" *HibJ* 8 (1910): 473–95.

Macintosh, Hugh R. "The Liberal Conception of Jesus in Its Strength and Weakness." *AJT* 16 (1912) 411–25.

Macgregor, G. H. C. "Recent Gospel Criticism and Our Approach to the Life of Jesus." *ExpTim* 45 (1933–34): 198–203, 283–86.

Manson, T. W. "Is It Possible to Write a Life of Christ?" *ExpTim* 53 (1941–42): 248–51.

Montgomery, James A. "Present Tasks of Biblical Scholarship." *JBL* 38 (1919): 1–14.

Montefiore, C. G. "The Originality of Jesus." *HibJ* 28 (1929–30): 98–111.

———. "The Significance of Jesus for His Own Age." *HibJ* 10 (1911–12): 766–79.

———. "What a Jew Thinks about Jesus." *HibJ* 33 (1934–35): 511–20.

Moore, George Foot. "Christian Writers on Judaism." *HTR* 14 (1921): 197–254.

Olmstead, A. T. "The Chronology of Jesus' Life." *ATR* 24 (1942): 1–26.

Parker, Pierson. "The Meaning of 'Son of Man.'" *JBL* 60 (1941): 151–57.

Patton, Carl. "Did Jesus Call Himself the Son of Man?" *JR* 2 (1922): 501–11.

Peabody, Francis. "New Testament Eschatology and New Testament Ethics." *HTR* 2 (1909): 50–57.

Roberts, Rev. R. "Jesus or Christ: An Appeal for Consistency." In *Hibbert Journal Supplement 1909*, 270–82. London: Williams and Norgate, 1909.

Sanday, William. "The Apocalyptic Element in the Gospels." *HibJ* 10 (1911–12): 83–109.

Schmidt, K. L. "Jesus Christ." In *Religion in Geschichte und Gegenwart* (1929).

Schmidt, Nathaniel. "The Origins of Jewish Eschatology." *JBL* 41 (1922): 102–14.

———. "Recent Study of the Term 'Son of Man.'" *JBL* 45 (1926): 326–49.

———. "Son of Man." In *Encyclopedia Biblica*, ed. T. K. Cheyne. London: A. and C. Black, 1899.

Scott, E. F. "The Originality of Jesus' Ethical Teaching." *JBL* 48 (1929): 109–15.

———. "The Significance of Jesus for Modern Religion in View of His Eschatological Teaching." *AJT* (1914): 225–40.

Taylor, Vincent. "Is It Possible to Write a Life of Christ? Some Aspects of the Modern Problem." *ExpTim* 53 (1941–42): 61–65.

———. "The 'Son of Man' Sayings Relating to the Parousia." *ExpTim* 58 (1946–47): 12–15.

Warschauer, Joseph. "The Present Position of Liberal Theology in Great Britain." *AJT* 16 (1912): 333–58.

"What Jesus Means to the Jews." *Literary Digest* (January 1926): 30–31.

Wilder, Amos. "The Eschatology of Jesus in Recent Criticism and Interpretation." *JR* 28 (1948): 177–85.

———. "The Nature of Jewish Eschatology." *JBL* 50 (1931): 201–6.

Windisch, Hans. "Das Problem der Geschichtlichkeit Jesu: Die Außerchristlichen Zeugnisse." *TRu*, n.f. 1 (1929): 266–88.

———. "Das Problem der Geschichtlichkeit Jesu: Die Christusmythe." *TRu*, n.f. 2 (1930): 207–52.

Reviews

Baldensperger, Wilhelm. Review of *The Life of Jesus Christ*, by James Stalker. *TRu* (1900): 342–44.

Bultmann, Rudolf. "Reich Gottes und Menschensohn." Review of *Reich Gottes und Menschensohn: Ein religionsgeschichtlicher Versuch*, by Rudolf Otto. *TRu*, n.f. 9 (1937): 1–35.

Cadbury, Henry J. Review of *Jesus: A New Biography*, by Shirley Jackson Case. *JR* 8 (1928): 130–36.

Case, Shirley Jackson. Reviews of E. F. Scott, *The Kingdom and the Messiah*, C. W. Emmet, *The Eschatological Question in the Gospels; and Other Studies in Recent New Testament Criticism*, and von Dobschütz's *The Eschatology of the Gospels*. *AJT* 16 (1912): 296–99.

Charnwood (Lord). Review of *The Historical Christ*, by Joseph Warschauer. *The Modern Churchman* 17 (1927–28): 132–38.

Davison, W. T. Review of *What Is Christianity?*, by Adolf von Harnack. *LQR* (1901): 168.

Easton, Burton Scott. Review of *Jesus: A New Biography*, by Shirley Jackson Case. *ATR* (1927–28): 250–57.

Ffrench, G. E. Review of *The Quest of the Historical Jesus: A Critical Study of Its Progress from Reimarus to Wrede*, by Albert Schweitzer. *HibJ* 9 (1910–11): 203–6.

Frick, Heinrich. "Wider die Skepsis in der Leben-Jesu-Forschung: R. Otto's Jesus-Buch." Review of *Reich Gottes und Menschensohn: Ein religionsgeschichtlicher Versuch*, by Rudolf Otto. *ZTK*, n.f. 16 (1935): 1–20.

Gookin, Warner F. Review of *The Eschatology of Jesus*, by H. Latimer Jackson. *HTR* 8 (1915): 559–61.

Grant, F. C. Review of *Die Gleichnisse Jesu*, by Joachim Jeremias. *ATR* 30 (1948): 118–21.

Hollmann, Georg. Review of *Das Messianitäts-und Leidensgeheimnis: Ein Skizze des Lebens Jesu*, by Albert Schweitzer. *TLZ* 27 (1902): 466–69.

Hoskyns, Edwyn. Review of *Jesus*, by Rudolf Bultmann. *JTS* 28 (1927): 106–9.

Lagrange, M.-J. Review of *Die Geschichte der synoptischen Tradition*, by Rudolf Bultmann. *RB* 31 (1922): 287–92.

Lloyd-Thomas, J. M. Review of *The Historical Christ*, by Joseph Warschauer. *HibJ* 25 (1927): 655–66.

Melhorn, D. Paul. Review of *Von Reimarus zu Wrede: Eine Geschichte der Leben Jesu Forschung*, by Albert Schweitzer. *Protestantische Monatshefte* 11 (1907): 372–75.

Porter, Frank. Review of *The Messianic Hope in the New Testament*, by Shailer Mathews. *AJT* 10 (1906): 111–15.

Sanday, William. "A New Work on the Parables." Review of *Die Gleichnisreden Jesu*, 2d ed., by Adolf Jülicher. *JTS* 1 (1900): 161–80.

Review of filmed life of Jesus. *Literary Digest* 45 (August 10, 1912): 227–28.

Review of *The Historical Christ*, by Joseph Warschauer. *Times Literary Supplement* 26 (1927): 754.

Troeltsch, Ernst. Review of *Jesus*, by Paul Wernle. *TLZ* (1916): 54–57.

Vos, Geerhardus. Review of *The Quest of the Historical Jesus: A Critical Study of Its Progress from Reimarus to Wrede*, by Albert Schweitzer. *PTR* 9 (1911): 132–41.

———. Review of *Die Reichsgotteshoffnung in den Ältesten Christlichen Dokumenten und bei Jesus*, by Paul Wernle. *PTR* 1 (1903): 298–303.

―――. Review of *The Messianic Hope in the Gospels*, by Shailer Mathews. *PTR* 4 (1906): 262.

Weinel, Heinrich. Review of *Das Messianitäts-und Leidensgeheimnis: Ein Skizze des Lebens Jesu*, by Albert Schweitzer. *TRu* 15 (1902): 242–45.

Wernle, Paul. Review of *Von Reimarus zu Wrede: Eine Geschichte der Leben Jesu Forschung*, by Albert Schweitzer. *TLZ* 31 (1906): 502–6.

Windisch, Hans. Review of *Von Reimarus zu Wrede: Eine Geschichte der Leben Jesu Forschung*, by Albert Schweitzer. *TRu* 12 (1909): 146–62.

―――. Review of *Jesus*, by Paul Wernle. *TRu* (1917): 42–49.

Newspapers

New York Times. Articles from January 1–2, 6, 1900, and January 2, 1901.

London Times. Articles from January 1, 1900, and January 1, 1901.

Miscellaneous

Bultmann, Rudolf. Bibliography of works. *TRu* n.f. 22 (1954): 3–20.

Case, Shirley Jackson. Lecture notes. Florida Southern College archives.

Cole, Stewart C. Letter to Shirley Jackson Case of May 30, 1920. Florida Southern College archives.

Flyer promoting William Benjamin Smith's *Ecce Deus: Studies of Primitive Christianity*. Chicago: Open Court Publishing Company, 1912.

"Spanish American War." *Compton's Interactive Encyclopedia* (CD-ROM, 1994).

Uncited Works, Annotated

Books

Anderson, Frederick L. *The Man of Nazareth*. New York: Macmillan, 1914. Popular and eulogistic. Utilizes liberal themes with a romantic touch from Renan.

Barnes, Harry Elmer. *The Twilight of Christianity*. New York: Vanguard Press, 1929. A secular humanist's look at a fading Christianity; the author wishes to vanquish all the old supernaturalism and allow only what is consistent with science. Little can be known of Jesus (who was nevertheless historical); his significance evaporated with Yahwism, whose son he was.

Bethune-Baker, J. F. *Early Traditions about Jesus*. Cambridge: University Press, 1929. Meant for younger students, but gives responsible information, treating Jesus as the suffering Servant-messiah who would come in the future in glory.

Bornhäuser, Karl. *The Sermon on the Mount Interpreted in the Light of Its Contemporaneous World of Creeds, Customs and Conditions*. Translated by Rev. and Mrs. C. Dandegren. 1935; Madras: The Christian Literature Society for India, 1951. Seems to be considered useful on the mission field; a kind of commentary on the text, with harsh treatment of the Pharisees, and references to the rabbinic parallels.

Caine, Hall. *Life of Christ*. New York: Doubleday, Doran, 1938. A massive work of some 1,320 pages, showing here and there acquaintance with critical issues. Most of the mass of the book comes from the recounting of history prior to the time of Jesus. The book represents the culmination of the life work of Sir Hall Caine, but was put together posthumously by his sons. The actual life of Jesus is largely a summary of the four gospels. An indication of its perspective is given in the evaluation of Mark, which "confines itself almost exclusively to a very simple purpose, namely that of narrating the actual facts of the life of Jesus" (258).

Carey, S. Pearce. *Jesus*. London: The Book Club, 1940. Literate, conservative, the work of a parish minister. Not critical, but rambling musings on the life of Jesus. Uses John in spite of critical opinion; knows scholarly views also, but tends to bypass them (two temple cleansings, two feedings, and so on); especially rejects Schweitzer's portrayal (use of Matt. 10:23, interim ethic).

Case, Shirley Jackson, ed. *Studies in Early Christianity*. New York: Century, 1928. A *festschrift* for Frank Porter and Benjamin W. Bacon. The essay by Frederick C. Grant on "Method in Studying Jesus' Social Teaching" is pertinent as window into the American sociohistorical approach.

Dushaw, Amos I. *The Man Called Jesus*. New York: Fleming H. Revell, 1939. A popular but uncritical book of the gee-whiz-Jesus type. It tries to unite all four gospels into a picture of Jesus, with expected strange results (two cleansings of the temple, many trips to Jerusalem).

Easton, Burton Scott. *Christ and His Teaching*. New York: Edwin S. Gorham, 1922. A study manual for students; offers text and commentary, but of little value for the scholar.

Eddy, Sherwood. *A Portrait of Jesus: A Twentieth-Century Interpretation of Christ*. New York: Association Press, 1943. A work dedicated to Schweitzer, but still bearing the marks of liberalism syncretized with other elements: a Jesus expecting to be the future ruler following his death as the suffering Servant messiah.

Einspruch, Henry. *A Jew Looks at Jesus*. Baltimore: The Mediator, n.d. [1930]. An appeal by a converted Jew directed to other Jews to accept Jesus as their messiah.

Enelow, H. G. *A Jewish View of Jesus*. New York: Macmillan, 1920. Jesus exemplified the prophetic tradition of Israel; he criticized people, but also loved them. He preached a non-political kingdom realizable internally. He attracted the poor and straying sinners. He did not intend to overthrow the Law or to found a new religion. He was condemned by the Romans with perhaps some collusion from the priests. His followers after his death made him into the suffering messiah; Paul was influential. Hostility with Judaism ensued, compounded eventually by the rise to power of Christians under Constantine.

Erskine, John. *The Human Life of Jesus*. New York: William Morrow, 1945. Reprinted twice. Based on all four gospels, has a degree of literary dressing. Conservative in outlook.

Fiske, Charles, and Burton Scott Easton. *The Real Jesus: What he Taught, What He Did, Who He Was*. New York: Harper, 1929. Easton's co-work with a bishop, combining popular and scholarly, with some romanticizing (the authors know that Jesus cried at his entrance into Jerusalem). Mainly of a liberal nature mixed with recognition of the eschatological kingdom, Jesus' self-awareness as messiah and expectation he would be elevated to ruler of the world.

Foakes-Jackson, F. J., and Kirsopp Lake. *The Beginnings of Christianity*. Part 1, *The Acts of the Apostles*. London: Macmillan, 1920. Part 3, chapter 1 (267–99) provides an extended essay on "The Public Teaching of Jesus and His Choice of the Twelve." Kingdom of God meant sovereignty, a present reality, and sometimes also a future Age to Come. We cannot say Jesus identified himself with either Son of Man or Davidic messiah; he claimed only the Spirit of God. Jesus' differences with the Pharisees rooted in his doctrine of nonresistance, in his association with sinners and interpretation of the Law. His choice of twelve was to support his message of the coming kingdom; it is doubtful he promised them thrones to occupy.

Gardner-Smith, Percy. *The Christ of the Gospels: A Study of the Gospel Records in the Light of Critical Research.* Cambridge: W. Heffner and Sons, 1938. A fairly conventional British presentation, seemingly aimed at those in the churches who need instruction in criticism. It constructs a picture of Jesus based largely, if not exclusively — John is used modestly — on Mark: Jesus knew himself messiah at the baptism, conducted a running contest with Pharisees, claimed the messiahship at Caesarea-Philippi, preached a transmuted eschatological kingdom, died a redemptive death at Jerusalem. "Apocalyptic" is disliked; Form Criticism exaggerates.

Gore, Charles. *Jesus of Nazareth.* London: Oxford University Press, 1929. Reprinted 13 times. A popular treatment by Bishop Gore, often cited. The picture is very conventional; Jesus took the Son of Man title and qualified it with the concept of suffering. Liberalism moderated by British caution.

Hunterberg, Max. *The Crucified Jew: Who Crucified Jesus?* New York: Bloch Publishing, 1927. Maintains the hypothesis that Jesus was killed by a malevolent, strictly limited high priestly family (Annas, Caiaphas) bent on saving its own power, with the compliance of Pilate and the Romans, who actualized the deed. The Jewish people had no role.

Hutton, John A. *The Proposal of Jesus.* London: Hodder and Stoughton, 1921. Advances the thesis that Jesus' activity was political and social, that he sought to save his people from disaster at the hands of Rome by communicating a message of a universal God, the Father of all persons, the kingdom as a new world order, Israel as the instrument of universal purpose. The author also recognized that the gospel material came out of community needs. Interesting propositions, though the book suffers a great deal from verbal overload.

James, Edward Holton. *Jesus for Jews: A History.* Concord, Mass.: Emerson Press, 1934. Wandering book with aimless chatter; trades on the loss of the historical Jesus when Constantine took over the church. The point of the title is unclear.

Keim, D. Karl. *Die Bergpredigt Jesu Für die heutige Zeit ausgelegt.* Tübingen: Furche-Verlag, 1946; 3d ed., 1949. Not a technical study, but a postwar piece looking for meaning from the Sermon on the Mount in the midst of chaotic conditions. Takes the position that the Sermon was meant for a "little flock" of like-minded persons, the salt of the earth, who could live by its commandments and so serve as leaven for the whole world. The Sermon is therefore not meant as rules by which to govern the world as it exists, but as commandments for the "shock troops" who will seek to permeate the whole. Examples are then taken (murder, retaliation, divorce, care).

Lyman, Mary Ely. *Jesus.* Hazen Books on Religion. New York: Association Press, 1937. A modest account of Jesus from a conventional liberal perspective, with some impact from the sociohistorical school: Jesus' "personality" is at the heart of his appeal for us; even though he claimed an apocalyptic element in his proclamation, the core is his personality and his message. Jesus' "estimate of human personality as the supreme value in our universe" (49) is vindicated by the centuries. Christological confessions are to be assessed by their functional value in the community holding them. Jesus matters because he embodied the ideal enshrined in his words (life lived in fellowship with God the Father and in community with other brothers).

Martin, A. D. *A Plain Man's Life of Christ.* New York: Macmillan, 1947. A work for general readers, showing some knowledge of critical scholarship and some literary skill as well. Some novelizing occurs, e.g., when Jesus was said to go out to pray, the author notes that "the cooling air of nightfall braced him for a long walk" (65). It is not clear whether the "plain man" of the title was the author or the intended audience.

Mathews, Basil. *A Life of Jesus.* London: Oxford University Press, 1930; 2d rev. ed., 1934. Fictionalized, with many photographs from modern Palestine and some pictures of paintings. Conversations are imagined, though Jesus' words are used. At the birth in Bethlehem "the donkey, his grey muzzle in the manger, contentedly munched his barley and broken straw" (5). Jesus preached a kingdom of love. The book shows knowledge of criticism, but uses John. Intended mainly for younger readers.

McDowell, Edward A. *Son of Man and Suffering Servant.* Nashville: Broadman Press, 1944. The author was at Southern Baptist Theological Seminary in Louisville, Kentucky. The work opposes Form Criticism, maintains that Jesus had a unique relation to God from which emerged a messianic consciousness as Servant and Son of Man (Enoch). Streeter's source theory is accepted.

Micklem, Nathaniel. *The Galilean: The Permanent Element in Religion.* London: James Clarke, 1920; 2d ed., 1921. A popular presentation of the "modernist" perspective. The kingdom is a right and filial relation to God and a brotherly relation to people; the realization of God as Father brings salvation.

Moffatt, James. *Everyman's Life of Jesus: The Gospel Story in the Moffatt Translation.* New York: Harper, 1937. Not a life in the usual sense, but a selection, presentation, and ordering of texts accompanied by a brief introduction. Intended for general audiences. Moderately conservative, utilizing critical data but also including material from John. Jesus preached the kingdom (realm of bliss), deepened the commandments, announced his messiahship at Caesarea-Philippi, died in Jerusalem by the chicanery of the priests forcing Pilate to act against a heretic and rebel.

Page, Kirby. *Jesus or Christianity: A Study in Contrasts.* Garden City, N.Y.: Doubleday, Doran, 1929. A liberal contrasting of Jesus' religion with that of Christianity. The kingdom is within; Jesus taught love and acceptance of everyone (social gospel).

Piepenbring, Charles. *The Historical Jesus.* Translated by Lilian A. Clare. New York: Macmillan, 1924. A work of liberal lineage with recognition of the eschatological element in Jesus' proclamation. Piepenbring was an Alsatian pastor of the Reformed tradition, but well acquainted with critical literature.

de Pina, Albert, and Stewart P. Maclennan. *The Galilean: A Life of Jesus.* Hollywood, Calif.: Murray and Gee, 1945. Novelistic. It is not encouraging when in the opening we read of Caiaphas contemplating his circumstances and that he "turned mentally to the Talmud" (14). There is also a certain overstretched effort at literary quality. Perhaps the authors aimed at a screen vehicle.

Porteous, John. *Studies in the Life and Teaching of Jesus.* Paisley: Alexander Gardner, 1922. The author was a minister of the United Free Church. The book has a misleading title; it consists of homiletical excursions into selected biblical texts and is of no real critical value.

Quimby, Chester Warren. *Jesus as They Remembered Him.* New York: Abingdon-Cokesbury Press, 1941. Written for the layperson with a degree of literary competence. It knows the scholarly discussion, but the interest lies elsewhere. The book often transgresses sensible limits; the author knows that Jesus had good digestion, for he was a welcome guest at meals; Jesus' "happy spirits" inclined him to receive invitations, his eyes "flashed" and he was "sensitive" and had a commanding voice that was, however, ordinarily well-modulated. Jesus preached salvation; little effort is expended on understanding the kingdom of God concept.

Raven, Charles E. and Eleanor Raven. *The Life and Teaching of Jesus Christ.* Cambridge: University Press, 1949. A work of joint authorship intended for use in secondary schools. Gives the historical background, sources, and a picture of Jesus in Mark, Q, M, and L. Some critical evaluation of miracles (healings, psychic, storm quieted by Jesus' courage), with Jesus as a suffering messiah.

Rawlinson, A. F. J. *Christ in the Gospels.* London: Oxford University Press, 1944; reprint, Westport, Conn.: Greenwood Press, 1970. An oft-cited work, perhaps because it was by the Bishop of Derby, for it contributed little not widely known. Addressed to those troubled by problems in the gospels and urged some familiar answers (all facts have to be interpreted, everyone has a perspective, the true alternative to faith is historical scepticism).

Ricciotti, Giuseppe. *The Life of Christ.* Trans. Alba I. Zizzamia. Milwaukee: Bruce Publishing, 1947. Roman Catholic version with all four gospels. Surveys critical work and condemns it all. Much learning demonstrated in regard to questions of background and context. Loisy is a particular target.

Robinson, Benjamin Willard. *The Sayings of Jesus: Their Background and Interpretation.* New York: Harper, 1930. A commentary on sayings following Goodspeed-Burton ("G" and "Pm" theories), setting the sayings in their Judaic historical context. The commentary runs along liberal lines: a kingdom present and future, not political but also social (an earthly commonwealth of justice and brotherhood, the "republic of God"), the ethics individual, no use of Son of Man.

Sawyer, Elbert. *Biography of Jesus.* Philadelphia: John C. Winston, 1927. Based on Matthew with supplements; an uncritical work.

Sharman, H. Burton. *Studies in the Life of Christ.* 1896; New York: Association Press, 1925; recopyrighted 1925 by the YMCA. A study guide with questions and application material.

Stewart, James S. *The Life and Teaching of Jesus Christ.* 1931; reprint, Nashville: Abingdon Press, n.d. Demonstrates a great capacity of the eminent Scottish minister-scholar to translate scholarly matters into an elegant and understandable language. Much is sermonic, but undergirded by a clearly wide learning, if also mostly conservative and conventional, e.g., the kingdom is moral and spiritual and actual, though also social, universal, and incomplete. Fatherhood looms large in the teaching, Caesarea-Philippi is a turning point.

Strachan, R. H. *The Historic Jesus in the New Testament.* London: SCM Press, 1931. Primarily theological, the book examines various New Testament sources for their christology and finds the "historic Jesus" of significance for all. ("Historic Jesus" was the one who went about in Galilee and "historical Jesus" is the one who is the object of adoration in the hearts of believers — the reverse of the usual usage).

Tasker, R. V. G. *The Nature and Purpose of the Gospels.* London: SCM Press, 1944. Aimed at students, teachers, and ministers. Grasps the importance of the oral tradition, but sees the life of Jesus as part of the transmitted tradition. Son of Man (Enoch) was used by Jesus; he was the first to see the role as including suffering. The religion of Judaism then was rigid and legal. Jesus' teaching was overlayed by apocalyptic thought to account for the delay of the Parousia. Neither Harnack nor Schweitzer is correct, but the kingdom is the rule in which the eternal breaks into the earthly. The ethics of Jesus remain an ideal not always susceptible of practice.

Woods, Ralph, ed. *Behold the Man*. New York: Macmillan, 1944. An anthology of essays from many writers; the essays are of a short nature. Extracts from people like Mary Austin, Shirley Jackson Case, Frederic Farrar, and F. C. Burkitt.

Yost, Casper S. *The Carpenter of Nazareth: A Study of Jesus in the Light of his Environment and Background*. St. Louis: Bethany Press, 1938. A layperson writing a popular book, though aware of technical literature. The treatment of Jesus is along modified liberal lines (a spiritual kingdom within, Fatherhood-brotherhood, Jesus as a suffering Servant-Son of Man messiah).

Zahn, Theodor. *Grundriß der Geschichte des Lebens Jesu*. Leipzig: A. Deichertsche Verlagsbuchhandlung, 1928. Conservative, utilizing all four gospels freely, engaging in some exegetical footwork to harmonize John and the synoptics (e.g., last supper dating).

Articles

Barr, Allan. "The Interpretation of the Parables." *ExpTim* 53 (1941): 20–25. Sees parables as weapons of conquest. Some dissent from Jülicher's single-point theory; a parable might have several subordinate points.

Bauer, Walter. "Jesus der Galiläer." In R. Bultmann and H. von Soden, *Festgabe für Adolf Jülicher zum 70. Geburtstag 26. Januar 1927*, 16–34. Tübingen: J. C. B. Mohr (Paul Siebeck), 1927. Based on a cautious appeal to Josephus. Sets forth the argument for a predominant gentile influence in Galilee; scribalism and Pharisaism were centered in Jerusalem, whereas the Galileans' environment lay largely outside their sphere of influence. Jesus was not against the law, but was concerned to set the coming Reign of God before persons and to attach them to himself as the one sent by God to prepare for the coming age. He only used the syncretistic title Son of Man, not the usual messianic predicates. Jesus' movement flowered in Jerusalem on the common basis of the resurrection-faith and expectation of Jesus' coming again. Jesus effectively practiced freedom from the law even without proclaiming it, a recollection that led to his community's bursting the boundaries of Judaism.

Bornhausen, Karl. "The Present Status of Liberal Theology in Germany." *AJT* (1914): 191–204. Defends a liberal position against criticism from orthodoxy; argues that the liberal position is the best because it seeks a way between Christian faith and the culture.

Cadbury, Henry J. "Motives of Biblical Scholarship." *JBL* 56 (1937): 1–16. Scholars are motivated both by devotion to truth and by concern for the consequences of their work. Both are appropriate.

Cadoux, C. J. "The Liberal-Modernist View of Jesus." *HibJ* 34 (1935–36): 288–99. Cadoux's answer to Edwards (below); defends the rights of criticism.

Cohon, Samuel S. "The Place of Jesus in the Religious Life of His Day." *JBL* 48 (1929): 82–107. Jesus had a unique consciousness of being the messiah; otherwise it is impossible to explain the faith of the disciples after the resurrection. His claims were the source of hostility to and from the Pharisees. Jesus was an *Am-ha-aretz*, a *Hasid*.

Cook, E. Albert. "The Kingdom of God as a Democratic Ideal." *JR* 1 (1921): 626–40. Enlists Jesus as an advocate of democratic ideals.

Craig, Clarence T. "Current Trends in New Testament Study." *JBL* 57 (1938): 359–75. Old research on the life of Jesus has come to an end; there are new understandings of Pharisaism and Form Criticism is growing in influence. Commentaries should concentrate on the faith of the writer; New Testament theology should probably be discarded.

———. "The Identification of Jesus with the Suffering Servant." *JR* 24 (1944): 240–45. Denies that Jesus combined Servant and messiah, but likely he did use Son of Man.

Davies, Paul E. "Jesus and the Role of the Prophet." *JBL* 64 (1945): 241–53. Makes a case for "prophet" as an early depiction of Jesus and as rooting in his actual ministry.

Edwards, R. A. "The Peasant Theory of Jesus." *HibJ* 33 (1934–35): 521–35. "Peasant Jesus" here seems to be the mostly liberal one; the author wishes to deny the liberal assumption that Jesus arose from the peasantry and was transformed into deity. His deity was rooted in himself.

Gilmour, S. MacLean. "How Relevant Is the Ethic of Jesus?" *JR* 21 (1941): 253–64. Jesus' ethic is not a norm for the world, but for Christians in the world.

Ginzberg, Louis. "Some Observations on the Attitude of the Synagogue Towards the Apocalyptic-Eschatological Writings." *JBL* 41 (1922): 115–36. Argues that basing the picture of Judaism on the apocalypses results in a distortion that would be a "visionary pseudo-history" (115).

Goguel, Maurice. "The Religious Situation in France." *JR* 1 (1921): 561–77. Reports on the law separating church and state, Protestant-Catholic relations, the hope of more French-American cooperation brought about by the recent war.

Lake, Kirsopp. "Jesus." *HibJ* 23 (1924–25): 1–20. Article argues that traditional orthodox faith in the Incarnation does not go back to Jesus, nor can much in his teaching simply be taken over into the present (eschatology, certain ethical injunctions).

Moore, George Foot. "A Jewish Life of Jesus." *HTR* 16 (1923): 93–103. Moore reviews Klausner's life of Jesus in the original Hebrew, contrasts it with a review by the American Jewish scholar Armand Kaminka, who was severely critical of it. Moore thought Kaminka's criticisms often sound.

McCown, C. C. "The Eschatology of Jesus Reconsidered." *JR* 16 (1936): 30–46. Critiques Schweitzer for posing polarities and for misrepresenting the eschatological material (Schweitzer did not know the work of R. H. Charles).

———. "Jesus, Son of Man." *JR* 28 (1948): 1–12. Says there has been nothing of an epoch-making character since von Dobschütz except perhaps Rudolf Otto. Others' views are recapitulated (R. Bultmann, M. Dibelius, A. T. Olmstead, H. B. Sharman, Paul Davies, C. H. Dodd, William Manson).

Riddle, Donald W. "The Central Problem of the Gospels." *JBL* 60 (1941): 97–111. The gospels have to be studied first for their own message and purpose and secondarily for what they portray of Jesus. The central problem is this double relationship. Both Form Criticism and sociohistorical method affirm the gospels as community writings.

Sanday, William. "The Injunction of Silence in the Gospels." *JTS* 5 (1905): 321–29. Sanday's review of Wrede. He found Wrede's hypothesis "unreal and artificial in the extreme. That any ancient should seek to cover the non-existence of certain presumed facts by asserting that they did exist, but that the persons affected were compelled to keep silence about them, is a hypothesis altogether too far-fetched to be credible" (324).

Scott, E. F. "The New Criticism of the Gospels." *HTR* 19 (1926): 143–63. Wishes still to see some biographical interest in the composition of the gospels.

———. "Recent Lives of Jesus." *HTR* 27 (1934): 1–31. Reviews a number of works, concentrating mostly on Goguel and Guignebert. Finds Goguel relying too much on literary criticism and psychologizing, Guignebert too negative.

BIBLIOGRAPHIC AND
RESEARCH HISTORY

Ayres, Samuel Gardiner. *Jesus Christ Our Lord: An English Bibliography of Christology Comprising over Five Thousand Titles Annotated and Classified*. New York: A. C. Armstrong and Son, 1906.

Burckhardt, A. E. "Moderne Richtungen im theologischen Denken Amerikas." *ZTK*, n.f. 8 (1927): 202–26.

von Dobschütz, Ernst. "Der heutige Stand der Leben-Jesu-Forschung." *ZTK*, n.f. (1924): 64–84.

Evans, Craig A. *Life of Jesus Research: An Annotated Bibliography*. New Testament Tools and Studies. Leiden: E. J. Brill, 1989; rev. ed., 1996.

Grant, Frederick C. "A New Testament Bibliography for 1914 to 1917 Inclusive." *ATR* 1 (1918–19): 58–83.

———. "A New Testament Bibliography for 1918 to 1922 Inclusive." *ATR* 6 (1923–24): 309–19.

———. "A New Testament Bibliography for 1918 to 1922 Inclusive." *ATR* 7 (1924–25): 40–47.

Grobel, Kendrick. "Amerikanische Literatur zum Neuen Testament seit 1938." *TRu*, n.f. (1948): 142–56.

Gutbrod, Walter. "Aus der neueren englischen Literatur zum Neuen Testament." *TRu*, n.f. 11 (1939): 263–77, and n.f. 12 (1940): 1–23.

Jones, Maurice. *The New Testament in the Twentieth Century: A Survey of Recent Christological and Historical Criticism of the New Testament*. London: Macmillan, 1914.

Kissinger, Warren S. *The Lives of Jesus: A History and Bibliography*. New York: Garland, 1985.

———. *The Parables of Jesus: A History of Interpretation and Bibliography*. ATLA Bibliography Series No. 4. Metuchen, N.J.: Scarecrow Press and the American Theological Library Association, 1979.

———. *The Sermon on the Mount: A History of Interpretation and Bibliography*. ATLA Bibliography Series 3. Metuchen, N.J.: Scarecrow Press and the American Theological Library Association, 1975.

Kümmel, Werner Georg. *Dreißig Jahre Jesusforschung (1950–1980)*. Herausgegeben von Helmut Merklein. Bonn: Peter Hanstein Verlag, 1985.

———. *The New Testament: The History of the Investigation of Its Problems*. Translated by S. McLean Gilmour and Howard C. Kee. Nashville: Abingdon Press, 1972.

McArthur, Harvey K. *The Quest through the Centuries: The Search for the Historical Jesus*. Philadelphia: Fortress Press, 1966.

Neill, Stephen. *The Interpretation of the New Testament 1861–1961*. London: Oxford University Press, 1964; 2d rev. ed. by N. T. Wright, 1988.

Purdy, Alexander. "Das Neue Testament in der amerikanischen Theologie." *TRu*, n.f. 3 (1931): 367–85.

Riches, John K. *A Century of New Testament Study*. Valley Forge, Pa.: Trinity Press International, 1993.

Riddle, D. W. "Jesus in Modern Research." *JR* 17 (1937): 170–82

Schrey, Heinz-Horst. "Die gegenwärtige Lage der amerikanischen Theologie." *TRu*, n.f. 10 (1938): 23–56.

Schweitzer, Albert. *Geschichte der Leben-Jesu-Forschung*. Tübingen: J. C. B. Mohr (Paul Siebeck), 1913.

———. *Von Reimarus zu Wrede: Eine Geschichte der Leben Jesu Forschung*. Tübingen: J. C. B. Mohr, 1906. English trans., *The Quest of the Historical Jesus: A Critical Study of its Progress from Reimarus to Wrede*. Translated by W. Montgomery. London: Adam & Charles Black, 1910.

Weinel, Heinrich, and Alban G. Widgery. *Jesus in the Nineteenth Century and After*. Edinburgh: T. & T. Clark, 1914. A translation and updating with additions by Widgery.

Windisch, Hans. "Englisch-amerikanische Literatur zum Neuen Testament in den Jahren 1914–1920." *ZNW* 20 (1921): 69–90.

———. "Literature on the New Testament in Germany, Austria, Switzerland, Holland, and the Scandinavian Countries, 1914–1920." *HTR* 15 (1922): 127–56.

INDEX OF NAMES

INDEX OF SUBJECTS